TARBELL'S
TEACHER'S GUIDE

TARBELL'S
TEACHER'S GUIDE

TO THE INTERNATIONAL BIBLE LESSONS
FOR CHRISTIAN TEACHING
OF THE UNIFORM COURSE
FOR SEPTEMBER 1980—AUGUST 1981

EDITED BY

FRANK S. MEAD

LITT. D., M. DIV.

SEVENTY-SIXTH
ANNUAL VOLUME

FLEMING H. REVELL COMPANY
OLD TAPPAN, NEW JERSEY

This volume is based on The International Sunday School Lessons; the International Bible Lessons for Christian Teaching, copyright © 1970 by the Committee on the Uniform Series.

The text of the Revised Standard Version of the Bible and quotations therefrom are copyright 1946 and 1952 by the Division of Christian Education, National Council of Churches, and used by permission.

Unless otherwise identified all biblical quotations in the material used by the author to illustrate the lesson are from the King James Version.

Printed in the United States of America

ISBN: 0-8007-1103-3
ISSN: 0082-1713

LIBRARY OF CONGRESS CATALOG CARD NUMBER: 5-40811

CONTENTS

A Word to the Teacher, by Frank S. Mead 9
The Lessons for September 1980–August 1981 11
Notes on the Printed Text by Frank S. Mead
Suggestions to Teachers and Illustrations by William P. Barker

LIST OF LESSONS
SEPTEMBER–NOVEMBER 1980:
GOD'S COVENANT WITH HIS PEOPLE

Lesson   Page

I. Sept. 7. *God: The Covenant Maker* .... Genesis 9:8–17 11

II. Sept. 14. *God's Covenant and Abraham* .... Genesis 12:1–4; 17:1–8 18

III. Sept. 21. *God's Covenant and Moses* .... Exodus 19:1–9 26

IV. Sept. 28. *God's Covenant and Joshua* .... Joshua 24:14–25 34

V. Oct. 5. *God's Covenant and David* .... 2 Samuel 7:8–16 41

VI. Oct. 12. *God's Covenant and Israel's Sin* .... 1 Kings 11:4–13 49

VII. Oct. 19. *God's Covenant and Jeremiah* .... Jeremiah 31:1–3, 29–34 57

VIII. Oct. 26. *God's Covenant and Ezra* .... Nehemiah 8:3; 9:32–38 64

IX. Nov. 2. *God's Covenant and Jesus Christ* .... Luke 4:16–21; Mark 14:22–25 71

X. Nov. 9. *God's Covenant and Peter* .... Acts 2:14–17; 3:18–26 . 78

XI. Nov. 16. *God's Covenant and Paul* .... Acts 13:44–52; 2 Corinthians 3:4–6 85

XII. Nov. 23. *God's Covenant and the New Israel* ..... 1 Peter 2:4–10 92

XIII. Nov. 30. *God's Covenant and the New Jerusalem* . Revelation 11:15–19; 21:10–14 99

5

DECEMBER 1980–FEBRUARY 1981
THE GOSPEL OF MATTHEW

Lesson   Page

I. Dec.   7. *Matthew Presents the Messiah* .... Matthew 1:1, 17; 5:17–20; 9:9; 13:51, 52 ...   107
II. Dec.   14. *John Prepares the Way*   Matthew 3:1–12   115
III. Dec. 21. *God Sends the Saviour*   Matthew 1:18–15   123
IV. Dec.   28. *Jesus Begins His Ministry* .... Matthew 3:13–17; 4:17–25   130
V. Jan.   4. *Let Your Light Shine* .   Matthew 5:1–16   138
VI. Jan.   11. *Build on the Solid Rock*   Matthew 7:13–29   145
VII. Jan. 18. *Proclaim the Kingdom*   Matthew 9:35–10:1, 5–15   152
VIII. Jan. 25. *Learn From the Lord* .   Matthew 11:2–6, 25–30   161
IX. Feb.   1. *Trust in God's Victory!*   Matthew 13:24–35   170
X. Feb.   8. *Have Compassion* ....   Matthew 15:29–39   178
XI. Feb.   15. *Live Your Faith* ......   Matthew 16:13–26   186
XII. Feb. 22. *Love One Another* ....   Matthew 18:1–6, 15–22   194

MARCH–MAY 1981
THE GOSPEL OF MATTHEW (COMPLETION)
THE BOOK OF HEBREWS

Lesson   Page

I. Mar.   1. *Relationships in the Kingdom* .... Matthew 19:1–15   202
II. Mar.   8. *God's Generosity* .....   Matthew 20:1–16   210
III. Mar. 15. *Questions of Priority* .   Matthew 22:15–32   218
IV. Mar.   22. *Signs of the End* .....   Matthew 23:37–24:14 .   226
V. Mar.   29. *Be Ready—Be Faithful*   Matthew 25:1–13   234
VI. Apr.   5. *Preparing for Difficult Times* .... Matthew 26:1–16   242
VII. Apr. 12. *They Crucified Him* ..   Matthew 27:33–50   250
VIII. Apr. 19. *Victory of the Resurrection* .... Matthew 27:62–28:10 .   259
IX. Apr.   26. *In Mission With the Victor* .... Matthew 28:11–20   268
X. May   3. *God's Ultimate Word* .   Hebrews 1:1–4; 2:1–8   276
XI. May   10. *Pioneer of Our Salvation* .... Hebrews 2:10–18   283
XII. May   17. *Our Great High Priest*   Hebrews 4:14–5:10 ...   291
XIII. May 24. *Mediator of a New Covenant* .... Hebrews 9:11–15, 24–28   299
XIV. May   31. *Perfecter of Our Faith*   Hebrews 12:1–13   306

JUNE–AUGUST 1981
THE BOOK OF DEUTERONOMY

Lesson   Page

I. June   7. *Hearing God's Com-*
               mands .... 2 Kings 23:1, 2; Deu-
                                       teronomy
                                       10:12–11:1   314

II. June   14. *Claiming God's Prom-*
               ise .... Deuteronomy 1:19–26,
                                       29–31   322

III. June   21. *Recalling God's Action* Deuteronomy 4:1, 2,
                                       5–10   330

IV. June   28. *Experiencing God's*
               Presence .... Deuteronomy 4:32–40   338

V. July   5. *Ten Commandments* . Deuteronomy 5:6–8,
                                       11–21   345

VI. July   12. *God's Words in Our*
               Hearts .... Deuteronomy 6:4–15 .   354

VII. July   19. *God Chose Israel* .... Deuteronomy 6:20–25;
                                       7:6–11   362

VIII. July 26. *Commitment in Wor-*
               ship .... Deuteronomy 12:5–12;
                                       14:27–29   370

IX. Aug.   2. *God Desires Justice* .. Deuteronomy 10:10–
                                       20; 24:10–15, 17–19   378

X. Aug.   9. *The Basis of Covenant*
               Renewal .... Deuteronomy 29:2–15   386

XI. Aug.   16. *Repentance and Resto-*
               ration .... Deuteronomy 30:1–10   393

XII. Aug.   23. *Choice and Its Conse-*
               quences .... Deuteronomy 30:11–
                                       20   401

XIII. Aug. 30. *God Is Faithful* ...... Deuteronomy 32:1–9 . 409

A WORD TO THE TEACHER

A good old friend who uses *TARBELL'S* regularly lately wrote us. "You have a good book here. I have only one criticism of it: it isn't a good enough crutch for the average church school teacher." We thanked him; criticism is always good for the ego, and it keeps us humble.

I replied, as humbly as possible, that the writers and publishers of *TARBELL'S*, using the Uniform Lessons outlines, are not in the crutch business, supplying props for the lame or lazy teacher. For seventy-six long years, our objectives (which are the objectives of all good Christian education) have been five in number:

1. To lead our readers to an awareness of God through His self-revelation in the Bible—that God was not only present at Eden and Sinai, but that in Christ He walks and wins in *our* world from Seattle to South Africa.
2. To know that He calls us to *respond* to Him in faith and love—a response in which action follows oral declaration of our faith or recitation of the Apostle's Creed.
3. To know who we are and what we are in fellowship with the God who gave us life.
4. To inspire growth in spirit and in knowledge of our Lord, maturing in development from the days when we spoke as children to the days of full spiritual maturity.
5. To lead us to *abide* with Him in Christian trust and faith, even unto the end.

An old, gnarled dead tree fell to the ground, just beyond my study window. Men came and took it away, leaving a part of the stump, hardly visible in the growing grass. And lo, as the months and years passed, I saw a totally new tree growing from the stump, and I sit in my study and watch it grow. If God can do that with a tree, what more can He do for us!

You are a sower of the seeds of the tree of faith, teacher! Your job, with the help of these lessons, is to teach *awareness* of this creative God, *response* to His love, *fellowship* with Him and His disciples, *growth*, and *trust* that with Him the old and outworn may be replaced with new and abiding faith. *TARBELL'S* may help you as you do this; God will help you more.

God bless you all,
Frank S. Mead.

SEPTEMBER, OCTOBER, NOVEMBER, 1980

GOD'S COVENANT WITH HIS PEOPLE

LESSON I—SEPTEMBER 7

GOD: THE COVENANT MAKER

Background Scripture: Genesis 6–9
Devotional Reading: Psalms 8.

KING JAMES VERSION	REVISED STANDARD VERSION
GENESIS 9 8 And God spake unto Noah, and to his sons with him, saying, 9 And I, behold, I establish my covenant with you, and with your seed after you; 10 And with every living creature that *is* with you, of the fowl, of the cattle, and of every beast of the earth with you; from all that go out of the ark, to every beast of the earth. 11 And I will establish my covenant with you; neither shall all flesh be cut off any more by the waters of a flood; neither shall there any more be a flood to destroy the earth. 12 And God said, This *is* the token of the covenant which I make between me and you and every living creature that *is* with you, for perpetual generations: 13 I do set my bow in the cloud, and it shall be for a token of a covenant between me and the earth. 14 And it shall come to pass, when I bring a cloud over the earth, that the bow shall be seen in the cloud: 15 And I will remember my covenant, which *is* between me and you and every living creature of all flesh; and the waters shall no more become a flood to destroy all flesh. 16 And the bow shall be in the cloud; and I will look upon it, that I	GENESIS 9 8 Then God said to Noah and to his sons with him, 9 "Behold, I establish my covenant with you and your descendants after you, 10 and with every living creature that is with you, the birds, the cattle, and every beast of the earth with you, as many as came out of the ark. 11 I establish my covenant with you, that never again shall all flesh be cut off by the waters of a flood, and never again shall there be a flood to destroy the earth." 12 And God said, "This is the sign of the covenant which I make between me and you and every living creature that is with you, for all future generations: 13 I set my bow in the cloud, and it shall be a sign of the covenant between me and the earth. 14 When I bring clouds over the earth and the bow is seen in the clouds, 15 I will remember my covenant which is between me and you and every living creature of all flesh; and the waters shall never again become a flood to destroy all flesh. 16 When the bow is in the clouds, I will look upon it and remember the everlasting covenant between God and every living creature of all flesh that is upon the earth." 17 God said to Noah, "This is the sign of the covenant which I have established between me and all flesh that is upon the earth."

11

may remember the everlasting covenant between God and every living
creature of all flesh that *is* upon the
earth.

17 And God said unto Noah, This *is*
the token of the covenant, which I
have established between me and all
flesh that *is* upon the earth.

*KEY VERSE: And I will remember my covenant, which is between me
and you and every living creature of all flesh* . . . . Genesis 9:15.

HOME DAILY BIBLE READINGS

Sept. *1.* M. *Sin Grieves God.* Genesis 6:5–13.
Sept. *2.* T. *God's Plan for Safety.* Genesis 6:14–22.
Sept. *3.* W. *Safety in the Flood.* Genesis 7:1–5, 17–23.
Sept. *4.* T. *Thanking God for Safety.* Genesis 8:6–12, 20–22.
Sept. *5.* F. *Living With God's Blessing.* Genesis 9:1–7.
Sept. *6.* S. *The Covenant of the Rainbow.* Genesis 9:8–17.
Sept. *7.* S. *The Majesty of God.* Psalms 8.

BACKGROUND

For the next month, we shall be studying covenants. Suppose we start
with a definition: a covenant is a promise, a contract, or an agreement. In
the Bible sense, it refers generally to a promise made by God and agreed
to by men. The covenant idea is a strong thread of unity running through
the entire Bible.

Now covenants are not all alike; they appear in different forms, for the
simple reason that they come in different periods of history at moments
when men faced different problems and/or crises. What we have in
these lessons is a chronological sequence of covenants in Jewish history,
from the first one in Genesis to the culmination covenant of the New
Testament—which, incidentally, is often called The New Covenant.

Our class sessions will become livelier and more meaningful if they
are taught against the background of the personalities involved; our first
lesson offers us a picture of one of the very first men to appear in the
Bible. Read the chapters leading up to chapter nine, and read 9:21, and
ask yourself what kind of man Noah was, and why he needed a covenant
with God.

NOTES ON THE PRINTED TEXT

*I. And I, behold, I establish my covenant with you, and with your
seed after you, And with every living creature that is with you* . . . .
Genesis 9:9, 10. This is a covenant of *promise*: God makes the promise,
and no requirement was laid upon man, as it was in covenants to come.
God doesn't ask Noah whether he wants a covenant or not; He simply
says, "This it the way it is to be!"

God is promising here that never again will there be a flood like the
one from which Noah has just been rescued—never again a deluge that
would "destroy all flesh." Think of what that must have meant to Noah
and his family. They had just come through a horrible experience, and
the memory of that experience would haunt them until they died. They

were terrified at the very thought of a disaster that threatened to put an end to *everything*, and even though they survived, the memory was to live on, as it always does. Primitive man was a human bundle of fear. When earthquakes shook their earth, they were sure that that was the end of everything; when lightning flashed and thunder roared, they cringed in hopeless fear. What they could not understand they dreaded. Let a volcano erupt, let there be an eclipse of the sun, let a river overflow, and terror took possession of them. All about them were gods and demons who were not good, but evil, vindictive, vengeful, destructive. They groveled hopelessly in what was apparently a hostile earth. The word *hope* was not in their dictionary.

But now, in the darkest moment they had ever experienced, they learn that it would never happen again, and that they have no cause for fear. This promise comes from the very lips of a God who not only created the earth, but a God who is the Sustainer of the earth and of all who dwell therein. Men might go on sinning, men might live in ignorance and folly, but this God of hope and mercy, in a great divine patience, will never again make such an attempt to destroy them.

So hope was to be written large and clear and indelibly in the hearts of those who believed in Him. It was a great milestone in the history of man.

Note that God applies this promise not to a chosen few, but to *all* men in every age. It was not a promise meant for Hebrew primitives, *but for us, now*. It was meant for those of us who live as the prisoners of fear. It was meant for the hopeless men of today who cry out in fear of atomic destruction, for those who in disappointment and misunderstanding cry, "What's the use? We are all doomed!" It is a promise for those who live in the black shadows of yesterday and who are terrified at the thought of what will—or may—happen tomorrow. It is for those who have shut their ears to the promise of a caring God who put upon the lips of Jesus Christ the promise that "I will not leave you desolate . . ." (John 14:18).

Hope! Faith in the universal and eternal goodness and mercy of God! Do you know the painting of G. F. Watts entitled *Hope*? In it, a woman sits blindfolded in what looks like a hopeless world, holding a lyre in her hands, her finger reaching for the only string left on that lyre, holding fast to hope in a world that looks like a deadly desert, trying to get just one more note of music when everything seems gone. Hope, undying, indestructible—hope took a new lease on life in this promise to Noah—and to us.

And have you read the words of James Russell Lowell? Here they are:

Truth for ever on the scaffold, Wrong for ever on the throne, Yet that scaffold sways the future, and, Behind the dim unknown, Standeth God within the shadow, Keeping watch above His own.

II. I set my bow in the cloud, and it shall be a sign of the covenant between me and the earth. Genesis 9:13 (RSV). There has been some confusion as to exactly what is meant by this, and why the figure of a bow is used, but there need not be to those who rightly divide (understand) the Scriptures. The symbolism of the bow—the Hebrew word is

always used as a weapon, not as an arc—goes back to the idea that the
lightnings are the Lord's arrows (*see* Psalms 7:13, 18:14, Habakkuk 3:11)
shot from His bow (Psalms 7:12, Habakkuk 3:9) which is laid aside when
His wrath is sated. But for the writer of Genesis 9, the lightnings of God
are no longer God's arrows shot from His bow; the bow becomes an arc
set in the cloud (skies), a *rain*bow, a symbol of peace between God and
man; God's anger has passed with the passing of the Flood, and He
points to the rainbow in the skies as a sign of His mercy and faithfulness.

Note, carefully, here, that God does not promise that there will never
again be *any* flood upon the earth, but that there will never again be
such a Flood as the one in Genesis, a Flood covering *all* the earth, and
all who lived upon it with the exception of Noah and his family. This
should be remembered by those who point to the floods of which we
read in our newspapers, and who scream as these flood waters rise,
"Where is God? Why does He permit it?" Such critics should understand that such modern floods may not at all be the work of God, but the
result of mankind's carelessness in stemming or controlling such floods
before they rise and roar.

The teaching here is that God has not, will never, forsake or deliberately destroy the earth, or those who are faithful to Him. He asks us to
believe that. He asks us to believe, as a Negro spiritual tells us, that He
holds us all "in the hollow of His hand." He asks us to look up and see
that rainbow. Some still refuse to look—but it is *there*. It is not an
accident of nature; it is the work, the sign of God, the reminder of the
covenant made by His eternal goodness. And that cannot, will not, fail.

As long as we see it in true spiritual perspective, we can have full faith
in the future, whatever has happened in the past. God lives, and cares,
and so should we.

Then there are these words, from Merv Rosel: "God could have kept
Daniel out of the lion's den . . . He could have kept Paul and Silas out
of jail—He could have kept the three Hebrew children out of the fiery
furnace . . . But God has never promised to keep us out of hard
places . . . What He has promised is to go with us through every hard
place, and to bring us through victoriously."

SUGGESTIONS TO TEACHERS

"*I'm ready to resign from the human race!*" Haven't you felt that
way? "*I feel like leaving the Church!*" Haven't you also been at this
point?

Every member of your class has also thought of writing off the world
and quitting the Church. That is why this lesson series is designed to get
to people "where they are."

The topic is God's Covenant. This theme is woven throughout the
entire Bible. Familiarize youself with the meaning of covenant. You will
be using the term often, and must understand how God has made a
solemn pact or covenanted with us.

Today's lesson centers on God's sacred pact with us through Noah.
The point of the Scripture in Genesis 6–9 is that God has made a promise with the human race that He will never wipe it out, no matter how

disgusted and disappointed He may be. Don't get pulled into pointless discussions over how Noah managed to care for the menagerie on his ark, or what happened to the fish during the flood, or where the ark came to rest, or whether archeological expeditions today will locate the ruins of the ark. Focus on God the Covenant Maker.

1. *GOD'S PERSEVERANCE.* Help your class to comprehend that God persists with the human race. He did not destroy everything or everyone. Comment that the Sign of the Rainbow means that God continues to persevere with our world. He will not quit on us. As teacher, bring the class discussion around to the way your people sometimes feel like giving up on others. You may ask your class to relate examples from personal experience. Stress that God insists on persisting with us. If this world is good enough for God, it is good enough for us!

2. *GOD'S PROMISE.* Call attention to the way God initiates the agreement or covenant. Also have your class take note how God remembers His covenant with humankind. Relate this to the evil, corruption, and violence around us today. God will not walk away from the human race. Nor will He scrap what He holds dear. Although God feels terribly disappointed in our perverse ways, He remembers His promise to us. Have your class offer reminiscences of times when God's promise that He means to stand by us has sustained them or others. Make sure you emphasize the way His promise is spelled out completely in Christ.

3. *GOD'S PATIENCE.* You won't need to look far for examples of human impatience. Contrast these with the mighty examples in today's Scripture reading of God's patience. God, the Covenant Maker, offers you and your class strength to endure patiently in the face of evil and disasters!

TOPIC FOR ADULTS
GOD: THE COVENANT MAKER

Pessimism Apart From God. To celebrate the Bicentennial, Michael O'Leary, president of Philadelphia Resident Astrologers Inc., decided to have various seers, psychics, and stargazers of his acquaintance predict the nation's next one hundred years. The prophecies were sealed in a three-and-a-half-foot steel cylinder and buried twenty-five feet beneath Chestnut Street.

Theosophist Kenneth Buzby predicted that war will become a thing of the past, that cancer will be cured and pollution overcome. But most prophets were decidedly gloomier. Several foresaw an end of the American presidency, perhaps by the year 2025. Tarot Card Reader Johanna Okovic predicted an earthquake in New York City in 1978 and a war between 2011 and 2016. Astrologer Leah O'Leary, Michael's wife, forecast a "naval conflict" in 1979, floods on both the East and West coasts, and a "nuclear mishap in 1983."

Taken as a whole, the seers were so pessimistic that one commentator remarked that it was a wonder that they thought anyone would be around in 2076 to retrieve their forecasts from the capsule!

Apart from God, however, such pessimism is inevitable. Only God's covenants keep us from giving up. The God who will not desert us gives us reasons for hope. Although psychics, and seers, and stargazers may predict nothing but gloom, Christians take their cue from the promises of God, beginning with the rainbow and continuing through the Resurrection!

God Not Acting as a Nazi. "May 21, 1940. It is said that while the Germans were desecrating a church somewhere in Poland, some German sergeant, cockeyed with the excitement, stood up in front of the altar and yelled out that if there was a God He would want to prove His existence at once by striking down such a bold and important and terrifying fellow as this sergeant. God did not strike him down. The sergeant went away still excited, and probably the unhappiest man in the world: God had not acted like a Nazi. God was not, in fact, a Nazi, and God's justice (which everybody obscurely knows about in his bones, no matter what he tries to say he thinks) is inexpressibly different from the petty bloodthirsty revenge of Nazis"—Thomas Merton, quoted in Henri Nouen, *Pray to Live.*

Venture for Thy Name! God's covenant tells how His Promise endures. That covenant also enables believers to persevere in face of impossible obstacles.

John Bunyan was in Bedford jail, imprisoned for his faith and facing a possible death sentence. He was afraid to die. But what bothered him more was that if he showed this fear to the public it might bring discredit on the Gospel. And he wrote:

"I thought with myself, if I should make a scrabbling shift to clamber up the Ladder, yet I should either with quaking, or other symptoms of fainting, give occasion to the Enemy to reproach the Way of God and his People for their timorousness. This therefore lay with great trouble upon me, for methought I was ashamed to die with a pale Face and tottering Knees, for such a cause as this."

He admitted also his uncertainty about his own salvation, even though he might be dying for his faith, but finally he concluded:

"I am for going on, and venturing my eternal state with Christ, whether I have comfort here or no. If God doth not come in, thought I, I will leap off the Ladder even blindfold into Eternity, sink or swim, come Heaven, come Hell. Lord Jesus, if thou wilt catch me, do; if not, I will venture for thy Name."

Questions to Pupils on the Next Lesson: 1. What are some of the risks incurred by God's challenges to Christians today? 2. Is it possible for Christians to mature in faith and trust without taking risks? 3. In what ways does knowing about God's covenant with Abraham help Christians today find greater meaning in their faith? 4. How do Christians in your congregation celebrate meaningful ways in which they are included in God's covenant? 5. What is the place of reminders in our lives to help us remember to obey God? 6. How was the heritage of the faith passed on to you, and how are you helping to pass it on to the next generation?

TOPIC FOR YOUTH
GOD THE COVENANT MAKER

Doomsday Community. A community calling itself the Stelle Group expects earthquakes, volcanic explosions, and tidal waves to destroy the earth in the year 2000. Situated on the prairie sixty miles south of Chicago, the Stelle Group plans to survive by airlifting members to safety, hovering over the destruction, then returning to build the Nation of God.

Founded by Richard Kieninger, but now led by Malcolm Carnahan, the community presently anticipates world monetary crises and prepares for the apocalypse by stockpiling grain and raising its own food.

The Stelle Group is one of hundreds that have sprung up throughout history. All share a pessimistic viewpoint. Conditions appear hopeless. A time of doom is imminent, each claims.

By contrast, we are part of the covenanted community. We live by God's promises! We are empowered to persevere with hope and patience!

Just Reigning? Your thoughts of God may well be ill formed and uninformed. You may regard God as the two little girls in the museum who came across a huge portrait of Queen Victoria. The youngsters studied the picture which showed the monarch in a stiff, formal pose. Finally, one girl whispered to the other, "What's she doing?" "Nothing," replied the first. "She's just reigning." You may have the same notion of God: aloof, silent, withdrawn.

God covenants with us that He acts in love on our behalf! He involves Himself. He makes promises to us. Unlike certain Eastern religions, the God revealing Himself in events in the Scriptures persists in serving us.

Poor Henry. Henry Ellsworth at one time was Director of the U.S. Patent Office. Shortly after he had been appointed to the position, he declared that the office should be closed. When asked why, Henry replied that he was convinced that everything had already been invented, and that there would be no need to continue the office. Henry said this before the Morse telegraph, the Colt revolver, the McCormack reaper, the Edison electric light, the Marconi radio, the Wright brothers' airplane, the Ford automobile, and literally thousands of other inventions which have drastically changed our lives. Poor Henry! His spiritual descendants are everywhere. Even in the Church! Poor Henrys today are convinced that everything is all over, that there is no future.

The poor Henrys reckon without God. They forget His covenant with humans, beginning with Noah. Just when the poor Henrys shake their heads and make pessimistic pronouncements, God reminds us that He keeps His word with this planet. God surprises us with startling futures!

Sentence Sermon to Remember:

> O holy trust! O endless sense of rest!
> Like the beloved John
> To lay his head upon the Saviour's breast
> And thus to journey on!
> —Henry Wadsworth Longfellow

Questions for Pupils on the Next Lesson. 1. How does God call people today? 2. Do you think God calls you? Why or why not? If so, how? 3. Why is faith risky? 4. What have you risked in order to be a Christian? 5. How does God accomplish His purposes in the world? 6. What are some of the blessings that come from following God's will?

LESSON II—SEPTEMBER 14

GOD'S COVENANT AND ABRAHAM

Background Scripture: Genesis 12:1–9 ;17:1–21
Devotional Reading: Romans 10:5–13

KING JAMES VERSION

GENESIS 12 1 Now the LORD had said unto Abram, Get thee out of thy country, and from thy kindred, and from thy father's house, unto a land that I will shew thee:

2 And I will make of thee a great nation, and I will bless thee, and make thy name great; and thou shalt be a blessing:

3 And I will bless them that bless thee, and curse him that curseth thee: and in thee shall all families of the earth be blessed.

4 So Abram departed, as the LORD had spoken unto him; and Lot went with him: and Abram *was* seventy and five years old when he departed out of Haran.

GENESIS 17 1 And when Abram was ninety years old and nine, the LORD appeared to Abram, and said unto him, I *am* the Almighty God; walk before me, and be thou perfect.

2 And I will make my covenant between me and thee, and will multiply thee exceedingly.

3 And Abram fell on his face: and God talked with him, saying,

4 As for me, behold, my covenant *is* with thee, and thou shalt be a father of many nations.

5 Neither shall thy name any more be called Abram, but thy name shall be Abraham; for a father of many nations have I made thee.

6 And I will make thee exceeding fruitful, and I will make nations of thee, and kings shall come out of thee.

7 And I will establish my covenant between me and thee and thy seed after thee in their generations for an everlasting covenant, to be a God unto thee and to thy seed after thee.

8 And I will give unto thee, and to thy seed after thee, the land wherein thou art a stranger, all the land of Canaan, for an everlasting possession; and I will be their God.

REVISED STANDARD VERSION

GENESIS 12 1 Now the LORD said to Abram, "Go from your country and your kindred and your father's house to the land that I will show you. 2 And I will make of you a great nation, and I will bless you, and make your name great, so that you will be a blessing. 3 I will bless those who bless you, and him who curses you I will curse; and by you all the families of the earth will bless themselves."

4 So Abram went, as the LORD had told him; and Lot went with him. Abram was seventy-five years old when he departed from Haran.

GENESIS 17 1 When Abram was ninety-nine years old the LORD appeared to Abram, and said to him, "I am God Almighty; walk before me, and be blameless. 2 And I will make my covenant between me and you, and will multiply you exceedingly." 3 Then Abram fell on his face; and God said to him, 4 "Behold, my covenant is with you, and you shall be the father of a multitude of nations. 5 No longer shall your name be Abram but your name shall be Abraham; for I have made you the father of a multitude of nations. 6 I will make you exceedingly fruitful; and I will make nations of you, and kings shall come forth from you. 7 And I will establish my covenant between me and you and your descendants after you throughout their generations for an everlasting covenant, to be God to you and to your descendants after you. 8 And I will give to you, and to your descendants after you, the land of your sojournings, all the land of Canaan, for an everlasting possession; and I will be their God."

KEY VERSE: And I will establish my covenant between me and you and your descendants after you throughout their generations for an everlasting covenant, to be God to you and to your descendants after you. Genesis 17:7 (RSV).

HOME DAILY BIBLE READINGS

Sept. *8.* M. *Going Out in Faith.* Genesis 12:1–9.
Sept. *9.* T. *Fear Causes Failure.* Genesis 12:10–20.
Sept. *10.* W. *A Parting and a Promise.* Genesis 13:1–16.
Sept. *11.* T. *Counted Righteous.* Genesis 15:1–6.
Sept. *12.* F. *Father of Many Nations.* Genesis 17:1–8.
Sept. *13.* S. *Promise of a Son.* Genesis 17:9–21.
Sept. *14.* S. *Righteousness Based on Faith.* Romans 10:5–13.

BACKGROUND

In Genesis 11, we read the story of Babel and of a people gone mad with pride and who in supreme arrogance planned to build a tower whose top "may reach unto heaven: and let us make us a name . . ." (Genesis 11:4); that was to be a proud monument to themselves, with no thought of God. God did not like it; He scattered "them abroad upon the face of all the earth" (11:9). Some of them were scattered as far away as the Land of Canaan.

In Ur of the Chaldeans, a city on the Euphrates in Lower Mesopotamia (today called Iraq) lived a man named Abram (later Abraham), a good and righteous man who was unhappy in this city famous for commerce and for a great temple of the pagan moon god. He left that city, thinking of a better way of life that might be found somewhere else—possibly in Canaan. He got as far as Haran, where life was not much better, inasmuch as the moon god was there, too. Abram's father died in Haran, which made matters still worse.

Then God stepped into the picture and laid His hand on Abram's shoulder, and the history of Israel began.

NOTES ON THE PRINTED TEXT

I. . . . Get thee out of thy country . . . and I will bless thee . . . . Genesis 12:1, 2. Here is a promise of inestimable value and meaning to a man lost in the company of men who had no faith in the true God. Go, Abram, go into Canaan, and I will *bless* you! That word *bless* occurs no less than five times in Genesis 12:2 and 3. God would bless this man Abram if he will go as God commanded him to go, bless him by making his name great in a great new land, bless him by making him father of a great new nation. Indeed, Abraham himself would be called blessed, if he obeyed this word from God.

So, the record says, "So Abram *went*" (verse 4). He did not hesitate for long— but could we blame him if he "had his doubts" about going on such an adventure? Must he leave the friends he had made in Haran? Must he cut himself off, with his family, from what little security he had and go into a land of which he knew nothing? He may have had questions in his mind and heart—but he went. Went, "not knowing whither he went" (Hebrews 11:8). That put him in the company of mankind's immortal heroes, into the ranks of those who expect great things from God and are ready to dare great things for God.

Most men stay in their Urs, where they are safe and comfortable, but Abram went. He went as Columbus went, sailing a sea that men called deadly and endless to a land of which he knew nothing; went as the colonists went out to Jamestown and Plymouth Rock; went as the American pioneers went West, while the faint-hearted stayed home. God was most wise in picking Abram as His man.

Note here that, unlike His covenant with Noah, God demanded action from His man. Go! Don't sit weeping in Ur. It isn't enough just to believe in God; He says, "Go"; He calls for action. And in this act of silent obedience, the course of world history was changed.

The world and mankind benefit greatly through the courage of men who are not content to paddle their little canoes in the shallow backwaters of a small river, but who have the courage to unfurl their sails upon the wideness of the sea. God can do little with the paddlers of little canoes; He builds His kingdom on the daring.

II. And I will make my covenant between me and thee, and will multiply thee exceedingly. Genesis 17:2. Abram was seventy-five years old when he left Haran; we find him now in Canaan, and aged ninety-nine! The ancients had a different method of counting time and people's ages, but that need not bother us. Apparently Abram and his people were settled in Canaan, in spite of all their difficulties on the long march and in spite of the presence of hostile people in Canaan. Now God rewards the leadership, the faith and humility and patience of Abram, in another covenant of great promise.

The whole history of Abram may be divided in four stages, each one of which began with a revelation of Jehovah: the first, when Abram was called to his work and mission (Genesis 12); the second, when he received the promise of an heir, and the covenant was made with him (Genesis 15, 16); the third, when that covenant was established in the change of his name from Abram to Abraham (Genesis 17); the fourth, when his faith was tried, proved, and perfected in the offering up of Isaac (Genesis 22).

Why was his name changed from Abram to Abraham? There are two explanations offered for this by Bible scholars; one is that both mean, practically, the same thing, that *Abraham* is used in some ancient documents, and that Abram and Abraham are actually variant spellings of the same name. But others see something more profound. As the *Living Bible* puts it, "God told him, I am changing your name. It is no longer Abram (Exalted Father) but Abraham (Father of Nations) for that is what you will be!" This sounds more like it, for this is exactly what Abraham became.

Father of nations, of a multitude of nations? This Abraham, at the moment, did not even have a son of his own, with which to perpetuate a "line"! God would take care of that, if Abram would "walk before me"—walk with me, live constantly in the knowledge that I am close to you, live a life completely dedicated to me (God), and I promise you that you will be great as the selfish, godless people of Babel could never be great.

Walk with me, and I, God, promise to "multiply thy seed"—"I will give you millions of descendants who will form many nations" (Living Bible). Not only the nation of Israel, but "all kindreds, and tongues, and nations."

If this boggles *our* minds, what do you suppose it did to the mind of Abraham? But there is no scriptural record of any confusion, any hesitancy in the mind of Abraham; lying there prostrate in the dust as God made His staggering promises (this was humility). Abraham *believed* that centuries after he was gone there would be kings in Israel who were men of his line (this was patience), and that this almighty, all-powerful God was *his* God, and with Him humble Abraham could believe and do the impossible (this was faith). Humility, patience, faith: this was Abraham.

God kept His promises, and Abraham walked with Him, and the descendants of Abraham wielded a tremendous influence upon all the nations of the world. Oh, yes, they broke many covenants with their God, but the purpose God had in them did not falter or disappear. God had a divine patience, too; He also had a persistent love for the people of Abraham from then until now. In that love, God sent to them the mediator of a yet greater Covenant, in the person of His only begotten Son—a still greater blessing to *all* the world.

SUGGESTIONS TO TEACHERS

A few years ago, the televised version of *Roots* drew the biggest audience in TV history. Millions, black and white, were fascinated by the saga of Kinte Kunta and his descendants. Millions also became interested in their own roots.

You should point out to your class that this series of lessons helps believers today to understand their spiritual roots. Abraham is our ancestor in the faith. Your class traces its roots back to this "founder" of the biblical "family."

Your key in understanding Abraham is the Covenant which God made with him. Refresh your memory of the meaning of *covenant.* You and your class must appropriate it into your vocabulary and into your lives, if you are to appreciate your roots!

1. *THE UNEXPECTED CALL.* Draw your class's attention to the way God singled out Abraham (*see* Genesis 12). Why Abraham? Well, why Saul of Tarsus? Or, why *you?* All that can be said is that God had an agenda in mind for Abraham and Saul. God also has an agenda for you and each person in your class. God summoned Abraham, and He summons your people. Emphasize that your class members who have heard something of the claims of God through Jesus Christ are "called" just as surely as Abraham was called. Take some time to think through how God calls people today. Let each one in your class grasp that he or she is called by God.

2. *THE IMPOSSIBLE COMMITMENT.* Continue your lesson by letting the story of Abraham tell itself. God insisted that Abraham move out from the security of his own homeland, and go on a life-long pilgrimage for God. God demanded Abraham live without proofs or rewards. God

offered him only a promise. Let your imagination roam, and consider how reckless Abraham must have seemed to everyone. Push this idea farther. Encourage your class to apply Abraham's call to their lives. God asks an impossible commitment of each! "When Christ calls a person," wrote Bonhoeffer before he was martyred by the Nazis, "He calls that person to come out and die."

3. *THE UNLIMITED CARING.* The saga of Abraham reveals that Abraham did not always live blamelessly or faithfully. Nevertheless, God lavished His mercy on Abraham. Those whom God calls also know God's astonishing goodness. Allow your class to bring up instances of God's undeserved caring in their personal stories.

4. *THE UNDESERVED COVENANT.* Check the number of times in the career of Abraham in which the Lord reiterates His promise that He will bless Abraham. Remind your class that Abraham had doubts that God would keep His word, especially the part about having a son. In fact, after hearing about God's covenant for so many years without having a child, Abraham and his wife literally laughed at God. Don't we sometimes laugh at His promise? Through Christ, we understand He has made a covenant with us although we do not deserve it!

TOPIC FOR ADULTS
GOD'S COVENANT AND ABRAHAM

Call and Covenant. How do we experience God's call today? How can we be aware of His covenant with us?

An overworked missionary nurse in a hospital in Angola told how she had complained to her superior that, after her twelve hours on duty with many extra calls beyond her routine tasks, she was simply too exhausted to pray, and that her interior life had ebbed away. She had gone on to explain with special bitterness the situation with which she was faced at that moment. At the close of the day, she still had twelve more African patients to wash before going off duty. After that all she would be able to do would be to throw herself on her bed in exhaustion when she came to her room. Her older colleague heard the outburst in love and suggested that it was not really necessary to wait until she got home to pray. If she washed each of these next twelve Africans as though each were the body of Christ, her praying could begin at once.

Human Covenants Mirror God's. Jim and Joan were newly married and very much in love. Both came from Christian homes. Jim's father was an Episcopal priest, and Joan's was a Methodist. The two frequently laughed about their upbringing as "P.K.s"—"preacher's kids." Joan and Jim quickly became active in the church near their new home. They joked with the young pastor in their new congregation, "Remember Roger, we're P.K.s; don't get too pious with us! We know all this church business backward and forward!" Roger, their pastor, enjoyed their contagious humor and spoofing the pomposity of clergy.

Jim and Joan grew older and more prosperous. They still retained their mild irreverence toward pastors and piety. Success in business seemed to stifle their church involvement, however, and they drifted to the margin of the congregation's life.

Some years later, Jim fell into a brief flirtation with a woman in his office. They had a few lunches together and met for drinks occasionally after work. Technically, it was not adultery, but Jim enjoyed the relationship and intended to cultivate it. Inevitably, Joan found out about it. She confronted Jim. Jim merely laughed it off as "harmless kicks."

Joan turned to Roger, their long-time friend and pastor, and insisted that she and Jim talk together with Roger.

"So what's the big deal?" laughed Jim when he and Joan sat down in Roger's study. "Okay, so maybe I acted a bit silly. But in this day of easy-going sexual morality, why get all worked up because I've enjoyed a few drinks with a woman? Joan should just forget it."

Joan, stung, replied heatedly, "How could you do this to me?" Joan played the role of an aggrieved wife, secretly congratulating herself on how nobly she was carrying on.

Roger tried to talk to them about God's covenant, and God's forgiveness. Jim and Joan both smiled cynically. Finally Jim interrupted, "C'mon, Roger. Knock off the covenant-and-charity stuff." Joan interjected that Jim was on probation before she'd ever forgive and take him back. Jim shrugged and laughed that he couldn't see what all the fuss was about. They stood up and departed. Roger sadly concluded that it was another pastoral care failure in his case-book.

Several months later, Joan's headaches were more severe and Jim's drinking was becoming a problem. Their family doctor told them to see either a psychiatrist, a divorce lawyer, or a pastor.

Jim called Roger. "You're cheaper than a shrink or an attorney," Jim quipped. They both laughed and arranged to meet.

Through prayer and counseling by Roger, Jim and Joan came to understand that a marriage covenant is mirrored on God's covenant. Several hours later, Jim quietly stood and walked over to Joan. Tenderly taking her hand, Jim said quietly, "Joan, please forgive me for hurting you so."

Joan stood and took Jim's two hands and answered, "Jim, please forgive me for not forgiving you."

That evening, in Roger's study, the two made a new covenant with God and with each other.

He Promised. Christy Mathewson was one of the greatest pitchers in big league baseball. He never pitched on Sunday. Once he almost was thrown out of the league because he was "*needed* on Sundays." When his teammates asked him why he was so stubborn about it, Matty said, "I promised my mother, once, that I would never do it. We prayed about it, and I promised both her and God that I'd never do it, and I never will." That's keeping a covenant, whether we agree with him or not!

Questions for Pupils on the Next Lesson. 1. How does God seem to call leaders from His covenant community in the Scriptures? 2. Does He call leaders today in these ways? 3. What is the nature of the authority of a spiritual leader? 4. How would you compare Moses' call from God with the experience of people today who claim His call? 5. What are the qualities which should be involved in a servant and priestly people, according to Exodus 19:4-8?

TOPIC FOR YOUTH
FOLLOWING GOD'S CALL

Hearing Something Else. Charles Ives, the great American composer (1874–1954), was a successful insurance executive who was known to his friends and business associates as a man who liked to dabble in music in his spare moments. His compositions contained unusual and seemingly unplayable music. No one seemed to be interested in listening seriously to his works. In fact, Ives was past fifty before anyone important performed his works. He finished his *Symphony No. 3*, for example, in 1904, but it was not performed until 1964. The following year, it earned Ives a Pulitzer Prize. He completed his *Symphony No. 4* in 1916, but it, too, was never performed in its entirety until 1965, eleven years after Ives's death. Acknowledged as the first American to pioneer a musical path outside the European tradition, he is acclaimed today as a genius. His polyrhythmic creations have spawned imitators and Ives Festivals.

Ives, asked how he could produce such exceptional sounds in a musical score which no one else had ever created, replied, "I heard something else."

"*I heard something else*"—so did Abraham. And so did Moses. Likewise Joshua, Jeremiah, and the prophets. They did not hear merely the noises and voices around them, but caught the message of God.

Have you heard something else? Have you heard of the covenant? Have you, like Abraham, heard the command to march out in lonely obedience?

The Loneliest Spot. Violence can flare quickly at the front line in Korea near Panmunjom where American and South Korean troops daily confront Communist North Koreans. The North Koreans create "incidents" without warning. Fifty Americans have died from these attacks in the area since the armistice was signed in 1953. The one-hundred-sixty American soldiers and the seventy-five South Korean guards are assigned to Panmunjom on one year tours of duty after being carefully screened and trained. So many premeditated outbreaks of violence by the North Korean Communists have been launched against this frontier force that all American and South Korean guardposts at Panmunjom are built within sight of one another for mutual protection. The farthest forward outpost is Checkpoint 3. The guards have dubbed this exposed truce site "the loneliest spot in the world."

Often, the covenanted man or woman feels that he or she is in the loneliest spot in the world. God calls each of us for duty. He places us in risky settings. Every one of us, however, is guarded by the knowledge that He keeps His word with us. Just as the people in Checkpoint 3 know that they are never abandoned, so we know we have God's assurance that He stands with us in our lonely assignments.

Promise to a Person. Contrary to what many people believe, the Christian faith is not a faith in a creed or a body of truth or a high ethical standard. The Christian faith is a covenant with a person—the Person— Jesus Christ. Perhaps the difference can be illustrated by an incident I once heard Dr. T. Z. Koo, a well-known Chinese Christian, tell of his own life.

He was raised in a Chinese village where the prevailing religion was Confucian. He and his family were the only Christians in the village. He early learned that the faith of his parents and the faith of the villagers were similar at many points. Both Christians and Confucianists held to the same virtues—honesty, integrity, tolerance. But he and his family believed in Jesus Christ and the others did not.

While a very young man, he became the purchasing agent for one of the Chinese railroads. One day a salesman offered him a handsome gold watch simply as a gift. Dr. Koo recognized it for what it was, an attractive bribe. Now came the test. Should he forego the ethics of honesty and accept the watch and its obligations, or should he remain true to the highest standard of conduct that he knew? It was an alluring temptation and a difficult decision. But he turned the watch down.

Why? Not because he wanted to be true to an ethical principle. He could have set that aside as many others were doing. But he could not be false to the Christ who dwelt in his heart. It was his personal loyalty to the personal Christ that was the deciding factor in his decision.

Sentence Sermon to Remember: If God sends us on stony paths, He provides strong shoes.—Corrie ten Boom.

Questions for Pupils on the Next Lesson. 1. Is freedom primarily liberty to do as you please? What does Scripture suggest? 2. How do you understand the meaning of sin as a form of slavery? 3. How do you explain the apparent paradox that living by God's law leads to freedom? 4. To what leadership roles do you think God is calling you and your associates? 5. What would be on your list of what you obey most in life? Why? Where is God's law on that list?

LESSON III—SEPTEMBER 21

GOD'S COVENANT AND MOSES

Background Scripture: Exodus 2:23–3:14; 19:1–9.
Devotional Reading: Jeremiah 17:7–13

KING JAMES VERSION

EXODUS 19 1 In the third month, when the children of Israel were gone forth out of the land of Egypt, the same day came they *into* the wilderness of Sinai.

2 For they were departed from Rephidim, and were come *to* the desert of Sinai, and had pitched in the wilderness; and there Israel camped before the mount.

3 And Moses went up unto God, and the LORD called unto him out of the mountain, saying, Thus shalt thou say to the house of Jacob, and tell the children of Israel;

4 Ye have seen what I did unto the Egyptians, and *how* I bare you on eagles' wings, and brought you unto myself.

5 Now therefore, if ye will obey my voice indeed, and keep my covenant, then ye shall be a peculiar treasure unto me above all people: for all the earth *is* mine:

6 And ye shall be unto me a kingdom of priests, and a holy nation. These *are* the words which thou shalt speak unto the children of Israel.

7 And Moses came and called for the elders of the people, and laid before their faces all these words which the Lord commanded him.

8 And all the people answered together, and said, All that the LORD hath spoken we will do. And Moses returned the words of the people unto the LORD.

9 And the LORD said unto Moses, Lo, I come unto thee in a thick cloud, that the people may hear when I speak with thee, and believe thee for ever. And Moses told the words of the people unto the LORD.

REVISED STANDARD VERSION

EXODUS 19 1 On the third new moon after the people of Israel had gone forth out of the land of Egypt, on that day they came into the wilderness of Sinai. 2 And when they set out from Rephidim and came into the wilderness of Sinai, they encamped in the wilderness; and there Israel encamped before the mountain. 3 And Moses went up to God, and the LORD called to him out of the mountain, saying, "Thus you shall say to the house of Jacob, and tell the people of Israel: 4 You have seen what I did to the Egyptians, and how I bore you on eagles' wings and brought you to myself. 5 Now therefore, if you will obey my voice and keep my covenant, you shall be my own possession among all peoples; for all the earth is mine, 6 and you shall be to me a kingdom of priests and a holy nation. These are the words which you shall speak to the children of Israel." 7 So Moses came and called the elders of the people, and set before them all these words which the LORD had commanded him. 8 And all the people answered together and said, "All that the LORD has spoken we will do." And Moses reported the words of the people to the LORD. 9 And the LORD said to Moses, "Lo, I am coming to you in a thick cloud, that the people may hear when I speak with you, and may also believe you for ever."

Then Moses told the words of the people to the LORD.

KEY VERSE. . . . *if you obey my voice and keep my covenant, you shall be my own possession among all peoples* . . . . Exodus 19:5 (RSV).

HOME DAILY BIBLE READINGS

Sept. *15.* M. *Drawn from the Water.* Exodus 2:1–10.
Sept. *16.* T. *Running from Danger.* Exodus 2:11–25.
Sept. *17.* W. *Hearing God's Call.* Exodus 3:1–10.
Sept. *18.* T. *Protest and Promise.* Exodus 3:11–22.
Sept. *19.* F. *The Song of Victory.* Exodus 15:1–13.
Sept. *20.* S. *Promising to Obey God.* Exodus 19:1–8.
Sept. *21.* S. *Learning God's Way.* Exodus 33:9–19.

BACKGROUND

Three months after they had left Egypt, the children of Israel, led by the great Moses, stood at the foot of Sinai. Think, now, what they had been through before they arrived here. They had suffered greatly in Egypt, and they had heard this courageous leader cry to Pharaoh in Egypt, "Let my people go!" With the scars of their taskmaster's whips on their backs, they had plunged into the desert and the wilderness, on what someone has called "the greatest labor march in history." They had suffered in the desert, too; here they were lashed with the whips of hunger and fear, and they longed to go back to Egypt where they had plenty to eat. This was anything but an orderly march; it was more like a loosely bound mob of runaway slaves fighting among themselves more often than fighting any strange desert enemy, complaining, bickering, making it as difficult as possible for Moses to bring them to the gates of the Promised Land.

There was little if any cohesion among them no sense of union in work or worship, no established code of laws to guide them. That's what they were like when they pitched camp at the foot of Sinai—a desert-worn people at the foot of a desert peak. And here it was that God called Moses to come up into the mountain for a conference.

NOTES ON THE PRINTED TEXT

I. . . . "Thus you shall say . . . and tell the people of Israel: You have seen . . . how I bore you on eagles' wings and brought you to myself. Exodus 19:3, 4 (RSV). Eagle's wings? That must have stunned them, for they seem never to have been conscious of being held up or empowered by any eagle's wings. That was the basic trouble with them, the reason for their disunity, their complaints. They forgot, on that march, that the march had been ordered of God through Moses. It was at His command that they had left Egypt, but they had forgotten that.

But never for a moment had God forgotten them. As an eagle dives under one of her offspring and comes up under him to stop his fall from the nest, so God had held up His children in every desert crisis. He had held them up when in fear they faced the crossing of the Red Sea with the troops of Pharaoh not far behind: it was God who had confused and driven off the Egyptians! When they were hungry, He gave them manna; when they thirsted, He gave them water. How could they ever forget *that?* It was God, with Moses as His intermediary, who had brought them to the foot of Sinai, where He awaited them with the promise of a new covenant.

The people may have been surprised at the sight of Moses going up the mountain to talk with God, but we can believe that Moses was not surprised, for Moses had never forgotten God. All down the road, he must have been brooding over the condition of his people, brooding and praying and wondering how to do what he had to do to make them a united people under God. This moment of inspiration was rooted in long years of labor. *Inspiration usually comes that way!*

II. *Now therefore, if ye will obey my voice indeed, and keep my covenant, then ye shall be a peculiar treasure unto me above all people . . . .* Exodus 19:5. This is the Mosaic covenant, instituted by a God who patiently sought after His people even when they had stopped seeking Him! God never gave up on Israel because He saw in them "a peculiar treasure."

All nations, as all men, are "called according to his purpose" (Romans 8:28). In the Greeks, God had a people gifted in the golden arts and philosophies. In the Romans, He had a nation strong in law and organization. Each nation had, and has, special gifts which God can use, provided the nations let Him use them. But He had something strangely beautiful, peculiar, in Israel: here was a classically *religious* nation. —

Have you ever wondered why God selected Israel as His precious and unique people? Dorothy Parker once wrote a biting little verse: "How odd/of God/To choose/The Jews." Odd? Why didn't He choose the Romans, or the Greeks? He chose the Jews because the Jews were a peculiarly *religious* nation, in spite of all their faults and errors. They were the one people most likely and the best equipped to spread the idea of one universal God across the world—and that is exactly what they did in ages to come. The religious ideas and ideals of the Jews have influenced the whole world.

That was God's aim with them: *if they would obey His voice,* He would make of them, in this new covenant, a nation of priests, a "priesthood of all believers." Whoever wrote this down in Exodus believed with all his heart that every man must become his own priest, that religion could not be left in the hands of a few leaders or officials or intensely religious men; it must be the life and work of *all* who believed in Him and obeyed His voice and will.

Note, here, that this covenant wasn't one just between Moses and God; it was a covenant that embraced *all the people,* and demanded allegiance from them.

III. *And all the people answered together, and said, All that the Lord hath spoken we will do.* Exodus 19:8. Give them credit! Their wilderness experience had been filled with error, filled with half-belief and often with a shameful incredulity, but the flame still burned even though at times it flickered weakly. A commentator says, "The people of Israel were not able to carry out in the coming years the resolve they here made, but they probably did better than they would have done if they had never reached for a moment this high peak of self-consecration."— J. Edgar Park, in *The Interpreters Bible.* They knew the right way, and they wanted to follow it, but, even as you and I, they had their bad moments.

IV. *. . . Lo, I am coming to you in a thick cloud, that the people may hear when I speak with you, and may also believe you for ever.* Exodus

19:9 (RSV). Surely, though the people agreed quickly to do as the Lord commanded, there were probably among the people certain ones who wanted proof that God had spoken directly to Moses. Here God promises yet another interview with Moses in a thick cloud, *within hearing of the people.* The people would not see God, any more than Moses had seen Him, but there would be that voice coming out of the cloud, proof eloquent that God had spoken to their leader. They were told to prepare themselves for that great moment to come, to wash their clothes, cleanse themselves of all defilement, so that they might appear clean and undefiled when the voice came.

In 1 John 4:12 we read that "No man hath *seen* God at any time." The *Living Bible* puts it, "For though we have never yet seen God, when we love each other God lives in us . . . ." That is well said. No man has seen Him, but all men can hear His voice, though it comes in a "cloud" from afar. We can hear it, if we have ears to hear— if we prepare ourselves to hear it.

Moses heard it, loud and clear, and he set about preparing for the great day when God would speak to him again and put His law in His servant's hands.

SUGGESTIONS TO TEACHERS

The idea of God's covenant, as we have seen, goes back to the earliest days of the Bible. And the covenant theme is woven into the tapestry of our lives as God's people. Although we are working in this lesson with the covenant and Moses, we are not studying this ancient story as history buffs. We are listening to Scripture to understand better how God's covenant applies to us.

As teacher, you should first let the biblical account (Exodus 2:23–3:14) confront you. The following salient parts will help you develop your lesson.

1. *PRESENCE.* Take note that the Lord confronts Moses. The symbolism of fire and flame are picture words to describe the awesome power and presence of God's Spirit. Any person who has ever been aware of the call and the nearness of the Lord recognizes the crackling energy His presence brings. "I felt my heart strangely warmed," John Wesley described his conversion encounter with God's presence. Pentecost in Acts 2 tells of the Spirit confronting them like tongues of fire. Point out to your class that God's presence persists, intrudes, and surprises His people today. Sometimes He interrupts us in our daily work, as He did with Moses (who was tending his sheep). The main thing to impress on your class is to be ready to respond to God's nudges, whenever He makes His presence known.

2. *PROTECTOR.* When God introduces Himself to a person, it is not for private "deals." Moses quickly discovered that the purpose of God presenting Himself to Moses was to send Moses to Egypt. The Lord makes it unmistakably clear that He hears the cries of the oppressed Hebrews. Furthermore, the Lord states that He remembers His commitments to Abraham's descendants (His covenant with them). Help your class to remember that God remembers the hurting and insists on being their Protector. Examine what this implies for your class today.

3. *PROOF.* "How can I go to the king of Egypt?" Moses complains; "I am nobody" (Exodus 3:11). Moses whimpers that he needs some positive proof that everything will turn out nicely. Don't we all? Remind your class that Moses gets only the assurance from God that He will be with Moses. The Lord's I-will-be-with-you is sufficient for whatever task He lays on us. Encourage your people to recall tough assignments they or others have had in which there were no proofs of success, but only God's promise of His presence.

4. *POWER.* Finally, in your lesson, call your class's attention to the name of God which is given to Moses: *"I am Who causes to be!"* What inexhaustible power that suggests! That power is still given faithful followers through the Risen Lord.

GOD'S COVENANT AND MOSES

Feeling Depends on Being Right With God. Russell Baker recently wrote about "the feel-good movement." Swamis, gurus, psychologists, writers, and "evangelists of sexual joy" try to persuade people that they have a right to feel good and happy. But Baker thinks the ability to feel good is "a matter of genes" rather than autosuggestion. Some persons are born to feel good, some are not.

Some think religion is designed to make people feel good. Smile, for God loves you. You are OK and I am OK. Think positively. Churchgoing families are the happiest.

Hellfire and brimstone sermons are out. Also out are words like *wrath* . . . *sin* . . . *eternal death* . . . *damnation,* for they do not make people happy.

One can hardly hope to feel elated every time God speaks. Jonah was not happy when he was commissioned to preach. Job was not pleased when he argued with God. Jesus said, "Blessed are the poor in spirit, those who mourn, those who are persecuted for my sake."

Being poor in spirit, mournful, and persecuted is what the "feel-good" preachers seek to avoid. But Jesus would have us believe that in spite of life's inconveniences, one can be blessed—blessed in the sense of believing God has spoken and that feeling that depends on being right with God even when all seems to go wrong.

The secular person seeks pleasure with freedom from problems. But in discomfort and pain, people of faith realize that only in a fool's paradise can they expect no trouble. A person of faith, like Job of old, has learned to accept the inconvenience of life because he realizes there is more to God than wisdom has imagined and that there is a divine control of the universe which cannot be understood—and all this will continue to be all right even though the Lord may slay him.—Rev. Joseph B. Mohr, Call Chronicle, Allentown, PA, August 6, 1977.

Key Link. Anniejean Moll never was able to attend the meetings of FISH (Friends in Service Helping) of Catasauqua, Pennsylvania, but she was considered a key link in the organization.

Although bedridden with multiple sclerosis, she was one of the original members of the group that started FISH two years earlier in her town.

And for over two years she was the group's answering service, taking calls for help and channeling them to the volunteers on duty who could best meet the caller's needs. She did this in bed from 7 A.M. to 7 P.M.

"Jeannie could have been down and pitying herself," board member Mary Heist said, "But she didn't. She was a catalyst for the organization."

Her duties involved answering the phone, learning what was needed (temporary child care, transportation, house checks, neighborhood aid in emergency situations, or delivery of Meals on Wheels) and transmitting the phone number and information to the volunteer on duty.

But she often went farther than that. According to Mrs. Heist, she often helped callers work out problems over the phone. "She buffered a lot of things."

Mrs. Moll was taken to the hospital, and died a few days later in the autumn of 1978. Those whose lives had been touched by her realized that in spite of pain and illness, Anniejean Moll had covenanted with God and others to be faithful as long as she had any strength. No wonder she was a key link.

God calls each of us to be such covenanted key links in His work of helping others. Regardless of how much or how little we may have, we can serve Him!

Burning Bush Experiences. Moses learned that being available to God meant being available to others. Furthermore, he discovered "holy ground" in the midst of being available to others in everyday life.

As parents, we find that such occasions and places come when we are busy but take time to be available to God and others. I remember occasions when the children were small and one of them would come rushing up, shouting excitedly, "Oh, Daddy! Come and see the sunset with me!" Often, I would be tempted to say, "Not now, Ellen. Can't you see that Daddy is busy preparing his sermon?" But I would drop the sermon preparation, and stand with a little girl for a few minutes by the window. I would feel a little hand reach up and take mine as we gazed silently at the beauty of the sunset. Together, we would experience what it was to be on holy ground. Almost invariably, the burning bush times in life seem to have been when I have allowed interruptions to make me available to God and other persons!

Questions to Pupils on the Next Lesson. 1. What did God do for His people from Abraham to Joshua? 2. How did Joshua challenge the people to serve God? 3. What were Joshua's doubts about the people's obedience to God? 4. What was the nature of the covenant between Joshua's contemporaries and God? 5. Is there still a relationship between apostasy, punishment, repentance, and deliverance from oppression?

TOPIC FOR YOUTH
THE WAY TO FREEDOM

"Thanks for Talking to Me." Sheri had been babysitting for days. Between responsibilities with the noisy, demanding children and taking dozens of telephone messages for others, she was weary. Sheri could hardly wait for a day by herself, away from people making demands on

her. She planned to go by herself to a secluded beach and spend the morning reading. It had been weeks, she remembered since she had got any time alone to read. She anticipated the luxury of not having to prepare lunches, answer telephones, or settle squabbles between children.

Sheri settled herself comfortably with her paperback on the beach. She sighed with pleasure. At last, she could relax alone, undisturbed, without responsibilities. Suddenly, a woman flopped down beside her on the beach. Sheri was tempted to get up and walk away. She resented the intrusion. Sheri tried to ignore her, and started to try to concentrate on her book. Before she could resume reading, however, the woman began to talk.

The woman poured out her story, a sad saga of a series of broken relationships, a divorce, a struggle for economic survival for herself and her baby, a lonely existence in a large city. After thirty-five minutes of monologue, during which Sheri had simply listened, the woman stopped. With tears in her eyes, she suddenly looked at Sheri gratefully and said, "Thank you so much for talking to me."

Sheri wondered. She had not said a word! The woman had done all the talking! But she was even more startled at the next comment by the woman.

The woman stood up and said quietly, "Thank you for giving me enough faith to go on."

Sheri began to understand that giving up some of her freedom for others' sakes was what gave meaning to her faith and the faith of others.

Free to Plunge on! Our freedom as the covenanted people is meant to be used to move ahead for God and for others. It may not be used selfishly. It means marching on with boldness, even when everything seems stacked against us. It often means not understanding the purposes or having proof of success.

There is an ancient Hebrew legend that when Moses struck the Red Sea with his rod nothing happened. It was only when the first man plunged in up to his shoulders that the sea parted.

Luther's remark is appropriate: "Had Moses waited until he understood how Israel could elude Pharaoh's armies, they might have been in Egypt still."

Pharaoh's Mummy Goes to Paris. The mummy of Pharaoh Ramses II has been shipped from Cairo to Paris, where it is to undergo possible treatment for a "disease."

A French physician examining the mummy last year found evidence that parts of it were being destroyed by mysterious growths, perhaps a fungus. The mummy is now to be tested and perhaps treated for the growths at the Musée de l'Homme in Paris.

Ramses II, who was the fourth king of the nineteenth dynasty of ancient Egypt, is considered by most experts to have been the Pharaoh mentioned in Exodus. He died in 1225 B.C. and examination of the mummy has shown that he had reached an advanced age.

Actually, however, the Pharaoh was "diseased" at the time of Moses! His refusal to recognize the Lord or to grant freedom to the oppressed children of Israel meant he was destroying himself even at the time of the Exodus. His mummy might have endured, but his life was decaying before 1225 B.C. The uncovenanted person is not free, but bound in the mummy cloth of greed, resentment, and fear. Moses, not the Pharaoh, knew a life with God which outlasts time itself!

Sentence Sermon to Remember: Moses served not only Israel, but left his mark on the social structure, thinking, ethics, and religion of all humanity. No man ever had more to contend with and no man, alone, has helped his brothers more.—J. C. Martin.

Questions for Pupils on the Next Lesson. 1. What do you recall that God has done for you during the years of your lifetime? 2. Why must your entire family obey and serve the Lord? 3. What happens when one's actions do not match one's words? 4. What are some examples of allowing bad habits to develop that you have observed in others or in yourself? 5. Is there a connection between disobedience and punishment, repentance and deliverance?

LESSON IV—SEPTEMBER 28

GOD'S COVENANT AND JOSHUA

Background Scripture: Joshua 24:1–31; Judges 2.
Devotional Reading: Psalms 15

KING JAMES VERSION

JOSHUA 24   14 Now therefore fear the LORD, and serve him in sincerity and in truth; and put away the gods which your fathers served on the other side of the flood, and in Egypt; and serve ye the LORD.

15 And if it seem evil unto you to serve the LORD, choose you this day whom ye will serve; whether the gods which your fathers served that *were* on the other side of the flood, or the gods of the Amorites, in whose land ye dwell: but as for me and my house, we will serve the LORD.

16 And the people answered and said, God forbid that we should forsake the LORD, to serve other gods;

17 For the LORD our God, he *it is* that brought us up and our fathers out of the land of Egypt, from the house of bondage, and which did those great signs in our sight, and preserved us in all the way wherein we went, and among all the people through whom we passed:

18 And the LORD drave out from before us all the people, even the Amorites which dwelt in the land: *therefore* will we also serve the LORD; for he is our God.

19 And Joshua said unto the people, Ye cannot serve the LORD: for he *is* a holy God; he *is* a jealous God; he will not forgive your transgressions nor your sins.

20 If ye forsake the LORD, and serve strange gods, then he will turn and do you hurt, and consume you, after that he hath done you good.

21 And the people said unto Joshua, Nay; but we will serve the LORD.

22 And Joshua said unto the people, Ye *are* witnesses against yourselves that ye have chosen you and Lord, to serve him. And they said, *We are* witnesses.

REVISED STANDARD VERSION

JOSHUA 24   14 "Now therefore fear the LORD, and serve him in sincerity and in faithfulness; put away the gods which your fathers served beyond the River, and in Egypt, and serve the LORD. 15 And if you be unwilling to serve the LORD, choose this day whom you will serve, whether the gods your fathers served in the region beyond the River, or the gods of the Amorites in whose land you dwell; but as for me and my house, we will serve the LORD."

16 Then the people answered, "Far be it from us that we should forsake the LORD, to serve other gods; 17 for it is the LORD our God who brought us and our fathers up from the land of Egypt, out of the house of bondage, and who did those great signs in our sight, and preserved us in all the way that we went, and among all the peoples through whom we passed; 18 and the LORD drove out before us all the peoples, the Amorites who lived in the land; therefore we also will serve the LORD, for he is our God."

19 But Joshua said to the people, "You cannot serve the LORD; for he is a holy God; he is a jealous God; he will not forgive your transgressions or your sins. 20 If you forsake the LORD and serve foreign gods, then he will turn and do you harm, and consume you, after having done you good." 21 And the people said to Joshua, "Nay; but we will serve the LORD." 22 Then Joshua said to the people, "You are witnesses against yourselves that you have chosen the LORD, to serve him." And they said, "We are witnesses." 23 He said, "Then put away the foreign gods which are among you, and incline

23 Now therefore put away, *said he,* the strange gods which *are* among you, and incline your heart unto the LORD God of Israel.

24 And the people said unto Joshua, The LORD our God will we serve, and his voice will we obey.

25 So Joshua made a covenant with the people that day, and set them a statute and an ordinance in Shechem.

your heart to the LORD, the God of Israel." 24 And the people said to Joshua, "The LORD our God we will serve, and his voice we will obey." 25 So Joshua made a covenant with the people that day, and made statutes and ordinances for them at Shechem.

KEY VERSE: . . . The Lord our God will we serve, and his voice will we obey. Joshua 24:24.

HOME DAILY BIBLE READINGS

Sept. 22. M. *Joshua's Good Advice.* Joshua 23:1-3, 11-16.
Sept. 23. T. *Joshua Remembers God's Blessing.* Joshua 24:1-8.
Sept. 24. W. *Joshua Gives an Example.* Joshua 24:9-18.
Sept. 25. T. *The People Choose God.* Joshua 24:19-31.
Sept. 26. F. *The People Forget God.* Judges 2:1-13.
Sept. 27. S. *Another Opportunity.* Judges 2:14-23.
Sept. 28. S. *God's Word to Joshua.* Joshua 1:1-9.

BACKGROUND

Joshua was a soldier and a gentleman. It was he who led the people of Israel in their conquest of Canaan, but, unlike most military heroes, he wanted no decorations for that, no credit. He had won great battles at Rephidim, Jericho, Gibeon, and Ai, and he insisted that it was not he who had won the battles, but God. After his wars were over, and his people settled in Canaan, we hear little about him, except that he divided the land among the tribes and preached two good sermons. We are reading one of those sermons in our Scripture for today's lesson, and it is Joshua's farewell to a people he loved—and a sermon that produced a strange covenant.

NOTES ON THE PRINTED TEXT

I. . . . fear the Lord, and serve him in sincerity . . . and put away the gods which your fathers served . . . . Joshua 24:14. The scene is laid in Shechem, the famous old shrine-city where Abraham had built an altar; in this sacred place, the old heroic leader has gathered the people, the elders, officers, and judges. He has brought them to present themselves before God, and to give them a few words of good advice.

He starts with an account of all that the Lord God has done for them, and for their fathers—for Father Abraham and his people, for Isaac and Jacob and Esau and their descendants, for Moses, who at the command of God had brought them out of Egypt and given them the land He had promised. And he tells them how God (not Joshua) had truly conquered the Amorites and the Moabites.

Dramatically, Joshua makes it seem that God Himself was talking to these Israelites. ". . . I [God] have given you a land for which you did not labour, and cities which ye built not . . ." (Joshua 24:13). "I, God, did this. *You* did not do it! By your own strength, you could never have done it. You speak of it as your land, your country, but it is *mine!"*

How often we make the same mistake; we talk as though through our own human ability we had built our country, or our Church, or our society, without any help whatever from God. We are blind if we do not see the hand of God working in our history, and in our lives.

II. . . . *choose you this day whom ye will serve* . . . . Joshua 24:15. Much as Joshua lauded the ancestors of Israel, he knew that they too often had been worshipers of pagan idols and heathen gods when they lived "beyond the flood" (beyond the Euphrates and in Egypt). Even settled in Canaan, they now and then bowed to the gods of the Amorites. If they wanted to survive, Joshua warns them, they must stop that *immediately*: "Choose ye this day . . ." whether you will put your trust in God or in the gods of the heathen. You may serve one or the other; you cannot serve both.

How often we have the same vital choice to make! How often we forget the God who has made and guided us, and gone off to worship the petty, false gods of gold, success, unrestrained pleasure that give back degradation and decay of the moral and spiritual self. Life is often just one alternative, one choice after another, and one has to be careful in his choosing between them.

"As for me and my house," Joshua told them, "we will serve the Lord." A good commander never orders his men to do anything he would not be willing to do himself. He and his house, said the old soldier, chose to serve the God of their fathers, the one true God. That is proof enough that Joshua was a man living a God-centered life. Such a life is a matter of choice; God does not *compel* any of us to live such a life. Salvation and the good life are a matter of choice with all of us: we can "go either way," but we must be ready to accept the results, however we go. Dale Evans put it well when she describes what happened to her when she stopped seeking fame and fortune and gave her life to God: "I sought happiness at the foot of a rainbow, and I found it at the foot of the cross." Choose ye . . . !

III. *And the people answered and said, God forbid that we should forsake the Lord, to serve other gods.* Joshua 24:16. How good that sounds! It might have been the eloquence and the example of God-centered Joshua that led them to say that in a burst of enthusiasm. It may also have been that they had been convinced by the experiences of their fathers long ago. They were admitting that without the mighty power of God, they would have failed, would have died in the wilderness; they wanted to serve a God born to them in the fires of hardship, suffering, and war. They were convinced. They would follow God, and Him only.

But—and what a but it is!—Joshua is not quite convinced that they understand what they are saying, and that they do not fully understand what they must *do*, as well as *promise*. God, he tells them, will *not* be satisfied with a promise to worship Him; He demands action after the promise, demands that they put aside once and forever any loyalty to any "foreign" god. God tolerates no rivals. God calls for enthusiasm *and* all-out devotion. God despises compromise.

IV. *But the people answered, "We choose the Lord!"* Joshua 24:21

(Living Bible Paraphrase). They shouted it. For the second time, they cried out that they were on the Lord's side all the way. Yes, they chose God; yes, they would both promise *and* obey Him *alone.* They wanted Joshua to understand that.

He understood; yet, knowing them as he did, he was still troubled about their actions in the future. All right, he says, you have said it. "You have heard yourselves say it (v. 22, *Living Bible*) and you will be witnesses against yourselves if you break that promise and fail to follow God. All right: *now break up your idols*, and see to it that you obey Him.

It might be good for all of us to look deep into the future when we promise God *anything* and ask ourselves if we can walk the narrow way with Him when the storms and the struggles come. Many a man, seriously ill, has promised God that if God will help him recover, he will serve God forever. But—when he is well again—somehow he forgets that and goes the old way again.

So Joshua led them into a covenant at Shechem; God did not have any part in *this* covenant; it was purely the will of the people. Then Joshua died, and they buried him in Mount Ephraim, and they were saddened as he left them, and they remembered the covenant, and they kept the covenant faithfully not only during the years he was with them but during the time of the elders who lived at the time (*see* Joshua 24:31). But now read the first two chapters of the Book of Judges and see what happened, so soon after Joshua was gone: "and there arose another generation . . . which knew not the Lord . . . And the children of Israel did evil in the sight of the Lord, and served Baalim" (Judges 2, 10–11).

How easily, how quickly, do so many of us become backsliders!

SUGGESTIONS TO TEACHERS

A pastor in Tennessee reported calling on a family which had grown inactive in his congregation. When he tactfully raised the topic of their absences, he inquired whether they had been offended or whether something had happened to cool their commitments. No, there had been nothing. The pastor, noting that the family seemed untroubled by the way it had been so inactive, bluntly asked what church membership meant. "Oh," gushed the wife, "Jim and I are born-again Christians all right, but you see we're just so busy with so many other things on Saturday nights and Sundays, you know, club parties, trips to the lake, our entertaining, well, Reverend, we just cannot do everything."

Choose! This is the key idea in the lesson for today. God's covenant with Joshua offers your class a prime opportunity to consider the choices which must be made in every person's busy life. "We just cannot do everything," as the Tennessee woman says. Study Joshua 24 and Judges 2 in the light of this thought.

1. *DEMAND FOR DECISION.* God chooses. Remind your class how He chose His people in the Old Testament stories. Also remind your class how God has chosen each member today. Furthermore, He empowers those He chooses to carry out their assignments. "Your swords and your bows had nothing to do with it . . . I give you a land," God tells Joshua's people (*see* Joshua 24:12). Joshua nails his followers with

the inevitable call for decision. "Choose this day whom you will serve!" (24:15).

2. *OBLIGATIONS OF OBEDIENCE.* Point your lesson toward the call for a response to God's choosing us. Insist that your class members grasp the requirement of *obeying* the Lord. You may wish to spark discussion by posing such a question as, "If arrested for being a Christian, would there be enough evidence to convict you?"

3. *SERIOUSNESS OF SERVICE.* Obeying God means serving Him and others. Point out that God's call is never to bestow a status, but to summon for service. God's people are a servant people. Tie in the covenant theme with the way Jesus Christ came to serve. Our covenant with Him calls for serious ministering to others.

4. *COMMITMENT TO COMMUNITY.* There are no hermit Christians. God's covenant with us puts in a community of those who are chosen, decided, and obligated to serve together. As teacher, you should also take time in this lesson to foster deeper understanding among your people that the Church is a covenanted family.

TOPIC FOR ADULTS
GOD'S COVENANT AND JOSHUA

First Things First. At the wedding dinner of the illustrious artist Francois Millet, his grandmother said to him. "Remember, my Francois, that you are a Christian before you are a painter. Never sacrifice on the altar of Baal."

Millet listened intently, then replied, "Even if they cover the canvass with gold and ask me to paint a 'St. Francis possessed by the devil,' I will never consent."

Have you chosen who you are? Are you a Christian before you are a painter, or whatever your profession may be? Have you made the decision that God comes first, even before fame or fortune?

God calls you to covenant with Him and each other, to keep those promises that He must be preeminent. First, you are a Christian, and you must live that choice in all areas of your life.

Ten Stepped Forward. Missionaries returning to the United States recently reported a revealing story about the Christian contribution in India, where only 2½ percent of the population are Christian. Government medical colleges in India graduate 10,000 new doctors annually. Christian medical colleges in India graduate 100 new doctors annually. When the government asked for volunteers among these graduates to work with the victims of leprosy, ten young doctors volunteered to serve . . . and all of them were graduates of the Christian medical colleges.

Christians understand that they are covenanted. Covenanted people realize that they are chosen and must choose! No surprise to believers that those who stepped forward were members of the covenanted community!

Choose to Stay! Rufus Mosely once met with a pastor who told him he was planning to resign becaue he felt his congregation needed a more able pastor, one with a deeper life of prayer and dedication. Rufus Mosely agreed with the Church's need, but asked the pastor why he was running away. "Instead," Mosely gently advised, "Why don't you stay and, with God's help, become that better pastor?"

The man stayed. The congregation and he grew together in their understanding of God's pledge of faithfulness as they faithfully tried to obey and serve Him.

Have your church and your pastor been helped to grow in the strength of God's covenant?

Questions for Pupils on the Next Lesson. 1. Why is it so necessary to have an identity and a heritage? 2. How much should God's people be concerned about the church building they erect for Him? 3. How may the dreams of adults be passed on in the activities of their children? Should they? 4. In what ways do you see God keeping His covenant with the Church today? With you personally? 5. What sense of historical continuity do you see in God's covenant with the patriarchs, David, and us?

TOPIC FOR YOUTH
DOING WHAT YOU SAY

Missing the Pass. Recently, a hard-fought high-school championship football game was lost in the closing seconds by a silly error by a star player. Ordinarily, the player had what sportscasters call "glue on his fingers" and seemed to snatch passes which were impossible to catch. He had a brilliant record and a winning season. College scouts were in the stands. In the waning seconds of the play-off, with his team trailing 13-10, this end streaked down the field. He was in the clear. A beautiful pass spiralled toward him. Player and football were timed to intersect perfectly; it would be an easy catch, and the field was open to the goal line. The game was as good as won. The fans screamed with joy. Suddenly, unexpectedly, the end bobbled the ball as it met his outstretched hands. It seemed impossible, but he dropped what should have been an easy pass. The post-game movies showed what had happened. For just a moment, the end took his eyes off the ball to take a look at a linebacker from the opposing team who was galloping toward him.

That's all it took to miss the pass.

That boy's failure to do what he had known and what he had said he would do cost him and his team a state championship. Instead of keeping his eye on the ball as he had been taught, he permitted himself to be diverted for a brief moment.

The moment we allow our attention to be distracted from God's commands, we will be in trouble. We may say that we will be covenanted to the Lord. The real question is *doing* what we say we believe!

Costly Hole. On production lines which manufacture today's aircraft, workers need a jeweler's touch to fit parts within supersonic tolerances. A single, one-inch hole in a wing can slow a modern jet by as much as 100 miles-per-hour!

In our lives, apparently trivial slips and lapses of not doing what we say may slow our progress as Christians. The God who covenants with us demands we covenant with Him and with each other for "precision living."

No Excuse Sunday. Realizing how often we choose to use weak excuses for not being part of the covenanted community on Sunday mornings, an anonymous wag decided to put together a "no excuse" Sunday worship service. Here is what appeared:

"To make it possible for everyone to attend church next Sunday, we are going to make it very special:

"A cot will be placed in the Sanctuary for those who say, 'Sunday is my only day for sleep.'

"Murine will be available for those with tired eyes from watching TV too late on Saturday night.

"We will have steel helmets for those who say, 'The roof would cave in if I came to church.'

"Blankets will be furnished for those who think the church is too cold and fans for those who say it is too hot.

"We will have hearing aids for those who think the Pastor speaks too softly and cotton for those who say he speaks too loudly.

"There will be score cards for listing the hypocrites present.

"One hundred TV dinners will be provided for those who can't go to church and cook dinner also.

"We will have a selection of trees and grass for those who like to see God in nature.

"A putting green will be placed near the altar for those who say, 'Sunday is my day for golf.'

"The Sanctuary will be decorated with both Christmas poinsettias and Easter lilies for those who have never seen the church without them."

(The above selection was copied from the Newsletter of Clinton Presbyterian Church, Clinton, Maryland.)

Sentence Sermon to Remember: Consecration is handing God a blank sheet to fill in with your name signed at the bottom.—M. H. Miller.

Questions for Pupils on the Next Lesson. 1. How does God bless people who allow Him to use them? 2. How does God promise us His presence? 3. Does God turn His back on us when we fall short of His expectations? Does He punish us? 4. When should Christians feel or not feel joy in their relationship with God? 5. Why do you think it is important to have a sense of identity and heritage? 6. In what ways does your faith help you have an identity and sense of heritage?

LESSON V—OCTOBER 5

GOD'S COVENANT AND DAVID

Background Scripture: 2 Samuel 7; 1 Chronicles 16:1–36
Devotional Reading: Romans 14:1–9

KING JAMES VERSION	REVISED STANDARD VERSION
2 SAMUEL 7 8 Now therefore so shalt thou say unto my servant David, Thus saith the LORD of hosts, I took thee from the sheepcote, from following the sheep, to be ruler over my people, over Israel:	2 SAMUEL 7 8 "Now therefore thus you shall say to my servant David, 'Thus says the LORD of hosts, I took you from the pasture, from following the sheep, that you should be prince over my people Israel; 9 and I have

2 SAMUEL 7 8 Now therefore so shalt thou say unto my servant David, Thus saith the LORD of hosts, I took thee from the sheepcote, from following the sheep, to be ruler over my people, over Israel:

9 And I was with thee whithersoever thou wentest, and have cut off all thine enemies out of thy sight, and have made thee a great name, like unto the name of the great *men* that *are* in the earth.

10 Moreover I will appoint a place for my people Israel, and will plant them, that they may dwell in a place of their own, and move no more; neither shall the children of wickedness afflict them any more, as beforetime,

11 And as since the time that I commanded judges *to be* over my people Israel, and have caused thee to rest from all thine enemies. Also the LORD telleth thee that he will make thee a house.

12 And when thy days be fulfilled, and thou shalt sleep with thy fathers, I will set up thy seed after thee, which shall proceed out of thy bowels, and I will establish his kingdom.

13 He shall build a house for my name, and I will stablish the throne of his kingdom for ever.

14 I will be his father, and he shall be my son. If he commit iniquity, I will chasten him with the rod of men, and with the stripes of the children of men:

15 But my mercy shall not depart away from him, as I took it from Saul, whom I put away before thee.

16 And thine house and thy kingdom shall be established for ever before thee: thy throne shall be established for ever.

2 SAMUEL 7 8 "Now therefore thus you shall say to my servant David, 'Thus says the LORD of hosts, I took you from the pasture, from following the sheep, that you should be prince over my people Israel; 9 and I have been with you wherever you went, and have cut off all your enemies from before you; and I will make for you a great name, like the name of the great ones of the earth. 10 And I will appoint a place for my people Israel, and will plant them, that they may dwell in their own place, and be disturbed no more; and violent men shall afflict them no more, as formerly, 11 from the time that I appointed judges over my people Israel; and I will give you rest from all your enemies. Moreover the LORD declares to you that the LORD will make you a house. 12 When your days are fulfilled and you lie down with your fathers, I will raise up your son after you, who shall come forth from your body, and I will establish his kingdom. 13 He shall build a house for my name, and I will establish the throne of his kingdom for ever. 14 I will be his father, and he shall be my son. When he commits iniquity, I will chasten him with the rod of men, with the stripes of the sons of men; 15 but I will not take my steadfast love from him, as I took it from Saul, whom I put away from before you. 16 And your house and your kingdom shall be made sure for ever before me; your throne shall be established for ever.' "

KEY VERSE: "And your house and your kingdom shall be made sure for ever before me; your throne shall be established for ever. 2 Samuel 7:16 (RSV).

41

HOME DAILY BIBLE READINGS

Sept. 29. M. *Desire to Honor God.* 2 Samuel 7:1–7.
Sept. 30. T. *God Honors and Reassures His Own.* 2 Samuel 8:8–17
Oct.   1. W. *Right Response to God's Goodness.* 2 Samuel 7:18–24.
Oct.   2. T. *A Plea for Blessing.* 2 Samuel 7:25–29.
Oct.   3. F. *Gratitude in Worship.* 1 Chronicles 1:1–7.
Oct.   4. S. *A God of Love to Proclaim.* 1 Chronicles 1:23, 24.
Oct.   5. S. *Honoring the Lord in Everything.* Romans 14:1–9.

BACKGROUND

David was a good man and a splendid king, but like all the rest of us,
he had his faults and his shortcomings. At times, as we read his record,
he seems to be a saint within whom a great faith lived and grew; or a
great warrior, winning great battles to the glory of God; or, alas, at other
times an adulterer and a tyrant who could stoop to murder. A many-
sided man, this David. He had a great heart and a fine mind.

Only occasionally did he stumble, rarely did he make a serious mistake. One of the most notable of his mistakes came, surprisingly, out of a
very good intention. He learned then, as some wise man wrote it down
much later in history, that the road to hell is paved with good
intentions—intentions that seem to be good but which are often not
good at all, and sometimes very dangerous.

One day he said to the Prophet Nathan, "I am ashamed, here I am
living in a palace, while the sacred ark of God is out there in a tent. That
isn't right." Certainly that didn't seem right, and when David planned to
build a great palace (Temple) for God to "dwell" in, he seemed to be
doing a great thing for God.

Actually, he was making a mistake—a mistake that most of us make, at
one time or another, in our relationship with God. David, thinking of
that Temple, was thinking of religion as an institution. And that, God
told him, was wrong.

NOTES ON THE PRINTED TEXT

I. ". . . *I took you from the pasture, from following the sheep, that
you should be prince over my people Israel; and I have been with you
wherever you went . . .* 2 Samuel 7:8, 9 (RSV). Speaking to David
through his Prophet Nathan, God reminds David that he had been chosen out of all men on earth for a peculiar but definite purpose and
mission. David hadn't made up his mind to become a king; God had
decided that, and God had guided him both as a shepherd boy and as
king. God had given him, "covenanted" him, not to work as a builder of
temples but as a king to lead Israel in the building of His Kingdom in the
hearts of men everywhere.

That did not mean that it was always wrong to build temples made
with human hands; it meant that God *needs* no particular house or temple or building in which He would live but that He would live in the
midst of His people wherever they were. He was a living, moving God;
He might speak to Moses in a tent in the wilderness, before there were
any temples at all in Israel. It has been said that the groves were God's
first temples, and that is true. God's true dwelling place is in His people,

not in a given geographical spot. We once heard a preacher try to justify
the often cruel and barbarous fighting of the Crusades on the ground
that it was right that the Holy Land be in the hands of Christians and not
Saracens. He was rebuked by another preacher who said, "We should be
interested not in gaining control of a geographical spot but in getting the
spirit of the Christ into the hearts of men." Good!

Too often, we move without consulting God as to what *He* would have
us do. Failing to do that, we have made some very bad mistakes all down
through history.

II. . . . *Moreover, the Lord declares to you that the Lord will make
you a house.* 2 Samuel 7:11 (RSV). This is a play on words, a pun with two
meanings. It can mean either "a dwelling place" or a "dynasty" and it
illustrates the main point in the attack on David's proposed temple. In
all probability, it was the Davidian dynasty that was in the mind of the
writer.

Having made it clear that God's dwelling place was in a people He
was shaping for Himself and His Kingdom, this writer puts stronger
emphasis on the promise that David's "seed" would rule Israel and that
there was to be an *eternal* covenant between God and the house (line,
dynasty) of David. That throne was established, once and for all; David's
family successors would rule after he was dead and gone, and God
would be with them, even when they were unfaithful to Him.

God has a purpose for all of us, and we are wise when we seek Him
and ask Him just what that purpose is, when we listen for His voice
instead of the voices of men or the voices of personal ambition. These
voices, at times, can be confusing, as they were to David. We are reminded here of the words spoken by an actor on a broadcast of the
"Mary Tyler Moore Show," playing the part of a priest. Asked why he
became a priest and why he gave up a career as a professional baseball
player to enter the priesthood, he said, "I had a vision in which I heard a
voice saying, 'I advise you to quit baseball immediately, and enter a
seminary to train for the priesthood.' But," said the priest, "that wasn't
the voice of God; it was the voice of my baseball manager."

Right! Some men are born athletes, some with what it takes to be a
successful businessman, or lawyer, or doctor, or dentist, or a carpenter,
or mechanic. Loud and clear came the voice to this priest: *that* was what
he should be, that was what he should do. Some are called to be priests,
ministers, evangelists, prophets, teachers, or just witnesses created to
win converts to His Kingdom. We cannot be everything, cannot be
equally skilled in all callings or professions, but we can "take account of
stock," account of our talents and abilities, and then do best what God
has equipped us to do and do it in His name and for His sake.

Now, as we read this scriptural account, we cannot help but hear a
note of conflict; we seem to see or hear not one writer, but two, telling
this story of David's problem and God's answer to him. One writer
seems to be playing down the importance of the temple—*any* temple—
and the other seems to be defending temple-building. It may just be that
there is more than one writer, here, as there is often more than one
writer involved in many places in the Old Testament (as, for instance, in
the two accounts of the Creation, in Genesis). But we should not be

confused by this, for in the end both writers seem to be saying the same thing. What both are pleading for is an awareness of the presence of God in the human heart and in human history. God is worshiped in the temple, in the Church, but He is not confined or locked up in the temple or church. We deny Him if we worship Him on Sunday in the pew, then lock the door of the church when the worship service is over and forget Him all the rest of the week! He is to be worshiped there, but He is not to be *hidden* there, "dwelling" there unseen and unnoticed in our daily lives and work.

They were not playing down the place and importance of temples and churches; they were Israelites, and the Israelites put great stress upon the centrality of their Temple as the headquarters, the place and stimulus of their religion and their religious living. But some of them, alas, lived as though He were not even *there* the other six days of the week.

We are wrong when we institutionalize our religious faith to the point at which the *institution* becomes of greater importance than the *practice.* It is only the church hypocrite who thinks he has done his whole duty to God in attending church services and dropping a quarter in the plate. When the institution becomes an end in itself, when the preservation of the structure, however hallowed it may be, becomes "all that is necessary," we are not in Christ, or of Him. It takes a lot of living beyond the walls of our beloved Church to truly become the friend of God.

Now turn to Acts 7:47, 48, and read it carefully: "But Solomon built him an house." It was Solomon who, was to build the temple! "Howbeit the most High dwelleth [does His work of love and redemption] not in the temples made with hands." There it is, in a nutshell. There is the covenant promise God made with His servant David. Do what has to be done *now*, David, wherever you are, and leave the rest to me, to God. God promised to use the seed (the descendants) of David to work out what had to be done *in the future.* Do what has to be done *now.*

God kept that covenant promise. The promise was fulfilled, finally, in the Person of our Lord and in His Church. God so loved His David that He gave him a house; he also gave him a Messiah for a son in the Davidic Line.

SUGGESTIONS TO TEACHERS

A Sunday-school class was discussing the various ways in which each member had united with the church. One or two had transferred from other congregations when they had moved to the area. Another person had come by reaffirmation of faith. One eager soul chirped, without intending to be witty, "Oh, I joined on confusion of faith."

You would probably agree that most of your class came into the covenanted community, the Church, with more confusion than confession of faith! You should gear your lesson today on the covenant with David and on God's saving us, His faith-filled people today. Remember that this is also World Communion Sunday. Remind your folks of the significance of the covenanted community throughout the earth remembering the Lord's faithfulness today. David's descendant, a greater King, brings salvation to your class and to His people everywhere.

1. *SAVED BY WHOM?* There are many cults, cures, and causes claiming to deliver people to new life. Have your class help you to list as many of these as possible. You will be surprised at the length of the list—from astrology to Zen. Without getting sidetracked into prolonged discussions on the relative merits of the claims of each of these, encourage your people to reflect on the "salvation" promises of each one of them. Next, ask if any of these reflect God's loving concern and faithfulness, such as He showed to David, and shows today through Jesus Christ?

2. *SAVED FROM WHAT?* Call attention to God's concern and faithfulness to David and his descendants. Be sure to mention the note of joy and thanks in the scriptural passages. God saves His people from hopelessness. His covenant means your class and everyone in Christ's community has an identity and a heritage!

3. *SAVED FOR WHAT?* It is important to note that God not only saves us *from* sin in all forms (hopelessness, futility, guilt, pride, etc.) but also saves us *for* something. Your lesson must also include the positive aspects of God's saving us. Since God's covenant with David in today's lesson mentions how David wanted to make David a "house," God has saved us for building Christ's "house" or rule everywhere!

TOPIC FOR ADULTS
GOD'S COVENANT AND DAVID

Treasures From Trash. A recent best-seller advertised dozens of ways to create objects of beauty from discarded materials. "In the trash box lie thrilling adventures," insisted the author. The writer told how to make artistic creations out of old newspapers, spools, rags, tin cans, gunny sacks, and cardboard boxes.

God's covenant with David and with us is somewhat like that. God may be relied upon to find ways to create meaningful existences out of the unpromising contents of our lives. He saves an obscure shepherd boy in order to make him a king of Israel. He saves us to induct us into His Kingdom.

Our heritage through the patriarchs and David informs us of our place in God's covenant. Celebrate it! Live it!

You Are Not Forgotten. Agnes Newton Keith and her infant son George were part of the European governmental personnel rounded up by the Japanese in Sandakan, Borneo, on January 19, 1942. Separated from her husband, she and George endured the hardships of a Japanese internment camp until September 11, 1945. Attempted rape, disease, overwork, and fear were but a few of the hardships that went along with hunger and malnutrition.

On August 24, 1945, a C-47 flew low over camp, circled, then dropped a torpedo-shaped object by parachute. The thirty-four children in the camp dragged the six-foot torpedo (which bore the printed word *BREAD*) into the center of camp. Said Mrs. Keith:

"People have asked me since if we raced for this first bundle of food, and tore it open, and fought over it. Such an action would have horrified us. We might have felt like it, but we could not have done it. Mean tricks we had learned in captivity, but an equal division of rations had become sacred.

"In any case, half starved though we were, that first parachute meant so much more to us than food that we were not even tempted. Even more than our bodies, our hearts had starved for contact with our own people, for a touch of the friendly hand. The word on that parachute spelled BREAD, but it meant, YOU ARE NOT FORGOTTEN."— *Three Came Home,* Little, Brown and Company, 1947.

World Communion demonstrates we are not forgotten. God remembered us in His great love to send His own Son whose body and blood were given for us. When we break bread and drink the cup, we recall, as a world, Christ's body broken for us and His blood spilled for us. God did not forget the world!

"World Communion gives us the opportunity as a church family to remember Him, to share His meal, and to commit ourselves to seeing that all people receive an equal ration of life-sustaining food."— John B. Barker.

How Time Is Spent. Just in case you have been wondering, by the time you reach seventy, you will have spent nearly a quarter of a century sleeping. Sleep is necessary, but the Bible warns of too much: "How long will you lie there, O sluggard?" (Proverbs 6:9 RSV).

The important thing is to spend the proper amount of time where it will count the most.

Here is how most Americans spend their waking hours during seventy years of life.

> 11 years working
> 8 years playing
> 6 years eating
> 5½ years grooming
> 3 years being educated
> 3 years reading
> 3 years talking
> ½ year worshiping God

If the above schedule is accurate, obviously something is out of balance. And if this is true of you, obviously now is the time to increase the time you spend reading the Bible, praying, and worshiping the Lord—before Jesus comes again.

Questions for Pupils on the Next Lesson. 1. What are some of the ways in which we turn away from God's spirit and covenant in mind, heart, or action? 2. What are some of the false gods which people in our culture are tempted to worship? 3. How does God react to human defiance and human irresponsibility? 4. What is the prophetic role of the Church today? 5. How does being a Christian relate to social-political action today?

TOPIC FOR YOUTH
CAN YOU RELY ON GOD?

What Covenant Means. The noted British philosopher Bertrand Russell had a cynical viewpoint of God, humans, and life. He once described that he imagined that the Creator, tired of associating with the angels, decided to make humans. But to entertain Himself, the Creator surrounded humans with tears and troubles. The Creator looked on, as Russell related it, watching how humans reacted with a certain gallantry. The Creator regarded the human struggle with amusement. Finally, He grew tired and bored. "A good play. Someday I must do it again. Meanwhile, enough! The jest is ended." And with a sweep of His hand, the Creator annihilated human life.

This fable by one of the brainiest twentieth century thinkers sums up the idea of many. But it is opposite the viewpoint expressed in the Bible. Reread the Scripture. Notice the frequent use of the word *Covenant*. God covenants with humans that He can be relied upon. This is the message of God's promise to David—and to us today!

Want to Argue? Instead of being willing to rely on God's promises, we are often like the aged and argumentative Highlander who knew he was dying. The dour old Scot on his deathbed was told by his wife that the minister was coming to pray with him. "I dinna want anybody tae pray wi' me, " he growled.

"Well then, he'll speak some words of comfort to you."

"I don't want tae hear words o' comfort," answered the gruff Scot.

"What then *do* you want?" asked his wife.

"I want tae *argue*."

Burden Bearers. "All of us have seen either personally or in a picture or by television, people of South East Asia and India carrying great loads balanced on either end of a long pole which is slung across the shoulders.

"Using the pole as both a balance and a distributor of weight, they seem to be able to travel at a jog trot for miles.

"In India and other hot humid climates, the strain is quite great and therefore it is no surprise to see at regular intervals along the highway *Soomai Tangi* or, 'the burden bearers.' These 'burden bearers' are two upright poles on which is mounted a flat slate-like table. It is a God-send to hot tired porters—as they ease their burdens upon it. What a great sense of relief they must experience!

"Significantly, the Communion Table at St. Christopher's Training College in Madras is shaped in the form of a burden bearer. Through the skill of its designer is echoed the words of our Lord, uttered often at Communion services, 'Come unto me all ye labouring and burdened and I will give you rest.'

"A better translation is 'I will refresh you.'

"Isn't this precisely what worship and communion is meant to do? It should be like coming to life. To worship was never meant to be a burden—a duty—though some people see it and make it that way.

"It is meant to refresh and to strengthen you; to save you in order to save others."— Douglas G. McKenzie.

Sentence Sermon to Remember: It is not the possession of extraordinary gifts that make extaordinary usefulness, but the dedication of what we have to the service of God.—Frederick William Robertson.

Questions for Pupils on the Next Lesson. 1. What are the principal temptations you see youth facing today? 2. What connection do you see between these temptations and false gods? 3. How can interest primarily in popularity, sex, money, success, possessions, alcohol, or drugs be a form of worship of idols? 4. How can the sins of our society lead us away from God? 5. What are some of the dangers and consequences of disobeying God?

LESSON VI—OCTOBER 12

GOD'S COVENANT AND ISRAEL'S SIN

Background Scripture: 1 Kings 11:1–13, 26–43; 12:25–33; 14
Devotional Reading: Isaiah 55:6–11

KING JAMES VERSION	REVISED STANDARD VERSION
I KINGS 11 4 For it came to pass, when Solomon was old, *that* his wives turned away his heart after other gods: and his heart was not perfect with the LORD his God, as *was* the heart of David his father.	I KINGS 11 4 For when Solomon was old his wives turned away his heart after other gods; and his heart was not wholly true to the LORD his God, as was the heart of David his father. 5 For Solomon went after Ashtoreth the goddess of the Sidonians, and after Milcom the abomination of the Ammonites. 6 So Solomon did what was evil in the sight of the LORD, and did not wholly follow the LORD, as David his father had done. 7 Then Solomon built a high place for Chemosh the abomination of Moab, and for Molech the abomination of the Ammonites, on the mountain east of Jerusalem. 8 And so he did for all his foreign wives, who burned incense and sacrificed to their gods. 9 And the LORD was angry with Solomon, becase his heart had turned away from the LORD, the God of Israel, who had appeared to him twice, 10 and had commanded him concerning this thing, that he should not go after other gods; but he did not keep what the LORD commanded. 11 Therefore the LORD said to Solomon, "Since this has been your mind and you have not kept my covenant and my statutes which I have commanded you, I will surely tear the kingdom from you and will give it to your servant. 12 Yet for the sake of David your father I will not do it in your days, but I will tear it out of the hand of your son. 13 However I will not tear away all the kingdom; but I will give one tribe to your son, for the sake of David my servant and for the sake of Jerusalem which I have chosen."
5 For Solomon went after Ashtoreth the goddess of the Zidonians, and after Milcom the abomination of the Ammonites.	
6 And Solomon did evil in the sight of the LORD, and went not fully after the LORD, as *did* David his father.	
7 Then did Solomon build a high place for Chemosh, the abomination of Moab, in the hill that *is* before Jerusalem, and for Molech, the abomination of the children of Ammon.	
8 And likewise did he for all his strange wives, which burnt incense and sacrificed unto their gods.	
9 And the LORD was angry with Solomon, because his heart was turned from the LORD God of Israel, which had appeared unto him twice,	
10 And had commanded him concerning this thing, that he should not go after other gods: but he kept not that which the LORD commanded.	
11 Wherefore the LORD said unto Solomon, Forasmuch as this is done of thee, and thou hast not kept my covenant and my statutes, which I have commanded thee, I will surely rend the kingdom from thee, and will give it to thy servant.	
12 Notwithstanding, in thy days I will not do it for David thy father's sake: *but* I will rend it out of the hand of thy son.	
13 Howbeit I will not rend away all the kingdom; *but* will give one tribe to thy son for David my servant's sake, and for Jerusalem's sake which I have chosen.	

KEY VERSE: "You shall have no other gods before me." Exodus 20:3.

49

HOME DAILY BIBLE READINGS

Oct. 6. M. *Dishonoring the Relationship With God.* 1 Kings 11:1–8.
Oct. 7. T. *God's Reaction to Faithlessness.* 1 Kings 11:9–13.
Oct. 8. W. *Preparation for Punishment.* 1 Kings 11:26–33.
Oct. 9. T. *The Promise Given to Another.* 1 Kings 11:34–40.
Oct. 10. F. *A Fatal Choice of Wordly Wisdom.* 1 Kings 12:25–33.
Oct. 11. S. *Judgment on Willfulness.* 1 Kings 14:1–10a.
Oct. 12. S. *The Faithful and Secure Way.* Isaiah 55:6–11.

BACKGROUND

Solomon was the brilliant son of David, and the third king of Israel. David preferred him as his successor rather than Adonijah, the eldest son of David and therefore the heir apparent to the throne. But with the help of Bath-sheba (remember her?) her son Solomon won the contest for the throne.

Solomon, next to his father, became a legend; he moved in an aura of greatness and power and wisdom. We call a brilliant man, even today, one who is "as wise as Solomon." They thought him wise because he brought to them what an American president once claimed for himself: "an unprecedented era of prosperity." He built a great Temple gleaming with silver and gold; he built great palaces for himself. His ships roamed the seas, laden with treasure. He sat on a throne of ivory overlaid with gold, and he brought Jerusalem up to the status of one of the capitals of the world's wealth. Whatever else we may think or say about him, in the days of his youth and middle age he was one of the ablest and most outstanding kings of his time.

But as he grew old and older, those who reveled in the Solomonic prosperity began to feel that there was something fatally wrong in their ivory-throned king. There were two serious revolts against him and his reign. The gold began to show signs of tarnish. Too many of his people lived in hovels. They groaned. The king called for more palaces, more golden drinking-cups. The king, they murmured, was not as wise as they had thought.

NOTES ON THE PRINTED TEXT

I. For it came to pass, when Solomon was old, that his wives turned away his heart after other gods: and his heart was not perfect with the Lord his God . . . . 1 Kings 11:4. Solomon had 12,000 horsemen and 1,400 chariots and a labor force building his great buildings made up of prisoners captured in war and his own people; he also had seven hundred wives and princesses, and three hundred concubines—and almost as many religions in the palace as he had wives and concubines! Now that was not exactly unusual among the kings of the day; other monarchs had similar establishments and such forced labor, if not in such profusion as Solomon had them. But while the other kings controlled their wives and their harems, Solomon did not! He was more than tolerant with them. He encouraged them to worship their (foreign) gods, and even worshiped those gods himself: "For Solomon went after Ashtoreth the goddess of the Zidonians, and after Milcom the abomination of the Ammonites" (1 Kings 11:3). He built high places (altars, temples) to the heathen gods of his wives and concubines. He was tolerant to a fault but there is a firm line to be drawn between tolerance and the surrender of one's religious convictions. Solomon's tolerance or broad-mindedness in marrying the daughter of an Egyptian pharaoh his people could forgive, and applaud it as clever statesmanship. But to set up altars to Israel's God—that they could not forgive. They hated that, and they came to hate the king who in his youth seemed to "have everything"—everything necessary to the great leader of a great nation. The ivory throne began to tremble; the aging king seemed a man in his dotage, irresponsible, weak, and above all unfaithful to his (and their) God.

There were other causes for his decline. His love of luxury was repulsive to the Hebrew people. He held banquets in his palace while his enslaved people who had built his palace nibbled on crumbs.

Again, while he might have had fleets of ships on the seas, other kings were to build larger fleets. (Doesn't that still happen today?) He had troops; other kings had larger troops. While Solomon the Wise never saw it, the tide of history was running against him; and so was geography. Israel's location between Egypt and Syria was a bad location, as the Israelites understood when these two great powers overran and ravished their land as they fought for domination of the Mediterranean world. It is always dangerous to ignore God and put our trust in princes!

Solomon was, in his best days, a man and a king of great strength and power. Give him credit for that. But on the debit side of the ledger, we read that strength and power are two of the most fearsome possessions of mankind. Absolute strength can corrupt absolutely; the abuse of power "plays havoc in every sphere of life," said Dr. Ralph Sockman. Power is safe in the hands of God-guided men; it is never safe in the hands of tyrants who think themselves as powerful as God. Solomon, with his power, might have done great things for God; he began his reign by praying to God for wisdom, but he forgot all that, in those terrible latter days of his reign. In those days, he glittered with bigness, and it hid his greater self. He was not wise then, not big at all, but pitifully small and weak. He lifted his kingdom high only to give it a greater fall.

There is food for thought in the fact that the fall and decay of this king was not sudden, but devastatingly slow and gradual. Little by little, the life of God's spirit oozed out of him. Sin grows like a cancer, hidden beneath the flesh; death comes not quickly with cancer, but fearfully slow. "In the life of the spirit," says Dr. Sockman, "slow changes need more to be watched than sudden shocks. Some sins are a rash, breaking out like measles in a single night. But the seven deadly sins, as traditional theology lists them, suggest slow decay rather than sudden outbreak. Pride, covetousness, lust, anger, envy, gluttony, and sloth are sins which gradually harden the arteries of the spirit and sap the energies of the will. For this reason, Jesus, in line with the record here, is more severe in condemning the sins of the mind and heart than the sins of physical passion and open shame. The latter beget boldly effects and a social disgrace which tend to awaken a spirit to repentance; but the former may be carried so secretly and respectably that there is no sting of conscience. Consequently, Jesus said to the chief priests and the

elders, whose sin-calloused minds were smugly complacent, 'The publicans and the harlots go into the kingdom of God before you'"
(Matthew 21:31). From *The Interpreter's Bible*, Vol. 3, p. 105, by permission of Abingdon Press, publishers.

II. . . . *I will surely tear the kingdom from you and will give it to
your servant.*" 1 Kings 11:11 (RSV). God was angry with Solomon; He
had twice warned against the breaking of their covenant, and twice
Solomon had ignored the warnings. For that, Solomon was told that he
would be punished.

All through the Old Testament, we find the Jewish people following a
principle of quick and immediate punishment for sin; only by the mercy
of God was it ever postponed. That is what happened here with Solomon. The old, failing, dying monarch was told that his kingdom would
be "rent" from him *after* he died! That may not seem to be adequate
punishment to some, but think of what such an announcement must
have meant to the old king. How high he had risen with the help of God!
How great was the early work he had done for God with these Hebrew
people. And how low had he fallen! What a horrible thing it must be for
a man of great power to be forced to sit for years thinking of how he had
failed, how far he had fallen. All those years of promise for Solomon—
and now he was condemned to sit in the ashes of his failure and think of
the collapse of his kingdom. Could any punishment be worse than that?

As God promised, he did: the kingdom—the only united kingdom
Israel ever knew, the kingdom and monarchy of David and Solomon—
came to an end. In infinite mercy, God still left His beloved city of
Jerusalem in the hands of the tribe of Judah (which included the tribe of
Benjamin, which was David's tribe), but the rest of the holy land was
given to the other ten tribes.

Thus ended the life and work of Solomon, the boy wonder, the king of
great promise who broke his promise to God and ignored his covenant
with the only power that might have saved him and his people. The
curtain fell upon Israel; there came Rehoboam, son of Solomon, who
was to be the last ruler of the United Kingdom and the first ruler of the
Southern Kingdom of Judah.

SUGGESTIONS TO TEACHERS

What is your mental picture when you think of an idol? A chunk of
stone shaped into human or animal form and worshiped by primitive
tribes?

We Christians can easily grow smug. We suppose we're too sophisticated to get caught up with worshiping false gods.

Today's lesson will aid your class in understanding the subtle ways
God's people stray from the covenant relationship with the Lord, and
the strong ways in which He persists in keeping trust with us.

1. *FOREIGN GODS AND FALSE SECURITY.* Urge your people to
state some of the "foreign gods" our society hankers after. In case they
are slow or manage to think only of the obvious, have them apply what
some Christian thinkers call the "temperature test." Briefly, that is
whatever warms your interest the most. Whatever you get most heated

about is what you worship, whether money, pleasure, a hobby, or whatever. Solomon's problem and your people's problem is that these
foreign gods can never deliver. They fail. Let the Scriptures for today
supply you excellent examples. Applying this to today, ask your class to
enumerate examples of the phony promises and false security which
idols in our society offer.

2. *FAITHFUL GOD AND FAMILIAR SECURITY.* Although Solomon
and his people proved to be unfaithful to the Lord, God appeared to the
mighty ruler twice (1 Kings 11:9–11) to warn him and command him not
to worship foreign deities. God also has covenant with us, remind your
people. Through Jesus, we know His fidelity. We also realize from the
long saga of His covenanted relationship with our spiritual ancestors
that He alone provides security.

3. *PROPHETIC VOICES AND PROPER WORSHIP.* Be sure to mention the Prophet Ahijah. Develop the lesson to ponder the place of
prophets in a nation. Who would your class describe as prophets today?
Why? Comment that a prophet in the Bible is one who speaks for the
Lord. Discuss who speaks for the Lord in our times. Does the Church?
Should it? Also consider the matter of worship, if prophetic voices tell us
to serve only the Lord. What would Ahijah and the prophets say to us
today about the meaning of true worship?

4. *PRIVATE SINS AND PUBLIC CONSEQUENCES.* Sin is never a
"personal matter." King Jeroboam, like so many, vainly imagined that
his disobedience was his own business. Note carefully how the Bible
insists that Jeroboam's sin led the people to sin, and ultimately brought
about the downfall of his country. Emphasize in your lesson that every
believer has a responsibility to others. The people of the covenant belong to each other!

TOPIC FOR ADULTS
GOD'S COVENANT AND ISRAEL'S SIN

"*I Want It All Now.*" This was the title of a television program shown
two summers ago in which producer-director-writer Joe De Cola did a
documentary on life in Marin County, California.

De Cola and his crew roved about the affluent communities of Mill
Valley, Tiburon, Belvedere, and Larkspur, where an overwhelming
majority of the residents have achieved the average American's goal, at
least on the material level.

Just fifteen minutes from San Francisco, Marin's 220,000 residents
drive high-priced sports cars, live in expensive homes, and generally
play "the good life" to the hilt. Yet, money isn't everything, and there
are a lot of unhappy people in Marin County, too. De Cola feels that
Marin may be giving an advance look at what might come in the '80s for
the rest of the country.

"I was struck by the incredible beauty of the place—its advantages in
terms of both nature and culture being so close to San Francisco," says
De Cola. "Yet, beneath the affluent security blanket, there's a frenetic
undercurrent. Marin has the highest divorce rate in the country, and 90
percent of all real estate transactions in some areas are the result of

broken marriages." Marin County's percentage of alcoholism and suicide is among the nation's highest.

De Cola, formerly a producer with "60 Minutes," researched hundreds of people in various professions all "doing their own thing" in this capital of the human-potential movement, where various gurus spend their sun-filled days teaching the unfulfilled how to find inner peace and happiness. He notes: "Their incomes are high, they live in one of the most beautiful areas in the country, and they have every mechanical convenience and recreational activity at their fingertips. They have leisure, they have freedom, yet there are more therapists in Marin County per capita than anywhere else in the country."

One particularly moving segment examines Kathy Burke, a divorcee with four children who has come to Marin to find herself. We see her in group therapy being advised to listen to feelings, not to the head—to trust impulses and forget judgment and criticism. She freely admits that "the whole parenting trip doesn't fit any more," and that her most important responsibility is to herself, not her kids. "I don't accept that I am responsible for my children—I'm responsible for me—yes, I'm selfish, and I like it—it's OK."

De Cola says he focused on these trends to point up what he believes is an advance look at what may lie ahead for the country. He feels that Marin County is not the only place in America where people are interested in the same set of values, where the "narcissism business" is commonplace. Where people are obsessed with the self and the elusive search for inner happiness.—From an interview reported in the Allentown, Pa., *Call Chronicle*, July 19, 1978.

Buying-Spree Junkie. The bumper sticker announced in bold letters: I STOP AT ALL GARAGE SALES. The people in the station wagon told a curious questioner that they hunted out all the weekend yard sales, porch sales, flea markets, pavement sales, and garage sales they could find. Why? "Well, we just enjoy accumulating things."

What did they do with all these things? Nothing, really. Besides, most of it, they admitted, was junk. They pointed to the accumulation of old books, dishes, tools and bric-a-brac in the car and in their garage. "Someday, we'll have to have a big garage sale and clear out all this stuff," they grinned.

A harmless pastime to this family (and thousands of others), but it is symptomatic of our interest in possessions. "Blessed are those who accumulate things," seems to be our motto.

We make this mistake of hugging our possessions and using persons. The covenanting God insists it be just the opposite. Israel's sin was frequently an obsession with "foreign gods," and our worship of material stuff puts us in as grave a danger as the prophets' contemporaries.

What Kind of Security? The nations of the world are now spending over $400 billion a year on armaments. That comes out to almost a million dollars a minute. To put that in perspective, think for a moment in these terms: if you gave away a dollar a minute, it would take you about two years to give away a million dollars!

The world's nations spend a million a minute on arms. That's twenty times as much as they spend on aid to poor nations.

Our stockpile of nuclear warheads in the world today has grown from 8,000 in 1970 to over 14,000 by 1978. There are well over 50,000 nuclear bombs in the hands of the two most powerful nations, the United States and Russia, and at least another 500 in Britain, China, France, India, and Israel. The world's inventories of nuclear weapons can destory every city in the world seven times over, but the world's major nations now want to up the kill-ratio to nine or ten.

The average family now pays more in the arms race than to educate its children. The cost of one new mobile intercontinental missile (the MX) would provide enough to feed 50 million undernourished children, open 65,000 health centers, and build 340,000 primary schools in developing countries.

In the light of the biblical claim that God's covenant is our only ultimate security, what do these statistics suggest? In the face of the human need in today's world, what is God's judgment on the nations today?

Questions for Pupils on the Next Lesson. 1. What does the phrase "having God's covenant written on the hearts" mean? 2. How do the covenants with Abraham and at Sinai relate to the new covenant promised in Jeremiah 31:31–34? 3. In what ways can the church help people to be more aware of their individual responsibilities in obeying God? 4. How does God's covenant tie in with changes (in relation to money, age, health, new worship experiences) which occur in life?

TOPIC FOR YOUTH
SERVING GOD ONLY

Beauty Worship. She was acclaimed "the most beautiful woman on earth." She had money, brains, and background to match her looks. Born Gladys Deacon, daughter of a wealthy Boston banking family, she was raised in France. Her beauty attracted attention everywhere. The ninth Duke of Marlborough, married to the former Consuelo Vanderbilt, was one of many men who fell in love with her. After his divorce in 1921, the Duke married Gladys and bestowed on her the title of the Duchess of Marlborough. Their marriage, however, was not happy, and when he died in 1934, the Duchess did not mourn his passing. Vain and concerned to preserve her reputation as the world's most beautiful woman, Gladys heard of a plastic surgeon who claimed to have special treatments to perpetuate her gorgeous appearance. The treatments consisted of injections of wax and paraffin in the skin in her forehead. The substances, however, wandered throughout her face, forming unsightly bumps. The woman who had been celebrated as the world's most beautiful, because of her worship of her appearance, had inadvertently caused herself to be disfigured! Afflicted with huge, ugly waxy blobs throughout her once-lovely face, the Duchess of Marlborough retired to her house near Banbury. She turned into a recluse, calling herself Mrs. Spencer, and refusing to see anyone except a few close friends. She lived for years, finally dying in October, 1977, at the age of 96, completely forgotten by a world which had once proclaimed her "the most beautiful woman on earth."

The irony of Gladys's worship of the idol of beauty, sex, and popularity succeeded in destroying what she most cherished.

God's covenant, not our looks or any other god, provides security!

What Then? Philip of Neri, the sixteenth century saint who founded the Orator, an Order in the Roman Catholic Church, listened one day to a bright young student of philosophy who described his ambitions. After the young man told how he was examining all branches of philosophy at the university, Philip Neri finally replied.

"What then?," he inquired.

"Then I shall study for my doctorate, and be competent and recognized in both canon and civil law."

"What them?" Philip Neri asked.

"Well, then I will come into a comfortable family inheritance, and will get married, raise a family and move along in my legal career."

"What then?" Philip Neri quietly repeated.

"I shall then achieve a brilliant career in law and will receive recognition and honors, probably even be elected an Orator of the Rota."

"And what then?"pursued Philip Neri.

"Why I then shall grow old and die the same as everyone else, I suppose."

"And what then?" Philip Neri asked, with significance.

Peer Pressures to Conform. Col. Buzz Aldrin, the astronaut who walked on the moon in 1969, acknowledges his long struggle with alcoholism because of the pressures of friends to "fit in." As a West Point cadet, Aldrin disclosed that he had been "caught in the alcohol trap." He realized that he was worshiping the bottle, and he resolved to quit. His abstinence ended when he was sent to Korea as a combat officer. There, he found that others measured his military image by the yardstick of "who could drink the most." Aldrin gave in, and started to drink again—heavily. His alcoholism, with God's help, was finally controlled shortly before the Apollo-11 launch, and Aldrin quit drinking.

The lure of the idols of drinking and conformity are powerful. They nearly claimed Buzz Aldrin. They threaten you. Only the strength of the God who wants you to covenant with Him can keep you from succumbing to the appeal of these false gods!

Sentence Sermon to Remember: Sin is man's declaration of independence of God.—Anonymous.

Questions for Pupils on the Next Lesson. 1. Why is it so much more important to have a personal commitment to God than simply lists of rules to follow? 2. How may your faith be more inner-motivated and inner-directed? 3. What could the church do to help youth understand better that God's law must be written on their hearts and involves a deep, personal level of obligation to God and others? 4. What are ways that you have found helpful to renew your commitment to the Lord?

LESSON VII—OCTOBER 19

GOD'S COVENANT AND JEREMIAH

Background Scripture: Jeremiah 31
Devotional Reading: Ezekiel 18:25–32

KING JAMES VERSION	REVISED STANDARD VERSION
JEREMIAH 31 1 At the same time, saith the LORD, will I be the God of all the families of Israel, and they shall be my people.	JEREMIAH 31 1 "At that time, says the LORD, I will be the God of all the families of Israel, and they shall be my people."
2 Thus saith the LORD, The people *which were* left of the sword found grace in the wilderness; even Israel, when I went to cause him to rest.	2 Thus says the LORD: "The people who survived the sword found grace in the wilderness; when Israel sought for rest,
3 The LORD hath appeared of old unto me, *saying,* Yea I have loved thee with an everlasting love: therefore with loving-kindness have I drawn thee.	3 the LORD appeared to him from afar. I have loved you with an everlasting love; therefore I have continued my faithfulness to you.
20 In those days they shall say no more, The fathers have eaten a sour grape, and the children's teeth are set on edge.	29 In those days they shall no longer say: 'The fathers have eaten sour grapes, and the children's teeth are set on edge.'
30 But every one shall die for his own iniquity: every man that eateth the sour grape, his teeth shall be set on edge.	30 But every one shall die for his own sin; each man who eats sour grapes, his teeth shall be set on edge.
31 Behold, the days come, saith the LORD, that I will make a new covenant with the house of Israel, and with the house of Judah:	31 "Behold, the days are coming, says the LORD, when I will make a new covenant with the house of Israel and the house of Judah, 32 not like the covenant which I made with their fathers when I took them by the hand to bring them out of the land of Egypt, my covenant which they broke, though I was their husband, says the LORD. 33 But this is the covenant which I will make with the house of Israel after those days, says the LORD: I will put my law within them, and I will write it upon their hearts; and I will be their God, and they shall be my people. 34 And no longer shall each man teach his neighbor and each his brother, saying, 'Know the LORD,' for they shall all know me, from the least of them to the greatest, says the LORD; for I will forgive their iniquity, and I will remember their sin no more."
32 Not according to the covenant that I made with their fathers, in the day that I took them by the hand to bring them out of the land of Egypt; which my covenant they brake, although I was a husband unto them, saith the LORD:	
33 But this *shall* be the covenant that I will make with the house of Israel; After those days, saith the LORD, I will put my law in their inward parts, and write it in their hearts; and will be their God, and they shall be my people.	
34 And they shall teach no more every man his neighbour, and every man his brother, saying, Know the LORD: for they shall all know me, from the least of them unto the greatest of them, saith the LORD: for I will forgive their iniquity, and I will remember their sin no more.	

KEY VERSE: I will put my law within them, and I will write it upon their hearts; and I will be their God, and they shall be my people. Jeremiah 31:33 (RSV).

HOME DAILY BIBLE READINGS

Oct. *13.* M. *The Faithfulness of God.* Jeremiah 31:1–6.
Oct. *14.* T. *The Reward of the Faithful.* Jeremiah 31:7–14.
Oct. *15.* W. *Hope for the Future.* Jeremiah 31:15–22.
Oct. *16.* T. *Each One Is Responsible.* Jeremiah 31:23–30.
Oct. *17.* F. *A Covenant in the Heart.* Jeremiah 31:31–40.
Oct. *18.* S. *A Promise to the Faithful.* Jeremiah 7:1–7.
Oct. *19.* S. *Call to Repentance.* Ezekiel 18:25–32.

BACKGROUND

The Prophet Jeremiah—one of the four major prophets of the Old Testament—was a mountain of a man. He could tower above all others in rage when his people turned their backs on God; he could blast them for making their Temple a fetish and their faith a farce. Like a minister appointed to watch a man die, he was appointed to watch his people march off to captivity; he pleaded and warned them of their coming Exile, but they paid no attention. In the bitter Exile years (in Babylon), he was still their great prophet, their comforting and inspiring preacher and teacher.

But his pre-Exile preaching and his later preaching and prophesying were different in content and purpose. Where he had scolded before the Babylonians put them in chains, now he talked of love and forgiveness and a new brand of religion. He came, he told his dishearted people to make an announcement for God: there would be a new and better Covenant between God and His people.

NOTES ON THE PRINTED TEXT

I. "The people who survived the sword found grace in the wilderness . . . . Jeremiah 31:2 (RSV). Jeremiah is represented here (probably in an account written by his secretary, Baruch) as preaching to the sad company of Israelites left to starve in the ruins of Jerusalem. They were a beaten, starving people, condemned to death (or so they thought) in a land laid waste by the invading Babylonians. It is not hard to believe that in such an hour some of them may have taken their own lives, or thought of doing just that. What had they to live for?

Jeremiah faced them and began his sermon with a challenge; he asked them to remember that they had been in similar situations before they had their Jerusalem; they (or their fathers) had been a terrified host of people stumbling through a wilderness; they have been a people who might easily have perished on the shores of the Red Sea with the Egyptians riding toward them. Had they forgotten that? Had they forgotten their escape from the Egyptians and that they had been saved at the Red Sea and in the wilderness *at the hand of their God and because of His undying mercy?* What made them think that God would desert them now?

From the lips of Jeremiah come the words of God: "Yea, I have loved thee with an everlasting love . . ." (verse 3). God had loved and protected them on their trek to Canaan. He had made a covenant with them at Sinai—a contract they had broken. He had made another covenant in the days of Joshua—and they had broken that one, too. But God, in a *steadfast* love, had never deserted them, never violated *His* part of the contract.

No matter how low a man may fall, he is never in a place where God cannot reach him if he has enough faith to reach out for God. Nothing mankind has ever done has been enough to make God say, "Go your own way; I am through with you!"

II. In those days they shall say no more. The fathers have eaten a sour grape, and the children's teeth are set on edge. Jeremiah 31:29. This was an old proverb in Israel and Judah; it was a ludicrous attempt to find an excuse for sin. It was a way of saying, "*We* did not sin; our fathers sinned, and we are being made to suffer for something *they* did!"

It is a lame excuse found in every age of man. We did not sin; someone else did it, and we are made to pay for it! We are born the debtors of sinning parents; we are the victims of heredity. We steal or lie or kill because our social environment makes us lie and kill. We are not to blame, Lord; we are only the victims of a sinful heritage or past.

Nonsense, says Jeremiah. *You have sinned, and you must pay the penalty for it.* "Every one shall die for his own iniquity" (verse 30). Ezekiel said the same thing: "The soul that sinneth, it shall die" (Ezekiel 18:4).

Let no man stand before God and say, "Lord, I have not sinned." God knows better.

This was a demand for personal responsibility. From this point on, Jeremiah says, each individual must understand that he is personally accountable to God: "Each man who eats sour grapes, his teeth shall be set on edge." *He* shall pay for his folly, pay the price for broken covenants with God. Jeremiah uses the words, "In those days . . ." What days? He is speaking of days in the future, days to come. Days in which yet another covenant shall come—a greater covenant than they (the Covenant People, as they were called) had yet known.

III. . . . I will put my law within them, and I will write it upon their hearts . . . . Jeremiah 31:33 (RSV). As they came out of Egypt, the children of Israel had to be led, as a father leads a child, through their wilderness experience. There was much they did not understand about God's hand, and God's laws. At Sinai, there were God's laws, or Commandments, cut into tablets of stone. The tablets were soon broken, and so were the laws! Now, thanks to the infinite wisdom and forgiveness of a loving God, they are promised a new covenant, a new promise: God henceforth would engrave His laws *in their hearts,* laws enforceable from *within,* not imposed from *without.*

"This was the very nerve of Jeremiah's vision and prayer and hope. Moses was the means of an *external* covenant; Jeremiah was the proclaimer of an *internal* covenant; Jesus the Messiah was to be the Creator of the *eternal* covenant, of which Jeremiah was a fit forerunner. Here is seen, therefore, the continuity of God's sovereign grace, conveying through covenant deep forgiveness for sin, a richer experience of God himself in such fellowship, issuing in a finer brotherhood among men. A vision and a dedication." *The New Bible Commentary,* Wm. B. Eerdmans Publishing Company. Used by permission.

Laws written deep in the heart are hard to disobey. We can cut laws in tablets of stone, and they will in time disappear; we can write them down in statute books, but books perish, too. But when we carve deep in the human heart the laws and the spirit of our Creator God, they are there forever. Laws, written laws, says someone, are written to be broken. But held in the heart, those who hold them there do not *want* to break them, do not *want* to sin. Once the heart is dedicated to God, once a man truly walks in close fellowship with God, there is a deep inner urge to obey the God who put them there.

Abraham Lincoln, as a young lawyer, was asked to defend a man who was clearly guilty of breaking the law. After listening to his would-be client's statement, he said, "Sir, you have a pretty good case in technical law, but a bad one in equity and justice. You'll have to get some other fellow to win this case for you. I couldn't do it. All that time while I was standing talking to that jury I'd be thinking, 'Lincoln, you're a liar,' and I believe I would forget myself and say it out loud."

Young Abe Lincoln, lawyer, had God's law firmly written on his heart, though he never had his name written on a church membership roll. But God was able to do great things for man with Abraham Lincoln, President of the United States.

One more item is described as it would appear in "those days" when the law guided men from within: it would not be necessary, then, for any man to admonish another man to know the Lord "For every one, both great and small," saith the Lord, "shall really know me then, and I will forgive and forget their sins."

Forever merciful, forever ready to forgive, is the God, who longs not for tributes from our mouths, but for tributes from the heart on which His name is written.

SUGGESTIONS TO TEACHERS

Following a week in which the news reports had described a severe earthquake in Iran killing thousands and the crash of an airliner taking over a hundred lives, a radio revivalist insisted that these events were God telling us He was tired of putting up with our sinful world.

This was one religious leader's interpretation of difficult times. Today's lesson examines another: Jeremiah's.

You should impress on your class that Jeremiah understood that God's covenant must be written on the heart of every believer. Every person in the covenanted community is related to the Lord. And everyone is responsible.

After you become familiar with the historical setting of Jeremiah, saturate yourself in Jeremiah 31. You will find that you may develop your lesson around three imperatives: Repent, Respond, and Renew.

1. *REPENT!* Jeremiah calls on his people to repent for their rebelliousness against God. Point out how John the Baptist and Jesus both opened their ministries by reiterating this prophetic call. Remind your

class that the word *repent* literally means *a change of mind*. Bring this notion into the present world. What do you and the members of your class believe that the Lord is calling us to repent of? In what ways is He calling us to change our minds today?

2. *RESPOND!* Help your class to grasp more clearly how Jeremiah called upon his countrymen to recognize their individual responsibility for obeying God. Furthermore, assist your people to understand that God does not punish us for the sins of others. Sin may have its consequences in the lives of others, but God holds each accountable. The covenant God makes with each means that *every* person has the ability to respond—or "response-ability!" Ask your class to discuss what forms responding to the covenant through Christ should take in the lives of faithful believers today.

3. *RENEW.* Be sure to call attention to the idea of the new covenant in this section of Jeremiah (31:31). Have your people trace the way this great idea appears in the New Testament (which, by the way, means *new covenant!*). Have them reread Matthew 26:26, where Jesus at the Last Supper announces that He is inaugurating the New Covenant. Do your class members grasp the mighty significance of the New Covenant through Jesus Christ? Help each member to renew his or her covenant-relationship to the Lord.

TOPIC FOR ADULTS
GOD'S COVENANT AND JEREMIAH

Indelible Mark. A recent P.T.A. program featured a speaker from the local police department who stressed the importance of marking belongings permanently in order to deter robbers from taking them. The speaker emphasized that an engraving tool could easily be used to put the owner's name or initials on household goods which are easily stolen and sold, such as television sets, typewriters, stereos, cameras, silver teapots, etc. He then demonstrated several devices which could be bought and used to scratch a permanent mark on metal, wood, or plastic. However, even these markings can be filed or sanded off by a clever and determined thief.

The most effective engraving tool of all time, however, was the point of the nails which crucified Jesus Christ, and God has used them to etch the memory and mark of the Cross on your memory. Through the New Covenant made in Christ, God has placed His signature on your life. He owns you! You belong to Him!

Each time you worship, each time you pray, each time you receive the Bread and the Cup, He manages to clear away the smudge and grime obscuring that mark and to disclose again the claim engraved on your soul which you have not noticed. He has covenanted with you. The Lord has written His law on your heart through the Cross!

God Replenishes. Those who claim the world is going to be destroyed reckon without the Spirit of God. In Bunyan's *Pilgrim's Progress*, once Pilgrim saw a fire burning brightly in spite of the water that was being thrown on it by a man who stood near. When he wondered why the fire was not extinguished, he was shown a man behind the wall who was casting oil upon the fire. Sometimes it seems the forces of evil will put out the fires of righteousness on this earth and that the world will be destroyed, but the Holy Spirit is pouring oil upon the fires of God to keep them burning.

Ask Not What God Can Do for You But What You Can Do for God. The uncovenanted person assumes that God owes him or her something. That person is like the Kentucky man which the late Senator Alben Barkley once encountered when running for reelection to the U.S. Senate.

Barkley was campaigning one day in Breathitt County, down around Hazard, when an old mountaineer told him straight-out that he was going to support Barkley's opponent in the next election. The Veep was outdone.

"Why Teecee," he said, "the first thing I did, once I got to be senator, was to make your Maw postmistress at Hardshell. I got your Uncle Jeb a job as deputy marshall in Lexington, and he can't even read. Last year I saw you got your crop loan, and when your Cousin Lily got in a family way a couple of months ago, I sent her the government baby book."

"That's all true," said Teecee, rolling his good eye, "and I don't want you to think I've forgotten. But, Senator, what have you done for me lately?"

How often our attitude toward God is, "What have you done for me lately?" As a matter of fact, He has covenanted with us in mercy. We should repent, respond, and rejoice!

Questions for Pupils on the Next Lesson. 1. Is there a point where an adult Christian no longer needs to be concerned about learning about the faith? 2. What to you are the most important ways a believer may respond to God's covenant? 3. How important do you think it is for a Christian to seek to find a continuity with the people of the Old Testament? Why or why not? 4. Can the Bible completely satisfy people's hunger for religious literature, or should they look for other materials? 5. What do the Scriptures of the Old Testament really mean to you? The New Testament?

TOPIC FOR YOUTH
A FAITH WITHIN

Dangerous to Make Commitments? A covenant is a commitment. God has made a commitment to you. He calls you to commit yourself to Him. Have you? Or are you skittish about making promises to Him? Are you like Angie Dickinson, who announced, "It is dangerous to give of yourself so completely to any one thing or one person. Your own individuality should come first."

Such a self-focus reflects a lack of thanks, a lack of trust. The person who cannot give himself or herself will suffocate in self. Only the committed person can take the risks of meaningful relationships with God and with others. The covenanted man or woman is the person who is able to give himself or herself completely to the Lord and to a partner in marriage. Angie to the contrary, your individuality is given only when you give yourself to God and others!

Doggy Diets. A faith within calls for concern for others. Generally, we Americans are more interested in our pets than we are in other persons. Recently, for example, it was disclosed that obesity has become a problem for many American dogs. Forty-one percent of our dogs are overweight. As a result, Ralston Purina and General Foods and other manufacturers of dog food are now marketing special "diet foods" for U.S. canines.

Meanwhile, a third of the world's babies die before they reach the age of five because of malnutrition, the head of the World Food Council reports. And unless drastic steps are taken, more than a quarter of those who do survive in the world's forty-three poorest countries will suffer from protein deficiency.

What is God's judgment on a society that overfeeds its pets while ignoring needy brothers and sisters? What does His covenant with us imply in regard to a lifestyle and eating habits?

A Faith Within Means Compassion Without. It is always a shameful thing to be concerned only for ourselves when others are in great distress and sorrow. One of the most callous and selfish expressions of such indifference is the entry in the journal of John Evalyn in London in 1660, when thousands were dying of the plague. He wrote, "Blessing and adoring the distinguishing mercy of God, to me and mine, that we, in the midst of this ruin, are safe and sound." No thought for others, suffering and dying, just thinking of himself and imagining that God cared only for him and his family.

Sentence Sermon to Remember: Belief is a truth held in the mind; faith is a fire in the heart. —Joseph Fort Newton.

Questions for Pupils on the Next Lesson. 1. How does the Bible give direction to your life? 2. Could the Church get along without the Bible? Why or why not? 3. When does a Christian stop being a learner? 4. What have you done recently to grow in your faith? 5. Why does the Christian faith stress the need for repentance?

LESSON VIII—OCTOBER 26

GOD'S COVENANT AND EZRA

Background Scriptures: Nehemiah 8, 9
Devotional Reading: Matthew 21:33–43

KING JAMES VERSION	REVISED STANDARD VERSION
NEHEMIAH 8 3 And he read therein before the street that *was* before the water gate from the morning until midday, before the men and the women, and those that could understand; and the ears of all the people were attentive unto the book of the law.	NEHEMIAH 8 3 And he read from it facing the square before the Water Gate from early morning until midday, in the presence of the men and the women and those who could understand; and the ears of all the people were attentive to the book of the law.
9 32 Now therefore, our God, the great, the mighty, and the terrible God, who keepest covenant and mercy, let not all the trouble seem little before thee, that hath come upon us, on our kings, on our princes, and on our priests, and on our prophets, and on our fathers, and on all thy people, since the time of the kings of Assyria unto this day.	9 32 "Now therefore, our God, the great and mighty and terrible God, who keepest covenant and steadfast love, let not all the hardship seem little to thee that has come upon us, upon our kings, our princes, our priests, our prophets, our fathers, and all thy people, since the time of the kings of Assyria until this day. 33 Yet thou hast been just in all that has come upon us, for thou hast dealt faithfully and we have acted wickedly; 34 our kings, our princes, our priests, and our fathers have not kept thy law or heeded thy commandments and thy warnings which thou didst give them. 35 They did not serve thee in their kingdom, and in thy great goodness which thou gavest them, and in the large and rich land which thou didst set before them; and they did not turn from their wicked works. 36 Behold, we are slaves this day; in the land that thou gavest to our fathers to enjoy its fruit and its good gifts, behold, we are slaves. 37 And its rich yield goes to the kings whom thou hast set over us because of our sins; they have power also over our bodies and over our cattle at their pleasure, and we are in great distress." 38 Because of all this we make a firm covenant and write it, and our princes, our Levites, and our priests set their seal to it.
33 Howbeit thou *art* just in all that is brought upon us; for thou hast done right, but we have done wickedly:	
34 Neither have our kings, our princes, our priests, nor our fathers, kept thy law, nor hearkened unto thy commandments and thy testimonies, wherewith thou didst testify against them.	
35 For they have not served thee in their kingdom, and in thy great goodness that thou gavest them, and in the large and fat land which thou gavest before them, neither turned they from their wicked works.	
36 Behold, we *are* servants this day, and *for* the land that thou gavest unto our fathers to eat the fruit thereof and the good thereof, behold, we *are* servants in it:	
37 And it yieldeth much increase unto the kings whom thou hast set over us because of our sins: also they have dominion over our bodies, and over our cattle, at their pleasure, and we *are* in great distress.	
38 And because of all this we make a sure *covenant,* and write *it;* and our princes, Levites, *and* priests, seal *unto* it.	

KEY VERSE: And they read from the book, from the law of God, clearly; and they gave the sense, so that the people understood the reading. Nehemiah 8:8 (RSV).

HOME DAILY BIBLE READINGS

Oct. 20. M. *Love for God's Word.* Nehemiah 8:1–12.
Oct. 21. T. *Learning From God's Word.* Nehemiah 8:13–18.
Oct. 22. W. *Confessing, a Part of Worship.* Nehemiah 9:1–8.
Oct. 23. T. *Remembering God's Loving Kindness.* Nehemiah 9:9–21.
Oct. 24. F. *God's Love and Patience.* Nehemiah 9:22–31.
Oct. 25. S. *A Resolve to Be Faithful.* Nehemiah 9:32–38.
Oct. 26. S. *"Thy Law Is My Delight."* Psalms 119:169–176.

BACKGROUND

Artaxerxes I (465–424 B.C.) ruled Babylon during the last days of the Exile; it was he who granted permission to his Hebrew cupbearer Nehemiah to return to Jerusalem and rebuild that city's walls—a political move on the part of this Persian king but, for the captive Jews, a good one. Nehemiah rebuilt the walls and changed Jerusalem from the status of an embittered colony to a quiet one, which pleased Artaxerxes very much indeed. It seemed to him to have been a good move.

It seemed so to the Jews in the restored city, too; they were free of Babylon—and they made the best of their freedom. Too many of them married heathen wives. Meanwhile, a priest named Ezra fumed in Babylon and at the court of Artaxerxes. Ezra was unhappy about Jews still captive in Babylon and in Persia and about certain rumors he had heard concerning the sad state of religion among the rebuilders in Jerusalem. He was, apparently, a man of some influence at the Persian court (he was a scribe to the king), and so he had little trouble in securing permission to lead another group of exiles home from Babylon. With 1,496 men and their families this priest marched four months across the desert to the homeland. By the time they got there, they knew that their leader had little interest in restoring a physical Jerusalem, but that he had almost a fanatical determination to restore it spiritually.

Nehemiah and Ezra dominated the Judean scene and development until they died; Nehemiah the layman, Ezra the priest. The two books bearing their names in the Bible were once one book.

Ezra looked about him, in restored Jerusalem, and said clearly that what he saw was not enough; one vital commodity was missing—a solid and sincere religious allegiance to the faith of their fathers.

NOTES ON THE PRINTED TEXT

I. And he read from it facing the square before the Water Gate . . . . Nehemiah 8:3 (RSV). In mid-September the people of Jerusalem—particularly those who had made the long trek with Ezra—gathered near the famous Water Gate. The scriptural record in the Book of Nehemiah doesn't say that they were *summoned* to meet there either by Ezra or Nehemiah; it simply says that "they gathered themselves together." There may have been some urging on the part of the priests and Levites under Ezra, whose duty it was to restore the Temple and a knowledge of the ancient faith, but all we know about it is that they came together of their own accord. For what?

They asked Ezra, whom they recognized as chief of all the priests returned to Jerusalem, to read to them the law of God as it had been revealed to Moses. This was a religious, not a political, gathering and occasion, a religious festival. ALL the people, says the record, were there—including the women; that was unusual, for the women had little to say in any religious meeting. They were men and women who could understand what was being read to them; The Vulgate and I Esdras call it "a multitude."

The reading began at daylight. Ezra mounted a platform erected for the occasion; on his left and right sides stood thirteen other priests, who took turns with him in reading from the sacred scrolls of the Mosaic law. And they read from dawn to midday, with the people standing and occasionally sobbing, and shouting, "Amen!" That was a long, long session, but not long enough to read *all* of the Law from beginning to end. Instead of reading the whole code, they probably read a series of selected passages to arouse in the people a repentance and to accept the law as binding upon them, plus a few new additions. It was a version of the law taken from the old Deuteronomic Code. We call it the Priestly Code, and that is probably correct; at least, it was based on the Holiness Code or Ezekiel's code, written in Babylon a century earlier.

The people *asked* for this because they knew how much they needed it. Who among us, living in a covenant with Christ, does not need reconsecration, from time to time? We forget too quickly and easily the day upon which we promised to follow Him.

II. And Ezra said . . . . Nehemiah 9:6. After the sermon, a minister prays; he uses the prayer to sum up what he has said in the sermon, and to call for reconsecration on the part of his hearers. Ezra used this prayer to call for repentance and a fresh devotion to the covenant of his people and their God. He speaks of troubles and hardships suffered by the people of Israel, back as far as Abraham, down through the flight from Egypt, the trials of the wilderness, and they are reminded that their suffering, while it came at the hand and the will of God, was their fault. They deserved it. They cried out to God in their days of trouble and suffering, and He heard them, and brought them through it—but once things went well again, they turned to their old sins (*see* verse 28) God punished them when they did that, and they acknowledged that He was justified and fair when He did it (verse 33).

Now they were back in the homeland—but still "slaves" in the land of plenty God had given their ancestors. That is too strong a word to describe their condition at that moment. They had indeed been slaves in Babylon, but, under the Persian kings who had crushed Babylon, their condition was far better that it was in the days when they wept and slaved in Babylonia. Life was never so severe under Persian rule, but they seemed to be forgetting that. Foreign domination rankled; there was always a fierce longing for independence in the Israelite. They were not yet as free as they wanted to be, even under the more tolerant rule of the Persians. They bemoaned the rule of their overlords, even though God had set the Persians over them because of their sins. They

resented paying tribute to Persia, resented the draining off of the produce (crops, food) of their land, resented the forced labor of the foreign
king. They were "in great distress" over all this (verse 37)—and in that
distress they once more threw themselves at the feet of their Lord and
begged once more for His mercy and guidance—and help.

Thus ends the prayer of Ezra.

III. *Because of all this we make a firm covenant and write it, and our
princes, our Levites, and our priests set their seals to it.* Nehemiah 9:38
(RSV). This verse is not a part of Ezra's prayer; it is a response to that
prayer on the part of the people. We must read on into the tenth chapter
of Nehemiah to get the full thrust and meaning of this new covenant. It
was, we might say, a one-way covenant, in that it was made by people
repenting of their sins and errors, asking God's forgiveness, and pledg-
ing themselves to follow His dictates and do His will in the future. God
had no direct part in the making of this covenant.

How well they kept the covenant is another matter. Some of the record is bad; there were those who forgot the covenant almost as soon as
they made it, but there were others who walked a straighter path, who
made an honest effort to keep their word with God. On the good side, a
new Code was established, and in a new temple there was a resuming of
worship and study of God's Word. And we who live long centuries after
Ezra and Nehemiah may find something helpful in what they did and
said. We, too, need a religious education along with our public school
education; we need to examine our faith; now and then, we need to
check up on ourselves; we need to ask questions when we are puzzled
about our God and His ways; we need to openly confess that we have
been wrong many times while God has never been wrong; we need to
repent and start a new leaf in our spiritual diaries.

Like the tanks on our automobiles, we need refilling, now and then.

SUGGESTIONS TO TEACHERS

Five Ohio couples claiming to be super-Christians of an avant-garde
variety announced smugly that their faith freed them from all regulations. They claimed they had the Holy Spirit's direction, and therefore
did not need to study the Bible anymore. Their insistence that Christ
brought them freedom from sexual restrictions, however, finally
wrecked the group.

What about the matter of rules? Are Christians subject to guidelines of
any kind? What is the place of the Scriptures? Can the Christian community get along without the Bible?

Today's lesson looks at these and other tough questions. God's covenant with Ezra will introduce these issues with clarity. The material in
Nehemiah 8 and 9 suggests at least three pegs on which to put your
lesson.

1. *REFORM.* God's covenant or agreement demands an on-going reformation by us. We are constantly being reshaped by His claims. We
may keep trust with the Lord as we live obediently. Out of love for us
and out of concern for our well-being, God has provided guidelines for
us. These guidelines help us to continue in our covenant relationship.

These guidelines assist us to live more responsibly. They re-form us; they bring us back to be and to do what God has in mind for us. As Ezra "explained the Law to them" (Nehemiah 8:7) leaders must call for reformation constantly. You, in the tradition of Ezra and other leaders of the faith, must call your class to allow obedience to God's guidelines in the Scriptures to reform each member.

2. *REJOICE.* Call attention to the way Ezra's people understood God's Law to be a cause for joy! Help your class to comprehend the way God will not permit us to do as we please. For our own safety, health, and well-being, He puts bounds on us. He lays down obligations for us because He loves us. Encourage your people to think and talk about the Good News of keeping the requirements Christ lays on us!

3. *REMEMBER.* Ezra and the people were told to remember God's covenant with their ancestors. Likewise, we must keep alive the corporate memory of God's promises. How? One crucial way is by regularly and carefully retelling the story of His involvement. Or, more properly, allow the story to tell itself by listening to Scripture. We remember God as we work with the Bible. Furthermore, we also remember who we are!

TOPIC FOR ADULTS
GOD'S COVENANT AND EZRA

Learning How to Remember. People sometimes speak of having a "poor memory." Actually, a memory is not something like an eye or an ear or a muscle that can be developed by exercise. *Memory* in actuality is the three processes of learning, retaining, and recalling. The first—learning—is the key to memory.

Some people can remember verses of poems learned thirty years ago, but cannot remember the names of two persons introduced to them two minutes ago. A man can recall the batting averages of ballplayers of two seasons ago, but has trouble remembering his wife's birthday. The late Jim Farley could remember names of workers in the Democratic party years after sitting with them at dinner and was an invaluable help to President Franklin D. Roosevelt. Oswald Jacoby, the bridge expert, could glance at his thirteen cards, put them in his pocket and play them one by one without looking at his hand again—and play a game of gin rummy on the side! Why is this?

Experts tell us that we learn what we are interested in. We learn what we like. We remember what has relevance to our concerns. Learning depends on motivation. Learning how to learn is the only way to improve memory. And this depends on wanting to remember.

How badly do you want to remember God? How much are you spurred to learn to grow in understanding His ways? How deeply do you desire to keep your commitments to Jesus Christ?

Essentially, Ezra's question to the returned exiles was one of *wanting* to remember God. Do you?

Spiritual Work. Our modern civilization has become quite flabby in matters of religion. Too many people simply accept religion as a natural part of their surroundings, without being religious themselves. They remind one of "father" in Clarence Day's humorous book, *God and My*

Father, who felt that he was doing enough by simply going to church and sitting in a pew: "Any spiritual work ought to be done by the clergy."

God's covenants mean that spiritual work is done by all of God's people. Ezra and Nehemiah insisted that called for a renewal on the part of every believer.

God summons each to undertaking His work where he or she lives!

Feelings in Cold Storage. During the height of the Russian Revolution and Civil War, Maxim Gorky took Lenin to a concert to hear a young Russian pianist. The musician performed superbly, concluding his concert with a beautiful rendition of Beethoven's *Appassianata Sonata.* Lenin was profoundly moved. He was so deeply affected that he sat for several seconds in his seat without speaking, his eyes downcast and misty. Finally he turned to Gorky, and told him how much he deplored having to live in a time when he was forced to be so cruel. Gorky looked surprised.

Lenin continued, "As long as the war lasts, I will listen to no more such music."

The mastermind of the Red takeover determined to put his finer feelings in cold storage for the time being.

How many people try to deal with the tragic "necessities" of life by "listening to no more such music."

The beauty and hope of God's merciful activity in our world must be heard again and again—especially in Scripture. We must listen frequently and attentively to God's Word if we are not to be desensitized and brutalized by the conditions of our age.

Questions for Pupils on the Next Lesson. 1. What is your congregation doing about conditions among the poor, the oppressed, and imprisoned? 2. What examples of discrimination based on sex, color, ethnic background do you notice in your community? 3. What is the connection between worship and service? 4. How is participation in the Lord's Supper an act of covenant renewal? 5. Are there exceptions in regard to those you should care for? Should you love hippies and communists, for example? 6. What does the New Covenant in Christ mean to you?

TOPIC FOR YOUTH
LIVING BY GOD'S WORD

Survival Rules. There is an old New England story about a farmer driving to town on a wintry, subzero morning. He passed a woman who had been walking and had sat down to rest on the edge of a bridge. The farmer also noticed a baby in the woman's arms. To his consternation, he saw that the woman, exhausted from the cold walk, showed signs of dropping off to sleep, which would have been fatal to the baby and her. The old Vermonter knew that he had to take drastic action to rouse her, certainly more than taking her up on his sledge where she would have dozed off again. Grabbing the baby suddenly from her arms, he shouted, climbed up on his sledge and whipped up the horses. To his relief, he looked back to see the woman stand startled, take a few steps, then push herself to running after the sledge. He slowed the sledge as her circulation restored and permitted her to catch up and climb on. Gruff, but considerate, he saved both the mother and child from freezing to death.

God must sometimes act the same way. For our own good, He establishes boundaries and basics. We must follow these. He covenants in love to be with us. We must contract in trust to obey.

Just as allowing oneself to fall asleep in freezing temperatures will bring destruction of one's life, so also disobeying God's Word will bring other forms of ruin and death.

Sometimes, God seems to act in a gruff way, but, like the Vermont farmer rescuing the freezing woman, He always does it out of wisdom and goodness!

No Easy Picture. When Holman Hunt set out to paint his famous painting, the *Light of the World,* he spent the major part of three years trying to get the proper atmosphere for depicting Christ at the door. In his effort to paint the wintry light in Christ's lantern, he spent many, many nights out in the wind, his feet wrapped in straw to keep them warm. If it took a great artist three years to catch the spirit of the presence of Christ, how can we expect to possess the "Light of the World" in an easy moment.

Jump With Joy. The covenant brings joy! Christians are meant to be joyful people. God's promises brought joy to Ezra and the people when He brought them back from captivity in Babylon to Jerusalem.

There was joy in the eyes of the apostles on the day of Pentecost as there is joy in the eyes of all who receive the Holy Spirit. The fruit of the Spirit is joy. Whenever the Holy Spirit is given, He brings joy. It was so with the early Franciscans. They were called "The Master's Merry Men." They were so happy that they had to be reproved for laughing in church. It was so with the early Methodists. They set their hymns to dance tunes.

It was so with the early Salvationist Army. The joy of the Holy Spirit was in them. General William Booth told his followers that, whenever they felt like jumping for joy, they were to jump. Sometimes in the middle of a meeting he would pause so that they could all jump together!

Sentence Sermon to Remember: We should not boast of having been born again unless we trim and light anew the candle of faith in our hearts, daily. —Anonymous.

Questions for Pupils on the Next Lesson. 1. How are you going about your search for a meaningful life's work? 2. What does Jesus Christ have to do with this search? 3. How does the Lord's Supper help you to understand your commitments in life to Jesus Christ? 4. How is your faith sensitizing you to the needs of the poor, the oppressed, the imprisoned? 5. What examples of discrimination do you see in your community and in your church? What do you think the church should do about any examples of discrimination?

LESSON IX—NOVEMBER 2

GOD'S COVENANT AND JESUS CHRIST

Background Scripture: Luke 4:16–30; John 13:31–35; Mark 14:22–25
Devotional Reading: Hebrews 6:1–12

KING JAMES VERSION

LUKE 4 16 And he came to Nazareth, where he had been brought up: and, as his custom was, he went into the synagogue on the sabbath day, and stood up for to read.

17 And there was delivered unto him the book of the prophet Esaias. And when he had opened the book, he found the place where it was written,

18 The Spirit of the Lord *is* upon me, because he hath anointed me to preach the gospel to the poor; he hath sent me to heal the broken-hearted, to preach deliverance to the captives, and recovering of sight to the blind, to set at liberty them that are bruised,

19 To preach the acceptable year of the Lord.

20 And he closed the book, and he gave *it* again to the minister, and sat down. And the eyes of all them that were in the synagogue were fastened on him.

21 And he began to say unto them, This day is this scripture fulfilled in your ears.

MARK 14 22 And as they did eat, Jesus took bread, and blessed, and brake *it*, and gave to them, and said, Take, eat; this is my body.

23 And he took the cup, and when he had given thanks, he gave *it* to them: and they all drank of it.

24 And he said unto them, This is my blood of the new testament, which is shed for many.

25 Verily I say unto you, I will drink no more of the fruit of the vine, until that day that I drink it new in the kingdom of God.

REVISED STANDARD VERSION

LUKE 4 16 And he came to Nazareth, where he had been brought up; and he went to the synagogue, as his custom was, on the sabbath day. And he stood up to read; 17 and there was given to him the book of the prophet Isaiah. He opened the book and found the place where it was written,

18 "The Spirit of the Lord is upon me,
because he has anointed me to
    preach good news to the poor.
He has sent me to proclaim release
    to the captives
and recovering of sight to the blind,
to set at liberty those who are op-
    pressed,
19 to proclaim the acceptable year of
    the Lord."

20 And he closed the book, and gave it back to the attendant, and sat down; and the eyes of all in the synagogue were fixed on him. 21 And he began to say to them, "Today this scripture has been fulfilled in your hearing."

MARK 14 22 And as they were eating, he took bread, and blessed, and broke it, and gave it to them, and said, "Take; this is my body." 23 And he took a cup, and when he had given thanks he gave it to them, and they all drank of it. 24 And he said to them, "This is my blood of the covenant, which is poured out for many. 25 Truly, I say to you, I shall not drink again of the fruit of the vine until that day when I drink it new in the kingdom of God."

KEY VERSE: By this all men will know that you are my disciples, if you have love for one another. John 13:35 (RSV).

71

HOME DAILY BIBLE READINGS

Oct. 27. M. A Covenant Needed. Genesis 3:9–15.
Oct. 28. T. A Renewed Covenant. Exodus 6:1–8.
Oct. 29. W. The Covenant Is Secure. 2 Samuel 23:1–5.
Oct. 30. T. God's Promise to His People. Psalm 147:1–11.
Oct. 31. F. God's Son Is Confirmed. Mark 1:1–11.
Nov. 1. S. The Living Covenant Is Coming. Isaiah 61:1–3.
Nov. 2. S. The Living Covenant. Luke 4:16–30.

BACKGROUND

Jesus of Nazareth, having been reared in a Jewish home, was well educated in the covenants of the Jewish people and their Scriptures—especially concerning the covenant of Jeremiah 31:31–34, which we studied in our lesson for October 19. As a well-established preacher and teacher, He was well qualified to talk and teach about the covenants of His people with God.

Luke 4:15 says that "he taught in their synagogues, being glorified of all." In the days following His temptations on the mount, He became a popular preacher, gladly heard and widely praised. And with this popularity, He faced another and greater temptation.

At this peak of His popularity, He came back to His home town of Nazareth to appear in the local synagogue, "And the eyes of all them that were in the synagogue were fastened on him" (Luke 4:20). These were indeed His own people; they knew Him well as "the carpenter's son" who had become famous all across the land. They settled down to listen to another "popular" sermon—and they were bitterly disappointed.

These people, too, knew of the promises of the old covenants; deep in them was the old expectancy of a great leader who would bring them freedom from Rome and reestablish their old power and glory,—a warrior-Messiah. That idea must have been a great temptation for Jesus—but He shook them badly when He got up to preach.

NOTES ON THE PRINTED TEXT

1. . . . and there was given to him the book of the prophet Isaiah. Luke 4:16 (RSV). Worship in the synagogue at the time of Jesus consisted of the recitation of the Shema, a prayer, readings from the Law and from the prophets, a talk based on the Scripture, and a final blessing. Any competent layman might be invited to read, or to teach (preach). Jesus, as the reader and preacher this Sabbath in the synagogue, chose to read Isaiah 61:1, 2, a passage in which the prophet pictures the deliverance of Israel from the exile in Babylon. The year in which this was to happen would be called "the year of the Lord's favor." "But," says a commentator, "the actual release from Babylonian captivity had not brought the fulfillment for which they hoped. Nor had the centuries since. Still they were an oppressed, conquered, broken people. The prophet, then, must have had a deeper meaning in mind. He must have been speaking of the Messianic Age, when the sin which had led to the Babylonian captivity would be dealt with."—Donald G. Miller in *The Layman's Bible Commentary,* Vol. 18, p. 58, by permission of John Knox Press, publishers.

Having read this prophecy of the Coming (Messianic) Age, Jesus closed the scroll and handed it back to the attendant (not the *minister*) who had given it to Him, and said boldly, "This day is this Scripture fulfilled in your ears" (verse 21). Today, that very day, the prophecy of Isaiah had come true. *He stood before them as the Messiah!* Can you imagine the silence that must have greeted that statement?

He had come, yes, but not as the sort of Messiah they had expected. Not as a great militant, perhaps even a great military leader, but as the Suffering Servant that Isaiah had predicted (Isaiah 52:12–53:12). As God's Servant He brought to earth the power of God—*the power of His love.* Love was the only weapon He would ever use. He came not preaching rebellion against Rome, but a better way: the way of sacrificial love.

He was a Messiah come to preach the Gospel to the poor, to those who so terribly needed understanding and compassion and not oppression and exploitation: that was Good News, great news, to the poverty-stricken who so desperately needed a little love. He came to heal the brokenhearted, to comfort and sustain those who mourn, to bring the presence and the uplifting arms to those who "walked with lame and weary feet upon a heavy road." He came not to magically prevent sorrow and suffering, but to give those who suffered a way to see through it all to a God of love who suffered with them.

He came to set the captives free; not political captives or captives who were criminals, but the captives of poverty and inequality, the captives enslaved by intolerance, the slaves of greed and avarice and hatred and prejudice and fear. He had come, this Messiah, to make the blind see—not necessarily the physically blind, although he healed many whom were blind physically—but those blind with lust and selfishness and the dust of the marketplace, so blind with all this that they could not see the glory and love and majesty of God. He came to give eyes to the mind and the heart and the soul to see clearly the truth and love and hope of their Creator.

Read it carefully, Christian, for this is what *you* are to do in His name. Ask yourself, "How much of this have I done lately—or at all?"

II. "This is my blood of the covenant, which is poured out for many." Mark 14:24 (RSV). Now we come to the Last Supper of Jesus, mere hours before He was to be arrested in Gethsemane. Actually, it was the occasion of the traditional Passover supper, long observed in Judaism. Jesus chose that moment, that supper, to make His dramatic statement that on this occasion He was instituting a new covenant, and in that sense it was something more than a casual celebration of the old Jewish Passover.

In the Judaistic Passover supper, a cup was passed not once but four times; they drank from cups which signified sanctification, explaining or proclaiming, thanksgiving, and consecration. Jesus gave the cup a new meaning and emphasis; as He passed the cup, after the breaking of the bread (symbolizing the breaking of His body), He reminded His disciples that the cup held "my blood of the new covenant." Up to this point, covenants in Israel meant an arrangement, a bargain, a relationship between God and the nation; but the new covenant of this Supper meant a new relationship between God and *man*, a covenant not dependent upon man's obedience to Jewish law but on *love*. It meant that men were no longer living under the law of God; they were living *within the love of God.* He was saying that in that love, man's sins would be conquered, overcome. He said that the cup contained His blood poured out for many (men), all men.

This, then, is the meaning of the Sacrament of the Last Supper which we celebrate in our churches. We say as we partake of this Sacrament that we do it in remembrance of Him. We like that word, *remembrance,* but to many of us it is something more. The Supper (Communion) is a reconsecration, a new vow of loyalty to Him; it is a reaffirmation of our faith in Him; it is a thanksgiving for the saving value of His death on Calvary's bloody cross.

We will do well, in this lesson, to keep in mind that statement of Jesus in which He tried to make it plain that His blood was offered up for the salvation of "many"; it was meant not only for those who understood that, but for those who did not. He knew that around that table there was one who would betray Him in Gethsemane; He knew that there were others there who would "fall away" from Him in days to come. He was about to die for those already fallen (Judas, for instance), and for those who would desert Him in fear, in the coming days of persecution. *But He loved them and still was ready to die for them.* Paul puts it well in Romans 5:8 (RSV).: "While we were yet sinners Christ died for us."

The Supper was meant for all sinners—and that includes all of us!

SUGGESTIONS TO TEACHERS

You need make no apologies about the fact that today's lesson will zero in on Jesus. You don't have to tiptoe around the subject, or hunt for catchy gimmicks. You have so much material in this week's Scripture that you should get down to business immediately.

1. *FULFILLMENT.* Emphasize that the fulfillment of all the old covenant takes place in Jesus Christ. He is God's new beginning. All of God's promises are summed up in Jesus' life, death, and Resurrection. Aid your class in understanding that they and others do not have to wonder if Jesus may be outdated or superseded. Jesus offers as complete a knowledge of God's plans and pledges that they will ever need!

2. *FULMINATION.* Take a few minutes to let the class comment on ways in which people resent Jesus today. Just as some fulminated against Him and finally murdered Him in the first century, some resist His claims in the twentieth century. As teacher, help your people to reexamine Jesus' extraordinary claims on their lives. What are some of these claims? Realizing these, no person may take Jesus for granted!

3. *FULCRUM.* Jesus insists that He is the one bringing a new age (read Luke 4:18, 19). He is the fulcrum of history. It is no accident that even the calendar relates all events in terms of before or after His coming! His covenant with each person is the most pivotal fact of his or her existence. Encourage each person in your class to reflect on the place of Jesus Christ in his or her life.

4. *FOLLOWERS.* The new covenant through Christ's death means a new commandment for His followers: "Love one another even as I have loved you" (*see* John 13:34). Love is the identity badge of the followers

of Christ. Unless you and your class grow in the terms of this covenant of love, you cannot presume to call yourselves His followers!

5. *FIDELITY*. The seal of the new covenant through Jesus Christ was His broken, bloodied body. The living Lord promises He keeps faith with us, and confirms His fidelity through the sacrament of bread and cup. His faithfulness, even to dying on a cross, is communicated afresh in communion.

TOPIC FOR ADULTS
GOD'S COVENANT AND JESUS CHRIST

The Christlike God. "There are unknown depths of God which must appear dark to us. Perhaps we can only make a negative statement and say, in some well-chosen words of Michael Ramsay, that in the Father 'there is no un-Christlikeness at all.' There are regions of the Godhead that must be veiled from finite understanding, but the Christian belief is that there is nothing in him that contradicts what has been revealed in his human face, Jesus Christ.

"But even to believe in this negative formulation that there is no un-Christlikeness in the primordial source of being is to believe much indeed. It is a belief that makes a great difference to the lives of those who hold it, and which enables them to live in this perplexing world with a hope that they could not otherwise have.

"Michael Ramsey was making his point about relating our thoughts about God to what we have seen in Christ in the course of a discussion in which he claimed that if the concept of God has come to seem incredible to many people nowadays, it may well be due to the fact that our concept of God has not been truly Christianized and that there are un-Christlike elements lurking in it. This has been very much my contention . . . . As Christians, we have to think of the Father in the light of Jesus Christ.

"When we ask how the passion and cross of Christ affect our understanding of the Father, then we can rule out some mistaken ideas right away. We cannot think, for instance, of the Father as a stern judge, exacting the death of the Son as a penalty for sin, though many Christians have in fact thought in that way. We cannot think either, I would say, of the Father remote and secure on his sapphire throne, himself untouched by the passion of the Son.

"Am I saying then that the Father, too, God in the very depth of his Godhood, is touched and affected by the passion? That is surely what we must say, if we are determined to know God through Jesus Christ, and not in some other way of our own choosing . . . ."—John MacQuarrie, *The Humility of God*, Westminster Press, 1978.

The Master's Mark. The ancient Greek artist Apelles was supreme in his day. Apelles also had the rare quality of being able to praise other painters. One day, he heard that his greatest rival, Protogenes, was living in poverty. Apelles sailed to Rhodes to visit him. Protogenes, however, had not known that Apelles was coming and was not in his studio when Apelles came. An old woman attendant asked Apelles whom she should announce had visited when her master returned. Apelles replied by taking a brush. Going to a panel, he traced with one stroke an outline of exceeding fineness and beauty. When Protogenes returned, the old woman told him that she was sorry that she did not know the name of a man who had called, but led Protogenes to the panel. Protogenes looked at the delicacy of the line and exclaimed, "Only Apelles could have drawn that line!"

When we see Jesus' life, we realize that He truly bears the mark of God. Only God could have lived that life! Through His covenanting presence, we realize that God has indeed visited us!

Working in the Living Flesh. Vincent Van Gogh, the brilliant painter, held to a devotion to Jesus Christ in spite of his emotional illnesses. In the later part of his life, he lived in Saint-Remy, where he was confined in an asylum. Between plunges into the depths of despair, Van Gogh painted brilliantly, and the turbulence of his own spirit is seen in the work of this period.

Van Gogh sank deeper and deeper into madness, and in the end committed suicide. But he never quite lost his religious feeling, which he once expressed in a painter's evaluation of Christ: "(He was) more of an artist than all the others, disdaining marble and clay and color, working in the living flesh."

Questions for Pupils on the Next Lesson. 1. Are you sometimes conscious of a lack of spiritual power? Does this trouble you? 2. What do you understand it is to be "filled with the Spirit?" 3.Have you been aware of the Spirit working through your life? Through your Church? 4. What relationship do you feel you have with the Old Testament people of God?

YOUTH TOPIC
NEW COVENANT IN CHRIST

Other Christs? "The uniqueness and finality of Jesus as the Christ are being challenged by the revitalization of old religions and the birth of new ones. Can Guatama Buddha or Sun Myung Moon be our savior too? Or does one of the myriad human potential movements point the way to self-fulfillment? The clearcut answer of the Christian faith is, No! Jesus is the unique and final Christ, God's anointed Savior and Lord. Interfaith dialogue . . . ought to be carried on from a stance *within* one particular faith. Only those who passionately believe in a particular faith can truly represent it to those of other faiths and can authentically judge how another faith challenges, differs from and supplements and enriches one's own faith."—Arnold B. Come, *Monday Morning,* Oct. 9, 1978.

Greatest Hero. Visitors to London's famous Madame Tusaaud's Wax Museum are treated to a display of life-size, lifelike models of many of the world's great personages. Most of the recent heroes and villains and dozens of notable historical personalities are depicted in astonishingly accurate detail. After looking at the figures in the museum, some visitors were recently polled.

The findings revealed that Uganda's mercurial dictator, Idi Amin, was rapidly gaining on Adolf Hitler as the most hated man in history.

The visitors polled considered Joan of Arc and Winston Churchill the greatest heroine and hero of all time. Tied for next place were John F. Kennedy, Jesus, and Admiral Horatio Nelson.

Where is Jesus in your list? Is He Lord, and therefore Number One? What does He mean to you?

Most important, are you covenanted with Him?

More Than Advice. Lucy comes up to Charlie Brown. Noticing his woebegone expression, she asks, "Discouraged again, eh, Charlie Brown?" Lucy continues, "You know what your trouble is? The whole trouble with you is that you're *you!*"

Charlie replies, "Well, what in the world can I do about that?"

Lucy states, "I don't pretend to be able to give advice. I merely point out the trouble."

Jesus does more than point out the trouble. He also does more than give advice. He even affirms that you are special to Him. His covenant with you underscores that He comes to bring a new relationship between you and God.

Sentence Sermon to Remember: Christ cannot be valued at all unless He be valued above all.—St. Augustine.

Questions for Pupils on the Next Lesson. 1. How do you think a person can find an exciting life? What does the leading of the Holy Spirit have to do with finding this? 2. Can you think of examples where God's Spirit filled a person's life with joy and meaning? Has this ever happened to you? 3. Are God's blessings primarily for older people, or for all ages? 4. What vision do you have of what you can do for God? 5. Is the new dimension in life which the Spirit brings primarily for individual believers or is it primarily for a Christian group?

LESSON X—NOVEMBER 9

GOD'S COVENANT AND PETER

Background Scripture: Acts 2, 3
Devotional Reading: 1 Thessalonians 4:1–12

KING JAMES VERSION

ACTS 2 14 But Peter, standing up with the eleven, lifted up his voice, and said unto them, Ye men of Judea, and all *ye* that dwell at Jerusalem, be this known unto you, and hearken to my words:

15 For these are not drunken, as ye suppose, seeing it is *but* the third hour of the day.

16 But this is that which was spoken by the prophet Joel;

17 And it shall come to pass in the last days, saith God, I will pour out of my Spirit upon all flesh: and your sons and your daughters shall prophesy, and your young men shall see visions, and your old men shall dream dreams:

3 18 But those things, which God before had shewed by the mouth of all his prophets, that Christ should suffer, he hath so fulfilled.

19 Repent ye therefore, and be converted, that your sins may be blotted out, when the times of refreshing shall come from the presence of the Lord;

20 And he shall send Jesus Christ, which before was preached unto you:

21 Whom the heaven must receive until the times of restitution of all things, which God hath spoken by the mouth of all his holy prophets since the world began.

22 For Moses truly said unto the fathers, A prophet shall the Lord your God raise up unto you of your brethren, like unto me; him shall ye hear in all things whatsoever he shall say unto you.

23 And it shall come to pass, *that* every soul, which will not hear that prophet, shall be destroyed from among the people.

24 Yea, and all the prophets from Samuel and those that follow after, as many as have spoken, have likewise foretold of these days.

REVISED STANDARD VERSION

ACTS 2 14 But Peter, standing with the eleven, lifted up his voice and addressed them, "Men of Judea and all who dwell in Jerusalem, let this be known to you, and give ear to my words. 15 For these men are not drunk, as you suppose, since it is only the third hour of the day; 16 but this is what was spoken by the prophet Joel: 17 'And in the last days it shall be, God declares,

that I will pour out my Spirit upon all flesh,

and your sons and your daughters shall prophesy,

and your young men shall see visions, and your old men shall dream dreams;

3 18 "But what God foretold by the mouth of all the prophets, that his Christ should suffer, he thus fulfilled. 19 Repent therefore, and turn again, that your sins may be blotted out, that times of refreshing may come from the presence of the Lord, 20 and that he may send the Christ appointed for you, Jesus, 21 whom heaven must receive until the time for establishing all that God spoke by the mouth of his holy prophets from of old. 22 Moses said, 'The Lord God will raise up for you a prophet from your brethren as he raised me up. You shall listen to him in whatever he tells you. 23 And it shall be that every soul that does not listen to that prophet shall be destroyed from the people.' 24 And all the prophets who have spoken, from Samuel and those who came afterwards, also proclaimed these days. 25 You are the sons of the prophets and of the covenant which God gave to your fathers, saying to Abraham, 'And in your posterity shall all the families of the earth be blessed.' 26 God, having raised up his servant, sent him to you first, to bless

25 Ye are the children of the prophets, and of the covenant which God made with our fathers, saying unto Abraham, And in thy seed shall all the kindreds of the earth be blessed.

26 Unto you first God, having raised up his Son Jesus, sent him to bless you, in turning away every one of you from his iniquities.

you in turning every one of you from your wickedness."

KEY VERSE: *And in the last days it shall be, God declares, that I will pour out my Spirit upon all flesh, and your sons and your daughters shall prophesy . . . .* Acts 2:17 (RSV).

HOME DAILY BIBLE READINGS

Nov. 3. M. Peter Encounters Jesus. John 1:35–42.
Nov. 4. T. A True Confession. Matthew 16:13–19.
Nov. 5. W. A Mountaintop Experience. Matthew 17:1–8.
Nov. 6. T. A Promise to Be Broken. Mark 14:26–31.
Nov. 7. F. A False Confession. Matthew 26:69–75.
Nov. 8. S. Peter's Challenge. John 21:15–19.
Nov. 9. S. Peter Proclaims. Acts 2:14–17.

BACKGROUND

Seven weeks after the Resurrection, on the day of Pentecost, a sizeable group of believers in Jesus (Acts 1:15 says that there were 120 of them), were gathered together, for what specific purpose we do not know. In all probability, they were wondering what they should do, now that Jesus was gone. They were people speaking in at least fifteen different languages (*see* verses 7–11 of Acts 2), and that meant confusion; There was even greater confusion; as Paul explains in Acts 2, there came the rushing of a mighty wind, and flames of tongues of fire settled on their heads. Desperately afraid, they all cried out together in their own languages; the record says that this was because they were filled with the Holy Spirit.

Peter was there—Peter who had not so long ago denied his Christ, but who now rose as a great leader with a great message for the hour—and for the ages. He preached the first of all Christian sermons; it is immortal; it set the guidelines of the Holy Spirit from that moment until today.

NOTES ON THE PRINTED TEXT

I. And it shall come to pass in the last days, saith God, I will pour out my Spirit upon all flesh . . . . Acts 2:17. Peter, typically, may have been a bit angry as he began to preach, for he prefaced his remarks with a condemnation of those who were saying that these confused people, speaking in (many) tongues, were drunk. Not so, said the gallant fisherman: no man gets drunk at nine o'clock in the morning! Those speaking in tongues were not stimulated by alcohol, but by the very Spirit of God.

He takes his text from Joel 2:28. He takes it from this prophet because he wants to make it clear that what was happening at this Pentecostal meeting was ordained of God, and a fulfillment of the prophecy of Joel, away back in the fourth century B.C. As far back as Joel, and perhaps even farther back, the people of Israel were longing and hoping for a time when God would send His Spirit not upon a few gifted people but upon His *whole* people. They looked forward to the day when that would happen; they called it "The Day of the Lord." For generations they had dreamed of this—of the Day when God would intervene in history through His Son's appearance on the earth. Peter cried out to them, "The Day has come; Jesus has come."

No, he said, these excited people were not drunk; they were people who understood that it was all a fulfillment of prophecy—people with vision enough to understand that the old ages of longing were over, and that a new day had come. Drunk? That allegation has always been made against men of great vision, against men not content to sit around dreaming of "the good old days," but younger, more farsighted men possessed of vision of a future in the hands of God. When Robert Fulton got the vision of steam-powered "steamboats," he was called crazy; when the Wright brothers flew their first airplane, they were called fools, crackpots: "If God had meant men to fly, He would have put wings on their bodies!" Said John Haynes Holmes, "It is the cracked people, historically, who have let the light through." It was not the past-bound Jewish rulers who fought the new Christian leaders, nor the Roman Nero who crucified the new Christians who were right; it was those who died for Christ who had a true, transforming vision in place of the old dreams of a yesterday that was dead. Old men dream; youth has visions—and tomorrow is in their hands.

Jesus was called mad by His own brothers; they did not see or understand the divine Spirit which in Him was to change the course of history. That was the central thought of Peter's sermon; that was the truth that God had sent, the truth that drove those who heard him into an ecstasy for which they were willing to die.

II. *"You are the sons of the prophets and of the covenant which God gave to your fathers; saying to Abraham, 'and in your posterity shall all the families of the earth be blessed.' "* Acts 3:25 (RSV). Now we are reading a second sermon of Peter. He preached it just outside the gate called The Beautiful Gate of the Temple, where, in company with John, he had just healed a man born lame. In the name of Jesus of Nazareth, the lame one had been healed; he went walking and leaping and praising God with them into the Temple. A crowd, gaping in awe, gathered around Peter, and he preached to them.

It was a sermon filled with spiritual dynamite. First, Peter told them that it was not he who had healed the lame one, but Jesus. "I refer to Jesus," he said, "the Jesus whom you rejected . . ." (verse 13, *The Living Bible*). This sermon deals with three generations—or, better with three ages of men and with their relationship to the Christ of the new covenant. And, more particularly, with what those in two of the ages should be doing for and about the Christ.

First, there are those who crucified Him. Paul says that *"you"* killed

Him; perhaps there were some in Paul's day who had approved of the Crucifixion; if so, the pronoun is justified. They crucified Him, but, as Peter says, they crucified Him in ignorance. The One they killed prayed God to forgive them, for they knew not what they did. But now they had no right to offer the weak excuse of ignorance, for the Risen Christ had been in their midst. This generation had seen Him and heard Him; they couldn't plead ignorance of *that!*

Then he speaks to a second group: those who may not have actively participated in approving of the Crucifixion, but who had denied Him nevertheless in giving the approval of silence. They did not approve publicly; neither did they object, and therein they sinned against Him. They were living in a day between Christ's Resurrection and His Second Coming. The prophecy of the Suffering Servant had been fulfilled before their very eyes, and it surely must have opened their eyes; it should have made them *want* to live in new covenant with Him. This was a time in which they should "Repent, turn again, that your sins may be blotted out" (3:19). They have a great opportunity to repent, *now.*

Peter, here, seems to be referring to the wholesale repentence of the Jewish *nation,* which should, by its repentance, hasten the return of Jesus. Unfortunately, the nation did no such thing; that has not happened yet. But *we* still live in the days between the death and the Resurrection. We are as much the sons of the prophets as they were!

The third age, to which Peter speaks, is the age of the future. It deals not only with those who lived in Christ's time, but those who lived after He had left the earth; it is a call to repentance on the part of those in the Church which had arisen in Israel and was to spread over the whole earth. Those in the Church *know* that He had come, and that He had died for them, and a great obligation is upon them: they must not only admit His living (resurrected) presence among them—they must keep His covenant, obey His commandments, follow Him in spirit and in truth.

But do we do that? Yes, a large percentage of us join the Church and attend its services in worship—but is that all that is required of us? Do we really have His Spirit and live by it, or do we merely pay Him lip service and do as we please? Do we crucify Him every day, in our lifestyles? Do we really know what we are doing when we partake of His Supper? Is repentance merely a case of saying "I'm sorry"?

What is your definition of repentance, and how do you practice it?

SUGGESTIONS TO TEACHERS

You probably have met church members who think that God stopped operating in people's lives about 1,900 years ago. Some, you perhaps noticed, have a wistful attitude of "How much easier it would have been if we'd lived back then." You may have some who secretly think this way in your class.

Your assignment today will emphasize the coming of the Holy Spirit into people's lives as the fulfillment of the covenant promise of God. You will help your people to understand that the same God who covenanted in love and power with Abraham, Moses, Joshua, David, Jeremiah, Ezra, and the rest of our ancestors in the faith, also covenants with believers in each age.

God's covenant and Peter (Acts 2, 3) provide a rich opportunity for exploring the meaning of the Spirit's coming.

1. *POWERFUL SPIRIT; POWERLESS SINNERS.* You will find that some in your class probably misunderstand what it is to be "filled with the Spirit." Refer to Acts 2, 3. The presence and the power of the Lord were known by ordinary folk like Peter. The same power and presence of God which had encountered these people in the person of Jesus confronted them at Pentecost. The same God who had entered into solemn agreements with His people in the old covenant, and had inaugurated a new covenant through Jesus Christ, made His promise a personal one with Peter and the other believers. Stress that this same God sends His Spirit to introduce His new covenant to people today. The coming of the Holy Spirit is not a religious luxury for a favored few. Powerless sinners today, you may remind your folks, find life through the powerful Risen Lord's Spirit.

2. *LIMITLESS SOURCE: LIMITED RESOURCES.* Focus also on the way the Spirit's coming impelled the early Christians to share. His coming to believers resulted in a community of power and a priesthood of companions. Peter and John shared the power given to that community of covenanted people by healing a cripple. These apostles also ministered to one another. The secret, of course, was the Spirit of Jesus in their lives. Silver and gold and other resources were in slender supply, but they had the promise of the Lord! That was enough! Discuss the meaning of Christ's promise of power through the Spirit now. Ask persons in your class to share ways in which they have been aware of the presence and power of the Lord in their personal lives.

TOPIC FOR ADULTS
GOD'S COVENANT AND PETER

Fire. "Several years ago, I read a novel entitled *Fire*, in which the author, George R. Stewart, described the birth and spread of a forest fire that had swept through 10,000 acres of giant pine trees in five days.

"As the story opened, a thunderstorm was raging in the Ponderosa National Forest. At the height of the storm, lightning struck a tall jeffrey pine tree whose roots penetrated a vein of underground moisture. Within a few seconds, the tree became tense with electrical pressure and pieces of charged bark were thrown through the air. At the base of the tree, the discharge ran along a buttress-root at the surface of the ground and heated some dry needles to kindling point. In the evening a thin column of smoke, as from a cigarette, rose faintly into the air.

"The fire barely lived through the night, for a chill descended upon the mountains, and the fire cooled until only a few glowing spots remained. During the first five days of its life, the fire came close to dying several times, but a pine cone or a dry twig gave fresh life to the cooling embers. It was not until the sixth day that the fire grew to noticeable size.

"But once the fire grew strong enough to sustain itself, it needed only some favorable wind of circumstance to enable it to sweep throughout the forest. Such a moment came, and the fire fighters were unable to conquer the fire until it had swept over 10,000 acres of pine trees.

"As I read Mr. Stewart's novel, I was impressed with the similarity between his account of the forest fire and the record of what takes place in the birth and development of the religious life."—Charles R. Woodson, *Pulpit Digest*.

Force Coming Down to Send Us Up. In Switzerland, you may go up in a funicular railway worked by hydraulic power, one of those engineering marvels that carries heavy loads almost perpendicularly up the mountainside. As you ascend you marvel at the mastery of man over nature. More than half-way up, when you look out of the window, you notice a waterfall pouring its cataracts over the mountainside. If the railway is the essence of modernity, the waterfall is no contrast but a complement. It is the source of the hydraulic power. It is the force of that water coming down that alone can send you up.

God's power came down at Pentecost that we might rise.

Luster Not Lighted. Do you recall the remark made by Sir Walter Scott as he stood before a statue of Robert Burns? He looked at it for a moment and then said: "Yes, the luster is there, but it is not lighted up." It seems to me that what Scott missed in the statue of the poet, we miss in our own lives and in the Church.

Questions for Pupils on the Next Lesson. 1. Why should Christians evaluate old and new methods in the sharing of God's message with unbelievers? 2. How can your congregation and your class help other Christians know that they can feel a special worth and acceptance by God? 3. How do you depend on the Holy Spirit for guidance? 4. Will faithful proclamation and living the Gospel necessarily mean a life of success and comfort? 5. What are circumstances which will provoke opposition to those trying to live obedient Christian lives in your community today?

TOPIC FOR YOUTH
LIFE'S NEW DIMENSION

Are You Present? In his autobiography, *Years of Fulfillment,* Dr. Norman Maclean tells a story of an examination at the Colinton Parish School. One teacher had taught a class to repeat the Apostles's Creed clause by clause, each pupil having his own clause. As the recitation began, the first boy said: "I believe in God the Father Almighty, Maker of heaven and earth." The second boy said: "I believe in Jesus Christ His only Son our Lord." So the recitation went on to the boy who said: "He ascended into heaven, and sitteth on the right hand of God the Father Almighty; from thence He shall come to judge the quick and the dead." Then there fell a silence, and it was broken by the next boy who said to the examiner: "Please sir, the boy who believes in the Holy Ghost is absent today." "Lots of folks are absent when it comes to that clause." is Dr. Maclean's comment.

What Plans Worth Making? In June, 1971, Dartmouth College held its commencement exercises. A young man by the name of David Levy said something that demands an answer by everyone.

David had the highest academic record of any of the 940 graduating seniors. On those credentials he was accorded speaking time on the commencement program. Imagine the shock on the faces of the old alumni gathered there, the mothers and fathers, the faculty, the dignitaries, and some of his own classmates when David Levy of New York City said:

"I have rejected graduate school offers because I could not worship black ink on white paper. I have made no plans because I have found no plans worth making.

"Take pity on me, those of you who can justify the air you breathe. Send me letters and tell me why life is worth living. Rich parents, write and tell me how money makes your life worthwhile. Dartmouth alumni, tell me how the Dartmouth experience has given value to your existence.

"And fellow graduates, fellow members of the Class of 1971, take pity on a student who did not think, but only studied. Tell me how you have justified your existence to yourself, or perhaps why you have not felt the need to do so. And if some one of you out there is also made like me, write a letter and tell me how you came to appreciate the absurdity of your life." —From the *New York Times*, June 14, 1971. © 1971 by The New York Times Company. Reprinted by permission.

How would you answer David Levy? What does the Holy Spirit's coming suggest to you for a reply?

From Chisel-Work to Dynamite. An old Welsh coal miner was converted to Jesus Christ. Filled with an awareness of the power of God through the Holy Spirit in his life, he said, "When I was a lad, we dug out the coal with chisels and picks, by hand. It was slow, and it was hard. After that came the dynamite. When we got dynamite, we could mine a much bigger quantity of coal. Until this week, I have seen nothing but chisel work in religion. But now here is God's dynamite at work!"

The coming of the Holy Spirit is God's dynamite at work in our churches and in our lives. In fact, the Greek word for *power* in the New Testament is *dynamis*, from which, of course, our English word *dynamite* is derived.

Are you and your class still in the chisel-and-pick kind of religion, or is your faith dynamic and power-packed?

Ask for the gift of His Spirit, and watch what happens!

Sentence Sermon to Remember: I should as soon attempt to raise flowers if there were no atmosphere, or produce fruits if there were neither light nor heat, as to regenerate men if I did not believe that there was a Holy Ghost.—Henry Ward Beecher.

Questions for Pupils on the Next Lesson. 1. How do you explain the fact that people respond to God's message in different ways? 2. What do you do when you meet someone who is indifferent to or opposed to the news of Jesus Christ? 3. How do you share the faith with others? 4. What does it mean to you when you are told that you share in the ministry of the new covenant? 5. How can you help others feel a personal sense of importance and acceptance by God? 6. Do you feel this sense of importance and acceptance by God?

LESSON XI—NOVEMBER 16

GOD'S COVENANT AND PAUL

Background Scripture: Acts 13:13–52; 2 Corinthians 3:1–6
Devotional Reading: Acts 26:9–18

KING JAMES VERSION

ACTS 13 44 And the next sabbath day came almost the whole city together to hear the word of God.

45 But when the Jews saw the multitudes, they were filled with envy, and spake against those things which were spoken by Paul, contradicting and blaspheming.

46 Then Paul and Barnabas waxed bold, and said, It was necessary that the word of God should first have been spoken to you: but seeing ye put it from you, and judge yourselves unworthy of everlasting life, lo, we turn to the Gentiles.

47 For so hath the Lord commanded us, *saying,* I have set thee to be a light of the Gentiles, that thou shouldest be for salvation unto the ends of the earth.

48 And when the Gentiles heard this, they were glad, and glorified the word of the Lord: and as many as were ordained to eternal life believed.

49 And the word of the Lord was published throughout all the region.

50 But the Jews stirred up the devout and honourable women, and the chief men of the city, and raised persecution against Paul and Barnabas, and expelled them out of their coasts.

51 But they shook off the dust of their feet against them, and came unto Iconium.

52 And the disciples were filled with joy, and with the Holy Ghost.

REVISED STANDARD VERSION

ACTS 13 44 The next sabbath almost the whole city gathered together to hear the word of God. 45 But when the Jews saw the multitudes, they were filled with jealousy, and contradicted what was spoken by Paul, and reviled him. 46 And Paul and Barnabas spoke out boldly, saying, "It was necessary that the word of God should be spoken first to you. Since you thrust it from you, and judge yourselves unworthy of eternal life, behold, we turn to the Gentiles. 47 For so the Lord has commanded us, saying,

'I have set you to be a light for the Gentiles,

that you may bring salvation to the uttermost parts of the earth.'"

48 And when the Gentiles heard this, they were glad and glorified the word of God; and as many as were ordained to eternal life believed. 49 And the word of the Lord spread throughout all the region. 50 But the Jews incited the devout women of high standing and the leading men of the city, and stirred up persecution against Paul and Barnabas, and drove them out of their district. 51 But they shook off the dust from their feet against them, and went to Iconium. 52 And the disciples were filled with joy and with the Holy Spirit.

KEY VERSE: *"I have set you to be a light for the Gentiles, that you may bring salvation to the uttermost parts of the earth."* Acts 13:47 (RSV).

HOME DAILY BIBLE READINGS

Nov. 10. M. *From Darkness to Light.* Acts 9:1–9, 19–22.
Nov. 11. T. *A Time for Living.* Galatians 2:16–20.
Nov. 12. W. *A Time for Suffering.* Romans 8:12–18.
Nov. 13. T. *A Time for Standing Fast.* Galatians 5:1–10.
Nov. 14. F. *A Time for Dying.* Romans 6:1–8
Nov. 15. S. *A Time for Hope.* 1 Thessalonians 4:13–18.
Nov. 16. S. *Sufficient in God.* 2 Corinthians 3:1–6.

BACKGROUND

There are two cities called Antioch in Acts 13. The first was Antioch in Syria, where there was a thriving Christian Church; the second was Antioch in Pisidia, known in Paul's day as the Roman province of Galatia. It was in Syrian Antioch that Paul and Barnabas were very successful in preaching and in building the famous church; it was also in this church that Paul and Barnabas were sent out as missionaries to spread the Good News of salvation. They journeyed through Cyprus, Paphos and Pamphylia (Turkey, as we call it now), to Antioch in Pisidia.

The population of this Antioch was a mad mixture of Jews, Romans, and Phrygians, who were a highly emotional, quarrelsome, and unstable people. Arguments and fights could start as spontaneously as a spark applied to gunpowder. Paul went into the local synagogue and preached to just such a mixture—and the explosion came.

He preached and taught as one called of God to preach and teach, as one who had a covenant (agreement) with God to speak His Word for Jesus Christ. It was a good sermon, but . . . . Well, let's see what happened *after* the sermon.

NOTES ON THE PRINTED TEXT

I. And the next sabbath day came almost the whole city together to hear the word of God. Acts 13:44. It must have been quite a crowd; "almost the whole city" must have been packed in to the point of suffication in that synagogue. But, whether this is an exageration or not, the point is that the synagogue was filled with Antiochians anxious to hear what this man Paul had to say. They had heard *of* him; now they were to hear him with their own ears.

It was a good sermon, well conceived and well delivered. Paul traced the history of God's relation with Israel from the days in Egypt to that sabbath in Antioch, through Canaan and the period of the Judges and the days of David to those of Jesus. This man Jesus, Paul said, "is one of King David's descendants (seed) . . . who is God's promised Savior of Israel . . . . Brothers—you sons of Abraham, and also all of you Gentiles here who reverence God—*this salvation is for all of us!*"

Then he reminded the congregation that the Romans and certain Jewish leaders had crucified Christ in ignorance of His Messiahship.

It struck fire, in this audience made up of Jews *and* Gentiles. There was many a Gentile in that crowd who had long hoped to hear such words as these, many honest and sincere "seekers" or "God-fearers" whose hearts ached and whose minds longed for just such a word and for just this concept of God and salvation. If it had not been in a synagogue, they could have cried aloud for joy. Their hearts went out to this man who told them that God had sent him to Antioch that he might be a light for the Gentiles; the very sight of him was like the sight of a sail to a storm-tossed ship after many days at sea.

Some of the more serious ones among the Gentiles crowded around Paul at the end of the service, and asked him to preach to them again on the next sabbath. That would have been good, but Paul was not in Antioch on the next Sabbath.

II. But when the Jews saw the multitudes, they were filled with jealousy, and contradicted what was spoken by Paul, and reviled him. Acts 13:45 (RSV). The Jews reviled him? Why?

They struck back at him because he had struck at one of their ancient prejudices: their hatred of the Gentiles. They, and not the Gentiles, were God's chosen people. Were they not His people, the heirs of His promise; His people, possessed of special privileges? If there was any one thing that would infuriate the strict and loyal Jew, it was the suggestion that God had any love for the Gentiles, or that any of God's privileges could be given to these uncircumcised "outsiders."

They reviled Paul because he was successful; he attracted crowds wherever he went, crowds who seldom if ever came to their synagogues. An unexpected success had come, not to the faithful few who had loyally been in their seats in the synagogue sabbath after sabbath and who had supported the synagogue year after year, but to *strangers*. This they could neither understand nor tolerate.

Jealousy is a fearful master; jealousy has destroyed many an individual's faith and divided many a church. Jealousy, sometimes called envy, is one of the most powerful of the seven deadly sins.

We once knew a fine lady who attended church every Sunday and sat in her assigned pew. She came late to an Easter Sunday service, found the church packed to the doors and total strangers occupying "her" pew. She turned away in anger and seldom came to church after that. We knew also a good minister who was so disappointed and bitter over his failure to be elected to a high office in his church that his preaching lost its power and beauty, and he spent his last days in shallow misery. Yes, envy can kill.

III. But the Jews incited the devout women of high standing and the leading men of the city, and stirred up persecution against Paul and Barnabas . . . . Acts 13:50 (RSV). Have you heard of "whispering campaigns" stirred up to ruin good and worthy men? The Jews of Antioch used that as a weapon against a Paul and a Barnabas who had driven them to desperation. They went further than whispering; they incited devout and honorable women, and prominent men of Antioch to move (riot?) against the preachers of the Christ.

The Judaism of the day had a special attraction for Jewish women. The worst sufferers of the sexual immorality of the Roman world were the women; they were too often the victims of pagan lust; they watched their families being broken; they saw their children growing up heedless of the high ethical standards and purity of the Jewish faith. So it is easy to believe that in the synagogue that day, and in the crowds surrounding the synagogue, there were women of high social standing. These women were approached by their Jewish leaders to rise in protest against Paul and Barnabas, whom they pictured as destroyers of their faith.

Certain "chief men of the city" also gave a helping hand to the persecutors. They may have been what we call "city fathers"—men in places of civic leadership, or they could have been the husbands of the "devout and honorable" women, or they could have been politicians who were anxious to keep things stable and quiet and who saw trouble for themselves in these two Jewish preachers who were, figuratively, rocking their boat.

It was too much; Paul and Barnabas, in words of delightful Oriental symbolism, "shook off the dust from their feet" and left the hostile town and went on to Iconium. And that is the most important part of this whole story. It was as if Paul were saying to the Jews, "All right; you have rejected me and rejected Christ; you have driven us from your town because you simply do not understand that the salvation we have been preaching here is meant for anyone who wants it, be he Jew or Gentile. If then you will not listen, we will go elsewhere—we will take the Gospel to the Gentiles." That was the most vital turn from one road to another, in the history of early Christianity: it meant the opening of the doors of the Gentile world to the Christian Gospel. If this had not happened at Antioch, Christianity would have become nothing more than a small sect of Judaism, and not a Good News that has reached out to the ends of the earth. Even a riot can be used of God for His good purpose.

There is one other lesson here worth remembering: that is, if a good preacher finds himself in a parish that is unresponsive and even hostile to him, there are other people to whom he may go and win men for Christ. We see that exemplified even in Jesus; when the people of His own country rejected Him as just a small-town carpenter's son (Matthew 13:55), when "he did not many mighty works there because of their unbelief," He went elsewhere to people and towns and cities in which it was possible for Him to do His mighty works.

Still, all was not lost when Paul and Barnabas left Antioch, for they left behind them, in that city, Gentiles who "were filled with joy, and with the Holy Ghost" (Acts 13:52). That made it abundantly clear that God's approval lay in the turning of the Gentiles to His Son. There was more victory in Antioch than failure!

SUGGESTIONS TO TEACHERS

There is an apocryphal story about a congregation in Texas which struck oil on its property—and promptly closed the membership! Laughs aside, there is a tendency toward exclusivism within every church. Your congregation has some members who feel little compulsion to reach out to others. So did some of the earliest Christians.

Today's lesson centers on God's covenant and the Apostle Paul, the great missionary to the Gentiles. The material discusses Paul, but it aims to impel believers in every age to share the Good News of Jesus with outsiders.

Examining the biblical material in Acts 13 and 1 Corinthians 3, you will discover that Jesus Christ, according to Paul's preaching, offers God's new covenant to all persons, Jews and Gentiles alike. Jesus Christ culminates, extricates, and illustrates.

1. *CULMINATES.* Call attention to Paul's sermon in Acts 13. Notice how Paul insists that Jesus is the apogee of everything God has promised. Jesus is not one of the two dozen flavors of "religions" to chose from. Before proceeding further in this lesson, make sure that your

people sense the exclusive claims of Jesus Christ. Paul and the early Christian leaders all insisted that Jesus Christ is the culmination of the covenant story which started with Abraham.

2. *EXTRICATES*. Take plenty of time in this lesson to give the idea of freedom through Christ the importance it deserves. Paul knew personally what forgiveness and freedom from the burdens of legalism meant. Jesus Christ extricates people! "By him everyone that believes is freed from everything from which you could not be freed by the law of Moses" (Acts 13:39 RSV). Ponder the ways people are enslaved and trapped today. What are some of the most oppressive things that people would like to be freed from? Have your class think together how the Gospel offers extrication from these burdens.

3. *ILLUMINATES*. Jesus, the Light, ignites us to be the beacon for others. Quoting Isaiah, who clearly understood God's covenant with Israel, Paul reminds his hearers (including us) that the Lord intends us to shed His light to skeptics, unbelievers, and outsiders. "I have set you to be a light for the Gentiles, that you may bring salvation to the uttermost parts of the earth," Paul insists (Acts 13:47 and Isaiah 49:6). Ask your class what kind of illumination your congregation is showing to the nonchurch people in your community!

TOPIC FOR ADULTS
GOD'S COVENANT AND PAUL

Lived Two Lives. Russell Conwell was a nineteen-year-old Yale law student and an avowed atheist when the War between the states broke out in 1861. He enlisted in the Union Army and was commissioned a captain in a Massachusetts regiment. Conwell, a tall, athletic man, was a hero to his men, particularly to a small, frail lad named John Ring who served as Conwell's orderly. Conwell noticed that Johnny Ring read his Bible each evening and prayed faithfully, and he often made fun of Johnny's faith. Johnny smiled and carried out his duties efficiently and uncomplainingly. He took particular pride in polishing Conwell's sword each day.

One day, Confederate troops surprised Conwell's regiment. The Union forces hastily withdrew across a river, setting fire to the bridges as they retreated. During the confusion, no one paid any attention to a slender figure racing back across the blazing bridge. It was Johnny Ring. Running past the Confederate soldiers, Ring hurried to Conwell's abandoned tents and grabbed the sword which Conwell had left behind in his haste to leave. Ring ran back to the bridge, clutching the sword. The bridge was a mass of flames by then. Suddenly, as soldiers from both sides noticed the figure stumbling through the fire, the gunfire stopped. Everyone stood transfixed, watching the boy struggling across the flaming span. "Come back, come back!" pleaded a Confederate officer, "You cannot make it!" Voices from the Massachusetts regiment joined in, "Go back, Johnny!"

Johnny Ring pushed through the worst, and emerged as a human torch on the other side, still clutching Conwell's sword. He collapsed as he reached his own buddies, and died a few days later.

Conwell was so affected that he made a vow to live out John Ring's life as well as his own. He made a promise to do his own work for eight hours every day, then do Johnny's for another eight.

Years later, Conwell, the founder of Temple University and Hospital in Philadelphia, confided, "You can't keep company with a good man that way, day in, day out, without finding yourself changed. Johnny's faith became my faith. Gradually I began to find I was using my hours differently. Still, I'd say Johnny's hours have been the best of the lot."

God's Call. "I've never forgotten the unsolicited advice I received from a layman long ago. I was waxing eloquent about all that was wrong with a prominent clergyman or program or something when my friend remarked, " 'Son, I hope that some day you'll learn that God called you to be in sales, not in management.' " Gary Demarest, *Monday Morning,* August 1978.

Live by the Light You Have. Abraham Lincoln put it this way: "I am not bound to succeed, but I am bound to live up to what light I have." Lincoln's story is one of endless recommencements, of the dispersal of doubts, and of the need, every once in a while, to examine whether he was measuring up to his own standards and those set for him by society.

We are called to live as beacons for the rest of the world, and are given a covenant relationship with the One who is the Light of the world. We are not called to succeed but to live that light!

Questions for Pupils on the Next Lesson. 1. What are the terms of your own personal covenant with God? 2. Must every Christian be covenanted with the Lord? 3. What are some of the consequences of rejecting or refusing to believe in Jesus Christ? 4. What do you understand it means to be "God's own people"? 5. How can your congregation better understand that all races and peoples who believe in Jesus Christ are "one body through the cross"?

TOPIC FOR YOUTH
SHARING GOD'S GOOD NEWS

Gave a Hand. One hundred ten miles off the northwest coast of Scotland lies a tiny, rocky island called St. Kilda. Today, it is preserved as a nature and bird sanctuary. At one time, it was inhabited and was fought over by rival Scottish clans.

The first owners, the MacLeods, won St. Kilda in a boat race against the MacDonalds. The boats of the two competing clans were churning the water as the two crews strove against each other. As the boat drew near to St. Kilda, the MacDonalds pulled ahead. It appeared that they would win, and would claim the island as a prize for their territories. Seeing that the MacDonalds would seize the island, at the last minute, the MacLeod leader named Coll MacLeod grabbed his axe and cut off his left hand, then hurled it onto the shore of St. Kilda, thereby winning the island for the MacLeods.

If a warrior would sacrifice a hand to claim a land for his cheiftain, a Christian would sacrifice life itself to claim the world for his Lord! The Apostle Paul understood this and lived his life in a covenant in which he gave up everything for Christ. What have you sacrificed? How zealous are you to claim the world for His rule?

What Are You Doing With Them? God gives you the gift of 86,400 seconds today. How are you using them? Will you use some of them to say, "Thank you!" by telling others about His goodness through Jesus Christ?

A covenant, after all, is a promise to Him to share your life with others in responsible ways.

See and Do the Needful. David Wells, M.D., a recent graduate of McGill University, volunteered his services as a physician to the Canadian "peace corps" and was sent to a remote area of Kenya in Africa.

One night, Wells was wakened by an emergency. As he entered the clinic, he noticed a badly battered African dressed in rags and caked with blood and dust, lying on a makeshift litter carried by two exhausted villagers. They had been traveling for two days. Wells approached the injured man and was surprised to see a note carefully pinned to the patient's rags. Written by a villager who was a Christian, the note read, "Please see and do the needful."

"Please see and do the needful"—isn't this what Christ calls us to do today in the world? Aren't we all meant to see the hurts of those around us, and then to "do the needful"?

Your covenant with Christ comes down to seeing and doing the needful in Africa, in America, or wherever!

Sentence Sermon to Remember: The most acceptable service of God is doing good to man.—Benjamin Franklin.

Questions for Pupils on the Next Lesson. 1. Do you really feel that you are part of Christ's Church? Why or why not? 2. What do you think are the consequences of rejecting Jesus Christ? 3. How can your church show that God's people includes people of all races, nationalities, and economic levels? 4. How can your church show that youth are also the stones with which Christ continues to build His church? 5. What kind of covenant have you made with God?

LESSON XII—NOVEMBER 23

GOD'S COVENANT AND THE NEW ISRAEL

Background Scripture: Ephesians 2; 1 Peter 2:4–10
Devotional Reading: Isaiah 2:1–5

KING JAMES VERSION	REVISED STANDARD VERSION

KING JAMES VERSION

1 PETER 2   4 To whom coming, *as unto* a living stone, disallowed indeed of men, but chosen of God, *and* precious,

5 Ye also, as lively stones, are built up a spiritual house, an holy priesthood, to offer up spiritual sacrifices, acceptable to God by Jesus Christ.

6 Wherefore also it is contained in the scripture, Behold, I lay in Sion a chief corner stone, elect, precious: and he that believeth on him shall not be confounded.

7 Unto you therefore which believe *he is* precious: but unto them which be disobedient, the stone which the builders disallowed, the same is made the head of the corner,

8 And a stone of stumbling, and a rock of offence, *even to them* which stumble at the word, being disobedient: whereunto also they were appointed.

9 But ye *are* a chosen generation, a royal priesthood, an holy nation, a peculiar people; that ye should shew forth the praises of him who hath called you out of darkness into his marvellous light:

10 Which in time past *were* not a people, but *are* now the people of God: which had not obtained mercy, but now have obtained mercy.

REVISED STANDARD VERSION

1 PETER 2   4 Come to him, to that living stone, rejected by men but in God's sight chosen and precious; 5 and like living stones be yourselves built into a spiritual house, to be a holy priesthood, to offer spiritual sacrifices acceptable to God through Jesus Christ. 6 For it stands in scripture:

"Behold, I am laying in Zion a stone,
   a cornerstone chosen and precious,
and he who believes in him will not
   be put to shame."

7 To you therefore who believe, he is precious, but for those who do not believe,

"The very stone which the builders
   rejected
has become the head of the corner,"

8 and

"A stone that will make men stumble,
   ble,
a rock that will make them fall";

for they stumble because they disobey the word, as they were destined to do.

9 But you are a chosen race, a royal priesthood, a holy nation, God's own people, that you may declare the wonderful deeds of him who called you out of darkness into his marvelous light. 10 Once you were no people but now you are God's people; once you had not received mercy but now you have received mercy.

KEY VERSE: But you are a chosen race, a royal priesthood, a holy nation, God's own people. 1 Peter 2:9.

HOME DAILY BIBLE READINGS

Nov. 17. M. *A New Direction.* Luke 5:36–39.
Nov. 18. T. *A New Helper.* Acts 1:6–14.
Nov. 19. W. *A New Challenge.* Acts 10:9–15, 28.
Nov. 20. T. *A New Openness.* Acts 15:13–23.
Nov. 21. F. *A New Community.* Ephesians 1:11–23.
Nov. 22. S. *A New People.* Ephesians 2:11–22.
Nov. 23. S. *A New Israel.* 1 Peter 2:2–10.

BACKGROUND

The First Letter of Peter was written about the year A.D. 64; it was written in Rome, or, as some scholars believe, it was dictated by Peter to Silas. Silas was a Roman citizen (as a Roman, it must have been difficult for him to write some of the passages in 1 Peter), who ministered to Peter after the death of Paul. The year was a hard one, for both Christians and for the Jews, for both of them had been scattered by persecution or other circumstances to various parts of Asia Minor. A cruel and wicked Nero ruled Rome, persecuted Christians, and in this very year of 64 the mad Emperor burned Rome and blamed the Christians for doing it!

At the peak of this persecution and death, Peter addressed his letter to the suffering Christians; in the letter, he gave to them—and to us—the most beautiful description of the nature and function of the Christian Church to be found anywhere in the New Testament. And it made very clear the nature of the covenant of the people of the Church with their God and their founder, Christ.

NOTES ON THE PRINTED TEXT

I. *Come to him, to that living stone, rejected by men but in God's sight chosen and precious* . . . . 1 Peter 2:4 (RSV). One of the most striking of the parables told by Jesus is the one telling of the wicked husbandmen who killed the servants of a vineyard owner and finally killed his son (Matthew 21:33–43). In this parable He was speaking to an Israel which had killed off many of her prophets, and which, He intimated, would in time kill Him, the Son of God. They would reject Him as they had rejected the prophets—but in the end He would triumph. He told them, quoting Psalms 118:22, that while they rejected Him, as a mason putting up a building rejected a good stone as its cornerstone. He (the Messiah) would become the "cornerstone" of a new "building"— the New Israel, the new Church.

Plainly, both Jesus and the Psalms were speaking here of Israel as "the head of the corner," as a nation and a people with a special mission and purpose. But both the early Christian writers and Jesus Himself took these words and applied them to Jesus Himself. Peter does this in this letter.

There are several quotations from the Old Testament about this "stone," this "head of the corner." *See* Isaiah 8:14, 15; Isaiah 28:16, and Isaiah 43:20, 21, and, particularly, Isaiah 28:16, in which God makes a covenant with Israel in the words, "Behold, I lay in Zion for a foundation a stone, a tried stone, a precious corner stone, a sure foundation . . . ." That precious stone to them was Israel, and that promise, that covenant, was based on the condition that Israel follow and obey God, His laws, His will, His purpose. That is exactly what Israel did *not* do—and so it was necessary to provide another cornerstone for the Church and the Kingdom—one called Jesus. Israel rejected Jesus as they had rejected the prophets, and so there came in Jesus what we might call The New Israel. This was not a national or racial unit or organization; it was a "spiritual house," a sanctuary and a salvation not limited to Israel but for all men everywhere who accepted and followed God as He appeared in Jesus Christ.

This is what the Church was meant to be.

II. *"A stone that will make men stumble, a rock that will make them fall"* . . . . 1 Peter 2:8 (RSV). That seems to contradict the positive, salvation-emphasizing words in the previous statement, but it doesn't. What God and Peter and Christ are saying here is that to *some*, to those who rejected Christ, *some* would find Jesus to be a stumbling block, a rock over which they would trip and fall. To those who rejected Him, an inevitable punishment would come: "They will stumble because they will not listen to God's Word, not obey it, and so this punishment must follow—that they will fall" (*see* verse 8). Punishment? Yes—but a punishment they had brought down on their own heads. No man is *forced* to accept Christ; he has the option to accept or deny. Some would fall of their own accord. They would be of no use in the New Israel, in the Church, for the Church is built on the faith of the loyal *believers*. Those who stumble over Him, those who think they can live without Him, those who want to go their way and not God's way—these are the true sinners. Sin has been described as "an absence from God." It is a good definition.

Back in verse 4, Peter speaks of those in the Church as "living stones." Not dead, insensible stones, but *living*, alive in the Spirit. Every Christian is a brick in the invisible temple of God, a brick among many bricks in a congregation, members of a "royal priesthood" performing "spiritual sacrifices." It was a new kind of sacrifice. The Old Testament tells of the sacrifice of lambs on the Temple altars; but in the Christian sense, the sacrifice God wants is that of lives lived in His service, whatever sacrifices may be involved.

This is the *nature* of the Church: a living, serving community of believers working together, as bricks work together to form a wall. The Christian makes of *himself* an offering to God.

III. *But you are a chosen race, a royal priesthood, a holy nation, God's own people* . . . . 1 Peter 2:9 (RSV). Here it is again: Peter takes the old idea of the people of Israel holding His power as a chosen race and makes it apply to Jesus Christ and His Church. Those in the Church are called and chosen as a *new* people of God. The promises once made in covenant to Israel are now given to the Church. But, again, those in the Church are called upon to *obey* His laws and walk His way; if they fail to do this, they are *not* His people!

Some of us have a strange idea: we think we are in the favor of God because we join a church. Not so! The Lamb's Book of Life is *not* copied from the Church records; it is made up of the names of those who take their Christianity seriously and live as active, militant, *serving* Christians. We forget too much the fact that while we may be "bricks" in the institution of the Church, *we have work to do along with the other bricks.* The Church is a bridge between men and God, a passageway to Him over the tempestuous tides of life which threaten destruction and death. And every one of us in the Church is called of God to act as a bridge in bringing others "out of the darkness into his wonderful light" (*The Living Bible*).

How long is it since you tried to bring someone out of the darkness of Godless living into the blazing light of the sacrificed Christ? We are poor Christian soldiers, if we bring no one, and we deserve a dishonorable discharge.

IV. *Once you were no people but now you are God's people* . . . . 1 Peter 2:10 (RSV). There was a bitter sting in that for the Jews to whom Peter preached. In their past the Jews had been a people wandering through not only a physical but a spiritual wilderness, searching, suffering, hoping for God's favor and protection, afraid, living in the dark. But now that Christ had come they need fear no longer, for while they were once "no people,"; now, in Christ, they are God's people, truly.

But—all this, to us, is past history. Bring it up to date; apply it to your "now." No man in our time and world need walk in darkness; in Christ he has, if he but have eyes to see it, a great light shining, guiding, saving, calling him out of uselessness and insignificance into significance. He is God's man, chosen of God to follow the light into a life more blessed, more purposeful, more Godly.

And that is the primary *function* of the Church: to hold the light high, to take it into every darkness. We put steeples on our churches to tell the world to look *up* to the light, to stop wandering through the night of human frailty, disappointment, and despair.

Does your Church do that?

SUGGESTIONS TO TEACHERS

A couple of years ago, a Minneapolis man tried to get his name legally changed to 1-0-6-9. The judge turned him down. the world is impersonal enough in a computer age, the judge reasoned, and the man should not be deprived of his sense of identity by giving up his name.

What is your real identity? You carry the "name" of Christian. What does that mean?

The matter of identity is the subject of your lesson. Many in your class, like so many church people, suffer from a spiritual identity crisis. You will strive to help each one grow to appreciate the sense of personhood that God's new covenant bestows.

Look over the background Scripture, noting what it has to say to us regarding who we are as Christ's people. God's new pact through Jesus Christ informs who we are! The New Testament writers suggest the following ideas, among others.

1. *FROM DEAD TO LIVING.* Apart from God, the biblical writers in your lesson insist, people are lost, are doomed. People following only their own interests and impulses are on a death trip. Have your class comment on the destructiveness of selfishness and disobedience. More important, help each person to understand that God through His new relationship with us in Christ has reversed the downward spiral. He resurrects us, "even when we were dead through our trespasses, (He) made us alive together with Christ . . . and raised us up with him . . ." (Ephesians 2:5, 6 RSV). Ask each person to consider how Christ brings a resurrection in his or her life.

2. *FROM ALIENS TO CITIZENS.* Every person at some time or

another feels like a stranger or foreigner from God and His community. The term *alienated* sums up these feelings of being such an alien. Allow your class members to recount times they felt like aliens before God. Remind them that all the barriers against outsiders have been flattened by the Cross. Jesus Christ brings a new covenant. Every person who acknowledged His authority is received as a citizen of His realm.

3. *FROM ORPHANS TO FAMILY MEMBERS.* Take time in this lesson to examine the hope that the new covenant brings to God's new Israel. Instead of being orphans in the universe, alone and friendless, homeless and frightened, we belong! In Christ, we are brought into a family relationship with each other. Is your congregation such a "family?"

4. *FROM NOBODIES TO SOMEBODIES.* Finally, use the 1 Peter 2 passage to illustrate the way God's new covenant makes us part of His priesthood. A priest, remind your class, mediates between God and humans and between humans and God. Does your class comprehend that each member is called to be such a priest?

TOPIC FOR ADULTS
GOD'S COVENANT AND HIS NEW PEOPLE

Not Good If Detached. "I held it in my hands some time ago. It was a piece of paper. I really do not remember what it was—perhaps a warranty or a guarantee? It makes little difference. But what I do remember about it would seem to make a difference. In any case, the words come clear now. They were bold and plain: 'Not Good If Detached.'

"Those words have run through my mind many times. I cannot quite shake them out. They seem to say something to me about my life and the way it must be lived. They seem to call me back to a truth about human existence. They seem to declare that I am 'Not Good If Detached.'

"Then I remember the times in my own experience when I was detached, and the memories are hard. They recall a measure of human misery. Indeed, the hardest days of my life have been those days when I was detached, or, at least, felt I was detached.

"There was the first time I was escorted to a police station by a firm policeman. It was in Detroit, Michigan. There I sat—in a barren room under the glare of harsh lights; surrounded by men in uniform; with strange voices coming from men I had never seen; with ringing telephones, shuffling feet, doors opening and closing. And I was three years old—a young lad who had wandered far from home and was lost. I was detached.

"There was another time. It was in Cincinnati, Ohio. The classroom was filled with sixth-grade children. All of them seemed to know everyone in the room—except me. I was the new boy, the boy whose haircut was a little bit different and whose clothes were not quite like the others. No one spoke to me; they were all busy visitng with friends. I sat at the last desk in the far corner of the room, I was detached.

"There have been other times, times not limited to childhood, when I knew both the agony and the anguish of being detached.

"There, then, is a truth about you and me. From the very beginning, we are 'Not Good If Detached.' We can only live in relationships."— Charles L. Copenhaver, *Pulpit Digest,* April 1971.

Palimpsests. "In the British Museum, you can see, if you have a mind to do so, a palimpsest known as Codex Nitriensis, so called because it was discovered in the Nitrian Desert in Egypt. A palimpsest is a document, usually of vellum, whose original message has been partly rubbed, scraped off, or otherwise obliterated in order that the scribe might reuse it for some other writing. In the centuries when vellum was in limited supply and high in cost, this practice was often followed. The word which describes the result is made up from two Greek words, *palin* (again) and *psao* (to rub smooth). Nitriensis, when it began its existence, was a manuscript of St. Luke's Gospel, but some time about the eighth century a minor theologian, Severus of Antioch, thought that the vellum could be put to better use and wrote a treatise of dubious value on it. Having removed a considerable portion of the original text, he inscribed his wisdom at right angles to it. Likewise in the history of art, canvases which were the work of some great master have been, on occasion, painted over by some inferior artist, thus concealing the treasure which lies beneath the amateur daub.

"So many valuable, old-Greek manuscripts were subjected to this type of reuse that, in A.D. 691, a decree was enacted prohibiting such treatment of intact manuscripts of the Scriptures. There was some real consternation when it was discovered that a work of St. John Chrysostom had been converted into a Grammar of the Latin language.

"We read in the Book of Genesis that God created man in His own image and likeness. That is, so to speak, the original imprint: 'Lord, Thou hast made us for Thyself,' wrote Augustine. The human tragedy lies in the fact that the intended purpose of life has been obscured by lesser objectives. We chose not to yield fully to the divine purpose for our lives, not to love the Lord with heart, mind, soul, and strength. Instead of being living epistles which reveal the Gospel, we demonstrate philosophies of life which are at variance with it.

"Fortunately, technicians are able to handle the problem of restoration and to make visible the initial script or picture. Modern photographic techniques have often proved useful in recovering hidden material. For man, too, there is a remedy. He also can be restored to what he was intended to be and to represent. 'If any man be in Christ,' says Paul, 'he is a new creature. Old things are passed away. Behold, all things become new.' "—Charles P. Robshaw, *East Liberty Church Bulletin,* April 6, 1975, East Liberty Presbyterian Church, Pittsburgh, PA 15206.

A Better Way. "I COME FROM GOD, I BELONG TO GOD, I RETURN TO GOD." What better way of describing your covenant with God?—Ignatius of Loyola.

Questions for Pupils on the Next Lesson. 1. Do you find genuine joy sometimes in being part of God's present and future Kingdom? 2. How does the promise of the New Jerusalem offer hope to us in time of pain, sorrow, hunger, and death? 3. Why is it that the covenant relationship and all that it entails cannot be enjoyed by those who refuse to believe in Jesus Christ? 4. What is the meaning of the symbolism of the "New Jerusalem"?

TOPIC FOR YOUTH
BEING GOD'S PEOPLE

Identity Crisis. Soon after World War I, at a national convention of the American Legion, a man walked to the center of the platform in the convention hall and faced thousands of delegates. As the spotlight played on him, he called out in a voice with tragic overtones that could be heard in the farthest corner of the hall. "Can anyone tell me who I am?" He was a victim of amnesia as a result of shell shock, and his presence there was dictated by the hope that one of his war-time buddies would recognize him and thus restore his personal identity. None did.

Do people know who you are? Do *you?* Are you aware that your real identity is being one of God's people?

Unified Self. "Nitroglycerin is explosive because it has a divided self. It is made up of nitric acid, sulphuric acid, and glycerin. These elements do not belong together and at the slightest jar they will pull apart and explode. So with a self that is not unified. When one is wholehearted, the same all the way through, he is happier, stable, secure."—Dr. Charles L. Allen, "The First Psalm," *Grace Pulpit.*

Why Not? Why Not the Best? The title of Jimmy Carter's biography comes from an experience he had as a young naval officer. Outlining his qualifications, he told Admiral Rickover that he ranked 59 in his class of 820 at Annapolis. "Did you do your best?" the Admiral asked. Startled, young Carter admitted that he probably had not done as well as he might have. "Why not?" came the disturbing reply.

God asks you the question, "Why not your best?" He invites you to be your best by covenanting with Him.

Sentence Sermon to Remember: We are, after all, like lumps of clay. There are brittle pieces, hard pieces. We have little shape or beauty. But we need not despair. If we are clay, let us remember that there is a Potter and His wheel.—Peter Marshall.

Questions for Pupils on the Next Lesson. 1. How can you get a proper perspective of the past, the present, and the future? 2. Do you see the future in terms of God's purposes being fulfilled? 3. How can you have a sense of security and confidence about the future when it looks so bleak? 4. Do you see yourself participating in the eternal plan of God? Why or why not?

LESSON XIII—NOVEMBER 30

GOD'S COVENANT AND THE NEW JERUSALEM

Background Scripture: Revelation 11:15–19; 21
Devotional Reading: Isaiah 11:1–9

KING JAMES VERSION

REVELATION 11 15 And the seventh angel sounded; and there were great voices in heaven, saying, The kingdoms of this world are become *the kingdoms* of our Lord, and of his Christ; and he shall reign for ever and ever.

16 And the four and twenty elders, which sat before God on their seats, fell upon their faces, and worshipped God,

17 Saying, We give thee thanks, O Lord God Almighty, which art, and wast, and art to come; because thou hast taken to thee thy great power, and hast reigned.

18 And the nations were angry, and thy wrath is come, and the time of the dead, that they should be judged, and that thou shouldest give reward unto thy servants the prophets, and to the saints, and them that fear thy name, small and great; and shouldest destroy them which destroy the earth.

19 And the temple of God was opened in heaven, and there was seen in his temple the ark of his testament: and there were lightnings, and voices, and thunderings, and an earthquake, and great hail.

21 10 And he carried me away in the spirit to a great and high mountain, and shewed me that great city, the holy Jerusalem, descending out of heaven from God,

11 Having the glory of God: and her light *was* like unto a stone most precious, even like a jasper stone, clear as crystal;

12 And had a wall great and high, *and* had twelve gates, and at the gates twelve angels, and names written thereon, which are *the names* of the twelve tribes of the children of Israel.

13 On the east three gates; on the north three gates; on the south three gates; and on the west three gates.

14 And the wall of the city had twelve foundations, and in them the names of the twelve apostles of the Lamb.

REVISED STANDARD VERSION

REVELATION 11 15 Then the seventh angel blew his trumpet, and there were loud voices in heaven, saying, "The kingdom of the world has become the kingdom of our Lord and of his Christ, and he shall reign for ever and ever." 16 And the twenty-four elders who sit on their thrones before God fell on their faces and worshiped God, 17 saying,

"We give thanks to thee, Lord God Almighty, who art and who wast, that thou hast taken thy great power and begun to reign.

18 The nations raged, but thy wrath came,
    and the time for the dead to be judged,
for rewarding thy servants, the prophets and saints,
    and those who fear thy name, both small and great,
    and for destroying the destroyers of the earth."

19 Then God's temple in heaven was opened, and the ark of his covenant was seen within his temple; and there were flashes of lightning, voices, peals of thunder, an earthquake, and heavy hail.

21 10 And in the Spirit he carried me away to a great, high mountain, and showed me the holy city Jerusalem coming down out of heaven from God, 11 having the glory of God, its radiance like a most rare jewel, like a jasper, clear as crystal. 12 It had a great, high wall, with twelve gates, and at the gates twelve angels, and on the gates the names of the twelve tribes of the sons of Israel were inscribed; 13 on the east three gates, on the north three gates, on the south three gates, and on the west three gates. 14 And the wall of the city had twelve foundations, and on them the twelve names of the twelve apostles of the Lamb.

KEY VERSE: . . . The kingdoms of this world are become the kingdoms of our Lord, and of his Christ; and he shall reign for ever and ever. Revelation 11:15.

HOME DAILY BIBLE READINGS

Nov. 24. M. *The Everlasting Kingdom.* Revelation 11:15–19.
Nov. 25. T. *Proclamations of the Angels.* Revelation 14:6–13.
Nov. 26. W. *Sing Praise to God.* Revelation 15:1–6.
Nov. 27. T. *The Marriage of the Lamb.* Revelation 19:6–10.
Nov. 28. F. *The Great Judgment.* Revelation 20:11–15.
Nov. 29. S. *The New Creation.* Revelation 21:1–8.
Nov. 30. S. *The New Jerusalem.* Revelation 21:10–14.

BACKGROUND

The book called the Revelation of St. John the Divine is one of the most bewildering of all books in the Bible; it is filled with visions and symbols which have called forth endless interpretations, explanations, and prophecies. The word *revelation* is derived from the Latin; the corresponding word in the Greek gives us our English word *apocalypse*, and that word describes not only the New Testament Revelation of St. John but a type of theology found in Jewish literature from the days of the Babylonian Exile to the early Christian era. It is at its best in the books of Daniel and Ezekiel in the Old Testament, and in the last book in the New Testament.

We can interpret what we read here in any one of three ways; (1) as a book referring to the past, a cryptographic accounting of the rise and fall of Rome and its aftermath; (2) as a book revealing events which occurred several times in history, or (3) as a book dealing with events that are still in the future. For our purpose, in this lesson, we will be using the third or "futuristic" method of interpretation, inasmuch as chapters 11 and 21 of Revelation deal with visions of the ultimate triumph of God.

Like most apocalyptic literature, this book was written in a time of persecution; it was the time of the Roman emperor Domitian. Its author is an old man (John, probably the same John who wrote a Gospel), a prisoner of the persecuting Romans on the island of Patmos. It is the work of a man who in his misery sees the cataclysmic end of the world and what he believes will follow the disaster—a terrible hour, but an hour in which the old theologian is ecstatically happy!

NOTES ON THE PRINTED TEXT

I. *Then the seventh angel blew his trumpet, and there were loud voices in heaven, saying, "The kingdom of the world has become the kingdom of our Lord and of his Christ, and he shall reign for ever and ever."* Revelation 11:15 (RSV). "Basic in apocalyptic writing is the cycle; a cycle is one of a number of intervals or spaces of time in which there is completed some round of happenings that is similar to other successive rounds."—Julian Price Love. Revelation is written in five cycles: The Cycle of the Seven Seals, of Seven Trumpets, of the Seven Mystic Signs, of the Seven Bowls, and of the Final Judgment. Our lesson deals only with the second cycle—with the seventh of the seven angels who announced the great Good News of the final state of man and his world.

The scene is laid in heaven; whence, says John, in a vision he had been summoned. Seated before God's throne are twenty-four Elders. Just who or what these "elders" were, we do not know. But we do know the purpose of the gathering: it was to make clear to John what was to happen in the near future. John has suffered, along with his people, under more than one earthly kingdom; he has seen such kingdoms rise and fall; he has seen his nation in chains and in exile. But now, here at the throne of God, he hears that soon all this will be no more than a passing phase of history; a better day is about to dawn. The kingdoms of this earth are about to become the kingdoms of God, and He shall rule over them for a thousand years. The Messianic age has begun, and the Millenium, a thousand years of peace and prosperity, has arrived.

This was the final fulfillment of God's covenant; it was to be a time of joy for the faithful. At the end of the Millenium, however, there was to come the final destruction of His enemies and a last and final judgment.

John is more than dramatic, as he tells this story. He tells us that in this moment in heaven he sees the heavenly Temple opened, and he sees in this Temple the ancient Ark of the Covenent. There is the flash of lightning in the place, and loud voices, and thunderings, and an earthquake, and heavy hail. We may call this overdramatization, or "imagery," but to John it was the unconquerable hope and faith in the ultimate rule of God.

II. *And he carried me away in the spirit . . . and shewed me that great city, the holy Jerusalem, descending out of heaven . . . .* Revelation 21:10. Back in the seventeenth chapter of Revelation, an angel takes John down into a "wilderness" to witness the final destruction of the harlot city of Babylon; why was it a wilderness? Perhaps it was called a wilderness in order to contrast this fall of a great earthly kingdom with the coming of the gleaming New Jerusalem, the City of God. Another angel (could it have been the same one?) comes now to take him out upon a mountaintop to see not destruction but the triumphant glory of God.

John says that the angel carried him out to see all things "in the spirit." Ezekiel had a similar experience; in Ezekiel 40:2 we read, "In the visions of God brought he me into the land of Israel, and set me upon a very high mountain . . . ." Like Ezekiel, John is speaking of a *vision*—and visions are mountaintop experiences. Some biblical scholars warn us not to take this poetic language dealing with visions too literally; they explain that this "lifting up" is a *spiritual* experience, and probably not a factual one. They may be right or wrong; all through the Book of Revelation we must be careful to distinguish between fact and symbolism. But that both John and Ezekiel were "in the spirit" we cannot doubt.

What John sees from that mountaintop is resplendently beautiful. He sees the great New Jerusalem as a city gleaming with light, flashing like a rare stone (jewel), like jasper, clear and clean and dazzling. But the real light of this city does not come from the reflection of rare jewels; it does not even come from the sun or the moon. It has no need of such light, *for God is its light.* Wherever God is, there is light. Within its limits live a multitude of His saints, whose saintly lives give it yet more light. There is a great lesson for us, here, however we may interpret the language of John: we who live in Christ are required to "shine as lights in the world" (Philippians 2:15). And in the first Epistle of John, we are told that "God *is* light." (Is this John the same John who wrote both the Epistle and Revelation and possibly the Fourth Gospel? All three of these writings stress the same theology and ideology!)

Around this New Jerusalem are four high walls. The interpretation of that, it is suggested, should be that this is the high wall of faith behind which the faithful are safe and secure. And the wall has twelve gates, three on each side. Could this represent the twelve tribes of Israel? Or does it mean that there is more than one gate through which a man may pass to God? And on the twelve foundations of the walls there is inscribed the names of the Twelve Apostles.

Numbers, numbers, numbers! Revelation is full of numbers. There is a tendency, in the Old Testament, to associate numbers with religion—sacred numbers, like seven heavens, seven great rivers, etc. In the New Testament, we find seven loaves and seven baskets, seven churches, seven candlesticks, and the seven seals and angels and trumpets and bowls and mystic signs in Revelation. There are other numbers—three, three and one half, five, forty, seventy, seven times seven, ten thousand, —the list is endless, and the cause of endless differences in interpreting what they may or may not mean. There is that mystic, mysterious, baffling number 666, in Revelation 13:18; that one has been used to an almost bizarre extent to prove any number of events or ideas. Many of us manipulate the numbers in Revelation to prove things and to stand for prophecies about the Second Coming and the end of the world; up to date, most if not all of such number-based predictions have *not* come true, but we go on guessing. Juggling numbers taken out of context, in Revelation, is not a very fruitful occupation.

What we need to do, and what John intended his readers to do, was not to spend their time working out mathematical numbers, but to believe and act as Christians believing in the ultimate victory of God and in the future life of the Christian in the resplendent City of God. The numbers are of secondary importance; living in Christ and living in eternity with Him are of primary importance.

SUGGESTIONS TO TEACHERS

As a hoax, a British newspaper ran an advertisement for settlers to ride a spaceship to establish a human colony on Mars. Hundreds responded. Some expressed a weariness with existence on earth. Most stated that their only hope lay in beginning over again on a different planet because of imminent world destruction.

People in your class have many of these same feelings. Some may be listening to radio broadcasts purportedly dealing with prophecies from the Bible, especially the Book of Revelation. Others may be reading literature claiming that we are in the final days.

Your lesson, taken from Revelation, will address many of the questions which persons are asking. God's covenant and the New Jerusalem,

as the biblical material suggestions, means they may continue to live in
the tension between hope and fulfillment—as the people of God always
have! Take some of those questions and work with them in the light of
the Revelation passages.

1. *WHAT TIME IS IT?* Notice how Revelation was written in a time of
terrible persecution yet expressed tremendous confidence in God's rule.
Point out to your class that Christians never give up on the world. In
spite of present hardship and an apparently hopeless future, the time is
still right for faithful service. Impress on your class that there is no need
to search Scripture for "secret signs" or to compile timetables for the last
days.

2. *WHAT'S HAPPENING?* Those unaware of the meaning of God's
covenant believe that the world is doomed and see only a descending
spiral toward destruction. Your class must be enlightened that God is
working to bring about a new creation. You and your class may not live
to see this, but God assures you that He will effect this. Take time to
ponder Revelation 21.

3. *WHO'S IN CHARGE HERE?* Let the impact of God's claim to be
the "Alpha and the Omega, the beginning and the end" (Revelation
21:6) sinks in. Events are not out of control. God insists that He remain
in command of the universe, of its history. His promise or covenant
through Christ steadies us when we are tempted to feel that He is helpless.

4. *WHERE DOES IT END? HOW WILL THINGS TURN OUT?
WHAT'S THE POINT?* Allow your people to talk about these profound
questions with the perspective of Revelation 11 and 21. The vision of
God's ultimate completion of His plan, in which there is no Temple and
all the gates of the celestial city remain perpetually open, offers a glorious glimpse into the way God will fulfill His commitment to us. What
should our commitments to Him be?

TOPIC FOR ADULTS
GOD'S COVENANT AND THE NEW JERUSALEM

Inheritance Claim. How responsible are you being about Christ and
the future? What does your covenant with Him mean in regard to the
days to come?

Ernest Digweed of England died in September, 1977, but left everything to Jesus—with certain provisions.

Jesus Christ will be eligible to inherit a substantial sum of money if
He returns to Earth within eighty years. The will of Ernest Digweed, a
retired schoolmaster, provided $44,000 to be invested and the proceeds
given to the Lord if and when He returns at the specified time. If He
does not return, the money will go to the Crown.

The will also stipulated that the Public Trustee, named as executor,
must obtain definite proof of Jesus' identity before giving the money.

Is this the way Christians should be anticipating the future? Is such an
action as Digweed's the way to live to celebrate the New Jerusalem?

End at Hand? He was the wisest man alive, and people took his words
seriously. Looking around him, he observed grim circumstances. As his

writings disclosed, his conclusions were that the end of the world would speedily come.

"Never was so much ignorance . . . . Far more sins reign in these days than in any past age . . . boundless corruption . . . lechery . . . gluttony . . . . Yet we have baptism and the revelation of Christ . . . which men cannot really believe in or revere, or they would not allow themselves to be so corrupted . . . . Therefore, many wise men believe that Antichrist is at hand, and the end of the world."

His name was Roger Bacon, and he lived from 1214 to 1294, and wrote the above words seven hundred years ago!

Do not jump to the conclusions that Bacon and others have. If conditions are bad, it does not necessarily follow that we are to assume that God has decided to wind up the human story in our time.

Besides, He calls us to be faithful, not to be doomsayers.

Shooting the Water Tower. Sometimes, God has to debunk our fears. We all are afraid of the unknown, especially the future. These fears can sometimes spur us to hasty or silly actions.

For example, on Halloween night, October 31, 1938, people in Grovers Mill, New Jersey were startled to hear that invaders from Mars had landed near their town. Strange-looking Martian creatures on long, spidery legs were described on the radio broadcast. It was all a hoax. The folks in Grovers Mill, along with millions of other Americans, were frightened by the superrealistic radio drama by Orson Welles of *"The War of the Worlds."*

The terrified townsfolk in Grovers Mill, where the radio reports stated the Martians were landing, looked out through the foggy night. Sure enough, appearing faintly in the gloom, was a tall thing on spindly legs. Panic-stricken, a number of people grabbed their guns and began to fire away.

It was not until the radio disclosed that the "invasion" was a Halloween trick and not until full daylight that the Grovers Mill people discovered that the Martian they had been shooting at was a water tower on thin, flimsy legs in a cornfield!

God debunks our terrors, He assures us that most of our fears are "shooting-at-the-water-tower" kind. Most of all, the Lord assures us that He is in control of the future. He covenants with us that we may trust Him with the days to come as well as in the present.

Questions for Pupils on the Next Lesson. 1. How do you try to interpret the Old Testament? 2. Do you feel you have any relationship to the Jewish people today? 3. What do you do to understand your ties to people who claim an inheritance to the Old Testament promises? 4. Why were the four Gospel accounts written? How do they relate to each other? 5. How do you understand Jesus as the Messiah?

TOPIC FOR YOUTH
LOOKING TO THE FUTURE

Scary, Spooky Stuff? How do you look to the future? With some uneasiness? Possibly, you have heard of some trying to allay that uneasiness by experiments in the occult.

Devotees of the long-departed escape artist Harry Houdini gathered in a dingy hospital room at exactly 1:26 P.M., on October 30, 1978. It was fifty-two years to the minute after the great Houdini had died of a ruptured appendix in 1926. It was also the last opportunity to gather in the exact place where he had died—Room 401 of Grace Hospital, Detroit, Michigan—because the aging hospital was torn down the following year. Seated around an old wooden desk in Room 401, a cluster of psychics attempted to make contact with the dead Houdini in a seance. Needless to say, the results were disappointing.

God does not encourage us to try to snoop into details of the future. He does, however, give us His promise that He will carry out His purposes. Our task is not to engage in seances and speculation. Rather we are to live faithfully and responsibly each day, and to entrust the future to Christ.

Gobble, Gobble. We are a nation of gobblers. We eat up, burn up, use up more than our share of the planet's bounty.

Since World War II, we Americans have consumed more natural resources than were consumed by all previous inhabitants of the globe in the entire previous history of humankind!

What does our covenant with Christ signify in the face of such gobbling? Are we being responsible for the futures of other persons?

Laughter in Adversity. In the Phantom Major (by Virginia Cowles, Harper and Row Publishers, Inc., N.Y., 1958, p. 218) the exploits of David Stirling and the S.A.S. (Secret Air Service) are related. Stirling, a six-foot-six youthful lieutenant from the Scots Guards in North Africa, conceived the idea of sending highly-trained, clever handfuls of men deep behind Rommel's lines to wreak havoc on enemy planes, communications, airfields.

They usually hid by day and struck by night. Over fourteen months, they inflicted phenominal damage with their unconventional, courageous, and even impudent raids.

Once, they captured Baron von Luttereti, a distinguished medical doctor from Hamburg serving with the Afrika Korps. Von Luttereti was held prisoner under a British Doctor, Malcolm Playdell, and he had several long conversations with Playdell. "He told him that he knew England quite well; in fact, he had spent several holidays at Clacton-on-Sea. Then Playdell asked him if he thought Germany would win the war. "Of course," said Luttereti in surprise, "don't you?" Playdell shook his head, Luttereti was genuinely puzzled. "But in that case you must think that you are going to win. How do you think you will do it?" "Well," said Playdell. "Well . . . ." It was a difficult question for him to answer when the Germans were only forty miles from Alexandria. "I became very much aware," he wrote, "that I had not got the faintest notion as to how we could win the war. Of a sudden the situation struck me as being very humorous and I rolled over on my back and laughed. 'I haven't the faintest idea,' I said, and at that he started laughing too. But I do not really think he understood what I was laughing about, and for the life of me I could not have explained it to anyone."

This is faith for the Future.

Sentence Sermon to Remember:

> The year goes wrong, and tares grow strong,
> Hope starves without a crumb;
> But God's time is our harvest time,
> And that is sure to come.
>
> —Lewis J. Bates

Questions for Pupils on the Next Lesson. 1. How do you understand the concept of Christ's Kingdom in your life? 2. Do you comprehend the claim that Jesus Christ is both human and divine? 3. Why is Matthew's Gospel so important if we are to understand the Old Testament? 4. How is Jesus the "Messiah"? 5. What is the relationship of Christians to the Jewish people today?

DECEMBER 1980—
FEBRUARY 1981

THE GOSPEL OF MATTHEW

LESSON I—DECEMBER 7

MATTHEW PRESENTS THE MESSIAH

Background Scripture: Matthew 1:1-17; 5:17-20; 9:9;
13:51, 52; 23:1-12
Devotional Reading: Isaiah 35

<table>
<tr><td>

KING JAMES VERSION

MATTHEW 1 1 The book of the generation of Jesus Christ, the son of David, the son of Abraham.

17 So all the generations from Abraham to David *are* fourteen generations; and from David until the carrying away into Babylon *are* fourteen generations; and from the carrying away into Babylon unto Christ *are* fourteen generations.

5 17 Think not that I am come to destroy the law, or the prophets: I am not come to destroy, but to fulfil.

18 For verily I say unto you, Till heaven and earth pass, one jot or one tittle shall in no wise pass from the law, till all be fulfilled.

19 Whosoever therefore shall break one of these least commandments, and shall teach men so, he shall be called the least in the kingdom of heaven: but whosoever shall do and teach *them*, the same shall be called great in the kingdom of heaven.

20 For I say unto you, That except your righteousness shall exceed the righteousness of the scribes and Pharisees, ye shall in no case enter into the kingdom of heaven.

9 9 And as Jesus passed forth from thence, he saw a man, named

</td><td>

REVISED STANDARD VERSION

MATTHEW 1 1 The book of the genealogy of Jesus Christ, the son of David, the son of Abraham.

17 So all the generations from Abraham to David were fourteen generations, and from David to the deportation to Babylon fourteen generations, and from the deportation to Babylon to the Christ fourteen generations.

5 17 "Think not that I have come to abolish the law and the prophets; I have come not to abolish them but to fulfil them. 18 For truly, I say to you, till heaven and earth pass away, not an iota, not a dot, will pass from the law until all is accomplished. 19 Whoever then relaxes one of the least of these commandments and teaches men so, shall be called least in the kingdom of heaven; but he who does them and teaches them shall be called great in the kingdom of heaven. 20 For I tell you, unless your righteousness exceeds that of the scribes and Pharisees, you will never enter the kingdom of heaven."

9 9 As Jesus passed on from there, he saw a man called Matthew sitting at

</td></tr>
</table>

Matthew, sitting at the receipt of custom: and he saith unto him, Follow me.
And he arose, and followed him.

13 51 Jesus saith unto them, Have
ye understood all these things? They
say unto him, Yea, Lord.

52 Then said he unto them, Therefore every scribe *which is* instructed
unto the kingdom of heaven is like
unto a man *that is* an householder,
which bringeth forth out of his treasure
things new and old.

the tax office; and he said to him, "Follow me." And he rose and followed
him.

13 51 "Have you understood all
this?" They said to him, "Yes." 52 And
he said to them, "Therefore every
scribe who has been trained for the
kingdom of heaven is like a householder who brings out of his treasure
what is new and what is old."

*KEY VERSE: Think not that I have come to destroy the law, or the
prophets. I am not come to destroy, but to fulfil.* Matthew 5:17.

HOME DAILY BIBLE READINGS

Dec. 1. M. *The Geneaology of Jesus.* Matthew 1:1–17.
Dec. 2. T. *Jesus and the Law.* Matthew 5:17–20.
Dec. 3. W. *The Intention of the Law.* Matthew 5:21–26.
Dec. 4. T. *Love for Enemies.* Matthew 5:43–48.
Dec. 5. F. *The Cost of Following Jesus.* Matthew 10:34–39.
Dec. 6. S. *Treasures Old and New.* Matthew 13:51, 52.
Dec. 7. S. *The One True Master.* Matthew 23:1–12.

BACKGROUND

Now we start on a study of the Gospel of Matthew, one of the most
interesting of the four Gospels which open the pages of the New Testament. Matthew is one of the three Gospels—Matthew, Mark, and
Luke— which we call the Synoptic Gospels. The word *Synoptic* means
"to see together," and it suggests that Mark, Matthew, and Luke all
wrote the same story with certain small differences and emphases, and
that they should be "viewed" together. The fourth Gospel, that of John,
is quite different; the author of this Gospel was a composer who wrote
his own, original story; Matthew, Mark, and Luke built their stories on
traditions already in existence in the Church.

Mark wrote first, about A.D. 70 or 75, and Matthew and Luke used
much that Mark wrote as the basis for *their* accounts of the work and
teaching of Jesus. (Matthew, for instance, reproduces no less than 606 of
Mark's verses.) But there are differences, in Matthew and Luke, as they
tell the story. Both of them borrowed from Mark, yes, but they added
much to Mark's account. And all three of these authors had different
approaches, different aims. Mark wrote for the Roman Christians;
Matthew wrote to convince the Jews of the Messiahship of Jesus; Luke
addressed himself to the Greeks. Mark wrote down what Jesus *did*;
Matthew wrote down what He *taught*.

Now let us see how Matthew starts to tell his story.

NOTES ON THE PRINTED TEXT

I. *The book of the generation of Jesus Christ, the son of David, the son
of Abraham.* Matthew 1:1. Why does Matthew start his story with a
genealogy? Mark starts his account with the baptism of Jesus; Luke

starts with the vision of Zacharias—both of which are more dramatic than starting with a genealogy. Matthew had a good reason for doing it his way. He was speaking to the Jews or the Jewish Christians, and the Jews put tremendous importance on a man's ancestors and forefathers. Both Luke and Matthew, however, make the genealogy of Jesus come down to Joseph, the father of Jesus. That was meaningful to a Jewish people who honored the father above the mother.

A priest in Israel had to prove that his ancestry went directly back to Aaron; if the priest married, his wife had to prove that she had been Jewish for four generations back. If there was just one non-Jew in a man's pedigree, he could not claim to be a Jew! So Matthew, in these opening genealogical verses, was proving that Jesus was a Jew of the Jews in His human parentage.

There is another good reason why Matthew starts with this genealogy of Jesus. The Jews to whom he was speaking had waited long for a descendant of David who would lead them back to their ancient glory—a Deliverer, a Messiah. The prophets had promised it; the people dreamed of it, and now this descendant had come, Matthew indicates by tracing the line back to David—no, to Abraham, to the forefather of David! What more, Matthew is asking, could the Jews want?

The fourteen generations mentioned in verse 17 are a little confusing, for there are only thirteen generations mentioned here, from the Babylonian captivity to Jesus. Probably, one name has been omitted or dropped out but fourteen still stands as a symbol for David. Historians were prone to error in those days, as well as in ours!

II. *Think not that I am come to destroy the law, or the prophets: I am not come to destroy, but to fulfil.* Matthew 5:17. This section is especially appropriate to Matthew's "Jewish" Gospel; He is speaking here of something that was considered eternal to the Jews: their Law, in itself, was considered by them to be eternal, and of first interest to those who loved God.

The Jews accused Him of ignoring, even breaking the Laws laid down by Moses. That He did not do. He thought of the new faith He brought as continuous with the Law. He said that the disciples should reverence and obey that Law; not one jot or tittle (not the least point or smallest detail) should be taken from it. But He also believed that eternal validity did not belong to the Law as Moses left it, but to the Law as "fulfilled," or developed and completed, by Himself. "He superseded the Law and the prophets by fulfilling them; He carried them forward to their ideal perfection. He fulfilled the old Law of Sacrifice in His own sacrificial death; circumcision in Him became Holy Baptism; the Passover became the Lord's Supper; the old Sabbath continued in Him as the Lord's Day. In regard to the prophets, He extended their idea of the Messiah from that of a conqueror to a Suffering Servant conquering by sacrificial love. This, and not slavish obedience to the written Law, or their predictions of it, was what He meant by "fulfilling the prophets."—Adapted from *A Commentary of the Holy Bible*, by J. R. Dummelow.

What men write in statute books is of secondary importance to what they do in His name.

III. As Jesus passed on from there, he saw a man called Matthew sitting at the tax office; and he said to him, "Follow me." And he rose and followed him. Matthew 9:9 (RSV). For Jesus to appoint or accept a man like Matthew as a disciple was nothing short of blasphemy to the orthodox Jews. Matthew was a collector of taxes in Capernaum, and tax collectors were hated as none other among men. They were, to put it in a nutshell, crooks and traitors, servants of the Romans, taking bribes and taking their illegal "cut" out of every tax paid by the suffering Jews. They were barred from the synagogue; they were not accepted as witnesses in court. How could Jesus bring Himself to call Matthew as one of His aides?

It offended the Jews no end that Jesus associated with publicans (tax collectors) and sinners (9:10). The Jews missed the whole point of the purpose of the ministry of Jesus: He came not to save the proudly righteous, but *sinners!* He was the Great Physician to those who were sinfully, spiritually, morally sick, and that is exactly what Matthew was. It is a great tribute to Jesus that He saw such tremendous possibilities in such a poor creature.

There was good as well as evil in this Matthew. Undoubtedly he had heard of Jesus long before he met Him; perhaps his guilty conscience had been torturing him, and perhaps he saw in this Man of Galilee one who could lift him from such torture and make of him something far better. At any rate, the despised tax collector got up and followed Jesus *immediately.* He left the seat of corruption, his tax-collectors table, and picked up his pen, or quill, and with it wrote his magnificent life of Jesus Christ.

Jesus still does it. He lifts the most insignificant, most unattractive of men to become men filled with the glory and love of God. This the Jews had been unable to do with Matthew, but Jesus could, and did.

IV. . . . Therefore every scribe who has been trained for the kingdom of heaven is like a householder who brings out of his treasure what is new and what is old. Matthew 13:52 (RSV). Jesus speaks here not of tax collectors, but of scribes. Scribes were men who knew all about the Law and the prophets. They had spent their lives studying all this. All right! That was not wasted time or study. Jesus says in effect, "Keep your knowledge of the commandments of Moses. Keep it—but try to see that knowledge in a new light, the very Light of God which I bring unto you. You need not throw away whatever you have found good in life, but use it in an enlarged faith and service."

No scholar need throw away what he has learned in the past; he does need to use his scholarship for Christ. No lawyer need give up his profession; let him apply it to the service of Christ, let him be a Christian lawyer. No businessman, no artist or clerk or construction worker or millionnaire need throw it all away; let him live as a Christian, whatever he has been. *Use your gifts* for Him!

"Jesus," says Dr. William Barclay, "did not come to empty life but to fill it, not to impoverish life but to enrich it."

As another commentator puts it, "It has been brilliantly suggested that this is a portrait of Matthew himself. It was the ideal of Jewish Christianity to preserve the best of the old religion together with the grace of the new." Amen!

SUGGESTIONS TO TEACHERS

The actor Charles Laughton used to insist that all the actresses and actors appearing with him in a long-running dramatic production gather from time to time to reread the play as if they were reading it for the first time. Laughton claimed that only by listening to the lines as if for the first time would they understand afresh what the author had in mind and would the players be kept from growing stale in their parts.

If helpful for a play, how much more so the Bible!

This series of twenty-one lessons from the Gospel of Matthew will give your class an opportunity to review the meaning of Jesus as the Messiah. Suggest to your people that they approach this series as if listening to Matthew for the first time. As a teacher, you are trying to help each person in your class to enlarge his or her understanding of Jesus Christ and encourage each to seek more faithfully to follow Him as Lord and Savior.

Today's lesson introduces the drama. Assist your people to grasp why Matthew wrote his account and what Matthew understood Jesus to be. From the background Scripture you will find several key points presenting themselves.

1. *FRUITION OF THE OLD.* The Messiah which Matthew presents is the culmination of the Old Testament. Tie in the theme of covenant which your class has been discussing during the past twelve weeks and point out that Jesus is the completion of the Old Covenant, or the Old Testament. Without being critical of Judaism or Jewish people today, allow time to discuss the ways in which Jesus is the fruition of the story of the people of God from Abraham until the first century.

2. *FULFILLMENT OF THE LAW.* Ethics is a key question for every believer. How does a Christian act? Remind your class that God does not offer recipes for behavior, or complete codes covering every contingency. Jesus embodies the ancient Jewish Law. He fulfills what God expects of your class and every other believer. Reread Matthew 5:17–20, and emphasize to your class that Jesus as our "Living Law" lays heavier demands on Christians than were placed on the Jewish Pharisees!

3. *FRIEND OF TAX COLLECTORS.* Focus for a while on Matthew's call by Jesus (Matthew 9:9). Have your people reflect on the fact that Jesus befriended a hated tax collector. Ask your people to comment on the implications of this episode. Are there any persons with whom Jesus would not associate? Who are "sinners" today who feel alienated from God's care? What should your class do about them?

4. *FLOWERING OF DISCIPLESHIP.* Turning to Matthew 13:51, 52, the close of a section on parables of the Kingdom, help your people to realize being a Christian means growing. Those in God's realm find themselves "trained" to find a "treasure" in God's promises. Are your class members learning Christians?

5. *FOCUS ON SERVICE.* Finally, stress that the Messiah Himself

suffered and served. He lived humbly. He came as a servant. Your people, your class, and your church are most authentically Christian when they go forth as servants in Christ's name!

TOPICS FOR ADULTS
MATTHEW PRESENTS THE MESSIAH

Through You. An old rabbi was walking down the village street. A member of his congregation came up and boasted loudly that he had read through all the volumes of the Talmud three times. The rabbi did not praise the man. Instead, he replied to the braggard, "The important thing is not how many times you have been through the Talmud, but whether the Talmud has been through you!"

Has the Gospel been through you? Perhaps you have read through Matthew and the other Gospel accounts before. Maybe you feel a vague sense of *deja vu* in starting a series of studies on Matthew.

Like Matthew, however, you will find that you can never completely understand the meaning of Jesus Christ. Read through Matthew's version of the Good News so that the Good News of Jesus may get into your living!

Dividing Point. "The life of Christ has the decisiveness of a supreme ideal, and that is why the history of the world divides at this point of time," wrote Alfred North Whitehead, the great British philosopher and mathematician.— *Religion in the Making.*

Whitehead reiterates what Matthew writes, Jesus Christ's coming is, in effect, the hinge of history, the dividing point for everything.

Are you living as an A.D. person, joyfully aware of the meaning of His coming? Or, are you living as if it is actually B.C.? During this series of lessons, reflect on how Jesus Christ divides everything in the human story, including yours, into longing and fulfillment.

Secret Parchment. Blaise Pascal, brilliant French intellectual of the seventeenth century, learned personally who Jesus Christ is. Although Pascal won renown for his magnificent treatises in scientific research (he was a mathematical genius at twelve, inventor of a computer at eighteen, and a pioneer in hydrostatics in physics and a developer of calculus in mathematics in his early twenties) he recognized Jesus Christ as the culmination of all his studies and insights.

Pascal's commitment to Jesus Christ led him to decide to "live only for God and to have no other aim than Him." He forsook his career in physics and mathematics to write to refute the claims of the French atheists. Never robust, and debilitated by illness from the time he was in his late teens, Pascal died in 1662 at the age of only thirty-nine.

When Pascal died, his friends found on his body a secret parchment which he had worn around his neck and kept near his heart. It read in part:

This year of Grace 1654, Monday, November 23rd . . . .
From about half past ten at night, to about half after midnight, Fire.
God of Abraham, God of Isaac, God of Jacob,
Not of the philosophers and the wise.
Security, security. Feeling, joy, peace.

God of Jesus Christ.
O righteous Father, the world hast not known thee,
But I have known thee.
Joy, joy, joy, tears of joy.

Questions for Pupils on the Next Lesson. 1. How was the ministry of
John the Baptist a bridge between the Old and the New Testament? 2.
How did John the Baptist fulfill the Jewish hope for the return of Elijah?
3. What are some of the ways in which John the Baptist prepared the
way for a mightier One whose mission would exceed his own? 4. What is
the relationship of John's baptism to Christian baptism? 5. How was
John a herald of repentance and of the imminent coming of the Kingdom?

TOPIC FOR YOUTH
MEETING THE MESSIAH

Warning Sticker. A young man in an Illinois High School understood
better than most what the New Testament is all about. Across the cover
of the New Testament he used regularly, he pasted a big sticker in
which the words stook in bold red letters: CAUTION—OPEN AT
YOUR OWN RISK!

You could well place this warning sticker over the cover of your Bible,
because when you open the Gospel According to Matthew, you run the
risk of meeting the Messiah! When you meet Him, you will never be the
same. You will find that Jesus the Christ changed Matthew's life. You
may find Him changing yours!

Where Do New Church Members Come From? How do other folks
come to meet the Messiah? What gets them to become part of His community?

Here are statistics as summarized by one expert in church studies:

Came because of Sunday School	3 to 6 percent
Walked into church on own initiative	3 to 8 percent
Came because of the program	4 to 10 percent
Came because of the Pastor	10 to 20 percent
Came in response to visitation evangelism	10 to 25 percent
Brought by a friend or relative	60 to 90 percent

What does that last line suggest, dear friend and relative? It should
mean that you are the key to others meeting the Messiah!

Whom have you invited and brought to church recently? How many of
your friends and family are waiting for you to show that Jesus is your
Messiah—and theirs also?

Incidentally, those same studies reveal that hardly anyone shows up
as a new church member because of a response to a radio-television
religious leader's ministry. It's people like you who bring in the new-
comers.

Best Sermon Ever Heard. Meeting the Messiah makes a difference.
Or, it *should.* Here's what Lois Gordon says in "God's Sword Thrusts,"
in *Christianity Today,* May 22, 1964 issue.

"David's prayer became mine: 'Search me, O God . . . . See if there be any wicked way in me . . . . Lead me . . .' (Psalms 139:23, 24). I arose feeling uncondemned; no sin stained our relationship—God's and mine. I hummed as I rolled my shiny washing machine from the corner. Suddenly panic seized me. I remembered another woman. She was struggling to coax a balky washer from its corner. Anxious to sell it before moving, I had assured her that it washed beautifully, failing to mention that the casters would scarcely roll.

"Had she been censuring me, I wondered? O well, that was done months ago and far away.

" 'Search me,' my prayer echoed!

"With trembling fingers I wrote, 'Forgive me for not telling you about the casters . . . . Check is enclosed for entire price.'

"My heart bowed as I read her answer: 'Your letter was the best sermon I ever heard . . . . Returning the check.' "—Lois Gordon, Fayetteville, Arkansas.

Sentence Sermon to Remember: Matthew presents Jesus as the Royal Saviour; Mark, as the Servant of man; Luke, as the Son of man; John, as the Son of God.—Anonymous.

Questions for Pupils on the Next Lesson. 1. What does it mean to repent? 2. How do Christians prepare others to hear and understand Christ's message in today's world of non-Christian culture? 3. How was John the Baptist the bridge between the Old Testament and the New? 4. What is the difference between John the Baptist's baptism and Christian baptism? 5. How can a Christian serve in a supporting role as well as in a leadership capacity?

LESSON II—DECEMBER 14

JOHN PREPARES THE WAY

Background Scripture: Malachi 3:1-5; 4:5, 6; Isaiah 40:1-11; Matthew 3:1-12; 11:7-15; 17:9-13
Devotional Reading: Isaiah 7:10-15

KING JAMES VERSION

MATTHEW 3 1 In those days came John the Baptist, preaching in the wilderness of Judea,

2 And saying, Repent ye: for the kingdom of heaven is at hand.

3 For this is he that was spoken of by the prophet Esaias, saying, The voice of one crying in the wilderness, Prepare ye the way of the Lord, make his paths straight.

4 And the same John had his raiment of camel's hair, and a leathern girdle about his loins; and his meat was locusts and wild honey.

5 Then went out to him Jerusalem, and all Judea, and all the region round about Jordan,

6 And were baptized of him in Jordan, confessing their sins.

7 But when he saw many of the Pharisees and Sadducees come to his baptism, he said unto them, O generation of vipers, who hath warned you to flee from the wrath to come?

8 Bring forth therefore fruits meet for repentance:

9 And think not to say within yourselves, We have Abraham to *our* father: for I say unto you, that God is able of these stones to raise up children unto Abraham.

10 And now also the axe is laid unto the root of the trees: therefore every tree which bringeth not forth good fruit is hewn down, and cast into the fire.

11 I indeed baptize you with water unto repentance: but he that cometh after me is mightier than I, whose shoes I am not worthy to bear: he shall baptize you with the Holy Ghost, and *with* fire:

12 Whose fan *is* in his hand, and he will thoroughly purge his floor, and gather his wheat into the garner; but he will burn up the chaff with unquenchable fire.

REVISED STANDARD VERSION

MATTHEW 3 1 In those days came John the Baptist, preaching in the wilderness of Judea, 2 "Repent, for the kingdom of heaven is at hand." 3 For this is he who was spoken of by the prophet Isaiah when he said,

"The voice of one crying in the wilderness:
Prepare the way of the Lord,
    make his paths straight."

4 Now John wore a garment of camel's hair, and a leather girdle around his waist; and his food was locusts and wild honey. 5 Then went out to him Jerusalem and all Judea and all the region about the Jordan, 6 and they were baptized by him in the river Jordan, confessing their sins.

7 But when he saw many of the Pharisees, and Sadducees coming for baptism, he said to them, "You brood of vipers! Who warned you to flee from the wrath to come? 8 Bear fruit that befits repentance, 9 and do not presume to say to yourselves, 'We have Abraham as our father'; for I tell you, God is able from these stones to raise up children to Abraham. 10 Even now the axe is laid to the root of the trees; every tree therefore that does not bear good fruit is cut down and thrown into the fire.

11 "I baptize you with water for repentance, but he who is coming after me is mightier than I, whose sandals I am not worthy to carry; he will baptize you with the Holy Spirit and with fire. 12 His winnowing fork is in his hand, and he will clear his threshing floor and gather his wheat into the granary, but the chaff he will burn with unquenchable fire."

115

KEY VERSE: . . . *Prepare ye the way of the Lord, make his paths straight.* Matthew 3:3.

HOME DAILY BIBLE READINGS

Dec.   8.   M.   *The Messenger of Good News.* Malachi 3:1–5.
Dec.   9.   T.   *The Day of Hope Comes.* Malachi 4:1–6.
Dec. 10.   W.   *The Voice in the Wilderness.* Isaiah 40:1–11.
Dec. 11.   T.   *A Song of Thanksgiving.* Isaiah 11:1–3.
Dec. 12.   F.   *The Roar of the Nations.* Isaiah 17:9–13.
Dec. 13.   S.   *Immanuel Promised.* Isaiah 7:10–15.
Dec. 14.   S.   *Prepare the Way.* Matthew 3:1–12.

BACKGROUND

Strangely, Matthew says nothing of the life of Jesus between His infancy and His baptism. We call these "the lost years"—the years in which Jesus grew to youth and manhood. While we are given no details as to what happened to Him in those years, it is fair to assume that they were years in which He was preparing Himself for the day when He came to be baptized by John the Baptist in the river Jordan.

We also know that for four hundred years there had been no prophets speaking in Israel. After Malachi, who wrote his prophetic book about 460 B.C., there was only silence. One wonders why. Was the day of prophecy over and done with? Had the people come to distrust the prophets, or had they only forgotten them?

If they had forgotten, or closed their ears to prophecy, God had not forgotten them. Down in the wild, desolate desert or wilderness near the Dead Sea, He was training a prophet so fiery and courageous that the people thought he was Elijah returned to earth. Out of the wilderness came John called The Baptizer, with the fierce heat and fire of the desert in his voice, crying out—what?

NOTES ON THE PRINTED TEXT

I. . . . *Repent ye: for the kingdom of heaven is at hand.* Matthew 3:2. He was a sight to behold; he wore clothes made of camel's hair; he ate locusts and wild honey. He was no preacher speaking softly; he roared, shouted. When people came out from Jerusalem to hear him preach, he didn't say what they might want him to say; he told them flatly that they were an errant, sinning people sadly in need of confession and repentance. He might have preached "popular" sermons, which would please everybody. But no—he preached what they *needed* to hear. Many did not like that; many thought he was crazy (wouldn't we think so if he appeared in our streets?). He had the courage of a lion.

He flattered no one when he cried, "Repent!" And he meant that for all of them, high and low. He saw the presence of evil in all of them. When Herod the king tried to stop him, John rebuked him. When the religious leaders opposed him, he scorched them with words of fire. Wherever he saw evil, he condemned it and called upon those possessed of evil to repent.

What does that mean? What *is* repentance? Repentance is confessing and it means a radical change of mind. It means asking for God's forgiveness, and it means turning around and going God's way. It isn't just saying, "I'm sorry." It means living an entirely different life from that which we have been living. Repenting is a summons to righteousness—active righteousness, practiced every day of our lives.

John won many to God—so many that the scribes and the Pharisees became alarmed lest they lose their hold on the people. They were more than angry when he called upon the people to "Prepare ye the way of the Lord, make his paths straight." The Lord? Did he mean that the Lord, in the presence of the expected Messiah, had come? He meant exactly that. He, John, was *not* this Messiah; he was no more than a slave, unworthy to carry the sandals of the Lord. He was the forerunner who himself was clearing the way for Jesus.

The Jews knew what he meant by that. Whenever a Jewish king went on a journey, the highways were repaired and cleansed for his passage. John was preparing the way for the King of Kings, and he was telling all of *us* to do the same thing. To make it possible for Christ to win the world, we must change the conditions that make it difficult for Him—the poverty, the injustice, the greed, the selfish wealth, the heedlessness of men who sin when they say, "I can sin, for I know God will forgive me!" John spoke not only to Israel, but to all who are guilty of sin, hypocrisy, and the worhsip of false gods.

II. . . . *O generation of vipers, who hath warned you to flee from the wrath to come?* Matthew 3:7. Many Pharisees and Sadducees came out to hear John preach. They were not exactly glad to hear him call them a generation of vipers. John knew his desert; he had seen vipers and scorpions flee in terror when a fire swept the wilderness, seeking a safe hiding-place—and he accused the Pharisees and the Sadducees of doing that when they came out to stand with the crowd in his open-air meetings. It was like a scheming politician coming to church not to worship, but because being seen in the church might impress the people!

Now all Pharisees and Sadducees were *not* evil people; many of them were good men, good scholars, well-meaning leaders of the historic faith. John was not condemning all of them, en masse; he was simply saying that the Pharisees and the Sadducees were wrong in trusting to their descent for salvation. They said proudly that they were the sons of Abraham, and so, automatically entitled to salvation. They were respected as such—but respectability is never enough. Nor is it enough for any of us to claim that we are Christians because our fathers were Christians, that religion is an affair of family or caste. It is not enough for us to go scurrying off to church when trouble or sadness comes. When we do that, we follow the pattern of the vipers running from the fire. The "good old time religion" which our fathers had is not enough, either; *we* must have a good new time religion, a faith of our own.

Put that ancestor worship behind you, says John, for now, with the coming of Jesus, the axe is put to the roots of that old tree (custom), and the tree (man) that does not bring forth good fruit shall be cast into the fire. The word *fire* is a good one, here; the Christ did come as a cleansing fire to burn out the dross, the useless, the evil in mankind. Malachi, long before John, had said the same thing: "But who may abide the day of his coming? and who shall stand when he appeareth? for he is like a refiners fire . . . " (Malachi 3:2). Many a man has had this holy fire burn all that is bad out of his heart and mind.

III. *"I baptize you with water for repentance, but he who is coming after me is mightier that I . . . he will baptize you with the Holy Spirit and with fire.* Matthew 3:11 (RSV). John baptized many converts with water; that was symbolic of the washing away of the old sin, the old character, of the convert, and of his devotion to Christ as a new creature. The Baptizer might have been proud of his success with the converts, up to this point, but he was not. He was not only great and courageous; he was astonishingly humble about his place in Christ's Kingdom, and so, repeatedly, he tried to make his converts understand that he was merely an announcer, a forerunner for Christ, doing the humble tasks of preparing others for His coming into their lives. And here he is saying that baptism with water is good but not the *final* baptism, that there are two baptisms necessary for the Christian: one with water, and one with the Spirit and with fire. The first baptism was introductory to the second, but the second was the most important. When that came, when the Spirit came to wholly possess the man, when he was "filled with Christ," then he was truly baptized.

Warden Lawes, of Sing Sing prison, was once asked how many of the convicts in his prison were church members. He said, "Ninety-nine percent of them!" Ninety-nine percent had been baptized, but they had never known the cleansing, refining fire of baptism at the hands of the redeeming Christ which would have given them access to a better life. They had not been purged of the old life, and so . . . they were in prison.

Humble John was saying that he could only *lead* men to Christ; Christ would do the rest. Christ would gather them into the Kingdom, as a farmer gathers his wheat in his barn; Christ, with a winnowing fork (the Spirit) would save them for His service, and the chaff (those who rejected or ignored the second baptism) would be cast out and burned with unquenchable fire (verse 12).

"So there are two baptisms—one the baptism of righteous fear, the other the baptism of redeeming love."—George A. Buttrick. The Christian must have both.

SUGGESTIONS TO TEACHERS

Your class members are undoubtedly caught up with the preparations for Christmas. Some are already feeling the effects of seasonal stress. Some may agree with the weary salesperson in Pittsburgh who sighed, "Sometimes I wish Christmas had never been invented."

Your lesson is to help your tired and tense folk realize that Christmas was not an invention as a seasonal spending spree, but the culmination of all history. Let your class appreciate the cosmic importance of Christ's coming!

1. *PREDICTION OF THE MESSIAH.* Work in the passage from Isaiah 40:1–11, reflecting the profound sense of longing for God's Deliverer. You may wish to spend a few minutes considering what the world would be if Jesus Christ had not come. How would we feel? What

longing we would have! Jesus fulfills a human's deepest desire for a sense of God. Encourage each member of your class to remark on what the Messiah's coming means to him or her.

2. *PREVIEW OF THE MESSENGER.* Switch to Malachi's announcement that "the Lord whom you seek will suddenly come . . . the messenger of the covenant" (Malachi 3:1–5). Jesus is the complete Messenger of all of God's promises because He embodies all of God's messages to humans. Your class should discuss this claim for Christ in the light of the claims of some cults which insist that Jesus Christ is not enough and their teachings must be added to His. Take a few minutes also to consider the particularities of God's message through Christ to the world today.

3. *PREACHER OF THE MESSAGE.* Your class needs to understand the person and the place of John the Baptist. Remind your people that John pointed to Jesus. Jesus fulfilled God's message. Furthermore, John the Baptist insisted that Jesus' coming meant the beginning of God's rule called for repentance and decision by every hearer. Have your class think about the demands for repentance and decision today. What do Christians need to repent of these days? What specific demands does God's rule lay on your people?

4. *PROPHET WITH THE MOST.* Continue the discussion on John the Baptist as the greatest of the prophets. Emphasize that he persisted in taking second place to Jesus. Introduce the subject of prophets today, especially the claims of cult leaders, those using mass media to preach, free-lance revivalists, etc. How can your class evaluate the claims of these people? One good clue, you should remind your class, is that a genuine prophet such as John the Baptist always emphasizes Jesus and deemphasizes himself.

5. *PREPARER OF THE MOMENT.* "History's Countdown to Zero Second" could be the subtitle of the biblical story leading up to the arrival of Jesus. Let the mystery, the splendor, and the significance of the cosmic story be spread in your lesson. Have each person in your class describe why and how Christ's coming makes such a difference. Ask whether each is living in a "B.C." viewpoint, or in an "A.D." lifestyle and outlook.

TOPIC FOR ADULTS
PREPARING THE WAY

Coming in on the Seventy-Fifth. Gerald Johnson, historian and writer, played the flute with the Baltimore orchestra for many years. In an article in a national magazine, he described the supportive role which flutists often play in orchestral pieces. Most of the time, the flute player, according to Johnson, is preparing the way for others to make dramatic contributions. Sometimes, the flutist will have to sit quietly, counting the measures, before taking up his instrument for a few notes.

Johnson describes a certain piece of music by Haydn, in which the flute player must wait for seventy-four measures without playing a note, then, on the seventy-fifth, come in precisely on the beat of the seventy-fifth. Johnson adds that a composer who expects a person to do that is asking for an individual with a rare and inestimable quality.

Like Johnson's flute player, John the Baptist had to play a supporting role. John counted the measures patiently until his brief appearance. His purpose was to introduce Another more illustrious than himself. He prepared the way for the climax of history, when God orchestrated events to bring the Messiah.

Sometimes, like John the Baptist and the flutists, we will be called upon to play supportive roles in God's production. We may have to wait quietly counting out the measures before we will be able to make our apparently minor contribution. We may merely seem to prepare the way for greater ones than we will be.

Each of us, however, can prepare the way for the One for whom God has intended all creation to celebrate, and around whom all history revolves.

Fifty-Two Strokes. For over 175 years, the old Church at the head of Orange Street in Nantucket has pealed fifty-two strokes at 9:00 P.M. each evening. The bell formerly tolled fifty-two at not only curfew time at 9:00 P.M. but also at rising time or 7:00 A.M. and at twelve noon each day. When the bell was electrified in 1958, townspeople agreed that once a day for the fifty-two strokes was sufficient.

The story behind the old bell chiming fifty-two, three times a day, each day of the year, is significant—and simple. The early town fathers, stern Puritans, wished to recall frequently that each person is granted only fifty-two weeks each year by God for serving, and that God holds each person accountable for using those fifty-two weeks responsibly. Furthermore, the tolling of the bell served as a sermon in tones that God came among humans in the midst of history, giving time a new dimension of meaning.

Perhaps no bell rings to remind you each day what God has done and who you are meant to be. This seaon of Advent, however, is intended to prepare the way for you to receive Christ in the midst of your time.

How will you use your time? How will you acknowledge that Jesus Christ is Lord of these times?

Prepared to Spend Time for Whom? "Computers have calculated that the average North American invests his seventy years in the following ways: twenty-four years sleeping, fourteen years working, six years eating, three years learning, three years convalescing, four years conversing, five years traveling, eight years amusing himself. What about worship? If you began on the day of your birth spending five minutes each morning and evening in praise and prayer (more than most people spend) and three hours per week in church, at the end of seventy years we would have invested only twenty months." Wesley Tuttle, *Eternity,* January 1975. Reprinted by permission of *Eternity* Magazine, Copyright © 1979, Evangelical Ministries, Inc., 1716 Spruce Street, Philadelphia, PA 19103.

Think about it! How did you spend your time this past year? How *do you* spend your time?

How will you spend your time this year?

Questions for Pupils on the Next Lesson: 1. What does it mean to be saved from our sins? 2. Does God guide us in specific ways today? How? 3. Do dreams matter spiritually? 4. Why is the doctrine of the virgin birth important for Christians today? 5. What can we learn from Joseph's faithful response to God? 6. How can we relate Christmas to salvation?

TOPIC FOR YOUTH
PREPARING THE WAY

Only Six Blank Pages. On July 12, 1493, a group of the wisest German scholars issued a book called the *Nuremburg Chronicle.* The learned men described the contents of the book in these words: "The events most worthy of notice from the beginning of the world to the calamity of our time."

The *Nuremburg Chronicle* listed what these wise professors felt were the significant milestones in the story of human history and ran to many pages.

The authors, however, were deeply pessimistic about the future. Conditions were nearly hopeless, they were convinced. Nothing much more could happen, they felt certain. In fact, at the end of the book, they left only six blank pages so that the reader might record any further important events that might occur before the Day of Judgment!

The writers of the *Chronicle* had not yet heard that Columbus had discovered the New World. At that very moment they thought that the story of humankind was almost concluded, when one of the most momentous events in history had taken place.

When we think that everything is over for humanity and its history, God surprises us with new chapters. The coming of Jesus was *the* new beginning by God with the human race.

John the Baptist, preparing the way, foretold His Coming. Jesus came as Lord, exactly as John promised.

Also as promised, Jesus assures us that, with Him, there are new beginnings. God has not written us off.

In the midst of the pessimism and cynicism today, we are called to be heralds of the new age of Christ's Coming. Like John the Baptist, we are to tell the great news of God's involvement in humanity and its history.

Human Condition. Herman Kahn, the brilliant futurologist, worked for many years for the Rand Corporation, one of the world's leading think tanks, before he formed his own, which he calls the Hudson Institute. Kahn lectures widely on what he sees happening during the coming years on this planet.

One of his best-known charts divides the twentieth century into four sections. Using French labels, Professor Kahn calls the first part of the twentieth century through the year 1913 *La Belle Epoque* ("the beautiful period"). From 1914 through 1947, Kahn states that we lived through *La Mauvaise Epoque* ("the bad time"). The era from 1948 to 1973 is defined as *La Deuxieme Belle Epoque* ("the second beautiful period"). The times we are presently in, beginning in 1974 and continuing at least until the turn of the century, A.D. 2000, Kahn says is *L'Epoque de Malaise.* Kahn himself answers that this is "the period of discontent and uneasiness."

The Good News, however, is that God has come into our world of discontent and uneasiness and claimed it as the world He loves. It was to an *Epoque de Mauvaise* that John the Baptist came, preparing the way for Christ's rule.

Jesus is still Lord! Get ready to tell others that Jesus the Messiah rules still!

Suitable Epitaph. A tombstone in remote mountain valley in Switzerland carries the simple inscription, "He Died Climbing." Old timers in the area recall that the man buried in the grave marked by the "He Died Climbing" epitaph was a noted Alpine guide who spent nearly sixty years ascending and descending peaks in this area. His skills as a guide and climber were legendary. The man perished during an attempt to rescue a foolhardy amateur who had recklessly become trapped on an icy ledge. Although he got the amateur to safety, the old Alpinist apparently suffered a heart attack from the exertion. He died climbing.

John the Baptist served as one blazing the trail for the Messiah. His epitaph could also read that he died climbing.

What will they say about you? Are you prepared to take risks for others? Are you willing to be a guide in the faith for others? Are you continuing to ascend the heights and to keep climbing to the very end of your days?

Sentence Sermon to Remember: John the Baptist was the first Christian, the morning star of the Kingdom of God.—Frank S. Mead.

Questions for Pupils on the Next Lesson: 1. How can you know that God is concerned for your redemption? 2. What is the role of the Holy Spirit in the birth of Jesus? 3. In what ways can you identify with Jesus in His family relationships and growth as a person? 4. In what specific ways can you show your response to Jesus Christ as your personal Lord and Savior?

LESSON III—DECEMBER 21

GOD SENDS THE SAVIOR

Background Scripture: Matthew 1:18–2:23
Devotional Reading: Isaiah 9:2–7

KING JAMES VERSION

MATTHEW 1 18 Now the birth of Jesus Christ was on this wise: When as his mother Mary was espoused to Joseph, before they came together, she was found with child of the Holy Ghost.

19 Then Joseph her husband, being a just *man*, and not willing to make her a publick example, was minded to put her away privily.

20 But while he thought on these things, behold, the angel of the Lord appeared unto him in a dream, saying, Joseph, thou son of David, fear not to take unto thee Mary thy wife: for that which is conceived in her is of the Holy Ghost.

21 And she shall bring forth a son, and thou shalt call his name JESUS: for he shall save his people from their sins.

22 Now all this was done, that it might be fulfilled which was spoken of the Lord by the prophet, saying,

23 Behold, a virgin shall be with child, and shall bring forth a son, and they shall call his name Emmanuel, which being interpreted is, God with us.

24 Then Joseph being raised from sleep did as the angel of the Lord had bidden him, and took unto him his wife:

25 And knew her not till she had brought forth her firstborn son: and he called his name JESUS.

REVISED STANDARD VERSION

MATTHEW 1 18 Now the birth of Jesus Christ took place in this way. When his mother Mary had been betrothed to Joseph, before they came together she was found to be with child of the Holy Spirit; 19 and her husband Joseph, being a just man and unwilling to put her to shame, resolved to divorce her quietly. 20 But as he considered this, behold, an angel of the Lord appeared to him in a dream, saying, "Joseph, son of David, do not fear to take Mary your wife, for that which is conceived in her is of the Holy Spirit; 21 she will bear a son, and you shall call his name Jesus, for he will save his people from their sins." 22 All this took place to fulfil what the Lord had spoken by the prophet:

23 "Behold, a virgin shall conceive and bear a son,
   and his name shall be called Emmanuel"
(which means, God with us). 24 When Joseph woke from sleep, he did as the angel of the Lord commanded him; he took his wife, 25 but knew her not until she had borne a son; and he called his name Jesus.

KEY VERSE: ". . . you shall call his name Jesus, for he will save his people from their sins." Matthew 1:21.

HOME DAILY BIBLE READINGS

Dec. 15. M. Jesus' Birth Announced. Luke 1:26–38.
Dec. 16. T. Mary Sings With Gladness. Luke 1:46–55.
Dec. 17. W. Born in a Manger. Luke 2:1–7.
Dec. 18. T. Angels and Shepherds Praise God. Luke 2:8–20.
Dec. 19. F. Simeon Sees God's Salvation. Luke 2:22, 23.
Dec. 20. S. The Wise Men Worship. Matthew 2:1–11.
Dec. 21. S. God's Son—Prince of Peace. Isaiah 9:2–7.

BACKGROUND

The Gospel by Matthew was written, as we have already said, to bring the Good News to those of Jewish birth and origin. Such readers, he well knew, would certainly cling to what they had been taught as Jews, and they would ask searching questions about the Christ who had won Matthew to His side and His cause. One question they would surely ask was this: "Just who is Jesus? Whose son is He?"

Matthew foresees the coming of that question, and he is ready for it when it comes. Before he begins to tell the story of Christ's ministry he demonstrates, using the Old Testament as his base and background, that Jesus Christ was definitely the son and heir of David and Abraham. Then he tells of another Father, greater than Joseph the son of David and Abraham, and of how that Father was in a greater and more profound sense the true father of the Man of Nazareth.

The teacher will wisely read the story of the birth of Jesus in both Matthew and Luke. Read Luke for perfect beauty; read Matthew for reasonable background in our belief that the One born in Bethlehem's stable was indeed both son of Joseph and Son of God.

NOTES ON THE PRINTED TEXT

1. Now the birth of Jesus Christ took place in this way. When his mother Mary had been betrothed to Joseph, before they came together she was found to be with child of the Holy Spirit. Matthew 1:18 (RSV). That may startle and even shock *us*, for to us it seems to mean that Jesus was born out of wedlock. He was not, according to Jewish belief and Jewish custom. For the Jew of the time, there were three steps in marriage.

First, there was the engagement; this was often the engagement of a couple in their childhood, an arrangement made by the parents without the child's consent. It is a custom, still, in some Eastern countries.

Second came the betrothal; that lasted for one year, during which the couple was known as man and wife. Mary was legally and legitimately Joseph's wife when they traveled to Bethlehem.

Then came the third step: the ceremony of marriage at the end of the year of betrothal. At this point, the betrothal might be broken if the girl did not want to be married, but it could be broken only by way of divorce, divorce by the husband. Joseph thought of getting a divorce, but not for long; he was a just and a good, compassionate man, and he could not do this to the one he loved.

Not only was he unwilling; he had a dream (vision?) in which the voice of God came to him through an angel who told him that Mary's child had been begotten or conceived by the Holy Spirit.

This, too, is puzzling to many a modern reader. Conceived of the Holy Spirit? To understand this, we must understand the Jewish thought concerning the Holy Spirit—not the Christian thought, for at that time there were no Christians. To the Hebrews, the Spirit of God was involved in every work of creation. It was through God that the heavens and the earth were made; it was by God's hand that the first inhabitants of the world were made. Said Job, "The spirit of God hath made me" (Job

33:4). The Spirit is the Creator and the Giver of life. Many, many times, this Creator intervened in the lives of men and through the working of the Spirit, moulded and changed them.

The essence of Matthew's thinking was this: in the birth of Jesus, the Spirit was operative in the world in a new way, in the coming of God in the person of Jesus Christ. It was the gift of One in whom, when men looked at Him and heard Him, saw and heard God. ". . . he that hath seen me," said Jesus, "hath seen the Father . . ." (John 14:9).

II. . . . *thou shalt call his name Jesus: for he will save his people from their sins.* Matthew 1:21. Why should He be given that name above all others? It was not so much above all others, literally, for the name *Jesus* is the Greek name for Joshua, which meant "Jehovah is salvation." This boy, the son of the carpenter Joseph and his wife Mary, was to stand above all other men ever born in performing a continuing miracle of which all others were incapable: He and He alone had the Spirit-power to forgive the most repulsive of sins in any and all men.

For centuries, Israel had longed for that. For centuries, Israel had struggled with her sins and hoped and prayed to be delivered from them, but for one reason or another, Israel went right on sinning and hoping for deliverance from it. Now Matthew tells them, the Deliverer had come! He came in fulfillment of the Prophet Isaiah: "Behold, a virgin shall conceive, and bear a son, and shall call his name Emmanuel" (Isaiah 7:14). That name, Emmanuel (or Immanuel) meant "God is with us." It was, in Isaiah, a name predicted to King Ahaz during the Syro-Ephraimitic war. God's enemies, Isaiah was saying, would not prevail against God's people. It is contended by many that this was not a Messianic prophecy, but Micah (5:2) interpreted it as applying to the Messiah. "Matthew used it as referring to the virgin birth of our Lord: Jesus the son of the Virgin Mary is the predicted Emmanuel, the true *God with us,* the Savior, the Christ. And Jesus is this to the Christian Church, whether predicted by Isaiah or not." *Harper's Bible Dictionary,* p. 278.

God is with us, and against Him the gates of hell will not prevail; the forces of hell *cannot* win, so long as God is with us. Or, as Abraham Lincoln put it, they shall not win so long as we are on God's side!

This, basically, is the meaning of Christmas. Christmas is the celebration of God coming into the world in the person of Jesus. Christmas is gift-time—the day upon which God sent us the greatest of gifts, the inestimable gift of His Son. God gave us Him to live in love among us, to die in love for us, to teach us how to live in love.

Gifts. What shall we give, this Christmas? Too many of us will be throwing our money away in the stores, on brutally expensive gadgets for friends and relatives who need them not! And when we do that, we completely miss what God meant Christmas to be. One little act of love is a far greater gift, in His sight, than all the gadgets that money can buy.

"We miss the spirit of Christmas if we consider the incarnation as an indistinct and doubtful, far-off event unrelated to our present problems. We miss the purport of Christ's birth if we do not accept it as a living link which joins us together as children of the ever-living and true God. In love alone—the love of God and the love of man—will be found the solution of all the ills which afflict the world today. Slowly, sometimes painfully, but always with increasing purpose, emerges the great message of Christianity: only with wisdom comes joy, and with greatness comes love."—Harry S. Truman.

SUGGESTIONS TO TEACHERS

A veteran of the Korean War who spent two Christmases in a prison camp recalls that those were the times when he seemed to celebrate the true meaning of Christ's birth. "We had none of the commercialism that surrounds us today. No frantic gift-buying, no tension and anxiety the season always brings to me now. The first time I really understood the real significance of Christmas was when I was a P.O.W., and all we had was the Christmas story and our memories."

Nearly everyone in your class is suffering from the seasonal-spending spasm. A few privately are finding it difficult to cope with the holiday. Against this backdrop, your lesson for today is appropriately called, "God Sends the Savior." He saves your class members from the anxieties, the guilt, the depression, and the fatigue which this holiday brings. Remind your class that the first Christmas happened to real live people, similar to your class's people!

1. *MIDST OF FAMILY.* Christmas is sometimes a trying time for families, but God is invested deeply in family life. He underscores the place and importance of family by coming into the home of Mary and Joseph. In spite of the frailties and fragility of relationships, God took the risk. He appeared in human form; He resided with humans. Take a few moments in your class to allow the class to consider afresh the need for relationships, both within the intimate circle of a home, and the larger circle of church family. Think also of ways in which God's presence may be "incarnated" through those relationships.

2. *MILIEU OF FEAR.* God sent the Savior in a time of anxieties. Have your class pick out examples of the anxieties the different persons had who were involved in the Christmas story, including Mary, Joseph, the shepherds, etc. Also have your class list some of the anxieties which they and others are feeling this season. Remark how the words in the original Christmas account repeat, "Fear not!" God sends a Savior to save us from fears!

3. *MINORITY FOR FUTURE.* In an age when "Big is Best" seems to be the motto, take a few minutes in today's lesson to point out that God also uses the apparently small and insignificant. Even the biblical account stresses that tiny Bethlehem was "by no means least" (Matthew 2:6). Those in your class who may be inclined to write off your community, your church, your class, or their own lives as being of no importance would be reminded that they are the minority for the future—with God!

4. *MODEL OF FAME.* Look at the coming of the Magi, and have your class remember that wisdom is still to be found at the manger when we kneel in awe. Wise men and women today as in the first century realize the source of their wisdom is in God sending the Savior!

5. *MATRIX OF FUTILITY.* Christ came into a world of brutality and

despair. Allow your class to understand the horror and cruelty of
Herod's massacre of the infants in Bethlehem. Proclaim the Good News
that God sent the Savior in such a setting. Tell it in a way that brings
hope to your class today!

TOPIC FOR ADULTS
GOD SENDS THE SAVIOR

Signal From Beyond. Scientists are concerned that our radio channels
from communications satellites are becoming so cluttered that we may
not be able to pick up signals from creatures from other galaxies. In fact,
the International Telecommunications Union has received a request
from twenty-one nations, including the United States, to keep several
cosmic radio channels open. The worried scientists say that they want
these channels kept clear in case radio messages are being beamed to us
from nearby star systems.

We all are inclined to overlook the fact that we have already received
the greatest message of all from beyond our world of time and space.
The Eternal and Almighty One has been signaling us earthlings for
years, and on every possible frequency of our life-experience.

This week, we celebrate God's supreme communication with the
human race—the coming of Jesus Christ! We recognize that we live on
"the visited planet."

The Star That Still Beams. In the Catacombs under the Appian Way,
where the early Christians met secretly to escape persecution and mar-
tyrdom, when every man's hand was against them, this inscription has
been found: "The roof hides our stars but they are shining still, and the
Star of Bethlehem will never set." However dark may be the outlook,
the uplook is always bright for the Christian.

No Jest. Bertrand Russell, the eccentric English philosopher, once
described an imaginary scenario of God's relationship with us humans.
The fantasy which he outlined revealed his own cynical view of the
Creator God, His Creation, and especially humans. Russell's imaginary
tale portrayed God, weary of Angels, finally making humans. According
to his story, the Lord surrounded them with tears and troubles, then
watched with detached amusement as humans struggled with a certain
gallantry. Then, Russell explained, God grew tired of watching. "A good
play. Some day I must do it again," God allegedly says. "Meanwhile—
enough! The jest is ended." And with a sweep of His hand, in Russell's
legend, God annihilates humans.

A brainy English thinker's notion, but hardly the Good News of
Bethlehem: God sends a Savior!

God has never grown tired of us. He cares so much for us, His creation, that He chose to come among us in human form.

Questions for Pupils on the Next Lesson. 1. Why does acceptance of
baptism imply commitment to share in Jesus' ministry? 2. What is the
most vital work for every Christian disciple? 3. How may you as a Christian carry out your responsibility to share the blessings of Christ's Kingdom with others? 4. In what ways may spiritual growth and maturity
come through the tensions and trials of life?

TOPIC FOR YOUTH
ACCEPTING THE SAVIOR

Merganthaller Waisleywillow. Merganthaller Waisleywillow is the name of a young Welshman who made a trip to Paris in 1935. His trip is remembered primarily because he succeeded in touring the Louvre, the magnificent museum housing such masterpieces as the *Venus de Milo,* the *Mona Lisa,* and the *Winged Victory of Samothrace*—in seven minutes! Others, hearing of Waisleywillow's "feat" of covering the enormous treasure house of art in seven minutes flat, set out to break the record. Tex Houston of Oklahoma knocked two seconds off Waisleywillow's time. More recently, another American, Peter Stone, used special track shoes and took the route via the Salle Daru rather than the Salle Sept Metres used by others. Stone "did the Louvre" in five minutes and fifty-six seconds.

Flushed with triumph, Stone announced his intentions of setting new records for covering the sights in the Tower of London and St. Peter's in Rome, hoping to break the four minute mark for both of these sights.

Perhaps Christmas has been the same thing for you—something "to do" as quickly as possible. Perhaps you, like Waisleywillow, Houston, Stone and others at the Louvre, have rushed through Advent Season without pausing to appreciate the beauty and meaning of what you are passing.

Until you have lingered long enough to accept the gift of the Savior, you are merely galloping recklessly and foolishly through life. Take time this season to reflect on God's superb gift!

Limited Range of Emotions? "What strikes me about our students, when we first meet them, is how limited is their range of emotions, their expectations of themselves. Having endured and survived the terrible trial of adolescence, they huddle together, bound within their own flat and narrow circle of permissible aspirations of career, not character. It is as if surviving is all that can be asked of humanity. Striking out on one's own is dangerous and demands courage. Imagination is for fools. Anguish, failure, self-doubt are to be dulled. Tears and laughter are permitted only in careful measure about some few things.

"It is for such as these . . . that Job speaks of his dead children. For them we tell the story of the Cross and all it stands for, for its part; and the suffering and enduring Israel, the Jewish people, for its part."— Jacob Neusner, "To Weep With Achilles," *The Chronicle of Higher Education,* January 29, 1979. Reprinted with permission. Copyright © 1979 by *The Chronicle of Higher Education.*

New National Anthem? An American businessman and a Syrian shared a table on a cruise ship in the Mediterranean. One evening, the ship's orchestra broke into the march tune, "The Parade of the Wooden Soldiers." The American was surprised to see the Syrian lay aside his napkin, rise to his feet, and stand politely at attention. When the American asked why the other was standing, the Syrian courteously replied, "Why, I thought it was your national anthem."

The Syrian was not being funny. He was quite serious. He sincerely believed that the music of "The Parade of the Wooden Soldiers" was the tune for the American national anthem!

In a sense, the Syrian's unintentional mistake is closer to the way we often act than we like to think. Aren't we often little wooden soldiers?

Christ frees us from marching lockstep with everyone else in society. Christ saves us from parading as mindless dummies. He empowers you to be the unique human which God intends you to be. Christmas is the celebration of His birth, and should be an occasion for your new birth!

Sentence Sermon to Remember: Christmas began in the heart of God; it is complete only when it reaches the heart of man.—*Religious Telescope.*

Questions for Pupils on the Next Lesson. 1. How can you find useful personal ways of ministering to the needs of others? 2. What is baptism supposed to mean to Christians? 3. How does spiritual growth and maturity frequently come in life? 4. How do you think younger members of Christ's community like yourself may show genuine faith and authentic ministry?

LESSON IV—DECEMBER 28

JESUS BEGINS HIS MINISTRY

Background Scripture: Matthew 3:13–4:25
Devotional Reading: Ephesians 1:3–14

KING JAMES VERSION

MATTHEW 3 13 Then cometh Jesus from Galilee to Jordan unto John, to be baptized of him.

14 But John forbade him, saying, I have need to be baptized of thee, and comest thou to me?

15 And Jesus answering said unto him, Suffer *it to be so* now; for thus it becometh us to fulfil all righteousness. Then he suffered him.

16 And Jesus, when he was baptized, went up straightway out of the water: and, lo, the heavens were opened unto him, and he saw the Spirit of God descending like a dove, and lighting upon him:

17 And lo a voice from heaven, saying, This is my beloved Son, in whom I am well pleased.

4 17 From that time Jesus began to preach, and to say, Repent: for the kingdom of heaven is at hand.

18 And Jesus, walking by the sea of Galilee, saw two brethren, Simon called Peter, and Andrew his brother, casting a net into the sea: for they were fishers.

19 And he saith unto them, Follow me, and I will make you fishers of men.

20 And they straightway left *their* nets, and followed him.

21 And going on from thence, he saw other two brethren, James *the son* of Zebedee, and John his brother, in a ship with Zebedee their father, mending their nets; and he called them.

22 And they immediately left the ship and their father, and followed him.

23 And Jesus went about all Galilee, teaching in their synagogues, and preaching the gospel of the kingdom, and healing all manner of sickness and all manner of disease among the people.

24 And his fame went throughout all Syria: and they brought unto him all sick people that were taken with divers

REVISED STANDARD VERSION

MATTHEW 3 13 Then Jesus came from Galilee to the Jordan to John, to be baptized by him. 14 John would have prevented him, saying, "I need to be baptized by you, and do you come to me?" 15 But Jesus answered him, "Let it be so now; for thus it is fitting for us to fulfil all righteousness." Then he consented. 16 And when Jesus was baptized, he went up immediately from the water, and behold, the heavens were opened and he saw the Spirit of God descending like a dove, and alighting on him; 17 and lo, a voice from heaven, saying, "This is my beloved Son, with whom I am well pleased."

4 17 From that time Jesus began to preach, saying, "Repent, for the kingdom of heaven is at hand."

18 As he walked by the Sea of Galilee, he saw two brothers, Simon who is called Peter and Andrew his brother, casting a net into the sea; for they were fishermen. 19 And he said to them, "Follow me, and I will make you fishers of men." 20 Immediately they left their nets and followed him. 21 And going on from there he saw two other brothers, James the son of Zebedee and John his brother, in the boat with Zebedee their father, mending their nets, and he called them. 22 Immediately they left the boat and their father, and followed him.

23 And he went about all Galilee, teaching in their synagogues and preaching the gospel of the kingdom and healing every disease and every infirmity among the people. 24 So his fame spread throughout all Syria, and they brought him all the sick, those afflicted with various diseases and pains, demoniacs, epileptics, and paralytics,

diseases and torments, and those which were possessed with devils, and those which were lunatick, and those that had the palsy; and he healed them.

24 And there followed him great multitudes of people from Galilee, and *from* Decapolis, and *from* Jerusalem, and *from* Judea, and *from* beyond Jordan.

and he healed them. 25 And great crowds followed him from Galilee and the Decapolis and Jerusalem and Judea and from beyond the Jordan.

KEY VERSE: From that time Jesus began to preach, saying, Repent, for the kingdom of heaven is at hand. Matthew 4:17.

HOME DAILY BIBLE READINGS

Dec. 22. M. *Jesus Is the Son of God.* John 1:29–34.
Dec. 23. T. *A Wedding Miracle.* John 2:1–11.
Dec. 24. W. *Opposing Corrupt Practices.* John 2:13–22.
Dec. 25. T. *Confidence in Jesus' Word.* John 4:46–54.
Dec. 26. F. *Jesus Declares His Mission.* Luke 4:16–21.
Dec. 27. S. *Preparing Fishers of Men.* Luke 5:1–11.
Dec. 28. S. *Faithful Though Tempted.* Matthew 4:1–11.

BACKGROUND

Jesus was thirty years old when he came to John to be baptized. For three long decades, He had lived a comparatively obscure life, doing at home with Joseph and Mary the humble little tasks as their loyal son. It is more than probable that He was also doing something of greater importance: He must have been meditating and working out in His mind just what He was to do with His life beyond the home. Over this period was developed in Him the conviction that His way of life must be the way of the Cross, of One called to serve and suffer for His suffering people.

Then the day came when He *knew* what He had to do; it was the day when John the Baptist came roaring out of the desert preaching repentance in Israel and calling upon her people to prepare the way for the Son of God, whose coming was imminent. For thirty years Jesus had waited for this, and now it had come. He went out to meet John in Jordan.

NOTES ON THE PRINTED TEXT

I. But John forbad him, saying, I have need to be baptized of thee, and comest thou to me? Matthew 3:14. John would say that! Here he was, the humblest of men, an unordained, free-lance preacher quite aware of his inexperience and shortcomings—and of his stature as just another sinner among sinners—here he was, asked to baptize the Christ! It was somehow like a young preacher just out of seminary being called upon to preach next Sunday in a vast cathedral. Why *me*, asked John? It is I who should be baptized by you!

Matthew is the only one of the Gospel writers who records this, and we wonder why. It was a high point in the story of Jesus—and it has a great lesson to teach. Why did Jesus ask John the Baptist to baptize

Him—He who was without sin? Good Christians still are puzzled by
this.

But Jesus made it clear. What He was doing in this baptism at the
hands of John was *identifying Himself with His people.* He was fulfilling all righteousness (*see* verse 15), or, to put it another way, He was
doing all that was righteous, or *right,* in this ceremony. By that He
meant the righteousness of God in the Covenant promises He had made
with His people. It was a baptism not of a sinner, but as an act to
reestablish the right relations between Him and His people.

Jesus identified Himself with the people He had come to save. It was
the first act by which He took upon Himself the sins of His people and
later died for them.

It was a startling thing to the Jews, for no Jew was required to submit
himself to baptism; that was a rite performed only for the proselytes of
Judaism, who needed to be "cleaned up" before they could be accepted
into that faith. But Jesus was making it clear as He stood in the waters of
Jordan that *all men,* high and low, Jew or Gentile, stood in need of the
cleansing rite of baptism.

It may not have been approved of by the Jews, as they saw Him there,
but it was approved of God: "This is my beloved Son, in whom I am well
pleased" (verse 17). This is a quotation from two Old Testament sources:
Psalms 2:7 and Isaiah 42:1, which is the description of the Suffering
Servant of God. Jesus stood there not as the conquering Messiah, but as
One chosen to win men back to God with the weapon of suffering love.
John could baptize a sinner with water, but this One greater than he
would baptize them with the Spirit; the Spirit descended upon Him that
day "like a dove"—a pure white dove, the eternal symbol of peace and
all that is beautiful in man's existence.

Jesus was consecrated to His work when He came up out of Jordan.
But now He had to find a method with which to do it.

II. *And Jesus, walking by the sea of Galilee, saw two brethren, Simon
called Peter, and Andrew his brother, casting a net into the sea . . . .*
Matthew 4:18. To do His work, He needed followers, disciples, men
with minds to understand Him and His mission and with hearts to follow and suffer with Him. He chose, first, Simon Peter, a man with a
quick temper and a burning heart. Peter was a man who rocked like a
skyscraper in a gale; skyscraper-like, too, he pointed ever heavenward,
came back to dead center when the gale had passed. He was rooted deep
in the bedrock of the Spirit; nay, his spirit was the rock on which Christ
built His church. He could promise to die for Christ one moment, and
deny Him the next; he was weak at times, but glorious in his declaration,
"Thou art the Christ!" He was perhaps the most human of the Twelve
and the most valuable to Jesus: a diamond in the rough, with great
polishing possibilities. He was transfigured and transformed.

And Andrew his brother? Actually, it was Andrew who brought Peter
to Christ. He was always bringing someone. He brought certain questioning Greeks who said to him, "Sir, we would see Jesus," and they
saw. He worked no spectacular miracles, but he was the first missionary
to the Gentiles. He brought others in: if we only had more Andrews,

more Christians willing to take second place to a more talented brother
in our trembling, fear-struck world, content to bring them in!

Then James and John, the sons of Zebedee, heard Him call and went
after Him. Jesus called them "the sons of thunder," but James was
hardly as noisy as that. He was one of the silent ones. Sometimes, when
he spoke, he said what was wrong—like suggesting that an inhospitable
village be burned, or when he asked for a prominent seat in the Kingdom (asked it, through his mother Salome). He was silent, but as strong
as Gibraltar. When Jesus needed help and support, he turned to
James—in the house of Jairus, on the Mount of Transfiguration, in
Gethesemane, he looked to James, James the silent, the mute sustaining
cooperator.

John his brother was all love. He is called in the Fourth Gospel "that
disciple whom Jesus loved." He left his fishing nets to fish for men with
Christ; in love he arranged the Last Supper; in love he stood at the cross
when the others had fled and heard Jesus commend His mother to his
care; in love he ran to the empty tomb with Easter's dawn; in love he
built the first church in Jerusalem. If we would know Jesus Christ, we
should study John, the most Christlike of the Apostles, the Galahad of
the Twelve.

Good men! Fishermen, yes, without the privilege of training in the
schools, but great men because they were patient men, courageous men
(all of them died in His service) ready to risk all for His sake. Great in
understanding that taking fish from the waters of Galilee was not to be
compared with taking men up out of the black waters of sin and death—
"catching them in the great net of God."—Suzanne de Dietrich. With
such men, Jesus started down the long, long road that led from
Bethlehem to Calvary.

III. *And Jesus went about all Galilee . . . . And his fame went
throughout all Syria . . . .* Matthew 4:23, 24. Verses 23–25 contain a
summary of the method that Jesus was to use in His subsequent ministry. It tells us where He went and what He did in that early ministry.
First of all, notice that He began in the synagogues. That was because
He found there the people He wanted to reach. The synagogue was, in a
way, the local school or "university" of the common people; it was a
teaching institution, and there His teaching began. Later, as we shall
see, He preached at open-air gatherings, when the synagogues could no
longer hold the crowds that came to listen.

We might summarize further in saying that His method was one of
preaching, teaching, and healing. The preaching was a proclaiming of
the Good News; the teaching was explaining it; and His healing was
proof of His power over sin, sickness, and death.

How quickly the crowds came! As we read Matthew's story, we find
that He was well known—no, famous, in a few weeks or months after
His baptism and after His temptations. How rapidly was He a successful
preacher, teacher, and healer far beyond the boundaries of Judea. All
across the Roman province of Syria, which included Palestine, they
flocked to Him, from both sides of Jordan, from Galilee south through
Perera on Jordan's far side and from Decapolis (a federation of ten Greek

Cities). He taught them all both in words and acts of healing. Taught those sick with divers (various) diseases, those tormented with illnesses of the body and the mind.

All down that long road, He taught His disciples how and what to preach, how to heal, and they passed along to us that faith in Him which includes teaching and preaching to those who do not believe in or even know the Christ, and that in our hands lies the healing of people and of nations for we, too, are His disciples.

SUGGESTIONS TO TEACHERS

Everyone approaches a new year with a mixture of groans and grins. Your class members are no exception. They will carry to your class their concerns (perhaps unspoken) about 1981.

Beginning a new year is a good place to think about Jesus beginning His ministry—the topic for today's lesson. Keep in mind that each Christian, as Jesus Christ's follower, will also be making a new beginning in his or her ministry.

Jesus' career opens with three distinct segments, and centers around three places: the Jordan River, where He was baptized; the wilderness, where He was tempted; and Galilee, where He began teaching and healing. Develop your lesson around these three foci. Remember that every person in your class also has a Jordan, a wilderness, and a Galilee.

1. *JORDAN.* At His baptism, Jesus understood that He was called, commissioned, and confirmed God's own Son. Baptism was Jesus' "ordination service," as some scholars put it. At the same time, He identified completely with all humans by submitting to the cleansing of baptism. In your lesson, you may well put heavier emphasis on the "ordination" of Jesus at His baptism. Note the words, "This is my beloved Son, with whom I am well pleased" (Matthew 3:17) which are quotations from the coronation ceremony in Psalm 2:7 and the suffering servant passages in Isaiah 42:1. Jesus understood His ministry would be one of serving as God's Anointed. Likewise, your class must be made to understand that the ministry of every Christian consists of sacrifice. Help your people to start the new year by remembering that they are called and commissioned. Let the beginning of a new year be a "Jordan experience" for each!

2. *WILDERNESS.* Jesus also was tempted. So are we. Appropriately, the place of temptation was "the wilderness," each Christian also faces such wildernesses. Enable your class to grasp the fact that being a Christian does not mean being free from temptation. Also suggest to your class that temptation takes many different forms, just as it did for Jesus. It would be worthwhile to take some time to share the temptations each faces, and discover what the various types are. It would also lower the guilt level in some to learn that others also are faced with temptations. Most important, put across the Good News that the Christ who was victorious over His temptations strengthens believers today to withstand the Tempter.

3. *GALILEE.* Jesus' ministry in Galilee meant decision and declaration and disciples. "Repent, for the kingdom of God is at hand"

(Matthew 4:17) was His call for decision by hearers. "Follow me, and I will make you fishers of men" (4:19), was His call for disciples. Each person in your class needs to understand that his or her ministry must contain these components. Each believer is intended to let others know that Christ's coming has inaugurated a new era. Each follower must invite others to follow Jesus. These are the "Galilee orders" for each Christian for the new year.

TOPIC FOR ADULTS
JESUS BEGINS HIS MINISTRY

Endured or Enjoyed? A few years ago, a book was published with the title *Coping With Christmas* by Gary Collins, (Bethany Press, 1975). The writer, a Pastor-Counselor, offers help for laypersons who find themselves depressed and angry during rush of the celebration this time of the year. These persons are trying to "cope" with Christmas.

Has this most blessed and joyous of all seasons merely been a time for "coping" for you?

Start with Jesus again, as He started His ministry. Let Him start again with you. Begin with His baptism, and go with Him into the wilderness. Continue to Galilee, and march with Him to Jerusalem. Repent and follow Him, and pass from victim to victor!

Rage Stops the Presses. An angry, frustrated printer in the press room at the Excello Press in Chicago finally had more than he could take one day in 1978, and in an explosion of temper hurled his lunch pail into one of the presses. The irate worker's outburst wrecked the press, causing $30,000 in damages.

Fortunately, the people at Excello Press sympathized with the man and have taken steps to introduce measures in the plant to lower tensions.

We all feel like heaving objects into the machinery at times. We all live under pressures and are tempted to let our rage burst out toward objects or, worse, toward persons near us. In fact, for many of us, our most serious temptation is to act destructively.

Whatever the pressures, and whatever the temptation, which you may feel, Christ experienced pressures and temptations. He triumphed over them. He also ministers to you in your times of pressure and temptation. Let Him begin His ministry to you!

New Era. There is no compelling reason to set aside January the first to celebrate the start of a new year. The ancient Egyptians began the cycle of a new year in September. The early Greeks began their new year in June. New Englanders for a time used Christmas Day, December 25th, as the start-up date for the new year. The Jewish New Year floats between September and October. It was only in the course of the seventeenth century that Germany, Russia, England, and Sweden finally officially adopted January the first as New Year's Day.

A small child, asked when the new year begins, will probably cite his or her own birthday as the most consequential turn of the yearly calendar.

In one sense, New Year's is an artificial contrivance, because life is a continuum. We move back and forth on that continuum until death. However, we need some device to break the continuity. Prisoners scratch the passing of time on their cell walls.

Christians understand New Year's as God's gift of a new ration of *time*. Christians also recognize that God has redeemed *time*. Our days are not a dreary procession of burnt-out yesterdays. God offers new start-ups.

Christ's ministry was God's new beginning with the human race— with us. His baptism, temptation, Galilean tour; His sufferings, death, and Resurrection; His entire career is God's serving us in love.

Questions for Pupils on the Next Lesson. 1. What does the word *Beatitude* mean? 2. How do the Beatitudes present a pattern for Christian discipleship to you? 3. In what ways do the Beatitudes speak to both a present reality and a future hope? 4. What is the relationship between the Beatitudes to the other teachings of Jesus in the Sermon on the Mount? 5. How does true happiness come to a Christian?

TOPIC FOR YOUTH
BEGINNING A MINISTRY

What You Are Created to Be. " 'God intends us to be what He created us to be and to know our proper role in life.'

"Robert McAfee Brown, a professor at the Pacific School of Religion in Berkeley, California, recently said, 'You are called upon to be who you are where you are, not to be somebody else somewhere else.' He quoted Rabbi Zushya, who said, as he contemplated death, 'When I approach the divine throne, I will not be asked, "Why were you not Moses?" but only, "Why were you not Zushya?" '

"Similarly, the Lord will ask a woman, 'Why did you want to be a man?' And a pupil, 'Why did you want to be a teacher?' And a man killed when he drove too fast on Route 100, 'Why did you want to be Mario Andretti?' And each one of us, 'Why did you not want to be what I created you to be?' "—Rev. Joseph B. Mohr, *Call Chronicle*, Allentown, Pennsylvania, February 3, 1978.

Time in Odd Moments. Jesus used His time well. He had a superb sense of timing. He made every minute count. Each hour was used as an opportunity for ministry, for serving.

Your life also is meant to be used for serving others. God gives you the gift of time to be used carefully.

You may say, "But I don't have enough time to serve others. I'm too busy with what I have to do at school and at the job."

God says that even the odd moments may be used for significant purposes. Longfellow translated Dante's *Inferno* while waiting during the odd moments for the water to boil each morning to make the coffee. Harriet Beecher Stowe made use of her odd moments in the midst of a busy life as a mother and homemaker to write *Uncle Tom's Cabin*, the book that shook the nation and signalled the end of slavery. Robert Burns used the odd moments while plowing his farm to compose many of his poems. Others have memorized Scripture verses—the point is that even the odd moments may be used as "valuable time." Your "ministry" can be carried out even in the odd moments as well as the even hours.

Begin serving Christ by serving others in His name this year!

Animals or Humans? Walt Whitman once wrote that he preferred animals to humans. He claimed that animals are calm and placid in comparison to people. Animals do not weep for their sins or whine about their condition. They do not discuss their obligations to God or their duties to others.

Whitman put it quite bluntly. He should have added, however, that animals are not concerned about the Spirit of God. They do not realize His call or His commands. Animals feel no guilt, but that does not make them superior. On the contrary, their very placidity is the sign of their inferiority.

You are created as a human, with all the potentialities for caring and serving, suffering for others and feeling their hurts. You, also, are meant to experience your own Jordan, your own wilderness, and your own Galilee. Remember, however, that the Living Lord stands with you as you face each of these.

Sentence Sermon to Remember: When a Baptist was asked about baptism, he replied, "It's all right, but you musn't hang around the river too long."—E. Stanley Jones.

Questions for Pupils on the Next Lesson. 1. In what way is your life a witness to others about the meaning of Jesus Christ? Specifically how do you let others know you are a Christian? 2. Is doing God's will a joy-filled or a glum experience? Give your reasons and offer examples. 3. Is Christian discipleship primarily to make you look good and to call attention to you? 4. What does the word *Beatitude* mean? 5. What are the clues to real happiness that Christ offers, and what are the clues to happiness that most television culture suggests?

LESSON V—JANUARY 4

LET YOUR LIGHT SHINE

Background Scripture: Matthew 5
Devotional Reading: Colossians 3:5–17

KING JAMES VERSION

MATTHEW 5 1 And seeing the multitudes, he went up into a mountain: and when he was set, his disciples came unto him:

2 And he opened his mouth, and taught them, saying,

3 Blessed *are* the poor in spirit: for theirs is the kingdom of heaven.

4 Blessed *are* they that mourn: for they shall be comforted.

5 Blessed *are* the meek: for they shall inherit the earth.

6 Blessed *are* they which do hunger and thirst after righteousness: for they shall be filled.

7 Blessed *are* the merciful: for they shall obtain mercy.

8 Blessed *are* the pure in heart: for they shall see God.

9 Blessed *are* the peacemakers: for they shall be called the children of God.

10 Blessed *are* they which are persecuted for righteousness' sake: for theirs is the kingdom of heaven.

11 Blessed are ye, when *men* shall revile you, and persecute *you*, and shall say all manner of evil against you falsely, for my sake.

12 Rejoice, and be exceeding glad: for great *is* your reward in heaven: for so persecuted they the prophets which were before you.

13 Ye are the salt of the earth: but if the salt have lost his savour, wherewith shall it be salted? it is thenceforth good for nothing, but to be cast out, and to be trodden under foot of men.

14 Ye are the light of the world. A city that is set on a hill cannot be hid.

15 Neither do men light a candle, and put it under a bushel, but on a candlestick; and it giveth light unto all that are in the house.

16 Let your light so shine before men, that they may see your good works, and glorify your Father which is in heaven.

REVISED STANDARD VERSION

MATTHEW 5 1 Seeing the crowds, he went up on the mountain, and when he sat down his disciples came to him. 2 And he opened his mouth and taught them, saying:

3 "Blessed are the poor in spirit, for theirs is the kingdom of heaven.

4 "Blessed are those who mourn, for they shall be comforted.

5 "Blessed are the meek, for they shall inherit the earth.

6 "Blessed are those who hunger and thirst for righteousness, for they shall be satisfied.

7 "Blessed are the merciful, for they shall obtain mercy.

8 "Blessed are the pure in heart, for they shall see God.

9 "Blessed are the peacemakers, for they shall be called sons of God.

10 "Blessed are those who are persecuted for righteousness' sake, for theirs is the kingdom of heaven.

11 "Blessed are you when men revile you and persecute you and utter all kinds of evil against you falsely on my account. 12 Rejoice and be glad, for your reward is great in heaven, for so men persecuted the prophets who were before you.

13 "You are the salt of the earth; but if salt has lost its taste, how shall its saltness be restored? It is no longer good for anything except to be thrown out and trodden under foot by men.

14 "You are the light of the world. A city set on a hill cannot be hid.

15 Nor do men light a lamp and put it under a bushel, but on a stand, and it gives light to all in the house.

16 Let your light so shine before men, that they may see your good works and give glory to your Father who is in heaven."

KEY VERSE: Let your light so shine before men, that they may see your good works, and glorify your Father which is in heaven. Matthew 5:16.

HOME DAILY BIBLE READINGS

Dec. 29. M. *God's Word Gives Light.* Psalms 119:129–136.
Dec. 30. T. *Called From Darkness to Light.* Ephesians 5:3–14.
Dec. 31. W. *Christians—Light in the World.* Philippians 2:12–18.
Jan. 1. T. *Living in Light Brings Freedom.* John 3:16–21.
Jan. 2. F. *Walk in the Light.* 1 John 1:5–10.
Jan. 3. S. *Love—Evidence of Walking in Light.* 1 John 2:7–11.
Jan. 4. S. *A Shining Light to Others.* Colossians 3:5–17.

BACKGROUND

Chapters five through seven, in Matthew's Gospel, contain the Sermon on the Mount, the greatest sermon in the history of Christianity. Someone has called it the Magna Charta of Christianity—of the New Age. In a sense, it can be said that in this sermon, Jesus was making known the terms of a new law. At some few points it reflects the Decalogue, at others it reminds of Sinai, but taken in its entirety it is something new, for it is a complete reversal of old standards, of the thinking of men, of the values by which they had been living, to a new set of values and judgments quite alien to the past.

The opening verse of Matthew 5 might lead us to think that it was a sermon, or a teaching, intended only for the disciples of Jesus. It would be so, but the word *multitudes* is there in verse 1, so He must have been speaking to the crowd as well as to His disciples. He "went up into a mountain (not much of a mountain, but more like two high hills near Galilee, as many scholars claim) and the disciples and the people followed Him up there to what we now call The Mount of Beatitudes. There He sat, and taught, and preached. There He told them what a disciple, *any* disciple, had to be in A.D. 30—and in A.D. 1981 and what the citizen of the Kingdom must be like.

NOTES ON THE PRINTED TEXT

I. Blessed are the poor in spirit . . . . Matthew 5:2. Both Matthew and Luke have a Sermon on the Mount; Luke has but four Beatitudes; Matthew has nine. Matthew seems to have Jesus talking to His disciples; Luke stresses the multitude. Both of them, it is believed, put together a number of the teachings of Jesus in this Sermon on the Mount, but it is possible that these teachings were not delivered at a single time or place. Both use the word *blessed* in introducing each Beatitude, and to be *blessed* meant to be happy. We may divide Matthew's Sermon into three parts: verses 3–5 indicate the contrasts between the world's standards of life, as opposed to God's; verses 6–9 point out the positive elements of the Christian life; verses 10–12 show the world's inevitable reaction to Him and His teachings in the Sermon.

Now let us look at the nine Beatitudes as we find them in Matthew, one by one, and see what they mean.

1. Blessed are the poor in spirit; for theirs is the kingdom of heaven. Jesus wasn't blessing *material* poverty here. He was saying that the

poverty of the *Spirit* was really a blessing, for when a man comes to realize his human helplessness and comes to put his trust in God, he comes to live in heaven. The prideful ones, the "strutters," cannot enter the gates of heaven or the Kingdom.

2. Blessed are they that mourn: for they shall be comforted. This does not mean that those who mourn the loss of a loved one should be happy about it; it means that the man who admits that he is a sinner and is sincerely sorry for it is on his way to the Kingdom; and he who pities the suffering people of the world and brings to them the compassion of God and thus brings to them and to himself the comfort of God. He who never knows suffering may never know God; desperate suffering often brings triumphant faith.

3. Blessed are the meek, for they shall inherit the earth. Meek, here, does not mean spinelessness; it means "the man who is always angry at the right time, and never angry at the wrong time."—Dr. William Barclay. Uncontrolled anger destroys; humility loves, sacrifices, and builds. He who is humble-minded and not brutally aggressive is a king among men.

4. Blessed are they which do hunger and thirst . . . . How much do we really want goodness? Only he who longs for it as a starving man, a thirsty man, longs for food and drink, only he can find *total* goodness and be truly satisfied. Occasional goodness is never enough; that is as ineffective as a mere drop of water to one dying of thirst.

5. Blessed are the merciful: for they shall obtain mercy. We are often too glib in asking God for mercy; we can receive mercy from Him only if we are ready to offer the mercy of forgiveness to others while we condemn others for committing sins which we ourselves commit. Happy is the man who forgives as God forgives.

6. Blessed are the pure in heart: for they shall see God. Nothing good can come out of a dirty heart or mind. Unhappy is the man who obeys false and unworthy impulses; happy is he who lives under the God-inspired commands of God. No man can see God clearly through hate-stained spectacles or low standards of life. No man is blessed when he makes a fortune through theft or trickery, and ignores God. Only the pure in heart can ever hope to see Him clearly.

7. Blessed are the peace-makers, for they shall be called the children of God. Happy men are men who have won the wars of the heart; happy is he who lives so peacefully that everyone he meets will want to live that way. Happy is he who knows that peace is an inner, not an outer force. He who brings peace among men is performing the work, the purpose of God, and God loves him as a son.

8. Blessed are they which are persecuted for righteousness' sake: for theirs is the kingdom of heaven. Men who are persecuted because they are good are close brothers to the persecuted Christ. Blessed is America because men of the past died for it. Blessed are the martyrs of the Church and blessed are we who have inherited their fidelity to God's righteousness.

9. Blessed are ye, when men shall revile, and . . . say all manner of evil against you falsely, for my sake. Men of His generation lied about Jesus, called Him blasphemer and traitor; we who know Him better call Him Savior, and we are blessed because He preferred to die rather than

accept the lies of His killers. To suffer persecution is to open the gate of heaven for others.

II. Ye are the salt of the earth . . . the light of the world . . . . Matthew 5:13, 14. The Beatitudes make it plain what Jesus expected His followers to *be;* now He turns to teach them what they should *do.* He used two illustrations of commonplace knowledge among the Jews: salt and light.

"Ye are the salt of the earth . . . ." What is salt? It is a substance which gives flavor to and which preserves our food; without salt in that food, we could scarcely enjoy eating it. But Jesus was using the word in a spiritual sense. The Jews, for centuries, had thrown salt on their sacrificial offerings, for salt was "a sign of the covenant" (Leviticus 2:13). To Jesus, the disciples spreading out across the world would be spreading the salt of His Gospel and thus purifying, giving new flavor to life and preserving the truth of God among men. They *were* salt, spiritually, "the salt of the earth." Without them, His work and message would die and be forgotten.

If they in any way lost this treasure thus put in their hands, if they became insipid and flavorless, then they would be thrown out of the Kingdom. That was a message to the Church: let any church become soft, or unsavory, let it become weak, diluted, then it is good only to be cast out, as a housewife would throw it out of her window, fit only to be "trodden under foot" of men. Many a church dies because those who pass its doors become disinterested and even disgusted with loss of the power to influence their lives. A church in one of our major cities recently closed its doors because it failed completely to reach out a helping hand to those who walked past it every day and night!

Salt of the world they were to be; they were also to be the light of the world—men carrying the lamp of God into the world's darkness. The Jews spoke often of God as the light of the world; now, in Christ, His promised Light had been lifted high in the presence of His Son. Jesus was God made visible to men. Those who followed Him were to be the bearers and witnesses of the light which shone in Him so brilliantly. It was the light of God's truth—something that could never be extinguished; it could no more be hidden than we can hide a city set on a hill. It was a guiding light, illuminating the path men must trod. His followers were called to reflect and radiate that light.

Christ challenges us to hold that light high, to spread it and not conceal it. Hold it up! Don't put it under a bushel (bowl), as some housewives did to keep their lamps from being blown out by the wind. Let it shine *out*, to guide and lead all who see it.

This is the only reason for the church's existence: to spread the light, the love, the truth that was in Christ and God. Let the light flicker and grow dim by ignoring the needs of the world, and the world will ignore it.

The Church is God's lighthouse.

SUGGESTIONS TO TEACHERS

How does your congregation train prospective members? What kind of instruction would you suggest? How many weeks or months would you propose? What should be stressed?

The Church of the Savior in Washington, D.C. insists on a year-long training program, followed by a year "probation" before being received into full membership, and then demands each member tithe and agree to specific forms of service for a certain number of hours each week. Membership is only for one year at a time, and must be renewed annually in order to remain on the rolls.

If this sounds too rigorous, examine again Matthew 5, the subject of today's lesson, and the opening of January's lesson series on "The Meaning of Discipleship."

1. *RECIPE FOR JOY.* Start with the Beatitudes. Remember that the Greek word for *Blessed* is "How happy!" or "How extremely fortunate!" Notice that these eight "how happy's" are the opposite of what most people think. In fact, your class members would profit from creating a list of the "Opposites" to Jesus' beatitudes, such as "Blessed are those who are smug and supercilious," instead of "Blessed are the meek," and "Blessed are those who never allow themselves to feel anyone's hurts" for "Blessed are those who mourn," etc. Jesus' list, He assures His followers, offers genuine joy. Christian discipleship is a joyous experience, based on letting His light shine through the believer's life.

2. *RESPONSIBILITY.* Examine the nuances of being "salt" and "light" in the notes. Have your people make suggestions about the way disciples are intended to be light and salt. Stress to your class that Jesus does not say "It would be nice if you were salt, and I hope you will shed some light." Rather, He said, "You *are* the salt. You *are* the light." He gives no option except obedience.

3. *RIGHTEOUSNESS.* Take time to understand Jesus' teaching on the higher righteousness (Matthew 5:20) in which disciples are to show they are right with God in a way superior even to the righteousness of the "scribes and Pharisees." Christians must keep the Commandments—and also observe the spirit and intent behind them. Christians reject the "anything goes" permissiveness of the swinging society. They also reject the self-righteous legalism of a rule book religion. Christian righteousness is being a mini-Christ.

4. *RECONCILIATION.* You could spend all of your lesson time on the ramifications of Jesus' teachings on murder, anger, adultery, divorce, oaths, and vengeance. Each of these topics deserves attention. In today's lesson, however, you may best remind your class that the basic theme of each of these subjects is reconciliation.

5. *RENUNCIATION* No *Numero Uno* philosophy in the New Testament. The pagan idea then and now may be "Do as you please," but the meaning of discipleship, you should remind your class, is renouncing self for the sake of others, even as Jesus Christ forsook everything for us.

TOPIC FOR ADULTS
LET YOUR LIGHT SHINE

Inward Happiness. Some years ago the sales manager of an American store engaged Mr. Joy B. Idden, the New York stage director, to teach his salesmen how to smile. He had come to the conclusion that a smiling assistant sold more goods. Mr. Idden took the men one by one, rehearsed their smiles, criticized them, pointed out their errors, embarrassed them, and finally gave them up. The experiment failed. The difference between the manufactured article and the real thing, they discovered, was in the eyes. When the smile is manufactured, it is only the mouth that smiles and it is really a smirk. The eyes don't light up. They remain hard and unfriendly. It is only real joy that can smile in the eyes.

The Beatitudes are Jesus' recipe for true joy. The Christ-life is the source of a genuine smile and inward happiness!

Reconciliation Needed. A reporter interviewing Professor Albert Einstein in 1948 at his Princeton laboratory asked, "Are you optimistic about the future of mankind?"

"Optimistic?" Einstein replied with compassion. "No. But if mankind fails to find a harmonious solution, then there will be disaster on a dimension beyond anyone's imagination."

Even Russian Premier Khrushchev was forced to make a similar statement, observing, "We need more than a hot line to save the world from chaos. We need a meeting of the minds."

For all their genius and for all their insights, however, apparently neither Einstein nor Khrushchev understood that true reconciliation must come from discipleship under Jesus Christ.

Christ's community, the Church, is intended to be the model community to exhibit the reconciling love of God between persons and groups, if the future of mankind is to be assured.

New Year's Message. "The future does more than judge. It summons us forward where we have a rendezvous with Christ. It is the source of the divine discontent with our achievements and our progress. It is the challenge to break camp, to give up a static and frozen way of life, and to move ahead again as pilgrims in the quest for 'a city' which hath foundations, whose builder and maker is God."—James I. McCord, Princeton Seminary Alumni News, Winter, 1977.

Questions for Pupils on the Next Lesson. 1. Is it possible to be a Christian and yet be a hearer and never a doer of God's Word? 2. What is the basis for Christians determining who is speaking and acting in Christ's name? 3. How can we encourage others to match their understanding of the Word of God with appropriate action? 4. What do you understand the phrase "Justification by faith" to mean? 5. What are the signs of real Christian discipleship, in your opinion? 6. Would a person meeting you for the first time be able to tell that you were a Christian within the first hour? How?

TOPIC FOR YOUTH
SET A GOOD EXAMPLE

Too Busy to Take Offense. Dr. Albert Schweitzer forsook brilliant careers in music and philosophy in Europe to study medicine and serve as a missionary doctor in Lambarene, Africa. For four decades, he let the light of the Gospel shine through his example of selfless service.

One day, Schweitzer was on the roof of his Lambarene hospital, nailing on a board during the course of some repairs. Schweitzer, although an intellectual who had held teaching positions at leading universities, never hesitated to get his hands dirty and clamber up ladders. Needing a hand for a couple of minutes while on the roof that particular day, he noticed an African idly standing by. Schweitzer called to him to come up and help him briefly.

The African, obviously not recognizing the great missionary doctor and not expecting him to be hammering on a roof on a hot day, haughtily refused. "I am able to read and write," he sniffed.

Schweitzer pulled himself over so that the African could see him, smiled, and replied, "My friend, I also have had a try at being an intellectual, but I haven't been able to make a go at it."

Schweitzer's example of service and humor immediately affected the African.

Your life is also intended to be a witness before others.

Jesus Meant It. A missionary who suffered the trials of the Japanese occupation of China described the example of a heroic Chinese Christian physician. During the Japanese persecution of the Chinese Church, a man in a neighboring town had been beaten by the Japanese police and urgently needed medical care. None of the doctors in the town dared to go. The missionary called his Chinese Christian doctor friend and explained the situation. Without waiting to be asked to go, the Chinese doctor said, "Of course I'll go. Jesus meant it."

"Let your light shine," Christ instructs us, His followers.

Without true discipleship in which the light of Christ is illumined through your life, your existence is merely a smooth approximation to what human life is intended to be.

Words to Ponder. "I have now reigned about fifty years in victory or peace, beloved by my subjects, dreaded by my enemies, and respected by my allies. Riches and honors, power and pleasure, have waited on my call, nor does any earthly blessing appear to have been wanting to my felicity. In this situation I have diligently numbered the days of pure and genuine happiness which have fallen to my lot: they amount to fourteen."—Abd-er-Rahman III of Spain, c. 960.

Sentence Sermon to Remember: Blessed are the valiant that have lived in the Lord.—Thomas Carlyle.

Questions for Pupils on the Next Lesson. 1. How can you tell true teachings from false teachings when the teachers all claim to be "Christian"? 2. In what ways does Christian discipleship help people to cope with the pressures of life? 3. Why is it that God's way is often not the easiest way? 4. Why must we both hear and act upon God's Word? 5. What is your basis for determining who is speaking and acting in God's name?

LESSON VI—JANUARY 11

BUILD ON THE SOLID ROCK

Background Scripture: Matthew 6, 7
Devotional Reading: Ephesians 3:1–12

KING JAMES VERSION

MATTHEW 7 13 Enter ye in at the strait gate: for wide *is* the gate, and broad *is* the way, that leadeth to destruction, and many there be which go in thereat:

14 Because strait *is* the gate, and narrow *is* the way, which leadeth unto life, and few there be that find it.

15 Beware of false prophets, which come to you in sheep's clothing, but inwardly they are ravening wolves.

16 Ye shall know them by their fruits. Do men gather grapes of thorns, or figs of thistles?

17 Even so every good tree bringeth forth good fruit; but a corrupt tree bringeth forth evil fruit.

18 A good tree cannot bring forth evil fruit, neither *can* a corrupt tree bring forth good fruit.

19 Every tree that bringeth not forth good fruit is hewn down, and cast into the fire.

20 Wherefore by their fruits ye shall know them.

21 Not every one that saith unto me, Lord, Lord, shall enter into the kingdom of heaven; but he that doeth the will of my Father which is in heaven.

22 Many will say to me in that day, Lord, Lord, have we not prophesied in thy name? and in thy name have cast out devils? and in thy name done many wonderful works?

23 And then will I profess unto them, I never knew you: depart from me, ye that work iniquity.

24 Therefore whosoever heareth these sayings of mine, and doeth them, I will liken him unto a wise man, which built his house upon a rock:

25 And the rain descended, and the floods came, and the winds blew, and beat upon that house; and it fell not: for it was founded upon a rock.

26 And every one that heareth these sayings of mine, and doeth them not, shall be likened unto a foolish man, which built his house upon the sand:

REVISED STANDARD VERSION

MATTHEW 7 13 "Enter by the narrow gate; for the gate is wide and the way is easy, that leads to destruction, and those who enter by it are many. 14 For the gate is narrow and way is hard, that leads to life, and those who find it are few.

15 "Beware of false prophets, who come to you in sheep's clothing but inwardly are ravenous wolves. 16 You will know them by their fruits. Are grapes gathered from thorns, or figs from thistles? 17 So, every sound tree bears good fruit, but the bad tree bears evil fruit. 18 A sound tree cannot bear evil fruit, nor can a bad tree bear good fruit. 19 Every tree that does not bear good fruit is cut down and thrown into the fire. 20 Thus you will know them by their fruits.

21 "Not every one who says to me, 'Lord, Lord,' shall enter the kingdom of heaven, but he who does the will of my Father who is in heaven. 22 On that day many will say to me, 'Lord, Lord, did we not prophesy in your name, and cast out demons in your name, and do many mighty works in your name?' 23 And then will I declare to them, 'I never knew you; depart from me, you evildoers.'

24 "Every one then who hears these words of mine and does them will be like a wise man who built his house upon the rock; 25 and the rain fell, and the floods came, and the winds blew and beat upon that house but it did not fall, because it had been founded on the rock. 26 And every one who hears these words of mine and does not do them will be like a foolish man who built his house upon the sand; 27 and the rain fell, and the floods came, and

27 And the rain descended, and the floods came, and the winds blew, and beat upon that house; and it fell: and great was the fall of it.

28 And it came to pass, when Jesus had ended these sayings, the people were astonished at his doctrine:

29 For he taught them as *one* having authority, and not as the scribes.

the winds blew and beat against that house, and it fell; and great was the fall of it."

28 And when Jesus finished these sayings, the crowds were astonished at his teaching, 29 for he taught them as one who had authority, and not as their scribes.

KEY VERSE: "Thus, you will know them by their fruits." Matthew 7:20 (RSV).

HOME DAILY BIBLE READINGS

Jan.   5. M. *Formula for Faith and Forgiveness.* Matthew 6:1–15.
Jan.   6. T. *Treasures of the Heart in Heaven.* Matthew 6:16–24.
Jan.   7. W. *Putting First Things First.* Matthew 6:25–34
Jan.   8. T. *Spiritual Nearsightedness.* Matthew 7:1–6.
Jan.   9. F. *Giving Good Things.* Matthew 7:7–12.
Jan. 10. S. *Way, Narrow, Hard.* Matthew 7:13–23.
Jan. 11. S. *Hearing and Doing.* Matthew 7:24–29.

BACKGROUND

The last seventeen verses of Matthew 7 are the verses of the conclusion of the Sermon on the Mount. In these verses, Jesus talked about decisions. In unbelievably few words, He pointed out the rights and wrongs of decision-making, and His words on how to go about making the right decisions about the great, basic problems of life were so true and sensible that the people who were listening to Him were "astonished at his doctrine" (7:28).

Decisions, decisions, decisions! We face them every day, every hour of our lives; man is forever at one crossroads after another, trying to decide which way to go, what to do. Jesus gives this harassed man certain guide lines which would solve his problems and set his feet on the road to an abundant, Christian life.

NOTES ON THE PRINTED TEXT

I. "Enter by the narrow gate; for the gate is wide and the way is easy, that leads to destruction, and those who enter by it are many." Matthew 7:13. This is a little double parable of two verses, dealing with two gates and two ways. One gate is the gate to heaven, to the Kingdom, to the Christian life; the other is the gate to hell. The way to hell is a broad and easy way; the way to the gate of the Kingdom of heaven is a hard and narrow way. Jesus says that few people ever find the way to heaven, but many travel the other way because it is easy.

Basically, He is teaching that *it is a matter of choice;* any man can choose either way and either gate. If he chooses the easy way, he says to himself, "I'll have a good time while I'm alive; I'll do as I please. I'll look out for number one, and let others look out for themselves. If I sin a little—so what? I can repent when I'm old, before I die, and God will forgive me." And so on, for threescore and ten years. We can travel that road, if we choose.

But the man who chooses the harder, narrower way of self-sacrifice and self-denial will, in the end, travel the better way, for it is on this road that men truly find God and give themselves to Him, and thus find the gates of heaven thrown wide open for him. It is the way of self-denial that makes a great lawyer or a great musician or a great doctor—or any truly great man. The road to greatness is not an easy one, but it leads straight to the right gate. So, man—choose which way you will go.

II. *Beware of false prophets, which come to you in sheep's clothing, but inwardly they are ravening wolves.* Matthew 7:15. Now Matthew is saying, "If you really want to live the good life and enter the right gate, be careful not to listen to false prophets—prophets, or teachers, who come to you like vicious wolves hiding their evil intent by wearing sheep's clothing. Look out for the "prophet" who comes to you with a hypnotic voice promising you everything you could ever want if you just follow him—*and* contribute your money to him! Jesus warned His people to beware of them; He had angry words for them (*see* Matthew 23 and 24:10, 11). He knew well that there would come liars who would make false claims and who would capitalize on His name. Like the poor, the false prophets will always be in our midst. There will always be those who preach a good sermon but live filthy lives, who come to make fortunes for themselves out of the pockets of the poor and the credulous. There have been some who claimed to be the Messiah Himself, returned to earth, in our own day. Beware of false prophets!

There is one infallible way in which to find out whether a prophet is true or false: *find out how he lives before you accept what he says.* Find out what he has done, what the "fruits of his ministry" have been. By his fruits shall you know whether he is good or bad. Just as you know a good tree by its fruits, know the good disciple by his works of faith. We know any real Christian not by his speech but by his actions.

III. *Not every one that saith unto me, Lord, Lord, shall enter the kingdom of heaven* . . . . Matthew 7:21. This passage is frightening in its severity. What Jesus is saying is that the most passionate and orthodox claims of faith have no value whatever in the eyes of God unless and until those claims are translated into obedience to Him. Let any man loudly profess his faith and then deny his Christ by even a *thought,* and Christ will reject him, because he does not *know* Him. Such a refusal to obey God is a greater sin than honest unbelief.

The statement about devils and mighty works (miracles), in verse 22, is rather confusing. To understand it, we must remember that the leaders of the early Church acknowledged that miracles could be and were performed by the heathen (*see* Acts 19:13). What Jesus was objecting to was the work of heathen charlatans who used His name in driving out demons while, in their hearts, they had no use for Jesus at all and paid Him no loyalty. They healed under false pretenses, and any man who lives in false pretense of loving Christ but not following Him will face a dismal day of judgment when the Lord shall say that he never knew such a man on earth. We can pray and sing and preach without end, but unless we have given ourselves to Christ, He does not even hear or know us! The very thought of that is devastating.

Some will say such punishment is just "too much"—that a Christ and a

God who love us could never do that. Maybe not—*but how do we know?* We have no right to make a judgment about that; it is not our place to judge, but God's. But this we do know: if we choose to follow Christ in every crossroad decision of our lives, we need not worry about any judgment, if we follow and *obey!*

IV. . . . *I will liken him unto a wise man, which built his house upon a rock.* Matthew 7:24. For many years of His life, Jesus Christ was a carpenter. He knew about houses, and their building. So when He used this parable of the two builders, He spoke out of His craftsman's experience, and with a builder's authority.

He also spoke of something that was familiar to the head of every Jewish family: houses. Many a Jewish householder had seen other Jewish householders build their houses on sandy land (easy to dig out for a foundation) close by a gulley or small stream that, most of the year, had only a trickle of water. Often, that gulley or rivulet bed was as dry as the Sahara. What they failed to take into consideration was the fact that there always came a wet season in winter or immediately following winter, when there came raging torrents of water in those dried-up stream beds that swept everything before them. Then the houses built on sand, with little or no protection against storms and floods, were often completely destroyed.

This editor once laughed at the sight of a deep cement-lined ditch which ran through a Western city; its bed was dry as a desert. What good was a thing like that? Later, when the snow on the mountains nearby melted and came roaring down upon the city, the ditch was filled almost to overflowing—but thanks to the people who dug it, no water rose beyond its cement banks, and no house was swept away. We thought then of this parable of Jesus.

Any man is a fool to build his house on shifting sand. And any man is a fool who fails to build his spiritual "house" on anything but the rocky truth of God in Christ.

Now Jesus may have gotten the inspiration for this parable of the rock from Proverbs 10:25; "As the whirlwind passeth, so is the wicked no more: but the righteous is an everlasting foundation." Certainly, He was familiar with the Old Testament conviction that God was the Rock of Israel (Psalms 18:3, 31, 46); and clearly He is saying in this Sermon that God is the rock of the new Israel, the new Christian community. The foundation of the Christian community is Jesus Christ and His Word (John 15:12–14). It is with these words that Jesus concludes His discourse.

We err when we think of this Sermon as an ethical treatise far removed from the spiritual truth incarnate in the Person of the Savior. It is not only an ethical ideal, it is a call from Jesus for spiritual as well as ethical obedience. It is a demand from Him that He be recognized as the sure, rocky foundation of life. It is a call from Him to be born again into a life of love, a call for day-by-day living in the consciousness of God in human life and in the grace and mercy of God through His Son. It is a demand that we take His commands seriously, that we live lives founded on obedience to Him—a life against which the storms may beat with no disastrous effect.

Christ is the Incarnation of the Rock of Ages, against which even the forces of Hell (evil) cannot win.

SUGGESTIONS TO TEACHERS

A young man who had been a nominal church member took his first job in a city distant from his home town and gradually became active in a local church. Through his associations in a group of Christian young people in that congregation, he discovered the excitement and challenge of serving as committed Christian. He referred to his previous church experience as "playing religious games" on "how to look good before God." Alluding to his newfound faith in his new congregation, the young man added brightly, "Here I really feel I'm built into something alive, and I'm really building something for other's lives."

His comments on being built into something and building something are appropriate. They are also the substance of today's lesson.

No religious games with Jesus! Instead of tips and hints on how to look good before God, Jesus taught and led followers to do good to others. Develop your lesson with these key points in mind:

1. *MEANINGFUL PIETY*. Jesus refused to play religious games when it came to giving, praying, or fasting. He helps us to have an authentic piety. Take time to study Matthew 6 and 7. Remind those who might have decided to give up all forms of piety for fear of being labelled a phony that Jesus insists that His followers must share and pray and adopt a distinctive life-style. Have your class talk about meaningful forms of piety for Christians today.

2. *MODEL PRAYER*. Allow time to go through the Lord's Prayer thoroughly. Remind your class that Jesus provides this model prayer for His model community. When believers are built into His community, they live as well as pray this prayer.

3. *MANDATED PARDON*. Budget sufficient time also to go over Matthew 6:14, 15 so that each person will comprehend Jesus' accent on forgiveness. Jesus, your people must grasp, insists that we are forgiven by God only as we in turn forgive others. Mercy is not an "extra." Forgiving and being forgiven is at the heart of the Gospel.

4. *MAIN PRIORITIES*. Part of your lesson should also be devoted to Matthew 6:19–34, Jesus' discussion of what comes first in life and how to live without anxiety. To keep this from wandering into an academic conversation, ask each person to list his or her main interests in life. After everyone has written his or her priorities, request each also to itemize his or her anxieties. Dissect these. Note any correlation between interests and anxieties. Compare these with the Sermon on the Mount in this lesson.

5. *MIGHTY PERSISTENCE*. Believers built on the solid rock of faith know that they must persevere. "Ask, and it will be given you; seek and you will find; knock, and it will be opened to you" (7:7 RSV) may be translated "Keep on asking and asking and asking, and keep right on seeking, and keep on and on knocking." Believers must also be wary of the claims of every prophet and be careful of how they build their lives. Help those in your class to persist in building on the Rock.

TOPIC FOR ADULTS
BUILD ON THE SOLID ROCK

Blood and Vessels. After the Battle of Adrianople, Ambrose, the Christian Bishop of Milan in the fourth century, used all his funds to buy freedom for captives taken into slavery. When those moneys gave out, he had the sacred communion ware melted down, and the precious metal rendered into coins. Critics charged him with being sacrilegious. The great Ambrose answered that those for whom the Lord's blood had been shed were more precious than the vessels that contained that blood!

Christians who build their lives on the Solid Rock will sometimes be faced with serious challenges and severe pressures. Through Christ, however, the proper priorities are shown. Allegiance to Him may even mean melting down the sacred communion ware, as it did with Ambrose, because humans are even more sacred.

Give the Pendulum a Push. Some time ago, the famed actress, Katharine Hepburn, was being interviewed by a reporter. During the interview, Miss Hepburn expressed her distaste for the increasing permissiveness in a society where character and moral strength are no longer honored. Finally, the journalist asked, "Miss Hepburn, do you think that this era will pass?" "Yes," she replied. "The pendulum will begin to swing back, but someone has to begin by giving it a push."

Christian commitment means taking the initiative to give the pendulum that push! Life with Christ demands a concern for the society in which we live.

Even His Scales Were Converted. In a town in eastern Poland a missionary went to buy a goose, for goose is the cheapest meat in Poland. The shop was surprisingly clean; the chickens and geese were fat and good looking.

When the missionary asked the shopkeeper about his salvation, his eyes lit up and his face beamed with joy as he answered, "Yes, I am a believer in the Lord Jesus Christ."

"How do you know that you are saved?" the missionary asked. "Becaused my life has been changed completely," he replied. "Now when I sell geese I give the correct weight and do not put my finger on the scales. Everything is right now. Even my scales are changed."

Questions for Pupils on the Next Lesson. 1. In what ways do your friendships and family connections offer an environment for sharing the faith? 2. What ways do you and your congregation minister to the harassed, the helpless, and the immature? 3. Has your witnessing for your faith in Christ ever cost you any great time or energy or hurt or money? If not, why not? 4. How could your experience of being helpless and being healed be used to help others know something of Christ's power and goodness?

TOPIC FOR YOUTH
BUILD A GOOD LIFE

True Piety. "Though you be caught up in the very rapture of God and there comes a sick man to demand of you a bowl of broth, descend again

from your seventh heaven and give him that which he comes to ask."—
Jan de Ruysbroeck quoted in *The Diary of a Country Priest.*

Eliminating Friction. "We are all proud of our ethnic and religious
heritages, although we personally lack any responsibility for them. We
are what we are by accident. One's blood is neither a cause for pride nor
a cause for a lack of it. In your school, club, office, factory, or community,
do what you can to reduce the unnecessary and often hurtful barriers
that divide us all into subcitizenries. There's enough reason for friction
on a one-to-one basis without invoking team spirit."—Edwin A. Roberts,
Jr., *National Observer*, January 1, 1977. © 1977 Dow Jones & Co., Inc.
All rights reserved.

Building the Good Life. Being a Christian sometimes seems undra-
matic. Often, no one seems to know— or to care. We ask, "Why bother?"

Building the Christian life is similar to building a gorgeous cathedral.
In the great Washington Cathedral, for example, eleven master stone
carvers carefully chisel the statuary and gargoyles for the magnificent
gothic edifice. One day, several years ago, a passer-by asked John Fanfani's father, who like his son was one of the artisans on the Washington
Cathedral, why he was working so painstakingly on the back of a figure.
After all, the onlooker pointed out, the back of the figure would never be
seen after it was installed.

Fanfani quietly laid aside his mallet and replied, "God will see it."

This is also true in your life. Perhaps no one will ever notice what you
do. Possibly most of your life will be spent in obscure areas. Remember,
however, that God will see it!

Sentence Sermon to Remember: You are going to worship something—the love of power or the power of love. Which?

Questions for Pupils on the Next Lesson. 1. Has being a Christian ever
really cost you anything beyond a few minor inconveniences? Should it?
Why, or why not? 2. In what ways do you see the Church should be
involved in reaching out in Christ's name to those who are hurting,
harassed and helpless? Who are some of the hurting, harassed and helpless in your community? 3. Why does doing God's will sometimes mean
being criticized, laughed at, or rejected by one's peers? Have you ever
felt this way? 4. Is ministry only for those who are ordained as clergy?

LESSON VII—JANUARY 18

PROCLAIM THE KINGDOM

Background Scripture: Matthew 8–10
Devotional Reading: Acts 10:34–43

KING JAMES VERSION

MATTHEW 9 35 And Jesus went about all the cities and villages, teaching in their synagogues, and preaching the gospel of the kingdom, and healing every sickness and every disease among the people.

36 But when he saw the multitudes, he was moved with compassion on them, because they fainted, and were scattered abroad, as sheep having no shepherd.

37 Then saith he unto his disciples, The harvest truly *is* plenteous, but the labourers *are* few;

38 Pray ye therefore the Lord of the harvest, that he will send forth labourers into his harvest.

10 1 And when he had called unto *him* his twelve disciples, he gave them power *against* unclean spirits, to cast them out, and to heal all manner of sickness and all manner of disease.

5 These twelve Jesus sent forth, and commanded them, saying, Go not into the way of the Gentiles, and into *any* city of the Samaritans enter ye not:

6 But go rather to the lost sheep of the house of Israel.

7 And as ye go, preach, saying, The kingdom of heaven is at hand.

8 Heal the sick, cleanse the lepers, raise the dead, cast out devils: freely ye have received, freely give.

9 Provide neither gold, nor silver, nor brass in your purses;

10 Nor scrip for *your* journey, neither two coats, neither shoes, nor yet staves: for the workman is worthy of his meat.

11 And into whatsoever city or town ye shall enter, inquire who in it is worthy; and there abide till ye go thence.

12 And when ye come into a house, salute it.

13 And if the house be worthy, let your peace come upon it: but if it be not worthy, let your peace return to you.

14 And whosoever shall not receive

REVISED STANDARD VERSION

MATTHEW 9 35 And Jesus went about all the cities and villages, teaching in their synagogues and preaching the gospel of the kingdom, and healing every disease and every infirmity. 36 When he saw the crowds, he had compassion for them, because they were harassed and helpless, like sheep without a shepherd. 37 Then he said to his disciples, "The harvest is plentiful, but the laborers are few; 38 pray therefore the Lord of the harvest to send out laborers into his harvest."

10 1 And he called to him his twelve disciples and gave them authority over unclean spirits, to cast them out, and to heal every disease and every infirmity.

5 These twelve Jesus sent out, charging them, "Go nowhere among the Gentiles, and enter no town of the Samaritans, 6 but go rather to the lost sheep of the house of Israel. 7 And preach as you go, saying, 'The kingdom of heaven is at hand.' 8 Heal the sick, raise the dead, cleanse lepers, cast out demons. You received without paying, give without pay. 9 Take no gold, nor silver, nor copper in your belts, 10 no bag for your journey, nor two tunics, nor sandals, nor a staff; for the laborer deserves his food. 11 And whatever town or village you enter, find out who is worthy in it, and stay with him until you depart. 12 As you enter the house, salute it. 13 And if the house is worthy, let your peace come upon it; but if it is not worthy, let your peace return to you. 14 And if any one will not receive you or listen to your words, shake off the dust from your feet as you leave that house or town. 15 Truly, I say to you, it shall be more tolerable on the day of judgment for the land of Sodom and Gomorrah than for that town."

you, nor hear your words, when ye depart out of that house or city, shake off the dust of your feet.

15 Verily I say unto you, It shall be more tolerable for the land of Sodom and Gomorrah in the day of judgment, than for that city.

KEY VERSE: . . . "The harvest is plentiful, but the laborers are few; pray therefore the Lord of the harvest to send out laborers into his harvest." Matthew 9:37, 38 (RSV).

HOME DAILY BIBLE READINGS

Jan. 12. M. *Action Based on Belief.* Matthew 8:1–13.
Jan. 13. T. *Following in Faith.* Matthew 8:14–27.
Jan. 14. W. *Time or Torment.* Matthew 8:28–34.
Jan. 15. T. *Glorifying God.* Matthew 9:1–13.
Jan. 16. F. *The Touch of Faith.* Matthew 9:1–13.
Jan 17 S *Compassion and Commitment* Matthew 9:27–38
Jan. 18. S. *The Call of the Kingdom.* Matthew 10:1–15.

BACKGROUND

Matthew, in writing his Gospel, is concerned with the past, present, and future: he keeps reaching back into Jewish history and religion as he strives to bring Jews to Christ; he is deeply concerned with the teaching and works of Jesus in the *present*, and he is anxious to make it clear that Jesus provided for the spread of His Kingdom in the *future* as the disciples labored to fulfill His work and teaching after He was gone physically from the earth.

Much depended upon these disciples; without them, there would have been no establishment or survival of the Kingdom on earth at all. So Jesus, according to Matthew, made it abundantly clear just what the disciples were to *do*, and what they were to *be*.

NOTES ON THE PRINTED TEXT

I. And Jesus went about . . . teaching . . . preaching . . . and healing . . . . Matthew 9:35. Concise, comprehensive, informative, and inspiring, no Christian scholar or writer has ever described so well the essence of Christianity and its discipleship as Matthew describes it here. Both the Christ and the disciples were, first of all, *proclaimers* of what Christian scholars call "the certainties of God." That certainty or assurance was something desperately needed in the Jewish world of the time of Jesus—and something equally needed in *our* world. We live in a world and a day of confusion and insecurity; a time in which it is often difficult to be certain about anything. Many of us shrug our shoulders and just try to "make the best of it," hoping that somehow "things will turn out for the best." Few there are who know in whom they believe and put their trust. We long for the assurance of a kindly God at the heart of the universe—something we can find only in Jesus Christ!

The disciple is a patient teacher; he is not dismayed at the indifference of his "pupils." He is a healer, a believer in a Christ who spent far more time healing, feeding, comforting than He did in just talking about God. Jesus called not for more words but for more love. No disciple can win anyone to Christ with mere words; he wins when he is a living example of the love of God.

There were too few, even in Jesus' time, who were willing to be such disciples. Jesus complained, wistfully, that the laborers in the Kingdom were few and He asked those who followed Him to pray for more helpers in the vineyard: "Pray ye therefore the Lord . . . that he will send forth labourers into his harvest." *It all began with that prayer.*

II. And when he had called unto him his twelve disciples . . . Matthew 10:1. Twelve very humble men, these men were. Not one of them was rich, not one was a member of the socially elite; not one was well educated. Jesus chose them not for what they were, but for the potential leadership and consecration that was within them. There were twelve—just as there had once been twelve tribes in Israel. They were twelve common men, but be careful not to criticize them for that, for their commonness gave them a bond with those Jesus wanted to reach—the poor, the socially abused. Twelve willing to die for Him, twelve whose hearts were open to God as the hearts of the rich and socially elite never were.

And He gave them instructions—marching orders. The orders are staggering, to us. Order 1: They were to work among their own people, not among the Gentiles. That sounds cruel, until we study and find out what it meant. A study of the background of the saying reveals to us that in this command to His disciples He was saying that they should recognize their limitations; that is, *they* could not possibly move out into the Gentile world in the short years that were given them. He is also telling them that the building of His Kingdom would be done by taking one step at a time, and the first step would be to spread the Word among their fellow Israelites. Their first duty was to work among "the lost sheep of the house of Israel" (verse 6). The Jews should have the first chance to accept the Gospel; after the disciples, others (Paul, for instance), would come better equipped to extend it into the Gentile world. This was, in short, a *temporary* command and a temporary arrangement. Jesus knew well that the disciples could not "do it all" at one attempt.

As we all know, Jesus Himself went into Samaria, but only for a very short time; in Samaria, he revealed Himself to a woman of that land, and from Samaria came His great parabolic hero, the Good Samaritan. He healed the daughter of a Syro-Phoenician woman (Matthew 15)—but He still did not spend much of His time on earth trying to win the Gentiles. He did bring God's message to them in what was primarily a ministry carried on only in Galilee and Judea. His *permanent* command to go out into Gentile country, into all the world, came later (Matthew 28).

Order 2: The disciples were to proclaim to all that the kingdom of heaven was "at hand"—imminent. The formation of the Kingdom society had begun with them in Christ.

Order 3: The disciples were to follow the plan of action that He had used: they were to proclaim, teach, preach, heal.

Order 4: They were not to go out with well-filled purses, not to preach for money. (The rabbis of Judaism were forbidden to take money for teaching the Law.) They were to carry no bags—no "beggar's bags"—on their persons, in which to collect money or even food. The wealthy find difficulty in preaching to the poor, but the preacher or missionary who is as poor as his hearers has a bond of interest with them which makes them hear him gladly.

Order 5: They were not to be burdened with such "excess baggage" as extra clothes or two pairs of shoes, or even a staff; there are people wherever you go who will give you these things if you need them; there will always be those who will take care of you. (We know of one present-day missionary who went out to India with fifteen dollars in his pocket; he is still in India!)

III. *And whatever town or village you enter, find out who is worthy in it, and stay with him until you depart.* Matthew 10:11 (RSV). Jesus says (verse 10) that the laborer (disciple) "is worthy of his meat." Worthy, that is, of food to eat from those to whom he comes with spiritual food. Here again, he is basing His command to His disciples on an old command in Judaism; no Jewish rabbi was to work for money, but every Jewish community was expected to support their Rabbi with whatever he needed. Let no Rabbi ask for pay— and let no community fail to support a *worthy* teacher of the law!

On entering a strange town, let the disciple find a friendly house where he may be welcome. He will have need of hospitality, of a resting-place, of conversation and prayer with fellow believers. Having found such a place, let him *stay* there until it is time to move on to another town—never leave that home for a better (wealthier) one. Bless the welcoming home, if you think it worthy; if you bless it and find it not worthy, take back the blessing (another old Jewish idea). If the strange city into which you come proves to be hostile to you, shake the dust of it from your feet and move on.

That does not sound like the meek and loving Jesus, does it? Jesus *did* enter homes of sinners and publicans and hostile Jewish leaders, but He did not spend *all* His time with them. His time was short; so was the time in which the disciples were to do their work for Him: they had to make the best possible use of that time. This, like the order to stay out of Gentile lands, was a *temporary* order, given to meet the necessities of a particular situation. Jesus never closed the door on anyone, Jew or Gentile; He was conducting a campaign to reach as many as possible, and in such a campaign, some "fields of battle" must be ignored for the sake of winning another battle. It was a matter of doing first what had to be done first.

The teacher of this lesson, and some of those he teaches, will be left with questions in their minds no matter how capable the teaching may be. Some will doubt that Jesus could have said some of the things involved here; some will think it "too Jewish and not Christian enough." It will take more than one lesson to answer those questions! But we must remember that Matthew was a converted Jew speaking to the Jews in his Gospel, and, naturally, he used Jewish illustrations and expressions. But his ultimate aim was Christian, and never Jewish; his purpose was to elevate Christ the Savior in the land of the Jews but with a message for every people and nation in the world.

Again, some students will say, "It's too much; we couldn't possibly follow these old rules Jesus gave to His disciples in our kind of world." That's a pretty lame excuse. What Jesus is calling us to do, as His disciples, is to live lives of unselfish, all-out service and compassion and love; to put our trust not in gold but in God, to at least try to offer whatever help we can to the sick and the desolate of mind and heart—to at least *try* to follow the example of a Christ who left nothing but His robe when He died—His robe and His offer of peace and salvation to the people sick with fear in a trembling, unclean, insecure world.

He who would be a disciple cannot even start being a disciple without accepting and practicing the humility which was in Christ. He must start there or never start at all!

SUGGESTIONS TO TEACHERS

In Bruton Parish Church, Williamsburg, at the time of the American Revolution, zealous patriots went through copies of the prayer book, scratching out the word *Kingdom* and substituting *Republic*. The revised version might have pleased those opposed to King George III and English monarchy, but the phrase "Republic of God" or "Republic of Heaven" hardly describes what Jesus had in mind. The Kingdom of God, as Jesus knew, meant the undisputed and absolute rule of God, not a democracy where humans have equal say with the Lord.

Today's lesson discusses God's rule. "Proclaim the Kingdom!" is the title. The same title also describes Jesus' ministry. It also summarizes the ministry of His people.

Working with Matthew 8–10, you will describe a quick series of vignettes dealing with the proclamation of the realm of God through Jesus Christ.

1. *THE AUTHOR OF OUR BELIEF.* Make certain that your class understands the significance of the phrase, "The Kingdom of God." God is the Activator of our faith. He has initialed this universe. He holds sway. Not humans. Nor "fate." Nor malevolent or mysterious "forces." Nor even events. "This is my Father's World" is still the theme song of New Testament-type Christians. Have your people discuss briefly various notions of the powers (versus The Power) running the universe. Point out that The Power has been actualized in human form through Jesus Christ.

2. *THE PROCLAIMER OF OUR BELIEF.* Go through the various episodes in today's Scripture, and have your class indicate ways in each of these in which Jesus proclaimed God's rule. Have your people grow in understanding that Jesus' healings, teachings, and dealings with persons were various forms of His proclaiming the reality of God's realm. Has Jesus Christ made the reality of that realm known to your people? Help your class members also to deepen their trust in Jesus Christ. Suggest that they share ways in which they have found security and serenity in recognizing God's rule in their lives.

3. *THE AUTHORITY OF US BELIEVERS.* Some in your class will assume that the age of "miracles" is past and will think, "What can God do today?" Many in the world think this. Stress in your lesson that God

deputizes His community, the Church, to be His authorized "Kingdom-proclaimers" today. Christians are people under divine orders. We bear the authority of Jesus Christ. In the light of this awesome fact, why are we timid? Why do we mute the message? Why do we flinch from serving as His agents?

4. *THE PROCLAMATION OF BELIEVERS.* Reread Matthew 10, and have your class pick up the clues offered on the subject of what Christians are to do. The proclamation of God's realm may take many forms. Encourage your class to name as many as possible, as a result of reflecting on today's Scripture material. What are the most important? How may your congregation "heal" as a way of proclaiming Christ's Lordship? What are some of the forms of "healing" which can be done in His name today?

TOPIC FOR ADULTS
PROCLAIM THE KINGDOM

Heaven-Sent Opportunities. "In 1271 the greatest empire in the world—the greatest empire the world has ever seen—was the empire of the Mongol Kublai Khan. It stretched from the Ural mountains to the Himalayas, and from the China Sea to the Danube. Kublai Khan in that year sent Nicolo and Maffeo Polo as his ambassadors to the pope with a request.

" 'You shall go to your high priest and shall pray him on our behalf to send me a hundred skilled in your religion . . . and so I shall be baptized, and when I shall be baptized all my barons and great men will be baptized, and then their subjects will receive baptism, and so there will be more Christians here than there are in your parts.'

"The East was wide open to Christ. But the pope was too busy playing politics. For eighteen long years precisely nothing was done, and not a man was sent. Then in 1289 a mere handful of missionaries was dispatched—too late and too few—and the chance was gone. Think of it. If the church had seized the chance, there would have been no such thing as Mohammedan Turkey, no such thing as pagan India, no such thing as Red China. The East would have been Christian from end to end. What a vision! What a tragedy! What a different world it might have been today!

"Today again there is a heaven-sent chance for the Christian to witness to the fact that he believes—and he proposes to act on the belief—that *only in Christ* can the world cohere."—William Barclay, *The All-Sufficient Christ.*

Social Responsibility. Is it only the task of government to be concerned with the hurting, the harassed, the helpless? Some business leaders say not. Some, such as William C. Norris, chairman of Control Data, a corporation which employs 46,000 people in thirty-four countries with annual sales topping $2.4 billion, have established plants where the hurting, harassed, and helpless live. Norris says his company does this because "It is the right thing to do."

Control Data, a giant technology company based in Minneapolis, deliberately goes into depressed areas to provide sorely needed jobs, attract small businesses, and encourage further renewal efforts in the inner city.

That's the aim of many of the company's projects, officials say: to stimulate further renewal and renovation efforts and attract businesses to depressed areas. As one executive put it, "If you can't get businessmen to build in the slum, you've got to get the slum out of the slum first. Then business will follow."

That credo underlies all of the company's programs, and explains why the major thrust of its efforts will continue in urban revitalization, which Mr. Norris calls the growth industry of the 1980s.

Scouting out potential projects for the company is the Social Responsibility Committee, comprised of fifteen people from all levels of the company. With a $3 million budget to fund its work, the committee is charged with developing programs once it has identified areas where the company can use its technology to alleviate problems.

Some of the projects which the Social Responsibilities Committee has got underway are:

Fair Break, a program that uses the company's sophisticated computer systems to offer remedial education, counseling, and paid work experience to inner-city youth between the ages of sixteen and twenty-two. The computer is often more effective in teaching these people than humans—a factor borne out by Fair Break enrollees. "I hated school," said one nineteen-year-old, with a minor criminal record, "But this is cool; I'm learning."

The success of the Fair Break program comes from its acceptance of the fact that "you don't just give a kid a job and let it go at that," as R. D. Connor, vice-president for business development, says. "You have to learn about that kid—who he is, where he's coming from, then start to deal with him as an individual."

An unusual attempt to make the workplace more accessible to ex-offenders, under which the company provides and finances used cars on liberal credit terms to newly released offenders through its finance and auto-leasing subsidiaries.

"One of the major hindrances in the ex-felon's attempt to secure and hold a job is his lack of transportation," Mr. Connor said. "Typically you find the man living downtown where he can afford lodging, but the jobs probably aren't there. Public transportation isn't there. Public transportation isn't thoroughly developed here yet, so the man has to have wheels if he's going to work." The Corporation undertakes some of its community-oriented projects because, as chairman William C. Norris puts it, "They are the right thing to do." But, he is quick to add, "We view the major, unmet needs of society as opportunities to pursue profitable business." These laymen proclaim the Kingdom by helping the forgottten.

Questions for Pupils on the Next Lesson. 1. What are some of the signposts which show that God is at work in our midst today? 2. What are some of the ways people today use to try to find inner peace and satisfaction in the face of opposition? What are the relative merits of these in the light of Christ's teaching? 3. Where do you see God at work today, making life whole? 4. How can the Church help others establish their life goals in the light of Christ's lordship over their lives? 5. What can the Church do to provide the spiritual blessings outlined in Matthew 11:25–30 when these seem to run counter to the characteristics exalted in our society?

TOPIC FOR YOUTH
SPEAK THE WORD

Relaying Information. Michael Davis, a thirteen-year-old ham radio operator, helped coordinate the rescue of three men whose boat was sinking a continent away. On the night of April 25, 1979, a fishing vessel with three Florida men aboard began to sink seventy-five miles south of Jamaica. Using a battery-powered radio, the crew issued an SOS which was picked up in New Zealand. Meanwhile, in Torrance, California, Michael Davis was trying to pick up signals from an East Coast point and heard the exchange.

Michael realized that the New Zealand operator couldn't do much, especially since the receiver "Down Under" had the wrong longitude and latitude. Michael asked the sender on the boat for the right location, then telephoned the Coast Guard in Long Beach, California. The Coast Guard relayed the call from California to Miami. However, the Miami Coast Guard could not make contact with the boat because they did not have any ham gear. Michael stayed on the air, keeping in contact with the boat and acting as a relay between the crew and the Coast Guard until the sun started to come up on the East Coast.

A Coast Guard cutter finally reached the foundering boat, rescued the crew, and towed the vessel to safety. Throughout the drama, Michael's mother had been asleep. The Coast Guard informed her of the incident the following day when it called to thank and congratulate Michael on the professional way in which he handled himself.

Michael himself modestly refused any praise. Said he, "I was just relaying information."

What a perfect description of what it is to proclaim the Kingdom! "*Relaying information!*" Each of us is expected to be ready to speak the word of hope and assurance, or to relay the information about Christ's rule. The opportunity usually comes unexpectedly, as with Michael Davis. God calls us to be co-workers in His great rescue operation!

"*National Scandal of Neglect.*" Who are some of the hurting, the harassed, and the helpless today? Children, that's who.

Here are a few statistics about kids in our nation from a recent study:

Twenty million never get complete medical care—immunizations and prompt treatment. Three million children in the U.S. (one out of six) live below the poverty line. Ten million children in the U.S. never have had any medical care at all. Half the youngsters in our nation have never seen a dentist. One million children were abused physically by parents or had their rights abused; one half million under seventeen years of age were imprisoned in adult jails. At least 2,000 children died from beatings by parents. Almost one third of all babies in the U.S. are born into families with financial strains so great that they will suffer deprivation.

President Carter, hearing of these shocking conditions correctly

called them "a national scandal of neglect." We Christians must speak
God's Word today!

Hidden People. "Christian missions means world evangelization. It is
the process of carrying out Christ's Great Commission, the expansion of
the Church into every dimension of humanity, 'not wishing any to
perish' (2 Peter 3:9). As such, world evangelization is the accomplish-
ment of the Spirit of God through the agency of the Church. Eventually,
it comes down to Spirit-filled people reaching lost people with the Good
News of Jesus Christ.

"Ralph D. Winter of the U.S. Center for World Mission has shown that
of the roughly three billion (out of 4.2 billion) people who do not claim
to be Christian, 84 percent of these non-Christians are 'hidden people.'
That is, they are hidden from the influence of the Christian world: there
are no churches among these people and there are no mission agencies
with active strategies for reaching them. These are the unreached, those
people who have never had a reasonable opportunity to respond to the
Good News.

"The Great Commission cannot be completed until these over 2.4
billion unreached people have a legitimate chance to turn to Christ.
What will it take to accomplish this 'task before us'? Our answer, in most
cases, is a growing army of people who will (1) bridge the cultural gaps
that separate the Church from these unreached millions and (2) persuade these people to become Christian."— *Acme Briefing,* October
1978, Association of Church Missions Committees.

Sentence Sermon to Remember: The Kingdom of God is a kingdom of
love, and love is never a stagnant pool.—Henry W. DuBose.

Questions for Pupils on the Next Lesson. 1. Is God still at work in the
world today? What signposts lead you to answer *yes* or *no?* What is the
New Testament claim in the lesson for this week? 2. Why is Jesus considered to be an offense to some people? 3. What does Christ expect of
you as a Christian in the face of the pressures you are under? 4. What
does the phrase of Christ, "Take my yoke," mean to you?

LESSON VIII—JANUARY 25

LEARN FROM THE LORD

Background Scripture: Matthew 11–12
Devotional Reading: 1 Samuel 3:10–21

KING JAMES VERSION

MATTHEW 11 2 Now when John had heard in the prison the works of Christ, he sent two of his disciples,

3 And said unto him, Art thou he that should come, or do we look for another?

4 Jesus answered and said unto them, Go and shew John again those things which ye do hear and see:

5 The blind receive their sight, and the lame walk, the lepers are cleansed, and the deaf hear, the dead are raised up, and the poor have the gospel preached to them.

6 And blessed is *he,* whosoever shall not be offended in me.

25 At that time Jesus answered and said, I thank thee, O Father, Lord of heaven and earth, because thou hast hid these things from the wise and prudent, and hast revealed them unto babes.

26 Even so, Father; for so it seemed good in thy sight.

27 All things are delivered unto me of my Father: and no man knoweth the Son, but the Father; neither knoweth any man the Father, save the Son, and *he* to whomsoever the Son will reveal *him.*

28 Come unto me, all *ye* that labor and are heavy laden, and I will give you rest.

29 Take my yoke upon you, and learn of me; for I am meek and lowly in heart: and ye shall find rest unto your souls.

30 For my yoke *is* easy, and my burden is light.

REVISED STANDARD VERSION

MATTHEW 2 Now when John heard in prison about the deeds of the Christ, he sent word by his disciples 3 and said to him, "Are you he who is to come, or shall we look for another?" 4 And Jesus answered them, "Go and tell John what you hear and see: 5 the blind receive their sight and the lame walk, lepers are cleansed and the deaf hear, and the dead are raised up, and the poor have good news preached to them. 6 And blessed is he who takes no offense at me."

25 At that time Jesus declared, "I thank thee, Father, Lord of heaven and earth, that thou hast hidden these things from the wise and understanding and revealed them to babes; 26 yea, Father, for such was thy gracious will. 27 All things have been delivered to me by my Father; and no one knows the Son except the Father, and no one knows the Father except the Son and any one to whom the Son chooses to reveal him. 28 Come to me, all who labor and are heavy-laden, and I will give you rest. 29 Take my yoke upon you, and learn from me; for I am gentle and lowly in heart, and you will find rest for your souls. 30 For my yoke is easy, and my burden is light."

KEY VERSE: *Take my yoke upon you, and learn of me; for I am meek and lowly in heart; and ye shall find rest unto your souls.* Matthew 11:29.

HOME DAILY BIBLE READINGS

Jan. 19. M. *Hear and See, Go and Tell.* Matthew 11:1–11..
Jan. 20. T. *Accepting the Yoke.* Matthew 11:12–30.
Jan. 21. W. *Lord of the Sabbath.* Matthew 12:1–8.
Jan. 22. T. *Restoring to Wholeness.* Matthew 12:9–21.
Jan. 23. F. *Standing United.* Matthew 12:22–32.
Jan. 24. S. *Be Careful of Careless Words!* Matthew 12:33–42.
Jan. 25. S. *When Evil Returns.* Matthew 12:43–50.

BACKGROUND

Having laid down "the rules of the road" to His disciples, Jesus set out on a preaching tour in the cities and countryside of Galilee, where He met more than a warm welcome. Crowds flocked to hear Him. His reputation as a miracle worker (a status He never wanted) spread far and wide. There was some opposition to Him on the part of Jewish leaders who saw their popularity among the masses threatened by this Man from Nazareth, but by and large Jesus was at the peak of His popularity.

But John the Baptist, that lowly and fiery one who had announced His coming and who had won many to His cause—John was in trouble. He was in prison for the crime of criticizing a king (a petty king named Herod). Had the Baptist only preached and baptized, he would never have been thrown in prison. But he was not the kind of man to ignore what he considered sin, even in a king. Quick to anger, he brought down the wrath of an immoral ruler and was thrown into a dungeon.

Men tortured by confinement in dungeons often lose heart; we cannot condemn them for that, for most of us could do the same thing. Poor John was so disconsolate that he sent one of his followers to ask Jesus why He was not helping him, there in the dungeon darkness.

NOTES ON THE PRINTED TEXT

I. . . . *Art thou he that should come, or do we look for another?* Matthew 11:3. John is a badly troubled man; in his dungeon, he is an eagle in a cage, longing for freedom. In effect, John was asking Jesus two questions: Is He truly the expected Messiah, and why doesn't Jesus help him now?

We may register astonishment at such a question, but we must remember that John was expecting the traditional Messiah, a miracle worker who would destroy His enemies in violence and fire. That idea was to coincide with the terror of the Last Judgment—and to John, it just wasn't working out that way. The wicked still held the upper hand; evil was still on the throne, and Jesus seemed to be helpless against it. Why? Was Jesus, after all, just another prophet, and not truly the Messiah? When, oh, when was Jesus going to wipe out the wicked with holy fire?

Jesus answers that question not with words but with proof of what He was doing. True to prophecy, He was preaching the Gospel to the poor; the lame were walking, the sick were healed, the deaf heard, the dead were raised. What more do we need as proof of His Messiahship? Jesus answers the question with proof of results, not with arguments of the mouth. Jesus was fulfilling the prophecy of Isaiah (Isaiah 35).

Why do we still argue about Jesus Christ? Can't we *see?* We can go on

debating until doomsday what and who He was, and get nowhere, but if
we have the courage and the good sense to consider what He *did*, and
what He can do for *us*, our questions will melt like snow in a July sun.

Was the Baptist satisfied with this answer? Quite probably, he was.
This man was not afraid to die; he only wanted confirmation for his hope
and belief in Jesus Christ, and here he got it.

These words of Jesus are climaxed in His statement: "And blessed is
he, whosoever shall not be offended in me" (verse 6). Blessed is he,
John, who does not *doubt* Me. Many of the Jews doubted that He was
the Messiah; to them He was a stumbling block, an offense to the ancient faith; to the Greeks, He was foolishness (1 Corinthians 1:24). His
teachings offended them— but to those who really knew Him, who saw
His deeds, He was the power and wisdom of God. We can doubt that
John doubted Him; John only made the mistake of wanting Jesus to be
One who agreed with his (John's) idea of Messiahship—and with Jesus'
answer, he knew that he was wrong.

II. . . . *I thank thee, O Father, Lord of heaven and earth, because
thou hast hid these things from the wise and prudent, and hast revealed
them unto babes.* Matthew 11:25. The life of Jesus was not made up of
constant conquest; He did not win to Himself all who heard and saw
Him. In Matthew 11:21-22, He tells of defeats in Chorazin, Bethraida,
Tyre and Sidon and Capernaum. In these cities, He had been rejected
and He thanks His Father that it had been so! Why?

Clearly, this is aimed at the scribes who prided themselves as "intellectuals"; they knew all about *everything;* they were, as one commentator puts it, "shut up in their own wisdom," so much so that they did not
recognize Him for what He was: the very Son of God the Father. The
scribes and the arrogant scholars and interpreters of the Law needed no
further wisdom than they already had, but their wisdom was human,
faulty, a detriment rather than an enlightenment. What Jesus was really
condemning here was not so much these "wise" *men*, but their intellectual *pride*. They did not know God when they saw Him, so how could
they be of any real help to either God or His Kingdom?

But to babes (children), He had revealed Himself successfully, and
they *knew* Him. By children, He meant the humble, the lowly, the
modest, and "unimportant"—those called "ignorant" by the scholars,
but known to God and loved by God for their humble faith.

Jesus was not saying "Put all learning, all education, all intellectual
reasoning aside." He was simply saying, if we may speak in the present
tense, that a Ph.D. is not necessarily a passport into the Kingdom of God,
and that faith in God is more a matter of the heart than of the brain. To
know Him, we must accept Him in the innocence of the childlike heart.

Jesus concludes this passage with words that strike deep to the heart
of Christian faith: " . . . no man knoweth the Son, but the Father;
neither knoweth any man the Father, save the Son, and he to whomsoever the Son will reveal him" (Matthew 11:27). This might be the
most important and revealing of the sayings of Jesus. Up to this point,
we have seen Him working and speaking with a divine authority, but
with this saying we find ourselves *seeing and understanding* the unique
Son of God to whom the Father has given all things and power, the One

the Father alone knows best and who alone knows the Father as no
other man can.

By "know," He meant not intellectual knowledge, but a living contact
and companionship with God. If we would know God, says Matthew,
we need only look at Jesus Christ, for in Him alone of all men who have
ever lived, we see what God is like. And Christ alone gives that knowledge to those who have the wisdom of humility.

This is Jesus Himself explaining the unrivaled character of His person. In these words, He solves the mystery of His divine Sonship. The
humbly wise among us will accept it as the final Word.

*III. Come unto me, all ye that labor and are heavy laden, and I will
give you rest.* Matthew 11:28. Two words sing out a note of comfort and
encouragement in verses 28 and 29. One word is *rest,* the other is *yoke.*
If the preceding words about the Sonship of Christ are deep and profound for the common mind, these two words are gloriously clear.
Speaking to a people who were often weary unto death in their search
for God and His truth, Jesus says, "Listen to Me, follow Me, and I will
rest you." To a people struggling under the weight of a Jewish Law,
complex and bewildering, He says, "I will help you to drop that burden,
that yoke around your neck; I will give you a yoke easier than easy to
carry—the yoke of *love." His* yoke is light; no, it is a song.

Love makes it easier to bear any burden men may inflict. Love made it
possible for Christ to die on Calvary for the overburdened; love makes
the road of life smoother for all of us.

Vergil, who died nineteen years before Jesus came, had a saying that
the Nazarene could have loved: "Omnia vincit amor." (Love conquers
all things.) Love is no burden; it is a joy.

SUGGESTIONS TO TEACHERS

Yokes on animals are rarely seen these days. Few in your class know
firsthand what yoking is all about. In fact, many do not even recognize a
yoke when they see one hanging in a museum or antique shop, or
decorating a home or restaurant.

Your first step in working up your lesson for today may be to educate
yourself about what Jesus had in mind about being yoked to Him. Ten
minutes with a good Bible dictionary and commentary will give you
helpful background material. Next, saturate yourself in the background
Scripture, Matthew 11, 12. Your lesson on accepting the yoke of Jesus
Christ may take the following parameters.

1. *CHALLENGES AND CHOICES.* Before we will accept Jesus'
yoke, we must learn from Him who He is. Examine what others thought
of Him in the background Scripture. Also scrutinize Jesus' words to the
followers of John the Baptist, to these critical of all prophets, to the
inhabitants of towns where Jesus had preached and healed. Ask whether
any of Jesus' words to any of these people would apply to religious
people today, and in what ways. Let the class see that Jesus often comes
as One who disturbs and makes difficult demands.

2. *CHAINS AND CLAIMS.* Being yoked means being joined. As ones
yoked to Jesus, we accept chains of service. Allow the class enough time

to reflect on the significance of yoking oneself to Jesus Christ. Comment that He pulls the load alongside of the one yoked to Him. Be sure to mention also that the word *yoke,* was a rabbinical term to refer to the Law, and that in Jesus' use of the word, it means accepting His claims as the embodiment of the Jewish Law. Note the example of those claims in Jesus' assuming He is Lord of the Sabbath (Matthew 12:1–14). Let your class steep itself in the enormity of Christ's claims!

3. *CHARGE AND CHARTER.* Have your class members go through the two chapters of Matthew in today's lesson and identify the specific ways in which Jesus intends His followers to learn from Him. Notice that He is bigger than mere "religion." He cannot be reduced to a book of rules. He cannot be described in traditional ways. The reason? He is more than just another religion, more than laws, more than observances. He embodies the Spirit of God. He introduces that Spirit into our lives so that "out of the abundance of the heart" (12:34) you and your class may live as His yoke fellows.

4. *CHARADES AND CHAMPION.* Compare the Pharisee with Jesus. Have your class comment on the contrast between the teachings of each. If Christians are yoked to Jesus, they will learn from Him and become like Him. They will move from a religion which is a pious charade to one of championing the rule of Christ.

5. *CHARY AND CHARITY.* Those who learn from the Lord have a wholesome skepticism of the claims of religious leaders who try to exploit the Lord, or who belittle Jesus' claims by inflating their own. Have your people discuss Jesus' ideas about blasphemy, and have them comment on the implications of Jesus' definition of the sin against the Holy Spirit. Note also Jesus' idea of who His real family is—those yoked to Him by doing the will of God.

TOPIC FOR ADULTS
TAKE MY YOKE

Hold of the Rope. As Christ's people, we are yoked together to Christ and to each other.

Virginians felt a special bond between themselves and General Robert E. Lee. Some years after Lee's death, funds were raised to have a large statue prepared to be placed in Richmond. Finally, the bronze statue of Lee mounted on his horse was delivered at the railroad station.

Someone commented how many horses it would take to pull the tons of metal to the side of the pedestal. "Horses?" replied someone else, "Never! We shall pull General Lee ourselves!"

The idea suddenly ignited the interest of people of all classes and ages in Richmond and nearby areas. Everyone, it seemed, wanted to take part in pulling General Lee's statue to its location. A special day was designated. Schools were let out, and a holiday was declared. People streamed into the city. In the middle of the main street, three wagons holding the huge statue were lashed together. In front of the first wagon stretched a heavy hawser over a city block in length. Without urging, people thronged to take hold of the rope cable. An ex-governor, some millionaires, housewives and working men, black people and whites, children and society women joined to tug the heavy burden.

When the statue was lifted into place, suddenly people began pulling out pocket knives to hack off pieces of the big rope. Soon the hawser was gone. For days afterward in Richmond, people would display a small piece of rope, hold it up, and proudly announce, "I had hold of the rope! Did you?"

Jesus calls us to take His yoke on our shoulders, to be joined with Him in the long pull of service. At the end of your life, will you be able to say, with pride and thanks, "I had hold of His yoke! Did you?"

Yoking Costs. Holiday Inns said it would build a casino-hotel in Atlantic City—a decision that led the company's president and chief executive officer, Ludwick M. Clymer, to announce his early retirement.

Clymer, fifty-five, a Presbyterian, announced he would retire because of "personal and religious objections" to the decision.

He said he disagreed with the Holiday Inns board's decision to pursue hotel-casino opportunities as they become available outside Las Vagas.

Some laughed at Clymer, regarding him as an idealistic fool who allowed his religion to interfere with business. Others sniffed that Clymer as head of a large conglomerate was being overly fussy, since the gambling operations at the Atlantic City location would be merely one small isolated portion of the overall business.

Ludwick Clymer, however, as a committed Christian, recognized that being yoked to Christ means placing Him ahead of title, power, wealth, and personal security. Clymer recognized that Christian living must apply to personal and business life.

What has being yoked to Christ ever cost you?

New Harmony. Being yoked to Christ implies being yoked together as congregations. Christ's people, without imposing uniformity on each other, strive for unity. In love, we are yoked together. Yoking means harmony.

A few years ago, in a small community called Salach, near Stuttgart, West Germany, the two churches—Protestant and Roman Catholic—repaired their bell systems in the two church steeples. Formerly, there had been clanging discord and confusion as each clashed with the other, and frequently nobody could tell exactly what the time was or what the occasion was. After the two congregations worked out the bell systems, the two towers of the churches toll together in a way so that each peals the tune of a different hymn, but the villagers, by the combination of the two tunes being pealed, can hear a greater and more beautiful melody. The tune which the two churches now produce is the centuries-old chant, "Praise Be to Thee, Lord Jesus Christ."

As we are yoked to our common Lord and to each other, the community around us hears the message that together Christians mean to extend praise to the Lord of all.

Questions for Pupils on the Next Lesson. 1. How did Jesus seem to prepare His followers? 2. Why do many Christians seem to be so pessimistic and gloomy about the way things seem to be going? How should Christians feel? 3. How do you think the New Testament helps Christians to endure and find courage today in the midst of the conflict be-

tween good and evil? 4. How do Christians make the distinction between indifference and tolerance toward those who differ from them?
5. What is our attitude supposed to be toward those who hold viewpoints at variance with ours? 6. Can we really be certain that God will
ultimately be victorious? On what do you base your answer?

TOPIC FOR YOUTH
TAKE MY YOKE

Yoking Means Helping. Being yoked to Christ is to take risks for
others. Glenn McDonald and Bill Kenney discovered this on the foggy
night of May 8, 1978, when they were piloting McDonald's tug and a
barge through Escambia Bay, near Pensacola, Florida.

"At 9:20 P.M., McDonald and Kenney, hearing a plane overhead,
looked up and spotted the massive Boeing 727 jetliner piercing the
dense fog. McDonald turned and shouted to Kenney, 'It's going to hit.'
Seconds later, National Airlines Flight 193 slammed into Escambia Bay
with a 'thunderous hiss' about 250 meters northeast of the barge. The
immense roar of the powerful jet engines churned up the muddy waters
of the bay, and then fizzled to a splashy halt.

" 'I alerted Kenney to start getting life jackets and ropes ready.'
McDonald says. 'I'd already made up my mind we were going to go after
them.'

"Minutes before the crash, McDonald had chastised himself for
traveling in foggy weather. 'It was really foolish to be out there. I could
have been home with my family, but I was trying to accomodate a cus-
tomer. When I saw that plane dive into the water, though, there was no
doubt in my mind as to why we were there. The Lord wanted us there.'

"Gritting his teeth, McDonald revved up his tug's engines to a top
speed of 10 kilometers per hour and headed toward the rapidly sub-
merging aircraft. Kenney quickly made a Mayday distress call on the
tug's citizen's band radio and then began gathering life preservers and
ropes to throw over the side.

" 'The lights went out inside the plane upon impact,' recalls
McDonald. 'My first thought was of explosion. When that didn't happen, I turned our only spotlight on the plane and ran it up and down
the fuselage, attempting to light the interior. Hatches began opening all over the plane and people were pouring out from all sorts of
places.'

"McDonald saw no rafts. Survivors, crying and screaming for help,
swarmed around the life-saving barge clutching life jackets, suitcases,
seat cushions, whatever they could hold onto. Maneuvering the awk-
ward 9 by 21 meter barge without running over anyone was now
McDonald's biggest concern.

" 'I was inching in, which was driving the passengers crazy. But I
knew if I hit the jet with that 180 metric ton steel barge, the plane would
rip open like an egg shell.'

"Ten thousand five hundred liters of jet fuel compounded problems.
The fumes which had spewed into the bay from the 727's ruptured fuel
tanks were overpowering; McDonald again feared an explosion. To most

passengers, McDonald was only a mysterious, reassuring voice behind a blinding white spotlight.

" 'I kept moving the spotlight back and forth, praying that I wouldn't overlook anyone. There was little panic—most people were just concerned that when I turned my spotlight in another direction they would be forgotten.'

"Kenney wrapped his legs around cleats and suspended himself face down off the side of the one-meter-high barge to pull survivors from the water. He dived into the fuel-filled waters several times to aid floundering passengers. Those who were able scrambled up the ropes he had tied to the barge.

"As the wing sank, McDonald piloted the cumbersome barge right over the spot where it had gone underwater, bringing the barge up alongside the aircraft's fuselage.

" 'We put wooden planks across from the barge deck to the top of the plane and rescued several people who were standing there. They were afraid to move at first, because the fuselage was so slippery with jet fuel,' McDonald recalls, 'but Bill walked across and carried them piggy-back to the barge.'

"After what seemed an eternity, U.S. Coast Guard, Search and Rescue, Marine Patrol, Florida Fish and Game Commission, private fishing trawlers, and pleasure boats approached the barge, lights flashing, and sirens wailing.

" 'It was extremely difficult to get people on to the smaller boats, especially the injured, but it all went in an orderly fashion and pretty quickly,' McDonald recalls.

"After the 55 survivors were safely aboard rescue vessels, McDonald and Kenney slipped away into the night fog and continued their trek to the railroad trestle, arriving shortly after 1 A.M. They walked one kilometer down the trestle to a truck and went home to an hour's sleep.

" 'I was just glad the Lord put us where he did,' says McDonald, 'and that we were able to help.' "—David Skipper, Reprinted from *The Rotarian,* December 1978.

Living Monument. Persons who are yoked to Christ do not care about making a big name for themselves. In fact, the only monument that yoke-fellows are interested in is spreading the Good News of Jesus Christ.

It reminds us of how James Hogg, Governor of Texas, felt about his grave.

On his deathbed, Governor James Stephen Hogg requested that no monument be placed on his grave. Rather, he asked that there be planted "at my head a pecan tree, and at my feet an old-fashioned walnut, and when these trees shall bear, let the pecans and walnuts be given out among the Plains people of Texas, so that they may plant them and make Texas a land of trees."

Yoked People Never Missing. Last year alone, 175,557 persons under the age of eighteen were reported missing, according to the Federal Bureau of Investigation's uniform crime report, which is compiled from statistics provided by 9,582 police departments. In the same period, the Chicago police received 19,000 reports of missing youths. Neither figure has varied significantly in recent years.

There are a lot of young people—some runaways, some wanderers—who maintain tenuous contacts with home. They are not so visible now, almost everyone agrees, as in the late 60s and early 70s, when their long hair and their clothes set them apart as hippies, street people, and Vietnam War protestors. But they are there, scarcely noticed by the police or by anybody else.

Christians know they are yoked to Christ and to a family of His people. Although Christ's people, like everyone, sometimes feel like dropping out or taking off, they realize that they can never be separated from Him. Therefore, they will remain faithful to life, to others, and to themselves.

Sentence Sermon to Remember: Nobody can teach you how to be a Christian; you learn it on the job.—Frank A. Clark.

Questions for Pupils on the Next Lesson. 1. What is the greatest and most demanding cause in the world today? What are you intending to do about it? 2. What are God's main concerns and interests at this time in your opinion? 3. Is the human situation and are world events so hopelessly out of control that even God can't handle them? 4. How can we be sure that God is still at work in our world today? 5. In what ways do you think God wants you and your generation to participate in the work of His Kingdom?

LESSON IX—FEBRUARY1

TRUST IN GOD'S VICTORY

Background Scripture: Matthew 13:1-52
Devotional Reading: Zephaniah 3:11-13

MATTHEW 13 24 Another parable put he forth unto them, saying, The kingdom of heaven is likened unto a man which sowed good seed in his field:

25 But while men slept, his enemy came and sowed tares among the wheat, and went his way.

26 But when the blade was sprung up, and brought forth fruit, then appeared the tares also.

27 So the servants of the householder came and said unto him, Sir, didst not thou sow good seed in thy field? from whence then hath it tares?

28 He said unto them, An enemy hath done this. The servants said unto him, Wilt thou then that we go and gather them up?

29 But he said, Nay; lest while ye gather up the tares, ye root up also the wheat with them.

30 Let both grow together until the harvest: and in the time of harvest I will say to the reapers, Gather ye together first the tares, and bind them in bundles to burn them: but gather the wheat into my barn.

31 Another parable put he forth unto them, saying, The kingdom of heaven is like to a grain of mustard seed, which a man took, and sowed in his field:

32 Which indeed is the least of all seeds: but when it is grown, it is the greatest among herbs, and becometh a tree, so that the birds of the air come and lodge in the branches thereof.

33 Another parable spake he unto them; The kingdom of heaven is like unto leaven, which a woman took, and hid in three measures of meal, till the whole was leavened.

34 All these things spake Jesus unto the multitude in parables; and without a parable spake he not unto them:

MATTHEW 13 24 Another parable he put before them, saying, "The kingdom of heaven may be compared to a man who sowed good seed in his field; 25 but while men were sleeping, his enemy came and sowed weeds among the wheat, and went away. 26 So when the plants came up and bore grain, then the weeds appeared also. 27 And the servants of the householder came and said to him, 'Sir, did you not sow good seed in your field? How then has it weeds?' 28 He said to them, 'An enemy has done this.' The servants said to him, 'Then do you want us to go and gather them?' 29 But he said, 'No; lest in gathering the weeds you root up the wheat along with them. 30 Let both grow together until the harvest; and at harvest time I will tell the reapers, Gather the weeds first and bind them in bundles to be burned, but gather the wheat into my barn.' "

31 Another parable he put before them, saying, "The kingdom of heaven is like a grain of mustard seed which a man took and sowed in his field; 32 it is the smallest of all seeds, but when it has grown it is the greatest of shrubs and becomes a tree, so that the birds of the air come and make nests in its branches."

33 He told them another parable. "The kingdom of heaven is like leaven which a woman took and hid in three measures of meal, till it was all leavened."

34 All this Jesus said to the crowds in parables; indeed he said nothing to them with out a parable. 35 This was to

35 That it might be fulfilled which was spoken by the prophet, saying, I will open my mouth in parables; I will utter things which have been kept secret from the foundation of the world.

fulfil what was spoken by the prophet: "I will open my mouth in parables, I will utter what has been hidden since the foundation of the world."

KEY VERSE: . . . "The kingdom of heaven is like leaven which a woman took and hid in three measures of flour, till it was all leavened." Matthew 13:33 (RSV).

HOME DAILY BIBLE READINGS

Jan. 26. M. *Responses to the Gospel.* Matthew 13:1–9.
Jan. 27. T. *Reasons for Parables.* Matthew 13:10–17.
Jan. 28. W. *Hearing and Understanding.* Matthew 13:18–23.
Jan. 29. T. *The Growth of the Kingdom.* Matthew 13:24–33.
Jan. 30. F. *The Time for Judgment.* Matthew 13:34–43.
Jan. 31. S. *Discovery and Discernment.* Matthew 13:44–50.
Feb. 1. S. *Judgment and Deliverance.* Zephaniah 3:8–13.

BACKGROUND

Matthew tells us that Jesus "spake many things unto them in parables" (13:3). A parable is a story, usually brief, intended to illustrate a single point. It is a literary form found in both Old and New Testaments.

Jesus used this parabolic method as an "attention getter," using words and objects that were easily understood by the rank and file of the people—such as wheat and tares, a lost coin, bread and leaven, the mustard seed, a bridal party, a fig tree, wise and foolish girls, new wine in old wineskins. The poorest of the poor, the most uneducated, could understand these inspired illustrations.

They are stories not to be taken as literal truth, but as illustrations. (Tourists in Palestine are still bewildered by guides who point out a house and tell them, "This is the house where the Good Samaritan lived"!) Jesus announced them as stories when He introduced them by saying, "The kingdom of God is likened unto [this]. . . ."
How dull a sermon can become without illustrations!

NOTES ON THE PRINTED TEXT

I. . . . The kingdom of heaven is likened unto a man which sowed good seed in his field: But while men slept, his enemy came. . . . Matthew 13:24, 25. There are two parables about the sowers of seed, in Matthew 13 (in verses 3–9 and in verses 24–30); the first one is known as the Parable of the Sower; the second, as the Parable of the Tares.

Tares were weeds. Anyone who plants a lawn or a garden hates a weed. In this story, the weed was known as darnel, a troublesome weed which, if it were ground up with kernels of wheat and eaten, produced a narcotic or stupefying effect. Jesus says that after the sower had sowed his wheat seed, an enemy came by night and sowed darnel "among the wheat." It was an old trick often played by quarreling farmers, or by one farmer jealous of another. Every man, woman, and child knew about darnel—and feared it.

As Jesus tells the story, He pictures the servants of the good farmer suggesting that they go out into the field and pull up the darnel plants. The farmer (householder) says no, for if they did that, they would be in danger of pulling up the wheat as well as the tare. It was almost impossible to tell one plant from the other, as they grew. So, they should wait until the time of harvest, when the tares could be separated from the wheat and burned.

This parable, like most of the others, has to do with the planting and growth of the Kingdom of heaven. The sowers were the disciples, the followers of Jesus who were to go about sowing the seeds of that Kingdom. The enemy is the evil one, Satan, who sneaks in by night, when men least expect it, or are in sleep and sows his seeds of doubt or suspicion or unbelief. The intelligent and wakeful disciples should prevent the evil sowing *before it starts*. But once it is sown, they should not fly off in rage to judge and kill the evil one. Judgment, indeed, is not a privilege of men; it is the concern and work of God, and it cannot come from God until the end, the last days, the Day of Judgment.

We tend to be too hasty in our human judgments. We are too quick to panic when disaster threatens us, to punish some who may be innocent. We should not run off into fear and acts of vengeance; "Vengeance is mine, saith the Lord" (Romans 12:19).

Neither should we be sleeping Christians, for it is while the Church sleeps that the seeds of evil are sown. The devil gets in his best work when the Church is busy not with action but with trifles. He is at work in the heart of the boy who, when he becomes a man, turns his back on Christ and goes Satan's way. That may be more our fault than the man's!

II. . . . *The kingdom of heaven is like to a grain of mustard seed* . . . Matthew 13:31. The seed of the mustard plant is a tiny thing. Some call it the smallest of all seeds, but it isn't quite that; the seed of the cypress tree is smaller. But it is still true that from this diminutive seed, huge plants, even trees, grow, trees filled with birds who feed on the little black seeds in its bark and branches. The Kingdom grows like that, like a tree. Some dedicated Christian comes along in a wicked neighborhood, preaches the Good News by simply living like a Christian, and he wins other Christians. We know a missionary who went up to live in an obscure mountain village; he could not speak the language of the people there; he did not start out by building a church. He merely lived the Christian life—and today the villagers have built their own church!

One man, Thomas A. Edison, sat in his laboratory for months and years experimenting with filaments which, burning, could give light; thanks to this one man, our world is filled with *electric* light! One man in Germany and another in Switzerland, brought on the Reformation. One man, Dr. Salk, conquered infantile paralysis. From little acorns, mighty oaks grow. Time and again, some one little individual got an idea that has changed the world.

So the Kingdom grows, like a tree, like a tiny mustard seed. So grows the Church. It all began with One in a carpenter shop in Nazareth; it was spread across the world by one man who was a fisherman, another who was a tax collector, another (Paul) who was once a pharisaical enemy of the Christian faith. Many a great Church has been built out of the dream of one enthusiastic, dedicated man; hardly a single soul would have been saved without the teaching of some one man who made the Good News of salvation plain. The Kingdom of heaven starts from the smallest of beginnings, or it does not start at all.

God cannot do it without the help of some one, some small one.

III. . . . *The kingdom of heaven is like unto leaven, which a woman took, and hid in three measures of meal, till the whole was leavened.* Matthew 13:33. This is a parable told in one verse, in twenty-four words. It is a parable of a *woman;* it comes out of a housewife's kitchen, and it is illustrative of the transforming power of Jesus Christ.

Baking bread in her kitchen, this woman took three measures of meal (flour), which would make enough bread for an ordinary family, and mixed in it a small lump of leaven. Leaven was sour dough, saved from a previous baking. That lump of sour dough "leavened" (changed the nature) of the whole mix. Actually, leaven was yeast. Jesus used this parable and made use of the power of leaven to illustrate the transforming power of Christ.

Unleavened bread turns out hard and dry; leavened bread is sweet to eat. Leaven causes a change in the dough; the coming of the Kingdom causes a change in life. The leaven of the Christian Gospel changed a baseball player into a Billy Sunday, one of our most famous evangelists; it took a young boy out of a mill in Scotland and made of him a David Livingstone, a great missionary; it took such men as Paul describes in 1 Corinthians 6 as fornicators, idolators, thieves, coveters, drunkards, revilers, and extortionists and made them fine men in Christ. It made saints out of sinners—and still does. It sanctified childhood in a day when children were abused and often murdered and made them children of God to be respected as such; he liberated women from a state of what was almost slavery to a status of equality with men. It has changed the world—a world which still stands in need of change with the application of yet more Gospel leaven.

Great things, great advances and improvement, come from the march of eleven men all down the ages; the twelve have become millions, and the end is not yet.

SUGGESTIONS TO TEACHERS

A cartoon in a magazine a few years ago depicted a self-important tycoon talking to a clergyman. Slamming his fist on the desk and blandishing an expensive cigar, Mr. big-shot bellows to the pastor, "When I pray, I want results!"

Like us, he wanted to see things happen. The tycoon wanted certainties NOW. He wanted to be assured of a satisfactory outcome for his efforts.

The humor of the cartoon is that the pompous businessman mirrors each of us to some extent. God's promise is that He brings meaning. He tells us that we may trust in His ultimate victory.

The lesson for today centers on our trust in God's victory. Jesus' string of parables recounted in Matthew 13:1-52 underscore this Good News. Each parable also, in a sense, asks a pointed question. Look at each of these questions to us.

1. *DO YOU LISTEN?* First look at the parable of the soils. Think of

this parable in terms of the parable of the hearers. Have your class consider carefully what type of hearer is suggested by each type of soil: the rocky ground, the thin topsoil, the thorny ground, and the rich, moist loam. Move on to the point that Jesus is making. "Do you *listen* to God's Word?" Jesus is asking. "How are you hearing My promise? What are you doing about it?" Let your class ponder whether or not each *listens* to God's voice through Jesus Christ.

2. *CAN YOU WAIT?* Proceed to the next parable in this string—the parable of the weeds growing in with the wheat (Matthew 13:24–30). Ultimately, the weeds are sorted out from the good grain at the time of harvest. Jesus makes it plain that finally in His own appropriate time and in His effective way, the Lord will distinguish and sift out the human "weeds." Our task is not to try to judge others. Nor is it to fret because God's harvest-time seems to take so long. Help your people to recognize that patient waiting for God's final victory is part of what trusting is.

3. *DO YOU TRUST?* Have your class members examine the mustard seed parable, the picture-story of the tiniest seed then known, flowering into a great, useful shrub (Matthew 13:31, 32). Have them also recall the activity of the pinch of yeast, making an entire batch of baking rise (Matthew 13:33). Out of apparently insignificant stuff astonishing things result. God's rule spreads the same way, Jesus assures us. Trust Him! His realm eventually grows, although we presently see little evidence of growth. Help your people to develop a kind of trust which perseveres in spite of seeing only the tiny seed or the blob of yeast at this stage of the Kingdom's spread.

4. *WILL YOU ACT?* Finally, call attention to the parables of buying the field (Matthew 13:44) and the pearl (13:45). Jesus makes the point that God's rule calls for the same intense, sacrificial effort on the part of each of us that the Galilean sharecropper or the jewelry salesman showed. Encourage your class people to consider Jesus' unspoken question: "What are you *doing* about God's rule and claim?"

TOPIC FOR ADULTS
TRUST IN GOD'S VICTORY

Perspective. "When I was in college, I was enthralled by the bells that would peal across the Wellesley campus at five every afternoon. One day I climbed up into the bell tower, hoping to find the source of this rich, harmonious sound. In the midst of the huge iron bells was a keyboard consisting of dozens of long wooden pegs. To produce the melody of the hymns the bellringer would pound ferociously on these pegs with the heel of her fist. At close range, the sound was atrocious— loud, clamorous, and out of key. I quickly turned and fled from this cacophony of noise—only to find once again that from the perspective of distance the melody was full and pure in tone. And so it can be with our lives—the sour, clamorous days when our feelings are out of tune are merely part of a larger whole—and when put into perspective, they add to the full harmony of living.

"If at certain points, we fail to hear God's promise, we must step back and look at the bigger picture. We must remember our history. For our history tells us that God's love never fails. The doubts are very real and important in our struggle with faith, but when we lose perspective and get lost in momentary despair, we are in essence calling God a liar, we are saying that God makes promises and then does not keep them. Let us hear the words again: 'I have promised that I will save and heal—and I will. I, the Lord have spoken.' "— From a sermon preached by the Rev. Susan R. Andrews.

Trust in God's Promise. "A Canadian author, Dr. Everek Storms, has counted the promises made in Holy Scripture and has come up with a total of 8,810. He confesses: 'I do not guarantee my count to be perfect, but it is the mst accurate one I know of.' Of these promises, 7,487 were made by God to man; 991 are promises made by one person to another; 290 are made by man to God; 28 by angels; nine by Satan. Only one book has none at all—Paul's letter to Titus. After fifty-three readings of the Bible, the writer designates the following as the most important: the promises of salvation, of the gift of the Holy Spirit, of answered prayer, of temporal help, of sustaining strength, and of heaven. He comments that we go to Church and sing 'Standing on the promises,' but that most of us are simply sitting on them.

"Sad to say, that observation is uncomfortably close to the truth. Maybe we are conditioned by experiencing so many human promises that are never implemented. Dr. Storms concludes his articles with a sensible plea: 'You can count on the promises of God. Why not try some of them and see for yourself?' "—Charles P. Robshaw, *East Liberty Church Bulletin*, November 19, 1978, East Liberty Presbyterian Church, Pittsburgh, PA 15206.

Any Hope? The following notice appeared in the Fremont Avenue United Presbyterian, Bellevue, Pennsylvania, Church bulletin: "The Dial-for-Hope machine has been repaired and is in operation, though not working well. The number is 761-7100. Please let us know if it malfunctions when you call."

Fortunately, God is not a mechanical device who fails us when we turn to Him for hope and help. Although we sometimes are inclined to think that our appeals to Him are unheard and unheeded, He assures us that we may trust in His victory. The Gospel is His assurance that we may trust Him, regardless of circumstances!

Questions to Pupils on the Next Lesson. 1. Why do many in churches seem to lack a wholeness in their lives? 2. Why is it easier to insulate ourselves from feeling the hurts and needs of others? 3. What does Jesus' compassion for hungry and hurting crowds mean for us today? 4. Can our excuses for not doing anything because of limited resources hold up in the light of Jesus' promises? 5. How does Jesus multiply the effectiveness of what we commit to Him today?

TOPIC FOR YOUTH
TRUST IN GOD'S VICTORY

Tragedy to Triumph Through Trust. Can a person trust God when tragedy strikes unexpectedly? Especially when it wipes out nearly all of one's immediate family?

This was the question faced by people in Willow Island, West Virginia. Fifty-one men were killed when the scaffolding on which they were working collapsed, hurling them to their deaths 168 feet below.

No one expected April 27, 1978, to be any different from any other work day when construction workers climbed up inside the half completed shell of a huge concrete cooling tower of Monongahela Power Company's plant. The workers were all friends or relatives. When the scaffolding tore loose from the inside of the great cylinder, nearly every family in the surrounding closely knit community experienced the loss of a loved one or close friend. Lee Steele's four sons, brother, two brothers-in-law, and three nephews were among those plunged to the floor of the tower in the jumbled wreckage.

The signs of grief are still noticeable in the homes in the community near Willow Island. Amos McVey, a local pastor, spends the afternoon with the bereaved. A reporter asks him what he is telling the families but he gives no reply. Later, he will say simply, "In an accident like this, you begin in faith with the question 'Why?' and you are led back to the same question 'Why?' "

Lee Steele, a strong and regular churchgoer, says, "I just trust in God. He'll never put more on me than I can bear, He gets me through rough spots."

Escape From World. Many people have not heard of God's promise of victory. Others who perhaps have heard do not believe that the news is true.

When the nation's space agency announced plans in September, 1976, to investigate ways of ferrying people to permanent space stations in orbit, many displayed keen interest. NASA stated that plans were being developed to have space colonists operate on these space stations for biological and medical research, manufacturing, exploration of deeper space, radio and optical astronomy, and beaming solar power to earth by laser. A new type of space shuttle, a cross between a rocket and an airplane, was built. This part of the space program would not require highly trained astronauts with extensive flight time and perfect physiques. NASA reported that the space shuttle would open space to reasonably healthy technicians of various kinds.

Perhaps to no one's surprise, hundreds of people wrote, asking to be considered as space colonists. Many were genuinely interested because of scientific backgrounds. Sadly, however, many others simply wanted to get away from planet earth. The latter's inquiries revealed a pathetic sense of despair over the future of the world and a desire to escape.

Christians, however, trust in God's ultimate victory! No escape-wishes among Christ's people. God's purposes prevail! Therefore, Christians persevere in the world.

Enough Reasons to Trust in God! "Can a modern person, rationally thinking, still believe in God?" Hans Küng, the controversial Roman Catholic theologian from Tuebingen, Germany, says that belief in God is a viable and rational choice for modern people.

"Many people have taken for granted that pure reason cannot prove the existence of God—that reason cannot bridge the distance from visible to the invisible, and I think basically, this is right. There is no single proof of God's existence accepted universally, but neither can God be rationally disproved.

"If God cannot be rationally eliminated nor rationally established, there is no conclusive argument for the necessity of atheism." But there is one for the existence of God, he notes.

"The fact that God exists can be accepted not on the basis of a rational proof but only on the basis of a reasonable trust. A trust rooted in reality. The reality of the senses is not the ultimate reality, but there is a primal reality that I can reasonably commit myself to. So though we have no clear proofs, we have enough reasons to have a trust in God."—Quoted from Religious News Service in *Presbyterian Outlook,* November 13, 1978, Outlook Publishers, Inc., 512 E. Main St., Richmond, VA 23219. Used by permission.

Sentence Sermon to Remember: Trust God for great things; with your five loaves and two fishes He will show you a way to feed thousands.— Horace Bushnell.

Questions for Pupils on the Next Lesson. 1. How can you best demonstrate the power and glory of God in your everyday life? 2. How can you be a whole person? 3. How can you help others become whole persons? 4. Is it possible to change social structures such as poverty, which hinder the growth, to wholeness of many persons? 5. Realizing that your resources are limited, how can you best use these creatively for others?

LESSON X—FEBRUARY 8

HAVE COMPASSION

Background Scripture: Matthew 13:53–15:39
Devotional Reading: Jonah 3:1–10

KING JAMES VERSION

KING JAMES VERSION

MATTHEW 15 29 And Jesus departed from thence, and came nigh unto the sea of Galilee; and went up into a mountain, and sat down there.

30 And great multitudes came unto him, having with them *those that were* lame, blind, dumb, maimed, and many others, and cast them down at Jesus' feet; and he healed them:

31 Insomuch that the multitude wondered, when they saw the dumb to speak, the maimed to be whole, the lame to walk, and the blind to see: and they glorified the God of Israel.

32 Then Jesus called his disciples *unto him,* and said, I have compassion on the multitude, because they continue with me now three days, and have nothing to eat: and I will not send them away fasting, lest they faint in the way.

33 And his disciples say unto him, Whence should we have so much bread in the wilderness, as to fill so great a multitude?

34 And Jesus saith unto them, How many loaves have ye? And they said, Seven, and a few little fishes.

35 And he commanded the multitude to sit down on the ground.

36 And he took the seven loaves and the fishes, and gave thanks, and brake *them,* and gave to his disciples, and the disciples to the multitude.

37 And they did all eat, and were filled: and they took up of the broken *meat* that was left seven baskets full.

38 And they that did eat were four thousand men, beside women and children.

39 And he sent away the multitude, and took ship, and came into the coasts of Magdala.

REVISED STANDARD VERSION

MATTHEW 15 29 And Jesus went on from there and passed along the Sea of Galilee. And he went up into the hills, and sat down there.

30 And great crowds came to him, bringing with them the lame, the maimed, the blind, the dumb, and many others, and they put them at his feet, and he healed them, 31 so that the throng wondered, when they saw the dumb speaking, the maimed whole, the lame walking, and the blind seeing; and they glorified the God of Israel.

32 Then Jesus called his disciples to him and said, "I have compassion on the crowd, because they have been with me now three days, and have nothing to eat; and I am unwilling to send them away hungry, lest they faint on the way." 33 And the disciples said to him, "Where are we to get bread enough in the desert to feed so great a crowd?" 34 And Jesus said to them, "How many loaves have you?" They said, "Seven, and a few small fish." 35 And commanding the crowd to sit down on the ground, 36 he took the seven loaves and the fish, and having given thanks he broke them and gave them to the disciples, and the disciples gave them to the crowds. 37 And they all ate and were satisfied; and they took up seven baskets full of the broken pieces left over. 38 Those who ate were four thousand men, besides women and children. 39 And sending away the crowds, he got into the boat and went to the region of Magadan.

KEY VERSE: . . . *he saw a great throng; and he had compassion on them, and healed their sick.* Matthew 14:14 (RSV).

HOME DAILY BIBLE READINGS

Feb. 2. M. Miracles That Did Not Happen. Matthew 13:53–58.
Feb. 3. T. Dinner for Five Thousand. Matthew 14:14–21.
Feb. 4. W. Walking on Water. Matthew 4:22–27.
Feb. 5. T. The Higher Law. Matthew 15:1–11.
Feb. 6. F. A Faith That Won. Matthew 15:21–28.
Feb. 7. S. The Making of a Miracle. Matthew 15:29–39.
Feb. 8. S. They Believed and Were Spared. Jonah 3:1–10.

BACKGROUND

Jesus and His disciples have been working along the coasts of (Gentile) Tyre and Sidon; they have returned to Galilee, tired out and in need of rest. To get that rest, they took a boat and crossed the Lake of Galilee to the desert hills near Bethsaida; this Bethsaida is on the eastern shore of Galilee. There they would have solitude for a while, far from the crowds with which they had been working.

But this was not to be. Somehow the people found out where He was, and "multitudes" of them followed Him; most of them probably walked around the northern end of the Lake to reach His "hiding place." It was the beginning of April, A.D. 29, just when the paschal feast (Passover) was beginning. That was an appropriate moment for what was to happen in those hills.

NOTES ON THE PRINTED TEXT

I. . . . I have compassion on the multitude, because they . . . have nothing to eat . . . . Matthew 15:32. Matthew has two accounts of Jesus feeding "multitudes": in chapter 14:13–21, He feeds "about five thousand men, beside women and children"; in 15:29–39, the number is four thousand. The question naturally arises: "Are both accounts describing the same event, or were there two separate feedings and miracles?" We cannot be certain about this, but generally it is believed that we have here two different events. The same story is told in all four Gospels, in Matthew 15:29–39, Mark 8:1–9, Luke 9:12–17, and John 6:1–14. It occurs no less than six times, under the names of these Gospel writer-evangelists.

Now there are three different interpretations of this story possible to the modern reader. The first interpretation is that it was indeed the account of a physical miracle. Jesus, in this view, literally took five loaves of barley bread and the two fish in His hands and with supernatural power transformed them into enough—more than enough—food to feed the multitude. But we cannot overlook the fact that in none of the four Gospels is Jesus pictured as multiplying the food *by touch*. But surely, in all humility, we cannot rule out the possibility that this did happen as just such a miracle. A second interpretation is that Jesus knew that there was enough food in that crowd to feed all of them, but that the individuals in the crowd showed no intention of sharing what they had with others. It is possible that Jesus may have instructed His disciples to sit down and share *their* food, after He had blessed it.

The third alternative view is that Jesus here was observing a sacrament, with the loaves and fishes as sacramental symbols. In John 6, we hear Jesus saying, "I am the bread of life; he that cometh to me shall never hunger; and he that believeth on me shall never thirst." Was He anticipating the symbolism of the bread and wine of the Last Supper—and of our Holy Communion? "Certainly," says Walter Russell Bowie, "the enduring miracle of Christ comes not through the temporary satisfaction of the flesh but through the invisible bread by which our souls are fed."

No matter which view we may hold about this, there are involved here more than one evidence of the compassion of Jesus for all in that crowd, Jew and Gentile alike. "I have compassion on the multitude . . . . I will not send them away fasting." Miracle or not, the whole great event teaches us that Jesus was deeply concerned with human hunger—physical as well as spiritual hunger.

II. . . . *those that were lame, blind, dumb, maimed, and many others . . . .* Matthew 15:30. First of all, during these three days with the multitude, Jesus turned His attention to the sick of mind, body, and spirit. Mark, who makes much of the healings of Jesus, records the reply of Jesus to certain scribes and Pharisees who criticized Him for eating with publicans and sinners: "They that are whole have no need of the physician, but they that are sick: I came not to call the righteous, but sinners to repentance" (Mark 2:17). He came as the Great Physician, with power to heal those who needed healing—healing of the longing heart, the questioning mind, the sick and ailing body. He caused the lame to walk, the blind to see the love and compassion of God. When General Booth of the Salvation Army was criticized for serving hot meals to the poor by some who claimed that the Christian's task was *only* to preach the Gospel, he replied, "How can you warm a man's heart with the love of Christ when his feet are perishing with cold?"

Right! Credit the Church with this: it has never turned its back on the poor, the sick, the underprivileged—and never can. Those who need Him most must be served first. Unfortunately, His disciples did not quite see that; they suggested that it was just too much for them to feed all that enormous crowd; they didn't have the food to do it, so why not just let them go home, or back to their cities, where they might find food enough. Besides, said Philip, *they* didn't have the money to do that right at the moment.

That was a lame excuse for doing nothing: they were saying, "Let's run away from it, and let somebody else do it." Perhaps the moral of this story is that we settle no problem by running away from it, by saying hopelessly, "Let George do it." Or, as Christians, saying, "Let Christ do it *all!*" He cannot do it all; He needs the help of His disciples. He needs the helping hands and hearts of every Christian; He has no hands, in our time, but our hands. The smallest and most "ordinary" of His followers have something to give. Let him give it! Let him be like the boy in John's story—the little lad who contributed what he had—only five barley loaves and two fish. We all have something, some talent, some compassion, to contribute. God forgive us if we withhold it!

Now there is a still greater lesson for us here. Jesus did *not* work this miracle to prove that He was a wonder-worker, performing miracles to gain for Himself a reputation like that. He came to us *as the Bread of*

Life; He came to satisfy the deeper hunger in our hearts and souls. He came to give contentment to the discontented, to give blessed assurance of the presence and power of God available to those living lives of frustration and emptiness; He came that the least and worst of us could, if we wished, in Him come to live lives that were more "abundant" and meaningful. We sin when we argue like children over the question of whether or not this was a miracle (would all four of the Gospel writers have told the story if there had not been an element of miracle in it?) and miss the greater miracle of Christ the Bread feeding the souls of men from A.D. 29 to A.D. 1981.

Matthew Arnold wrote this, about Christ the Bread:

> 'Twas August, and the fierce sun overhead
> Smote on the squalid streets of Bethnal Green,
> And the pale weaver, through his windows seen
> In Spitalfields, look'd thrice dispirited.
>
> I met a preacher there I knew, and said,
> "Ill and o'erworked, how fare you in this scene?"
> "Bravely?" said he, "for I of late have been
> Much cheer'd with thoughts of Christ, the living bread."
>   That's it!

SUGGESTIONS TO TEACHERS

The beloved Fred Rogers of *Mister Rogers' Neighborhood* has a beautiful song which states that there are many ways of saying, "I love you." Fred Rogers reminds his audience that there is more than the "telling" way of saying these important words.

So with God. Through Jesus, God's I-Love-You has been communicated in various ways. In today's lesson, you will consider four different ways God has told us of His love in Jesus' life. Use these also as a means of deepening your class members' understanding of ways of showing compassion on others.

1. *THE FEEDING WAY.* "Having compassion" is not like having brown eyes or having a high-school diploma. Having compassion is actively, intelligently, sensitively showing care for others. Look at the two stories of feeding the multitudes in this light. Note that having compassion does not necessarily depend on having much (the disciples could find only a few fish and loaves). Point out that there are always excuses to be found not to show care. (Why didn't the people bring their own food? Such forgetfulness deserved to have them go home hungry. Besides, there were so many 5,000 of them one time, 4,000 another. And how did the disciples know they'd have enough for themselves?)

2. *THE JOINING WAY.* Move your lesson to the way Jesus came into the boat with frightened followers, and to the way He lifted Peter from the waters. Jesus was present when they needed Him. Isn't this another way of saying, "I love you"? Discuss in your class ways in which being present with others when they need someone is a way of showing compassion. What about the forgotten elderly in your congregation? Or the lonely singles, the widows, the divorced? Think also of neighbors and

remember one's own family. What do your people do to be "present" as Christ's representatives to these?

3. *THE HEALING WAY.* Have your class look at the extraordinary patience and concern Jesus had for those who were hurting physically, mentally, emotionally, and spiritually as seen in Matthew 14:34–36 and 15:29–31. Have your class list reasons why Jesus *could* have decided to ignore these people. (Too many of them. I'm tired. I'm busy. They're not my type. I've other things to do.) Think how these excuses apply to us. Think also of the form of healing which Christ wants to bring to others through us.

4. *THE TEACHING WAY.* Jesus also used the teaching way to demonstrate His compassion to others. His teachings might have seemed stern and uncompromising, but they were also a form of love. Furthermore, note the teachings in this section in Matthew 15 about "clean" and "unclean." Jesus teaches that ritual and diet are not what make someone unclean, but rather evil thoughts and attitudes. Our ideas and our outlook toward others are what instruct our hands and our voices. And our acts and our words in turn teach others in so many ways!

TOPIC FOR ADULTS
HAVE COMPASSION

Breakthrough of Love. We understand compassion only when the biblical story gets hold of us. The life, the death, and the Resurrection of Jesus Christ are God's compassion in action—for *us*. No other philosophy or no other teaching can approach the significance of God's caring shown in Jesus.

The German philosopher-scholar Heine, for example, cannot bring himself to accept the wholeness which God's compassion brings. Heine sarcastically writes, "Mine is a most peaceable disposition. My wishes are: a humble cottage with a thatched roof, but a good bed, good food, the freshest milk and butter, flowers before my window, and a few fine trees before my door; and if God wants to make my happiness complete, He will grant me the joy of seeing some six or seven of my enemies hanging from those trees. Before their death I shall, moved in my heart, forgive them all the wrong they did me in their lifetime. One must, it is true, forgive one's enemies—but not before they have been hanged."— Godanken and Einfalle Section I.

Wholeness Through Spending. Compassion needs to be translated into specific forms of action. Caring is more than nice feelings. Love is even more than personal acts of kindness. Compassion has to do with national priorities.

Consider the following statistics, and reflect on what they suggest about showing compassion.

$1 billion of military spending creates 75,710 jobs, But . . . .
$1 billion spent on mass transit creates 92,071 jobs;
$1 billion spent on construction creates 100,072 jobs;
$1 billion spent on health care creates 138,939 jobs;
$1 billion spent on education creates 187,299 jobs.

Figures from Bureau of Labor Statistics, *Structure of U.S. Economy in 1980 and 1985.*

A Passing Kindness. "I expect to pass through life but once," wrote William Penn. "If therefore, there be any kindness I can show, or any good thing I can do to any fellow being, let me do it now, and not defer or neglect it, as I shall not pass this way again."

Crowded Phone Booths. "If we discovered that we had only five minutes left to say, all we wanted to say, every telephone booth would be occupied by people calling other people to stammer that they loved them. Why wait until the last five minutes?"—Christopher Morley.

Questions for Pupils on the Next Lesson. 1. What does it mean for us to confess Christ as preeminent when we live in a pluralistic society of many faiths? 2. Why does God call us to experience the Christian life with others? Why doesn't He allow us to be in isolation from other people? 3. What does it mean to lose oneself in order to find one's life in a personal quest for identity? 4. In what ways do Christians sometimes misunderstand God's will when they think only in terms of traditional ideas of success?

TOPIC FOR YOUTH
CARE!

Pastor's Conversion Through Policeman's Caring. The Reverend A. L. Reynolds is a black pastor in Chicago's south side. Years of experiencing hatred and bigotry had left deep emotional scars on A. L. Reynolds.

Years before A. L. Reynolds had been forced to confront his personal racial attitude: "When I went into the ministry, I hated the white man," he said. "I preached about love, and it was good . . . but I hated the white man."

He told of an incident when he was five years old, shopping with his father in the general store of a small Missouri town. He noticed a white girl, younger than he, had dropped her all-day sucker. "I was taught to be nice to people. I reached down to pick it up and I was going to give it to her. But her father saw me doing it and he kicked my leg out of joint—and it's out of joint today." This and other incidents while growing up confirmed A.L.'s hatred, which he carried within himself.

A change in attitude came through the help of a white assistant chief of police who took care of the Reynolds family after they had spent a night in jail. A.L., his wife, and two young sons had resorted to sleeping in their car when they could not find a motel that would accept them. The police picked them up. The chief's assistant found them the next day behind bars, weary, and hungry. The assistant released the family and invited them to his home for breakfast. The Reynolds were shocked to learn that the policeman's son had been murdered by blacks.

"He treated us royally," said A.L. "He even drove with us to see us safely out of town. This was the first time I had been helped by a white man.

"The next Sunday, while preparing to preach to my congregation, I knew I had to confront a deep emotional conflict between the love I had been preaching and the hate I had been feeling." That morning, contrite and broken, A.L. begged God's forgiveness from the pulpit.

Family of Man. "Man is a family. If any member of the family hurts, we all hurt. If any member is shut out by the family, the whole family is diminished. Last year the family of man spent four hundred billion dollars—$400,000,000,000—for armaments, four times the amount spent on public health around the world. In a nuclear family, if no one was threatening the house and Dad kept buying guns and ammunition and grenades till they filled the whole downstairs, while upstairs the baby was crying for food and his sister needed an operation and Mommy was wearing rags, we'd lock Dad up, since he was obviously mad. But we go on selling fighter planes and bombs and guns with impartiality to Arabs and Israelis, black and white Africans, and anybody with the money to buy.

"Meanwhile, hunger and poverty, inflation and illness, continue to stalk the world. The physical handicaps and the mental pressures of the modern world remain a tremendous challenge. They demand the time and talent and treasure of the family of man, freed from a $400,000,000,000 arms drain."—Richard Steiner, *Call Chronicle*, Allentown, PA, July 29, 1978.

The Fight for Food.

1. World food production increased in 1979 and 1980, yet a third to a half of the world's population remains seriously undernourished. Why?

2. Each American consumes about 101 grams of protein a day roughly; 500 million people on three-fourths of the globe receive under 50 grams a day. Why?

3. Almost a third of the world's babies die of malnutrition before they reach the age of five. Why?

4. Most of the people who are malnourished live in developing countries in which the average income per person is below $200 a year. Yet more than 40 percent of U.S. food aid goes to richer countries that are important to the U.S. for military and political reasons. Why?

5. India has about 16 million tons of food grains in reserve, the largest surplus in its history. Yet millions of Indian people still suffer from malnutrition and hunger. Why?

6. Despite production increases, global food reserves are insufficient to prevent widespread famine if drought or bad weather causes a year of poor crop yields. Why?

7. Over 56 percent of U.S. agricultural exports go to highly industrialized countries, not to developing nations. In 1974 when many developing nations, including India, were experiencing famine conditions, 1145 pounds of wheat per person was exported to Japan, but only 75 pounds per person went to india. Why?

8. Because of an inadequate diet, more than 300 million children will never in their lives feel alert or energetic, they will never have the ability to learn, the desire to succeed, or the will to make an effort. Why?

Sentence Sermon to Remember: Without compassion, no man can call himself a Christian.— Anonymous.

Questions for Pupils on the Next Lesson. 1. How can you claim that Christ comes first when we live in a pluralistic society in which many faiths are tolerated? 2. Is it possible, in your opinion, for the Church to be a warm, nourishing community of trust and caring? Is your congregation such a "family"? What are you doing to help make it so? 3. Does every decision have long-range consequences? 4. What does it mean "to lose one's life in order to find it"? Are you experiencing this?

LESSON XI—FEBRUARY 15

LIVE YOUR FAITH

Background Scripture: Matthew 16, 17
Devotional Reading: Isaiah 58:5–12

KING JAMES VERSION

MATTHEW 16 13 When J sus came into the coasts of Caesarea Philippi, he asked his disciples, saying, Whom do men say that I, the Son of man, am?

14 And they said, Some *say that thou art* John the Baptist; some, Elias; and others, Jeremias, or one of the prophets.

15 He saith unto them, But whom say ye that I am?

16 And Simon Peter answered and said, Thou art the Christ, the Son of the living God.

17 And Jesus answered and said unto him, Blessed art thou, Simon Bar-jona: for flesh and blood hath not revealed *it* unto thee, but my Father which is in heaven.

18 And I say also unto thee, That thou art Peter, and upon this rock I will build my church; and the gates of hell shall not prevail against it.

19 And I will give unto thee the keys of the kingdom of heaven: and whatsoever thou shalt bind on earth shall be bound in heaven; and whatsoever thou shalt loose on earth shall be loosed in heaven.

20 Then charged he his disciples that they should tell no man that he was Jesus the Christ.

21 From that time forth began Jesus to shew his disciples, how that he must go unto Jerusalem, and suffer many things of the elders and chief priests and scribes, and be killed, and be raised again the third day.

22 Then Peter took him, and began to rebuke him, saying, Be it far from thee, Lord: this shall not be unto thee.

23 But he turned, and said unto Peter, Get thee behind me, Satan: thou art an offense unto me: for thou savourest not the things that be of God, but those that be of men.

REVISED STANDARD VERSION

MATTHEW 16 13 Now when Jesus came into the district of Caesarea Philippi, he asked his disciples, "Who do men say that the Son of man is?" 14 And they said, "Some say John the Baptist, others say Elijah, and others Jeremiah or one of the prophets." 15 He said to them, "But who do you say that I am?" 16 Simon Peter replied, "You are the Christ, the Son of the living God." 17 And Jesus answered him, "Blessed are you, Simon Bar-Jona! For flesh and blood has not revealed this to you, but my Father who is in heaven. 18 And I tell you, you are Peter, and on this rock I will build my church, and the powers of death shall not prevail against it. 19 I will give you the keys of the kingdom of heaven, and whatever you bind on earth shall be bound in heaven, and whatever you loose on earth shall be loosed in heaven." 20 Then he strictly charged the disciples to tell no one that he was the Christ.

21 From that time Jesus began to show his disciples that he must go to Jerusalem and suffer many things from the elders and chief priests and scribes, and be killed, and on the third day be raised. 22 And Peter took him and began to rebuke him, saying, "God forbid, Lord! This shall never happen to you." 23 But he turned and said to Peter, "Get behind me, Satan! You are a hindrance to me; for you are not on the side of God, but of men."

24 Then said Jesus unto his disciples, If any *man* will come after me, let him deny himself, and take up his cross, and follow me.

25 For whosoever will save his life shall lose it: and whosoever will lose his life for my sake shall find it.

26 For what is a man profited, if he shall gain the whole world, and lose his own soul? or what shall a man give in exchange for his soul?

24 Then Jesus told his disciples, "If any man would come after me, let him deny himself and take up his cross and follow me. 25 For whoever would save his life will lose it, and whoever loses his life for my sake will find it. 26 For what will it profit a man, if he gains the whole world and forfeits his life? Or what shall a man give in return for his life?

KEY VERSE: . . . *"If any man would come after me, let him deny himself and take up his cross and follow me.* Matthew 16:24 (RSV).

HOME DAILY BIBLE READINGS

Feb.   9. M. *Blind to the Signs.* Matthew 16:1–12.
Feb. 10. T. *The Great Promise.* Matthew 16:13–20.
Feb. 11. W. *Losing and Finding Life.* Matthew 16:21–26.
Feb. 12. T. *Blessing Out of the Past.* Matthew 17:1–8.
Feb. 13. F. *The Way of the Cross.* Matthew 17:9–13.
Feb. 14. S. *The Essential Faith.* Matthew 17:14–23.
Feb. 15. S. *The Lord Will Answer.* Isaiah 58:8–12.

BACKGROUND

Jesus, at this time in His ministry, senses something that His disciples did not sense: He knew that the end of His life on earth was near, and He was anxious that His disciples should know, beyond the shadow of a doubt just who and what He was. If they did not know this, His Kingdom could not survive and His work and hopes were lost. It was a crucial moment. To talk with them He took them out to Caesarea Philippi, twenty-five miles northeast of the Sea of Galilee. Here they would be far removed from the pressure of crowds and beyond the reach of Herod Antipas, who was His bitter enemy. In Caesarea, too, they would be surrounded by pagan Syrian gods and the gods of Greece; high on a hill, in this place, was a splended temple dedicated to the worship of Caesar. That was a good place to hold such a "retreat"; here the disciples might be led to understand that while there were many gods, there was but one true Christ of one true God. Here they could choose which they would serve, at whatever cost.

He starts talking with them by way of a stunning question.

NOTES ON THE PRINTED TEXT

I. . . . Whom do men say that I the Son of man am? Matthew 16:13. This was His first question; it produced a babel of answers. The disciples said that some men believed He was John the Baptist brought back to life; some said He was Elijah returned to earth—Elijah, the greatest of the prophets, expected by the Jews to return before the Messiah should come; still others said He was Jeremiah, who had denounced the established religion of his day and who was also to come back before the Messiah arrived.

These were wild answers, based on blind and persistent hope. Other wild answers claimed that Jesus was just another prophet, a wonder-worker with mysterious, mystic powers, a good man who went about doing good, or a rebel going about upsetting people and condemning His "superiors." Ask any ten men this question, and you are likely to get ten different answers—none of which may be satisfactory or even intelligent. These are all *human* conclusions, human categories which fall far short of the truth. Napoleon, who was no model Christian, once remarked that, "I know men, and Jesus Christ is more than a man."

Peter knew that, as none of the others seemed to know it. When Jesus turned to him and asked, "But who do *you* say that I am?" (verse 15), Peter *knew:* he broke out with a cry, "Thou art the Christ, the Son of the Living God." Peter was no great theologian or philosopher, but Peter *knew.* He knew that no merely human description of Jesus could possibly be enough. Peter spoke the truth about Jesus *because he spoke out of a great faith* and out of a great spiritual experience. To him, Christ was a personal discovery.

Knowing Christ is a personal, individual matter. Never mind what other men say—others with faint knowledge and little faith—never mind what others say: who do *you* think He is? Being a Christian does *not* mean knowing about the Master but knowing Him intimately because He lives in our hearts.

That was the answer Jesus was seeking as He probed their minds and hearts with His question. There must have been tears in His eyes as He turned to Peter and blessed him for saying it and, in a play on words, called him the rock on which he would build His church. In Greek Peter is *Petros*, and a rock is *petra*. Exactly what did Jesus mean by "the rock"? Protestant and Roman Catholics hold different ideas about that; the Catholic claim that Peter was the *literal* rock, the first pope, the first great leader of Christ's Church; Protestants hold that it was Peter's *faith* that was the foundation stone of the Church. Augustine said that it was Jesus Himself who was the rock; others have claimed that God the Father was the rock.

It is confusing. There are good arguments for either of these conclusions. Generally, we might sum it all up in the belief that Peter was the first one among the Twelve who seems to have understood that Jesus was beyond question the Son of the Living God, and upon that *conviction* the Church has been built. Certainly Peter was a leader of tremendous influence in the early Church. But the faith and the power which brought the Church through its days of persecution was its faith in Jesus as Living Lord. Peter was the first of the fellowship of Christians who believed *that.*

This fellowship of believers (or the Church), Jesus tells Peter, will prevail against the gates of hell. Read *Hades*, here, instead of hell; for Hades was the place of punishment for sinners in Jewish belief. Gates shut the sinners in, hopelessly—and the only key able to open those gates was the key of faith in the redeeming Christ. Jesus gave this key to Peter, as leader of the fellowship. As the *Good News for Modern Man* translates this, "I will give you the keys of the Kingdom of heaven: what you prohibit on earth will be prohibited in heaven; what you permit on earth will be permitted in heaven." Hades cannot hold within its gates those who live in Christ.

II. . . . Get thee behind me, Satan . . . . Matthew 16:23. Hardly was the great declaration of "Thou art the Christ, the Son of the living God" out of Peter's mouth, and hardly had Jesus blessed him for saying it, when He calls him Satan! Why? It was because Peter was displaying his usual impatience and impetuosity; he was shocked at Jesus' announcement that He would soon suffer crucifixion at the hands of His enemies. Peter just couldn't accept that; in *love* he blurts out his objection to such a prospect. And in love, Jesus corrected him.

Jesus must have thought of the temptations of Satan in the days of His temptations in the wilderness. One of those temptations was to compromise with the world; that wilderness temptation was now repeated, unconsciously, by Peter. On his lips was not the Word of God which had led him to make his great declaration that Jesus was the Christ, but the words of the devil. Peter couldn't understand how one with the power of a Messiah could let such a fate befall Him. Quite probably Jesus corrected Peter's false conception not in anger, but gently, even sadly.

The word *Satan* meant "Adversary"—any influence that would deny the concept and truth of Jesus as the suffering Servant of God. Peter still had to learn that lesson, and learn it he did, when he offered himself up to be crucified in Rome.

Both Peter and Jesus spoke in love for each other, but Peter's love was an overprotective love; such love can at times do more harm than good, if it gets in the way of God's love for men. That was Peter's error.

III. . . . If any man will come after me, let him deny himself, and take up his cross, and follow me. Matthew 16:24. There are two kinds of men and women in this world: those who think first of themselves and live lives of selfishness, and those who deny themselves the material luxuries of the world and live lives of service to others. Some of them say, "I'll look out for myself; let others look out for themselves." These self-servers never know Christ, never follow Him even though they call themselves Christians. Some prefer to paddle their canoes through life in little ponds; others launch out into the deep, living adventurous, unselfish lives. You can have it either way, but not both ways.

The man who serves only himself wastes his years, and his whole life. But the man who denies "himself"—his selfish ambitions—and truly follows Christ, lives well. Once having wasted his years and his life, *a man cannot get those years back*. He may get everything he selfishly wants, but he will one day come to the realization that he has sold his soul too cheaply. Elizabeth I, Queen of England, cried out on her deathbed, "One more inch of life; give me just one more inch." It's sad, but none of us can get that, none can correct the lost years.

How much of a bribe do you pay Satan for going his way? How much would you take for your soul?

SUGGESTIONS TO TEACHERS

Suppose you were asked to design a training manual for new converts to the Christian faith. What would you want them to know? How would you expect them to live?

The Gospel According to Matthew was, among other things, a manual for new Christians. It may be read as a practical guide for Christian discipleship for both the first century A.D. and the twentieth.

Develop your lesson from Matthew 16, 17 for today with the idea that Matthew is presenting specifics for living the faith. In fact, you might want to put the point in chapters 16, 17 in the blunt imperatives of a military command!

1. *BE ON GUARD!* Jesus warns followers against lusting after signs or proofs on the one hand, and after legalism or Pharisaism on the other. Be on guard against allowing yourself to get caught up in wanting the faith to be "proven" to you by irrefutable evidence. The Christian lives by faith! And be on guard against permitting youself to reduce the Gospel to a list of rules to keep. Give your class time to explore the pitfalls of each of these viewpoints.

2. *ANSWER THE QUESTION!* Let the impact of the question Jesus asked the disciples on the road to Caesarea Philippi sink in. "Who do *you* say that I am?" is the ultimate question in everyone's life. Leave sufficient time in your lesson period to have your people think and discuss Jesus' claims on them.

3. *CARRY YOUR CROSS!* Stress the call to sacrifice which Jesus issues to every follower. Point out that bearing a cross meant laying down life and no longer thinking of self. Let your class consider the fact that the average Christian in our country spends more for cigarettes, liquor, and sports than for following Jesus Christ. Ask what living the faith has cost your class members.

4. *CLIMB THE MOUNTAIN!* Center everyone's attention on Matthew 17, the Transfiguration account. Remind them that it was in worship that Peter, James, and John came to comprehend who Jesus was. On the mountaintop, these disciples understood that Jesus surpasses Moses, symbolic of the Law, and Elijah, symbolic of the prophets, in the Old Testament. What is the place of worship in the life of your people? Remind them that recognition of Jesus' true identity comes when we reverence Him. They will understand Jesus when they "stand under" Him! Vision comes from being with Him.

5. *TRUST ALWAYS!* The disciples had to leave the mountaintop, and so must we. Matthew's training manual reminded followers of this. Back in the valley, they encountered a "hopeless case," an epileptic boy which they decided they couldn't help. Jesus ordered them to believe and serve. Likewise, He commands us to trust, in spite of everything, and to do for others, in spite of everything!

TOPIC FOR ADULTS
LIVE YOUR FAITH

At Home, 11 A.M. Sunday. George Bernard Shaw once received an invitation from an aristocratic "celebrity hunter." "Lady _____ will be at home Thursday between four and six P.M." He returned the card to the sender with the notation: "Bernard Shaw likewise." Such a response was hardly the height of courtesy. Indeed, the anecdote comes from a small volume entitled *The Little Book of Famous Insults.* On the other hand, the famous are often besieged by people trying to gain secondhand glory at their expense, so G.B.S. may have had some justification.

There are times, however, when the rejection of a gracious invitation is much less excusable. Take, for example, the invitation to the public worship of God which is as much a command as an invitation. Going to church is a minimum responsibility of the Christian. In a recent publication, the writer, Eliot Porter, observes: "There is more to being a Christian than going to church, but if you unnecessarily stop going to church, your interest in church will very probably die. You will in all likelihood become dead wood on the church roll, and it would have been better if you never made your confession at all. One minister insists that the principal reason why church members discontinue regular attendance at church is because they have bad consciences—not necessarily that their consciences are burdened with sensational sins, but that they know their lives to be unspiritual and unchristian. If you find yourself disinclined to attend church, examine yourself to see whether this is true. Recall your vow of allegiance to Christ, attend church regularly, and strive to bring your life into conformity with what Christian worship implies." He continues: "Moreover, by going to church, you vote for the survival of Christianity. . . . Pray for the worship when you have entered—for yourself, for your fellow-worshippers, and those who minister; and pray with the minister when he prays. . . . Above all other services of the church, observe the Lord's Supper by unfailing attendance after prayerful preparation. 'This do in remembrance of me,' our Lord has said. Almost invariably those members who neglect the Communion drift away from the church."— Charles P. Robshaw, *East Liberty Church Bulletin*, September 17, 1978, East Liberty Presbyterian Church, Pittsburgh, PA 15206.

What We Have in Common. Several years ago, when George W. Webber directed East Harlem Parish, the men of an upper-class, well-to-do, all-white suburban church invited the relatively poor, black men of the East Harlem Parish to a church supper. The men from the comfortable white suburb thought and thought. What could they find in common with the men in the city from Harlem? What could the two groups talk about? The two groups were completely different in background and outlook. What kind of a program could they share?

Fortunately, someone in the suburban congregation received an inspired idea. No, they would not try to sing fun songs. No, they would not try to manufacture "fellowship" with tricks and games. They would not seek some harmless general meeting ground, such as sports. They would not discuss the stockmarket. They simply went around the circle and asked each man present, black and white, rich and poor, to tell in his own words the response to one question: How had he become a Christian?

That was the reason for their being together. That was the basis for their fellowship.

Needless to say, the meeting was one of the most profoundly meaningful any man had ever attended!

Action and Passion. A person's faith must be lived and shared. Otherwise, it is pious theory.

Oliver Wendell Holmes put this truth pithily. Said he in a speech in 1884, "I think that, as life is action and passion, it is required of a man that he should share the passion and action of his time at peril of being judged not to have lived."—Quoted by Charles Alan Wright, *Legal Eagle News*.

Are you sharing the passion and action of your faith? Will others, using Holmes criteria, judge you to have lived?

Questions for Pupils on the Next Lesson. 1. In your relationships with others, are you mostly accepting or are you mostly judgmental? 2. How can Christians deal with the concept of leadership in the church in the light of Jesus' words? 3. How does the Scripture in this lesson challenge the popular notion of "Live and let live." 4. In the light of the Scripture passage in this lesson, what is the Christian approach to conflict in the Church?

TOPIC FOR YOUTH
LIVE YOUR FAITH

Who Do You Fear More? A Midwestern father gave this piece of advice to a son leaving for boot camp: "Be quiet—and get in the middle." We know what he meant. Don't stick your neck out. Don't call attention to yourself. If you're the first man at formation or the last man to stumble out of the barracks, they'll notice you. Adopt the protective coloration of the majority. Keep the herd around you.

Eminently sensible. But if the fathers of Joshua, David, Paul, Luther, Washington, Wilberforce, Churchill et al ever said to their sons, "Be quiet—and get in the middle," we can be thankful the boys paid no attention.

Contrast this to the way Alan Osmond, one of the Osmond Brothers, was taught. Osmond is not ashamed of his religion and tries to live his faith. Alan, who handles the Osmond enterprise finances, used the spiritual strength inbred by his family when he went through Army basic training. "The first night when the lights went out," he said, "I wanted to kneel down next to my bed and say my prayers. But I was afraid I would be ridiculed. After a while I found myself asking: 'Who do you fear more, man or God?' So I got down on my knees. It caught on pretty fast, and in the nights that followed, some of the guys would tell everyone to quiet down so Osmond could say his prayers."

Will you live your faith when you are away from home? Will you "be quiet and get in the middle," or will you let others know you are a Christian?

Live Your Faith at Church! Margaret Thomas set out to survey accurately some of the things that are going on in adult classes in the Presbyterian Church, U.S.: "Most of the things documented by 2,600 questionnaires turned out to be about what would be expected. Students do more homework if the teacher makes assignments. Small classes are likely to have more discussion, better attendance, and a better percentage of members preparing during the week. The men's Bible class studies least of all.

"A few of the discoveries were perhaps surprising. Young adults discuss more but study less. Older adults are likely to study more. Younger teachers are not necessarily better liked than older ones, nor are men regarded as better teachers than women. The women's Bible class is likely to study hardest.

"But one of the most interesting findings came in response to the question, 'Why do you attend this class?' Five percent said they chose that class because they liked its subject matter. Eighteen percent said that they went to the class to which they were assigned by age group or because it was the only adult class in the church. Eighteen percent said they went because they learned something in that class. But by far the largest number (43 percent) said they chose a class and attended it because they liked the people in it, the teacher and/or the other class members. Even in the church's school the most important thing to most adults is the Christian fellowship!"—William M. Ramsay, *Presbyterian Outlook*, Nov. 13, 1978, Outlook Publishers, Inc., 512 Main St., Richmond, VA. 23219. Used by permission.

Saturday Night in Madison Square Garden. Faith must be lived, not in general terms, but in down-to-earth ways in the here-and-now. It's something like the way Jack Dempsey once described being a champion fighter to a person trying to promote a promising newcomer to the ring.

Dempsey listened for a long time as the new boxer was described. The newcomer seemed to have all the makings of a champion. He was big, fast, muscular. He worked out daily. He kept in training. He showed good form at the punching bag. "This boy can sure box!"

Dempsey finally broke in. "It's not so much what you can do but that you can do it on Saturday night at ten o'clock in Madison Square Garden."

Living your faith means showing that you are Christ's at 9:00 A.M. tomorrow morning in school or on the job among the group you associate with!

Sentence Sermon to Remember: Faith is kept alive in us and gathers strength, more from practice than from speculation.—Joseph Addison.

Questions for Pupils on the Next Lesson. 1. How are you helping others to grow as Christians? 2. Who are those who have helped you the most to grow in the faith? 3. Why does serving others in Christ's name help people in their search for identity? 4. Where is it hardest for you to extend forgiveness? 5. Why is it often hard to receive forgiveness from others? 6. Is it necessary for a Christian to be humble?

LESSON XII—FEBRUARY 22

LOVE ONE ANOTHER

Background Scripture: Matthew 18
Devotional Reading: 1 Corinthians 1:26–2:5

KING JAMES VERSION	REVISED STANDARD VERSION
MATTHEW 18 1 At the same time came the disciples unto Jesus, saying, Who is the greatest in the kingdom of heaven?	MATTHEW 18 1 At that time the disciples came to Jesus, saying, "Who is the greatest in the kingdom of heaven?" 2 And calling to him a child,
2 And Jesus called a little child unto him, and set him in the midst of them,	he put him in the midst of them, 3 and said, "Truly, I say to you, unless you
3 And said, Verily I say unto you, Except ye be converted, and become as little children, ye shall not enter into the kingdom of heaven.	turn and become like children, you will never enter the kingdom of heaven. 4 Whoever humbles himself
4 Whosoever therefore shall humble himself as this little child, the same is greatest in the kingdom of heaven.	like this child, he is the greatest in the kingdom of heaven.
5 And whoso shall receive one such little child in my name receiveth me.	5 "Whoever receives one such child in my name receives me; 6 but whoever causes one of these little ones
6 But whoso shall offend one of these little ones which believe in me, it were better for him that a millstone were hanged about his neck, and *that* he were drowned in the depth of the sea.	who believe in me to sin, it would be better for him to have a great millstone fastened round his neck and to be drowned in the depth of the sea
15 Moreover if thy brother shall trespass against thee, go and tell him his fault between thee and him alone: if he shall hear thee, thou hast gained thy brother.	15 "If your brother sins against you, go and tell him his fault, between you and him alone. If he listens to you, you have gained your brother. 16 But if he
16 But if he will not hear *thee, then* take with thee one or two more, that in the mouth of two or three witnesses every word may be established.	does not listen, take one or two others along with you, that every word may be confirmed by the evidence of two or three witnesses. 17 If he refuses to lis-
17 And if he shall neglect to hear them, tell *it* to the church: but if he neglect to hear the church, let him be unto thee as a heathen man and a publican.	ten to them, tell it to the church; and if he refuses to listen even to the church, let him be to you as a Gentile and a tax collector. 18 Truly, I say to you, what-
18 Verily I say unto you, Whatsoever ye shall bind on earth shall be bound in heaven; and whatsoever ye shall loose on earth shall be loosed in heaven.	ever you bind on earth shall be bound in heaven, and whatever you loose on earth shall be loosed in heaven. 19 Again I say to you, if two of you agree
19 Again I say unto you, That if two of you shall agree on earth as touching any thing that they shall ask, it shall be done for them of my Father which is in heaven.	on earth about anything they ask, it will be done for them by my Father in heaven. 20 For where two or three are gathered in my name, there am I in the midst of them."

194

20 For where two or three are gathered together in my name, there am I in the midst of them.

21 Then came Peter to him, and said, Lord, how oft shall my brother sin against me, and I forgive him? till seven times?

22 Jesus saith unto him, I say not unto thee, Until seven times: but, Until seventy times seven.

21 Then Peter came up and said to him, "Lord, how often shall my brother sin against me, and I forgive him? As many as seven times?" 22 Jesus said to him, "I do not say to you seven times, but seventy times seven."

KEY VERSE: "Whoever humbles himself like this child, he is the greatest in the kingdom of heaven." Matthew 18:4 (RSV).

HOME DAILY BIBLE READINGS

Feb. 16. M. Who Is Greatest? Matthew 18:1–6.
Feb. 17. T. The Terrible Responsibility. Matthew 18:7–11.
Feb. 18. W. Not One Shall Perish. Matthew 18:12–17.
Feb. 19. T. The Power of the Fellowship. Matthew 18:18–22.
Feb. 20. F. How to Forgive. Matthew 23–35.
Feb. 21. S. Thanks for Your Partnership. Philippians 1:3–11.
Feb. 22. S. Faith by the Power of God. 1 Corinthians 1:26–2:5

BACKGROUND

In our New England, there is an institution known as "The Town Meeting"—a gathering of the citizens of a community sitting down together to discuss their civic problems. This meeting of the disciples with Jesus in Matthew 18 was such a meeting; they sat down together to discuss two problems of primary interest: the leadership of the Twelve, and the conduct of Christ's Church. There was at that moment no "Church" but only a community of believers. We need to keep in mind the fact that in the writing of Matthew, we have both the words of Jesus and the words and decisions of the early Church, which was then in process of being founded to carry on the work of the Christ.

Their main problem was a simple one: how were they to select their leaders, and how were they to maintain a unity and cohesion in a community which contained both Jews and Gentiles? Both Mark (9:33–49) and Matthew give us w,rd pictures of this meeting and discussion; Mark gives us more detail than Matthew, who was an artist in emphasizing main points and condensing Christ's truths and teachings in the fewest possible words. Read both accounts as you start preparing this lesson.

NOTES ON THE PRINTED TEXT

I. . . . Who is the greatest in the kingdom of heaven? Matthew 18:1. Take any organization, sacred or secular, and sooner or later you find someone who wants to be "Number One" in that organization; as Carl Sandburg said, "We all want to play Hamlet"—to play the leading part. The disciples were wondering which one of them would stand in the center of the stage, which would be considered the best among them, the most talented, the one in command.

Jesus must have been hurt when He heard them ask that, but He displayed no hurt, no indignation. He merely said that unless they "became as little children," they would not *even* enter the Kingdom; whoever humbled himself as a child would be the greatest among them. He said this in a day when children were chattels, when male children were loved and reared lovingly, but unwanted girl babies were often allowed to die in infancy. Children had a hard time of it in the heathen world.

But Jesus loved children so much that He made them symbols of His Kingdom leadership. Turn from your sins and become as little children, if you want *any* place in the Kingdom. Why children?

Children have the characteristics that should be shown in men good enough for the Kingdom. They are small, and they know it and accept it; they do not try to become business leaders or bishops; they have an innocence which leads them to forgive and forget easily. They are dependent upon the love of their parents for their very existence, and they accept that. The child has deep trust in his or her parents—"My father can lick your father!" And above all, the child has *humility;* it is only when he grows to man's estate and enters the "rat race" of overambitious men that he becomes unworthy of the Kingdom.

So, you who are disciples be humble and not selfishly ambitious. Put your dependence in God's hands, in Christ's. Don't be childish (immature), be child*like* in your trust and humility. Only the humble can be called great. (Is this the standard by which *you* determine who is greatest in your town?)

Actually, by the word *children,* Jesus was including more than *young* children; He was thinking of those young in the faith, of the grown men who were just beginning to be Christians, of those who were at the moment *weak* in their understanding of what the Kingdom was all about. When the author of the First Epistle of John wrote his fellow-Christians (1 John 2:1), "My little children, these things I write unto you . . . . "— he was speaking not to teenagers but to grown men. The "little ones" were those who *resembled* children—the weak, the young in the faith, the humble in heart—often, the disciples.

Jesus strikes out at the heartlessness of the pagans in their child abuse; those who follow Him *welcome* (receive) their children in His name, in His love, and when they do that, they welcome Christ into their lives. Those who do not treat the child so, who defile his mind or soul, who weaken his faith, deserve to be drowned to death. Harsh words: they express the horror of Jesus as He sees *any* child, young or old, denied the right to grow in Him.

II. Moreover, if thy brother shall trespass against thee . . . . Matthew 18:15. Verses 15–22 deal with discipline in the early Church; many scholars believe that the content of the verses is made up of more of the words of Matthew than the words of Christ. Matthew is writing about a Church which did not exist while Jesus lived.

It all sounds harsh; perhaps, in those difficult days, it had to be. If a brother in the Church sins or falls away from the faith, let a friend visit and counsel with him; if he does not listen to the friend, let the friend try again with two or three witnesses; if he still refuses to listen, let him be brought before the whole Church for judgment; if he is still obdurate, then let him be cast out and treated as a Gentile or a tax collector.

Somehow, it doesn't sound like the Jesus who healed Gentiles and who ate in the house of Zacchaeus the tax collector.

This is a reflection of the thought and practice of the early Church; it is also indicative of the problems that Church had to face. They had some unattractive members—had some scandal, some gluttony, etc., that had to be dealt with. We might not use such stern measures with *our* unworthy members, but *we* live in a Christian world, and they did not. They had to determine which practices would be forbidden (bound) and which should be sanctioned (loosed). They had to excommunicate in order to keep the unity and purity of their community; *excommunication* is a word almost dropped from *our* Christian dictionary, except in very rare cases.

They were a very *small* Church, with small memberships; they found great cheer and hope in words credited to Jesus—that wherever two or three (more than one), were gathered for prayer in His name, He would be in their midst, offering understanding and hope. That was a plea for corporate, collective prayer. Personal, private intercessional prayer is good and necessary, but private, closet prayer without collective prayer "would wither like a leaf without its tree."—George A. Buttrick. Small churches, small prayer groups, have a way of growing into great churches and widely influential prayer groups, if they have faith in the Man in their Midst!

III. . . . Lord, how oft shall my brother sin against me, and I forgive him? Matthew 18:21. This is Peter speaking, Peter asking still another question! The Big Fisherman had a quick tongue; he often let his tongue run wild when he should have been working out his problems in his mind. But it is good that we have Peter, for *we* speak too often in the same impatient way.

How many times should a man forgive someone who had wronged him, or hurt him? Peter asked Jesus if forgiving seven times wasn't enough; he thought he was being generous when he said seven times, for most of the Old Testament rabbis taught that three times was enough. But, Jesus informed him, even seven times was *not* enough; we should forgive seventy times seven—490 times! That was another way of saying that we should *always* forgive times without number. The Christian never closes the door on forgiveness, for if he does *he* may not be forgiven for *his* trespasses. And which of us does not trespass?

Jesus may have had the words of Genesis 4:24 in mind, when he said seventy times seven; in that verse Lamech avenged himself "seventy-sevenfold." Against this idea of endless hate and vengeance, Jesus puts the endlessness of pardon, forgiveness, and love. Forgive without end, without counting the times, lest in vengeance you destroy yourself! Whatever else you do or fail to do, *love one another*.

SUGGESTIONS TO TEACHERS

Love is one of the most abused, overworked words in the English language. The Greeks had three separate words to differentiate between lust, friendship, and sacrificial concern for another. New Testament use of *love* refers to the latter. Jesus Christ, of course, is God's sacrificial concern for us in action.

Today's lesson examines what this means for us, Christ's people. Matthew's Gospel, sometimes described as a manual for recent converts, helps us to understand the practical implications of love.

In your lesson, remember that love is not mere feelings, nor is love mere theory. It is *doing*. Jesus lived love.

Furthermore, love is other-directed. Love involves interaction with persons.

Using Matthew 18 as the basis for your lesson on loving one another, note that there are at least six facets of caring for others suggested in this chapter.

1. *HUMBLE YOURSELF.* Consider yourself still a child in the faith. Only those who realize they are kindergartners in Christian maturity can receive the Father's guidance. The childlike faith means also a sense of dependency on the Lord, exactly as a youngster must depend on a parent. Are you and your class members sometimes exhibiting an arrogance of acting as if you have all the answers and do not need God?

2. *HELP THE WEAKER TO GROW.* Turn to Matthew 18:6, and remind your people that love means, among other things, encouraging the weaker ones in the faith to become stronger. Discuss ways in which the example of an older Christian may help or may hinder others.

3. *DISCIPLINE YOURSELF.* Make sure that your class understands that love is more than mushy feelings, but calls for immense self-discipline. Reread Matthew 18:8, and ask each person to react by commenting in what ways he or she should lead a more disciplined life as a Christian.

4. *SEEK THE LOST.* Get away from romanticizing the story of the Lost Sheep (Matthew 18:10) by insisting that your class determine who the "lost" are in your community. What are you as Christians doing specifically to seek these? Or, are you avoiding them because they are "different," or "dirty," or "dangerous"?

5. *SETTLE SQUABBLES.* Take some time to talk about church fights. How do Christians disagree without quarreling? Can Christians love each other and also not see eye-to-eye? Call particular attention to the way Matthew suggests handling serious squabbles between believers. How are you and your people bringing reconciliation within the Church?

6. *RECEIVE AND SHARE MERCY.* Love means first receiving love, then giving it. List ways in which Christians are given love, starting with what God has done through Christ. Stress that the "bottom line" of love is being a *forgiven* person and being a *forgiving* person.

TOPIC FOR ADULTS
LOVE ONE ANOTHER

Love Means Sacrifice. A clergyman told the story of the man in his congregation who joined the Navy when World War II began. One night when the man's ship was in Boston, he stopped to see his friend and pastor. He was captain of a large transport, and he told his pastor how he had been guiding his ship in a convoy across the Atlantic during a submarine attack. In one fateful moment, he had seen the white mark of a torpedo coming directly toward his ship. The ship was loaded with hundreds of boys. He had no time to change course. Through a loud speaker he shouted, "Boys, this is it."

Nearby was a destroyer, whose captain also had seen the submarine and the torpedo. Without hesitation he gave the order, "Full speed ahead." The destroyer swiftly maneuvered into the path of the torpedo and took the full impact of the deadly missile. It sank with all hands.

After the story, the man remained silent. Then he looked at his pastor and said, "Reverend, the skipper of that destroyer was my best friend." Again he was quiet for a time, then slowly he remarked, "You know, there is a verse in the Bible which has special meaning for me now. It is: 'Greater love hath no man than this, that a man lay down his life for his friend.'"

Definition of Hell. "Hell is not to love anymore, madame. Not to love anymore! That sounds quite ordinary to you. To a human being still alive, it means to love less or love elsewhere . . . .

"Hell is not to love anymore. As long as we remain in this life we can still deceive ourselves, think that we love by our own will, that we love independently of God. But we're like madmen stretching our hands to grasp the moon reflected in water."— Georges Bernanos, *The Diary of a Country Priest,* translated by Pamela Morris. Copyright 1937 and renewed 1965 by Macmillan Publishing Co., Inc.

Councilman Turns Other Cheek. Allentown, Pennsylvania, City Councilman Benjamin F. Howells, Jr., was quietly touring one of his city's depressed neighborhoods on a hot day in July, 1978, seeking ways to improve his city. When he returned to his car, he found it hemmed in by another car illegally double parked. Howells politely asked the man to move his car. The other refused, and got out of his car and began to berate Howells.

Suddenly, the man began assaulting Howells. Police were called. The other man, Catalino Morales, a twenty-five-year-old Hispanic newcomer, was placed under arrest.

Howells was urged to take steps to "throw the book" at Morales, and to "teach young Puerto Rican toughs a lesson." Instead, Howells tried a caring tactic.

- He said he would not file charges against the twenty-five-year-old Riverview Terrace man on the condition that Morales work with the neighborhood group to promote a better understanding between the community and its Hispanic residents.

"I don't know if I'm offering a solution to any problems, but I'm offering a first step," said Howells. "If Morales agrees to cooperate— he can become a very useful communication bridge in this community if you want him to," he said.

Catalino Morales put himself at the disposal of Neighbors in Cooperation, and the group agreed to use him to work toward greater community understanding in that neighborhood.

After lengthy discussion on the matter, President Richard Dougherty said, "We'll use him. I plan to walk through the neighborhood with

Morales and talk to people about problems and solutions."

Howells said he could have filed felony, misdemeanor, or summary offenses against Morales, but he added he felt nothing would be accomplished by making Morales a ward of the state and his wife and three children a welfare case.

Questions for Pupils on the Next Lesson. 1. How would you have handled this as a Christian? What are some prime causes of marital strife? 2. What are some of the needs and concerns of persons who have never married? 3. What are some of the attitudes of adults toward children which inhibit good child development? 4. What should Christians understand about divorce in the light of Jesus' teachings on forgiveness? 5. How may communications be improved between husband and wife? 6. What are some of the factors in our society which undermine and threaten relationships between people?

TOPIC FOR YOUTH
LOVE ONE ANOTHER

Other Ways of Handling Problems. How do you cope with conflict? Dr. Eugene Sharpe, a Harvard University Professor, has researched the subject for years. His massive, three-volume study of conflict concludes that there are 193 ways of resolving conflict.

How many of these involve war or force? One, yes, only *one!*

Another way of putting it may be that there are 192 ways of handling conflict situations other than trying to destroy the other with the use of physical power.

What are the caring ways of resolving conflict? What ways do you use?

Envy's Effects. Are you able to be loving when someone else has defeated you or has been shown to be better than you? Does jealousy sometimes keep you from caring?

Ponder the true story which is reported in an account in Greek history. A young man excelled in the Greek public games. He was so outstanding that grateful, admiring fellow citizens erected a statue to him to perpetuate his most glorious victory.

The youth he had beaten out of top honors, however, was disgruntled and envious. Jealous of the champion, the runner-up went out one evening after dark to destroy the statue of his competitor, the famous victor. He rigged ropes and used crowbars to try to move it from its pedestal. After prolonged straining, he finally succeeded. But when the statue came crashing down, it fell on the envious lad, crushing him to death.

Here is a parable for all of us. Anything less than love toward others ultimately destroys!

Love Lets Go. The Rev. Eugene Jerome Dupuis, a Tampa, Florida, revivalist, has named all six of his children, including his recently born third daughter, after himself. His sixth child, a little girl, like the others, is called Eugene Jerome Dupuis, Jr. "I love me," explained Dupuis. He insists that the children do not have nicknames, although "I just have to call, '1-2-3-4-5-6' and they all come running." The girls—3, 5 and 6—don't mind having a male name because they are called by their number, and, besides, 1 and 2 are twins.

Although Dupuis claims to be a born-again Christian, his "I-love-me" answer hints at a cult of self. Naming all of his children after himself is name-cloning, and a kind of conceit. When children are reduced to being merely a number, they are hardly being given the freedom and individuality which Christ can bring.

Love means letting go, and encouraging each other to grow to be the unique person with a special name and special place in the larger human family!

Sentence Sermon to Remember: If you haven't love in your heart, you should throw your hope to the four winds.—Dwight L. Moody.

Questions for Pupils on the Next Lesson: 1. How can Jesus' teachings help your family have more harmonious relationships? 2. What are the implications of Jesus' teachings on sexual relations and marriage, to dating, courtship, and marriage today? 3. What rights and responsibilities do you think you should have as a Christian in your family? 4. What are some of the problems and conflicts in family life which lead to broken marriages? 5. Can a single as well as a married person consider himself/herself carrying out the will of God?

MARCH, APRIL, MAY 1981

THE GOSPEL OF MATTHEW (continued)
THE BOOK OF HEBREWS

LESSON I—MARCH 1

RELATIONSHIPS ON THE KINGDOM

Background Scripture: Matthew 19
Devotional Reading: Deuteronomy 30:15–20

KING JAMES VERSION

MATTHEW 19 1 And it came to pass, *that* when Jesus had finished these sayings, he departed from Galilee, and came into the coasts of Judea beyond Jordan;

2 And great multitudes followed him; and he healed them there.

3 The Pharisees also came unto him, tempting him, and saying unto him, Is it lawful for a man to put away his wife for every cause?

4 And he answered and said unto them, Have ye not read, that he which made *them* at the beginning made them male and female,

5 And said, For this cause shall a man leave father and mother, and shall cleave to his wife: and they twain shall be one flesh?

6 Wherefore they are no more twain, but one flesh. What therefore God hath joined together, let not man put asunder.

7 They say unto him, Why did Moses then command to give a writing of divorcement, and to put her away?

8 He saith unto them, Moses because of the hardness of your hearts suffered you to put away your wives; but from the beginning it was not so.

9 And I say unto you, Whosoever shall put away his wife, except *it be* for fornication, and shall marry another, committeth adultery: and whoso marrieth her which is put away doth commit adultery.

REVISED STANDARD VERSION

MATTHEW 19 1 Now when Jesus had finished these sayings, he went away from Galilee and entered the region of Judea beyond the Jordan; 2 and large crowds followed him, and he healed them there.

3 And Pharisees came up to him and tested him by asking, "Is it lawful to divorce one's wife for any cause?" 4 He answered, "Have you not read that he who made them from the beginning made them male and female, 5 and said, 'For this reason a man shall leave his father and mother and be joined to his wife, and the two shall become one flesh'? 6 So they are no longer two but one flesh. What therefore God has joined together, let not man put asunder." 7 They said to him, "Why then did Moses command one to give a certificate of divorce, and to put her away?" 8 He said to them, "For your hardness of heart Moses allowed you to divorce your wives, but from the beginning it was not so, 9 And I say to you: whosoever divorces his wife, except for unchastity, and marries another, commits adultery."

10 His disciples say unto him, If the case of the man be so with *his* wife, it is not good to marry.

11 But he said unto them, All *men* cannot receive this saying, save *they* to whom it is given.

12 For there are some eunuchs, which were so born from their mother's womb: and there are some eunuchs, which were made eunuchs of men: and there be eunuchs, which have made themselves eunuchs for the kingdom of heaven's sake. He that is able to receive *it*, let him receive *it*.

13 Then were there brought unto him little children, that he should put *his* hands on them, and pray: and the disciples rebuked them.

14 But Jesus said, Suffer little children, and forbid them not, to come unto me; for of such is the kingdom of heaven.

15 And he laid *his* hands on them, and departed thence.

10 The disciples said to him, "If such is the case of a man with his wife, it is not expedient to marry." 11 But he said to them, "Not all men can receive this saying, but only those to whom it is given. 12 For there are eunuchs who have been so from birth, and there are eunuchs who have been made eunuchs by men, and there are eunuchs who have made themselves eunuchs for the sake of the kingdom of heaven. He who is able to receive this, let him receive it."

13 Then children were brought to him that he might lay his hands on them and pray. The disciples rebuked the people; 14 but Jesus said, "Let the children come to me, and do not hinder them; for to such belongs the kingdom of heaven." 15 And he laid his hands on them and went away.

KEY VERSE: With men this is impossible, but with God all things are possible. Matthew 19:26.

HOME DAILY BIBLE READINGS

Feb. 23. M. *Those Whom God Has Joined Together.* Matthew 19:1-12.
Feb. 24. T. *Putting Christ First.* Matthew 19:13-22.
Feb. 25. W. *Forsaking All to Follow Jesus.* Matthew 19:23-30.
Feb. 26. T. *Living Together as Christians.* Romans 12:9-21.
Feb. 27. F. *Transformed Relationships.* Colossians 3:18-24.
Feb. 28. S. *The Unity of the Spirit.* Ephesians 4:1-6.
Mar. 1. S. *Obedience to the Commandments.* Deuteronomy 30:15-20.

BACKGROUND

Jesus has been teaching and healing in Galilee for some time; now we find Him starting for Jerusalem, some sixty or sixty-five miles away. He circles Samaria and walks through Perea, moving southward through Jericho to Jerusalem. That is a long way to walk and in walking it, Matthew says that "great multitudes" met Him, listened to Him, and were healed by Him. Jesus was popular in Perea and Judea, as well as in His own Galilee.

But—there were some who wanted no healing, some with whom He was not popular—some who were busy setting traps for Him and even beginning to make plans for His assassination. Jesus knew that He was walking toward His own death in Jerusalem, and along that road to death He met many who made the way as hard for Him as they could. Somewhere on that road He was met by a group of Pharisees who asked Him a trick question which they thought might destroy His popularity with the common people. It was somewhat like people in our times asking a politician a question which would cost him votes no matter *how* he answered it.

NOTES ON THE PRINTED TEXT

I. . . . "Is it lawful to divorce one's wife for any cause?" Matthew
19:3 (RSV). This was a question that struck to the roots of Jewish life:
marriage and divorce. Marriage was a sacred institution to the Jews;
marriage meant families, and families were the strong basic unit at the
heart of the Jewish nation. Divorce was frowned upon, hated, discouraged as something evil, and there were endless arguments over the
grounds for divorce that were or were not legal and respectable. The
Pharisees questioning Jesus were trying to involve Him in a bitter controversy.

We must understand that among these Jews, at this time, divorce was
something secured by the man, and definitely not by the woman. The
wife had no legal rights; she could be divorced for the most trivial
reasons—for burning a meal, if she went about the house with her hair
unbound, or spoke to men in the street—and *always* because she was
"unclean," a word which, in the hands of the lawyers, could be twisted
around to mean almost anything.

There were two schools of thought or two different ideas about just
what "uncleanliness" was. The school of Shammai said that it had but
one meaning: uncleanliness was fornication or adultery. The school of
Hillel claimed that it meant a lot more than adultery: divorce should be
sought by the husband when the wife committed the unpardonable sin
of criticizing his parents, or when she quarreled with him in a voice that
could be heard next door. Another rabbi thought divorce was justified
when the husband found another woman he liked better than his
spouse. (We in the present century like that one and use it!)

So, the Pharisees asked Jesus, where do *you* stand, with Shammai or
with Hillel? Jesus did not fall into their trap; He simply reminded them
of the law of Creation as God Himself had laid it down: "Therefore shall
a man leave his father and his mother, and shall cleave unto his wife:
and they shall be one flesh" (Genesis 2:24). Based on that, He said,
"What therefore *God* hath joined together, let not man put asunder"
(Matthew 19:6). That meant, plainly, that marriage meant the total giving of two persons to each other. Marriage is a love which thinks more
often of the love of others (love of man and woman, love of their children) than it thinks of love for one's self. Marriage is not an "arrangement": it is a vow made in the presence of God to have such a love for
each other "until death shall us part." Jesus laid this down not as a *law*,
but as a *principle*.

If any generation of Christians ever needed to hear and follow that,
our generation does. Marriage in our day has too often been considered
a joke; indeed, we have come to a time when men and women live
together in open adultery, as if the institution of marriage were an old
useless relic to be cast aside like a pair of old shoes. Marriage is not that
at all in the view of Jesus, who left open the door to divorce only on
grounds of adultery.

It is a high standard, not practiced faithfully today, but it is the *Christian* standard. If we even *tried* to live by His standard, we might not
have had 1,090,000 divorces in the United States last year!

II. They said to him, "Why then did Moses command one to give a certificate of divorce, and to put her away?" Matthew 19:7 (RSV). This was another tricky question. The critics of Jesus often reached back to some declaration of Moses made away back in wilderness days, when they could think of no other argument. Whatever Moses said, they held, *must* be true! To quote a Mosaic law was to settle everything, even in a generation thousands of years removed from Sinai.

The Living Bible has an interesting restatement of this question: "Then why did Moses say a man may divorce his wife by merely writing her a letter of dismissal?" Moses said that because that was the custom in his primitive day—a custom Moses did not like. He did it in order to correct an evil situation—promiscuity and "the hardness of your hearts." In fact, he laid this down not so much as a law but as a concession to fallen nature. "But," said Jesus, "it was not what *God* had originally intended" (verse 8, the Living Bible). Even if Moses said this, the guilt of promiscuity was not wiped out, and the true ideal, the unbreakable eternal truth of the statement in Genesis 2:24 still remained, still was what God meant marriage should be.

III. . . . If the case of the man be so with his wife, it is not good to marry. Matthew 19:10. The disciples had difficulty trying to understand Jesus' ideal of marriage; accustomed to the granting of divorce for a number of reasons or on a number of "grounds," they were stunned at His claim that there was only one ground that should be accepted—that of adultery. If this were true, they said, if a man cannot escape from an unhappy or unfortunate marriage, wouldn't it be better if he never married at all?

Jesus has two answers to that. First, it is only the Christian who can accept this ideal, this ethic of marriage. Without the help of Christ, *any* marriage can fail; with it, any marriage can be a good marriage. Non-Christians do not accept this; Christians *do*, and therefore have a better chance to make their marriages succeed.

Jesus' second answer was also confusing; it dealt with eunuchs—the unsexed men in Jewish society—in, as a matter of fact, many other societies. Some of them were born eunuchs—sexually impotent; others were made eunuchs by men (often these were palace servants in charge of the king's harem). And there was a third class or group in which men "have made themselves eunuchs for the kingdom of heaven's sake" (verse 12). That is, they denied themselves marriage and all sexual activities in order to devote themselves completely to the work of the Kingdom. This is the principle of chastity.

The Roman Catholic Church holds chastity as the perfect condition of Christian work and existence; the Protestants deny this and teach that marriage is "the normal vocation" of *all* men and women. What Jesus is saying here is that it may be necessary for *some* Christian workers or leaders to deny themselves the pleasures of marriage. Sometimes, certainly, it may be necessary for a man engaged in dangerous work to forbid himself the joys of taking unto himself a wife and even leave his parents, to accomplish more for the Kingdom of God. Such a man must choose between two loves—the love of home, wife, and parents and the love of serving Christ. Fortunately, few men have to make such a choice.

So we must choose which way we want, which way we will go. Most Christians are sympathetic to Paul's declaration that "it is better to marry than to burn" (1 Corinthians 7:9). But *if* we marry, let us remember that we are committed, as Christians, to an indissoluble union. Many of us today do *not* believe that. Are we right, or wrong?

The passage concludes with a short (two verses) dissertation on children and the Kingdom of God. We have already discussed this in a previous lesson.

SUGGESTIONS TO TEACHERS

Little Jimmy was uneasy when his mother told him that he would be left with a neighbor for a few days because of a death in the mother's family. Jimmy pondered the news for a few moments, then asked, "Is Mrs. McIlhenny a hugger?" Assured that Mrs. McIlhenny was, indeed, a hugger, Jimmy's anxieties subsided.

God means for us to hug persons and use possessions. Unfortunately, we tend to hug our possessions and use persons. Relationships in God's Kingdom call for an ordering of priorities in which we learn how and what to "hug."

Today's lesson from Matthew 19 discusses the crucial matter of such relationships. Remember that Jesus is not giving tips on etiquette. He is laying it on the line that through Him, God has entered into a new relationship with humans. In a sense, God is a "hugger." Jesus makes it clear that those who have understood the new relationship God has with them also must have a supportive, caring relationship with each other.

Your lesson from today's Scripture falls into three sections: relationships with spouses, with children, and with possessions. Consider each of these relationships in the light of what God has done for you and your class, and in the light of what He intends us to hug most closely.

1. *SPOUSES.* Jesus does not mince words on the subject of marriage and divorce. In an era of permissive attitudes toward the casual affair and alternate lifestyles, His words will probably seem stern to some. Study them carefully. Do not try to water down the meaning. Let your class reflect on their significance. You won't need to spend much time on commenting on the alarming statistics of divorces and marriage breakups; your class already knows something about these. Nearly everyone has his or her own sad tale of a relative or close friend whose marriage has foundered. Some in your class may be divorced, and you must not appear to treat them or anyone judgmentally. You must, however, hold up the norms for Christians in the realm of marriage.

2. *CHILDREN.* Various historians, anthropologists, and sociologists have pointed out that Jesus was the first to accord personhood to children. Just as He gave dignity to women, as Matthew 19 also notes, Jesus also welcomed children and young people and made clear that they, too, had a status equal to adult males in God's realm. Take time in your lesson to reflect on the implications of this. What is your congregation doing to reach out to the younger generation? How do children and

young people perceive the older members of Christ's community to be? How can the relationships be improved in families within your church?

3. *POSSESSIONS*. Christian visitors from the Third World almost always express astonishment at the way North Americans are so obsessed with things and sex. Both articles and others are mistakenly regarded as objects to be hoarded and possessed. In your lesson, give plenty of time to discuss Jesus' comments on riches in Matthew 19. Insist that your class consider the hard implications of these verses. Stress that people are to be hugged, not possessions.

TOPIC FOR ADULTS
DIGNITY OF PERSONS

Fabric of the Universe. "Our gifts are not for ourselves alone, or for our own little tribe—the people we know. They are the means by which our energy and personality are released into life—the means of our giving to others what they lack, and of receiving from them what we lack. . . . None of us is complete alone. To recognize that we are complete only in community is to realize that we need not be threatened by the gifts of others. How else, save through their gifts, can others serve us, bear our burdens, give us new thoughts? When I hold the other down, or put him too high up, community is damaged, and gifts are not offered and received.

"An inner truth always has a corresponding outer reality. Our interdependence is woven through the fabric of the universe. . . ." —Elizabeth O'Connor, *THE NEW COMMUNITY*, Harper & Row.

Deprived of a Parent. About 45 percent of the babies born last year in the United States will spend much of their childhood with only one parent because of the high divorce rate. According to U.S. Census Bureau statistics, because of the rising divorce rate in the overall population, 45 percent of all babies born will be members of one-parent households for some time before they reach the age of eighteen years.

What is your congregation doing to strengthen marriage ties for couples in your Church family? What is it doing to reach out to the single parents in your church and in your community? What is your congregation doing to welcome kids from one-parent households? What are specific ways in which you bestow greater dignity of persons to the victims of such homes?

Drive for Dignity. Jane Addams was a dedicated Christian whose "ministry" led her into social work. For many years, she directed Hull House, in Chicago, where persons of diverse backgrounds in the windy, brawling city were helped to acquire a sense of worth through aid in finding jobs, study courses, training programs, and social assistance.

Jane Addams not only established Hull House, one of the first social settlement houses in the United States, but she also helped found both the National Association for the Advancement of Colored People and the Women's International League for Peace. During World War I, she presided over an International Congress of Women held at The Hague. Delegations were sent to neutral and warring nations urging negotia-

tions to establish peace. Her drive for human dignity for all persons won
her the Nobel Peace Prize in 1931—the first American woman to be so
honored.

As a Christian, Jane Addams once summed up her concern for dignity
for others in the words, "The good we secure for ourselves is precarious
and uncertain . . . until it is secured for all of us and incorporated into
our common life . . . . Nothing could be worse than the fear that one
had given up too soon and left one effort unexpended which might have
saved the world."

Questions for Pupils on the Next Lesson. 1. Is God's love impartial
and constant to those who answer His call? 2. Is the claim that God's
generosity always exceeds one's expectations true in your experience?
3. How do Christians deal with envy and self-righteousness? 4. Is grace
a gift of God or a reward? 5. How do you interpret the parable of the
Laborers in the Vineyard?

TOPIC FOR YOUTH
YOU AND FAMILY RELATIONSHIP

One-Man Band. Don Davis of Hollywood, California, prides himself
on being able to play Beethoven's *Fifth Symphony* alone on four
melody and two percussion instruments at the same time. Davis plunks
a banjo while one arm is strapped to a perpendicular eight-pronged
pendular piano pounder, and uses a semicircular chromatic radially operated centrifugally sliding left-handed glockenspiel. A mouth organ is
held in place by an ingenious device on Davis's neck. Each foot manipu-
lates drums, cymbals, blocks, and other musical instruments. Davis's
"Totalmedia Orchestra," as he calls it, produces a barrage of musical
sounds as he labors mightily to play many instruments simultaneously.

Some listeners question whether it is music. Especially when Davis
attempts classics such as Beethoven's *Fifth*, those who know music
insist that it is impossible for one person, regardless of how talented he
or she may be, to render such a piece as a solo by a one-man band.

Sometimes, we get the notion that we can be "one-man bands" when
it comes to living. We think we can do it all ourselves and do not need
others. As young people, we assume that we don't need our families.
We'll strike up the music our own way, and pride ourselves on playing it
on our own. Like Davis's "orchestra," however, our efforts may be
amusing for a time and even bring us a certain amount of attention.

The real harmony comes from interacting with others, especially in a
family. Family relationships alone can orchestrate many differing personalities into a meaningful whole. God intends for us all, youth, children, and grown-ups to blend our unique talents into a symphony of
mutual concern and support. No "one-man band" Christianity for us in
our families!

The Me-Oriented Society. Department store executives and retail
merchandisers keep a close watch on buying trends. They report a drastic change in emphasis during the past few years. Today, they say, we
live in a "me-oriented" society. Consequently, most sellers espouse a

marketing emphasis known as "ego-intensive selling." They aim to cash in on the me-oriented society.

Ego-intensive selling in the me-oriented society means a hard sell to appeal to your selfishness and vanity. It means putting your comfort and whims ahead of everyone else. It suggests that things take precedence over people.

What does this mean for you and your family? What does this philosophy do to relationships? How do you stand up to the pressures of this kind of sales pitch?

Covenanted in Community for Keeps. Christ's people have a different idea about sex, marriage, and family than the rest of society. Christians think of family relationships in terms of permanent commitments. Christian men and women will not be swayed by comments of those who think it's "square" or "unnecessary" to be covenanted with a husband or wife for life.

For instance, we Christians are not impressed when Francesca Annis, Broadway actress who played Lillie Langtry, the mistress of Edward VII in the "Lillie" TV series, sniffs at marriage and family relationships. Miss Annis arrived in New York with her baby daughter, laughing that the baby's father, Pat Wiseman, and she will not marry. "What's the obsession everybody in America has about getting married?" she asked. Referring to Lillie Langtry's seven "relationships" with various lovers, including Edward VII, Miss Annis was asked if she could imagine having seven "relationships"? Miss Annis said, "I'd hate to limit myself to seven."

Contrast this remark and this attitude to the biblical norms for relationships in marriage and families. Christians affirm that Christ's rule applies to dating, courtship, marriage, and having children.

Sentence Sermon to Remember: A house without a roof can scarcely be a more different home than a family unsheltered by God's friendship and the sense of being always rested in His providential care and guidance.—Horace Bushnell.

Questions for Pupils on the Next Lesson. 1. How can you help others to see that God never plays favorites among those who serve Him? 2. Do you think that God's goodness to you is based on your being good? 3. What does Scripture say about envy? How do you deal with tendencies to be envious? 4. How does an awareness of God's love help you to discover self-acceptance?

GOD'S GENEROSITY

Background Scripture: Matthew 20.
Devotional Reading: Leviticus 20:22–26.

KING JAMES VERSION

MATTHEW 20 1 For the kingdom of heaven is like unto a man *that is* a householder, which went out early in the morning to hire labourers into his vineyard.

2 And when he had agreed with the labourers for a penny a day, he sent them into his vineyard.

3 And he went out about the third hour, and saw others standing idle in the market place,

4 And said unto them; Go ye also into the vineyard, and whatsoever is right I will give you. And they went their way.

5 Again he went out about the sixth and ninth hour, and did likewise.

6 And about the eleventh hour he went out, and found others standing idle, and saith unto them, Why stand ye here all the day idle?

7 They say unto him, Because no man hath hired us. He saith unto them, Go ye also into the vineyard; and whatsoever is right, *that* shall ye receive.

8 So when even was come, the lord of the vineyard saith unto his steward, Call the labourers, and give them *their* hire, beginning from the last unto the first.

9 And when they came that *were hired* about the eleventh hour, they received every man a penny.

10 But when the first came, they supposed that they should have received more; and they likewise received every man a penny.

11 And when they had received *it,* they murmured against the goodman of the house,

12 Saying, These last have wrought *but* one hour, and thou hast made them equal unto us, which have borne the burden and heat of the day.

13 But he answered one of them, and said, Friend, I do thee no wrong: didst not thou agree with me for a penny?

REVISED STANDARD VERSION

MATTHEW 20 1 "For the kingdom of heaven is like a householder who went out early in the morning to hire laborers for his vineyard. 2 After agreeing with the laborers for a denarius a day, he sent them into his vineyard. 3 And going out about the third hour he saw others standing idle in the market place; 4 and to them he said, 'You go into the vineyard too, and whatever is right I will give you.' So they went. 5 Going out again about the sixth hour and the ninth hour, he did the same. 6 And about the eleventh hour he went out and found others standing; and he said to them, 'Why do you stand here idle all day?' 7 They said to him, 'Because no one has hired us.' He said to them, 'You go into the vineyard too.' 8 And when evening came, the owner of the vineyard said to his steward, 'Call the laborers and pay them their wages, beginning with the last, up to the first.' 9 And when those hired about the eleventh hour came, each of them received a denarius. 10 Now when the first came, they thought they would receive more; but each of them also received a denarius. 11 And on receiving it they grumbled at the householder, 12 saying, 'These last worked only one hour, and you have made them equal to us who have borne the burden of the day and the scorching heat.' 13 But he replied to one of them, 'Friend, I am doing you no wrong; did you not agree with me for a denarius? 14 Take what belongs to you, and go; I choose to give to this last as I give to you. 15 Am I not allowed to do what I choose with what belongs to me? Or do you begrudge my generosity?' 16 So the last will be first, and the first last."

14 Take *that* thine *is,* and go thy
way: I will give unto this last, even as
unto thee.

15 Is it not lawful for me to do what I
will with mine own? Is thine eye evil,
because I am good?

16 So the last shall be first, and the
first last: for many be called, but few
chosen.

KEY VERSE: . . . *The Son of man came not to be served but to serve,
and to give his life as a ransom for many.*

Matthew 20:28 (RSV).

HOME DAILY BIBLE READINGS

Mar. 2. M. *Laborers in the Kingdom.* Matthew 20:1–16.
Mar. 3. T. *Greatness in the Kingdom.* Matthew 20:17–28.
Mar. 4. W. *God's Love in Our Hearts.* Romans 5:1–5.
Mar. 5. T. *Reconciliation Through Christ.* Romans 5:6–11.
Mar. 6. F. *The Free Gift.* Romans 5:12–21.
Mar. 7. S. *God's Gift to Believers.* John 1:9–13.
Mar. 8. S. *A Separated People.* Leviticus 20:22–26.

BACKGROUND

The number of parables in the New Testament depends upon what a
parable *is;* lists of what the Bible writers thought to be parables vary
from twenty-seven to fifty-nine, but the generally accepted number is
set at thirty-nine. Eleven of these parables appear in Matthew's Gospel.
He explained that Jesus used parables in His teaching to reveal more
and more of the mysteries of the Kingdom of God—but in the parable we
have for today's lesson, we have a parable almost impossible for the
ordinary man to understand. It has been called "the wallflower of the
parables"—one too often ignored or passed over lightly because its
meaning is not as plain as in other parables. Indeed, there were those—
and there are still those—who understood the parable, but disbelieved
it!

It takes some study to understand it, but when we do understand, it
becomes one of the most revealing and noteworthy of all His parables.

NOTES ON THE PRINTED TEXT

*I. For the kingdom of heaven is like unto a man that is an house-
holder, which went out early in the morning to hire labourers into his
vineyard.* Matthew 20:1. The grape harvest, in Palestine, was taken in
late in September; early in October, the rains came and whatever was
left in the fields was ruined. So the householder was in a hurry to get his
crop under cover; he went out to the marketplace of his town—the place
where the unemployed (not the lazy) stood waiting for someone to hire
them for an hour or a week. Not once did he go to the marketplace, but
five times: early in the morning, then two hours later, then at noon, three
o'clock, and five o'clock. He offered them all the same pay—one denarius (about twenty cents, today) a day. They were all hired for that,
and they all agreed to accept that rate of pay.

But the last of these laborers were hired at "the eleventh hour," or at five o'clock; these had only one hour to work, but they were paid the same wage as those who had worked since six o'clock in the morning! Naturally, the laborers who had worked the full day objected. This wasn't fair!

At first glance, it certainly does not seem to be fair; no self-respecting laborer today would accept any such proposition or inequality of wages, and no modern contractor would accept it, either! But there are several points to be understood here. First of all, the householder was well within his "rights" when he set the wage; it was *his* vineyard not the workers'. Second, the workers agreed to the contract; they were not forced to accept it. And, third, those who objected to the late-hour workers were men interested only in "what they could get out of it"; they didn't care what happened to anyone but themselves, and Jesus in this parable was condemning that attitude.

And He was answering a question put by Peter (Matthew 19:27 RSV): "Lo, we [the disciples] have left everything and followed you. What then shall we have?" He might as well have asked, "What do we get out of the Kingdom?" Jesus told him how wrong he was—and that he had to take another view of work in the Kingdom.

We cannot understand this parable at all until we understand that, parabolically speaking, the householder is God Himself—and that God gives the rewards of life in the Kingdom. *All that we have, comes out of His mercy.* "This story is saying that the great Landowner (God) has every right to reward men any way He wishes. That is His business. Who are we to question Him about heaven's wage scale?"—David A. Redding. His ways may not be the ways of labor and management in our world, but they are still His ways, whether we like it or not.

What else does the story say?

It says much of the compassion of God and of Jesus who was more interested in the plight of the men who were hired at the last hour than He was in the prosperity of the men who worked all day. He came to us not to applaud the successful but to help the poor. He gave us a Church which must be concerned with both spiritual and material need.

It tells us that there is a place in the Kingdom for *every* man, whatever his place and talents may be. There is a place in the Kingdom not only for life-time Christians but for those whom society has rejected, or who come to know Christ late in life. He implies that it is never too late to come and labor in God's vineyard. Come early or late, the door of the Kingdom is always open. There was a thief on a cross beside the cross of Jesus who repented at the very door of death, and Jesus in His infinite compassion said to him, *"To day* shalt thou be with me in paradise" (Luke 23:43). There is joy in heaven over one sinner who repents, and that sinner may be among the first to enter heaven, before the wealthy and the highly placed on earth who had lesser faith than the penitent one. The door is forever open; the arms of God are held open, too, to the prodigals who come late to the Kingdom door. "Many a man in this world whom, as the world counts reward, will be great in the Kingdom, because he never thought in terms of reward but worked for the thrill of the working and for the joy of serving."—William Barclay.

Last but never least, the parable makes clear the *generosity* of God. In the Sermon on the Mount, Jesus reminded His hearers that God "maketh his sun to rise on the evil and on the good, and sendeth rain on the just and the unjust" (Matthew 5:45). That is generosity beyond most human understanding. God gives more: He gives us life itself, He gives us minds and hearts capable of putting ourselves "in tune with the infinite"; He gives us rich soil to catch the rain and give us wheat with which to make bread. He opens for us, through Christ, the gates of the Kingdom, through which we may walk to abundant life on earth and life eternal beyond earth. He opens those gates to *all men,* whatever their race, color, or condition. He gives us gifts beyond reckoning, *and whatever He gives us is unmerited grace.*

Keep it clear: there are no "wages" paid in the Kingdom. Those who really know God never think of wages, or "pay" in the human sense. They work for the sheer joy of working with God; their purpose is not to become rich in gold and silver but to *serve,* to do all that they possibly can do with the talents He has put in their hands. As Bishop Gerald Kennedy puts it, "It (this parable) is our Lord's way of telling us that wages are an inadequate concept altogether when we are being dealt with by God. It is not the rate of pay that is the ultimate consideration, but the generosity of God."

How many of us really realize what we are saying when we repeat the Humble Access to the Communion Services in our Church? Say it slowly, and think deeply, when you take that wine and bread:

> We do not presume to come to this thy table,
> O merciful Lord, trusting in our own
> righteousness, but in thy manifold and
> great mercies. We are not worthy so much as
> gather up the crumbs under thy table. But
> thou art the same Lord, whose mercy is unfailing.

Crumbs, like the poor widow's mite, may be the stuff of which the Kingdom is made—and maintained.

SUGGESTIONS TO TEACHERS

To get this lesson on God's generosity off the launching pad, have your class ponder the most outstanding act of generosity that has been shown to each. Have two or three share the who-how-why-and-what of the act of generosity in his or her personal experience that has most deeply affected him or her. Recall a couple of occasions in your own life where someone has shown exceptional generosity toward you.

If a human can be as generous as these personal reminiscences shown, imagine how much more generous God is! No stingy grouch He! Evidence? Look at some of the incredible news of divine generosity in Matthew 20.

1. *KINDNESS THAT BREAKS THE RULES.* Work with the class on the Parable of the Laborers in the Vineyard. Remember that this is not a lesson in labor-management techniques, nor a treatise on economic

theory, so don't get bogged down in fruitless discussions on how fair or unfair the boss is in the parable. And don't allegorize; the boss is not to be equated with God. The point of the parable is the sheer kindness of the employer, who recognized that men going home without a full day's pay will not have enough to feed their families that night. God's realm is similar to such an act of generosity, says Jesus. Have your class recount more of the "parables" from their own experiences of human generosity, and tie these in with the biblical claim of God's generosity by pointing out that God is the great Giver.

2. *CHRIST WHO SACRIFICES HIS LIFE.* Take time in your lesson to think about the verses about Jesus going to Jerusalem to the Cross (20:17–19). Since you are coming into the Lenten season, you should help your class to understand the supreme act of generosity in history— Jesus Christ's death. Ask our class to comment on why the Cross is paramount in the Christian faith. Urge your people to talk aloud how Christ's sacrifice exemplifies God's generosity toward us.

3. *CONCERN THAT SURMOUNTS SELFISHNESS.* Direct the class's attention also to the scene in which the mother of James and John tries to get preferential treatment in God's realm for her boys (20:20–28). Here is human "generosity" in its most typical form—an enlightened self-interest. Nudge your class into commenting on the way Jesus insists that generosity means serving others rather than contriving to be served. True generosity consists in humility and caring. Relate this truth to the examples of generosity which persons in your class have recounted earlier in the lesson period.

4. *CARING THAT SEES THE NEEDS.* Finally, work with the story of Jesus healing the two blind beggars (20:20–34). Point out how obnoxious these two were. Others saw them as noisy nuisances. Jesus saw them as persons in need. He overlooked their objectionable characteristics. He generously extended new life. God's generosity, remind your class, never regards people as "problems" or objects, but as subjects for His service. Ask your class to offer instances of human need—especially among some people who are unlovely, unloving, and unloveable—in their own experience at this time. What kind of divine generosity is called for in these cases?

TOPIC FOR ADULTS
GOD'S GENEROSITY

Drink Deep! Immediately after World War II, a Quaker relief worker went into a war-torn area of Poland which had been scoured by fighting, death, and famine. Holding out a glass of milk to a little boy whose eyes seemed to fill his face because his little face was so gaunt from starvation, the relief worker offered the milk to the child. The boy reflected on the times he remembered when many had to drink out of one cup and asked, "How deep shall I drink?" The worker, moved by the question, revealing such desperate need, huskily answered, "Drink as deep as you can, son, as deep as you can."

How deep shall I drink of the cup of Christ's mercy?

"As deep as you can, son or daughter," He replies. "As deep as you can." His generosity is greater than you expect!

Compelling Response. A preacher went to the shop of one of his parishioners to get a haircut. The conversation drifted around to the matter of showing our love for the Lord in tangible ways. The preacher suggested rather pointedly that since his business was prospering, he hoped they could count on the barber to contribute liberally to the new missionary budget.

Irritated, the barber replied, "The church is always asking me for help," he exclaimed. "All I hear is money, money, money! I think a person should give what he pleases instead of hearing about all those systematic and proportionate amounts you're always stressing in your sermons."

The pastor said nothing, but when the haircut was finished, he gave his barber friend fifty cents. The barber declared with some anger that it wasn't nearly enough. The pastor replied, "I thought I should give as I felt inclined." "But," the barber protested, "I can't pay the rent or take care of my other expenses if people just give me any amount they happen to have in their pockets."

Producing the rest of his fee, the preacher said, "Nor can the Lord's work be carried on if we don't appreciate His blessings and give back to Him what is rightly His."

Expression of Thanks. A women client of the famous attorney Clarence Darrow felt grateful to Darrow for his efforts on her behalf at the close of a case. She hurried up to Darrow and gushed, "Oh, Mr. Darrow, I don't know how I can ever thank you for what you have done for me!"

Darrow courteously nodded, then replied, "Madame, ever since the Phoenicians invented money, there has been a wonderful way to express your thanks!"

The same words might be applied to God whenever we feel thankful for His generosity toward us. A wonderful way to express our gratitude is through our generous giving of our money to share in His ministry!

Questions to Pupils on the Next Lesson. 1. How can adults at various life stages understand and express responsible citizenship? 2. How can grown-ups be more responsible stewards? 3. How can your congregation help persons find reassurance in Jesus' teaching about God? 4. What does the Great Commandment mean specifically in your everyday life? 5. When might controversy help and when might it hinder our understanding of priorities?

TOPIC FOR YOUTH
GOD IS GENEROUS

From Death House. In 1961, Walter Sher shot and killed a jewelry store owner in Manhasset, Long Island during an armed robbery. He was caught and sentenced to death. After six years in the death house at Sing Sing, his sentence was commuted, and a sentence of life imprisonment was imposed. For the next seventeen years, Sher lived in the harsh world of maximum security state prisons.

"In the first years of confinement," reports Sher, "I was a real tough guy." Then he began to have a change in attitude.

Walter Sher began to study. He secured a high school equivalency diploma. Then he worked toward a B.A. degree through Empire State

College in New York. In 1978, Sher completed a graduate program and was awarded a master's degree in psychological counseling from Goddard College in Plainfield, Vermont. Walter Sher became the first inmate in New York State correctional history to earn an accredited graduate degree while confined to a maximum-security prison.

Walter Sher, however, does not credit the corrections system for his success. "Prison hasn't rehabilitated me," he states. What Sher has learned and what he wants to share with other prisoners is "how a change in attitude may be a possible solution for the peculiar problems of those confined in our prisons."

And how did Walter Sher learn to change in attitude? He gives the credit for his attitudinal change to a generous prison chaplain, the late Rev. Cormac Walsh. Sher describes working for Walsh while Walsh was ministering at the Clinton, New York correctional institution. Walsh's example profoundly affected Sher, and Sher responded to Walsh's generosity in a positive way. Sher hopes to use his counseling degree to help other prisoners.

God's generosity to us through Jesus Christ also produces a powerful, positive response. Anyone who realizes anything of His generosity is impelled to live generously for others.

Failure to Be Generous Costs. God is generous. He expects us, in turn, to be generous with each other. Failure to live generously with others ultimately hurts everyone.

For example, in 1938 U. S. and British oil companies owned or controlled most of the oil deposits in Mexico. These companies greedily refused to pay their Mexican workers decent wages. When the Mexican Supreme Court ruled that the companies had to increase their pay scales, the oil companies would not comply. The Mexican government nationalized the foreign petroleum companies operations in Mexico. Petulantly, the American and British companies removed or destroyed their own equipment, and for years refused to share their advanced drilling techniques with the Mexicans. Consequently, the Mexicans lagged far behind in oil-finding and producing technology for many years.

Today, with huge new oil discoveries on central Mexico's southeast coast, some estimates claim that Mexico may have twice as much oil as Saudi Arabia. Had it not been for the lack of generosity on the part of oil company officials over forty years ago, Mexican oil might well be more cheaply and readily available to us today.

Only the generous person or group, reflecting God's generosity, survives.

"All I Hear Is Money!" The concept of giving *is so important that the Bible refers to it no less than 1,520 times!* Because of all that God has bestowed upon us as His children, gratitude demands that we happily reach into our pockets to further His work in this needy world.

Bumper Sticker Lesson. Seen on street of Illinois town: PLEASE BE PATIENT—GOD ISN'T FINISHED WITH ME YET.

In His generosity, He never is!

Sentence Sermon to Remember: God loveth a cheerful giver.—2 Corinthians 9:7.

Questions for Pupils on the Next Lesson. 1. How may Jesus' teachings be used as a guideline in making moral choices? 2. When it is necessary to disagree, how is it possible to do so without being disagreeable? 3. In a time of conflicting loyalties, how do you establish what your top loyalty is? 4. Where do you find guidance in making commitments consistent with God's requirements? 5. In what specific ways does the Great Commandment apply to your everyday life?

LESSON III—MARCH 15

QUESTIONS OF PRIORITY

Background Scripture: Matthew 21:45–22:46.
Devotional Reading: Psalms 119:169–176.

MATTHEW 22 15 Then went the Pharisees, and took counsel how they might entangle him in *his* talk.

16 And they sent out unto him their disciples with the Herodians, saying, Master, we know that thou art true, and teachest the way of God in truth, neither carest thou for any man: for thou regardest not the person of men.

17 Tell us therefore, What thinkest thou? Is it lawful to give tribute unto Caesar, or not?

18 But Jesus perceived their wickedness, and said, Why tempt ye me, *ye* hypocrites?

19 Shew me the tribute money. And they brought unto him a penny.

20 And he saith unto them Whose is this image and superscription?

21 They say unto him, Caesar's. Then saith he unto them, Render therefore unto Caesar the things which are Caesar's; and unto God the things that are God's.

22 When they had heard *these words,* they marveled, and left him, and went their way.

23 The same day came to him the Sadducees which say that there is no resurrection, and asked him,

24 Saying, Master, Moses said, If a man die, having no children, his brother shall marry his wife, and raise up seed unto his brother.

25 Now there were with us seven brethren: and the first, when he had married a wife, deceased, and having no issue, left his wife unto his brother:

26 Likewise the second also, and the third, unto the seventh.

27 And last of all the woman died also.

28 Therefore in the resurrection, whose wife shall she be of the seven? for they all had her.

29 Jesus answered and said unto them, Ye do err, not knowing the Scriptures, nor the power of God.

MATTHEW 22 15 Then the Pharisees went and took counsel how to entangle him in his talk. 16 And they sent their disciples to him, along with the Herodians, saying, "Teacher, we know that you are true, and teach the way of God truthfully, and care for no man; for you do not regard the position of men. 17 Tell us, then, what you think. Is it lawful to pay taxes to Caesar, or not?" 18 But Jesus, aware of their malice, said, "Why put me to the test, you hypocrites? 19 Show me the money for the tax." And they brought him a coin. 20 And Jesus said to them, "Whose likeness and inscription is this?" 21 They said, "Caesar's." Then he said to them, "Render therefore to Caesar the things that are Caesar's, and to God the things that are God's." 22 When they heard it, they marveled; and they left him and went away.

23 The same day Sadducees came to him, who say that there is no resurrection; and they asked him a question, 24 saying, "Teacher, Moses said, 'If a man dies, having no children, his brother must marry the widow, and raise up children for his brother.' 25 Now there were seven brothers among us; the first married, and died, and having no children left his wife to his brother. 26 So too the second and third, down to the seventh. 27 After them all, the woman died. 28 In the resurrection, therefore, to which of the seven will she be wife? For they all had her."

29 But Jesus answered them, "You are wrong, because you know neither the scriptures nor the power of God. 30

30 For in the resurrection they neither marry, nor are given in marriage, but are as the angels of God in heaven.

31 But as touching the resurrection of the dead, have ye not read that which was spoken unto you by God, saying,

32 I am the God of Abraham, and the God of Isaac, and the God of Jacob? God is not the God of the dead, but of the living.

For in the resurrection they neither marry nor are given in marriage, but are like angels in heaven. 31 And as for the resurrection of the dead, have you not read what was said to you by God, 32 'I am the God of Abraham, and the God of Isaac, and the God of Jacob'? He is not God of the dead, but of the living."

KEY VERSE: . . . Render therefore to Caesar the things which are Caesar's; and to God the things that are God's. Matthew 22:21.

HOME DAILY BIBLE READINGS

Mar. 9. M. *The Priority of Faith.* Matthew 21:18–22.
Mar. 10. T. *"By What Authority . . .?"* Matthew 21:23–27.
Mar. 11. W. *The Priority of Deeds Over Words.* Matthew 21:28–32.
Mar. 12. T. *The Stone the Builders Rejected.* Matthew 21:33–44.
Mar. 13. F. *Those Who Enter the Kingdom.* Matthew 22:1–14.
Mar. 14. S. *Render to God His Dues.* Matthew 22:15–22.
Mar. 15. S. *Sacrificing All for Christ.* Philippians 3:7–11.

BACKGROUND

This lesson marks a turning point in the life and ministry of Jesus. Up to this point, His preaching had been successful; more and more came to hear Him, and to love what they heard. But there were some in Palestine who did not agree with Him, who were frightened by what He said. These were certain Pharisees and Sadducees, who felt that Jesus was questioning their faith and their sincerity and—worst of all—threatening their authority. These Jewish leaders had no intention of allowing a carpenter's son to challenge their leadership or destroy their power and control in the religious establishment of Israel.

But—how? How could they stop this Man of Nazareth? There were two ways open to them: the way of violence, and the way of defamation or ridicule. If you can make an opponent look ridiculous, or ignorant, or confused about what he is saying, you have him in a trap and at a disadvantage. If they could trick Jesus into saying something that even *seemed* ridiculous, or which stood in opposition of normally accepted ideas or procedures, *that* might defeat Him and ruin His popularity.

And that was exactly what the Pharisees and the Sadducees were doing in our lesson. They laid what they thought were clever traps in which Jesus might destroy Himself by giving wrong answers to their questions.

NOTES ON THE PRINTED TEXT

I. ". . . Is it lawful to pay taxes to Caesar, or not? Matthew 22:17 (RSV). This, they thought, was clever; it turned out to be a boomerang. First, the Pharisees and Herodians (Jewish collaborators who pretended to be loyal Jews but who actually were serving the Roman puppet

Herod) flattered Him. Like a modern Senator who will address another
Senator whom he would destroy as "The Honorable Senator from . . ."
these opponents of Jesus addressed Him as One who spoke the way of
God in truth, regardless of the positions of men. Jesus called them hypocrites for saying that, for they lied when they said it.

Was it lawful to pay tribute—taxes—to Rome? They struck a sensitive
nerve when they mentioned taxes; every Jew in Palestine struggled
under a heavy Roman-levied system of taxation. (Has there *ever* been a
happy taxpayer, anywhere?) They paid crop taxes, oil and wine taxes,
income taxes, and a poll tax that was paid by every male Jew from age
fourteen to age sixty-five and every female from age twelve to sixty-five.
Now see the dilemma in which they put Jesus. If He approved of such
taxation, every Jew in the land would turn from Him. If he disapproved
of it, the Romans would throw Him in jail. How could He answer it?

He answered by having them produce a coin; on that coin was
stamped the image of Caesar. "All right," said Jesus; "then give it to
Caesar, for it is his. Give him what belongs to him; and give God what
belongs to *Him!*" That was a way of saying that the citizen of the state
owes a debt to the heads of State who are appointed to keep the peace,
and to render other necessary public services. The Christian has a duty
to "Caesar" then and now. But there are times when, as Peter said at a
later time, "We ought to obey God rather than men" (Acts 5:29). Times,
that is, when allegiance to God must overrule allegiance to an *oppressive* Caesar. There are times and circumstances in which conscience and
faith and principle *must* prevail. (Such as "No taxation without repre-
sentation.")

You see, we live in two worlds at once: Caesar's (material, political)
world, and God's (spiritual) world. We *must* have government in
Caesar's world, lest we fall into anarchy—but Jesus never suggested that
any man was obligated to support a corrupt or evil government. The final
authority and sovereignty is that of God; the State can justly demand our
money and our services, but it can never demand our souls or the obedience which we owe only to God.

How do we determine what is God's and what is Caesar's? Jesus
leaves that to the individual conscience.

*II. "In the resurrection, therefore, to which of the seven will she be
wife?"* Matthew 22:28 (rsv). The Pharisees had put to Jesus the question of Caesar and taxes; now the Sadducees spoke up. They asked
questions about the resurrection and about a man who had seven
wives—an odd combination, and rather ridiculous questions about both.

We must understand the thinking of both Pharisees and Sadducees, in
this matter of resurrection. On this subject, there was a great deal of
controversy among the Jews, although belief in resurrection does not
appear often in the Old Testament, and when it does, is usually in its
later books, like the Book of Daniel. The Pharisees believed in it; the
Sadducees did not—they accepted only the authority of the Pentateuch,
or the original Mosaic Law. They claimed that life after death could not
be proved by any quotation from the Pentateuch, and they put to Jesus a
question which they thought would make the doctrine of the resurrection a false and absurd doctrine. They put a question that was absurd.

The Sadducees tried to base their question on a quotation from Moses (in the Pentateuch): if a man died and left no children, his brother should marry the widow and raise children for his brother. Now, they said, suppose she married *seven* of her husbands brothers (a large order, even in *our* times!). In the resurrection, if there be any resurrection, whose wife would she be? To which of the seven would she "belong?" It was another "catch" question, and it was nonsense.

Jesus turned their reference to Scripture back upon them; He told them that they were sadly wrong, sadly ignorant of the Scriptures *and of the power of God.* How, he asked, could they explain the words of God in their precious Pentateuch, "I am . . . . the God of Abraham, the God of Isaac, and the God of Jacob" (Exodus 3:6)? If these three fathers of Israel, dead for so long, were not alive in the presence of God, then God would have said, "I *was* the God of Abraham, . . ." God said, "I *am* not the God of the dead, but of *the living.*" They had no recorded answer to *that;* they knew that they had blundered. They did not understand that life after death cannot be thought of in earthly terms and that life in heaven is not the same as life on earth. Marriage and the production of children are a part of this world, not of the next, where there is no marriage or giving in marriage. By their very nature, the angels are not concerned with such idle questions as to whose wife the poor woman would be.

Resurrection is resurrection to a wholly new form of existence. We once saw a man who was just about the homeliest man in the world get up in a conference in which the delegates were trying to prove that we would all be exactly the same in the next world as we are in this world; he pointed to his poor ugly face and asked them, "Are you saying that I will have to wear this face through all eternity?" The answer must be *No.* In eternity we are raised a *better* being than we are on this earth. Said the Apostle Paul of the Resurrection and the body: "It is sown a natural body; it is raised a spiritual body"—a transformed body—and still *alive.*

Thus ended the Sadducean debate—thus ends all debates on the resurrection for those who truly know and believe in the power of God to transform.

SUGGESTIONS TO TEACHERS

In the last fifty years, a new field of expertise known as *Management* has evolved. Management experts draw upon scientific studies in many disciplines, including behavioral sciences and engineering, to offer sound principles for the efficient and effective operation of an enterprise. Nearly every organization, from giants like General Motors to midgets like a church-school class, use these management principles. One of the key components of responsible management is Priority-Setting. Long before the studies and books on management were done, Jesus was insisting that His followers keep proper priorities in life. Your lesson today is to facilitate the process of making priorities among your class members.

The Scriptural material offers many examples of arranging priorities.

Jesus emphasizes that God and His realm must come out at the top of the list. His parables and conversations are graphic illustrations of how a disciple must sort out his or her life so that nothing will edge out serving in His Kingdom.

You will find at least six down-to-earth cases of where the question of priorities often causes difficulties.

1. *BUSINESS.* In the parable of the king's son's wedding, guests turn down royal invitations on the grounds of being too preoccupied with their own affairs. Such discourtesy shocked Jesus' hearers. Our refusal to celebrate the joy of God's rule is equally rude, Jesus lets us know. Not even business may be placed ahead of God!

2. *TIME.* The wedding guest without the proper garment had not taken time to pick up suitable attire at the door. This guest's effrontery also shocked Jesus' hearers. Jesus' parable is a startling lesson in priority-setting in regard to time. Have your class work carefully on how each one uses the gift of each twenty-four hours, perhaps doing "time studies." How much time is given to Christ?

3. *STATE.* Everyone is familiar with "Render unto Caesar the things that are Caesar's," but not everyone remembers that Jesus goes on to command His followers to give to God His due. In fact, Jesus insists that His people must put loyalty to God even ahead of loyalty to the State.

4. *CUSTOM.* The absurd trick question about the hypothetical woman who was wife to each of seven brothers also reflected how many wanted to put custom ahead of trust. Custom can be good, but if it becomes an end in itself, it can edge out God. What are customs which have been allowed to become almost "sacred" in your church, or in your community, or in your life?

5. *RELIGION.* Strangely, the forms of faith may take over for faith. Religion can be put ahead of God! The question about which is the greatest commandment (21:34–40) displays a man who had his priorities mixed up. Give examples where rules and systems, discussions and dogma may be placed in first position, rather than the living Lord.

6. *TRADITION.* Jesus' comments about the place of David in His hearers' lives point up the way that following tradition can take higher priority than obeying God. Many traditions, of course, are helpful, but they must always be used as aids to faith and never objects of faith!

TOPIC FOR ADULTS
QUESTIONS OF PRIORITY

Give Yourself What? "The self-denial pattern of Lent stands in vivid contrast to the prevailing pattern of our society, which is that you really owe it to yourself to buy this or that. Over against this, we feel a certain embarrassment over Jesus' reminder that a man's life does not consist in the abundance of his possessions.

"The issue is not one of few or many possessions. The issue is whether or not we recognize that possessions were meant to serve life, and that life comes first. We make it the other way around: Man serving possessions, being mastered by his possessions.

"It is conceded that if we are to have an expanding economy based on mass production we cannot deny the necessity for mass consumption of new goods. For this, advertising is obviously essential. Yet there is a dilemma. We are being carried along by a process that is becoming an end in itself and which threatens to overwhelm us. There is a loss in proportion in living when we become so easily and so quickly dissatisfied with last year's models."—Vance Packard, *The Hidden Persuaders*.

Peace Priorities. "Defense Secretary Howard Brown and Secretary of Energy James Schlesinger recently said the U.S. would 'defend its vital interest in the Middle East and Persian Gulf with military force if necessary.' Vital interest, of course, is oil.

"It seems we are willing to defend whatever business we have anywhere.

"Much like the ancient Roman Empire that dominated militarily its world.

"What does it all mean? According to Matthew Spetter, associate professor at the Peace Institute, Manhattan College, Bronx: 'Ever since we assumed the role of empire, seeking our "manifest destiny" by entanglement on foreign shores, we have simply fallen into the classic trap of believing our own propaganda. Our propaganda image is that our aims and actions are clean and the aims and actions of our adversaries are foul. Of course, our opponents see us in a similar fashion.'

"The argument that peace can be preserved by being more mightily armed than any enemy is hardly plausible when we consider Hitler. His Germany was the most heavily prepared-for-war nation on earth, but that neither preserved peace nor achieved victory.

"Hitler left a legacy of violence, according to Jacques Ellul. Many nations fell into the trap of adopting Hitler's god, his propaganda. Said Ellul: 'There can be no doubt that it was the Hitler movement that loosed the reign of violence in the world. . . . Hilter won his war after all: his enemies imitate him.'

"Jesus wept over Jerusalem because it did not know the 'things that make for peace,' anticipating the complete destruction of the city.

"This old world of ours does not seem to know what makes for peace, cannot make up its mind whether it be guns, bullets, oil, power, or hearts washed clean of avarice, prejudice, lust, idolatry, violence. While most people profess faith in what they consider the true God, they nevertheless pay homage, like Amaziah, to lesser deities, idols, superstitions.

"That our troops are all over the world indicates that what happens elsewhere affects us, whether in Iran or Diego Garcia. We must sorrowfully confess our involvement in a humanity needing salvation—this humanity to which God comes again and again through His Spirit with warnings of dire consequences to unbelievers but also with promises of blessedness to all who change their minds and believe truly in Him." By Rev. Joseph B. Mohr, *Call Chronicle*, Allentown, Pennsylvania, March 3, 1979.

Business Priorities. A chemical company which dumped tons of toxic chemicals into waste sites at Niagara Falls, New York, knew the health of nearby residents was threatened twenty years before pregnant women and young children were evacuated.

An official of the Hooker Chemical Corporation said residents of the

Love Canal area of Niagara Falls were not warned because the company was afraid of legal action. If Hooker had acted, residents of Love Canal would have been spared exposure to the chemicals.

Six present or former Hooker executives testified about various internal company documents demonstrating the firm was aware of serious pollution problems long before their dangers were publicly known.

One Hooker document dated June 18, 1958, reported that children were using the dump site as a playground. Some children had been burned by the chemicals.

According to another memo, the company knew by June 21, 1977, that the chemicals had substantially leaked from the site, yet no action was taken.

The priorities of business and industry must always be those of human concern. Ironically, the name of the area contaminated by the Hooker Chemical Company's callousness is called the "Love Canal." The business of everyone is to keep the channels of caring—the "love canals" between humans in all areas of society—pure and open.

Questions for Pupils on the Next Lesson. 1. What actions could adults take to foster hope in the light of population, nuclear, and environmental crises? 2. How are Christians to understand natural disasters in the light of the scriptural material in this lesson? 3. How do Christians assess the speculation about signs of the end of the world? 4. How can Christians avoid the extremes regarding the promise of Christ's return? 5. How can a Christian be realistic without being pessimistic about the times in which he or she lives?

TOPIC FOR YOUTH
PUTTING GOD FIRST

Emotional Drop-Out. Putting God first means permitting God to help you keep growing. Putting anything else first means preventing the maturing process to take place.

Ralph Waite, for example, once allowed drinking to be put first in his life.

Waite, who plays John Walton on the television series "The Waltons," says he's a "recovering alcoholic" who missed a great deal of what life has to offer because of drinking. "If they had taken attendance for my life, I'd have been marked absent," he said. Waite, fifty, said he began drinking at seventeen "behind the gym at high school dances" and continued until age forty-four. "One characteristic of the disease is that when you start drinking, you stop growing emotionally and spiritually. And when I stopped drinking at the age of forty-four, I was emotionally seventeen."

Sympathy for the Suffering. Abraham Lincoln is loved because, in putting God first, he had priorities which he felt for the hurting and oppressed.

One of the most characteristic incidents in the life of Abraham Lincoln occurred when he was a young lawyer riding home from court with a company of lawyers. He spied two little birds by the roadside that had been blown out of their nest. He dismounted and searched for the nest and the mother. Half an hour afterwards he overtook his brother lawyers, who laughed at him. In a most serious tone Lincoln said to them, "Gentlemen, I could not have slept tonight if I had not given those little birds back to their mother."

There spoke out the big loving heart which afterwards throbbed in sympathy for a whole race that lay suffering by the wayside—wronged and wounded by years of bondage. We count that one of the finest of Lincoln's innumerable strokes of heart eloquence.

Paper Idols. You may think you put God first, but you actually find yourself pressured and tempted to serve paper gods, each one 2/5⁄8 inches wide by 6⅛ inches long, and .0043 inches thick. Each of these idols has a life span of about eighteen months. It takes 490 of them to weigh one pound. Two hundred thirty-three of them stacked together measure exactly one inch in height. There are over two billion of them in circulation.

What are these paper idols which claim such a disproportionate amount of your time, energy, interest?

Give up?

Dollar bills!

Remember to put God first, not these paper gods!

Sentence Sermon to Remember: Choose you this day whom ye will serve.—Joshua 24:15.

Questions for Pupils on the Next Lesson. 1. What are the dangers of a life uncommitted to God? 2. Are Christians exempt from suffering simply because they are Christians? 3. How can you prepare yourself to adjust to changes in life? 4. What are the dangers of being led astray by false prophets? 5. How can you tell the difference between a false prophet and a true one?

LESSON IV—MARCH 22

SIGNS OF THE END

Background Scripture: Matthew 23–24:35.
Devotional Reading: Joshua 23:14–16.

KING JAMES VERSION

MATTHEW 23 37 O Jerusalem, Jerusalem, *thou* that killest the prophets, and stonest them which are sent unto thee, how often would I have gathered thy children together, even as a hen gathereth her chickens under *her* wings, and ye would not!

38 Behold, your house is left unto you desolate.

39 For I say unto you, Ye shall not see me henceforth, till ye shall say, Blessed *is* he that cometh in the name of the Lord.

24 1 And Jesus went out, and departed from the temple: and his disciples came to *him* for to shew him the buildings of the temple.

2 And Jesus said unto them, See ye not all these things? verily I say unto you, There shall not be left here one stone upon another, that shall not be thrown down.

3 And as he sat upon the mount of Olives, the disciples came unto him privately, saying, Tell us, when shall these things be? and what *shall be* the sign of thy coming, and of the end of the world?

4 And Jesus answered and said unto them, Take heed that no man deceive you.

5 For many shall come in my name, saying, I am Christ; and shall deceive many.

6 And ye shall hear of wars and rumours of wars: see that ye be not troubled: for all *these things* must come to pass, but the end is not yet.

7 For nation shall rise against nation, and kingdom against kingdom: and there shall be famines, and pestilences, and earthquakes, in divers places.

8 All these *are* the beginning of sorrows.

9 Then shall they deliver you up to be afflicted, and shall kill you: and ye shall be hated of all nations for my name's sake.

REVISED STANDARD VERSION

MATTHEW 23 37 "O Jerusalem, Jerusalem, killing the prophets and stoning those who are sent to you! How often would I have gathered your children together as a hen gathers her brood under her wings, and you would not! 38 Behold, your house is forsaken and desolate. 39 For I tell you, you will not see me again, until you say, 'Blessed is he who comes in the name of the Lord.' "

24 1 Jesus left the temple and was going away, when his disciples came to point out to him the buildings of the temple. 2 But he answered them, "You see all these, do you not? Truly, I say to you, there will not be left here one stone upon another, that will not be thrown down."

3 As he sat on the Mount of Olives, the disciples came to him privately, saying, "Tell us, when will this be, and what will be the sign of your coming and of the close of the age?" 4 And Jesus answered them, "Take heed that no one leads you astray. 5 For many will come in my name, saying, 'I am the Christ,' and they will lead many astray. 6 And you will hear of wars and rumors of wars; see that you are not alarmed; for this must take place, but the end is not yet. 7 For nation will rise against nation, and kingdom against kingdom, and there will be famines and earthquakes in various places: 8 all this is but the beginning of the birth-pangs.

9 "Then they will deliver you up to tribulation, and put you to death; and you will be hated by all nations for my name's sake. 10 And then many will

10 And then shall many be offended, and shall betray one another, and shall hate one another.

11 And many false prophets shall rise, and shall deceive many.

12 And because iniquity shall abound, the love of many shall wax cold.

13 But he that shall endure unto the end, the same shall be saved.

14 And this gospel of the kingdom shall be preached in all the world for a witness unto all nations; and then shall the end come.

fall away, and betray one another, and hate one another. 11 And many false prophets will arise and lead many astray. 12 And because wickedness is multiplied, most men's love will grow cold. 13 But he who endures to the end will be saved. 14 And this gospel of the kingdom will be preached throughout the whole world, as a testimony to all nations; and then the end will come.

KEY VERSE: *Heaven and earth shall pass away, but my words shall not pass away.* Matthew 24:35.

HOME DAILY BIBLE READINGS

Mar. 16. M. *The Greatest in the Kingdom.* Matthew 23:1–12.
Mar. 17. T. *Blind Guides.* Matthew 23:13–22.
Mar. 18. W. *Leaders Who Are Hypocrites.* Matthew 23:23–32.
Mar. 19. T. *Sufferings Before the End.* Matthew 24:1–14.
Mar. 20. F. *False Christs.* Matthew 24:15–28.
Mar. 21. S. *The Last Days.* Matthew 24:29–35.
Mar. 22. S. *Keeping the Covenant.* Joshua 23:14–16.

BACKGROUND

Jesus has just come through one of His most severe controversies with the scribes and the Pharisees (23:13–36). In righteous anger, He calls them hypocrites, fools, serpents of a generation of vipers, and blind guides of the blind. His anger was aroused over their sin of refusing to accept Him for what He is, and for attempting to lead men not to God but to Phariseeism. That is still a sin too common among those of us who claim a monopoly on God and His truth.

His condemnation reaches its peak when He prophesies bitter punishment to fall upon them. Seldom has Jesus been as angry as this, and yet there is a note of heartbreaking sorrow in it all—sorrow for the people of Jerusalem who have suffered at the hands of these false, blind leaders of the innocent. He speaks not only to them, but to those of us who may have a bit of the Pharisee in our hearts and minds without knowing it. So we must listen to His words as though He were speaking directly to us.

NOTES ON THE PRINTED TEXT

I. "O Jerusalem, Jerusalem, killing the prophets and stoning those who are sent to you! How often would I have gathered your children together as a hen gathers her brood under her wings, and you would not! Matthew 23:37 (RSV). Jesus loved this Jerusalem, these people in the Holy City. Strangely, Matthew, Mark, and Luke mention no visits of Jesus to Jerusalem between the beginning of His ministry to the day of the Last Supper, but John mentions five visits: see John 2:13, 5:1, 7:14, 10:22, 23 and 12:12. John must be right: Jesus must have known this city and people well to cry out in tears, "How often would I . . . *and you would not!*

That was the reason for His agonized cry. He had offered salvation to the city and the people—*and they had rejected Him.* God loves New York City, in spite of its fearful crime and immorality. God loves Paris, Rome, Moscow, Berlin, Tokyo, London—because He loves their *people.* He offers all of them entry into His Kingdom, and it is their choice whether to accept or reject. We do not have to look far, from Iran to anywhere to find Him more generally rejected than accepted. Jesus must be weeping over it.

He predicts disaster when they reject, but not permanent destruction. God bears with their sinning, in unlimited love. They may turn their backs on Him now, but they will see Him again, coming as their King, and they will applaud Him then. We may not deserve it, but that is His promise.

II. . . . *There shall not be left here one stone upon another, that shall not be thrown down.* Matthew 24:2. The disciples "came to point out to him the buildings of the temple" (verse 1 RSV). We wonder why, what was in their minds when they did that? He had surely seen those buildings before this. Perhaps it was because of the ancient pride of the Jews in the beauty and glory of the Temple. Naturally the disciples were astounded when He told them that the day would come when this Temple would be brought down in ruins.

This was a prophecy which literally became true; the Temple Jesus was looking at, that day, was completely destroyed forty years after His Crucifixion—destroyed by the Romans under Titus, in A.D. 70, and never rebuilt. Just for the record, another, previous temple had been destroyed in 587 B.C. But it is more than probable that Jesus was not speaking of the ruin of Temple *buildings* but rather of the end of what we might call the Temple age. He was saying that no longer would the temple be the central place of worship or the place in which the divine will of God was revealed to men. In Matthew 12:6, He says that "in this place is one greater than the temple," meaning Himself. In John 2, we have a clarification of this prophecy; here Jesus says, "Destroy this temple, and in three days (after the Resurrection) I will raise it up" (John 2:19). John makes clear what was behind that statement when he adds, "But he spoke of the temple of his body" (John 2:21). His body, and His person.

In other words, this was the end of an *age.* The Jews believed that all time was divided into two ages: the present age and the golden age in which God would intervene and rule. At the end of the first wicked age, there would come The Day of the Lord, a day of terror and destruction in which all that was wrong and evil would be wiped out and all that was good and Godly would be established. It was this far-off day of the coming of the Messiah that Jesus was speaking, not of the imminent destruction of the Temple on Mount Moriah.

Many a temple in many a polluted heart must be destroyed before many of us can even hope to see Jesus in proper perspective, and to worship Him in spirit and in truth. This is not to downgrade our temple of the Church; it is to upgrade the necessity of finding and worshiping Christ in the temple of the human, cleansed and forgiven heart.

III. . . . Tell us, when shall these things be? and what shall be the sign of thy coming, and of the end of the world? Matthew 24:3. The Jews had a tradition that on the last day of the first age God would appear on the Mount of Olives, and from that "headquarters" lead a final war against the nations of the world (*see* Zechariah 14). They believed that and they looked forward to it, but they did not know just *when* God would so appear. Daniel wrote at great length about it and confusingly; even as great a prophet as he could not accurately or finally set the exact date. Men have been trying to "pinpoint" the exact date without much success ever since. We still ask "when," and by what signs shall we know that the great event is upon us?

Jesus gave His disciples two signs. The first would be the appearance of false messiahs. There would come scheming men who could claim that they were the promised Messiah, and they would preach false doctrine and, often they would use religion as a cover for political gains. Just before Titus came to burn Jerusalem, there were many national leaders with Messianic pretensions deceiving the people, calling for insurrections and piling up fortunes for themselves. We who live in 1981 are plagued with them, too; more than one living "evangelist" is drawing crowds and telling them that he is the reincarnation of Jesus. We can meet their followers on the streets of our larger cities, begging contributions for the work of their new "Jesus" who lives in luxury on huge estates while his poor duped followers eat humble bread and live in dormitories far from luxurious. Beware the false Messiah! (Is this a sign in our times that we have come "to the end of an age?")

Sign No. 2.: There will be wars and rumors of wars, famines, catastrophes, tremblings of the earth, whole nations in revolt against God, crisis after crisis. We have all of this, in our times, with many crying "The end is near!" Probably some in every generation in history have uttered that cry—but the end is not yet. Jesus warns us not to be alarmed, not to go into panic, not let it trouble our faith. It is not our privilege to set a date on the end of things; that is God's privilege.

It is a dismal outlook, but Jesus sounds a hopeful note in Matthew 24:13 RSV: "But he who endures to the end will be saved." "He" is the believer who puts his trust in God whatever happens; he is one who goes about his Father's business regardless of threats of disaster. Verse 14 contains an eloquent plea for missionaries who will go out when the sky is darkest to preach the saving Christ to all the world. When all nations have heard that, the end will come.

Yes, we have the same "signs" today, but we still have no right just to sit down and wait for the end: there is work for us to do! The world must know this message of salvation, for its proclamation is a necessary prelude to the end of the world.

SUGGESTIONS TO TEACHERS

The horrible episode in Jonestown, Guyana in 1978, when over 900 disciples of the Rev. James Jones gulped Kool-aid laced with potassium cyanide, brought a shudder to every thinking person. Why had members of Jones's Peoples' Temple passively followed him to a hideaway in the

South American jungle and to their deaths? Why do the sects and cults (over 3,000 in the U.S. today according to the count) attract so many?

In the face of difficult times, how do we keep our balance? Where do we get our bearings? What does Scripture tell us about the future?

These are some of the many questions which will surface in today's lesson. As teacher, you may find some of these issues steering the lesson instead of the other way around.

As always, begin with Jesus Christ and His teachings in the scriptural material. Today's lesson from Matthew 23, 24 takes up signs of the end. Jesus warns His followers to be wary. Specifically, He warns about three dangers when the subject of the signs of the end comes up.

1. *PHARISAICAL RELIGION.* Make a list of the woes pronounced by Jesus against the scribes and Pharisees. Pharisaism, your class should note, consists of a pose versus piety, haughtiness versus humility. It is a religion of meticulously straining out gnats but gulping down camels, or stressing minor stuff while neglecting the major matters. Pharisaism remembers the externals, but forgets the internal. Don't let your class think that Pharisaism stopped in New Testament times. Evoke thinking and example-giving of emphasizing the insignificant while overlooking the significant in the life of the Church, the nation, your congregation, your community, and each person's family and person.

2. *FAINT-HEARTED COMMITMENT.* Jesus minces no words about how Christians may face rough times. He promises no easy time of it for His followers. "Remain faithful!" is the sense of His words in this passage for today. The faithless or faint-hearted believer will not be able to survive, He warns.

Insist that your class discuss the urgency of having a rugged faith in order to survive whatever the future may bring for Christians. Have your group comment on the threats to remaining faithful in their own personal experience. What will be the chief rivals to the Gospel in the next five years? How will your people cope with the attempts to undermine their trust in Christ?

3. *FALSE DELIVERERS.* Emphasize Jesus' blunt warnings about phony messiahs. Remind your people that Jesus particularly warns against those who try to set dates for the End. Note also that He cautions against following those who try to establish personality cults, revolving around themselves instead of Him. In days of bleak headlines, big talkers with extravagant and egocentric claims always appear.

Most important, enable your class to understand that Jesus Christ is *the* Deliverer. His death and Resurrection already have dealt with the fears of the unknown so that we can face the future with calm and confidence!

TOPIC FOR ADULTS
FACING THE FUTURE WITH GOD

Kon-Tiki Reminder. The late Jean Monnet was the father of European unity. Born in the days of Queen Victoria, when Grover Cleveland was President of the United States and Alexander III was Czar of the old Russia, this great Frenchman served France in critical missions during both World Wars. However, Monnet loved France too much to be a nationalist. Jean Monnet realized that common problems called for common policies to defend a common civilization. His vision grew out of the united Allied Commands of the two World Wars, and resulted in the European Common Market. He saw human problems but he also saw human possibilities.

On Monnet's desk was a photograph of the *Kon-Tiki.* The *Kon-Tiki* was a strange sea-going craft which explorers under Heyerdahl used. The *Kon-Tiki's* progress depended not upon the troubled surface of the waters of the world, but on the deep-running tides. Monnet believed that there are other kinds of deep-running tides in life, and that his task and all nations' task was to hitch themselves to those tides.

Christians know that God has His own tides operating in human affairs. Christians do not despair, but ride out all storms with confidence.

As Monnet kept the *Kon-Tiki* as a symbol, let Christ's people look to the empty Cross as a reminder of God's ultimate victory. His people also continue to face the future with hope. The tide of Christ is running!

Stress-Filled Days. Recent studies disclose that stress is taking a greater toll on Americans than most acknowledge. One survey, conducted by the research firm of Yankelovich, Skelly, and White, Inc. for General Mills Inc., of a cross section of America's 58 million families in 1979, revealed that just living apparently can be hazardous to one's health. More than eight out of ten cited the need for less stress in their lives. Most acknowledged that it is harder to cope now with the problems of daily living than it was a few years ago. In addition to inflation, money worries, fear of crime, concern over personal safety, family problems and pressures of juggling demands of family, job, and personal leisure, most cited uneasiness about the future as a major source of stress in their lives.

According to the President's Commission on Mental Health, over 20 million people—15 percent of the population—are under such severe stress that they experience symptoms of depression and anxiety requiring mental health care.

Jesus prepares His followers to be prepared for days of tension and trials. He does not promise His disciples that they will be exempt from problems. He realistically states that there will be difficult times. However, Jesus Christ also enables His people to maintain an emotional and spiritual equilibrium.

"Ani-Ma-Anim." Part of the liturgy of the Jewish synagogue is the ancient Hebrew chant, the *Ani-Ma-anim.* Translated from Hebrew, the beautiful prayer means; "I affirm, with unbroken firmness, that the Messiah will come. And even if He tarries, even so, I affirm it."

During the terrible days in which the entire Jewish populations of Nazi-controlled cities were rounded up, on countless occasions the men, women, and children marched to the freight cars carrying them to the death camps with the *Ani-Ma-anim* on their lips.

As people for whom the Messiah has already come, how much more can we sing with confidence during difficult times! Even though we may not always feel His presence, we can trust that He walks with us. The Cross and the Resurrection announce that God has not faltered or tarried. Christ has come! We can affirm life, regardless of the times we live in, because He lives and triumphs.

Questions for Pupils on the Next Lesson. 1. How do you think you could be helped to be more open to God's will? 2. How may you use God's gifts more effectively? 3. How may you help others use their God-given gifts more effectively? 4. How may Christians prepare themselves more effectively as faithful disciples? 5. In what ways do even insignificant matters sometimes prepare the way for helping or hurting others?

TOPIC FOR YOUTH
FACING THE FUTURE WITH GOD

Salty Nonsense. Many people view the future with dread. Some try to cope with the terrors of the unknown by resorting to superstition.

Alfred Gwynne Vanderbilt, for example, was such a person. Although a millionaire many times over, Vanderbilt feared evil spirits which could affect him in the future. The rich playboy was so superstitious about the future that he always slept with the legs of his bed resting in dishes of salt. The salt, he felt confident, would succeed in warding off the evil powers.

Vanderbilt's carefully maintained efforts to protect himself through the use of the salt, however, failed. He died in 1915 when the liner, the *Lusitania,* was torpedoed, by drowning in salt water!

What are some of the superstitions you see others resorting to? How seriously do you take some of the superstitions people talk about? Will relying on these superstitious practices get a person through difficult days? What is the claim of Christ in contrast to the false hopes raised by reliance on such hokum as dishes of salt?

Future Fantasies. Everyone is curious about the future. Some try to probe its secrets by weird ways. Psychics and astrologers claim to have powers to unlock the mysteries of what the coming year will bring. Susceptible people, anxious about the difficulties of today and fearful of the problems of tomorrow, pay close heed to such psychics and stargazers.

What's the record of those who allege to be able to predict the future? *These Times,* a publication of the Seventh Day Adventist Church kept tabs on them. For 1978, there were 250 specifically published predictions for that one year. How many could be said to be reasonably fulfilled? Less than 3 percent, and even these in nearly every case could be attributed to coincidence rather than clairvoyance. The psychics and astrologers, in other words, bombed out.

Christians do not have to probe into the future anxiously. We can take the difficult times today or tomorrow with the knowledge that Jesus has already been through the worst. He steels us to "take it." We can forget the spooky, scary stuff, such as the psychic and occult, and concentrate on the important matters of relying on God and serving others.

Lady Luck or Lord Jesus? Close to 23 billion dollars will be spent on gambling this year, according to an exhaustive survey of gambling in the United States by the Institute for Social Research at the University of Michigan, Ann Arbor. An estimated three out of five American adults plunked down money in pursuit of Lady Luck. Ninety million people make bets—17 billion dollars in legal betting, and over 5 billion in illegal gambling.

The reasons why people bet? "To have a good time," "to pass the time," "nothing else to do," "to try to make some money," "to be challenged," are the answers most often given.

However, there seem to be deeper reasons. Ultimately, the gambler puts his trust—and his money—on luck. The bettor is unconsciously stating that God does not control the future. The difficult times to come cannot be controlled or addressed in a meaningful way since life is at heart an existence on a cosmic roulette wheel.

Christ affirms differently. Think again of the significance of His death on the Cross and His Resurrection from the grave. God promises that He manages the future!

Sentence Sermon to Remember: God's golden age is before us, not behind us.—Anonymous.

Questions for Pupils on the Next Lesson. 1. How are you preparing to be more faithful as a Christian? 2. Why is preparation necessary in order to do one's best as a Christian? 3. What are some examples of lack of preparedness in your experience? 4. How are you seeking God's guidance in selecting what kind of vocation you will pursue in the future? 5. How can you be helped to become more faithful in fulfilling your commitments to others?

LESSON V—MARCH 29

BE READY—BE FAITHFUL

Background Scripture: Matthew 24:36–25:46
Devotional Reading: Joshua 24:16–24

KING JAMES VERSION

MATTHEW 25 1 Then shall the kingdom of heaven be likened unto ten virgins, which took their lamps, and went forth to meet the bridegroom.

2 And five of them were wise, and five *were* foolish.

3 They that *were* foolish took their lamps, and took no oil with them:

4 But the wise took oil in their vessels with their lamps.

5 While the bridegroom tarried, they all slumbered and slept.

6 And at midnight there was a cry made, Behold, the bridegroom cometh; go ye out to meet him.

7 Then all those virgins arose, and trimmed their lamps.

8 And the foolish said unto the wise, Give us of your oil; for our lamps are gone out.

9 But the wise answered, saying, *Not so;* lest there be not enough for us and you: but go ye rather to them that sell, and buy for yourselves.

10 And while they went to buy, the bridegroom came; and they that were ready went in with him to the marriage: and the door was shut.

11 Afterward came also the other virgins, saying, Lord, Lord, open to us.

12 But he answered and said, Verily I say unto you, I know you not.

13 Watch therefore; for ye know neither the day nor the hour wherein the Son of man cometh.

REVISED STANDARD VERSION

MATTHEW 25 1 "Then the kingdom of heaven shall be compared to ten maidens who took their lamps and went to meet the bridegroom. 2 Five of them were foolish, and five were wise. 3 For when the foolish took their lamps, they took no oil with them; 4 but the wise took flasks of oil with their lamps. 5 As the bridegroom was delayed, they all slumbered and slept. 6 But at midnight there was a cry, 'Behold, the bridegroom! Come out to meet him.' 7 Then all those maidens rose and trimmed their lamps. 8 And the foolish said to the wise, 'Give us some of your oil, for our lamps are going out.' 9 But the wise replied, 'Perhaps there will not be enough for us and for you; go rather to the dealers and buy for yourselves.' 10 And while they went to buy, the bridegroom came, and those who were ready went in with him to the marriage feast; and the door was shut. 11 Afterward the other maidens came also, saying, 'Lord, lord, open to us.' 12 But he replied, 'Truly, I say to you, I do not know you.' 13 Watch therefore, for you know neither the day nor the hour.

KEY VERSE: Watch therefore; for ye know neither the day nor the hour. . . . Matthew 25:13.

HOME DAILY BIBLE READINGS

Mar. 23. M. *Watch and Be Ready.* Matthew 24:36–44.
Mar. 24. T. *Be Faithful Servants.* Matthew 24:45–51.
Mar. 25. W. *When the Bridegroom Comes.* Matthew 25:1–13.
Mar. 26. T. *Talents Are to Be Used.* Matthew 25:14–30.
Mar. 27. F. *Those Who Inherit the Kingdom.* Matthew 25:31–40.
Mar. 28. S. *Those Who Fail to Help.* Matthew 25:41–46.
Mar. 29. S. *Choosing to Serve the Lord.* Joshua 24:16–24.

BACKGROUND

A wedding party was one of the happiest festivities in a Palestinian village; the people of the town literally "pulled out all the stops," in celebrating a marriage. Scholars put their books aside; the whole town turned out to celebrate and even religious duties and services were put temporarily aside.

Actually, the couple had been married from the moment of their betrothal, and not simply engaged. But there was an interval before they began to live together; the actual wedding *ceremony* consisted of the bridegroom's bringing the bride to his home; properly dressed for the occasion, he went in a procession with his friends to meet the bride at her father's house. No one knew exactly *when* the bridegroom would start on that little journey, but they knew approximately and were usually prepared to join him in the procession. Through the streets they went, singing and dancing in the light of the lamps they carried. Everyone from seven to seventy, "followed the marriage drum" and joined the happy procession.

Jesus used this illustration, this parable, to teach a profound truth about Himself and about His coming among men — and about those who believed in His coming but who foolishly failed to prepare themselves for it.

NOTES ON THE PRINTED TEXT

I. "Then the kingdom of heaven shall be compared to ten maidens who took their lamps and went to meet the bridegroom. Matthew 25:1 RSV. Here were ten young girls who looked forward to the happy day when the bridegroom would come to claim his bride. But the girls waited and waited and *waited,* and the bridegroom didn't appear; they waited so long as he "tarried" and delayed his appearance that they fell asleep. Now there was nothing wrong with that, nothing foolish about it; they were just tired, and they fell asleep. What was wrong was that they were not ready for his appearance when it finally came. That is, *five* of them had failed to be really ready to join the procession when it came. (Could the bridegroom have been playing a joke on them?)

They all had oil lamps—but only half of them had thought to provide oil for those lamps. So when the shout went up at midnight, "The bridegroom cometh," they all rushed out into the village street to walk with him to the home of the bride, the careless five saw their lamps go out. No oil! They rushed out to buy oil, but the shops were closed at midnight, and when the unhappy maidens ran back to the bride's house, they found the door shut against them.

It is a good story, with a comic twist. Many of us only see the comedy in it and so miss the whole point Jesus was trying to make. There was nothing funny about it to the Master, for He had great truths to tell in this parable. What were those truths?

First, He was telling of the need of preparation for entrance into His Kingdom and for His Second Coming. Certainly, to the early Church, the parable dealt with the Second Advent. To that Church, Jesus Christ was the "Bridegroom" who should come, no man knew when. There is here a reference to the expectation of the Messiah in Jewish faith and thought. The Jewish people were the Chosen People; above all other people, they should have been a nation prepared for the Coming of the Son of God—but prepared they were *not*. There is in this parable a clear reference to the unpreparedness of Israel, and a warning to the Christians to make themselves ready for the Coming of the Lord. The Jews were as the five foolish virgins who had waited too long.

Preparedness! Not long ago there was a Roman Catholic pope named John XXIII, who was probably the most brilliant pope of modern times. He was an old man when he came to that high office, and too soon, he became ill. Realizing that he was going to die, he said, "I have my bags packed for the journey." John was ready to meet his Maker—and that is a claim that few of us can honestly make.

But Jesus wasn't talking about death; He was talking about life and a living God, about preparation while we live to know Him and live with Him, about people who wait too long before accepting Him, about those of us who put off any real commitment to Him until the last moment— and then find the door of a more abundant life in Him closed against them. Life consists of about three-quarters preparation and one-quarter realization; a good minister, for instance, does not become a good minister without long preparation; he spends, from childhood to manhood, nearly twenty years being educated before he is ordained. We know a baseball player in the major leagues who spent fifteen years in the minor leagues before becoming famous in the major leagues—where he spent only ten years. Life is mostly preparation.

We know many divorced men and women; many of them explain that "We just weren't *ready* for marriage," and so there came disaster. We know of no sensible student who waits until the last minute to prepare for an examination; that way lies failure. We read in our newspapers of whole countries which have suddenly become "democratic," and free—and which did not know what to do with their freedom when they got it! Without preparation, we have no oil in our lamps.

The foolish virgins in this parable made the mistake of thinking that they could borrow oil from their wiser companions, and the wiser ones refused to help them. There is great hidden truth in that; *there are some very important things in life which cannot be borrowed.* We cannot borrow wisdom; we must get that by and for ourselves. We cannot borrow faith; that is a possession not to be handed down to us from our fathers but won by struggles within ourselves. We cannot borrow honor, respect, or skill. These qualities we must win for ourselves.

II. *Watch, therefore, for ye know neither the day nor the hour wherein the Son of man cometh.* Matthew 25:13. This is the deeper and more important meaning of the parable. Jesus was disturbed over the questioning of His disciples concerning His return to earth in the golden age, and He sets them straight in advising them to stop asking for a definite date of His return and to hold fast to their faith in Him and go about the work of preparing others for His coming, whenever that might be. Back in Matthew 24:12, He calls on them for fidelity and perseverance and warns against the danger of "growing cold" (discouraged, doubtful) in their love and allegiance. This slow process of growing cold remains in all too many of us. We have a great experience of conversion, a moment in which our love of Him overwhelms all else in our lives; but then comes the testing as the world and its demands close in on us, as slowly but surely we forget that blazing moment of faith and drift back to what we were before it came. "The world," said the poet Wordsworth, "is too much with us; late and soon, getting and spending, we lay waste our powers. . . ." Getting and spending, the Great Dream, the Great Hope, wither and die.

In Revelation 2:4, 5, we find John picking up this thought as he cautions: "Yet there is one thing wrong: you don't love me as at first! Think about those times of your first love (how different now!) and turn back to me again and work as you did before; or else I will come and remove your candlestick from its place among the churches" (The Living Bible).

Perseverance! Does your faith in His Coming flicker and go out in the face of opposition or persecution? We come to Church to witness to our faith in Him—but how is it with us in the street? Has even the possibly second birth become meaningless and neglected because of the lack of the oil of love? If we have not persevered in that love, can His Second Coming really mean very much to us? It is good that we remember the day and hour of our conversion and acceptance of Christ, but—after that, what? What have we done for Him *since then?* Does the candle you have lighted for Him in your heart still burn, or not?

SUGGESTIONS TO TEACHERS

Christians, like guards, must be constantly alert. History is filled with examples of which both believers and belligerents allowed themselves to be lulled into a relaxed, careless state—with disastrous results.

The scriptural material for today's lesson carries Jesus' words regarding watchfulness. They crackle with authority. They also snap His hearers to attention. Behind all the picture-stories rings the stern command, "Be ready! Be faithful!"

Your assignment is to remind your class that each member is summoned to "shape up." Lent, indeed, is a spiritual fitness program for flabby, indifferent believers. The teachings and parables in today's lesson suggest four dangers.

1. *UNSUSPECTED EVENTS.* As Jesus' followers we must be prepared for the unexpected. We are constantly to be on the alert. The "enemy" mounts sneak attacks in ways, times, and places we may least expect. Likewise, the Lord presents opportunities to serve in surprising ways, times, and places. Christ's Coming can be understood both in an "end-of-the-age" way, and in a "today-and-every-day" way. The Christian disciple must live each day as if it is the last—and the first! Preparedness is what counts. Point out to your class how the figures Jesus mentions in the Scripture lived a business-as-usual existence and did not realize what was happening until it was too late. How may Christians today discern what's happening? What is God doing these days? What are some of the unsuspected ways through which He has been operating in both mercy and justice in our times?

2. *UNEXPECTED ARRIVAL.* Christ's intrusion into life is frequently unexpected. Go over the slice-of-life examples of unexpected arrivals of

a thief, a landlord on a trip, a bridegroom, etc. which Jesus tells to illustrate the need for watchfulness. Emphasize to your class that Christ's Coming will be unexpected. Sometimes, His approach is so quiet and unnoticed, like the birth scene at Bethlehem, that few pay much attention. Help your class to comprehend the call for bein9 4eady for Christ's whispers as well as His shouts.

3. *UNAFFECTED SERVANTS.* In some of the parables, people behaved irresponsibly by being unprepared. They were unaffected by the urgency of their duties. They grew sleepy or sloppy. Stress to your class that every Christian is on a constant Twenty-Four Hour Alert—each believer to look after his or her assignment, wherever it may be. Christ never asks any person how "successful" he or she was. He only asks how faithful! Have your class comment on what Christ would ask each one to be busy doing this week when He comes.

4. *UNDETECTED RESPONSIBILITY.* Give ample time to discuss the parable of the last judgment (Matthew 25:31-46). Let the weight of the words of the surprised people saying, "When did we see *you?*" sink in. Reaching out in acts of service to the refugees, the homeless, the prisoner, the hungry, the sick is serving Jesus Himself! The basis for divine judgment lies in how faithful we are in shouldering our responsibilities of practical caring!

TOPIC FOR ADULTS
BE PREPARED

Costly Carelessness. Dr. Wilfred Grenfell, the famous missionary doctor in Labrador, once received a new motorboat from friends in England to help him in his ministry to isolated areas. On the very night in which the new boat arrived, Grenfell received an emergency call to rush to a desperately ill woman on an ice-bound island. Grenfell jumped into the boat and set out, grateful for the powerful engine that would hurry him to the bedside of the stricken woman in time to save her. The night was black and the seas were running high. Grenfell, however, kept his flashlight on the compass and steered confidently.

Hours later, Grenfell realized that he was lost. Although he had carefully watched the compass and followed his navigation chart, he had missed the island. He finally took sightings from the stars and found his bearings. Plowing through the icy waters in the frigid darkness, he finally chugged in to the tiny island. The woman, however, had died shortly before. Grenfell examined her body, and felt certain that he would have been able to save her life if he had arrived earlier.

Later, Grenfell and his associates examined the new boat and discovered that the compass was being deflected from its proper position. Checking further, they found that a steel screw instead of a brass screw had been used to fasten the compass to the boat. A careless workman in the boatyard in England had been in a hurry to quit work and had substituted a steel screw, which, of course, threw the magnetic needle off course. One minor act of unpreparedness cost the life of a woman in faraway Labrador and almost cost the life of Dr. Grenfell.

We are constantly called to preparedness, not knowing the effects of apparently minor actions. Like the steel screw, our small contributions may seem unimportant but have tremendous importance. Who but God knows the way our insignificant words and deeds may affect others in difficult times!

The Risk of Faithfulness. "One of the most common metaphors used in the New Testament to describe the relation of the church to the gospel is that of stewardship. The church, and especially those called to any kind of leadership in the church, are servants entrusted with that which is not their property but is the property of their Lord.

"A steward can fall into several kinds of temptation. All of them are illustrated in the history of the church and in the parables of Jesus. He can forget that he is only the steward and imagine that he is the proprietor. When this happens the church supposes itself to be the saved while the nations ("the heathen") are the lost. Or he can be lazy, drowsy, and slack, and so allow the treasure to be stolen. When this happens the church falls into a worldly slumber and the world is left without the sound of the gospel. Or the steward may forget the purpose for which the treasure was entrusted to him and keep it wrapped up or buried in the ground. It is to such an unprofitable servant that the master in Jesus' parable says: "You wicked and slothful servant. . . . You ought to have invested my money with the bankers, and at my coming I should have received what was my own with interest." To invest the money with a view to a high rate of interest is to risk the capital. The church has often been afraid to do this, thinking that the faith once delivered to the saints is to be preserved inviolate and without the change of a comma. Verbal orthodoxy then becomes the supreme virtue and syncretism becomes the most feared enemy. When this is the mood real dialogue becomes impossible. And so does real mission. If such a church is strong there can be a kind of proselytism, but there is not that kind of mission which seriously expects the Holy Spirit to take what belongs to Christ and show it to the church, thus leading the church into new truth. The mystery of the gospel is not entrusted to the church to be buried in the ground. It is entrusted to the church in order to be risked in the change and interchange of the spiritual commerce of humanity."—Leslie Newbigin, *The Open Secret*, Grand Rapids: Wm. B. Eerdmans Co. 1979. Used by permission.

Questions for Pupils on the Next Lesson. 1. How did Jesus show sensitivity to the woman in the scriptural material for this lesson? 2. What were the motives of Judas and Peter in relationship to Jesus' announcement of His coming death? 3. What was the significance of the Last Supper to the disciples? To Jesus? 4. How does the story of Jesus' passion help us to learn to deal with opposition?

TOPIC FOR YOUTH
BE PREPARED

Turning Point. Christmas Eve, 1777. The cause for American Independence was almost finished. Washington's few ragged survivors had been chased out of New Jersey and were dying of starvation and exposure. Most knowledgeable persons stated that by spring, the British would reassert control over the rebellious colonies. Meanwhile, with heavy snows and subfreezing temperatures, no armies would be expected to move.

Colonel Rahl, commander of the Hessians employed as mercenaries by the British, relaxed in the warmth of his comfortable headquarters in Trenton. It was Christmas Eve, and he knew it was an occasion when no action would occur, no enemy would attack, no precautions would be necessary. His officers had organized a party and dance to celebrate. The orchestra was playing, the guests were laughing, his men were enjoying the good food and drink. The holiday spirit brought a pleasant feeling to everyone. Rahl was dancing when someone slipped up to hand him a message. He smiled as he tucked the paper inside his pocket, indicating he would read it later.

Meanwhile, on the icy roads outside of Trenton, columns of lean, grim men overpowered the few sentries posted by Colonel Rahl that December 24th. Washington and his veterans had boldly crossed the Delaware River that cold night, and advanced toward the unsuspecting Hessians and British. The battle of Trenton itself was a brilliant surprise move and turned the tide of the American cause.

The following day, the defeated Rahl dejectedly reached into his jacket pocket and pulled out the message he had been handed while on the dance floor the previous evening. It was a paper warning him that the Americans were advancing on Trenton.

Rahl the unprepared lost, while Washington, the prepared, won the battle. So also with Christian disciples in their battles in life!

Preparedness Parable. "There is a parable in the story of an eagle on the Niagara River. It lived high above the river on a cliff. From here it could watch the swirling waters of the stream below. One day it saw the carcass of some animal moving downstream, and so it lifted those great eagle wings and soared down to satisfy its hunger. It drove its claws into that carcass, and proceeded to enjoy the feast, as eagle and carcass floated down the river. Soon it could hear the rush of the waters where the river flows over Niagara Falls, but he knew he had nothing to worry about. Those great wings had always supported the eagle. At the very last minute he could always rise up from the falls and fly away. The eagle said to itself, 'I am free. I am an eagle. When this carcass goes over the falls, I can simply fly leisurely back to my own nest.' So that moment came, and the eagle spread his mighty wings and prepared to fly out of danger, only to discover that his feet were frozen into that carcass. He struggled in vain, but could not rise. Both eagle and carcass went over the falls."—Hoover Rupert, *Presbyterian Outlook*, May 9, 1977, Outlook Publishers, Inc., 512 E. Main St., Richmond, VA 23219. Used by permission.

Ready for Action. General Douglas MacArthur won many of his brilliant World War II battles years earlier by preparing himself for all contingencies. Realizing that he would have to be physically robust, he toughened himself and constantly kept in training. Instead of indulging himself in idle talk and harmless diversions during off-duty hours, MacArthur read widely in books of history and military tactics. He even insisted that doctors remove his appendix, although he had never had any trouble with it, lest he have an appendicitis attack during a time of national crisis. Probably no American commander ever prepared himself so carefully for leadership for the years ahead.

Each Christian must also prepare himself or herself with the same kind of thoroughness.

How carefully are you preparing yourself for service as Christ's person for the years to come?

Sentence Sermon to Remember: Those who fear the dark day of judgment need only to find the lamp of faith, and follow its gleam into the brightness of heaven.—George Wooster.

Questions for Pupils on the Next Lesson. 1. How does Jesus help us to be more sensitive to the needs and feelings of those around us? 2. How do you show empathy with those who are suffering? 3. What is the difference between empathizing and sympathizing with someone? 4. In what ways do you think your class can help you and others to develop an unselfish life-style? 5. Why must you evaluate the source as well as the content of criticism?

LESSON VI—APRIL 5

PREPARING FOR DIFFICULT TIMES

Background Scripture: Matthew 26
Devotional Reading: Isaiah 51:4–6

MATTHEW 26 1 And it came to pass, when Jesus had finished all these sayings, he said unto his disciples,

2 Ye know that after two days is *the feast of* the passover, and the Son of man is betrayed to be crucified.

3 Then assembled together the chief priests, and the scribes, and the elders of the people, unto the palace of the high priest, who was called Caiaphas,

4 And consulted that they might take Jesus by subtility, and kill *him.*

5 But they said, Not on the feast *day,* lest there be an uproar among the people.

6 Now when Jesus was in Bethany, in the house of Simon the leper,

7 There came unto him a woman having an alabaster box of very precious ointment, and poured it on his head, as he sat at meat.

8 But when his disciples saw *it,* they had indignation, saying, To what purpose *is* this waste?

9 For this ointment might have been sold for much, and given to the poor.

10 When Jesus understood *it,* he said unto them, Why trouble ye the woman? for she hath wrought a good work upon me.

11 For ye have the poor always with you; but me ye have not always.

12 For in that she hath poured this ointment on my body, she did *it* for my burial.

13 Verily I say unto you, Wheresoever this gospel shall be preached in the whole world, *there* shall also this, that this woman hath done, be told for a memorial of her.

14 Then one of the twelve, called Judas Iscariot, went unto the chief priests,

15 And said *unto them,* What will ye give me, and I will deliver him unto you? And they covenanted with him for thirty pieces of silver.

16 And from that time he sought opportunity to betray him.

MATTHEW 26 1 When Jesus had finished all these sayings, he said to his disciples, 2 "You know that after two days the Passover is coming, and the Son of man will be delivered up to be crucified."

3 Then the chief priests and the elders of the people gathered in the palace of the high priest, who was called Caiaphas, 4 and took counsel together in order to arrest Jesus by stealth and kill him. 5 But they said, "Not during the feast, lest there be a tumult among the people."

6 Now when Jesus was at Bethany in the house of Simon the leper, 7 a woman came up to him with an alabaster jar of very expensive ointment, and she poured it on his head, as he sat at table. 8 But when the disciples saw it, they were indignant, saying; "Why this waste? 9 For this ointment might have been sold for a large sum, and given to the poor." 10 But Jesus, aware of this, said to them, "Why do you trouble the woman? For she has done a beautiful thing to me. 11 For you always have the poor with you, but you will not always have me. 12 In pouring this ointment on my body she has done it to prepare me for burial. 13 Truly, I say to you, wherever this gospel is preached in the whole world, what she has done will be told in memory of her."

14 Then one of the twelve, Who was called Judas Iscariot, went to the chief priests 15 and said, "What will you give me if I deliver him to you?" And they paid him thirty pieces of silver. 16 And from that moment he sought an opportunity to betray him.

KEY VERSE: . . . *O my Father, if it be possible, let this cup pass from me; nevertheless not as I will, but as thou wilt.* Matthew 26:39.

HOME DAILY BIBLE READINGS

Mar. 30. M. *News Difficult to Accept.* Mark 8:31–37.
Mar. 31. T. *High-Level Consultation.* Matthew 26:1–5.
Apr. 1. W. *Costly Devotion.* Matthew 26:6–13.
Apr. 2. T. *Betrayed by a Friend.* Matthew 26:14–16, 21–25.
Apr. 3. F. *The Last Supper.* Matthew 26:20–29.
Apr. 4. S. *Breaking Under Pressure.* Matthew 26:31–35.
Apr. 5. S. *Finding Strength Through Pressure.* Matthew 26:36–46.

BACKGROUND

We come now to the last act of the divine drama. Jesus has just finished a long discourse (chapter 5)—one of the most inspiring in all of Matthew's Gospel. But with the opening verses of the next chapter, the disciples are hushed into sad silence as Jesus says that within the short space of only two days He will be "betrayed to be crucified."

Up to this point, He had been attacking His enemies among the Jewish leaders; now He announces that these very enemies will put Him on a cross.

As Matthew tells the story (a story also told by Mark and John), there were three people playing "leading parts" in this last act: Caiaphas, the woman with a vial of precious ointment (perfume), and Judas Iscariot.

NOTES ON THE PRINTED TEXT

I. Then the chief priests and the elders of the people gathered in the palace of the high priest, who was called Caiaphas, and took counsel together in order to arrest Jesus by stealth and kill him. Matthew 26:3 (RSV). The Sadducees and the temple leaders had reached a fearful decision; baffled in their attempts to silence Jesus, they decided to kill Him. They went about it in a secret meeting, behind closed doors; that is usually the procedure of murderers. They did not want the people to know what they were planning; this all happened during the celebration of the Jewish Passover, and Jerusalem was overcrowded with both people who hated Jesus and others who loved Him. To stir their anger with a public arrest could start riot and insurrection, and if there was anything feared by their chief priest Caiaphas, it was insurrection. The Romans just might crucify Caiaphas, if that happened.

This Caiaphas was a man possessed of the strength of the devil. He was the puppet of the Roman conquerors—a collaborator. In the days before Caiaphas, the priesthood was hereditary; under Rome, they were appointed by the Romans, who saw to it that they "stayed in line" and did the will of Caesar. Now the wheel of fortune had put Caiaphas in a dangerous position; he either had to defy Rome and let Jesus live, or arrange His murder in such a way that it could be accomplished before any followers of the Master could organize opposition. He chose to bow to Rome.

Jesus, in these two days before His arrest, knew exactly what Caiaphas was about to do; He knew that the chief priest was nothing more than a man involved in working out God's plan for His Son. Caiaphas was not aware of this, but Jesus knew the very day and hour in which His cross would be raised on Calvary.

Jesus knows the minds of His opposition, in our twentieth century. He knows why and how they oppose Him, and crucify Him either in violence or in just walking past Calvary and never seeing what was happening—for *their* sakes—on that hill.

II. *Now when Jesus was at Bethany in the house of Simon the leper, a woman came up to him with an alabaster flask of very expensive ointment, and she poured it on his head* . . . . Matthew 26:6, 7 (RSV). Matthew says that this happened at Bethany in the house of Simon, a leper. Mark tells the same story; John a similar story, adding the statement that the woman was Mary, the sister of Lazarus. Luke tells a story which probably was built not around the same occasion but on another "anointing"; Luke says that the Simon mentioned here is actually Simon the Pharisee, and the woman is a notorious sinner. These four stories could be identified as one and the same story, but probably they are two different stories of two different events.

Be that as it may, wherever and whenever it occurred, it was to both Matthew and Jesus a moment of perfect beauty and love and a deeply penetrating meaning and lesson. This woman, whoever she was, poured out her perfume—the most expensive possession she had—upon the head of One she had come to love with a priceless devotion. It was not an act; it was consecration. She took the most precious thing she owned (valued at three hundred denarii, which amounted to nearly a year's wages of a working man) and with it anointed her King! What a love that was! It was a love that never counted the cost. She never stopped to ask herself, "Can I *afford* this?"

Matthew gives the gesture of the woman a Messianic significance; to him, the woman was royally anointing One who was to become a crucified King. And Jesus Himself tells the disciples that "she did it for my burial" (verse 12). Whether or not the woman had this in her mind when she broke the vial, we will never know; but we do know that Jesus called it "a beautiful thing." Interpret it as we may, the scent of that perfume is still to be found in the modern Christian's acts of love.

The disciples apparently didn't understand the underlying meaning of this sacrificial perfume. One of them (Judas?) called it a waste! Why was the perfume not sold, and the proceeds given to the poor? (Why spend money building a great cathedral when there are poor living in its shadow?) That question is a familiar one, now as then. We find the answer to it in Christ's reply: "The poor will always be with you, but you will not always have *me!*" Poverty may be a stubborn if not a necessary evil in human society—but the poor have needs which money cannot meet. They hunger for more than bread made of wheat; they hunger for the presence of a Jesus who was the very bread of life—the bread of the soul. As one writer says, "A Beethoven must not forsake his music, except in direst emergencies, to run a soup kitchen." Christ fed the poor on the mountainside, yes, but that was secondary to His spiritual mission. Now He was about to die: who then would carry on that (beautiful) mission? His church is called to feed the poor in emergency, but what bread shall they give the poverty-stricken, day in and day out, without *Him?*

III. . . . *And they paid him thirty pieces of silver.* Matthew 26:15 (RSV). Enter Judas, the greatest of all history's traitors. For a handful of silver he betrayed his Christ and gave Him to the soldiers of Rome in Gethsemane. *Why?* Three reasons have been offered to explain the treachery of Judas: greed, hatred, and disappointment.

It couldn't have been greed; Judas got only thirty sheckles from the Romans for this "deal," and that is less than fifteen dollars in our money! Judas had no need of such small money. In John 12:6 we learn that he had long been a plain thief; as treasurer of the Twelve he took money out of their treasury bag for his own purposes. It couldn't have been money that stimulated his betrayal. One so money-conscious as Judas was would never have settled for a mere thirty shekels. But if it *was* greed, it stands as a horrible example of what the lust for money can do to a man.

Some others explain that Judas betrayed in hatred, or in disillusionment. It is argued that Judas loved power, that he saw Jesus as One with superhuman power and with the ability to lead His people in a great rebellion to drive out the Romans and establish the promised Kingdom of God. Jesus refused to do that. He *may* have done it because this Christ was not the kind of Christ he wanted Him to be. It sounds like good reasoning, but could even a thief have spent three years with Jesus and not absorbed His *love?* We wonder?

By far the better explanation is that Judas never intended to see Jesus die. Isn't it more probable that he wanted only to force Jesus' hand, wanted only to force Him to lead that great rebellion? That seems more likely.

We might give him credit for one thing: unlike Pilate, who was the one who actually sent Jesus to His death, Judas went out and hung himself after it was all over. Pilate was the kind of man who could forget, in later life, that he ever sentenced this Man to die, but Judas was overcome with remorse, and in penitence, killed himself. Which do we prefer—Judas or Pilate?

SUGGESTIONS TO TEACHERS

A. E. Housman has a poem in which he depicts Jesus as a naive country boy who finds Himself caught up in idealism. The idealism quickly sets off events which He cannot control. In over His head, Jesus becomes a helpless dupe. He is carted off to His execution, waving a pathetic farewell, perplexed and victimized.

The poet's Jesus, however, is not the Gospels' Jesus. Far from being overwhelmed by events which propelled Him to His doom, Jesus confidently marched through suffering to victory. Your next four lessons, covering Matthew 26–28, cover His trials and triumph. These lessons are also intended to help each person in your class to endure life's Calvaries confident of God's resurrecting power.

Today's lesson focuses on Matthew 26. Use it as a diary of Jesus' progress toward the Cross for us.

1. *DETECTION*. Make sure your class understands what Jesus thought of Himself. Point out how His enemies understood what His claims were, and how they were so threatened by these claims that they plotted to kill Him. Jesus was no placid, well-mannered English butler to these people, but a dangerous menace to everything for which they stood. Do your people detect the ways that Jesus undermines greedy, cruel, exploitive interests?

2. *DEFECTION*. Pause for a few minutes to let your class talk over Judas's deeds. Don't let the class simply shrug off Judas as the mean "heavy" in the drama, but suggest that each person examine the Judas-like traits in his or her own relationship to the Lord. What are ways in which traitorous attitudes and acts appear among believers today? How may your people help keep themselves from betraying Jesus today?

3. *DEJECTION*. Shift your class's attention next to the Upper Room. Let your class ponder the enormity of the disappointment Jesus must have felt as He looked around at His disciples. One had already arranged to betray Him. Another would deny Him. The three closest to Him would doze off when He would ask them to sit with Him. All would desert Him. Yet, Jesus celebrates the banquet of God's new age! He shared the cup of the New Covenant.

4. *REJECTION*. Move to the Gethsemane scene, where Jesus feels abandoned by His friends. Urge your class to share "Gethsemane experiences" the members of your group have known. Difficult times in a believer's life are made worse by a sense of loneliness and rejection. Nevertheless, "Not my will but thine" prayers get a Christian through these times.

5. *ELECTION*. Next, direct your class to the Trial of Jesus. Notice that instead of Jesus being on trial, it seems that His acsusers and judges are the ones who seem to be tried. No bewildered peasant boy from Nazareth here! Instead, Jesus boldly acknowledges that He is "the Christ, the Son of God," and adds that He is to be recognized as God's unique, Chosen One (Matthew 26:64)! Do your people grasp the significance of Jesus' claims for Himself?

6. *PROTECTION*. Finally, mention how Jesus, although aware of the Father's strength, chooses not to make a show of divine might or to overwhelm with the miraculous. Jesus refuses to appeal to raw power to crush His critics. Instead, He steadfastly advances toward Calvary with the certainty of God's ultimate victory! Enable your class to be bolstered with this same confidence.

TOPIC FOR ADULTS
PREPARING FOR DIFFICULT TIMES

Painless Discipleship. A weekly magazine aimed at sophisticated highbrows carried the following advertisement in its personal columns a couple of years ago: "BECOME A LEGALLY ORDAINED MINISTER AND HONORARY DOCTOR OF DIVINITY. Complete professional package $25. No future obligations. Church of Universal Brotherhood." An address followed.

Mail order ordination is bad enough, but the phrase, "No future obligations" is too much!

No future obligations with Jesus? Never! Look again at Matthew 26. As He passed through suffering to victory, He warned disciples then and now to prepare for difficult times. That means obligations, and lots of them!

Preparing in Personal Caring. Dr. Elizabeth Kubler-Ross, author of the well-known *Death and Dying,* recounts a touching story of a little girl suffering from a terminal illness and confined to an oxygen tent. One night, the little girl became terrified and called out. The nurse rushed to her bedside. "What would happen," the child asked between her sobs, "if the oxygen tent caught on fire?" The nurse on duty could not cope with this situation, and immediately summoned her supervisor. The nursing supervisor turned out to be a seasoned but sensitive woman. She quickly detected what the little girl was wanting to know. With motherly compassion, the supervisor half-crawled inside the oxygen tent beside the little girl and held her in her motherly arms. "Does this help?" the nursing supervisor inquired.

The small girl broke into sobs and began to tell what was actually bothering her. She knew that she was going to die, and she wanted to talk about it. What she wanted and needed was not the assurance that she would not die (she did die in a few days) but that she would not be alone when death came. When the nursing supervisor promised her that she would not be forgotten, the girl's sobs subsided. The child knew that the nurse holding her would be there.

This supervisor helping to prepare a little girl for a difficult time is, in a sense, what every Christian is called to do in whatever ways possible. Every person is called to be a "preparer" in the name of the Christ who prepares each for all difficult days.

Prepared to Stick. Two hundred feet above the East River, workmen were constructing the Manhattan Tower of the Queensboro Bridge.

Some feet below the two men working at the top, others were at work, and still farther down, more were at work. A steel beam of several tons' weight was lowered to its position, the business of the two at the top was to guide the beam into position.

Before the great mass of steel could be fastened, it began to slip, and the efforts of the two men were powerless to keep it from sliding toward their comrades below. They had only to stand out of the way to see many of them crushed to death.

An instant for decision, and one brave fellow gasped, "I'll stick to it if you will." The other nodded, and they held on grimly until their fellow workmen could swarm up the ladder to attach the derricks. In the meantime, a hand of each of the heroes had been ground off at the wrist.

Questions for Pupils on the Next Lesson. 1. How do Christians often show indifference for Jesus? 2. What are times when you have felt abandoned by God? 3. Why do we tend to rationalize our behavior to fit our situations? 4. What are ways in which we crucify Christ today? 5. How can we avoid sentimentalizing the cross and see it as the event which changes lives?

TOPIC FOR YOUTH
PREPARING FOR DIFFICULT TIMES

Coping with Criticism. Ignace Jan Paderewski, one of the greatest
pianists of all time, practiced diligently during his youth to fulfill his
dream of becoming a concert musician. Family and friends tried to dis-
courage him from continuing, pointing out how difficult a time a musician had in making a living. Even his teachers tried to dissuade him.
One noted artist-teacher advised him to take up the cornet because he
had a protruding upper lip, and he might be able to find a job in a band.
Paderewski's own instructors told him that his hands were too small and
that he could never become a concert artist. Paderewski persevered.
With an indominable faith, the young Polish pianist refused to permit
criticism to stop him. Finally, at the age of twenty-four, Paderweski
showed his critics that he had the gifts, drive, and skills to become a
pianist. He went on to become the most acclaimed piano performer of
his time. As a youth, he had prepared for difficult times and had endured.

Used Difficult Times. The artist was a minister's son, and had early
learned to identify with people with hurts and sorrows. He was also
desperately poor. Nonetheless, he continued his art studies. His young
wife was not able to join him. Transportation was poor in the early
nineteenth century, and mails traveled slowly. The young artist was
frequently forced to wait long periods for word from his beloved.

One day, a letter arrived. Opening it, the artist was shocked to read
that his wife had taken ill and had died. The mail with the tragic news
had arrived seven days late. The grief-stricken husband resolved that he
would discover a means by which messages could be transmitted more
quickly than by the mails.

A few years later that artist, who had received word too late of his
wife's death, designed the telegraph and the code that still bears his
name. His name was Samuel F. B. Morse. Morse used his difficult days
of heartbreaking grief to contrive a way to spare others the anguish he
had experienced.

With God's help, we also may use difficult times as a way to reach out
to others. We can be sensitive to the hurts of others and use our experience to help other sufferers.

Ready for Slights and Suffering. We must prepare now for difficult
times. The school of Christian living starts *now*. The lessons need to be
mastered painfully and carefully.

Booker T. Washington, the great black educator, was born a slave but
rose to become one of America's most outstanding citizens because he
early learned to prepare himself for difficult days. Dr. Washington
seemed to be able to endure incredible hurts, snubs, and setbacks.

Once arriving by train to give a speech at a university in a certain city,
Booker T. Washington was pressed for time to arrive to keep his appointment. He rushed up to a taxi and asked the white driver to take him
to the university. The man glared at Dr. Washington and muttered, "I
don't drive niggers."

Washington merely smiled and answered, "Okay, then you jump in back and let me drive."

Sentence Sermon to Remember: For if the trumpet give an uncertain sound, who shall prepare himself to the battle?— 1 Corinthians 14:8.

Questions for Pupils on the Next Lesson. 1. What exactly does Christ's Crucifixion mean to you? 2. How do you deal with the times when you feel rejected by others? 3. How do you react when others make false accusations against you? 4. What are ways in which people "crucify" Christ today?

LESSON VII—APRIL 12

THEY CRUCIFIED HIM

Background Scripture: Matthew 21:1-13; 27:1-61
Devotional Reading: Isaiah 53:7-12

KING JAMES VERSION

MATTHEW 27 33 And when they were come unto a place called Golgotha, that is to say, a place of a skull,

34 They gave him vinegar to drink mingled with gall: and when he had tasted *thereof*, he would not drink.

35 And they crucified him, and parted his garments, casting lots: that it might be fulfilled which was spoken by the prophet, They parted my garments among them, and upon my vesture did they cast lots.

36 And sitting down they watched him there;

37 And set up over his head his accusation written, THIS IS JESUS THE KING OF THE JEWS.

38 Then were there two thieves crucified with him; one on the right hand, and another on the left.

39 And they that passed by reviled him, wagging their heads,

40 And saying, Thou that destroyest the temple, and buildest *it* in three days, save thyself. If thou be the Son of God, come down from the cross.

41 Likewise also the chief priests mocking *him*, with the scribes and elders, said,

42 He saved others; himself he cannot save. If he be the King of Israel, let him now come down from the cross, and we will believe him.

43 He trusted in God; let him deliver him now, if he will have him: for he said, I am the Son of God.

44 The thieves also, which were crucified with him, cast the same in his teeth.

45 Now from the sixth hour there was darkness over all the land unto the ninth hour.

46 And about the ninth hour Jesus cried with a loud voice, saying, Eli, Eli, lama sabach-thani? that is to say, My God, my God, why hast thou forsaken me?

47 Some of them that stood there, when they heard *that*, said, This *man* calleth for Elias.

REVISED STANDARD VERSION

MATTHEW 27 33 And when they came to a place called Golgotha (which means the place of a skull), 34 they offered him wine to drink, mingled with gall; but when he tasted it, he would not drink it. 35 And when they had crucified him, they divided his garments among them by casting lots; 36 then they sat down and kept watch over him there. 37 And over his head they put the charge against him, which read, "This is Jesus the King of the Jews." 38 Then two robbers were crucified with him, one on the right and one on the left. 39 And those who passed by derided him, wagging their heads 40 and saying,"You who would destroy the temple and build it in three days, save yourself! If you are the Son of God, come down from the cross." 41 So also the chief priests, with the scribes and elders, mocked him, saying, 42 "He saved others; he cannot save himself. He is the King of Israel; let him come down now from the cross, and we will believe in him. 43 He trusts in God; let God deliver him now, if he desires him; for he said, 'I am the Son of God.'" 44 And the robbers who were crucified with him also reviled him in the same way.

45 Now from the sixth hour there was darkness over all the land until the ninth hour. 46 And about the ninth hour Jesus cried with a loud voice, "Eli, Eli, lama sabach-thani?" that is, "My God, my God, why hast thou forsaken me?" 47 And some of the bystanders hearing it said, "This man is calling Elijah."

48 And straightway one of them ran, and took a sponge, and filled *it* with vinegar, and put *it* on a reed, and gave him to drink.

49 The rest said, Let be, let us see whether Elias will come to save him.

50 Jesus, when he had cried again with a loud voice, yielded up the ghost.

48 And one of them at once ran and took a sponge, filled it with vinegar, and put it on a reed, and gave it to him to drink.

49 But the others said, "Wait, let us see whether Elijah will come to save him."

50 And Jesus cried again with a loud voice and yielded up his spirit.

KEY VERSE: . . . they were filled with awe, and said, "Truly this was the Son of God!"

Matthew 27:54.

HOME DAILY BIBLE READINGS

Apr. 6. M. *They Praised Him.* Matthew 21:1-13.
Apr. 7. T. *They Arrested Him.* Matthew 26:47-56.
Apr. 8. W. *They Tried Him.* Matthew 27:1,2,11-14.
Apr. 9. T. *They Rejected Him.* Matthew 27:15-25.
Apr. 10. F. *They Mocked Him.* Matthew 27:27-39.
Apr. 11. S. *They Killed Him.* Matthew 27:35-44.
Apr. 12. S. *"He Makes Himself an Offering for Sin."* Isaiah 53:7-12.

BACKGROUND

Following the final discourses at the Last Supper, Jesus was arrested in Gethsemane, subjected to hearings and trials before Caiaphas and Pilate and condemned to death. Then the Roman soldiers scourged (whipped) Him until the blood streamed from His face and body and finally marched Him through the streets bearing the cross beam of the cross. The march was made along the longest route, so that as many people as possible could see it and be stricken with fear of Rome as they saw it. Atop the hill called Calvary, He was crucified.

Matthew's record of this gruesome and sadistic event is told with great restraint, as though he were writing in an agony second only to the agony of Jesus. He omits many of the details mentioned by Mark, Luke, and John. The cross was raised at nine o'clock in the morning; Jesus died at three o'clock in the afternoon; that was a very short time of suffering, comparatively; many a criminal hung on his cross for days before death came.

Before teaching this lesson, the teacher should read Psalms 22; quotations from this Psalm run all through the Crucifixion story.

NOTES ON THE PRINTED TEXT

I. And they crucified him . . . . Matthew 27:35. Surrounding the cross were six groups of people come to the scene for different purposes: the soldiers who "guarded" Him (lest His friends might try to take Him down), the cynics who mocked, the indifferent, the hostile, two thieves on crosses beside His—and a few women. Before He was even nailed to the cross, He was offered a drink of wine mixed with an opiate which would make His pain easier to bear (that was a custom followed by certain wealthy women of Jerusalem) and "he would not drink it." We can only guess why He did that. It could have been that He was determined to meet death with open eyes; it could also have been that He wanted to share to the very end the agony and pain of those He was dying to save, in obedience to the purpose of God in His death on the cross. However it was, whatever His reasoning, there was in this a sign of the compassion of the women—of *wealthy* women—who put sympathy for the suffering above the law.

The soldiers at the foot of the cross were indifferent; this was a military assignment, just another execution of troublesome Jews. They had probably seen hundreds of such executions; this one was no different from the others. They knew not who or what this Man was, and they did not care. They had already whipped Him into exhaustion that would bring death within a few hours. Gleefully they threw dice for His only earthly possession: His purple robe.

Occasionally they might have glanced up at the sign nailed above His head: "This is Jesus, The King of the Jews." Such a sign was always fastened to the cross of those crucified for whatever crimes they may have committed; it was also the final insult offered by Pilate (John 19:14)—but now, on Calvary, it was an insult direct at the Jews. It was Pilate and Rome saying to them, "This is what will happen to you, if you defy Rome." It was the Romans and not the Jews who put Him to death; the Jews of the time could not inflict capital punishment, so they brought the charge of treason to Pilate, and for treason Pilate condemned Him.

II. *And they that passed by reviled him . . . .* Matthew 27:39. These were the cynics, the scorners, the servants of the high priest (Caiaphas lacked the courage to see his victim die!), the sadistic and the curious who came just to see a man die, the passers-by in the street. They "wagged their heads"—a gesture of scorn. They shouted at Him to come down from the cross; if He was really the Son of God, He could surely do that! He had claimed the power to save others, and He couldn't even save Himself! Mockery! Some of us still mock Him with the words, "After all, He was only a *man*."

Poor fools they were; they never understood that He was dying for *them*. Certainly He could have come down from the cross if He willed to do so—but that was not in the divine plan of Calvary. General Booth of the Salvation Army once put it in these words: "It is precisely because He would not come down that we believe in Him." The mockers saw God in Him only as a powerful warrior building His Kingdom on the point of a sword; Jesus was dying to lead men into recognizing God in sacrificial love.

Matthew makes no mention of the penitent thief who died beside Jesus; he says that both thieves "cast the same (mockery) in his teeth." If that be true, it would have been just another agony for Jesus, but John has a repentant thief who was saved at the door of death. Love might help us to prefer John's version, but it could have been either way.

III. *Now from the sixth hour there was darkness over all the land unto the ninth hour.* Matthew 27:45. It says "over all the land," not "over all the earth." Now read the 22nd Psalm, from which Jesus seems to be quoting. In this Psalm we read the words: "All they that see me laugh me to scorn . . . they shake the head, saying, He trusted on the

Lord that he would deliver him . . . . They part my garments among them, and cast lots upon my vesture (a prophecy terribly come true on Calvary) . . . . " And, most poignant of all, the words, "My God, my God, why hast thou forsaken me?" Many believers feel that Jesus, in a coma or subconscious state due to His long sufferings, was repeating these words from the psalmist—words, incidentally, which end in a hymn of victory. Certainly it was His darkest moment, His "midnight" on the cross.

Luke says that at this moment there was an eclipse of the sun—hardly possible during the period of the pascal full moon. Matthew thinks of it as a miracle, a sign of the divine displeasure. All we know is that this was the darkest hour ever to fall upon the earth as well as upon Palestine, and that in this hour Jesus was sharing the depths of pain suffered by all men. But we may well doubt that it was a cry of despair; crucified among two sinners, just as He had lived with and for sinners, in these last moments, He led one of them to the door of heaven in victory.

Those who stood there and heard it did not understand it fully, as we do not always understand. Some of them had a final taunt to throw at Him; they said that these last sad words meant that He was calling on Elijah for help. The Jews had a tradition about Elijah: he was the rescuer of pious, believing Jews, and to them Jesus was calling out to the great old prophet to deliver Him from pain and death. Let us wait and see now whether Elijah will help Him! To mockery, they added blasphemy.

The end came swiftly now. Someone in the watching crowd filled a sponge with vinegar and lifted it on a reed to His lips. This may have been not pure vinegar but posca, a drink made of water, sour wine and egg popular among Roman soldiers; if it were that, it was a startling deed of mercy from an unexpected source. But the authors of the Gospels saw it as another, final torture—"In my thirst they gave me vinegar to drink." (Psalms 69:21). Then Jesus, with a loud voice, bowed His head in death. It was finished—no, *accomplished!*

When Joan of Arc was burned to death at Rouen in 1431, a soldier said, "Well, that's the end of her." It was not the end; she still lives in the hearts of Christians around the world. When Jesus died, the Roman soldiers who had crucified Him thought that their murder had put an end to Him. It had not. "Actually, it is only the beginning. . . . What is unique about Jesus is that, on the testimony, and in the experience of innumerable people, of all sorts and conditions, of all races and nationalities from the simplest and most primitive to the most sophisticated and cultivated, he remains alive."—Malcolm Muggeridge, *Jesus, The Man Who Lives*, by permission of Harper & Row, publishers.

SUGGESTIONS TO TEACHERS

There is simply no way to sum up the meaning of Christ's Crucifixion. Surprisingly, the Church has never promulgated an orthodox view of the Cross. Perhaps the poets and artists come closer. But even John Milton, trying to pen a sonnet on the significance of Christ's death on the Cross as a sequel to his graceful lines on His birth, finally gave up the attempt.

Nobody can say adequately or completely what the death of Jesus means.

Your assignment in today's lesson is not to try to "teach" what the Cross is all about. Rather, it can best be described as pointing each person to Calvary, then asking, "Now what are you going to do about it?" You do not need to worry about programing; the crucified Lord speaks for Himself.

Your lesson could well be structured around the series of questions and taunts directed at Jesus during His final days. Let these be means of making each person in your class come to deeper terms with Christ's sacrifice.

1. *WHO IS HE?* (Matthew 21:10.) Some in the Palm Sunday throng wondered. Perhaps some in your class privately are also bewildered about Jesus. Who *is* He? How would each person describe Jesus to a child? To a stranger from a non-Christian culture? To an associate at work or school who is only a nominal church member? Who is He to you as teacher?

2. *ARE YOU KING?* (Matthew 27:11.) Who rules your life? (Or, is it "What rules your life?") If Jesus is King, what does His kingship demand? Remind your class that Jesus' claims of being King do not permit rivals on the throne. What are some of the rivals to His rule?

3. *"WHICH ONE DO YOU WANT?"* (Matthew 27:17.) Pilate's question to the crowd still holds. Jesus or Barabbas? Stress the place of choices in the life of a Christian. Remind your class that ultimately it is the choice of someone ahead of Jesus that resulted in the Crucifixion. In what ways do we "crucify" Him afresh in our times through poor choices?

4. *"WHAT SHALL I DO WITH JESUS?"* (Matthew 27:22.) No one can remain neutral about Jesus. It finally comes down to crowning Him or crucifying Him. Even the most mature Christian, however, comes to realize that he or she never completely resolves the matter of what to do about Jesus. Life presents so many challenges which call for a fresh assessment of one's commitment. Help your people to ponder what to do with Jesus during the next few days' decision-making.

5. *"SAVE YOURSELF!"* (Matthew 27:40.) The taunt of the crowd to Jesus, "Come down from the cross!" could have been answered with a bit of dazzling theatrics. He *could* have come down from the Cross and saved Himself. But He did not. And that is precisely why He is our Savior. He chose not to save Himself, but to save us. He died so that we could have life. Take time in your lesson to allow the mystery and paradox of Christ's death to provoke whatever response the Spirit leads your people to make.

TOPIC FOR ADULTS
THEY CRUCIFIED HIM

Bought at Pain. In the best-selling novel by Colleen McCullough, *The Thornbirds*, she frames the story that spans three generations with the Australian legend from which the book's name is derived:

"There is a legend about a bird which sings just once in its life more sweetly than any other creature on the face of the earth. From the moment it leaves the nest, it searches for a thorn tree, and does not rest until it has found one. Then, singing among the savage branches, it impales itself upon the longest, sharpest spine. And, dying, it rises above its own agony to outcarol the lark and the nightingale. One superlative song, existence the price. But the whole world stills to listen, and God in his heaven smiles. For the best is only bought at great pain . . . or so says the legend."

Show Us the One. "I once heard one of the greatest chaplains the British Army ever had tell a story about that great soldier Field Marshal Slim. The thing happened in the Burma campaign. Slim asked the senior chaplain to arrange for a visit to one of his soldiers who was going through a bad time. News had come to Burma that his wife was behaving, to say the least of it, indiscreetly at home. A chaplain was duly sent to see the man. After the visit Slim sent for the senior chaplain. 'Padre,' he said, 'about that visit I asked you to get one of your chaplains to pay.' 'Well, sir,' said the senior chaplain, 'what about it?' 'Well, padre,' said Slim, 'your chaplain went to see the man. He was very nice to him. He smoked a cigarette with him, and drank a cup of tea with him. But he never showed that soldier the one thing he wanted to see.' 'What was that?' said the senior chaplain. And Slim answered: 'The man on the Cross. Padre,' said Slim, 'when are you going to show us the one thing we want to see—the man on the Cross?' Don't mistake me. I'm not saying that at every visit the minister must talk religion; I'm not saying that at every visit he must say a prayer. But I am saying that somehow or other he must acquire the spiritual awareness which will enable him to see when these things have to be spoken about. And there lies the problem—and the problem is the terrible possibility of failing your people just when they need you most, and of paying a social visit, when they want the man on the Cross."—William Barclay, *Testament of Faith* London:Mowbrays, 1975.

Costly Rudeness. Chou En-Lai, Prime Minister of the People's Republic of China, in 1945 pleaded with friends at the Embassy in Peking to be allowed to fly to the United States to visit President Franklin D. Roosevelt and try to explain the Chinese Revolution to him. He was repeatedly turned down. In 1954, Chou helped design the Geneva conference, which temporarily halted the Vietnam fighting. In Geneva shortly afterward, he saw John Foster Dulles approaching him and courteously extended his hand in friendship to the American Secretary of State.

Dulles refused to shake the proffered hand, humiliating Chou En-Lai in front of the entire gathering. Observers such as Theodore White later remarked that this was probably the costliest display of rudeness by any diplomat anywhere. Smarting under the deliberate insult, Chou became an implacable enemy of American diplomacy for many years.

Dulles's inability to allow his pride to be crucified in order to shake hands with Chou might have seemed an insignificant matter to some. But to others, it helped bring on the bloody debacles in Vietnam.

Christ's Crucifixion must elicit the response in us whereby we will allow our pride to be crucified. Until we permit this crucifixion, Christ's death will be meaningless and in vain in our lives.

Questions for Pupils on the Next Lesson. 1. Do you agree with the statement that the Resurrection of Jesus is the heart of the Christian faith? Why or why not? 2. What should be our attitude toward those who doubt Jesus' Resurrection? 3. How does faith in the Resurection affect Christian living today? 4. How can believers today affirm victorious living in spite of opposition and unbelief? 5. Why do some people want the assurance that death is not the final arbiter of human affairs? 6. How can adults be helped to prepare for death?

TOPIC FOR YOUTH
JESUS GAVE HIS LIFE

Reluctant to Risk. Jesus sacrificed His life for others. The meaning of that cannot be understood unless we measure His willingness to give up what is most precious to a person with others' willingness to make sacrifices. For example, a couple of years ago in Pittsburgh, a thirty-nine year-old asbestos worker named Robert McFall was suffering from aplastic anemia, a rare blood disease which prevented his bone marrow from making new red blood cells. McFall was told that his disease would be fatal unless he receive a bone marrow transplant from someone whose own marrow would be compatible with his. Tests showed that McFall's cousin, David Shimp, had such bone marrow. No one else in McFall's family was able to be considered as a donor except David Shimp. McFall and Shimp had grown up together and were like brothers. McFall approached Shimp and asked him if he would be willing to provide the transplant of bone marrow which could save his cousin's life.

Shimp refused. McFall pleaded. Shimp continued to turn down McFall. Desperate for the life-saving transplant, McFall filed a legal suit to force his cousin to share some of his bone marrow. Fearful of the risks involved, David Shimp protested that he should not have to help his cousin. The court upheld Shimp. "In our law, there's no duty to rescue someone or save someone's life," ruled the Judge. McFall died a few weeks later.

True, there is no civil law compelling anyone to sacrifice for others. Jesus did not have to go to the Cross. He could have taken the attitude of Shimp. He could have pointed out the risks and refused to lay down His life for others.

The Cross is God's own rule of life spelled out in blood and tears. He has sacrificed for us. Christ risked everything. He gave more than a transplant of bone marrow. He gave life itself!

Love so amazing, so divine, demands your life, your soul, your all!

Took the Sting. A little boy was once riding in a car with his father when a bee flew in the window. The boy was terrified; somehow, he had been led to think that if a bee stung him, he would die. As the bee buzzed around him, the youngster became hysterical with fright.

The father quickly pulled the car over to the side of the road and caught the bee in his hand. The father winced slightly as the bee stung him, but released the insect. He noticed that his young son became frantic when the bee began to fly again. The father finally learned that the little boy had mistakenly thought that the bee sting would be fatal, that the father would quickly die, and that the bee might sting again. Showing the red swollen place, the father explained quietly that the bee could not harm anyone again because it had left its stinger in him. The father then held the boy in his arms, and explained further that he loved the little fellow so much that he could accept such a sting, even if it were true that it would be fatal!

Christ's death on the Cross is like that. He accepted the sting of death for us.

Modern Kind of Crucifixion. Beyers Naude is a Christian who lives in South Africa. He was born an Afrikaner, was an ordained minister of the Dutch Reformed Church in South Africa, and a member of the secret *Broederbond* or brotherhood sworn to uphold white supremacy in South Africa. He became chaplain of prestigious Pretoria University, and was honored by being elected the Moderator of the Transvaal Synod. Highly respected in governmental, church, and educational circles, young Dr. Naude had a brilliant career waiting for him.

As a Christian, however, Beyers Naude became increasingly convinced that apartheid was contrary to the Gospel. He began to challenge the restrictive policies directed toward black people. In December, 1960, then forty-five years old, he spoke out firmly against his government's harsh racial policies at a meeting of the World Council of Churches in Johannesburg. Naude's own synod demanded he retract his statements and confess his "error." He refused. Since 1961, Beyers Naude's life had been made increasingly miserable.

His status as a pastor has been "withdrawn" and he has not been allowed to preach a sermon in a Dutch Reformed Church since 1963. His friends have fallen away. His wife and children have been harassed and threatened. His pension has been cancelled and his salary dropped.

In 1963, Naude tried to organize a Christian Institute to foster black-white dialogue and encourage black initiative. His Church accused anyone associating with the Institute of "heresy." In 1977, the South African government "banned" the Institute and placed Naude under house arrest. He is not allowed today to meet with more than one person at a time, to publish anything, to visit any educational institution, to set foot in any African, colored or Asian, area.

Beyers Naude, however, is undismayed. In spite of his "crucifixion" by his Church and his government and friends, he is confident of God's ultimate victory.

Crucifixions come in many forms. Christ's people are expected to bear a cross. Beyers Naude's cross means being labelled a "subversive" and "heretic." Yours will bring you your own kind of pain. In the name of the One who was crucified for us, however, you and I are called to endure whatever types of suffering for others our loyalty to the crucified Lord may bring.

Sentence Sermon to Remember:
> The moon of Mahomet
> Arose, and it shall set:
> While, blazoned as on heaven is immortal noon,
> > The cross leads generations on.
> > —Percy Bysshe Shelley.

Questions for Pupils on the Next Lesson. 1. Do you think that there would be any Church or Bible if the Resurrection had not occurred? On what do you base your answer? 2. How does the fact of the Living Christ help us to deal with fears of existence beyond death? 3. What exactly does the Resurrection mean to you? 4. How can you live victoriously despite opposition and disbelief?

LESSON VIII—APRIL 19

VICTORY OF THE RESURRECTION

Background Scripture: Matthew 27:62–28:10
Devotional Reading: 1 Peter 1:3–9

KING JAMES VERSION

MATTHEW 27 62 Now the next day, that followed the day of the preparation, the chief priests and Pharisees came together unto Pilate,

63 Saying, Sir, we remember that that deceiver said, while he was yet alive, After three days I will rise again.

64 Command therefore that the sepulchre be made sure until the third day, lest his disciples come by night, and steal him away, and say unto the people, He is risen from the dead: so the last error shall be worse than the first.

65 Pilate said unto them, Ye have a watch: go your way, make it as sure as ye can.

66 So they went, and made the sepulchre sure, sealing the stone, and setting a watch.

28 1 In the end of the sabbath, as it began to dawn toward the first *day* of the week, came Mary Magdalene and the other Mary to see the sepulchre.

2 And, behold, there was a great earthquake: for the angel of the Lord descended from heaven, and came and rolled back the stone from the door, and sat upon it.

3 His countenance was like lightning, and his raiment white as snow:

4 And for fear of him the keepers did shake, and became as dead *men.*

5 And the angel answered and said unto the women, Fear not ye: for I know that ye seek Jesus, which was crucified.

6 He is not here: for he is risen, as he said. Come, see the place where the Lord lay.

7 And go quickly, and tell his disciples that he is risen from the dead; and, behold, he goeth before you into Galilee; there shall ye see him: lo, I have told you.

8 And they departed quickly from the sepulchre with fear and great joy; and did run to bring his disciples word.

REVISED STANDARD VERSION

MATTHEW 27 62 Next day, that is, after the day of Preparation, the chief priests and the Pharisees gathered before Pilate 63 and said, "Sir, we remember how that impostor said, while he was still alive, 'After three days I will rise again.' 64 Therefore order the sepulchre to be made secure until the third day, lest his disciples go and steal him away, and tell the people, 'He has risen from the dead,' and the last fraud will be worse than the first." 65 Pilate said to them, "You have a guard of soldiers; go, make it as secure as you can." 66 So they went and made the sepulchre secure by sealing the stone and setting a guard.

28 1 Now after the sabbath, toward the dawn of the first day of the week, Mary Magdalene and the other Mary went to see the sepulchre. 2 And behold, there was a great earthquake; for an angel of the Lord descended from heaven and came and rolled back the stone, and sat upon it. 3 His appearance was like lightning, and his raiment white as snow. 4 And for fear of him the guards trembled and became like dead men. 5 But the angel said to the women, "Do not be afraid; for I know that you seek Jesus who was crucified. 6 He is not here; for he has risen, as he said. Come, see the place where he lay. 7 Then go quickly and tell his disciples that he has risen from the dead, and behold, he is going before you to Galilee; there you will see him. Lo, I have told you." 8 So they departed quickly from the tomb with fear and great joy, and ran to tell his disciples. 9 And behold, Jesus met them and said, "Hail!" And they came up and took hold of his feet and worshiped him. 10 Then Jesus said to them, "Do not be afraid; go and tell my

9 And as they went to tell his disciples, behold, Jesus met them, saying,
All hail. And they came and held him
by the feet, and worshipped him.
10. Then said Jesus unto them, Be
not afraid: go tell my brethren that they
go into Galilee, and there shall they
see me.

brethren to go to Galilee, and there
they will see me."

KEY VERSE: *He is not here; for he has risen, as he said . . . .* Matthew
28:6

HOME DAILY BIBLE READINGS

Apr. *13.* M. *The Burial of Jesus.* Matthew 27:57–61.
Apr. *14.* T. *The Tomb Sealed and Guarded.* Matthew 27:62–66.
Apr. *15.* W. *Vainly They Watched the Tomb.* Matthew 28:1–4.
Apr. *16.* T. *"He Has Risen."* Matthew 28:6–10.
Apr. *17.* F. *Sorrow Turned to Joy.* John 20:11–18.
Apr. *18.* S. *"My Lord and My God."* John 20:24–29.
Apr. *19.* S. *Resources for Victorious Living.* 1 Peter 1:3–9.

BACKGROUND

The body of Jesus, taken down from the cross, was claimed by a
newcomer: Joseph of Arimathea, thought to have been a member of the
Sanhedrin or of the council in his home town. If it was the Sanhedrin,
then this Joseph did nothing to help Jesus after His arrest. But now he
comes to Pilate to ask for the body of the Lord. With him is another who
had known Jesus but not followed Him: Nicodemus (John 19:39), who
had once talked with Jesus about being born again. These two: none of
the family of Jesus, none of His disciples, came to claim and bury the
body. Nicodemus brought myrrh and aloes, to be used in the embalm-
ing; Joseph wrapped the body in a linen sheet and placed it in a tomb in
his garden—a tomb perhaps intended for himself! They rolled a great
stone across the door of the sepulchre, and left.

Nearby unable to do anything but watch and weep, were Mary Mag-
dalene and "the other Mary" (Mary of Bethany or Mary the mother?).
Two seeking men, two mourning women; these alone followed Him to
His tomb in Joseph's garden.

The next day—our Saturday, others came, sent by worrying Pilate.

NOTES ON THE PRINTED TEXT

*I. Next day, that is, after the day of Preparation, the chief priests and
the Pharisees gathered before Pilate . . . .* Matthew 27:62 (RSV). Jesus
died on Friday, at three o'clock in the afternoon. Now the hours from 3
P.M. to 6 P.M. on Friday were called The Eve, or The Preparation—
preparation for the Sabbath, which actually began at 6 o'clock on Friday.
In doing that, the priests and the Pharisees broke the Sabbath Law.
They were so anxious to make sure that Jesus was dead and out of their
way that they violated one of their most sacred laws.

Curious, isn't it, that they did that? What made them do it? They came
to Pilate saying that Jesus had said that after three days He would rise
from the dead. That worried them; if the disciples could steal the poor

broken body from its tomb and hide it elsewhere, they might go up and down the land claiming that Jesus was resurrected from the dead—and how would the chief priests and Pharisees deny that if they could not produce the body?

This absurdity of suggesting that the body of Jesus might have been stolen is not unusual, or limited to the Pharisees of the times. We still have novelists and somewhat hysterical "historians" who tell us that it *was* stolen, even from the cross; they tell us that Jesus was not quite dead when His body was taken down, and that He was revived then and there! But the spectacle of a torn and mutilated Jesus living on and wandering over the land, an emaciated wreck, is hard to believe. In such a condition, how could He have influenced His disciples to go up and down the land preaching His *Resurrection?*

Pilate was too clever a diplomat to get involved with the priests and the Pharisees after all that had happened. This was the Pilate who so recently had washed his hands of the whole thing (*see* Matthew 27:24). Now, again, he dodged, he said to the chiefs and Pharisees, "You have soldiers available to guard the tomb; use them." Soldiers went out and sealed the tomb, and sat down to watch. It was a foolish move. They did not know that there was no tomb in the world that could imprison the Son of God. Neither is there a tomb or a prison that can hold a faith, or a love, or a redemptive idea, simply by imprisoning a body.

II. He is not here; for he is risen . . . . Matthew 28:6. The story of the Resurrection needs no repetition here; we know it well, and we know that, historically, that this Resurrection is the foundation of the Christian church. So, rather than engage in a discussion of the details of the event, it may be better to think of this greatest of all history's moments as a whole; let us see it through the eyes of those who witnessed it.

The mood of the moment was one of *fear*. Those who had put Him on Calvary's cross were frightened. It was like this: "A clay-cold wind moaned 'round the hill, and clouds of furious black drove down the sky like chariots out of hell, with the devil's fiends driving. Demons on holiday, they frightened the earth; the watchers on the hill pretended not to see or hear or be afraid, but the housewives of Jerusalem drew their shutters and barred their doors and sat pale at their supper-tables, listening. A sense of doom, of death, was in the air. For love was in eclipse this night, and hope hung lifeless on a cross atop the hill. Jesus Christ was dead."—Frank S. Mead, *The Ten Decisive Battles of Christianity*.

Fear! So frightened were His enemies that they set a guard to prevent the kidnapping of a dead body in a tomb! At three o'clock in the morning following the Crucifixion, the two Marys who had watched Him die came to see the sepulchre, came in fear born of overwhelming sorrow. The record in Matthew says that they came "toward the dawn" (RSV), a greater dawn than they realized, for these first two to go out to the tomb did not yet expect a resurrection to come. Neither did the disciples who remained in hiding through it all, struck numb with fear. The guards at the tomb were in anything but a courageous frame of mind; they collapsed like dead men before the dawn came. And when an earthquake shook the earth at this same hour, the whole city trembled. Fear! Humanity still clings to fear; Christian or otherwise, we all have a fear of death. We are like the innocent child who asked his father, "What is there beyond the sunset?" If a man die, shall he live again? Many of us ask that all through life, but there are those who understand that on this first Easter morning Jesus Christ held out His pierced hand to lead us toward a *sunrise* of immortality. We bring flowers to our funerals, for flowers are evidence of an eternal springtime.

Then there was love at the empty tomb. Fearful as they were, the two Marys came in love for One who had loved them. They may have been afraid that the guards at the tomb might drive them away, but they came. Mark says that they "fled from the sepulchre" (Mark 16:8) and said nothing about it to any man, but John (20:2) says that Mary Magdalene ran and told Peter of what she had seen, and that Peter and another disciple (John?) came *running*. John got there first, but impetuous Peter was the first to enter the tomb. John, in that moment, "believed"; of the thoughts and reaction of Peter, we are not told. Perhaps fear still held him.

In love, too, God sent an angel who rolled back the sealing rock at the tomb door, and sat upon it. We are intrigued by that word *sat*. The angel sat upon it as one might sit on a broken bench in a public park, listening to the singing of the birds; sat to demonstrate that sealed doors which keep men away from Crhist can be broken as easily as a twig is broken by human fingers—*when we have faith*.

Belief! Who among these who came out to the tomb in the garden that Easter morning was the first to believe? It was Mary Magdalene. With the other Mary, says Matthew, she left the sepulchre with fear *and great joy*, and ran to tell the disciples about it. She who had sinned much and had been forgiven much knew first what it all meant in spite of her first fears. Then the disciples believed. "That," said George A. Buttrick, "is the face behind the resurrection stories. The proof of the stories is not in the letter of the Scripture, but in the change which befell his disciples, and in the change that may befall us." The Magdalene believed it because she *saw* it. Those cynics among us who are agnostic or atheistic about the Resurrection would better spend their time explaining to us how belief in His Resurrection became objectified in the minds of His disciples and in the hearts of long ages of disciples who *know* that their Redeemer lives.

"He is not here; for he is risen!" So said the angel at the empty tomb. Believing that, fear is changed into joy, into rejoicing. Belief in His rising robs death of its sting, the grave of its false victory. In all the words of all the men who ever lived there has never been such a hope that meant so much as this: *we* shall rise again; *we* shall not die; *we* shall live. That is the triumphant shout which we call Easter.

Go, said Jesus to His disciples—go tell thy brethren of this Resurrection. Do not hide it; say it in courage and full belief; say it to *all* men. . . . Tell them that an angel sits beside every tomb.

SUGGESTIONS TO TEACHERS

About 800 years ago, the Spanish city of Valencia was besieged by the Moors. The small Spanish garrison was able to hold off the assaults of the Moors because of the inspired leadership of a military hero named Ruy Diaz de Bivar, usually remembered as *"el Cid."* Finally, *el Cid* died of old age and battle fatigue. His lieutenants, however, dressed up the body in armor, strapped his sword to his right hand, and by a cleverly designed and carefully concealed wicker framework, propped up *el Cid's* corpse on his horse. With the mounted cadaver leading the procession, the Spanish forces surged out of the gates of Valencia.

Some critics of the Church think that Easter is much the same. They allege that Jesus' disciples wanted to perpetuate the Master's life, and tried to con people into thinking He was not actually dead. Easter, in effect, was like the charge of *el Cid's* corpse: propping up a departed hero to rally frightened followers.

Your task today is to help your class to deepen each member's understanding of the Resurrection announcement. The key note is *Victory!*

Reread the account in Matthew. Note again how the victory of the Resurrection brought victory for Jesus' followers. The emphasis, of couse, is on Jesus alive.

Incidentally, when the Spaniards galloped out of Valencia behind *el Cid's* body, they were quickly defeated. Their hearts were not in the battle. They knew their leader was dead. A corpse could not inspire or lead.

The Victory of the Resurrection is exactly the opposite from the hoax of Valencia. Easter was no bold stunt staged by disciples, but God's mighty act of deliverance.

1. *KEEP HIM A CORPSE?* Pilate and the guards and the authorities thought they could dispose of Jesus by shutting Him up in a tomb. They even tried to suppress the Easter news. Enemies of the Lord still try to reduce Jesus to a lifeless has-been. Sometimes, Church folks do also! Take some moments today to have your class members think how their lives sometimes deny the Resurrection victory, and encourage others to assume that Jesus is dead. How does your congregation sometimes appear to outsiders to be a Pilate or one of the guards, keeping Christ a corpse, rather than living triumphantly in the light of the Victory of Easter?

2. *MOURN FOR A MARTYR?* Examine the account of Mary Magdalene and Mary coming to Jesus' tomb to "pay their last respects." How similar that is to some Christians' attitudes toward Jesus today! Is this how some in your class regard Easter—as a sort of memorial service for a departed leader? Does worship take on the mournful tone of a funeral on too many Sundays in your church? Nudge your class to ponder the Victory's meaning in their own lives, and in the life of your congregation's worship.

3. *MEET THE MASTER!* Easter is the experience the women had of encountering the Living Lord! They met the Master! The climax of today's lesson must be the need of each believer to know personally the Risen Christ. Easter is more than secondhand report; it is firsthand experience.

TOPIC FOR ADULTS
BECAUSE HE LIVES!

Where Is He? John Masefield, near the end of his play, *The Trial of Jesus*, has a fine passage in which he in imagination records a conversation between Procula, the wife of Pilate, and Longinus, the centurion who stood by the cross.

"Longinus says: 'He wasn't a strong man. The scourging must have nearly killed him. I thought he was dead by morning and then suddenly he began to sing in a loud clear voice that he was giving back his spirit to God. I looked to see God come to take him. He died, singing. Truly, lady, that man was the Son of God, if one may say that.'"

A little later, the play goes on:

"Longinus: 'He was a fine young fellow, my lady, not past the middle age. And he was all alone and defied all the Jews and all the Romans, and when we had done with him, he was a poor broken-down thing, dead on the cross.'

"Procula: 'Do you think he is dead?'

"Longinus: 'No, lady, I don't.'

"Procula: 'Then where is he?'

"Longinus: 'Let loose in the world, lady, where neither Roman nor Jew can stop his truth.'"

Resurrection in Ward M-1-2. In 1929, a thirty-three-year-old woman was admitted to Allentown State Hospital with a nervous breakdown. Hospital officials tried to communicate with her, but could not understand the language she spoke. For the next forty-eight years, the woman remained in the institution, isolated and almost forgotten because no one could speak with her.

Finally, in December, 1977, an interpreter named John Kurz, a multilingual case worker from the Bureau of the Aging, was asked to try to make contact with the woman. Kurz, an active Christian layperson who knows firsthand the meaning of Christ's life in his own from having survived the war, displacement, and loss of loved ones, visited the woman.

Kurz listened intently, and discovered that the woman was speaking a heavy Austrian dialect of the German language. He repeated the Lord's Prayer in her native dialect, and elicited a response. Gently, Kurz made a conversational breakthrough.

For the first time in all the years she had been in the public institution, the woman was able to talk with someone. She gradually disclosed her troubled story to John Kurz. She said that her name was Mary Peischl, and her home was in the former Austro-Hungarian Empire when Franz Joseph I was ruler. She had come to America and had five children.

Kurz's efforts succeeded in attracting a news story about Mary Peischl. That story helped locate her children who, unknown to hospital authorities a half-century earlier, had been scattered throughout foster homes in the Philadelphia area. Mary Peischl and her family had a joyful reunion.

The meaning of the Resurrection of Jesus Christ is that He continues to make contact with us when we may think we are isolated and unheard. Just as John Kurz broke through to Mary Peischl that she was known and understood, so the risen Lord breaks through to our consciousness that God knows us and understands us.

Resurrections take place at Allentown State Hospital Ward M-1-2 with Mary Peischl, and also where you live. Because He lives, you shall live also! Let the Risen Lord bring you new life!

"*Cu Lao Vu Vong.*" Over 30,000 refugees who have fled Vietnam have been forced to resettle on Pulau Bidong off the Malaysian coast. The refugees are regarded as illegal immigrants. The world has dubbed them the "boat people." They are not wanted in Malaysia, or in any other country. These hapless people have no future. They squat in misery day after day.

The Vietnamese on this steep, isolated bit of rock and sand eighteen miles off the Malaysian coast call it Cu Lao Vu Vong—"the island of the hopeless."

Many people feel that they are living on an island of the hopeless. After the Crucifixion of Jesus, His followers regarded themselves as inhabitants of a bleak, miserable world. They had no hope. They were changed by the Resurrection. Because He lived, they came alive.

Thousands of men and women today can testify to the power of Jesus' life in their lives. They have been rescued from their islands of hopelessness by the vital presence of the risen Lord.

Perhaps you think that you are marooned in a hopeless situation. Easter is the news that God has not forgotten you. He has come to you with life. He offers new beginnings. You may live with hope! You may also stretch out toward others on their islands and bring resurrections in His power.

Questions for Pupils on the Next Lesson. 1. In what ways do you think other areas in life besides church could be permeated with the message of the Gospel? 2. What are some of the ways by which people deny the truth of the Christian message today? 3. What are some of the obstacles to belief for people who genuinely want to believe? 4. What is the responsibility of every individual Christian in carrying out Christ's commission? 5. What are some of the ways in which Christ is working with us as we carry out His work?

TOPIC FOR YOUTH
CHRIST IS ALIVE!

New Beginning From Bad Ending. A sudden flash. Searing pain, then merciful oblivion. When young Jay Armes awoke in the Texas hospital, he looked down at the bandaged stumps. He began to realize that the exploding dynamite cap had blown off both of his hands.

Jay cried bitterly. His life was over, he told himself. He thought mostly of suicide.

Jay Armes conquered the temptation to end his life—with the help of the Lord. With the power of God, Jay also resolved to do everything he could with a pair of hooks that any other person could do with hands.

Today, J. J. Armes is one of the great private investigators in the world, selected by Marlon Brando to locate his missing son, and solver of dozens of cases on which police had closed their books. J. J. Armes delights in attempting impossible situations. The loss of his hands became a challenge instead of a tomb.

The Risen Christ enables anyone to begin again. He resurrects you from the tomb of despair. Jesus Christ is alive. He makes you alive, as He made Jay Armes alive, even after the loss of his hands and his thoughts of suicide. Ask Him for the new beginnings He has in mind for you! Let Easter be in your life.

Lost Tribe. Many people go through life without ever personally realizing that Christ is alive and present. They are like the Tasadays and the moon.

Who are the Tasadays?

The Tasadays are a lost tribe recently found in the rain forest of Mindanao in the Philippines. They live under such a thick growth of trees that they had never seen the moon. Anthropologists who discovered the Tasadays showed the surprised tribesmen the sight of the moon for the first time in 1971!

Are you a "Tasaday Christian"—a person who has never noticed the beauty and light of Jesus Christ? Are you aware of His presence?

Has the "jungle" of everyday distractions obscured the reality of His existence in your life? Are you part of a lost tribe of those who don't know about the Resurrection?

Easter is the awareness that Christ is alive. Come out of the jungle!

Your Tombstone Epitaph. "Does it worry you? I mean what they may carve into a granite grave marker which stands on your grave? With cremation becoming more widespread in its usage, that could be a way out from that anticipatory fear! Here's one in Ft. Wallace, Kansas, 'He tried to make 2 jacks beat a pair of aces.' (While that's the story of many a life even today in the post-Gunsmoke Era, few want that as a carved memory!)

"There's more than humor in such epitaphs. In many of them, there is a dreary drama which flippancy seeks to alleviate. In others, there are probably words thought up by his old buddies down at the Long Branch saloon. But there they stand, readable after a century or two or three—or more. And that's all we know about the person whose remains lie beneath that sod.

"That's a great deal more of a tragedy if one believes that death has the final answer, that the grave is a dead end, that the casket or rough coffin contains all there was, there wasn't any more. In these days of mass suicides which horrify us, even though we have been used to wars with 'body-counts,' in a day when human life seems cheap on many of the commodity markets of the world—what a terrifying thought that this is all there is, there isn't any more!

"Yet, I have to believe that Jesus was no scoundrel, that he was not the world's greatest con artist, that he was who he said he was, and whom the world has acknowledged across 20 centuries. In fact I believe him even when he said, 'He who believes in me shall never die.'

"How about that quotation for an epitaph for your grave? It beats two jacks and even four aces!"—Hoover Rupert, *Presbyterian Outlook*, January 22, 1979, Outlook Publishers, Inc., 512 E. Main St., Richmond, VA 23219. Used by permission.

Sentence Sermon to Remember: Once accepted as fact (the Resurrection) tells more about the universe, about history, and about man's state and fate than all the mountains of other facts in the human accumulation.—Editorial in *Life,* 1965, Time, Inc.

Questions for Pupils on the Next Lesson. 1. What is the authority of the Risen Christ in your life? How is His authority shown in your life? 2. What do you see to be the biggest problem or difficulty in your congregation in working for Christ in mission? 3. Do you really think that God promises to be with us always? Why or why not? 4. Where do you go or what do you do when you have religious doubts?

LESSON IX—APRIL 26

IN MISSION WITH THE VICTOR

Background Scripture: Matthew 17:1–9; 28:11–20
Devotional Reading: 1 Peter 1:13–25

KING JAMES VERSION

MATTHEW 28   11 Now when they were going, behold, some of the watch came into the city, and shewed unto the chief priests all the things that were done.

12 And when they were assembled with the elders, and had taken counsel, they gave large money unto the soldiers,

13 Saying, Say ye, His disciples came by night, and stole him *away* while we slept.

14 And if this come to the governor's ears, we will persuade him, and secure you.

15 So they took the money, and did as they were taught: and this saying is commonly reported among the Jews until this day.

16 Then the eleven disciples went away into Galilee, into a mountain where Jesus had appointed them.

17 And when they saw him, they worshipped him: but some doubted.

18 And Jesus came and spake unto them, saying, All power is given unto me in heaven and in earth.

19 Go ye therefore, and teach all nations, baptizing them in the name of the Father, and of the Son, and of the Holy Ghost:

20 Teaching them to observe all things whatsoever I have commanded you: and, lo, I am with you alway, *even* unto the end of the world. Amen.

REVISED STANDARD VERSION

MATTHEW 28   11 While they were going, behold, some of the guard went into the city and told the chief priests all that had taken place. 12 And when they had assembled with the elders and taken counsel, they gave a sum of money to the soldiers 13 and said, "Tell people, 'His disciples came by night and stole him away while we were asleep.' 14 And if this comes to the governor's ears, we will satisfy him and keep you out of trouble." 15 So they took the money and did as they were directed; and this story has been spread among the Jews to this day.

16 Now the eleven desciples went to Galilee, to the mountain to which Jesus had directed them. 17 And when they saw him they worshiped him; but some doubted. 18 And Jesus came and said to them, "All authority in heaven and on earth has been given to me. 19 Go therefore and make disciples of all nations, baptizing them in the name of the Father and of the Son and of the Holy Spirit, 20 teaching them to observe all that I have commanded you; and lo, I am with you always, to the close of the age."

KEY VERSE: . . . *lo, I am with you always, to the close of the age.*
Matthew 28:20. (RSV)

HOME DAILY BIBLE READINGS

Apr.   20.   M. *Three Disciples See Jesus' Glory.* Matthew 17:1–12.
Apr.   21.   T. *The Transfiguration.* Luke 9:28–36.
Apr.   22.   W. *The Great Commission.* Matthew 28:16–20.
Apr.   23.   T. *The Heart of the Good News.* Mark 12:28–34.
Apr.   24.   F. *Spreading False Reports.* Matthew 28:11–15.
Apr.   25.   S. *A Promise of Help.* John 14:8–21.
Apr.   26.   S. *"Be Holy . . . in All Your Conduct."* 1 Peter 1:13–25.

BACKGROUND

What happened *after* the crucifixion of Jesus should be studied as carefully as we study what happened on the cross. It was the custom of the executioners to cast the bodies of the criminals they had crucified into a ditch, or to bury them somewhere in a hidden grave; that is undoubtedly what happened to the bodies of the two thieves who died beside Jesus.

But it was not what happened to Him who died on the center cross. There were those who knew the location of His tomb—and His body was *not* in that tomb now. There was darkness and an earthquake that spread fright among believers and nonbelievers. There were people in and beyond Jerusalem spreading a story that there had been a Resurrection, and that Jesus Christ was *alive*. Other stories said that He had appeared to certain women near the tomb, and later to certain of His disciples.

A fresh hope flared up in the hearts of those who loved Him; a new fear struck at the hearts of those who had killed him. To both Roman officials and Hebrew leaders, this was gossip that had to be stopped, quickly. So once more the chief priests met in a hastily called meeting to discuss what they might do to silence the story brought down from the garden tomb by those women who had first claimed to have actually *seen* Him, and about those disciples who were coming out of hiding to hear that Good News—and to claim, later, that they had seen Him, too. They panicked at the thought of what these rumors might do to both Roman authority and established religion.

NOTES ON THE PRINTED TEXT

I. So they took the money, and did as they were taught . . . .
Matthew 28:15. Whether the guards at the tomb were Jewish or Roman, we do not know. Whatever they were, they came swiftly into Jerusalem to officially report that the tomb they had been commissioned to "protect" was now empty. They said nothing about any Resurrection. They came to the chief priests, as Matthew tells it, and not to their Roman commander, which seems strange. They may have been too frightened to report to their military superior, for any Roman soldier who allowed a prisoner to escape paid for it with his life, and such a penalty could have been inflicted for their negligence at the tomb.

Now what, chief priests? They had used a traitor to arrest Him; they had lied about Him in the courts; they had slandered Him falsely before the people, and all that had failed to stop or silence Him. What now, that He was dead?

Now came the crowning infamy. They offered the guardsmen "large money"—a bribe—to spread the word that the disciples had come and stolen the body while they slept. Bribery!

It doesn't make sense. If those guards, or soldiers, had fallen asleep at that tomb, they would have been executed within twenty-four hours, just as a guard or sentinel in time of modern war would be shot if he fell asleep while on duty. Matthew alone, among the four Gospel writers, tells of this attempt at a bribe and he adds to the story the words,

". . . this saying is commonly reported among the Jews until this day"(verse 15).

Now Matthew was a Jew, writing for the Jews and condemning the Jews. Involved, here, is the echo of a long dispute between the Jews and the first Christian churches on the subject of the empty tomb. It was a war of words that continued through the second century: by that time, the Church had the courage and the power to publicly contradict the fabricated story by which the Jews hoped to beat down the Resurrection joy that was sweeping the land. The synagogue fought the new faith; the Christians belabored the Jews. Perhaps it had to be, but—did our anti-Semitism come out of this dispute, at least in part?

The Jews fought a lost cause; the Resurrection evidence was too strong for them. The Romans had a saying to which they should have listened: "Great is the truth, and it will prevail." No slander, no lie, no bribe can prevail against it.

Winston Churchill once said, "Truth is incontrovertible. Panic may resent it; ignorance may deride it; malice may distrot it; but there it is."

II. *And when they saw him, they worshipped him* . . . . Matthew 28:17. Here we come to the end of Matthew's account of the Christ who was about to depart from this earth. Matthew says that Jesus had "appointed them" to meet Him on a mountaintop in Galilee; that is, Jesus planned this meeting for His farewell appearance. That the meeting was on a mountain is significant; this was to be another mountaintop experience for those who came; they would be lifted up above the plain, above and beyond the marketplaces of men. Eleven disciples came, but this does not mean that no others were there. Matthew leaves this possibility open when he says that "some doubted" when they saw Him there, risen from the dead.

"They worshipped him." That is to say that they (at least the disciples who were present) recognized Him at last for what He was: the Son of God. That others present may not have come to the conclusion, that they still "doubted," is quite likely, for doubt is a persistent master. Indeed, it is probably true that no Christian has ever become a Christian without his moments of doubt, and Tennyson may have been more than half right when he wrote, "There lives more faith in honest doubt, believe me, than in half the creeds." Honest doubt—or wonder about the mystery of Jesus Christ—is nothing of which one need be ashamed. The disciples had their moments of nagging doubt, but now, in this last meeting with their Master, all doubts vanished. Now they *knew*!

Certain that these eleven men now knew exactly what He was and what He must be to all men, Jesus proceeds to give them three great gifts as arms in the battle for His Kingdom which was to begin with them. First, He gave them *power*. It was the very power of God, enough to face a pagan, hostile world and evangelize it. To these eleven disciples, who had so recently deserted Him (He never reminded them of that!), He gives not only power to overcome their own weaknesses and doubts, but enough to overcome the weaknesses and doubt of any man to whom they might speak. He gave them *His* power; with that, they could not lose.

Second, He gave them what we call the Great Commission: they were to go out beyond the Jewish world into the nations of the Gentiles and *teach* them. Teach, and baptize, in the name of the Father, and of the Son, and of the Holy Ghost. This trinitarian baptismal formula is found only in Matthew, and not elsewhere in the New Testament, but it is accepted and used in all of the great creeds of Christianity. Baptism was to be the seal of the teaching, or the sign of the convert passing into the new life in Christ.

Third, He gave them the greatest promise in all of the Bible: the promise of His Presence in their midst as they fanned out across the earth. "Lo, I am with you alway, even unto the end of the world." *They would never be alone*, whenever they went or whatever happened to them.

To the first Christians, this promise meant that when the end of the "age" came, when the universal catastrophe long predicted and believed to be imminent, Christ would still be there as Lord and Savior; later, when the expected end was delayed and delayed and delayed, they gradually came to believe that *whenever* it came it would be the day when in a Second Coming He would reveal Himself as the King of a new age, a new creation.

The modern Christian does not deny this Second Coming, but he also puts his faith in a Christ *still alive in the Spirit*, still searching out the hearts and allegiance of men. In this concept, they live and walk with Him, and will do that in spite of the threat of a possible end of it all in a final all-consuming burst of atomic dust.

As Jerry Lewis put it, in his telethon for sick or abandoned children, "You never walk alone!"

SUGGESTIONS TO TEACHERS

Easter Island is a speck in the Pacific Ocean rarely visited by tourists, it is noted mostly as a point on navigational charts.

Easter for many church people is also an "island." Once a year, it's "All ashore!" For the other fifty-one Sundays, the day is reduced to a date on the calendar.

Today, the Sunday after Easter, there will be no crowds surging to services. For many, it's back to the same old Sunday-as-usual slump. Some in your class will be inclined to regard this week's class time and worship as simply "the Sunday after Easter."

Your topic today is appropriately called, "In Mission With the Victor." It stresses personal response to the Risen Lord. This lesson is not intended to hype-up folks for another brief Easter-island excursion. Rather, your lesson should prepare people for long-term mission as members of the Resurrection community. By reflecting on today's Scripture in Matthew 17 and 28, you will find that people can respond in at least four forms to Jesus Christ

1. *THOSE WHO RECOGNIZE THE REVELATION.* Work for part of your lesson time with the Transfiguration account (Matthew 17:1–9). Point out how the trio of followers present with Jesus understood that He was greater than Moses and Elijah. In other words, the three disciples had the insight of realizing that Jesus is the fulfillment of the Law

(the *Torah*, as delivered by Moses) and all prophecy. Help your class to understand what the claims of Jesus are. The key notion is the *finality* of Jesus Christ.

2. *THOSE WHO REPUDIATE THE RESURRECTION.* Some, according to Matthew 28, did not take seriously the announcement of Jesus' Resurrection. In fact, some people accepted bribes to spread rumor that the disciples had snatched Jesus' body and hidden it. Denying the Easter news, however, is tantamount to living a life of deceit. It ultimately becomes morally debilitating. The Risen Lord instills life! He brings a life of openness and integrity.

3. *THOSE WHO RESPOND TO THE REALITY.* Make sure that you devote enough time on the theme of going and making disciples. To be with the Risen Lord means to be in mission for Him. Impress on your people that "going" may mean reaching out across the nation, across the world—and across the street to evangelize. Ask your class members to make lists of those they know who understand little of the meaning of the Gospel. Next, ask the class what can be done to share the Good News of Jesus Christ with those they have listed.

4. *THOSE WHO RELY ON THE RISEN LORD.* "I will be with you always!" Jesus promised. David Livingstone, the intrepid missionary to Africa who suffered great privations, called this promise "the Gentleman's word" of Christ. Help your class people to comprehend that they may trust Christ as one who keeps his word. Share instances where His Word has sustained you, and ask others to relate occasions when they have relied on the Risen Lord.

TOPIC FOR ADULTS
INTO ALL THE WORLD

Target Audience. The National Conference of Catholic Bishops commissioned Gallup poll experts to survey the need for evangelism. The polls revealed that 41 percent of over-eighteen Americans are functionally unchurched, which leaves a "market" of 61,000,000 people, most of whom are now overlooked by aggressive evangelizers, who keep raiding the 59 percent functionally churched, getting them to shift loyalties. There are no signs of mass conversion in America today. Evangelization of the unchurched will be a one-by-one process, greatly dependent on peer to peer ministry. In other words, don't believe the claims you hear about mass conversion on "Christian" television. Finally, 68 percent of the unchurched believe in the Resurrection of Chirst, 64 percent of the unchurched believe that Christ is God. They just don't believe that the Church is His body.

What do these findings suggest to you? Is your congregation in mission with the Victor to welcome these unchurched to Christ's community? Are you going into "all the world"—including your own street and all your community?

Big Spender. The cost of the international arms race exceeds $400 billion each year. Knowing Christ's commission to us, we cannot sit idly at this diversion of resources from human need to military production. $400 billion.

To put this figure in understandable terms, imagine that Jesus was given one-fourth of that sum for programs of social service. If He spent that $400 billion in allotments of $100,000 a day, He would have spent it throughout His lifetime, past the year 1000, past 1978 and still have some 760 years left to spend that $100,000 a day.

They'll Know We Are Christians by Our Love. Evangelism by example is perhaps the most powerful form of witness to many in our nation today. People have seen too much internal bickering in congregations and denominational backbiting.

For example, in April 1865, five days after the surrender of General Robert E. Lee, President Lincoln was assassinated. One month later the Northern Presbyterian General Assembly (Old School), which throughout the war had retained on its rolls its Southern synods and presbyteries, convened in Pittsburgh. Instead of forgetting the past and looking forward, it declared that to be readmitted each Southern minister must confess the "sin" of secession and renounce the error of considering slavery a divinely sanctioned institution. Church sessions were commanded to apply these same tests for readmission of members to communion. That Assembly also told its Board of Domestic Missions that the South was now a missionary territory.

This action not only prevented an early reunion of the Northern and Southern churches but also caused the withdrawal of synods in the border states to join the Southern Presbyterian Church. Thus, two seperate denominational organizations became firmly established. Despite later withdrawal of the bitter things that each had said about the other, attempts at reconciliation did not succeed.

This is the kind of picture we Christians seem to project to many. No wonder outsiders are turned off by the Church.

When we are in mission with the Risen Lord, we will exemplify a caring and forbearance within the community of Christ's people. They will know we are Christians by our love!

Questions for Pupils on the Next Lesson. 1. How do you accept Christ's claim of superiority in the light of conflicting contemporary claims for allegiance? 2. How may Old Testament passages help people to understand the work of Christ? 3. Looking at the Book of Hebrews, how would you translate its imagery into present-day terms? 4. What are the manifestations of the Holy Spirit today?

TOPIC FOR YOUTH
WORKING WITH CHRIST

Parable of Interdependence. When we accept the fact that we Christians are meant to work with Christ throughout the world, we have a different perspective toward ourselves, toward others, and toward the world's resources. Working with Christ especially means remembering to distribute the food.

John Conner invented a Hunger Simulation Experience (Please don't call it a game.) for people in earnest about learning how food is distributed—indeed, maldistributed—around the world.

Compressed, the event may be described as follows. Each participant draws from a container a slip of paper telling him or her what continent is home. Presiding at a meal, John—anyone can learn how—begins to pass out food, divided in each case according to the availability or lack of food, in the respective continents. Those representing poor and hungry continents get precious little. The affluent nations, in accord with fact, get plenty. Protein is a diet essential. A long loaf of bread is cut in portions that represent the amount of animal protein the average individual in each continent receives daily. Silverware is distributed on another unequal basis to represent resources other than food.

Not only the amounts of food but the reactions of the people are interesting. They negotiate. They bargain. They barter. They move into roles they began only to represent. Finally, some become angry. It is then that light shines on the world situation.

Conner does not seek an interdependent world. He affirms that the world now is, and irrevocably, interdependent. He notes that America has the reputation, particularly at home, of feeding the world. He then notes the degree to which we are dependent on certain countries for some minerals; on others for fossil fuels; and on others for technology. He sees the people of the world sitting at a vast round table, each reaching for that which is wanted, or needed. Some are more successful than others at grasping, but that is not the point. The point is that all are around one table and all the resources are there to be shared more equitably. What one brings another needs. It is a picture of interdependence. It may be a parable of relief from hunger.

Aquarium Keepers. George G. Hunter, III, national evangelism executive of the United Methodist Church, told a gathering of evangelism leaders that many clergy and lay people have ceased being "fishers of men," and have become merely "keepers of the aquarium."

In the keynote address of the United Methodist Council on Evangelism, the head of the Board of Discipleship's evangelism section asserted that many United Methodists "equate the church with the building. They assume you do the will of God by coming to the building."

Do you agree? Is this the way it seems to be in your congregation? Or, is Hunter being too hard on church people?

More important, is George Hunter on target when it comes to you? Which are you: "fishers of men" or aquarium keepers?

Christ's Kind of People. During a discussion on the floor of a church meeting concerning the future of a local church, a statement was made by an ecclesiastical executive that the particular church being discussed should be dissolved. One of the reasons which he gave was, "The people moving into the neighborhood where the church is located are not our kind of people."

One observer in response to this statement had an explosive desire within to stand and cry out, "My God, what kind of people are our kind of people?" That particular church was dissolved and the property was sold to a denomination who no doubt looked upon the people in the neighborhood as their kind of people.

The words, "They aren't our kind of people!" have been stated over and over again by many people in the church, especially when any emphasis was placed on reaching out, beyond the local church family, for boys and girls, men and women who were not members of any church. Yet, the decline and decrease of the membership of the mainline churches continue. Those around every church are Christ's kind of people. Are you and your fellow-church members welcoming everyone?

Sentence Sermon to Remember: I have but one candle of life to burn, and I would rather burn it out where people are dying in darkness than in a land which is flooded with light. With the risen Christ, I intend to do just that.—A Missionary.

Questions for Pupils on the Next Lesson. 1. Do the young people you know understand the meaning of the claim that God revealed Himself in Jesus Christ? Do you? 2. How can you relate to Christ in an age dominated by science and technology? 3. Are you getting a good religious foundation now so that you can cope with various ideas you are encountering? 4. What are some of the present-day manifestations of the Holy Spirit?

LESSON X—MAY 3

GOD'S ULTIMATE WORD

Background Scripture: Hebrews 1:1–2:9
Devotional Reading: John 10:1–10

KING JAMES VERSION

HEBREWS 1 1 God, who at sundry times and in divers manners spake in time past unto the fathers by the prophets,

2 Hath in these last days spoken unto us by his Son, whom he hath appointed heir of all things, by whom also he made the worlds;

3 Who being the brightness of his glory, and the express image of his person, and upholding all things by the word of his power, when he had by himself purged our sins, sat down on the right hand of the Majesty on high;

4 Being made so much better than the angels, as he hath by inheritance obtained a more excellent name than they.

2 1 Therefore we ought to give the more earnest heed to the things which we have heard, lest at any time we should let *them* slip.

2 For if the word spoken by the angels was stedfast, and every transgression and disobedience received a just recompense of reward;

3 How shall we escape, if we neglect so great salvation; which at the first began to be spoken by the Lord, and was confirmed unto us by them that heard *him;*

4 God also bearing *them* witness, both with signs and wonders, and with divers miracles, and gifts of the Holy Ghost, according to his own will?

5 For unto the angels hath he not put in subjection the world to come, whereof we speak.

6 But one in a certain place testified, saying, What is man, that thou art mindful of him? or the son of man, that thou visitest him?

7 Thou madest him a little lower than the angels; thou crownedst him with glory and honour, and didst set him over the works of thy hands:

8 Thou hast put all things in subjection under his feet. For in that he put all in subjection under him, he left nothing *that is* not put under him. But now we see not yet all things put under him.

REVISED STANDARD VERSION

HEBREWS 1 1 In many and various ways God spoke of old to our fathers by the prophets; 2 but in these last days he has spoken to us by a Son, whom he appointed the heir of all things, through whom also he created the world. 3 He reflects the glory of God and bears the very stamp of his nature, upholding the universe by his word of power. When he had made purification for sins, he sat down at the right hand of the Majesty on high, 4 having become as much superior to angels as the name he has obtained is more excellent than theirs.

2 1 Therefore we must pay the closer attention to what we have heard, lest we drift away from it. 2 For if the message declared by angels was valid and every transgression or disobedience received a just retribution, 3 how shall we escape if we neglect such a great salvation? It was declared at first by the Lord, and it was attested to us by those who heard him, 4 while God also bore witness by signs and wonders and various miracles and by gifts of the Holy Spirit distributed according to his own will. 5 For it was not to angels that God subjected the world to come, of which we are speaking. 6 It has been testified somewhere,

"What is man that thou art mindful of him,
or the son of man, that thou carest for him?

7 Thou didst make him for a little while lower than the angels,
thou hast crowned him with glory and honor,
8 putting everything in subjection under his feet."

Now in putting everything in subjection to man, he left nothing outside his control. As it is, we do not yet see everything in subjection to him.

KEY VERSE: In many and various ways God spoke of old to our fathers by the prophets; but in these last days he has spoken to us by a Son . . . . Hebrews 1:1, 2 (RSV).

HOME DAILY BIBLE READINGS

Apr. 27. M. *The Eternal God.* Hebrews 1:10–14.
Apr. 28. T. *God the Creator.* Psalms 8.
Apr. 29. W. *God's Word Becomes Flesh.* John 1:1–5, 14–18.
Apr. 30. T. *God's Son.* Hebrews 1:5–9.
May 1. F. *God Reveals Through His Spirit.* 1 Corinthians 2:6–13
May 2. S. *The Eternal Christ.* Colossians 1:15–23.
May 3. S. *The Good Shepherd.* John 10:1–11.

BACKGROUND

Now we have a short series of lessons based on the Epistle to the Hebrews. While the King James Version calls this "The Epistle of Paul to the Hebrews," it is widely agreed that it was not all written by Paul but, perhaps, by Paul and Apollos—and it might better have been entitled "The Epistle to the Jewish *Christians.*" Written possibly about A.D. 67 just before the fall of Jerusalem, its main purpose is to prove that "Jesus fulfilled the highest conception of the Jewish religion, and is infinitely superior to any predecessors. Christian Jews must realize that Christ has fulfilled and surpassed all their old ideas, and they must not therefore relapse into the old Jewish religion."—J. B. Phillips.

This study of the Epistle also seeks to challenge modern Christians to steadfastness of faith on the basis of the superiority of God's revelation in Christ.

NOTES ON THE PRINTED TEXT

I. *In many and various ways God spoke of old to our fathers by the prophets; but in these last days he has spoken to us by a Son . . . .* Hebrews 1:1 (RSV). Some unknown writer has said that "By many different ways does man come unto God," and he was partly right; that is truth, but not all of the truth. Men had heard *about* God from the prophets of Israel, but that was only an *incomplete* picture. The prophets spoke to their times; Amos spoke of the social justice of God; Isaiah spoke of the holiness of God; Hosea concentrated on the love of God. All this was good, but we must remember that these prophets spoke as men who had a message from God to the men of their day. They gave those men a partial revelation of what God was like, and of what His will was for men. That was good—but not enough, not the final revelation; at best, if was piecemeal, fragmentary, and lacking in unity. It was given in various ways—by dreams, visions, through a burning bush, by angels or an angel, and in other ways.

The prophets spoke and spoke well for God. *But* (and this is a big "but") but *now* God "hath in these last days spoken unto us by his Son" (verse 2). As we have explained in previous lessons, the Jews divided time into two "ages"—the present age and the age to come or "the golden age," and the author of Hebrews is saying that the new age has begun with the coming of Jesus. He had not come as just another prophet (some, like the Mohammedans, *still* think of Jesus as just another prophet) but as the final revelation of God and as One (the only One) who could bring men directly into the presence of God. Jesus was in the direct line of the prophetic revelations, but superior to the prophets. They were men, inspired men, intelligent and consecrated men; *Jesus was the Son of God,* greater than all of the prophets put together, greater than the angels of heaven.

This divine Son is described in two ways: in His being, and in His functions or work. Upon this Jesus there was a lightness of glory, outshining all who had gone before, as the sun outshines all the other planets that whirl about it. In 2 Corinthians 4:6, Paul speaks of "the glory of God in the face of Jesus Christ." No other face on earth reflected such glory. He is so much more than a prophet: *they* were comparatively short-lived in their lives and prophecies, but *Jesus* was the *eternal* light of God come to shine upon mankind.

He is described as one who "bears the very stamp of His (God's) nature," which meant that Jesus was the exact image and expression of God. In another sense, as the Son, He stamped His image upon the human heart, and those hearts, this world, was never the same again. We know that He was the superior Son not only because of His nature, but because of what He *did:* He had within Himself the very power of God to cleanse men of their sins. He brought to man not only a "message"; He brought the new great Good News of salvation. And having done that through His labors and through Calvary, He ascended into heaven to sit at the right hand of God the Father.

No other man can make such a claim. As Sholem Asch, the famous Jewish author, once said to this editor, "To me, Jesus Christ was the greatest man ever to walk this earth." Right!

II. *Therefore we must pay the closer attention to what we have heard, lest we drift away from it.* Hebrews 2:1 (RSV). The author of Hebrews is speaking to the second and possibly the third generation of Christians. These generations had not *seen* Jesus; they had only *heard* about Him, and they were in danger of neglecting what they had heard. They were drifting, as a ship without a pilot will drift from the great open sea to rocks upon which the ship could be wrecked.

The author has in mind two revelations of God: the first came through the angels of the Lord, and was written down in the Ten Commandments; the second came through Jesus Christ the Son, and it was vastly more important than the first. Both were valid revelations, but not of equal importance. The point here is that the Hebrews had "drifted away" from the revelation of the prophets and angels—and they had suffered for that; "every transgression or disobedience received a just retribution (punishment)" (verse 2). So, the author asks, what makes you think that you can allow yourself to drift away from the greater revelation of salvation through Christ and not be punished for *that?*

It is a necessary warning put into good words. Most men do not break away from God with one terrible sin; they just drift away from Him, gradually, bit by bit, slowly. But in spite of their drifting, God still loves them and seeks their return.

The teacher should pause here and read Psalms 8, for this Psalm runs all through this chapter of Hebrews. "What is man," the Psalms asks, "that thou (God) art mindful of him?" Why should God be so everlastingly interested in what man is or does? He is mindful because God has made man as something "a little lower than the angels," and has given man dominion over all the earth. That is a great dominion, but God trusted man with it, and He knew that man was capable of exercising that dominion faithfully and under His guidance. Oh, yes, He knew that man would sin, but man could be saved from his sins and born again into a finer, more reverent man; this whole Psalm is "a great cry of the glory of man as God meant it to be." Made only a little less than the angels, man could *become* angelic through the sacrifice of His Son. God loves us not for what we *are*, but for what we *might* be.

Horace Walpole, the great British author and letterwriter, once wrote to his friend the Earl of Strafford, "We are poor silly animals; we live for an instant upon a particle of a boundless universe . . . ." and then, presumably, we die like animals. It seems unlikely, as we read this, that Walpole ever read the eighth Psalm. But St. Augustine, who knew the Psalm, wrote of man in these words: An earthly animal, *but worthy of Heaven.*" Augustine, like the writer of Hebrews, saw the evil (animal) in man, but he also saw in man the molding hand of God shaping him into a being crowned with glory and honor and lifted high above the form of the animal and in control of everything on earth.

The passage ends with a jolting bit of warning: "As it is, we do not yet see everything in subjection to him" (see verse 8). Men are proud of their powers, of their advancement toward a better world, of their progress in science, but men have not yet learned how to put all that under subjection. Men crave power in order to rule other men—and that is power running wild. Men fly faster than the speed of light and use their airplanes to drop bombs and set cities afire. Not yet have we moved very far up the ladder toward the status of the angels. As G. K. Chesterton says, "This one thing is certain: man is not what he was meant to be."

Not yet do men see clearly the glory offered them in the uplifting, ennobling Christ. That is not God's fault; it is ours.

SUGGESTIONS TO TEACHERS

In the ancient days in the Speyside area of the Scottish Highlands, every person belonged to the Clan Grant. The Grants were proud of their heritage, and successfully withstood many enemy attacks. Whenever danger presented itself, the chief sent a messenger carrying a fiery cross throughout the glens. At each village or lonely cottage, the cry, "Stand Fast, Craigellachie!" would be shouted. Craigellachie, the name of a mountain in the heart of Grant country, symbolized the steadfast qualities which the Grants needed in times of trouble. To this day, the motto of the Clan is, "Stand Fast, Craigellachie."

The Book of Hebrews is an attempt to rally faltering Christians. "*Stand fast!*" could well be its subtitle. Hebrews was circulated as a kind of fiery cross to steady shaky believers in the first century.

God's ultimate Word, the writer shouts, is in Jesus Christ. Today's lesson, the first of five from Hebrews, emphasizes that God's revelation in Jesus Christ is supreme and is sufficient for any danger.

Construct your lesson with the end in mind that your class members, like early Christians, often feel bewildered and uneasy. Some privately wonder whether their faith is strong enough. Others secretly question whether Christ is enough to help them. Others may tend to relegate Christ to the area of life marked "sacred," and regard everything outside of that small compartment to be beyond Christ's control or interest.

1. *EXACT LIKENESS OF GOD'S OWN BEING.* Spend enough time on the Scripture material to catch the flavor of Hebrews' claims about Jesus Christ. The author claims that Jesus "bears the very stamp of his (God's) nature" (1:3). Let the significance of this assertion about Christ sink in. Impress on your class that Jesus is more than another holy man or leader. Others may say, "I will try to teach you something about God's nature." Jesus is, in effect, the embodiment of God's own nature.

2. *PLACE OF HONOR IN GOD'S UNIVERSE.* The words about Jesus sitting on God's right hand are picturesque images from the ancient Middle Eastern courts, and emphasize that Jesus ranks with the Creator-God. Provoke some soul-searching among your people by asking what or who gets the place of honor in their personal universes.

3. *ETERNAL RULER IN EVERY AGE.* Jesus is greater than any angel, any power, any supernatural force. A society which seeks for directions from astrology and tea leaves, for answers from millionaire swamis and cult leaders, for stability from a drink or a joint, will founder. Direct your class discussion to encompass the awesome breadth of the claims about Jesus in Hebrews. He is sufficient. Although the world may seem to be going through frightening changes, Christ's claim still stands!

TOPIC FOR ADULTS
GOD'S ULTIMATE WORD

Inescapable Christ. Katherine Mansfield, the gifted shortstory writer, had lost her faith somewhere in a doctor's waiting room in her losing battle with tuberculosis. To her best friend she wrote: "God is now gone for all of us. Yet we must believe; and not only that—we must carry our weakness, and our sin, and our devilishness to somebody." She toyed with the idea that love between lovers might take the place of the religious relationship, but then dropped it with a sigh, saying, "It's no good." Even human love, she knew, could not atone for sin. Katherine Mansfield, who tried but gave up the idea of forgiving, got a note from her lover, "Cheer up, Kate, Jesus is a back number."

But is He? We still date our years from His birth. By all odds He should now be the forgotten man, but He is not. Time is not "like an ever-rolling stream" that "bears all its sons away." Christ, like the sun, is the center, and like the sun gives light, guidance, forgiveness, reconciliation. He is "the Way, the Truth, and the Life."

Fashioning God to Suit My Taste. The famous writer, Isaac Bashevis Singer, writes for many when it comes to trying to describe the Diety.

He is frequently asked if he is a religious man, Isaac Bashevis Singer said, and it is true that he believes in God.

Singer's God possesses many desirable traits, although "He has burdened Himself with so many tasks that one eternity is not enough for

Him." Not surprisingly, this God is also something of a writer. Maybe what He sets down isn't always clear, Mr. Singer said, but then, "What is God to do—discuss His book with every reader?"

But since he has no clear idea what God has in mind, "I have fashioned Him precisely to suit my taste." What this means, said the Nobel Prize-Winning Yiddish author, is that "Mine is an eclectic God."

Is this what you are doing—fashioning God precisely to suit your taste? Do you have a merely vague, "eclectic God"?

Christians claim that Christ is God's ultimate Word, God's unique revelation of Himself.

Reread the Book of Hebrews. "In many and various ways God spoke of old to our fathers by the prophets; but in these last days He has spoken to us by a son" (1:1, 2 RSV).

Genuine Poverty. "Very often we have real poverty in very well-to-do families. I am not speaking about the lack of material things. The real poverty is the poverty of the heart. They have a hunger for God. I've talked to big people. I've talked to small people. They all want to know 'what is poverty? What is charity?' It always comes back to religious life.

"You must remember we all belong to Christ."— Mother Theresa, of Calcutta.

Questions for Pupils on the Next Lesson. 1. What are some of the ways you have discovered for putting faith into action? 2. Why do we need to reach out to those in bondage? 3. How do you deal with temptation? In what ways does your faith help? 4. How does Christ's example give you assurance for daily living? 5. How may the Church encourage a pioneering spirit in your faith and instill the joy of confident living? 6. How may the help of Christ enable people to overcome the reluctance they have to risk involvement?

TOPIC FOR YOUTH
CHRIST REVEALS GOD TO US

Too Smart. An eight-year-old boy had been listening to his father and a friend discuss some of computer technology of today's world. The little fellow was awed by the description of what computers could do. As the two men disclosed more of the wondrous achievements of these electronic instruments, the youngster grew more and more impressed. Finally in excitement he shrilled, "Nowadays, we know more than God, don't we Daddy?"

This is the attitude many persons hold.

Hebrews states unequivocally that we are *not* wiser than God. It continues that God's plans and wisdom are spelled out through Jesus Christ's life. Christ is the ultimate Word, not scientific gadgetry, not human achievement.

Abraham Lincoln writing for his day also speaks to our times when he warned, "Intoxicated with unbroken success, we have become too self-sufficient to feel the necessity of redeeming and preserving grace, too proud to pray to the God that made us."

God's Priorities. If Christ reveals God to us, we must arrange our priorities and values to be in line with Jesus Christ. What about your priorities? Is the number one the "Me" priority?

The "Me" priority has gotten out of hand, if a study issued by the Carnegie Council on Policy Studies in Higher Education is any indication. The study indicates that college campuses face an ethics crisis, involving student cheating, vandalism, and theft. It's complicated, on the other hand, by faculty escalation of grades and dishonest advertising by colleges seeking students at a time when the pool of college-age persons is diminishing.

The report cited a survey that said 8.8 percent of undergraduates considered cheating necessary to attain the grades they aspired to, compared with 7.5 percent in 1969. Among graduate students, the figure was 9.8 percent in 1976, up from 5.4 percent in 1969.

The study expressed concern that student and institutional abuses "may indicate a larger and more deep-seated problem: A general loss of self-confidence and . . . mutual trust, and a general decline in integrity of conduct on campus."

If Christ is God's ultimate Word in your life, it must affect what you do in the classroom and on the campus. Your priorities? "Me" or Jesus, which?

Who Reveals. Whom do you turn to when you want answers about the heavier, deeper mysteries of life? Do you truly believe that Christ is the One who shows us what we want to know about God and the future?

Maybe. But you perhaps have some interest in what the seers and psychics are saying. Maybe you even do a lot of reading about what crystal-ball gazers and people who go into trances and claim to be the mouthpieces for someone in another world are saying. You may privately take their predictions and pronouncements more seriously than Jesus Christ's.

Let's look at the record of one such psychic for just one year. Religious News Service kept the score on Jeane Dixon, one of the favorites of many. Here's a list of some of her predictions for 1978:

"The American people will be stunned in 1978 by the resignation of President Carter, the finding of relics which prove aliens have visited earth—and by an amazing discovery that nearly wipes out cancer . . . President Carter's Panama Canal Treaties will never go into effect. Pope Paul VI will survive, to surprise the world with his vigor and determination."

Needless to say, not one of these came true.

Christ reveals God to us. Christ is still the Way, the Truth, the Life. Rely on Him, not the charlatan-saviours who pretend to be ultimate. Jesus Christ is God's complete message to us!

Sentence Sermon to Remember: In his life, Christ is an example, showing us how to live; in his death, he is a sacrifice, satisfying for our sins; in his resurrection, a conqueror; in his ascension, a king; in his intercession, a high priest.—Martin Luther.

Questions for Pupils on the Next Lesson. 1. How exactly is Christ the "pioneer" of our salvation? 2. When confronted with temptations of sex, drugs, and pressures from peer groups, how does Christ help believers to find help? 3. Is God really concerned with every phase of our lives now, or is He mostly interested in the future? 4. What are some of the risks of being a Christian that you are finding?

LESSON XI—MAY 10

PIONEER OF OUR SALVATION

Background Scripture: Hebrews 2:10–4:13
Devotional Reading: John 6:35–41, 44, 45

KING JAMES VERSION

HEBREWS 2 10 For it became him, for whom *are* all things, and by whom *are* all things, in bringing many sons unto glory, to make the captain of their salvation perfect through sufferings.

11 For both he that sanctifieth and they who are sanctified *are* all of one: for which cause he is not ashamed to call them brethren,

12 Saying, I will declare thy name unto my brethren, in the midst of the church will I sing praise unto thee.

13 And again, I will put my trust in him. And again, Behold I and the children which God hath given me.

14 Forasmuch then as the children are partakers of flesh and blood, he also himself likewise took part of the same; that through death he might destroy him that had the power of death, that is, the devil;

15 And deliver them who through fear of death were all their lifetime subject to bondage.

16 For verily he took not on *him the nature of* angels; but he took on *him* the seed of Abraham.

17 Wherefore in all things it behoved him to be made like unto *his* brethren, that he might be a merciful and faithful high priest in things *pertaining* to God, to make reconciliation for the sins of the people.

18 For in that he himself hath suffered being tempted, he is able to succour them that are tempted.

REVISED STANDARD VERSION

HEBREWS 2 10 For it was fitting that he, for whom and by whom all things exist, in bringing many sons to glory, should make the pioneer of their salvation perfect through suffering. 11 For he who sanctifies and those who are sanctified have all one origin. That is why he is not ashamed to call them brethren, 12 saying,

"I will proclaim thy name to my brethren,

in the midst of the congregation I will praise thee."

13 And again,

"I will put my trust in him."

And again,

"Here am I, and the children God has given me."

14 Since therefore the children share in flesh and blood, he himself likewise partook of the same nature, that through death he might destroy him who has the power of death, that is, the devil, 15 and deliver all those who through fear of death were subject to lifelong bondage. 16 For surely it is not with angels that he is concerned but with the descendants of Abraham. 17 Therefore he had to be made like his brethren in every respect, so that he might become a merciful and faithful high priest in the service of God, to make expiation for the sins of the people. 18 For because he himself has suffered and been tempted, he is able to help those who are tempted.

KEY VERSE: For because he himself has suffered and been tempted, he is able to help those who are tempted. Hebrews 2:18 (RSV).

HOME DAILY BIBLE READINGS

May 4. M. *Sending of the Son.* John 3:16-21.
May 5. T. *Salvation Through Jesus Christ.* 2 Timothy 2:8–13.
May 6. W. *Salvation Is at Hand.* Psalms 85:7–13.
May 7. T. *The Day of Salvation.* 2 Corinthians 6:1–10.
May 8. F. *No Longer Strangers.* Ephesians 3:11–22.
May 9. S. *Salvation Belongs to . . . the Lamb.* Revelation 7:9–11.
May 10. S. *I Am the Bread of Life.* John 6:35–41, 44, 45.

BACKGROUND

We have a very interesting problem on our hands with this lesson. The problem is: why did Jesus Christ have to die on a cross? This is not a new problem—something disturbing only your generation; men have been talking about it for centuries, and most of them have come up with no satisfactory answers. There is only one answer, and many miss it completely.

Some men claim that He was foolish to die that way when He didn't have to. Others say it was His own fault because He outraged the Jewish people and their leaders, and did great harm to their faith. Still others tell us that it was not the Jews who crucified Him, but the Romans (and there is truth in that) because to the Romans He was guilty of treason. Which of these answers is the right answer?

None of them are right. They are only half-answers, containing a few half-truths but missing completely its greater, basic, and divine truth as it is explained in the second chapter of Hebrews, which is our Scripture for today. Read this Scripture carefully. Hebrews is not always easy to understand.

NOTES ON THE PRINTED TEXT

I. *For it was fitting that he . . . should make the pioneer of their salvation perfect through suffering.* Hebrews 2:10 (RSV). This word *pioneer* is used in the Revised Standard Version of the Bible; in the King James Version the word is *captain;* both words come from the same Greek word *archegos,* which can also mean founder, or head. Socrates founded a school of philosophy. Moses was a captain of Israel who led his people through the wars of the wilderness; Gideon was the leader of the hosts of the Lord. All of these "captains" led their followers into something that was new. The American pioneers who took their wagon-trains into the new West in our country, fighting off the opposition of the Indians, led their people into a land and a culture and a civilization that was something new in history. And Jesus was a greater pioneer than all of them, a spiritual captain of the soul, the founder of a fellowship of believers who were to turn the tide of history and create a new brand or kind of man never known before He came.

Pioneer! The word smacks of *trail-breakers.* The word makes us think of Columbus sailing an unknown sea, breaking the way out of an old world into one entirely new, of Galileo with his telescope discovering a new universe, of Livingstone and Stanley opening up an unexplored continent in Africa, of Peary at the North Pole. All these were great trailblazers, but pygmies in comparison with the Pioneer Christ.

Just how and of what was Jesus a pioneer? He was, Hebrews says, the pioneer of *salvation.* He broke a new pathway to God. He broke with old, tired religions that just were not enough and gave mankind a faith to live by in this life and an assurance of eternal life in a world beyond this one. He made a final conquering attack upon the problem of men's sins which had left men unhappy and insecure and opened to them the gates to the Kingdom of God. He offered Himself as a sacrifice for their sins, dying in their place: He gave them *salvation.* No man, no pioneer before

Him, had ever been able to give men the confidence to believe that beyond the shadow of a doubt.

Pioneers are men who know the trail over which they lead others; they are also men who understand those who follow them—their strengths, their weaknesses. Jesus fulfilled that requirement as the leader and deliverer of men: He knew, as verse 11 of this chapter of Hebrews puts it, that both He and His people were of "one origin"— that is, both Jesus and His followers had one common father—God! *The Living Bible* clarifies this in a beautiful paraphrase of the verse: "We who have been made holy by Jesus, now have the same Father he has. *That is why Jesus is not ashamed to call us his brothers."*

That is a tremendous statement. Before Jesus came, the nations of the world had galaxies of gods *who were remote from men:* they lived on some "Olympus," some mountain so high in the sky that no human being could reach them—far, far away from the homes and cities of men. But Jesus came down to earth to live in the midst of men, to wear their flesh, to talk face to face with men, to put His hands upon them. He lives among us as a brother, and He is not ashamed to *call* us brothers.

This is all important, when we read the words that follow—words that tell us *why* Jesus identified Himself with us, and why He *had* to suffer on His cross.

II. For because he himself has suffered and been tempted, he is able to help those who are tempted. Hebrews 2:18 (RSV). Jesus was the *perfect* spiritual pioneer; He was perfectly equipped to bring to men freedom (salvation) from man's two worst enemies: the power and influence of the devil over the lives of men, and the last great enemy of all mankind—the fear of death. No absentee God, far removed from men, could do that; such a God (or god) could only shout his commands from afar. But Jesus, wearing the flesh and in the body of man, could know at firsthand all the fears and temptations of man. "Jesus could not be a perfect mediator between God and man unless he shared in the sorrows and tribulations of his brethren."— H. T. Andrews, in *The Abingdon Bible Commentary.*

The King James Version says that it was God who made Jesus "perfect through suffering," and there is profound truth in that statement. The ideal counsellor for a man tempted to steal is a man who has also been tempted to steal, and who knows the consequences of stealing. The man most able to bring comfort to one in sorrow is a man who has walked through the darkness of sorrow himself. The best doctors are those who have suffered the pain of their patients. He who does not know the tortures of temptation is usually of little help to others who are tempted.

Recently, on TV, we saw a group of young (teen aged) potential criminals taken for a visit to a state prison. They were confronted by hardened convicts serving long sentences, who talked with them (often shouted at them) about what life was like behind prison walls. It was horrible—and it horrified the tough little would-be criminals who came strutting into the prison. They came out of it "scared straight"; only one of their group committed crime again. When they saw the suffering that faced them if they did not change their ways, they *changed* their ways. Only hardened criminals could have made them do that, because hardened criminals knew what it was all about.

Jesus was able to lead men out of temptation for the simple reason that He had put on their flesh and clothes and submitted to temptation Himself. As a brother, He could understand their sorrows and sufferings. When He went to the cross, He suffered the pain of others who die on crosses; on Calvary, *in dying,* and in coming back from His tomb, *He proved to men that death could be conquered.*

Jesus did not want to die on that cross, but He knew that He *had* to die so, if we were to fully understand that He was truly the Suffering Servant who in dying and rising again could take from us all fear of death and all temptation. If He had not died so, He would have been quickly forgotten. On the cross, He proved to all of us that He is wonderfully able to save us from the sins of life and the false fear and despair of death.

Some unknown Christian has said, "We bring the atoms of sin to the cross where they are smashed."

SUGGESTIONS TO TEACHERS

Today's lesson centers on Jesus as the Pioneer of our slavation. You may be helped to prepare your lesson by knowing more about the Greek word for *pioneer* in the scriptural passage from Hebrews. It is the word for one who blazed a trail through uncharted wilderness. It refers to one who opened a passage so others could follow safely. The same Greek word was also used to refer to a powerful swimmer who would make his way out through the dangerous surf to a shipwrecked vessel, carrying the end of a rope, and who would fasten the rope to the wreck, thereby assisting passengers and crew to make their way to safety before the ship broke apart. Jesus as the Pioneer of our salvation may be understood to embody all of these notions. He blazed the trail; He opened the passage; He effected the rescue.

With the notion of Jesus' pioneering for us in mind, have your class examine the rest of the biblical material in today's lesson.

1. *PROTOTYPE.* Jesus is the prototype of what God intends each of us to be. His pioneering has made it possible for us to grow into His likeness. Hebrews notes that Jesus has acted to destroy the power of death (2:14) and fear of death (2:15). He enables us to withstand the destructive effects of anxiety about ourselves and our future. Jesus Christ helps us when tempted. Hebrews takes considerable pains to point out that Jesus endured the same fears and frustrations which we and all humans suffer, but pioneered a new life for us. Ask your class what it thinks God intends us to be. How does each member see himself or herself in the light of God's intentions for the human race, as revealed in the prototype, Jesus?

2. *PARTNER.* Jesus is more than a pattern to be followed. He goes with us in our struggles. Or, as Hebrews puts it, "we share in Christ" (3:14). He wants to be our partner. Do your people really share their troubles with Him and with each other? Or do they hold back? Do they share their time and their money with Him? Do they regard Jesus as

Just like ... if he ... is sitting ... to JS. ... class

partner in their decision-making? Consider the ramifications of allowing Jesus Christ to take His place as partner in your class members' lives. Ask if there are any areas where one cannot or should not share in Christ.

3. *PROMISER.* If you are a person who puts pencil marks in your Bible, and if you would underline the words *faith* or *believe* or *trust* every time they appear in Hebrews, you would find nearly every page heavily marked. Be full of faith (or "faith-full") *now*—this very day—is the constant plea in Hebrews. Trust! Discover that Christ keeps His word. Furthermore, such trust means receiving "rest" or a sense of calm and confidence from the Promiser!

4. *PROBER.* Call attention to the way Hebrews describes the way that God's Word is like a scalpel in the hands of a master surgeon (4:13), dissecting and laying bare the most secret thoughts and motives of each of us. Nothing is hidden from the Lord! Since He already knows us better than we know ourselves, He is able to pioneer a new life for us. Also, if God knows firsthand exactly who we are, yet accepts us, He is astonishingly merciful! Encourage your class to think about the meaning of God's knowledge of our private lives, including those matters which even spouses or our closest friends are not aware of.

TOPIC FOR ADULTS
THE PIONEERING SPIRIT

Unheralded Pioneer. Remember Charles E. Yeager? On October 14, 1947, he made aviation history, and pioneered the space-travel age, when he became the first person to fly faster than the speed of sound. Until his historic flight in 1947, however, many scientists had theorized that flight at such speeds would demolish any aircraft used to achieve it.

People told Yeager that he was crazy to risk trying to fly faster than sound. Yeager, however, knew that someone had to pioneer to break the space barrier. He succeeded and opened the way for incredible developments in aeronautics. Yeager is also credited with being the first person to fly at twice the speed of sound.

As so often happens, however, no one remembered Charlie Yeager's pioneering efforts. It wasn't until nearly thirty years later that someone thought to acknowledge him. Congress had a special medal struck for Yeager, "the noncombatant equivalent of the Medal of Honor," and had the President present it to him to express the nation's gratitude.

Christ was an even greater pioneer. He opened the way to us to God. Like most pioneers, Jesus Christ was (and is) also neglected by many. He, however, risked everything for us. Thanks to His pioneering spirit, we also may risk for God and for others!

Christ's pioneering for us impels us also to be pioneers. Frequently, this exacts a heavy cost for us. Christ's pioneering demanded that He sacrifice His life.

Costly Pioneering. For years, fans had packed the stands to watch the bloody gladiatorial contests. These contests pitted two combatants to fight until one of them died. Sometimes teams of gladiators were forced to battle each other until only one survivor was left. The Roman spec-

SEE 3

tators called this bloody slaughter "sport." Few voices protested the practice. Meanwhile, the Roman arenas were filled regularly for the gladiatorial contests.

One day in the fifth century A.D., a sensitive Syrian monk by the name of Telemachus decided to protest the grisly sport of compelling humans to butcher each other. Telemachus went to the Colosseum in Rome. When the gladiators were starting to fight, the little monk leaped into the ring and stopped the contest.

Telemachus's pioneering act infuriated the sports fans. They poured out of the stands onto the floor of the arena and attacked him. Telemachus's battered body was found lying on the pavement after order was restored. Telemachus's pioneering spirit, however, deeply affected the people of Rome. His sacrifice in protest against the carnage in the arena persuaded Emperor Honorius to do away with the bloody gladiatorial contests.

Would that our society had more such pioneers who had such a conscience!

Pioneers for Freedom Today. Leaders of the Presbyterian Church in Taiwan recognize that the Church must serve as the pioneer for religious freedom and civil liberties for all Taiwanese citizens. They have also learned that such pioneering is never easy.

These intrepid Christians have long been subjected to pressures by the Taiwan government to cease their pioneering for freedom. For instance, the Taiwan Department of Interior Affairs censured the Presbyterian Church because of its support for Human Rights. Leaders of the Church had gathered for a consultation in December, 1978. Government representatives offered each delegate $1,361 if the general secretary, Dr. Kao, were not reelected and if a statement on human rights were not passed. In spite of the bribes, Dr. Kao was reelected and the resolution passed, each by about a five to one majority.

Questions for Pupils on the Next Lesson. 1. What are ways in which you and other adults can develop confidence in prayer which is willing to share everything with Jesus? 2. What are some of the ways in which Jesus enables us to know God and the wholeness of salvation? 3. What is meant by the "priesthood of all believers?" 4. What are some of the principal developmental stages in Christian faith? What are ways to make progress in them?

TOPIC FOR YOUTH
PIONEER OF YOUR SALVATION

Run Down the Road. Lorado Taft was a great person as well as a great sculptor. He had a cottage in New England where he loved to spend the summers. He would invite friends to come just to sit on the porch with him and watch the sunsets. One guest described the experience in these words. "He pointed out the infinite variety of colors, changing and shifting on the horizon, his trained senses enabling him to perceive more than an average man would have seen in this sunset."

The maid who had been serving them, interrupted after a few moments to say, "Mr. Taft, may I run down the road? I want to go home a minute."

"Bless your heart," Mr. Taft replied, "why do you want to go home at this time?"

She said, "I want to show Mother the sunset."

"Your mother has lived here a good many years," Mr. Taft said; "she must have seen many sunsets."

"Oh, no," was the earnest reply. "We never saw the sunsets here until you came."

Life looked different to everyone after they met Jesus Christ. They never saw life the right way until He came. He pioneered a new understanding of God, of their place in His universe, of the future. No one had really seen reality or beauty until Jesus came among them.

Is this also true for you? Has Jesus Christ opened up an entirely new perspective for you? If so, "run down the road" and tell others!

Pain of Pioneering. Just as Christ is the Pioneer, so you must be a pioneer for justice, for truth, for caring. Such pioneering usually costs.

William Dick was the pioneer for excellence in veterinary medicine.

Willie Dick was born in 1793. His father, John Dick, was a Scottish blacksmith. In those days before cars, taxis, buses, and tractors were invented, people used horses to ride on and to pull carriages and farm carts and ploughs. This made the blacksmith's job very necessary and important. As well as other things, smiths made and fitted shoes on the horses' hooves to protect them from hard stony roads and cobbled streets.

John Dick knew a good deal about the ailments and diseases of horses, and how to treat them. And not only about horses, for farmers who came to his smith talked about their cows and sheep and pigs and dogs and cats, too.

Young Willie worked with his father, and listened, and learned. He soon realized, however, that some men just pretended that they knew how to cure or heal sick animals, and in fact caused suffering and death by their ignorance. Willie felt he must do something to help them.

Even after he had left school to work in the forge, he spent his spare time attending classes in mathematics and other subjects. An opportunity came to join a class for medical students. Just what he wanted. Learning about people's anatomy and diseases was a step towards knowing more about animals.

Some of the young men laughed at him—a blacksmith's son, a working lad, studying along with young gentlemen of the medical profession! Willie let them laugh. He worked all the harder.

By chance, he heard that there was a veterinary college in London. Off he went, and in a very short time gained its diploma of veterinary surgeon.

Back to Edinburgh. He lectured at first to smiths and farriers. Gradually people recognized that here was a man who really knew how to care for horses and other animals in health and in sickness.

When the Highland Society at Edinburgh set up its Veterinary School in 1823, Mr. William Dick was appointed as Lecturer. The "School" was really a forge, with the shoeing of horses one of the subjects! At his own expense, Willie added a stable as a hospital where poor people's animals could be kept and treated free of charge.

Later, new buildings were opened and improvements made. Soon students were coming from all over this country and even from America. Queen Victoria appointed Mr. William Dick to be her vet in Scotland.

William Dick died in 1866. By that time, more than 800 men had been trained at his school. Just think how much animal suffering had been prevented or relieved!

Pew-Sitter or Pioneer? "Too often in their church-life people adopt an attitude of the theater, imagining that the preacher is an actor and they his critics, praising and blaming the performance. Actually, the people are the actors on the stage of life; the preacher is merely the prompter, reminding the people of their lost lines; and they, the people listening, in truth, act before God."— *Purity of Heart,* Soren Kierkegaard.

Sentence Sermon to Remember: Feed on Christ, and then go and live your life, and it is Christ in you that lives your life, that helps the poor, that tells the truth, that fights the battle, and that wins the crown.— Phillips Brooks.

Questions for Pupils on the Next Lesson. 1. What is the place of prayer in your life? 2. What are the principal stumbling blocks to spiritual growth in the lives of people your age? 3. What exactly is meant by the phrase "the priesthood of all believers"? 4. What are some of the stages of Christian growth? What stage are you on? What are you doing to mature to a higher stage of Christian faith?

LESSON XII—MAY 17

OUR GREAT HIGH PRIEST

Background Scripture: Hebrews 4:14–7:28
Devotional Reading: John 14:15–24

KING JAMES VERSION

HEBREWS 4 14 Seeing then that we have a great high priest, that is passed into the heavens, Jesus the Son of God, let us hold fast *our* profession.

15 For we have not a high priest which cannot be touched with the feeling of our infirmities; but was in all points tempted like as *we are,* yet without sin.

16 Let us therefore come boldly unto the throne of grace, that we may obtain mercy, and find grace to help in time of need.

5 1 For every high priest taken from among men is ordained for men in things *pertaining* to God, that he may offer both gifts and sacrifices for sins:

2 Who can have compassion on the ignorant, and on them that are out of the way; for that he himself also is compassed with infirmity.

3 And by reason hereof he ought, as for the people, so also for himself, to offer for sins.

4 And no man taketh this honour unto himself, but he that is called of God, as *was* Aaron.

5 So also Christ glorified not himself to be made a high priest; but he that said unto him, Thou art my Son, to day have I begotten thee.

6 As he saith also in another *place,* Thou *art* a priest for ever after the order of Melchizedek.

7 Who in the days of his flesh, when he had offered up prayers and supplications with strong crying and tears unto him that was able to save him from death, and was heard in that he feared;

8 Though he were a Son, yet learned he obedience by the things which he suffered;

9 And being made perfect, he became the author of eternal salvation unto all them that obey him;

10 Called of God an high priest after the order of Melchizedek.

REVISED STANDARD VERSION

HEBREWS 4 14 Since then we have a great high priest who has passed through the heavens, Jesus, the Son of God, let us hold fast our confession.

15 For we have not a high priest who is unable to sympathize with our weaknesses, but one who in every respect has been tempted as we are, yet without sin.

16 Let us then with confidence draw near to the throne of grace, that we may receive mercy and find grace to help in time of need.

5 1 For every high priest chosen from among men is appointed to act on behalf of men in relation to God, to offer gifts and sacrifices for sins.

2 He can deal gently with the ignorant and wayward, since he himself is beset with weakness.

3 Because of this he is bound to offer sacrifice for his own sins as well as for those of the people.

4 And one does not take the honor upon himself, but he is called by God, just as Aaron was.

5 So also Christ did not exalt himself to be made a high priest, but was appointed by him who said to him,

"Thou art my Son,
   today I have begotten thee";

6 as he says also in another place,

"Thou art a priest for ever, after the
   order of Melchizedek."

7 In the days of his flesh, Jesus offered up prayers and supplications, with loud cries and tears, to him who was able to save him from death, and he was heard for his godly fear. 8 Although he was a Son, he learned obedience through what he suffered; 9 and being made perfect he became the source of eternal salvation to all who obey him, 10 being designated by God a high priest after the order of Melchizedek.

KEY VERSE: Let us then with confidence draw near to the throne of grace, that we may receive mercy and find grace to help in time of need. Hebrews 4:16 (RSV).

HOME DAILY BIBLE READINGS

May *11.* M. *The Source of Eternal Salvation.* Hebrews 5:7–14.
May *12.* T. *"Offer Right Sacrifices."* Psalms 4.
May *13.* W. *"Offer Spiritual Sacrifices."* 1 Peter 2:1–10.
May *14.* T. *"A Living Sacrifice."* Romans 12:1–8.
May *15.* F. *The Sacrificial Love.* John 15:12–17.
May *16.* S. *The Priest Who Offered Himself.* Hebrews 7:23–28.
May *17.* S. *The Spirit of Truth.* John 14:15–24.

BACKGROUND

Far, far back in the early history of Israel, we meet priests and high priests. The father-in-law of Joseph was an Egyptian priest; the priests of that period had the power to make or break kings—to set them up on thrones or drive them from their thrones. Jethro, the father-in-law of Moses, was a good priest. In Israel, no other class wielded such power and influence. Traditionally, the formal priesthood of Israel began with Levi, the third son of Jacob and head of the tribe of Levites, who were known as the priestly tribe. The early Levites were the early priests— and high priests; they were assigned to work in the Hebrew Tabernacle. Thus, the priesthood was a matter of heredity. Some who inherited the position of priests were good priests, and some others were not good at all. Good or bad, they were "born to the office."

The highest priestly position was held by one called the high priest; he was viewed as the holiest man in Israel and the spiritual head of the people, and he had authority over the highest lay officials. He was the only priest who was anointed.

Now let us see what all this priestly background had to do with Jesus Christ.

NOTES ON THE PRINTED TEXT

I. Since then we have a great high priest who has passed through the heavens, Jesus, the Son of God, let us hold fast our confession. Hebrews 4:14 (RSV). Up to the arrival of Jesus among us, the high priests of Israel were men, and only men, like all the rest of us. They were priests by way of heredity—priests who were fortunate enough to have been born within the priestly tribe, priests who inherited their position as members of the Aaronic line. But Jesus has a qualification for the high priesthood that the others never had; He came as the Son of God, and He had "passed through the heavens."

What does that word *heavens* mean? It could mean the heavens, or heaven, above the starry firmament, or it could mean the heaven of the angels; more probably it meant the heaven of the very presence of God. *The Living Bible* suggests that Jesus is our High Priest "because he has gone to heaven itself to help us." We like that. Jesus was no mere man who wanted to be a high priest; *He was One who was in closest touch with God in heaven.* Knowing that, let us *never* lose our trust in Him; no other priest, high or low, has such credentials, or is more worthy of our trust and faith.

That alone "entitled" Jesus to the position of the greatest high priest of all time. But there was something else. Jesus was not only in closest touch with God; He was in closest touch with *man.* He not only knew the power of God; He knew the weaknesses of men because He had become one of them. He knew the meaning of human temptation—knew it better than men knew it, for He had been tempted as no other on earth had ever been tempted. Think of it: here was One who, possessing the very nature and power of God, never needed to subject Himself to temptation at all, but who in His desire to help men into the presence of God laid Himself wide open to every temptation known among men. He was "in all points tempted as we are, yet without sin" (verse 15). He went the limit in sympathy for sinning men, and when He did that He showed men just how merciful God is.

To the pagans, the gods were untouchable; in Jesus men found a God who reached down to touch *them.* There is no greater mercy, no greater love. Jesus is indeed our greatest high priest, for with His sympathy and love of men He brought men into intimate acquaintance with a God who was closer than a brother to mankind.

II. For every high priest chosen from among men is appointed . . . to offer gifts and sacrifices for sins. Hebrews 5:1 (RSV). In Israel, the high priest's "headquarters" was in the Temple. He was in charge of all that went on in that Temple—including the sacrifices that were offered up on its altars. He superintended the offering of the blood of *animals* as a sacrifice which would bring about a reconciliation with God. It was a sacrifice intended to "cover" not only the sins of the people, but the sins of the priest himself. The high priest was chosen for this work, chosen of all men, elected by men for this all important work. But Jesus was not elected by men to become high priest; He never sought such election. He did not choose this task; God chose Him to do it; God says to His Son, "Thou art my Son, today I have begotten (honored) thee" (verse 5). Honored, that is, to offer Himself, His blood, as the final and complete sacrifice for the saving of sinful men. Honored, that is, as the greatest of all high priests "after the order (with the same rank) of Melchizedek" (verse 6).

Do you know Melchizedek? You miss a great man, if you do not know him. He was not only a priest; he was king of Salem (Jerusalem?) who worshiped God in a day of terror and decline; he was so noble a priest that he would be honored as the model for the Christ—the perfect minister!

Christ became perfect, too, in a greater sense. He did not want this role, did not ask for it. He saw the great dangers in it. He prayed, in tears, that this cup of suffering might not be given Him to drink—but He *did* drink it, in superb obedience. Through this suffering, through the sacrifice of His own body and blood, He won His place as deathless high priest.

Now, looking at all this from our twentieth-century perspective, we learn much about the perfect minister, be he cleric or layman. We learn that the true priest or minister is appointed of God, or chosen of God.

The sincere and successful minister does not choose to become a minister as others choose to be lawyers or physicians; he has a divine *call* to become a minister. The real priest is never one who strives to distinguish himself as one who can put pretty words together in a pulpit oration; he is one who understands that he is a bridge between man and God and that he must bring others across that bridge with a language as simple and plain as the words of the Sermon on the Mount. He is never to pose as a "superior" man; he should be another Paul—"less than the least of all saints."

Above all, the ideal minister is one whose labors are not limited to office hours in the temple, or the church: he is a man involved in all the grief and gladness of the people who come to his temple to pray and to seek the touch of the Master's hand on their hearts. He is one whose Sunday prayers become action in the community on Monday.

We once knew a minister who never won a prize for great preaching, but his sermons lived on in the hearts of his people long after he was gone. He never got an honorary degree from any college or seminary. He never had a big church (if you determine what a big church is in terms of its membership). But there was a saying in the town where he labored for twenty years: "When there is a death in any house in this town, he gets to that house before the undertaker . . . ."

Divine call—and human sympathy. That does it!

SUGGESTIONS TO TEACHERS

The term *Priest* probably doesn't excite you. If you come from certain Protestant denominations, you may be turned off by the word. You may question how you can construct an entire lesson around the theme of Jesus as our great High Priest.

The word for *priest* in Latin is *pontifex*. Literally, it means "bridge builder." A priest is a bridge-builder. In the case of Jesus, He is the bridge-builder between God and humans, and between humans. Jesus Christ opens new communications between the separated.

Think of Jesus as the Bridge-Builder as you work with Hebrews 4:14—7:28 for today's lesson. Recall that Jesus Christ establishes new relationships between God and us.

1. *PERSON.* Devote some time in your lesson to the person of Christ. Most people have a hazy notion of what He was like. Remind your class that He was tempted like us, yet remained steadfast. Jesus Christ identified completely with us, yet lived without sinning. As a Melchizedek-like priest, He had no priestly pedigree. He was constantly faithful and obedient. Jesus is the only priest who is completely credible. Everything about His person inspires trust. He may be accepted as the Bridge-Builder.

2. *PURPOSE.* Assist your class in understanding that Jesus Christ as the great High Priest helps us to mature in the faith. His purpose is to enable us to grow. He wants us to grow up. He wants us to move "from milk to meat," to move from the "bottle" stage to heftier, more substantial fare. How often, however, we want to remain in the toddler stage of discipleship! Discuss with your class ways in which each can be aided

to progress in his/her Christian growth. Have each comment what he/she perceives Christ's purpose for him or her to be.

3. *PROMISE.* As High Priest, Christ assures each believer that He does indeed build a living relationship with the Creator-God. Hebrews stresses that Christ keeps His Word. Therefore, each Christian may patiently endure anything. Everyone in your class had difficulty on occasion in being patient with God. Ask for examples. Emphasize that every one may find patience in life through confidence in Christ's promise that God remains trustworthy.

4. *POWER.* Allow some time to handle that phrase about how Christ "anchors our lives" (6:19). With Him, we have holding power. We will not be pushed around or swept away. With Jesus Christ as "anchor," we will not be pulled loose or shipwrecked. Recall instances in your experiences in which your faith has helped you to keep a grip on reality. As the great Priest or Bridge-Builder, Jesus Christ firmly connects you to the power of God.

5. *PARDON.* Hebrews states repeatedly that Jesus brings complete and unconditional forgiveness. We are told that through His sacrifice, God has once-and-for-all assured all humans that He pardons. There is no need to try to repeat efforts to wheedle mercy, as in the case of other priesthoods. Christ our great High Priest announces God's forgiveness with a finality! Let your class think about the way God has ended the cycle of guilt.

TOPIC FOR ADULTS
OUR GREAT HIGH PRIEST

Bridge-Builders. Christ, our great High Priest or Bridge-Builder, established new communication between us and God. We in turn, are called to be bridge-builders or priests in the world today.

A story from the Napoleonic era in French history describes a heroic example of bridge-building which hints at what Christ's is like.

It was the depth of winter, and the French army, pressed on all sides by the Cossacks, had to cross a river. The enemy had destroyed all the bridges, and Napoleon was almost at his wit's end. Suddenly came the order that a bridge of some sort must be thrown across the river, and the men nearest the water, of course, were the first to carry out the almost impossible task. Several were swept away by the furious tide. Others, after a few minutes, sank through cold and exhaustion; but more came and the work proceeded as fast as possible. At last the bridge, of sorts, was completed, and the army reached the opposite bank in safety. Then followed a dramatic scene, one of the most horrible recorded in the annals of any nation. When the men who had built the bridge were called out of the water, not one moved. Clinging to pillars, there they stood, silent and motionless—frozen to death. Napoleon, who witnessed the awful scene, could not, in spite of his impassive temperament, restrain his tears.

No Need to Mind. William Temple, Archbishop of Canterbury, once assigned a young curate to a difficult parish. The young clergyman, who had a reputation for complaining, came to see Dr. Temple to ask for an

easier assignment. Dr. Temple was firm but gentle. The curate expostu-
lated, "But if I go there, it will kill me!"

William Temple smiled benignly. "Well," he said pleasantly, "you
and I don't mind a little thing like that, do we?"

As priests sent to build relationships in Christ's world, we look to
Christ our great High Priest, who endured a cross as a cost to His priesthood.

Personal Safety Consideration. Jesus, our Great High Priest, thought
nothing of His personal security or safety in order to mediate God's
mercy to us. In contrast, most human rulers think primarily of themselves. Some, such as King James II of England, have presumed that
they have a divine right to look after themselves.

England felt no love for James II. Yet he was proclaimed king without
disturbance, and accepted by the nation without a murmur.

Scottish Presbyterians and English Puritans suffered much during his
reign. John Bunyan, jailed for a dozen years, produced *Pilgrim's Progress* within prison walls, and the brutal Claverhouse remorselessly
hunted the Covenanters. Monmouth, the king's nephew, mounted an
ill-fated rebellion and despite pleas for clemency was sentenced to die.
His Majesty's infamous henchman, "Hanging Judge Jeffrys," sent many
a nonconformist to the gallows.

William Penn was much moved when one of his honor's victims, a
devout young woman, was burnt at the stake, noting that the crowd
melted into tears around her.

To the Duke of Somerset, who was in disagreement with many of
James's policies, the sovereign haughtily said: "I know how to make
myself feared as well as the law; don't you know that I am above the
law?" When the Universities of Oxford and Cambridge refused to ac-
cede to some of his autocratic requests, he was infuriated. "I will make
you feel the weight of my hand," he promised, thereupon dismissing
several of the higher dignitaries, including a Vice-Chancellor.

Eventually, his people grew weary of his arbitrary ways and appealed
to William, Prince of Orange, to become their ruler. James fled to Ireland and raised an army there. On July 12, 1690, on the banks of the
River Boyne, half-way between Dublin and Belfast, the two forces, each
about 30,000 strong, met in battle array. King James, unlike his opposite,
William, took no part in the conflict. When news came to him at his
observation point from the hill of Dunmore that the day was lost, he fled
with a few loyal cavaliers to Dublin. "I have nothing to think of now but
my personal safety," he said.

Contrast these words with Christ's attitude!

Questions for Pupils on the Next Lesson. 1. What are some of the
experiences you and others have had as persons living in the new covenant? 2. What is the relationship of the promises of the new covenant to
some of the contemporary concerns and needs in your community? 3.
How can adults be freed from the attitudes and actions which hinder
their ministry? 4. What are some of the possibilities for expressing the
reality of our new covenant freedom? 5. How can you make it clearer
that God forgives even though some adults find it difficult to forgive
themselves?

TOPIC FOR YOUTH
CHRIST, YOUR GREAT HIGH PRIEST

Little Joe's Priesthood. On the campus of the Barium Springs Home for Children in Barium Springs, North Carolina there is a beautiful church with a huge porch and a high steeple. Toward dusk on clear days the shadow of the steeple falls across a small grave in the cemetery nearby. Within the grave sleeps a little boy whose dream came true after he died.

In the early, 1900s, a small crippled boy was brought to the home and left there. He was an attractive and winsome child, with a ready smile for all. Even when the children of the home on Sundays left him to walk the railroad tracks to church in Troutman, two miles away, Joe Gilleland was happy.

Each Sunday he would wave to his friends before they left the campus and call out, "Some day I will build a church with a porch on it." Everybody smiled indulgently at the little boy's dream. A companion at the home, Oscar Mann, told the crippled youngster, "You build the church and I'll preach in it."

One night little Joe died, suddenly.

When the supervisors of the home went through his pitifully few effects, they found forty cents he had saved and marked for his church.

The story of the boy's dream became known, and the people of North Carolina started to send money to the home so that a church could be built with a porch on it.

A small brick church, large enough to seat 300 children, was completed. Almost instinctively everyone called the building Little Joe's Presbyterian Church. Years later Joe's friend, who had become a Presbyterian minister, returned to the home to preach in Little Joe's Church.

The original building has since been replaced by a new structure, with a huge porch and a high steeple whose shadow falls across the grave nearby, and is officially named Little Joe's Presbyterian Church, a lasting memorial to the "priesthood" of a crippled child who mediated for the Great High Priest.

Mediator of Mercy. Starr Daily, living amid criminals in the underworld, looked with eyes of yearning envy upon the gold of the wealthy, but every attempt to make their gold his ended in frustration, defeat, and failure. He longed for health, but dissipation deprived him of the health that he sought. In his most normal moments, he yearned for true friends, but the kind of friends drawn to him were those that would leave him whenever misfortune loomed.

Then one day in the solitary cell of a great penitentiary he found Christ. Or, more properly, Christ found Starr Daily. Christ mediated mercy to this hardened criminal. Starr Daily prayed. He began to grow as a Christian. He allowed Christ to be his companion in the cellblock. Starr Daily started to share the Good News of the new relationship Christ brought him with God. He surrendered himself to Jesus Christ.

All his desires fell away except one—the desire to belong to Christ. From a notorious outlaw known by every prison authority in America, he suddenly became so poor in spirit that he would gladly have remained in that cell for the rest of his life if that were the price he must pay to remain with Christ.

Starr Daily became one of the most effective witnesses for Christ, the Great High Priest, of this century.

Is Christ your Great High Priest? Are you growing in your understanding of His mercy mediated to you?

Priestly Act on Olympic Bike Track. We are meant to be mediators of God's justice and mercy wherever we are. A group of British cyclists were such "priests" a few years ago at the 1973 Olympics.

The British cycling pursuit team was trailing the Germans. The German leader was streaking toward the finish line. Suddenly, for no reason, an Olympic official moved from the edge of the track. The German was forced to swerve. Although the German tried desperately to maintain control of his bicycle, he fell. His British competitor rushed past him and crossed the finish line. Officials announced that the British were the victors.

The British team, however, refused the gold medal. Although it was the undisputed winner by having crossed the finish line first, the British insisted the Germans would have won if it had not been for the untoward movement of the official at the moment the German cyclist was about to take first place. The British cyclists finally convinced the jury to change its decision.

Sentence Sermon to Remember: . . . No man cometh unto the Father, but by me.—John 14:6.

Questions for Pupils on the Next Lesson. 1. How do you understand the meaning of Christ's sacrifice for you? 2. What is the significance of Christ's dying for others on the Cross to the youth culture today? 3. What does it mean to be "covenanted" with Christ? 4. Do you sometimes find it hard to forgive yourself even though you have been told that God forgives you? 5. How is your relationship to Christ deepening?

LESSON XIII—MAY 24

MEDIATOR OF A NEW COVENANT

Background Scripture: Hebrews 8–9
Devotional Reading: Ephesians 1:15–23

KING JAMES VERSION

HEBREWS 9 11 But Christ being come a high priest of good things to come, by a greater and more perfect tabernacle, not made with hands, that is to say, not of this building;

12 Neither by the blood of goats and calves, but by his own blood he entered in once into the holy place, having obtained eternal redemption *for us*.

13 For if the blood of bulls and of goats, and the ashes of a heifer sprinkling the unclean, sanctifieth to the purifying of the flesh:

14 How much more shall the blood of Christ, who through the eternal Spirit offered himself without spot to God, purge your conscience from dead works to serve the living God?

15 And for this cause he is the mediator of the new testament, that by means of death, for the redemption of the transgressions *that were* under the first testament, they which are called might receive the promise of eternal inheritance.

24 For Christ is not entered into the holy places made with hands, *which are* the figures of the true; but into heaven itself, now to appear in the presence of God for us:

25 Nor yet that he should offer himself often, as the high priest entereth into the holy place every year with blood of others;

26 For then must he often have suffered since the foundation of the world: but now once in the end of the world hath he appeared to put away sin by the sacrifice of himself.

27 And as it is appointed unto men once to die, but after this the judgment:

28 So Christ was once offered to bear the sins of many; and unto them that look for him shall he appear the second time without sin unto salvation.

REVISED STANDARD VERSION

HEBREWS 9 11 But when Christ appeared as a high priest of the good things that have come, then through the greater and more perfect tent (not made with hands, that is, not of this creation) 12 he entered once for all into the Holy Place, taking not the blood of goats and calves but his own blood, thus securing an eternal redemption. 13 For if the sprinkling of defiled persons with the blood of goats and bulls and with the ashes of a heifer sanctifies for the purification of the flesh, 14 how much more shall the blood of Christ, who through the eternal Spirit offered himself without blemish to God, purify your conscience from dead works to serve the living God.

15 Therefore he is the mediator of a new covenant, so that those who are called may receive the promised eternal inheritance, since a death has occurred which redeems them from the transgressions under the first covenant.

24 For Christ has entered, not into a sanctuary made with hands, a copy of the true one, but into heaven itself, now to appear in the presence of God on our behalf. 25 Nor was it to offer himself repeatedly, as the high priest enters the Holy Place yearly with blood not his own; 26 for then he would have had to suffer repeatedly since the foundation of the world. But as it is, he has appeared once for all at the end of the age to put away sin by the sacrifice of himself. 27 And just as it is appointed for men to die once, and after that comes judgment, 28 so Christ, having been offered once to bear the sins of many, will appear a second time, not to deal with sin but to save those who are eagerly waiting for him.

KEY VERSE: Therefore he is the mediator of a new covenant, so that those who are called may receive the promised eternal inheritance. . . . Hebrews 9:15 (RSV).

HOME DAILY BIBLE READINGS

May 18. M. *Mindful of His Covenant.* Psalms 105:1–11.
May 19. T. *End of the Law.* Romans 10:1–11.
May 20. W. *The Law Was Our Custodian.* Galatians 3:23–29.
May 21. T. *A New Covenant.* Hebrews 8:6–13.
May 22. F. *Ministers of a New Covenant.* 2 Corinthians 3:1–6.
May 23. S. *Blood of the New Covenant.* 1 Corinthians 11:23–26.
May 24. S. *Lord of the Church.* Ephesians 1:15–23.

BACKGROUND

There is a great deal of repetition in the Epistle of Paul to the Hebrews; the teacher will be almost painfully aware of that, as he moves along from one lesson to another. There is a very good reason for this: one great theme runs through the whole epistle, and is stressed again and again because of its extreme importance. This theme is that Christ has fulfilled and surpassed the deepest concepts of the old Jewish faith. It was certainly written by one who had been brought up in Judaism. While there is some doubt that Paul, alone, wrote the Epistle (some say it was Paul and Apollos together), it was surely written by a man or men of Jewish origin and training, and who knew the virtues as well as the shortcomings of the Jewish faith.

One of the basic Judaistic concepts was that of sacrifice. They may have inherited that from any number of religions of ancient times. The idea of sacrifice, we might say, was as old as Eden. It was practiced in many forms and for different purposes, and its ceremonies meant a great deal to the pre-Christian Hebrews. Major services in the Temple, involving sacrifices, were held regularly, in connection with the yearly festivals, and held more often outside the Temple by the people, who thought of constantly burnt offerings as a sign of God's presence among them.

Jesus accepted the practice of sacrifice, but He gave it a vastly different meaning that had little to do with Temple ceremonies. And when He did that, He brought God's people into a new covenant.

NOTES ON THE PRINTED TEXT

I. He entered once for all into the Holy Place, taking not the blood of goats and calves but his own blood. . . . Hebrews 9:12 (RSV). Sacrifice in its various forms, as we have said, was practiced far, far back into primitive times. The pagan nations surrounding Israel often sacrificed, or executed, their prisoners of war as an act of vengeance. To win favorable winds for the ships he was sending against Troy, the Greek Agamemnon offered the sacrifice of his daughter Iphigenia. And who can forget Abraham making ready to sacrifice his son Isaac? These were cruel and barbaric sacrifices, but the scene in which Isaac was saved from death by firstborn sacrifice may be the scene in which human sacrifice was banned forever in Israel (with the possible exception of

Jeththah's daughter!) Human sacrifice was exceptionally rare, even in earliest Jewish history. But for a long time, there was a constant sacrifice of animals for one purpose: to bring men into fellowship and into the presence of God.

In Hebrews 9:13, we read of the sacrifice of calves (young bulls) and goats. Goats were "scapegoats," driven out into the wilderness bearing the sins of the people. But bullocks were sacrificed in the Jewish tabernacle on the Day of Atonement, and it was a sacrifice offered up by the High Priest for his own sins. On this holy day, the High Priest parted the curtains of the Holy of Holies (a room which only he could enter), and sprinkled the altar there with the blood of the slain bullock. This High Priest also performed another sacrificial duty outside the tabernacle: he spread the blood of a sacrificed heifer "before the Tabernacle, seven times." Under Jewish law, any man who touched a dead body was shunned as "unclean" and barred from the worship of God. Everything he touched became unclean. The ashes of the heifer were spread outside the camp in a clean place, and were regarded as a purification for the sin of touching a dead body.

This was all done by way of keeping the old covenants between God and Israel—and as time wore on these offerings of animals seemed to become of less and less interest. Amos stormed against them: "Though ye offer me burnt offerings and your meat offerings, I will not accept them: neither will I regard the peace offerings of your fat beasts" (Amos 5:22). Then, in God's good time, came Jesus. The author or authors of Hebrews saw clearly that with His coming, the days of sacrifice in the old Tabernacles were over; these sacrifices may have cleansed the body, but they did not cleanse the *soul*. This earthly Tabernacle had been built with human hands, but on the body of Jesus there was a new *heavenly* Tabernacle. While the old Tabernacle might cleanse a man of sins against the Law, the body and shed blood of the sacrificed Christ washed clean the hearts, the souls, the consciences of men. While the ancient High Priest, alone in the Holy of Holies, might believe that he stood there in the presence of God, Jesus was a living, *visible* pesonification of God come down among men. To see Jesus was to *see* God. Jesus parted the curtain between God and men, and let all men pass into a living, personal, eternal life in His presence.

It had to come. Men *cannot* find salvation by sacrificing an animal, or by unloading his sins on an innocent scapegoat. Yes, sacrifice is necessary in *all* religion, but it is the sacrifice of placing one's life completely in the hands of the redeeming Christ, the putting away of all else in life that keeps him from God in Christ. The old Tabernacle sacrifice was a mechanical affair; the sacrifice evident in the blood of Christ is an affair of love—sacrificial love.

At the Last Supper, Jesus held up the cup and bade His disciples to drink of it, and He said, "This is my blood, sealing the New Covenant. It is poured out to forgive the sins of multitudes . . . " (*Living Bible*). That said it all, in so few words!

II. *So Christ, having been offered once to bear the sins of many, will appear a second time, not to deal with sin but to save those who are eagerly waiting for him.* Hebrews 9:28 (RSV). The High Priest entered the Holy of Holies in the old Tabernacle to sprinkle the blood of dead animals on the altar once every year. Jesus offered His blood only once, and He will never be seen on a cross, offering *His* blood again. He died once and for all to save men from their sins—and He will never die so, again. But He will return; there will be a Second Coming, and at the time of this Coming He will bring *others* into salvation. Of this, the early Christians were sure; again and again and again, all through the various Epistles, this belief is evident; it has the sound of a song of victory.

He would come again, but this second time would be different from the first. As He lived among men at the time of His first coming, He was judged by men, and crucified by them; at the Second Coming He would be among us as One who judges *us*. For those who have believed in Him, the Second Coming will be a day of glory; for those who had refused to believe in Him even after His Resurrection, it will be a day of fear and even terror.

This word *judge* need not be a word filled with terror for any of us, for between the time of His first and next appearances on earth, God gives us time in which we may turn to Him and in Him find salvation. This second time "he will come bringing salvation to all those who are eagerly and patiently waiting for him" (verse 28, *Living Bible*).

How many of us, would you say, are waiting for Him eagerly and patiently? Or are too many of us not waiting at all?

SUGGESTIONS TO TEACHERS

Your class worked with the theme of God's covenant last September through November. This, however, does not mean that you may drop it. God as Covenanter persists in reminding His people of the solemn agreement between them. The writer of Hebrews reiterates this. In fact, your lesson today centers on how Jesus Christ mediates a new solemn agreement between God and your class members, and between your class members and God.

The lesson will compare the New Covenant with the Old. One note of caution: do not get off on tangents whereby people criticize Jews or Judaism. It is easy to think that because we Christians are the inheritors of the new covenant we are the good guys and the Jews are the bad guys. Don't get sucked into this arrogant, prideful attitude. The point of today's lesson is not to score points against the synagogue, but to grasp the meaning of Christ's covenant with us, the Church.

1. *INNER VS. OUTER.* Jesus Christ, the Mediator of a new covenant, writes the Law in our minds and hearts. We live not so much by outer regulations as by inner compulsion. As the embodiment of God's will, the Living Lord calls us to a harder obedience than merely keeping some rules. We are to be like Jesus Himself. Does your class understand the distinction between a religion of keeping outward rules and a dynamic relationship of living with Christ?

2. *LEADERS VS. FOLLOWERS.* Commit some class time to the meaning of the claim in Hebrews that everyone is a leader-teacher because "they all shall know me" (8:11). This means that everyone share the responsibilities of being the people of God. What does this suggest

in regard to our usual thoughts about the place of clergy and laity? If everyone is intended to be a leader-teacher, how can everyone in your class be trained and equipped for the work? Where is it carried out? When?

3. *OPEN VS. CLOSED*. Hebrews claims that Christ opened the way to God's presnece for us. We now have access to God. The curtain, so to speak, was ripped aside. Why do some Christians still think that God is hidden or remote? Why do we sometimes imagine that prayers are not heard? Help your people to advance boldly before God! Through Christ, we know the way is open!

4. *SERVICE VS. CEREMONY*. Encourage your class to reflect on the meaning of a new covenant as a call to responsibility rather than ritual. You may wish to criticize worship in your congregation. Does it sometimes seem empty and formal? Stress above all that service to others in Christ's World is the purpose of all worship. Ceremonies are not necessarily bad except when they fail to strengthen believers for serving.

5. *COMPLETE VS. INCOMPLETE*. Have your class think through the implications of Christ's death and Resurrection. His sacrifice is sufficient. No one needs to punish himself. Furthermore, no person needs to think that God must be placated or appeased by special sacrificial efforts. Christ has already made us right with God!

TOPIC FOR ADULTS
BETWEEN YOU AND GOD

Quaint Ceremonial. Once each year a robed and bewigged delegation strides purposefully into London's Royal Court of Justice and seeks out that specialist in matters ceremonial, Queen Elizabeth's Remembrancer. With a grave bow of acknowledgement, the Remembrancer accepts in Her Majesty's behalf these items: six horseshoes ("suitable for the forefeet of a great Flemish warhorse"), sixty-one horseshoe nails, a hatchet, and a billhook.

Warrants attesting receipt of the token hardware are recorded. Then presumably, the Lord Mayor of London can breathe a bit easier. Once again his resolutely independent City of London, a self-governing domain of one square mile in the heart of Greater London's 720 square miles, will have paid its annual land rents to the Crown.

Some would say that the Bible, Christian worship and all religious symbolism, including mention of the covenant, are as empty and outmoded as the rent-paying ceremony by the Lord Mayor of London.

God did not come among us to inaugurate quaint rituals. Through Jesus Christ, He instituted a new relationship. He stated His solemn promise of faithfulness. The new covenant through Christ is God's assurance of His peronsal concern for you. There is a new relationship between God and you. No mere ceremonial, this!

Last Resort Religion. The new covenant is intended to mean that you and God are to live as intimate friends. Such a relationship implies trust and respect.

Does your prayer life reflect such trust and respect? Or, is praying a sort of last-ditch effort when every thing else has failed?

Some folks in Cleveland, Ohio, felt that prayer for their city had become a last resort a couple of winters ago, during the city's financial crisis. Unable to resolve the fiscal problems, a group of downtown business and civic people called "Prayer on the Square" decided to sponsor weekly prayer breakfasts "to help dispel the malaise that now encompasses Cleveland."

Other devout people in Cleveland were not so sure about turning prayer into a gimmicky whimper to get the Lord to bail out Cleveland's money woes. Not that these folks were against praying, or questioned God's interest in Cleveland. They had misgivings about neglecting the covenant relationship which Christians recall whenever they pray. These church people were more anxious that Clevelanders try to serve God rather than to get God to serve Cleveland.

As a covenanted Christian, what do you think?

Between You and God and Third World Little Ones. The new covenant is not a private "deal" between just you and God. The new covenant instituted by Christ means that you are involved in the lives of the hurting and forgotten, regardless of who they are or where they live. You see, Christ's covenant means you are commissioned to represent Him to bring help and healing.

It is estimated, for example, that of one hundred children born every minute in developing countries, twenty will die within the year. Of the eighty who survive, sixty will have no access to modern medical care in childhood. An equal number will suffer from malnutrition during the crucial weaning age with the possibility of permanent physical or mental damage. During this period their chance of dying will be twenty to forty times higher than if they lived in Europe or North America. Of those who live to school age, only a few more than half will ever enter a classroom. Fewer than four out of ten who do will complete their elementary schooling.

As a person who has a covenant between you and God, what will you do on behalf of these children?

Questions for Pupils on the Next Lesson. 1. What are some of the best examples of Christian living you have seen in you lifetime? 2. Why must we emphasize the need for discipline in Christian living? 3. What is the meaning of Christ as the Author and Finisher of our faith? 4. What is the role of both the individual and the community of faith in sharing the Gospel?

TOPIC FOR YOUTH
BETWEEN YOU AND GOD

First Things First. When Leon Spinks won the heavyweight boxing championship, he said this: "I don't listen to other people anyway . . . because when I get in the ring they won't be doing my fighting for me. I don't care what they say. I know where I'm at, and I know where I came from. I'll never forget, either. I came from poorness to try and find some meaning of life, and I'll never forget where I came from because I never want to go back." Later, in his dressing room, he said this: "Celebrate later, but now, first things first. Before anyone starts jiving, we must give our thanks to the Lord. 'Dear God, thank you for answering my prayers. Thank you for my not getting hurt, and for my man not getting hurt. Thank you for the miracle. All praise sweet Jesus. Amen.' "

Sneaky Celebrity. The covenant between you and God means you live a life of honesty. You cannot be sneaky with God. And you cannot be dishonest with others.

A young man in Tokyo named Yusuke Shikauchi learned the hard way that you cannot cheat secretly. Yusuke decided to sneak away from his job one day. He felt pleased with himself for having fooled the supervisor and for collecting his pay without working.

Yusuke went to a baseball game that day when he was supposed to have been at work. Enjoying the ball game on company time, he decided to buy a raffle ticket on an automobile. To his delight, Yusuke held the winning ticket.

Imagine his chagrin when he found his picture on the front pages of all the Tokyo newspapers later that afternoon and the following day!

Cheap Talk or Costly Promise. The high-school senior had a faint curl on her pretty mouth as she told her church-going friend that "all that Christian stuff is so trivial. *Such trivia.*"

Trivial? Trivia? Did this high-school senior know the origin of these words?

In Virgil's day, a peasant built an inn at the place where three roads met—*Tri Via* ("three roads" in Latin). It was the meeting place for soldiers, who told the kind of stories and indulged in the kind of talk men are known for when under the influence of liquor. Soon surrounding families were talking about the Tri Via and warning their children to stay away from this place where crude, cheap, worthless talk took place. And so the root of the word *trivia* or *trivial* leaped from life into language.

Trivial, in other words, has to do with cheap worthless talk. The Christian faith, on the other hand, is God's sacred Word, God's never-to-be-broken promise to you. God has never gone back on His Word, nor will He ever. He assures you that a special relationship will always be in effect between you and Him.

Sentence Sermon to Remember: For there is one God, and one mediator between God and men, the man Christ Jesus.—1 Timothy 2:5.

Questions for Pupils on the Next Lesson. 1. Who are the people who have inspired you the most as examples of Christian living? Why these persons? What did they do? 2. In what ways can Christians profit from experiences which are difficult and trying for them? 3. Have you tried reading biographies of great Christian people? 4. What are some ways of publically expressing gratitude to God?

LESSON XIV—MAY 31

PERFECTOR OF OUR FAITH

Background Scripture: Hebrews 10–13
Devotional Reading: John 17:1–11

KING JAMES VERSION

HEBREWS 12 1 Wherefore, seeing we also are compassed about with so great a cloud of witnesses, let us lay aside every weight, and the sin which doth so easily beset *us,* and let us run with patience the race that is set before us,

2 Looking unto Jesus the author and finisher of *our* faith; who for the joy that was set before him endured the cross, despising the shame, and is set down at the right hand of the throne of God.

3 For consider him that endured such contradiction of sinners against himself, lest ye be wearied and faint in your minds.

4 Ye have not yet resisted unto blood, striving against sin.

5 And ye have forgotten the exhortation which speaketh unto you as unto children, My son, despise not thou the chastening of the Lord, nor faint when thou art rebuked of him:

6 For whom the Lord loveth he chasteneth, and scourgeth every son whom he receiveth.

7 If ye endure chastening, God dealeth with you as with sons; for what son is he whom the father chasteneth not?

8 But if ye be without chastisement, whereof all are partakers, then are ye bastards, and not sons.

9 Furthermore, we have had fathers of our flesh which corrected *us,* and we gave *them* reverence: shall we not much rather be in subjection unto the Father of spirits, and live?

10 For they verily for a few days chastened *us* after their own pleasure; but he for *our* profit, that *we* might be partakers of his holiness.

11 Now no chastening for the present seemeth to be joyous, but grievous: nevertheless, afterword it yieldeth the peaceable fruit of righteousness unto them which are exercised thereby.

REVISED STANDARD VERSION

HEBREWS 12 1 Therefore, since we are surrounded by so great a cloud of witnesses, let us also lay aside every weight, and sin which clings so closely, and let us run with perseverance the race that is set before us, 2 looking to Jesus the pioneer and perfecter of our faith, who for the joy that was set before him endured the cross, despising the shame, and is seated at the right hand of the throne of God.

3 Consider him who endured from sinners such hostility against himself, so that you may not grow weary or fainthearted. 4 In your struggle against sin you have not yet resisted to the point of shedding your blood. 5 And have you forgotten the exhortation which addresses you as sons?—

"My son, do not regard lightly the discipline of the Lord,
nor lose courage when you are punished by him.
6 For the Lord disciplines him whom he loves,
and chastises every son whom he receives."

7 It is for discipline that you have to endure. God is treating you as sons; for what son is there whom his father does not discipline? 8 If you are left without discipline, in which all have participated, then you are illegitimate children and not sons. 9 Besides this, we have had earthly fathers to discipline us and we respected them. Shall we not much more be subject to the Father of spirits and live? 10 For they disciplined us for a short time at their pleasure, but he disciplines us for our good, that we may share his holiness. 11 For the moment all discipline seems painful rather than pleasant; later it yields the peaceful fruit of righteousness to those who have been trained by it. 12 Therefore lift your drooping hands and strengthen your weak

12 Wherefore lift up the hands which hang down, and the feeble knees;

13 And make straight paths for your feet, lest that which is lame be turned out of the way; but let it rather be healed.

knees, 13 and make straight paths for your feet, so that what is lame may not be put out of joint but rather be healed.

KEY VERSE: . . . let us run with perseverance the race that is set before us, looking to Jesus the pioneer and perfecter of our faith . . . . Hebrews 12:1,2 (RSV).

HOME DAILY BIBLE READINGS

May 25. M. "Eyewitnesses of His Majesty." 2 Peter 1:3–7,16–19.
May 26. T. "Every Knee Should Bow." Philippians 2:1–11.
May 27. W. Reconciled Through Christ. 2 Corinthians 5:17–21.
May 28. T. "He Who Promised Is Faithful." Hebrews 10:19–25
May 29. F. The Unchanging Christ. Hebrews 13:7, 8, 18–21.
May 30. S. "Dying in Faith." Hebrews 11:13–16.
May 31. S. "Keeping Them in Thy Name." John 17:1–11.

BACKGROUND

This is our final lesson based on Hebrews, and it is the most exciting lesson of all. There have been lessons, in this series, which are difficult to teach, even to understand, as we try to make clear the place of Jesus Christ as our High Priest. Now we turn to think of what response is required from us to the work of Jesus.

Just what is a Christian, anyway? A Christian has different meanings to different people. Some think of him simply as one who believes in Jesus Christ. Others think he is one who knows his Bible well sometimes to the point of almost worshiping the Bible rather than the Christ. Or he is thought to be someone who joins a Christian Church and goes regularly to attend its services. Edward Young said that a Christian is the highest type of man, but Voltaire calls Christians the most intolerant of men. Which one would you vote for: Young or Voltaire—and what makes the Christian a high type of man or a low type? How does he "get that way?"

Hebrews 12 is one of the most inspired and inspiring chapters in our whole Bible; it tells us in brief, summarized form what it means to be a Christian, and what we have to do to *stay* a Christian. Whoever wrote it turns from pointing his finger at Jesus and turns it upon us who call ourselves Christians but have no guidelines to help us live the Christian life. It is easy reading—and it can both shock and inspire us.

NOTES ON THE PRINTED TEXT

I. *. . . since we are surrounded by so great a cloud of witnesses . . . .* Hebrews 12:1 (RSV). *The Living Bible* paraphrases these words and says, "Since we have such a huge crowd of men of faith watching us from the grandstands . . ." That helps make it clear. All through the epistles of Paul we find reference to some form of athletics: the writer is a man who evidently loved athletic events. So in this verse he pictures the Christian as someone running a race before a great crowd of "witnesses," or spectators. These spectators are people who have run other races—who have already won their race and their crown. They are the saints of old, the pioneers, the "veterans" of the faith. The very sight of them up there in the grandstands galvanizes the runner down on the track; he goes all-out to win; he will not let them down! We have all heard the Texans sing, "The eyes of Texas are upon you . . ."; the eyes of the saints of yesterday are upon the Christians of today. They have put their faith in us, so we try harder.

Christianity, said Wendell Phillips, is a battle and not a dream. We might say that Christianity is a race and not a rest-camp. Sometimes we call life "a rat race"—a race to beat our fellowmen to fame and wealth and the admiration of men; life for the Christian is a race against those who believe that, a race of good against evil, a race toward God and heaven.

To win that race we must put away from us anything that will hinder us in the running—laziness, for instance, or the refusal to train long and hard for the race. Olympic champions train for months, even for years, to win a race that takes less than five minutes to run! No runner ever runs with a pack on his back, or in shoes made of lead; he "lays aside every weight," if he hopes to win.

And the runner, the Christian, *concentrates* and runs with "patience." Have you ever watched a great golfer "set himself" to put that little ball in that little hole on the green? He takes his time, he will not be rushed, and he will not be disturbed by any spectator; if his concentration is distrubed, he backs off and sets the whole thing up again, before he strokes the ball.

The Christian has a goal, and he concentrates on that goal and thinks of nothing else: *his* goal is Christ, and life in the imitation of Christ, and he will let nothing take his eyes from that goal. He may fail, at times, but then he starts all over again, gets his eye on his Christ—and finally reaches his goal.

II. Ye have not yet resisted unto blood, striving against sin. Hebrews 12:4. That shocks us. We all make sacrifices, in this life, in one way or another, but—*blood*? Is the Christian obligated to give his blood—to serve Christ even unto death? Few of us would accept that. Yes, we give of our blood to our hospitals, in transfusions but that is only such blood as we feel we can spare. The giving of it does us no harm and does not have any bad effect upon our health. But the blood given by Jesus Christ cost Him His earthly life. He gave *all* of it, even unto death. He died bleeding, on a cross, patient, even praying in unbelievable patience for His executioners!

These martyred saints up in the grandstand did the same thing! Think of that holy patience of the crucified ones when you become weary and fainthearted in the race of life. If Jesus could endure the shame of death on a criminal's cross, *we* can at least take up our cross and follow Him. Great victories are won at great cost: at the sweating of blood. What He paid for that victory on Calvary we should be willing to pay if we are to win His crown and glory in the race.

III. It is for discipline that you have to endure. Hebrews 12:7 (RSV). Discipline! Some of us hate that word. We heard a famous Olympic champion say, "I know many men who could be better athletes than I am, but they will not go through the discipline necessary to win." We shun discipline—or any form of "punishment." He who will not run five miles a day before competing in a marathon never wins a marathon.

God disciplines us as a father disciplines his child—not as a punishment, but in love. In the view of the early Christians the troubles and afflictions and hardships of life were sent to us as a discipline from God. We may not like to believe that, but they were.

In the day in which this was written, fathers had absolute and continuing authority to punish a child in any way they saw fit; they could whip a child, sell him into slavery, even execute him. That was still the law, even when the child became a man; his father still had the right to discipline. We have long since thrown that idea into the trash heap of history—but the modern child *still* needs the corrections of discipline if he is to become anything resembling a good man or woman. Without it, we have anarchy in all directions. No author ever became a good author without the practice of grim discipline; no doctor ever hung out his shingle until he had gone through years of strict discipline in years of learning, in both school and internship in a hospital. If we are willing to accept such discipline for such purposes, why should we not accept God's discipline for His purposes with every man? "God's correction is always right and for our best good, that we may share his holiness" (verse 11, *Living Bible*).

IV. Wherefore lift up the hands which hang down, and the feeble knees. . . . Hebrews 12:12. The Christian can be rightfully happy and perhaps even proud when he wins his race and receives his prize—but, says Hebrews, while that is good it is not good enough: the Christian has a duty to perform for those others who do not win the race. Only one can win, can "come in first"; behind him are those whose strength has left them—people with weak knees and tired legs, people who have stopped trying, who have given up. The Christian has an obligation to reach out and help those who have fallen in despair. One of the great satisfactions of the Christian life lies in our strengthening of those who are for one reason or another weaker than we are. The author of this Scripture may have been thinking of the days of the Jews wandering in the wilderness: the strong, in the long wilderness march, helped the weaker ones who wanted to give up the marching and wandering and go back to slavery in Egypt. The strong ones helped them to fight on toward the Promised Land.

A Christian has two responsibilities to God: one, to win through the struggles of life to live in Christ, and, two, to reach out and help others find that Christ. Nothing can be more sinful than the selfishness of one who claims to be born again but who does nothing to lift his fellowman out of the depths of failure, trouble, and despair. Just winning the prize for one's self is good but not enough in the eyes of God; He has given us the strength to help others win.

SUGGESTIONS TO TEACHERS

Last June, a seventy-nine-year-old grandmother received a bachelor of arts degree in English literature from a leading southern university. Reporters interviewed her before the graduation exercises.

"Why," they asked, "did you go to college after all these years?"

With a twinkle, the woman brightly replied, "When you stop growin', you stop livin', and I just wanted to make sure I was still growin'."

Her answer could also apply to Christian discipleship. Christ works to make sure believers are still growing.

Your lesson should bear in mind that Jesus Christ is the Perfecter of our faith, and also that every person in your class must be growing in that faith. For lesson starters, spotlight these points raised in today's scriptural material in Hebrews 10-13.

1. *ACCEPT YOUR ACCEPTANCE.* Do your class members understand that they need have no more uncertainty about their standing before God? That they are conclusively forgiven? Point out that being accepted by God through Christ means they no longer need to be reminded of failure (*see* 10:13). The guilt of the past has been dealt with by Christ. They need not be preoccupied with self, but can be directed toward others. Suggest that they share examples of how understanding God's mercy has enabled people to accept their acceptance, and have grown.

2. *KEEP THE FAITH.* Christ as the perfecter bestows a sense of trust in God. Look at the "roll call of the faithfull" in chapter 11. Ask your folks to add to that list persons in their own experience who have lived by their trust in Christ. Have your people give definitions of trust from their own lives (one teenage boy recounted a superb example of trust from his experience as a junior volunteer fireman in which he had to depend completely on a buddy in the fire company during a dangerous situation!).

3. *LIVE BETWEEN PROMISE AND FULFILLMENT.* Remind your class that the Christian sometimes has no proof that the final outcome will be good, and that the Christian may not necessarily live to see the final outcome with God. Hebrews makes it clear that Christians live in the midst of hardships and suffering. Let your class mull over what it means to live in the era between God's promise and the fulfillment of His promise.

4. *KEEP ON KEEPING ON.* As how many in your class were ready to quit during the past week, or the past month. Encourage your class members to share times when they privately wondered whether they could face another setback or problem. Remind them that Christians are tough, because Jesus Christ keeps on helping faithful followers to keep on keeping on.

5. *SHOW YOUR FAITH.* Christ helps us to grow as Christians by prodding us to show His love to others in tangible ways. Loving others, Hebrews suggests, happens especially in areas such as keeping marriage vows and remembering fellow church-members. In the words of the song in *My Fair Lady,* "Don't talk to me of love; *show* me!" is the plea of Hebrews to us!

TOPIC FOR ADULTS

PERFECTER OF OUR FAITH

No Ladder. "A little girl had asked her father what faith meant, and he had told her to wait for his answer. One day he was doing something in a cellar, the entrance to which was a trap door in a passage. The child called out to him. 'May I come down to you, Father?' 'Yes,' he said. The little girl was going to descend, when she found that the ladder had been taken away. 'I can't get down' she called out. 'There is no ladder.' 'Jump down,' her father answered, 'and I will catch you.' The child hesitated; she could not see her father, and below her everything seemed dark. 'But I can't see you, Father. I can't see anything,' she said. 'I can see you,' was the reply. 'Jump, and I shall be sure to catch you. My arms are wide open now.' The child hesitated no longer; she was sure that her father was there ready to catch her, though she could not see him. She jumped into the darkness and was safely caught."—J. R. Gregory, in *One Thousand Evangelistic Illustrations*, by Aquilla Webb, Harper & Row.

Grow Up! "For unless a man has acquired the character of an adult, he is a lost soul no matter how good his technical equipment. The world unhappily contains many such lost souls . . . . It is full of semiadult persons who secretly nurse the idea that they are, or that by rights they ought to be, Don Juan, Croesus, Napoleon, or the Messiah . . . . Their purposes are merely the relics of an infancy when their wishes were law and they knew neither neccessity nor change. When a childish disposition is carried over into an adult environment, the result is a radically false valuation of that environment . . . . The childish pattern appears also as a deep sense that life owes him something, that somehow it is the duty of the universe to look after him and to listen sharply when he speaks to it. . . . The childish pattern appears also as a disposition to believe that he may reach out for anything in sight and take it, and that having gotten it nobody must ever under any circumstances take it away."—From A PREFACE TO MORALS by Walter Lippmann. (Copyright 1929 and renewed 1957 by Walter Lippman), Macmillan Publishing Co., Inc.

Chain Reaction of Kindness. One of the laws of life seems to be that no kindness is ever in vain. This was discovered by a man who was waiting for an important letter. On Saturday, the letter had still not arrived at his office. He went home Saturday afternoon, exasperated because the mail had apparently been so slow and inefficient. Precious hours would be lost until the next mail delivery on Monday. To the man's surprise, the post office delivered the letter marked "Special Delivery" to his home early Sunday morning, although the letter carried his office address. He knew that the post-office personnel would have carried out their responsibilities by trying to deliver it to his office, and, finding no one there, waiting until Monday to return. Grateful for the post-office people's thoughtfulness, the businessman wrote a note of appreciation to the local postmaster. Many months later, the same man required a post-office box for a new business and learned at the post office that no boxes were available. There was a long waiting list. Discouraged, the businessman was leaving when the postmaster walked up. "I overheard your conversation and remembered your name," the post-master explained. He then related how he recalled the businessman's thank-you letter a year earlier. The postmaster also told him how much that letter had meant. Pausing for a moment, he added, "We'll find you a box here in this post office, even if I have to build it for you, myself! After all the complaints we get, you have no idea how much your letter meant."

Kindness always seems to set off a chain reaction.

Question for Pupils on the Next Lesson. 1. How can you rediscover the Word of God which sometimes gets lost in cultural and religious trappings? 2. Why is response to God's Word tied so closely with a hearer's readings? 3. Do you allow remembrance of your childhood and youth to influence positively the way in which you exercise justice? 4. With whom do you have covenanted relationships today?

TOPIC FOR YOUTH

CHRIST—FROM START TO FINISH

Feed the Enemy. Autumn, 1944. The Lower Rhine, Der HexenKessel (The Witches' Caldron) was a name coined during the bloody siege of Arnhem. During the siege, Hendrike van der Vliet served in a makeshift hospital in the old Schoonoord Hotel.

Hendrike had slept in her clothes only a few hours each night, getting up to assist as fresh casualties were carried in. Fluent in English and German, she had noted a pessimism among the Germans in contrast to the patient cheerfulness of the British paratroopers. The Red Devils seemed stoically prepared to accept their fate. As she brought one trooper the miniscule portion of soup and a biscuit that constituted the only meal the hospital could provide, he pointed to a newly arrived casualty. "Give it to him," he told Hendrike. Pulling down the blanket, she saw he wore a German uniform. "German, eh?" the trooper asked. She nodded. "Give him the food anyway," the Britisher said. "I ate yesterday."

The Important Thing. Jesus Christ, the Perfecter of our faith, calls us to persevere. It's not too important whether we make headlines or win applause. The important thing is to continue with Christ from start to finish of life.

In 1896, Baron de Coubertin of France revived the ancient practice of the finest amateur athletes of each state competing against each other as the Olympic Games had been in the Greek city-states. The Baron op-posed the emphasis on victory. "The important thing in the Olympic Games is not winning but taking part. The essential thing in life is not conquering but fighting well."

Jailed for Christian Stand. Standing with Christ from start to finish is not always easy or pleasant. Christians in other lands know this better than we.

Three Protestant Ministers have been jailed by South Korean au-thorities. The three include two Presbyterians, Hyung Kyu Park of the First Church in Seoul who is under indictment for the fifth time, and

Ik-Whan (Timothy) Moon, a theologian and poet who was recently re-arrested and sentenced to serve out the remaining three years and two months of an original five-year term and citizenship suspension. Mr. Hyung had also been sentenced to five years in prison and "suspension of citizenship" for an additional five years. The third, another outspoken champion of human rights, Cho Hwa-soon, a Methodist woman minister and a leader of the Urban Industrial Mission in Inchon, was rearrested for the third time. The two men were charged under the Presidential Emergency Decree No. 9, which among other things, forbids any criticism of President Park or even of the decree itself.

Sentence Sermon to Remember: A simple, childlike faith in the Divine Friend solves all the problems that come to us by land or sea.—Helen Keller.

Questions for Pupils on the Nest Lesson. 1. What are you and your church doing to counteract the injustice you see around you? 2. In your list of commitments, what place do your spiritual commitments have? 3. Do you see that God is involved in history? On what do you base your answer? 4. Do you understand that God is at work in human affairs today? 5. How do you experience covenant relationship today? Whom are you covenanted with?

JUNE, JULY, AUGUST 1981

THE BOOK OF DEUTERONOMY

LESSON I—JUNE 7

HEARING GOD'S COMMANDS

Background Scripture: 2 Kings 22, 23; Deuteronomy 10:12–11:1
Devotional Reading: Acts 2:1–13

KING JAMES VERSION

2 KINGS 23 1 And the king sent, and they gathered unto him all the elders of Judah and of Jerusalem.

2 And the king went up into the house of the LORD, and all the men of Judah and all the inhabitants of Jerusalem with him, and the priests, and the prophets, and all the people, both small and great; and he read in their ears all the words of the book of the covenant which was found in the house of the LORD.

DEUTERONOMY 10 12 And now, Israel, what doth the LORD thy God require of thee, but to fear the LORD thy God, to walk in all his ways, and to love him, and to serve the LORD thy God with all thy heart and with all thy soul,

13 To keep the commandments of the LORD, and his statutes, which I command thee this day for thy good?

14 Behold, the heaven and the heaven of heavens *is* the LORD's thy God, the earth *also*, with all that therein is.

15 Only the LORD had a delight in thy fathers to love them, and he chose their seed after them, *even* you above all people, as *it is* this day.

16 Circumcise therefore the foreskin of your heart, and be no more stiffnecked.

17 For the LORD your God *is* God of gods, and Lord of lords, a great God, a mighty, and a terrible, which regardeth not persons, nor taketh reward:

REVISED STANDARD VERSION

2 KINGS 23 1 Then the king sent, and all the elders of Judah and Jerusalem were gathered to him. 2 And the king went up to the house of the LORD, and with him all the men of Judah and all the inhabitants of Jerusalem, and the priests and the prophets, all the people, both small and great; and he read in their hearing all the words of the book of the covenant which had been found in the house of the LORD.

DEUTERONOMY 10 12 "And now, Israel, what does the LORD your God require of you, but to fear the LORD your God, to walk in all his ways, to love him, to serve the LORD your God with all your heart and with all your soul, 13 and to keep the commandments and statutes of the LORD, which I command you this day for your good? 14 Behold, to the LORD your God belong heaven and the heaven of heavens, the earth with all that is in it; 15 yet the LORD set his heart in love upon your fathers and chose their descendants after them, you above all peoples, as at this day. 16 Circumcise therefore the foreskin of your heart, and be no longer stubborn. 17 For the LORD your God is God of gods and Lord of lords, the great, the mighty, and the terrible God, who is not partial and takes no bribe. 18 He executes justice for the fatherless and the widow, and loves the sojourner, giving him food and clothing. 19 Love the

18 He doth execute the judgment of the fatherless and widow, and loveth the stranger, in giving him food and raiment.

19 Love ye therefore the stranger: for ye were strangers in the land of Egypt.

20 Thou shalt fear the LORD thy God; him shalt thou serve, and to him shalt thou cleave, and swear by his name.

21 He *is* thy praise, and he *is* thy God, that hath done for thee these great and terrible things, which thine eyes have seen.

22 Thy fathers went down into Egypt with threescore and ten persons; and now the LORD thy God hath made thee as the stars of heaven for multitude.

11 1 Therefore thou shalt love the LORD thy God, and keep his charge, and his statutes, and his judgments, and his commandments, alway.

sojourner therefore; for you were sojourners in the land of Egypt. 20 You shall fear the LORD your God; you shall serve him and cleave to him, and by his name you shall swear. 21 He is your praise; he is your God, who has done for you these great and terrible things which your eyes have seen. 22 Your fathers went down to Egypt seventy persons; and now the LORD your God has made you as the stars of heaven for multitude.

11 1 "You shall therefore love the LORD your God, and keep his charge, his statutes, his ordinances, and his commandments always."

KEY VERSE: *"You shall therefore love the Lord your God, and keep his charge, his statutes, his ordinances, and his commandments always*. Deuteronomy 11:1 (RSV).

HOME DAILY BIBLE READINGS

June 1. M. *Finding the Book of Law.* 2 Kings 22:3-10.
June 2. T. *Huldah Prophesies.* 2 Kings 22:11-20.
June 3. W. *Renewing the Covenant.* 2 Kings 23:1-3, 21, 22.
June 4. T. *The Wrath of the Lord.* 2 Kings 23:24-30.
June 5. F. *Stone Tables for the Ark.* Deuteronomy 10:1-5.
June 6. S. *God of Love and Justice.* Deuteronomy 10:12-22.
June 7. S. *Coming of the Spirit.* Acts 2:1-13.

BACKGROUND

The teacher may be almost frightened at the thought of a full quarter of lessons based on the Book of Deuteronomy; this is one of the least read—and least understood—of all the books of the Bible. He should not approach it as a dry law book, but he should know, at the start, that it is one of the most important of all biblical books, that the early Christians put great value upon it and studied it carefully, and based much of their faith and living upon it. It deals with ancient times, with the old basic truths of their faith. Alexander Solzhenitsyn has said that "A people that no longer remembers (its history) has lost its history and its soul." In reading and remembering, with this book, we know better from where faith came, and into what it has developed.

The word *Deuteronomy* means literally second law-giving according to the Greek. But that does not adequately describe it: *Deuteronomy* is more aptly called "a *copy* of the existing law." It is more a book of three sermons or orations preached by Moses in an effort to make clear the meaning of God's authority in national and personal life.

Jesus quoted it often; He had great respect for it, and so did the people who were to become "a people of the Book." (*See* Matthew 4:4, 7, 10.) So should we who follow Him discover the hidden gold of the faith contained in this revealing, inspiring book.

We start with an account of the "finding" of the book in 622 B.C.

NOTES ON THE PRINTED TEXT

I. And the king went up into the house of the Lord . . . . and he read in their ears all the words of the book of the covenant which was found in the house of the Lord. 2 Kings 23:2. King Amon of Judah was murdered in 640 B.C; he was followed by his son Josiah, as king (at the age of eight!). The first thing the young king did was to punish (execute) the assassins of his young father; then, as he matured, he turned to lead his people to new spiritual heights where the ethical character of God, God's love of man and man's duty to God were emphasized. He was made king not so much by way of royal succession but "by the people of the land," who came to love him as they had not loved before.

The most important event of his reign was the discovery during Temple repairs of the lost Book of the Law. Hilkiah the high priest found it and brought it to Staphan the scribe, who took it to the king (2 Kings 22:8). Just what this precious book was and where it came from is fundamental question long discussed by students of the Old Testament; the most common view is that it was "a compendium of ancient laws, traditionally ascribed to Moses, but collected, revised, and edited in a new spirit by the prophetic party during the reign of Manasseh, and then deposited in the Temple library with the hope that sometime it would be discovered and used as a program of national reform."—Richard C. Dentan. New editors took over at the request of Josiah; we call them "the Deuteronomists," and they wrote in the light of the revolution which Josiah led on the basis of the principles set forth in the Book of Deuteronomy.

It was quite a revolution—a revolution based not so much on renewal as on a basic *reformation* which changed every aspect of Israel's life and character. The reform was based on the conviction that, under the Law, they were "one nation with one God and one sanctuary." The Temple was cleansed and made the only sanctuary in which sacrifices might be made; worship of foreign gods anywhere was forbidden and their shrines were destroyed; witchcraft was abolished and the use of household images known as seraphim was condemned.

One wonders: while the condemnation of all other faiths than the Christian faith might be impossible today, it might be good for us to reevaluate our Christian faith and its shortcomings in our society, and to move toward the Deuteronomic principle of absolute loyalty to God. We seem to have drifted far away from that!

II. . . . . what does the Lord your God require of you, but to fear the Lord your God, to walk in all his ways, to love him, to serve the Lord your God with all your heart and with all your soul, and to keep his commandments . . . . Deuteronomy 10:12, 13 (RSV). A long century before Josiah, a prophet named Micah asked the people of Judah a blunt and beautiful question: "What doth the Lord require of thee, but to do justly, and to love mercy, and to walk humbly with thy God? (Micah 6:8). That amazingly concise verse and description of true religion should be memorized by every Christian. The Deuteronomist is doubtlessly repeating the question in his own words, and he had good reason to ask it of the people among whom he lived. All about him he saw exactly what Micah had seen: landowners oppressing the poor, social injustices, corrupt religious leaders, a lack of true justice and —above all—an atmosphere of pious platitudes and loud praises *of* God without service *to* God. To this the Deuteronomists added another national and individual sin: the neglect and abuse of the strangers within their midst and the keeping of God's commandments. The people had not changed much in the long years between Micah and Josiah. (How much has human nature and sin changed between Josiah and the year of our Lord 1981?)

What this preacher in Deuteronomy is doing is to make an appeal to his readers and to the national conscience to move out in a new direction toward the God of their fathers. He bases his appeal on two expressions of faith: fear and love. No, there is no contradiction in the use of these words. By *fear* he means reverence to the God who has brought them from Egypt to Jerusalem. He is not picturing God as an avenger or a criminal court judge but as a majestically divine creator and lover of mankind. We have no reason to be frightened about God; we do have an obligation to reverence and love Him even as He loves us, to honor Him for what He is and for what He has done for us. He had led Israel out of Egypt; Israel in Egypt had only seventy persons; led to freedom in the Land of Promise, they had become "as the stars of heaven for multitude." Just so, God led a handful of Pilgrims to Plymouth Rock and today we have a nation of over 200,000,000! We should at least remember that!

What had to be done in Josiah's time was to bring his people back to a love of the God who had done so much for them. By *love,* he did not mean a sentimental homage paid to God at Christmas and Easter, but a love that was obedient *service.* Love that is only lip-service is not love but shameful pretense. We say, "I love God." God say, "Prove it!"

There was a lot of proving to be done in Josiah's kingdom. There is a lot of it waiting to be done in the kingdoms of the twentieth century. We call ourselves a Christian America. We engrave on our coins the words, "In God We Trust." But are we Christian when we become arms merchant to the world, to friend and foe alike? Are we serving Him in love when we donate fortunes in money to charlatans who have turned religion into a racket while main-line church denominations show a steady decline in support and membership? Are we acting in loving service when policemen, firemen, nurses, and even doctors go out on strike? Can we honestly say that we are giving God first priority in our lives? Think on these things!

"Circumcise therefore the foreskin of your heart, and be no more stiffnecked" (verse 16). Circumcision was a Jewish rite which marked a man as a Jew. Applied to the Christian, it means that a man is marked as a Christian when he opens his heart to God, opens his ears to His Word. (Read what Jeremiah has to say about uncircumcised ears, in Jeremiah

6:10, and what Moses says about uncircumcised lips in Exodus 6:12.) Opening the ears, lips, and heart to God means loving what He loves and that His will, not ours, be done.

SUGGESTIONS TO TEACHERS

A high-school boy querulously asked his teacher why he should be forced to study history.

"Do you know what happens to a man who loses his memory?" the teacher replied.

Your lesson today is, in part, about the time God's people forgot to study their history and lost their memory until it was almost too late. Deuteronomy is a reremembering of both what God has done and what He expects of His people.

Don't think that you are merely teaching a history lesson about Josiah. Your purpose is to help your class to understand what God has in mind today. When you and your students respond to Scripture—the history and the covenant—you will discover startling evidence that the Spirit is at work in your lives! As with Josiah, the Lord also has surprises in store for you.

1. *CHOSEN PEOPLE WHO CHOOSE GOD.* Rehearse with your class what it means to be "chosen." Remind your people that being "chosen" in no way means being God's mascots or pampered favorites. By examining the scriptural background material, you will observe that God chooses His people to serve. God's people are selected to choose God ahead of every other choice. Take time in your class to let your class thresh out the misconceptions your people have about being the "chosen people."

2. *OBEDIENT PEOPLE WHO OBEY COMMANDS.* Ask your folks to ponder carefully what obedience to God implies today. Prod them to consider the implications of being obedient not only individually, but also corporately as a congregation. Have each write on a card, "To be obedient to God today, He specifically would want my church to do these things:" (List these). Furthermore, nudge your class members to think about what God commands. Dissect the key verse, Deuteronomy 11:1, and suggest what particular orders God is issuing to society today.

3. *SERVANT PEOPLE WHO SERVE OTHERS.* The theme of *servant people* runs through the entire Bible. Call your class's attention to the emphasis on serving in the Scripture in today's lesson. Ask pointed questions about what it means for the Church to be a servant community in these days. What is your congregation doing to serve minorities and refugees? Is your church effectively serving the needs of children and teenagers, of elderly and lonely, of divorced and singles? Who are the "sojourners, the fatherless and widows" today around you?

4. *COVENANTED PEOPLE WHO COVENANT TOGETHER.* Finally, allot a portion of your lesson period to consider the nature of the bond which you and every member of your class shares. Emphasize the meaning of being "covenanted" with each other. If you wish, use analogies such as the marriage covenant to illustrate the way all Christians are joined together in an unbreakable relationship. You and each

person in your class—and every other member of Christ's community—have covenanted to be faithful to each other! Explore the significance of such a covenanted relationship. What does the covenant mean in respect to your attitudes and actions toward other congregations in your community? Toward Roman Catholics? Toward other denominations?

TOPIC FOR ADULTS
HEARING GOD'S COMMANDS

Using the Well. A writer recounts how he returned to the one hundred-fifty-year old farmhouse in which his grandparents had lived. He had particularly pleasant memories of the old well on the property. As a boy, he had often paused to drink of the pure, refreshing water from that well. For over a century, year in and year out, even in the midst of droughts, that well had supplied plenty of good water.

The writer found that someone had boarded up the old well. Nevertheless, he felt certain that there would be an ample supply of delicious cold water in the ancient well and tore off the rotting boards and lowered a bucket on a rope. Nothing happened. The bucket clunked to the depths of the dark hole, and came to rest in dry debris at the bottom. No friendly splash. No brimming bucket. No cool drink. What had gone wrong? The writer was perplexed. The well had always produced sufficient water and had never been known to go dry.

The answer was simple. Several years earlier, someone had modernized the old farmhouse and had sunk a pipe for an artesian well beside the house. The old well was boarded up and abandoned. The old well, fed by hundreds of tiny rivelets, had provided ample water as long as it was used. When no water was taken out, however, the tiny rivelets eventually became clogged. These little springs could no longer drip their replenishing droplets into the well, and the well simply dried up.

When we no longer hear and do God's commands, eventually, like those small rivelets ceasing to feed water into the well, we find that we no longer can appropriate the covenant-promise into our lives. The covenant must be lived, just as the well had to be used.

Deuteronomy, in a sense, is the story of Israel "redigging the well of faith" by rediscovering the covenant. Even today, the community of God's people must reclaim the promise of God. Understanding the foundations for faith means uncovering the debris preventing us from hearing God's commands.

Holy Worldliness. Sir George MacLeod, the energetic Scottish pastor-theologian who founded the Iona Community, once described the results when a small Glasgow-slum lad threw a stone through a window of a Church. The stone smashed one of the letters in the inscription, "Glory to God in the Highest," so that the inscription was changed to read GLORY TO GOD IN THE HIGH ST. (In Scotland, the main street of nearly every town is called the High Street). MacLeod was reluctant to have the window repaired. He made quite a point of how the stone thrown by the boy had provided unintentionally what could be the motto of that parish, and, indeed, every congregation. "Glory to God in the High Street" means hearing God's commands and applying them to every life situation.

MacLeod tried unsuccessfully to have the new letter, the "E" in *HIGHEST,* mounted on a swivel so that no one could read either inscription without being reminded of the other.

Is your church aware that hearing God's commands means glorifying Him on Main Street?

Heeding the Call of Duty. The foundations for faith mean hearing God's commands. Often, those commands will be understood only in the context of doing one's duty. Admittedly, the word *duty* is not heard much these days. Our age emphasizes doing your own thing, expressing yourself, finding the real you. Duty? That sounds repressive.

God's people, however, do not shrink from the idea of hearing God's command meaning accepting certain duties. Many of these may be chores. Others may not be exiciting or challenging. Washing the dishes may not be the most creative act in the world, but for the good of everyone, someone must accept that duty. That same is true with many of the tasks God lays on us.

"Duty is the sublimest word in the language," said Robert E. Lee. "You can never do more than your duty; you should never wish to do less." And Ralph Waldo Emerson wrote in his *Journals:* "Don't tell me to get ready to die, I know not what shall be. The only preparation I can make is by fulfilling my present duties."

Questions for Pupils on the Next Lesson. 1. Do you think that there are unclaimed promises by God which you have not yet realized? 2. Why do some adults lose their sense of adventure and willingness to risk? 3. How do mistakes of the past sometimes prevent people from living for God today? What can be done to help such persons to make efforts to adventure for God? 4. How can you and your congregation move forward in new ways by trusting that God will fulfill His promises?

TOPIC FOR YOUTH
HEARING GOD'S COMMANDS

Brown-Bag Sermon. "Once I was in Vienna, after a two-week illness in a little Austrian village. I had spent most of my travel money on medicine and doctors and used my last bit to take a train to Vienna. I had no clue as to where I could find my friends who had been waiting for me earlier. I was lost and hungry and depressed. As I was standing in one of the streetcar stations in central Vienna, tired, discouraged and trying to figure out what to do, a little, old wrinkled woman (whose job it was to sweep out the station) came over to me and asked if I was hungry. Even before I could answer, she took her lunch from a brown bag and offered me half! I was moved. She not only helped my aching hunger, but lifted my spirit in an unforgettable way.

"I have never forgtten her—the warmth of her face, the graciousness of her gift, the youthful sparkle in her eyes. We talked for more than an hour about her life. It had not been easy. She was raised in the country, knowing nothing but hard work on a farm. She had lost her husband and two sons in the Resistance to the Nazis. Only her daughter survived. But she was thankful, she said, for many things. She was at peace with her story. Finally, I asked her why she offered me her lunch. She said simply, 'Jesu ist mein Herrn. Gott ist gut.' (Jesus is my Lord. God is good.) She understood and lived in the story of Jesus in a way that most sophisticated scholars could never do. Her faith touched mine. Who was it, after all, that I met that day in Vienna?

"Her life, with all its hurts, she saw as a pilgrimage, a faith journey, full of meaning."—Roy Fairchild, *Concern*, July 1978.

Obscuring the Word. Sometimes the commands of God get lost in the cultural or religious trappings of our society.

Some large American corporations have discovered that some of their favorite slogans got twisted or smothered in the course of translation into other languages and cultures. The Chevrolet Nova, for example, wasn't selling well in Latin America. Someone pointed out finally that *nova* sounds like the words for "No-go" in Spanish, and the name had to be changed. The slogan "Come Alive With Pepsi" was somehow rendered into Chinese in Taiwan to state, "Pepsi brings your ancestors back from the grave." General Motors's famous "Body by Fisher" was somehow being called "Corpse by Fisher" in some countries until the negative nuance was discovered and corrected. These corporations see little amusing in such malapropisms.

God's commands get muffled and mangled by our culture. We must rediscover the original message He gives us. Only careful Bible study and disciplined living by a faithful community of God's people will permit His commands to be heard today. Are you prepared to try to hear His commands?

Reward in Seeking. Albert Einstein once told the National Academy of Sciences that awards should not be showered on those who discover the fundamental laws of nature. "When a man, after long years of searching, chances upon a thought which discloses something of the beauty of this mysterious universe, he should not therefore be personally celebrated. He is already sufficiently paid by his experience of seeking and finding."

The same holds for those trying to hear God's commands and to do them. They do not look for any rewards. They expect no acclaim. Like Einstein's scientists, they are already paid sufficiently by the experience of seeking and finding God's commands in the life of the Church today.

Sentence Sermon to Remember:

> I'll go where you want me to go, dear Lord,
> O'er mountain or plain or sea;
> I'll say what you want me to say, dear Lord,
> I'll be what you want me to be.
> > Mary Brown: Hymn.

Questions for Pupils on the Next Lesson. 1. Does God have a plan for your life? 2. If God does have such a plan, do your choices influence the working out of that plan? 3. Is God's love consistent? 4. Is God's love the same or different from the parent/child relationship which you have experienced in your home? 5. How may fear be handled in a positive manner? 6. Do you sometimes act impetuously rather than waiting on God to work out His purposes in His own time?

LESSON II—JUNE 14

CLAIMING GOD'S PROMISE

Background Scripture: Deuteronomy 1.
Devotional Reading: 2 Corinthians 13:5–13

KING JAMES VERSION

Deuteronomy 1 19 And when we departed from Horeb, we went through all that great and terrible wilderness, which ye saw by the way of the mountain of the Amorites, as the LORD our God commanded us; and we came to Kadesh-barnea.

20 And I said unto you, Ye are come unto the mountain of the Amorites, which the LORD our God doth give unto us.

21 Behold, the LORD thy God hath set the land before thee: go up *and* possess *it*, as the LORD God of thy fathers hath said unto thee; fear not, neither be discouraged.

22 And ye came near unto me every one of you, and said, We will send men before us, and they shall search us out the land, and bring us word again by what way we must go up, and into what cities we shall come.

23 And the saying pleased me well; and I took twelve men of you, one of a tribe:

24 And they turned and went up into the mountain, and came unto the valley of Eshcol, and searched it out.

25 And they took of the fruit of the land in their hands, and brought it down unto us, and brought us word again, and said, It is a good land which the LORD our God doth give us.

26 Notwithstanding ye would not go up, but rebelled against the commandment of the LORD your God:

29 Then I said unto you, Dread not, neither be afraid of them.

30 The LORD your God which goeth before you, he shall fight for you, according to all that he did for you in Egypt before your eyes;

31 And in the wilderness, where thou hast seen how that the LORD thy God bare thee, as a man doth bear his son, in all the way that ye went, until ye came into this place.

REVISED STANDARD VERSION

Deuteronomy 1 19 "And we set out from Horeb, and went through all that great and terrible wilderness which you saw, on the way to the hill country of the Amorites, as the LORD our God commanded us; and we came to Kadesh-barnea. 20 And I said to you, 'You have come to the hill country of the Amorites, which the LORD our God gives us. 21 Behold, the LORD your God has set the land before you; go up, take possession, as the LORD, the God of your fathers, has told you; do not fear or be dismayed.' 22 Then all of you came near me, and said, 'Let us send men before us, that they may explore the land for us, and bring us word again of the way by which we must go up and the cities into which we shall come.' 23 The thing seemed good to me, and I took twelve men of you, one man for each tribe; 24 and they turned and went up into the hill country, and came to the Valley of Eshcol and spied it out. 25 And they took in their hands some of the fruit of the land and brought it down to us, and brought us word again, and said, 'It is a good land which the LORD our God gives us.'

26 "Yet you would not go up, but rebelled against the command of the LORD your God; 29 Then I said to you, 'Do not be in dread or afraid of them. 30 The LORD your God who goes before you will himself fight for you, just as he did for you in Egypt before your eyes, 31 and in the wilderness, where you have seen how the LORD your God bore you, as a man bears his son, in all the way that you went until you came to this place.'"

322

KEY VERSE: " 'Behold, the Lord your God has set the land before you; go up, take possession, as the Lord, the God of your fathers, has told you . . . .' " Deuteronomy 1:21 (RSV).

HOME DAILY BIBLE READINGS

June 8. M. *Moses Speaks in the Wilderness.* Deuteronomy 1:3–9.
June 9. T. *Moses Speaks About Judges.* Deuteronomy 1:9–18.
June 10. W. *Moses Speaks About the Spies.* Deuteronomy 1:19–25.
June 11. T. *Moses Speaks of God's Care.* Deuteronomy 1:26–33.
June 12. F. *Moses Speaks of God's Denial.* Deuteronomy 1:34–40.
June 13. S. *Moses Speaks of Disobedience.* Deuteronomy 1:41–46.
June 14. S. *Do What Is Right.* 2 Corinthians 13:5–13.

BACKGROUND

For forty years, the children of Israel, led by the indomitable Moses, struggled through the wilderness. They had left Egypt in high spirits, for they had a promise from the Lord: He promised to give the great rich land between Egypt and the Euphrates (the "Promised Land") to Abraham, Isaac, and Jacob and their descendants. God told them to go and take possession of this land with His almighty help.

They moved toward this Promised Land through a wilderness; there were good days and bad days on this long journey; there were hope and despair, victories and defeats, hesitation and courage, fear and faith, as they moved on. They came to the mount called Horeb (Sinai), and here Moses had had his great experience with his God, had given the great Commandments to his people, and had prepared them for their next move toward the land promised of God. He had led a mob of slaves out of Egypt; at Sinai they were a well-disciplined army—a nation—ready for the final battle with the Amorites.

So now they marched from Sinai to Kadesh-barnea, the southern gateway through which they would enter and take over the Land. It was only an eleven-day march, and they sang in enthusiasm as they moved along, all the way to Kadesh. They marched in confidence—no, in over-confidence, for in Kadesh something happened that cost them forty years more in the wilderness. Only a year had passed since they had left Egypt, and on the whole they had done well, but now!

NOTES ON THE PRINTED TEXT

I. . . . Ye are come unto the mountain of the Amorites . . . . Deuteronomy 1:20. Who were these Amorites? Originally they were the inhabitants of a land called Amurru, which may have been Syria, and at least a part of Palestine. The term *Amorite*, it is believed, refers to the general pre-Israelite population of Palestine. Jerusalem was quite likely an Amorite town in these times.

Thanks to the existence of reliable historic records, we actually know little about them, except that they fought more than their share of battles and wars, trying to establish themselves as a dominant kingdom; they conquered the last Sumerian kingdom, fought with Egyptians, Hurrians, and Hittites, but succeeded only in establishing a number a small kingdoms which existed only until Hammurabi of Babylon put an end to them. (It is ironic that Hammurabi himself had an Amorite background.)

Now the Israelites coming up to the gates of Kadesh probably knew of all this; but what they "knew" was less history than myth. They knew that the Amorites were a people who never ran from a fight. When they thought of the Amorite conquests, they thought of big, strong men in a formidable army. Legends were woven about them; as late as Amos, this prophet said that the Amorites were as tall as cedars, and as strong as oaks (Amos 2:9). How good were the chances of the Israelites if they had to fight such giants as these? They began to wonder—on this land they would invade, there were not only Amorites; there were also Hittites and Jebusites and Amalekites and Canaanites living in fortified towns and cities, and they had to be conquered, too! It would not be easy!

Turn now and read the more detailed story of what happened at this point, in Numbers 13, 14.

II. "'. . . Let us send men before us, that they may explore the land for us, and bring us word again of the way by which we must go up and the cities into which we shall come.'" Deuteronomy 1:22 (RSV). It sounds like common sense; this is an accepted prebattle procedure, even among modern nations. (The United States had spies working in most countries abroad, and those countries have spies in *our* country right now!). Even Moses thought it was a good idea; he named twelve spies, one for each tribe, to go into Canaan and "search it out." But it was a mistake for which he paid dearly.

When they reached Kadesh and pitched their camp there at Canaan's gate, Moses said to them, "Behold, the Lord your God has set the land before you; go up, take possession, as the Lord, the God of your fathers, has told you; do not fear or be dismayed" (verse, 21 RSV). The Lord had promised them that He would bring them victory over the Amorites: *go and possess their land!* If God were with them, who could be against them? Who could withstand or defeat the *Lord*? In view of that promise, they had no need to send in their spies; God already knew their enemies and their fortified cities, and He had given His word that they could be taken. When they sent out their spies, they distrusted God and broke their covenant with Him.

The spies went in, looked it over, and came back to add terror to the hesitation of the Israelites. Ten out of the twelve of them said *yes*, this was a land of milk and honey, a rich, fertile land; they brought back a cluster of grapes so large that it had to be carried on a pole by two men. That was true, but . . . *but* it was also a land of men who were "the children of Anak"—Anak of the Anakims, a race of monstrous giants. They were entrenched in cities with great high walls, in cities that could never be taken by the smaller, weaker men of Israel. Only two of the spies, Caleb and Joshua, told another story; these two said that the Amorites were not giants, that "their defense is departed from them" (Numbers 14:9), and that the land could be taken: "The Lord is with us: fear them not."

But they did fear; they went into panic. They sat in their tents murmuring against God, even accusing Him of hating them and bringing them out of Egypt to die in a wilderness (Deuteronomy 1:27). They turned their backs on Canaan and ran back into the wilderness.

Fear may be the greatest enemy of God in so many of us. *Human* fear, that we allow to overwhelm our fear (reverence for, trust it) of God! We fear failure; we hesitate to accept the challange to do great things—we hesitate, and we are lost. We fear the loss of our jobs; we fear the influence of wicked men, of tyrants. We fear taking a stand for God against them. In the fear of hesitation, we put off until tomorrow that which we should do today. We live little, ineffective lives, afraid to venture out upon crusades for righteousness; we sit in our tents and murmur that we should "let God do it"; and we doubt too much that God is *able* to do it! We plead that "the time is not ready for it." We are too much like General McClellan, of the Union army. McClellan was forever pleading that "the (Union) Army is not yet ready for aggressive action." He spent his time getting ready—and he had to be removed from his command. It was not until General Grant took over that the army moved into action.

Above all, we fear the unknown, the darkness of things unseen. Someone has said of the men who drove their wagons across the mountains into the unknown West of our country that "The heroes drove those wagon-trains; the fearful stayed at home." It took heroic men to possess the American West.

Or we are like the man who woke up in the middle of the night and thought he saw a burglar coming in his bedroom window; he took a revolver from under his pillow and shot off his two big toes! Fear can do that and often does.

Hesitance and fear to take the bold step which God had commanded almost cost Israel the Promised Land. Hesitancy and human fear of other humans can cost us fellowship with God. He has promised us abundant life in His Kingdom—but we must take the long step toward Him in complete and fearless faith. There is no other gate to the Kingdom.

SUGGESTIONS TO TEACHERS

Take a poll in your class on what faith is. Chances are you will find that most think that faith is "believing." Faith, in other words, is regarded as an intellectual exercise; "swallowing what you know t'ain't so," as Tom Sawyer put it!

The Bible insists that faith is adventuring with God. Faith is a pilgrimage. Faith is trusting God enough to step out into the unknown. Faith means going on even when you don't know what's ahead. Faith is claiming God's promise!

The problem is—as you will explore in this lesson—that we don't want to be pilgrims. We're shy about adventuring. Claiming God's promise? Well, sometime, perhaps, but not right now when things look so bleak.

This is what the scriptural material in today's lesson states that God's people were experiencing. Look again at Deuteronomy 1. Doesn't it sound like you and your class? Your lesson this week can well be a catalogue of refusals on the part of God's people then and now to claim His promise.

1. *STALLED ON THE MOUNTAIN.* Moses and the people of God seem to be bogged down in their journey toward the promised land.

They had stopped at the mountain. They were not progressing any nearer their destination. Finally, God firmly barks orders for them, "You have stayed long enough at this mountain; turn and take your journey, and go . . . " (Deuteronomy 1:6). God's people are sometimes reluctant to move out. However, when we claim God's promise, we can move forward! Have your class talk over whether or not your class and your congregation seems to be stuck on dead center. Is God trying to nudge your church to going in some new directions?

2. *SLOWED NEAR THE AMORITES.* God's people not only have reluctance to adventure in faith but also have doubts. In Moses's time, they had misgivings because of the wild clan of warlike Amorites which blocked their entrance to the promised land. Their doubts made the Amorites into bigger-than-life adversaries. Isn't it always this way when doubt takes over? What are the matters which create doubts (today's "Amorites") in the lives of your class members? Allow each person to relate what are the biggest causes of misgivings about God in his or her life.

3. *SCARED BY THE GIANTS.* God's people could not start to claim His promise because they were scared by the giants, ("greater and taller than we"—Deuteronomy 1:28). Fear prevents God's people from appropriating His assurance of His plans, His presence, His power, His ultimate victory. Christians are sometimes the most timid anywhere! What are the fears which inhibit your church from risking boldly? Fear of losing some members or alienating folks? Fear of upsetting leaders or powerful people in the community? Fear of getting hurt? Fear of getting in over your head? Remind your class that when they claim God's promise through Christ, they can face any terrors!

4. *SMITTEN BY THE IMPETUOUS.* Look for a few minutes at the time when some of Moses' followers "rebelled against the command of the Lord and were presumptuous and went up into the hill country" (Deuteronomy 1:43). Those who impulsively decide to try to move forward by relying only on their own wisdom and strength are doomed. Caution your class there is always the danger that God's people will act rebelliously and smugly. The congregation that engineers its programs by human schemes without claiming the divine promise will soon experience defeats!

TOPIC FOR ADULTS
CLAIMING GOD'S PROMISE

Confident of God. On April 28, 1979, Georgi P. Vins, one of five Soviet dissidents released in exchange for two convicted Russian spies, arrived in New York. Georgi Vins, a Ukrainian Baptist leader, had been sentenced by a court in Kiev in 1975 to five years in prison, to be followed by five years in Siberian exile for his activities in preaching the Gospel in the Soviet Union. Vins and his fellow prisoners described harsh conditions, of being denied medical treatment and the right to religious worship, of abuse and of beatings.

In his first interview after landing in New York a few hours earlier, Vins picked up a copy of Scriptures and smiled. "I was delighted that the first book I saw in this hotel in New York was the Bible," he said, "For five years, I was deprived of this Book. There is no Book I cherish more," he added, his voice rising.

In spite of being denied access to Scripture, Vins strengthened himself and his fellow prisoners by quoting passages from memory. Through the horrors of the Gulag, Vins and fellow believers claimed God's promise.

Is your faith based on Scripture's promise? Are you confident of God in spite of the threats and terrors which assail you?

Uncowed by Power. The only clergyman to sign the Declaration of Independence was the Rev. John Witherspoon, President of Princeton College. Witherspoon also was a fervent American patriot. His speeches and writings instilled hope into the oft-faltering American cause in the grim days of the Revolution.

Someone asked Dr. Witherspoon in 1777 how he could possibly continue to have dreams for the American republic when it seemed obvious that British military might was invincible. "How can you continue to have any faith for America when the Redcoats are so powerful?"

Witherspoon recounted that he had been present at the battle of Falkirk in 1746, when he was a youngster in Scotland, and had seen the redcoats beaten into retreating. English redcoats could not threaten or intimidate a man who had seen them defeated.

God's promise is like that. People who know the Good News of God through His works are aware that nothing need daunt them. Christians have already known that the powers of evil have been defeated. God has already demonstrated His power. Believers in Him will never be cowed by any earthly powers. As His people, members of the Church may claim God's promise of ultimate victory!

Always a Future With God. In 1933, George Marshall of the United States Army was certain that he was a washed-up, burnt-out has-been. He seriously contemplated retiring from the Army. He felt that his career had run its course. "I am fast getting too old to have any future of importance," he wrote to friends. Promotions were painfully slow in those days, and Marshall privately wondered what God's plans were for him.

Fortunately, George Marshall dutifully continued in the Army. For several years, however, he had no assurance of God's promise of big plans for his own life. He knew how hard it was to believe that there was any point in keeping on in his career. His perseverance and faith were vindicated in 1941. Marshall was selected to serve as Chief of Staff for the wartime Army and engineered military victories over the Axis. Following the war, he was named Secretary of State. As the architect of the humane and generous American program to rebuild the devastated countries of Europe (now remembered as the Marshall Plan), George Marshall claimed God's promise and put it into practice on an international scale!

Questions for Pupils on the Next Lesson. 1. Do you sense that much of the responsibility for understanding, preserving, and teaching God's commandments rests upon adults like you? Why or why not? 2. How can you recall and interpret the lessons of the past to others? 3. How are the ways in which you live helping to shape the attitudes others have toward God and righteousness? 4. How do you interpret the contradictions between the claims and the conduct of our nation? 5. How does God's Word give direction to your life?

TOPIC FOR YOUTH
CLAIMING GOD'S PROMISE

Mad Dreamers. When the people of Seville, Spain, decided to erect a cathedral, they called in architects for ideas. One man presented such a grand plan that everyone gasped.

"It is too big," some protested. Others shook their heads, stating that they could never afford to build it. "How can we be certain it won't collapse?" asked those doubting the engineering skills of the architect. Still another group examined the plans and announced that they were too ambitious and too big to be feasible.

The architect heard all of the critics patiently before he replied. With the fire born of faith in God's promise, he exclaimed, "We must build a cathedral so great that they will think us mad!"

Because of his claim on the promise of God, the people of Seville embarked on the venture of faith that produced one of medieval Europe's grandest and loveliest architectural masterpieces.

Likewise, we as God's community today must build so ambitiously and fearlessly that people in years to come will think us mad!

Costly Glance Backward. Although Roger Bannister set the world's record for the first mile run under four minutes in 1954, he was soon challenged. John Landy broke Bannister's record, and the world watched breathlessly for the two champion sub-four-minute milers to compete at a track meet.

The famous encounter took place at the Empire Games at Vancouver in August of 1954. Landy, the powerful Australian titleholder, went to the front soon after the starting gun. Bannister, determined not to knock himself out in the first half of the race let him take a fifteen yard lead. Finally, Bannister gambled and went on past. As he swept by on Landy's right, Landy glanced back over his left shoulder to see where his rival was. In that instant, Bannister snatched the lead. That did it. Time: 3:58:8. If Landy had not looked back as Bannister passed him on the blind side, Landy would have won the race! Ruefully, the losing Landy commented later, "Lot's wife was turned into a pillar of salt for looking over her shoulder. I am the first person to be turned into bronze to commemorate that."

Claim God's promise! Don't look back over your shoulder to see what others are doing. You only break pace and lose the race when you give way to fear about others. Move forward with confidence and trust in God.

Fear Causes Flood. Art treasures of twenty centuries were nearly lost when a disastrous flood swept through Florence, Italy in 1966. Investigations followed. Experts could not understand how such massive flooding could occur.

The cause finally came to light. A dam official was afraid that the flood waters filling up behind his dam would cause his dam to collapse. Instead of holding the rising tide behind the powerful walls of the dam, however, this fearful official decided to open the gates. The crest roared through the valley and hit the beautiful city of Florence. The dam remained intact, but the ancient beauty and irreplaceable art work of the famous city were almost destroyed.

Those who fail to claim God's promise will fall prey to panic. And fear can destroy. God's promise also steadies and strengthens His people to face any threats.

Sentence Sermon to Remember:

The promises of God are certain, but they do not all mature in ninety days.

—Adoniram J. Gordon.

Questions for Pupils on the Next Lesson. 1. Why is it that disciplined living in obeying God's Word actually brings freedom? Isn't this a contradiction? 2. How actively involved are you in sharing your faith with others? 3. What happens when people fail to remember and interpret the lessons of the past? 4. What actions of God can you recall in your life or the life of the nation? 5. How do you interpret the contradictions between the claims and the conduct of our nation?

LESSON III—JUNE 21

RECALLING GOD'S ACTION

Background Scripture: Deuteronomy 3:12–4:14
Devotional Reading: Romans 4:13–25

<table>
<tr><th>KING JAMES VERSION</th><th>REVISED STANDARD VERSION</th></tr>
</table>

KING JAMES VERSION

DEUTERONOMY 4 1 Now therefore hearken, O Israel unto the statutes and unto the judgments, which I teach you, for to do *them*, that ye may live, and go in and possess the land which the LORD God of your fathers giveth you.

2 Ye shall not add unto the word which I command you, neither shall ye diminish *aught* from it, that ye may keep the commandments of the LORD your God which I command you.

5 Behold, I have taught you statutes and judgments, even as the LORD my God commanded me, that ye should do so in the land whither ye go to possess it.

6 Keep therefore and do *them;* for this *is* your wisdom and your understanding in the sight of the nations, which shall hear all these statutes, and say, Surely this great nation *is* a wise and understanding people.

7 For what nation *is there so* great, who *hath* God *so* nigh unto them, as the LORD our God *is* in all *things that* we call upon him *for?*

8 And what nation *is there so* great, that hath statutes and judgments *so* righteous as all this law, which I set before you this day?

9 Only take heed to thyself, and keep thy soul diligently, lest thou forget the things which thine eyes have seen, and lest they depart from thy heart all the days of thy life: but teach them thy sons, and thy sons' sons;

10 *Specially* the day that thou stoodest before the LORD thy God in Horeb, when the LORD said unto me, Gather me the people together, and I will make them hear my words, that they may learn to fear me all the days that they shall live upon the earth, and *that* they may teach their children.

REVISED STANDARD VERSION

DEUTERONOMY 4 1 "And now, O Israel, give heed to the statutes and the ordinances which I teach you, and do them; that you may live, and go in and take possession of the land which the LORD, the God of your fathers, gives you. 2 You shall not add to the word which I command you, nor take from it; that you may keep the commandments of the Lord your God which I command you. 5 Behold, I have taught you statues and ordinances, as the LORD my God commanded me, that you should do them in the land which you are entering to take possession of it. 6 Keep them and do them; for that will be your wisdom and your understanding in the sight of the peoples, who, when they hear all these statutes, will say, 'Surely this great nation is a wise and understanding people.' 7 For what great nation is there that has a god so near to it as the LORD our God is to us, whenever we call upon him? 8 And what great nation is there, that has statutes and ordinances so righteous as all this law which I set before you this day?

9 "Only take heed, and keep your soul diligently, lest you forget the things which your eyes have seen, and lest they depart from your heart all the days of your life; make them known to your children and your children's children— 10 how on the day that you stood before the LORD your God at Horeb, the LORD said to me, 'Gather the people to me, that I may let them hear my words, so that they may learn to fear me all the days that they live upon the earth, and that they may teach their children so.' "

KEY VERSE: *"Only take heed, and keep your soul diligently, lest you forget the things which your eyes have seen, and lest they depart from your heart all the days of your life; make them known to your children and your children's children. . . ."* Deuteronomy 4:9 (RSV).

HOME DAILY BIBLE READINGS

June 15. M. *Pass Through Esau's Territory.* Deuteronomy 2:1–8.
June 16. T. *A Hardened Spirit Brings Defeat.* Deuteronomy 2:24–31.
June 17. W. *God Fights for You.* Deuteronomy 3:18–22.
June 18. T. *Look But Don't Cross.* Deuteronomy 3:23–28.
June 19. F. *Keep God's Statutes and Ordinances.* Deuteronomy 4:1–8.
June 20. S. *Teach Your Children God's Commands.* Deuteronomy 4:9–14.
June 21. S. *Faith in the Promise.* Romans 4:13–25.

BACKGROUND

The Book of Deuteronomy, as we have earlier stated, is really a book of sermons or orations delivered by Moses. For the sake of the record, let us keep it clear that there are three orations here: the first in Deuteronomy 1–4; the second, in Deuteronomy 5–26; the third, in Deuteronomy 27–30. Chapters 31–34 are a record of the last days of Moses, and not, literally, an oration. Today we come to the closing words of Moses' first oration.

Following the needless defeat and disaster at Kadesh, the Jews fled back into the shelter of the wilderness, and for the next thirty-eight years there is a complete silence about them in the Bible. We do not know what they did in those lost years, but we do know that Moses and his captains must have worked overtime restoring the spirit and the whole attitude of their people, and must have led them once more to accept the guidance of a God they had betrayed at Kadesh. They come out of their hiding in a fighting mood. Sihon, a king of the Amorites, refused to let them pass though his territory as they moved toward the Jordan Valley and he was killed, along with his sons, in a battle at Jahaz. Then there was Og, king of Bashan, a huge man ruling a powerfully built people who should have frightened the Israelites but didn't: Israel whipped them in another battle, annihilated them, and burst through all other obstacles to occupy the country east of Jordan.

Moses made good use of this moment of victory: he made an eloquent plea for devotion and loyalty. His people looked back with pride at what they had accomplished; wise Moses looks ahead to what will happen and tries to prepare Israel for its future.

NOTES ON THE PRINTED TEXT

I. Now therefore hearken, O Israel, unto the statutes and unto the judgments, which I teach you . . . . Deuteronomy 4:1. The words and teachings of this section and chapter of Deuteronomy are based on two deeply significant historical events. If the people wanted to go on living, Moses says, they must never forget these two events, and never wander from their teachings.

The first event was shocking and sad to remember. At a place called Beth-peor, in the Jordan Valley, "some of the young (Israelite) men began going to wild parties with the local Moabite girls . . . ," says *The Living Bible.* It was bad enough for an Israelite to be seen in the company of a Moabite; it was worse when the young Israelites, under the coy influence of the girls, allowed themselves to engage in the worship of Baal (Beth-peor is also known as Beth-Baal). Other Israelites were soon doing the same thing: "Israel (all of Israel?) joined himself unto Baal-peor" (Numbers 25:3). That roused the anger of Israel's God, who ordered the execution of every last one of the worshipers of Baal. The record says that 24,000 died in that purge and in the plague that followed.

We gasp at the horror of it, but we must remember that this happened at a very early age in Hebrew history. The figures of the slain may be exaggerated, but the main point is clear: the Deuteronomist was anxious to make it clear that to disobey God is to court destruction. To flaunt God is to die; to obey Him is to live. The people of Israel, at Sinai, had accepted the commandment of God to worship Him and no other—and they had broken their promise to do just that at Beth-peor. They knew that by the statutes (laws) and the judgments that was something more than ordinary sin. The lesson God was teaching, the writer suggests, is that the God who had given Israel could destroy it if it defied Him.

Such a massacre would be impossible today; in our time we can understand that anyone defing God causes his own spiritual death.

II. Specially (remember) the day that thou stoodest before the Lord thy God in Horeb . . . . Deuteronomy 4:10. The "statutes and judgments," the Law, were in the Ten Commandments, and in the explanations Moses put upon them. This Law was given on the greatest day in Hebrew history, and the giving of that day on Sinai is the second event behind the words of Deuteronomy 4. Let Israel never forget *this* day; let Israel, all down the future, teach these Commandments to their children and their children's children.

Recently we heard a Jewish rabbi make a statement that "The purpose and work of Judaism is to teach obedience to the Ten Commandmants." We hesitated to accept that, at the time, but now we realize that the good rabbi has scriptual proof of his statement here in Deuteronomy.

There was another aspect involved here. What was really vital in this account of the giving of the Commandments was the fact that Israel actually heard the voice of God: "You heard the sound of words, but saw no form; there was only a voice" (verse 12). God offered, on Sinai, and the people accepted, and in accepting the Law they made a covenant with Him. Never before had such a thing happened between God and men. Never before had God come so close to men. This is what made Israel unique among the nations of the world. Moses is eloquent about this greatness: "For what nation is there so great, who hath God so nigh unto them, as the Lord our God is in all things that we call upon him for?" (verse 7).

See to it, Israel, that you never forget this day and this covenant; see to it that you do not add to the commandments I have given you, and never take any of them away. Teach all this to your sons, and to generations to come.

Israel has seen to it. Every Jewish boy and girl is well instructed in the faith; each child repeats the Shema and knows the meaning of Passover and the Commandments at a very early age. Israel has not forgotten, though generations of persecution have tried to make them forget.

Nor has the non-Jewish world forgotten Sinai and the giving of the Law. A prominent lawyer recently said at a banquet of judges and lawyers in our country, "Sometimes I think it would be a good idea to throw all our multitudinous books of confusing laws into the ocean and start all over again with the Ten Commandments!" He said it in jest, and he knew it couldn't happen, but the truth is that we have not improved very much on the Decalogue of Sinai. And the modern Copyright League has as its motto the words written by a great poet:

> In vain we call our notions fudge
> And bend our conscience to our dealing.
> The Ten Commandments will not budge
> And stealing will continue stealing.

That day on Sinai should be of interest to the Gentiles as well as to the Jews.

SUGGESTIONS TO TEACHERS

"Do you remember the time we. . . ?"

Every person, every group, must take time to recall. Children love to hear their parents reminisce about experiences involving both children and parents a few years earlier. Old war buddies and college classmates retell the same yarns and laugh over them for the hundredth time. A couple married for thirty-five years smiles and recounts experiences shared early in their struggle, and feels even closer and more in love. We must remember our history. The search for roots leads everyone to remember what has happened.

God's family also must recall God's action. Loss of memory of what God has done—spiritual amensia—means being disoriented. (Perhaps this is what is afflicting the Church sometimes!)

Your lesson today is to recall God's action, especially as shown in Deuteronomy 3:12 through 4:14. Try arranging the material as follows:

1. *DELAY TO SETTLEMENT.* The scriptural account states that those given territory east of the Jordan were told to delay occupying it until they had helped their brothers conquer their areas west of the Jordan. In other words, God told some of the tribes. "Not yet!" No permanent home yet. Not until they aided others to get their promised land.

In recalling God's action, it is important to remember that God sometimes says, "Not yet!" Enumerate times when He has said, "Not yet" in your life. Have your class share experiences when God has seemed to delay things for them. Help your class to see that God's "Not yet's" are always for a good reason. Often, the reason is His concern for others—as in the case of the tribes of Gad, Reuben, and Manassah.

2. *REPAY IN SATISFACTION.* Retell the account of Moses pleading with God to be allowed to enter the promised land and being turned down (Dueteronomy 3:25). God sometimes says, "No."

Let those in your class recall God's action in their lives which took the form of saying *No* to a request. Undoubtedly, some bring up the question *Why?* Without becoming tied up in speculation, call attention to the way in which God took Moses up to the top of Mount Pisgah for a glimpse of the promised land. Although we may not live to receive every request, God blesses us with glimpses and visions of His ultimate victory!

3. *RELAY TO SUCCESSOR.* Point out that Moses was told to anoint Joshua as his successor. God's action in history is like a relay race in which each person runs his or her lap, than passes on the baton to another. Moses serves, then must prepare another to take his place. You and your class, and every part of Christ's community, must continually make provision for others to take up the responsibilities of leadership. What steps is your congregation taking to discover and nurture the "Joshuas" among the coming generation? Who will recall God's action when you are gone?

4. *REMEMBER BAALPEOR.* "Remember Baalpeor" is shorthand for "Obey God if you expect to survive." Reread the biblical story of God's people and Baalpeor. Discuss the high cost of disobedience. Recalling God's action means retelling the times of disobedience and suffering, and also means reminding God's people of His mercy!

TOPIC FOR ADULTS
RECALLING GOD's ACTION

Participant Instead Spectator of God's Action. In Elie Wiesel's book, *The Town Beyond the Wall,* he tells the story of a Holocaust survivor who, several years after the war, is obsessed with the need to return to the small village in Hungary where he grew up. The village where, at the age of fourteen, he had been herded one morning, along with all the other Jews, into the village square, then into the box cars for the trip to the concentration camp. He doesn't know why he feels he must return, but he cannot rest until he has done so.

When he at last stands in that village square he suddenly remembers why he had to come back. On that morning so long ago, he had glanced up and had seen a face in the window. It was an impassive face, devoid of any emotion, of any caring, of any involvement in the tragic events which were taking place just below. It was the face of the Spectator. Turning now, he looks up again, and the face is still there! This the author cannot comprehend: to stand in the presence of evil and not care. To have one's eyes fall on cruelty and inhumanity and not cry out. To see suffering and remain aloof and uninvolved. This is how he puts his inability to understand:

"How could one remain indifferent? The executioner I understood. The victims I understood, but with more difficulty. But those others, all those others, who were neither for nor against; who sprawled in passive patience; those who said the storm would blow over and all would be normal again; those who thought themselves above the battle; those who were permanently merely spectators; those were all closed to me. How can one remain a spectator indefinitely? How can one continue to embrace the woman he loves, to pray to God with fervor if not faith, to dream of a better tomorrow, after having seen all this?"

A generation ago, the church was that face at the window. We must return to make certain that the face of Christianity is on longer a mere spectator. "The meaning of the Holocaust for Christians must be built into the confessions of faith and remembered in the hymns and prayers. That was the turn in the road that most of the churches missed, and

many of them are still plodding down a dead-end trail that leads away
from the Kingdom of God. We Christians must go back to the turn in the
road and reject the signs and signals which, expressing a spiritual and
intellectual teaching which was false though familiar, turned us toward
Auschwitz." —From a sermon on the Holocaust by Robert I. Doom,
First Church, Ste. Genevieve, Mo.

Character Like a Photograph. Possibly the world's greatest protrait
photographer is a short, balding Canadian named Yousuf Karsh. Karsh
has traveled nearly everywhere in the world to snap pictures of the
world's great men and women. His famous 1941 photo of a scowling
Winston Churchill captured the bulldog spirit of Britain's wartime
Prime Minister.

Statesmen, tycoons, artists, musicians, actors, physicians, kings,
popes, and presidents have been "Karshed" for all time in their own
environments, with an uncanny light seeming to play against their facial
features, hands and clothing. Albert Einstein, Nikita Khrushchev,
George Bernard Shaw, Pablo Picasso, Charles de Gaulle, Ernest
Hemingway, Fidel Castro, Albert Schweitzer, Pablo Casals, Igor
Travinsky—all have had their images caught by his camera.

He tries to capture the "inward power" of his subjects. He waits for
them to drop their "masks" in unguarded moments. With President
Franklin D. Roosevelt, he clicked a gadget attached to his camera to
make it appear that he'd tripped the shutter. When FDR relaxed, he took
the real picture.

A reporter once interviewed Karsh, asking for his observations on
great leaders. Karsh replied, "I have found that great people do have
some things in common. One is an immense belief in themselves and in
their mission. They also have great determinations as well as an ability
to work hard. At the crucial moment of decision, they draw on their
accumulated wisdom. But above all, they have integrity.

"I've also seen that great men are often lonely. This is understandable, because they have built such high standards for themselves that
they often feel alone. But that same loneliness is part of their ability to
create. Character, like a photograph develops in darkness."

Remembering God's Involvement. "Life is a series of opportunities
brilliantly disguised as insoluble problems," stated former United
States Vice-President John Nance Garner. Garner was born in a log
cabin to poverty-stricken tenant farmer parents. "Cactus Jack" Garner,
however, knew his Bible. He could recall God's action. With little
money and with no connections, he studied. His bedrock sense of remembering God's involvement in the lives of poor Israelites impelled
him to plod ahead with a career in law and politics which eventually led
him to the nation's second highest office.

Questions for Pupils on the Next Lesson. 1. How can anxious, guilt-
ridden people receive assurance that God is present with them? 2. Is
God truly concerned with our every day well-being? 3. What are some of
the gods we tend to make of our concerns and interests? 4. How does a
strong faith in God's purposes for life help to overcome feelings of
meaninglessness and emptiness?

TOPIC FOR YOUTH
RECALLING GOD'S ACTION

Throwing the Torch. Year after year, the Montreal Canadiens play championship hockey. More than any other team, the Flying Frenchmen have carried off the coveted Stanley Cup.

How do they do it? What is their "secret"?

There is, of course, the tradition in Quebec that the French skaters are faster and have more flair. That may be part of the reason for the invulnerability of the Canadiens.

Others maintain that each Canadien player has been so deeply imbued with a sense of the illustrious past of the team that he remembers that he is part of an on-going saga of victory. In their locker room, off limits to all but the players, they dress in front of plaques of the old greats: Maurice (Rocket) Richard, Jean Beliveau, Doug Harvey, Toe Blake, while above the portraits is this saying from a Rudyard Kipling poem: "To you from failing hands we throw the torch—be yours to hold it high."

This is the setting in which the Montreal Canadiens play hockey.

We Christians live in a setting in which we remember what God has done with and through and for those ancestors in the faith who have lived before us. Likewise, we know that these have thrown the torch to us, and that we, in turn, must pass it on to others.

Retrain Memory Bank. "The memory bank of the human mind has a tendency to remember the bad longer than the good and to recall it with ease. Perhaps we should train our minds to recall the good times and to forget the bad."—C. Neil Strait.

Recall God's Action. The Constitutional Convention, in 1787, was going poorly. The delegates were weary. For five weeks, they had argued, but hadn't been able to agree on a single line. Then Franklin rose, addressed himself to a point of order:

"Mr. Washington, the small progress we have made is melancholy proof of the imperfections of the human understanding. In this situation of the assembly, groping as it were in the dark to find political truth, and scarce able to distinguish it when presented to us, how has it happened, Sir, that we have not hitherto once thought of humbly applying to the Father of Lights to illumine our understanding . . . . I have lived, Sir, a long time; and the longer I live the more convincing proofs I see of this truth, that God governs in the affairs of man . . . . We have been assured, Sir, in the Sacred Writings that 'Except the Lord build the house, they labor in vain that build it.' I firmly believe this. I therefore beg leave to move that hereafter prayers, imploring the assistance of heaven and its blessings on our deliberations, be held every morning before we proceed to business."

The delegates rose and cheered. The motion was unanimously passed. Is it strange that from that moment on, progress was rapid in the framing and adoption of the Constitution of the United States?

Sentence Sermon to Remember: Remember now thy Creator in the days of thy youth . . . . —Ecclesiastes 12:1.

Questions for Pupils on the Next Lesson. 1. Why does the Christian faith claim that God is the one true God? 2. What place do you plan to give God in your future? 3. How do you understand God to be present in your life? 4. What do you think God's purpose is for human life? How do you think you can go about understranding better what His purpose is for your life? 5. How may people overcome feelings of meaninglessness and emptiness in their lives?

LESSON IV—JUNE 28

EXPERIENCING GOD'S PRESENCE

Background Scripture: Deuteronomy 4:15–49
Devotional Reading: Hosea 6:1–6

KING JAMES VERSION

DEUTERONOMY 4 32 For ask now of the days that are past, which were before thee, since the day that God created man upon the earth, and *ask* from the one side of heaven unto the other, whether there hath been *any such thing* as this great thing *is*, or hath been heard like it?

33 Did *ever* people hear the voice of God speaking out of the midst of the fire, as thou hast heard, and live?

34 Or hath God assayed to go *and* take him a nation from the midst of *another* nation, by temptations, by signs, and by wonders, and by war, and by a mighty hand, and by a stretched out arm, and by great terrors, according to all that the LORD your God did for you in Egypt before your eyes?

35 Unto thee it was shewed, that thou mightest know that the LORD he *is* God; *there is* none else beside him.

36 Out of heaven he made thee to hear his voice, that he might instruct thee: and upon earth he shewed thee his great fire; and thou heardest his words out of the midst of the fire.

37 And because he loved thy fathers, therefore he chose their seed after them, and brought thee out in his sight with his mighty power out f Egypt;

38 To drive out nations from before thee greater and mightier than thou *art*, to bring thee in, to give thee their land for an inheritance, as *it is* this day.

39 Know therefore this day, and consider *it* in thine heart, that the LORD he *is* God in heaven above, and upon the earth beneath: *there is* none else.

40 Thou shalt keep therefore his statutes, and his commandments, which I command thee this day, that it may go well with thee, and with thy children after thee, and that thou mayest prolong *thy* days upon the earth, which the LORD thy God giveth thee, for ever.

REVISED STANDARD VERSION

DEUTERONOMY 4 32 "For ask now of the days that are past, which were before you, since the day that God created man upon the earth, and ask from one end of heaven to the other, whether such a great thing as this has ever happened or was ever heard of. 33 Did any people ever hear the voice of a god speaking out of the midst of the fire, as you have heard, and still live? 34 Or has any god ever attempted to go and take a nation for himself from the midst of another nation, by trials, by signs, by wonders, and by war, by a mighty hand and an outstretched arm, and by great terrors, according to all that the LORD your God did for you in Egypt before your eyes? 35 To you it was shown, that you might know that the LORD is God; there is no other besides him. 36 Out of heaven he let you hear his voice, that he might discipline you; and on earth he let you see his great fire, and you heard his words out of the midst of the fire. 37 And because he loved your fathers and chose their descendants after them, and brought you out of Egypt with his own presence, by his great power, 38 driving out before you nations greater and mightier than yourselves, to bring you in, to give you their land for an inheritance, as at this day; 39 know therefore this day, and lay it to your heart, that the LORD is God in heaven above and on the earth beneath; there is no other. 40 Therefore you shall keep his statutes and his commandments, which I command you this day, that it may go well with you, and with your children after you, and that you may prolong your days in the land which the LORD your God gives you for ever."

KEY VERSE: *Thou wilt shew me the path of life: in thy presence there is fulness of joy* . . . . Psalms 16:11.

HOME DAILY BIBLE READINGS

June 22. M. *The Lord's Name Proclaimed.* Exodus 34:1–10.
June 23. T. *The Glory of God's Presence.* Exodus 34:29–35.
June 24. W. *God Is a Jealous God.* Deuteronomy 4:15–24.
June 25. T. *God Is a Merciful God.* Deuteronomy 4:25–31.
June 26. F. *God of Heaven and Earth.* Deuteronomy 4:32–40.
June 27. S. *Summary of Moses' Speech.* Deuteronomy 4:41–49.
June 28. S. *Return and Be Revived.* Hosea 6:1–6.

BACKGROUND

The world of Moses and the early Hebrews was full of Gods—no, *overfull* of gods! Every Egyptian city had its gods and goddesses: atin, Ptah, Psiris, Isis, Apis, Horus, Hathor, Temu, Set—there were countless pagan gods and godesses surrounding Israel in Egypt and among the tribes in the wilderness. In Canaan, they had to contend with the gods and cults of Baal in a long struggle to establish their God as superior to this god of fertility of the heathen. Out of these struggles in Egypt and Canaan came the unique concept of God held by the Israelites, which we call monotheism.

Now *monotheism* is a big word; let the teacher beware, as he considers the word, and make sure that he knows what it means before lesson time comes! This lesson will take more consideration and study than usual; there are other big, confusing words here that take some pondering. The lesson cannot be taught by our usual verse-by-verse method, for we have talked about many of the verses in Deuteronomy 4:32–40 in previous lessons. Now we need to get an overall view of what the writer in talking about, and that involves a different approach.

Start slowly, and have patience! When the work is done, you will have a clearer picture of the God you worship.

NOTES ON THE PRINTED TEXT

Moses is winding up his first oration by reemphasizing what he has said before about the great revelation that has been given by God to His people and to no other people on the face of the earth. Now a good sermon is often built in the form of a wheel; the preacher gets hold of one great central thought or theme, and uses it as the center or hub of the wheel; while he may make little excursions from the hub, he comes back again and again to make other excursions off toward the rim of the wheel, but he always comes back to the hub. Moses makes his hub out of the words, "You shall have no other god before *me*" (Deuteronomy 5:7). That is, no other gods beside me, or apart from me. He repeats this (goes back to the hub) twice, in verses 4:35 and 4:39.

Right here, we need to look at some of these big, confusing words used to describe our concepts of God. We have just said that the unique concept of God held by the Israelites was *monotheism*. That word is made up of two words from the Greek *mono*, meaning one, and *theos*, meaning God. One God! Then there was a concept called *pantheism*; this was the belief that the universe, as a whole, was God. There was nothing personal about this "God"; it was simply a belief in all the laws, forces, and matter that make up the universe, like the sun, the stars, the winds that blew, and the grass that grew! The word also means "the worship of all gods." Non-Hebrews of Moses' time worshiped God in rocks and trees and clouds and storms and they had idols of other gods who they though might give them good crops, or many children or anything else their hearts desired.

There was *polytheism*, which also meant the worship of two or more gods. And there was *Deism*, which was a belief in a God who created the world and set man free in that world to go where he pleased without God's guidance—like the driver of an automobile who started the engine, put the car in gear and then jumped out of the car to let it go wherever it pleased!

There was *theism*, too; this was the belief that God is an existent, unified, and perfect Being who not only created the universe but who guides it by providential care. And there was *henotheism*, or faith in only one God among many gods. This *henotheism* did not deny the existence of other gods, however good or bad they might be; the people of early Israel was typical henotheists, believing that each nation or race of people had its own god.

All right: now we know something of the "vast confusion of having many gods." Israel did not flatly deny the existence of other gods, but it denied their *power*. (*See* Judges 11:24, 1 Samuel 26:19, Psalms 95:13.) "Israel was forbidden to worship these lesser beings (gods), although the nations, because of their lack of knowledge, might be allowed to do so. The realm of God's authority was universal, but His unique revelation was given to the people of Israel. Here only, among His Chosen People, were His true nature and purposes known. The gods of the nations were no gods in any proper sense of that term, and the idols of these nations were creations of the hands of men."—Edward P. Blair, *The Layman's Bible Commentary*, Vol. 5.

So, surrounded by little ineffective gods and false images of false gods, Israel at Sinai became monotheists—the worshipers of one great, supreme, almighty God who stood high above the little lesser ones *invented by men*. Here a whole nation heard the voice of the true God speaking out of a column of fire on the Mount. They listened, trembled, and saw plainly that this God of Sinai was the God who had delivered them from slavery, *and taken them for Himself. They* were bidden to possess a land; now they knew that they could do that only if God possessed *them*. One God, one people! Now God was in the very midst of them; He was no absentee God living in a far away place called heaven, but a living Presence down here on earth.

What has all this to do with *us?* It has a great deal to do with us. We still have polytheists in 1981; we have semilunatic sects and cults led by leaders who claim to be a reincarnation of Jesus Christ; we have millions of people who worship nature, but who are looking through the wrong end of the telescope when they fail to see the God *behind* nature; we have many who worship Mammon (money) first, and God second; too many of us think of God as being a divine magician living somewhere beyond the clouds; we go our own way, and only when we get into trouble do we call upon Him! All about us are a multitude of little, lesser, false gods who are impotent and unable to help or inspire or lift us an inch above the common and the base. "The world," said Seneca, "is the temple of the gods."

Like Israel, *we* must choose which we shall serve: these gods, or the God above them all, Who is "Closer . . . than breathing, and nearer than hands and feet." The only important decision we have to make is to live with God; He will make the rest.

SUGGESTIONS TO TEACHERS

Some gulp hallucinogenic drugs. Otheres try to train themselves to sink into trances. Still others hope to hype themselves into a spiritual "high" through surrendering to a cult. Whatever the method (and the three preceding are not only futile but ultimately destructive) they reflect a desire to experience God's presence. You have people in your class who also long for an awareness of His nearness.

Your lesson for today, "Experiencing God's Presence," will be particularly appropriate. It will not give simplistic answers or easy shortcuts or cute recipes. Working with the background Scripture, you will raise important questions.

1. *WHAT DO YOU WORSHIP?* Deuteronomy 4:15 discusses idolatry. Ask your class to note what is idolized in contemporary society, such as security, pleasure, material possessions, sexual fulfillment, power, etc. Have them give examples of how these are worshiped. Remind your class also that an idol is what each person puts first in life. On that basis, what heads the list in your life? In your class members' lives? If God is to be experienced, He must be the One worshiped. He must top the list of what is important in life before He will be real or be significant.

2. *WHAT DO YOU REMEMBER?* Experiencing God for Christians will be in the context of also understanding the biblical story. Deuteronomy 4:20 stresses this fact. In fact, trying to experience God without remembering God's covenanting with us, especially through Christ, will lead to a distorted view of God. Have your class recall the highlights of the biblical story of God's covenanting.

3. *WHOM DO YOU SEEK?* The scriptural material (4:29) advises those who would experience God to search with all one's heart and soul, especially in times of tribulation. In other words, God will be appreciated as personal Friend by those who actively pursue the friendship. Remember also that God is to be sought particularly in the rough times. Here is a good occasion for members of your class to recount the times when God seemed most close and caring. In addition, suggest that searching after God with all one's heart and with all one's soul calls for a determined, disciplined prayer life. Allow time in your class to work through the implication of actively experiencing God through praying regularly.

4. *HOW DO YOU COMPARE?* Deuteronomy 4:35 insists that "the Lord is God; there is no other besides him." How often, however, there are other authorities besides God to depend on for help. For example, astrology is allowed to become a coauthority with God for some. With

others, it is a human leader, or a book, or a philosophy. What others can you and your class list? Ask your class, "Are any of these ultimately able to help as God promises He does?"

5. *WHEN WILL YOU TURN?* "Keep his statutes," this scriptural material admonishes us (Deuteronomy 4:30). Eventually, each person must make a conscious act of his or her will. Each must *will* to turn toward the God who has already turned toward us. In Jesus Christ's life, death, and Resurrection, we already know how God has willed it that He be near us. Each of us, in turn, must respond by living obediently.

TOPIC FOR ADULTS
EXPERIENCING GOD'S PRESENCE

God-Controlled. Frank Laubach, missionary to the Philippines, desired to become president of the Union Theological Seminary in Manila. He yearned for it, and when he lost the appointment by one vote, he found himself filled with resentment. He mourned over his great disappointment. His health began to fail, his work became inefficient. And then one day he turned to God. He turned to Him completely. He utterly abandoned his longing to be president of the Seminary, he relinquished all desire for high position of any kind. He tried practicing the presence of God every minute of the day. He tried to erase himself totally from the picture, to make himself so poor in spirit that people would not see *him*, that they would see only the Christ shining through him. As a step toward relinquishing all desire for fame and for position, he went to the Moros, the headhunters, an illiterate people that no missionary had hitherto been able to reach. He buried himself for months and years in a wilderness. Then it was that God took the deep yearning that had turned into mourning, and the mourning which had triumphed into relinquishment, and out of this yearning and relinquishment brought into birth, first, a reborn, meek, God-controlled Frank Laubach; second, a vital Christian church in a former stronghold of Islam; and finally, a miraculous new and simple method of teaching backward races to read, by which Frank Laubach is today still making more people literate than any man who ever lived.

Century for Discovery. Many scientists point out that future generations may well look upon the twentieth century with appreciation and respect because of what we have managed to learn about ourselves and our universe. Many scholars insist that there has never been a period of comparable scientific discovery. It began at the turn of the century with Einstein's creation of the theory of relativity and Max Planck's invention of the quantum of action, followed by Neils Bohr's discovery of the mechanics of the atom. Ernest Rutherford's discovery of the atomic nucleus and the grand synthesis of all these developments in the quantum theory.

This is simply in physics. In astronomy, just to skim the surface, there was the discovery of the expanding universe, the understanding of why and how stars shine, the identification of quasars and pulsars. In mathematics, entirely new fields were invented, such as the theory of distributions and the proof by Kurt Gödel that the consistency of mathematics itself cannot be proven. In medicine, tuberculosis, once a virtually epidemic and incurable disease, has been all but eliminated in advanced industrial societies.

Within the past century, our entire view of how species reproduce and how these processes can be altered has been changed. The discovery of DNA in the area of biology by Watson and Crick by the use of the double helix model in the last twenty-five years opened new understanding of genetic molecular engineering.

These outstanding intellectual achievements deserve praise. However, why can we not use the closing years of this great century to spiritual growth? Why don't we church people show the same dedication to experiencing God's presence which researchers have been using to bring scientific advances? If Christians like us wished, we could make this century truly one of renaissance in awareness of God's presence as much as in discoveries in biology, physics, astronomy, medicine, and mathematics.

Special Training to Hear. About one in a thousand school-age children have a severe enough hearing loss to require special educational services. These deaf children are victims of a world where there is no language. They cannot hear their parents talking. They do not listen to bedtime stories. Televison is merely pictures. Radios and telephones are useless. They do not know how to ask for a drink of water or to say that they are afraid. They do not even know that they have a name. Educators of the deaf must try to close the language gap between deaf children and the hearing world.

Fortunately, sign language (now called American Sign Language or A.S.L. or Amesian) is now recognized by linguistic experts as a legitimate language of its own. However, learning sign language takes discipline and training. The deaf student must apply himself or herself diligently.

To experience God's presence, we must also submit ourselves to discipline and training. Most of us are deaf to His voice. We have not been able to listen to His claims. There is a hearing-gap. His language is not understood.

Only the man or woman who desires to experience God's presence will be able to make the effort to learn the language of love and to detect the signs of His presence. It means starting with a commitment to Jesus Christ and a covenanted relationship with the rest of His community.

Questions for Pupils on the Next Lesson. 1. In an age like ours, can adults really benefit from the ethical guidelines provided by the Ten Commandments? 2. What exactly do you understand the ethical guidelines of the Ten Commandments to be? 3. Does obedience to God's law bring the sense of satisfaction and harmony to your life which is promised? 4. Why do the Commandments depend upon a covenanted people's relationship to God?

TOPIC FOR YOUTH
EXPERIENCING GOD'S PRESENCE

Searcher. A Japanese veteran of World War II is searching a rugged Philippine mountain area for a friend he believes has been hiding there for thirty-five years disguised as a primitive tribesman and unaware that the war is over.

The Japanese Embassy said that the veteran, Isao Miyazawa, a grocer, and two helpers were on Mindoro Island looking for a man they believe to be Komiyo Nakaharu, who was a sergeant in intelligence.

Between 200 and 300 Japanese soldiers appeared in 1944 after American troops occupied Mindoro, a mountainous island seventy miles southwest of Manila.

The three-man party began its search after reports that a man with Japanese features had been seen living with a tribe called the Mangyan in the village of Rototuko. The man, known in the village as Mondoka, is married to a Mangyan woman and has seven children, the embassy said. He makes his living by farming.

At last report, Komiyo Nakaharu, the Japanese war recluse, had not been found. His friend promises to press the search.

If a war buddy will patiently comb the jungles to locate a missing friend, how much more God searches for us! In the person of Jesus, He finds us. "I have come to seek and to save those who are lost," Jesus announces (Luke 19:10).

Perhaps you have been hiding from Him, living in the jungle of loneliness, guilt, and separation. You need no longer flee. The "war" is over. God wants you to enjoy a new relationship with Him!

Real Person. Small children experience some disillusionment when they learn that there is no Santa Claus or Easter Bunny. For some adults, the experience comes when they find that many well-known names are fictitious.

For example, Betty Crocker, the smiling personality on the back of boxes of General Mills baking mixes and cookbooks, was created in 1921 to personalize a large, anonymous corporation and its product. Betty Crocker quickly became famous. She once took second place to Eleanor Roosevelt as the best-known woman in the country, and she still receives almost 300,000 letters each year. When some persons learn that Betty Crocker does not actually exist, they feel disappointed.

God, however, is no illusion. The Lord is not manufactured by the Church. Jesus is not an attempt to personalize religion.

It is not we who have created God, but God who has created us. He persists in introducing Himself through the story of our forebearers, the Hebrews, and through the events of Jesus Christ's life and death and Resurrection. Through the Holy Spirit, He makes possible an experience of His goodness and nearness today to believers.

Sentence Sermon To Remember: When I am operating, I feel the presence of God so real that I cannot tell where His skill ends and mine begins.

—A famous surgeon, name unknown.

Questions for Pupils on the Next Lesson. 1. Is it necessary to make commitments in life before there can be meaningful relationships? Why? How? 2. What exactly do you understand the meaning of each of the Ten Commandments to be? 3. What do you think of the claim that God's law make human relationships better? 4. Why do Christians claim that obedience to God's gracious law brings satisfaction and a sense of harmony to life?

LESSON V—JULY 5

THE TEN COMMANDMENTS

Background Scripture: Deuteronomy 5
Devotional Reading: Romans 5:6–11

KING JAMES VERSION

DEUTERONOMY 5 6 I *am* the LORD thy God, which brought thee out of the land of Egypt, from the house of bondage.

7 Thou shalt have none other gods before me.

8 Thou shalt not make thee *any* graven image, *or* any likeness of *any thing* that *is* in heaven above, or that *is* in the earth beneath, or that *is* in the waters beneath the earth:

11 Thou shalt not take the name of the LORD thy God in vain: for the LORD will not hold *him* guiltless that taketh his name in vain.

12 Keep the sabbath day to sanctify it, as the LORD thy God hath commanded thee.

13 Six days thou shalt labour, and do all thy work:

14 But the seventh day *is* the sabbath of the LORD thy God: *in it* thou shalt not do any work, thou, nor thy son, nor thy daughter, nor thy manservant, nor thy maidservant, nor thine ox, nor thine ass, nor any of thy cattle, nor thy stranger that *is* within thy gates: that thy manservant and thy maidservant may rest as well as thou.

15 And remember that thou wast a servant in the land of Egypt, and *that* the LORD thy God brought thee out thence through a mighty hand and by a stretched out arm: therefore the LORD thy God commanded thee to keep the sabbath day.

16 Honour thy father and thy mother, as the LORD thy God hath commanded thee; that thy days may be prolonged, and that it may go well with thee, in the land which the LORD thy God giveth thee.

17 Thou shalt not kill.

18 Neither shalt thou commit adultery.

19 Neither shalt thou steal.

20 Neither shalt thou bear false witness against thy neighbour.

REVISED STANDARD VERSION

DEUTERONOMY 5 6 " 'I am the LORD your God, who brought you out of the land of Egypt, out of the house of bondage.

7 " 'You shall have no other gods before me.

8 " 'You shall not make for yourself a graven image, or any likeness of anything that is in heaven above, or that is on the earth beneath, or that is in the water under the earth;

11 " 'You shall not take the name of the LORD your God in vain: for the LORD will not hold him guiltless who takes his name in vain.

12 " 'Observe the sabbath day, to keep it holy, as the LORD your God commanded you. 13 Six days you shall labor, and do all your work; 14 but the seventh day is a sabbath to the LORD your God; in it you shall not do any work, you, or your son, or your daughter, or your manservant, or your maidservant, or your ox, or your ass, or any of your cattle, or the sojourner who is within your gates, that your manservant and your maidservant may rest as well as you. 15 You shall remember that you were a servant in the land of Egypt, and the LORD your God brought you out thence with a mighty hand and an outstretched arm; therefore the LORD your God commanded you to keep the sabbath day.

16 " 'Honor your father and your mother, as the LORD your God commanded you; that your days may be prolonged, and that it may go well with you, in the land wh ch the LORD your God gives you.

17 " 'You shall not kill.

18 " 'Neither shall you commit adultery.

19 " 'Neither shall you steal.

20 " 'Neither shall you bear false witness against your neighbor.

21 Neither shalt thou desire thy neighbour's wife, neither shalt thou covet thy neighbour's house, his field, or his manservant, or his maidservant, his ox, or his ass, or any *thing* that *is* thy neighbour's.

21 " 'Neither shall you covet your neighbor's wife; and you shall not desire your neighbor's house, his field, or his manservant, or his maidservant, his ox, or his ass, or anything that is your neighbor's.' "

KEY VERSE: You shall walk in all the way the Lord your God has commanded you, that you may live, and that it may go well with you, and that you may live in the land which you shall possess. Deuteronomy 5:33 (RSV).

HOME DAILY BIBLE READINGS

June   29.   M. *Laws About God.* Deuteronomy 5:1–15.
June   30.   T. *Laws About Others.* Deuteronomy 5:16–21.
July   1.   W. *The Voice of God.* Deuteronomy 5:22–27.
July   2.   T. *Obey God's Laws.* Deuteronomy 5:28–33.
July   3.   F. *God's Perfect Law.* Psalms 19:7–14.
July   4.   S. *"How I Love Thy Law."* Psalms 119:97–104.
July   5.   S. *Love Fulfills the Law.* Romans 13:8–10.

BACKGROUND

The Ten Commandments are recorded twice in the Old Testament, in Exodus 20 and in Deuteronomy 5. They both come, apparently, from the same source, and while some scholars express doubts that they came at the time of Moses, it is generally accepted that they are basically Mosaic and reflect the spirit and the work of Moses. In their earliest form they were probably laid down in shorter statements, like "Thou shalt not steal . . ." etc.

In studying the Commandments, we find that they are divided into two parts: Commandments dealing with man's relationship to God (Deuteronomy 5:11–15) and those dealing with man's relationship with his neighbors (16–21). We also notice that the Commandments are addressed not so much to the nation as to individual Israelites: "The Lord made not this covenant with our fathers, but with *us*, even us . . ." (verse 3). The Commandments were given not just for one generation but for all generations; they put a personal responsibility that is ageless, permanent, on the shoulders and in the hearts of all men. The Commandments are a summary of all the duties which God requires of men. Jesus realized this when He held them to be perfect, and that to disobey them would be not only an injury to men but a defiance of God.

And in very recent years the Supreme Court of West Virginia called them "Absolutely flawless, negative in terms but positive in meaning, they easily stand at the head of our whole moral system." They give us a code of behavior for *every* age.

NOTES ON THE PRINTED TEXT

I. I am the Lord thy God, which brought thee out of the land of Egypt . . . . Deuteronomy 5:6. When we read the words of Moses on the Commandments, we are reading the words of his second oration; he begins his discussion of the Commandments with this reminder that the

God who gave them to Israel was the God who brought them out of Egypt—a land in which the people worshiped little gods in nature, in the sun, moon, stars, and the cycle of the seasons. But in the historic experience of Israel in the wilderness, Israel found a God whose demands were both spiritual *and moral.* "Judaism . . . while recognizing the creative power of God in nature, found the morality of God in the unfolding drama of human life. They believed that all mankind's history is subject to God's control."—Robert I. Kahn, *The Ten Commandments for Today.*

II. *Thou shalt have none other gods before me.* Deuteronomy 5:7. Now, having established the fact that God is both a spiritual and a moral God demanding certain moral behavior in men, let us look at the Commandments, one by one, and see what such a demand means to those of us who live three thousand years after Moses.

The first and second Commandments must be studied as one; they interlock, and they both say the same thing. First, we shall worship but *one* God, because the universe in which we live can be governed by only one God. Imagine the confusion if we had a dozen different creators (Gods) all doing something different, all in separate departments and with different responsibilities. That would be utter confusion, positive anarchy. Or imagine what confusion would settle upon us if some of us worshiped a God of war and others worshiped a God of peace! We can't have it both ways.

These Commandments are also saying, "Put first things first." Put God first, all else second. Martin Niemoller, a pastor in Nazi Germany, was thrown into jail for preaching a sermon entitled, "You Shall Have No Other Gods Before Me." Hitler thought differently; he put the State first—and the Nordic race first—and he brought on a war that cost millions of lives. Others put science first, made a god of it. But science, lest we forget it, has given us bombing airplanes, and a build-up of nuclear power that has the world frightened out of its wits. Reliance on science and the rejection of religious faith is a dangerous form of idolatry.

"Thou shalt not take the name of the Lord thy God in vain . . . ." This prohibition was directed against perjury and lying in the courts, but in time it was directed against the breaking of any oath, in court or in daily life. The breaking of oaths was so common that both the Jews and Jesus urged people not to swear by God, lest they outraged Him by breaking the oath. But the Commandment is levelled at much more than this: against profanity in speech, blasphemy, hypocrisy, and two-faced religion. Does this mean anything to us today? Profanity has become accepted custom among us; both men and woman break the Commandment with no sense of guilt whatever. We think hypocrisy is funny; we laught at corrupt politicians and at money-mad "evangelists", at children cheating on examinations and fathers cheating on their income tax on Saturday and "worshiping" God on Sunday, at crooked scheming in business and misleading advertising, at senators breaking their oaths of office. God will hold guilty those who profane His name!

The fourth Commandment calls for the observance of the Sabbath. The Sabbath to the Jew was the seventh day; to the Christian, remembering the Resurrection, it was the first day of the week. *We* should

remember that Jesus called for one day in seven to be observed as a day
of worship and rest, to be broken only by deeds of necessity and mercy.
To quibble like children over which is the right day is indeed childlike;
what we need to know is that rest is God's order, on any day. We need
more rest on the rest-day than we have today; too many of us are "work-
oholics" working ourselves to death and giving little of any time in the
week to God. God rested after six days of labor and He expects man to
rest, too! Rest and re-create. There was a time when we used Sunday to
rest and create, but it seems to be almost gone now, and that is *not* good,
for man should not live by work alone. At least one day a week given to
God is not asking too much. We who are tied up six days a week with
work should welcome a chance to become untied, to think about God
and to reach out to others.

"Honor thy father and thy mother"—the fifth Commandment. It is at
this point that the Commandments turn from our duties to God to our
obligations to men. The Jews have put high priority on this fifth Commandment, for the reason that they realized that the family was the
cornerstone of their existence and survival. Do *we* believe that? Someone has said that the home and the family exist today as a place to eat
and sleep and get away from as soon as possible. That is a dishonor to
parents. It isn't enough to send mother or father a card on Mother's Day
and Father's Day; God *commands* us to honor them *every* day. To respect them, to love them. To honor one's parents means *action based on
attitude.*

"Thou shalt not kill." Does this one need any explanation or commentary? It seems clear enough that killing should be forbidden, as it *has*
been forbidden ever since Cain killed Abel. But there are complications
in the word *kill.* Does it mean that we can *never* kill? The Bible does not
say that, nor did the Mosaic Hebrews. They approved of one man killing
another to save his own life when attacked. They approved of killing in
war, and as capital punishment, and the killing of animals for food. What
they did condemn was killing for revenge, killing innocent babies and
children (infanticide) as the pagan tribes killed them, or the killing of
the aged. The Hebrews also condemned suicide. In other words, they
condemned unauthorized wilful, unjustified *murder.* But we are still
confused when we try to determine *which* killing to condone and which
killing to condemn. In a way, says one commentator, "the sixth Commandment represents the unfinished business of civilization." Are *we* to
refuse to kill in defensive war? Are we justified in hastening the death of
one with an incurable disease—in "mercy" death? We are deeply troubled right now about capital punishment: is this really trying to punish
one killing by committing another? Unfinished business!

"Thou shalt not commit adultery." This Commandment stresses the
sanctity of marriage, a state instituted by God; it relates here to the
conduct of married couples, and not to the unmarried (fornication).
Sodomy, bestiality, and incest were punished by death. Israel stood
opposed to the sexual license practiced by the (pagan) fertility cults of
the day. We wonder what they might say if they were to come back and
see our flaunting of this Commandment in our unbridled, repulsive
approval of adulterous sexual activity. We not only approve of it; we

boast of it in the newspaper headlines, and we write best-selling books about it!

"Neither shalt thou steal." This applies to the sacredness of property, just as the preceding sixth Commandment applies to the sacredness of life. The right of a man to enjoy his property as the fruit of his labor is defended here. Private property is not a privilege, but a *right*. Jesus had respect for this Commandment: He taught stewardship—that all property or wealth is a sacred *trust*. But He would surely disapprove of some of our tendencies to steal property in the payment of unjust wages, dishonest gains, and unfair labor practices.

"Neither shalt thou bear false witness against thy neighbor." This refers to witnessing in courts of law. "It applies to any untrue statement affecting the good name of a neighbor (gossip); but it also clearly prohibits all falsehood, untruth, and deception as contrary to the revealed will of God."—Dr. Charles R. Erdman. Stand up, all who have never told a lie, either white or black!

And finally, "Neither shalt thou covet . . . ." This is last, but not least, for it shows the superiority of the Jewish Decalogue over any and all other codes of law and morality ever ever conceived on this earth. Here, we get down to the "bottom line"—we find that this code deals not only with acts but with intentions of the human mind and hearts. It strikes a blow at evil *desire*, which is the forerunner of committed sin. It was Jesus who built upon this Commandment in His statement that "Whosoever looketh on a woman to lust after her hath committed adultery with her already in his heart" (Matthew 5:28). Stealing, killing, and false witness begin in the *heart;* covetousness is the wicked thought that precedes the wicked act, and covetousness is the basic cause of most of the sins of mankind. Only one thing should we covet: a closer fellowship with the Christ who coveted only us, and our redemption.

SUGGESTIONS TO TEACHERS

A distraught father who had spent two hours trying to assemble a new tricycle for his daughter's birthday laid down his wrench and mumbled a few choice words to himself. In exasperation, he picked up the carton in which the tricycle parts had been packed and shook it. Out fell a folder. Across the top, in large type, was written: WHEN ALL ELSE FAILS, READ THE DIRECTIONS.

Today's lesson could carry this message as title. Like the father pridefully trying to put together the tricycle without checking the basic steps outlined by the manufacturer, we often attempt to put together our lives without reading the directions set down by our "Manufacturer." The Ten Commandments are the basic guidelines which God has given us for our own good.

Your lesson has so much material that your main difficulty in preparing it will be to select what to include. You should consider some of these points:

1. *PEOPLE UNDER CONTRACT.* The Lord our God made a covenant with *us* . . . (*see* Deuteronomy 5:3). We have entered into solemn agreements with God. The reason we take the Ten Commandments

seriously is because of the covenant with God. The Commandments are special requirements for the special people. Make sure that your class understands that these are non-negotiable as far as Christians are concerned. Others outside the community of God's people may wish to argue their purpose or validity, but your class members as ones under contract with God may not!

2. *GOD IN ACTION*. The Commandments are given by a good God for our own good. He acts on our behalf. The Scripture nails down the facts about God: "who brought you out of the land of Egypt, out of the house of bondage" (Deuteronomy 5:6). In other words, you are not talking about any old god, but about *the* Lord who has already shown His concern for you and your class. Take time to air the "complaints" about the Commandments as being "too negative" or "too harsh for today's world." Help your class to recognize that the Commandments are part of God's acting in love for His people.

3. *COMMUNITY UNDER OBLIGATION*. Needless to say, you could develop at least one entire lesson on each one of the Ten Commandments. Although time will not permit you to look as thoroughly at each as you or the class might like, devote a substantial chunk of the lesson period on covering the list. Don't slide over the first ones. These are the basic obligations of members of God's community toward God Himself. Reflect with your class on the meaning of "no other gods," "no graven images," upholding God's good name, and Sabbath observance.

4. *PEOPLE IN COMMUNITY*. The last in the list of Commandments deals with how members of God's community act toward other persons. Be sure to touch on each of the ones addressing the topics of family, murder, sex and marriage, property, truth-telling, and greed without getting stuck on any one Commandment for too long.

5. *GOD WITH WARNING*. Finally, take note of the closing verses of Deuteronomy 5. God solemnly warns us to take heed that we obey—or else! At the same time, God assures us that keeping faith with Him brings joy and life! Encourage members of the class to relate ways in which obedience to God has eventually brough a sense of His promise.

TOPIC FOR ADULTS
TEN LAWS

Pointed Truths. The Ten Commandments are not merely general advice or tips of etiquette. They are pointed commands to us, today. Frequently, these laws cause us to squirm.

For example, some years ago in the Pacific Northwest, a small community stood downstream from a large logging camp. The people in the town regularly fished logs out of the river, sawed off the ends bearing the stamp of the lumber company, and used the logs for their own building purposes. The young, newly-arrived pastor quickly got wind of this practice. The following Sunday, he preached an eloquent sermon on "Thou Shalt Not Steal."

After worship services, the young man was warmly greeted and thanked for his fine preaching. Conditions continued, however, as they had before.

On the next Sunday, the preacher spoke pointedly on the topic, "Thou Shalt Not Cut Off The Ends of Other People's Logs."

It was reported that he was asked to leave town after that sermon!

Banks to the River. God provides laws for us to live by. These are for our own good. God does not grant us complete freedom, but insists upon limits or boundaries.

Christian freedom is like a river. If the water does not have strong banks to support and guide it, the river soon spreads out in all directions at once. The river loses both its direction and its power. It begins "to spread itself thin" and finally seeps down into the earth and disappears. Without banks, the river ceases to be a river, becomes aimless, shapeless, and gradually disappears. But with firm and strong banks a river goes somewhere, has power and direction, becomes creative and useful, and remains vigorous and purposeful.

Need for Norms. The Ten Commandments are God's answer to our need for standards. We must have ways of measuring right and wrong. The Decalogue offers norms for our actions and attitudes within God's community, both toward God and toward others.

It is true throughout life. Take the matter of standardized time. We take for granted that there are time zones in which every clock is set exactly to conform with official time. It was not always so. In fact, up until November 18, 1883, there was no "official time," either nationally or internationally. Each town, city, and village operated on its own time. This system brought havoc to railroad schedules since each line operated on its own time, but had to pass through hundreds of differing places, each with its own time.

Finally, a Saratoga, New York, school principal named Dr. Charles Ferdinand Dowd began to campaign to end the confusion by establishing standard time. Dowd's proposal finally won acceptance, and in 1883 Congress required clocks to be reset on November 18, 1883, to conform with "standard time" as set in various zones.

The immediate popular success of standard zones led to the convening of the Washington Meridian Conference by President Chester Arthur in 1884. At this conference, it was agreed to set up standard time zones around the world and to recognize Greenwich Mean Time as the Standard for the so-called "Prime Meridian" which runs through the town of Greenwich, near London.

God long before recognized our need for moral and ethical standards. He wisely and graciously established the Ten Commandments as His provision of a measuring device for our behavior as His people.

Questions for Pupils on the Next Lesson. 1. Why is it so important for you to have personal loyalty toward God? 2. What practical suggestions can you make in regard to teaching the young the meaning of the faith? 3. What kinds of disobedience result from forgetting that land is a gift? 4. Why must God's law pervade our entire lives? 5. Why are we in danger whenever we think we are self-sufficient and "self-made"?

TOPIC FOR YOUTH
GOD ACTS/DEMANDS!

Honesty in Sports. Both team and individual sports, amateur and professional, are vulnerable to scandal. Baseball had its Black Sox Scandal of 1919, when eight Chicago White Sox' players were barred for life from the sport after throwing the World Series to Cincinnati. The point-shaving scandals of the early 1950s damaged the image of collegiate baseball.

Recent years have been bad ones for the reputation of sports. Outright cheating was uncovered at the Olympic Games in Montreal. Allegations of spying surfaced on the major college football level. Phrases such as judge-fixing and blood-doping joined probation and even scandal in the day-to-day reporting on sports contests.

Even so seemingly innocent an episode as the Great Walkie-Talkie Affair, when the Yankees were caught with their antenna up during the 1976 World Series, has serious overtones.

Penn State's football coach, Joe Paterno, thinks society is to blame for any trend toward dishonesty. "Sports won't change society," Paterno said, "If there is a trend toward less morality in the world, sports will go that way, too. It is naive to think that sports can exist in a vacuum. It has the same problems as society."

Paterno isn't the only one who believes sports reflect society.

"There is a high level of cynicism in our society today," says Jonathan Cole, professor of sociology at Columbia University. "The old image of sports as an escape from social realities is dying. People tend to consider bending the rules a general condition of sports today." Cole contends that some organizations feel they have to cheat to keep up with the competition.

"It's not a matter of evil individuals, for the most part," added Cole, an avid sports fan. "The programs are corrupted. The structural and social pressures on coaches and programs to be successful, competitive from a business standpoint in order to survive, cause the deviant behavior.

"Sports institutions, amateur or professional, sometimes feel they must play illegal games in order to survive."

Will sports fans stand still for that sort of thing? It depends on who does it.

"Your view depends on which side of the incident you're on," said Adrian Avani, associate professor in the Ohio State sociology department. "As an analogy, it's like integration. People may be all for it until someone moves next door. If you turn a violator in," he added, "then it's a good thing. As long as it doesn't happen to you."

How do the Ten Commandments apply to your attitudes and acts in sports, whether as a spectator or as a participant?

Sticky Fingers Where You Work. Employee theft continues to rise. Industry and business have long been plagued with the problem of trying to curb sticky-fingered help by both blue-collar and white-collar types. Last year, employees carried away more than $6 billion in merchandise, tools, and materials from their jobs—20% more than the previous year. New strategies by employers such as surveillance techniques have not stemmed the tide of employee larceny.

How do you as a Christian see the Commandment, "Thou Shalt Not Steal," as God's rule for you when it comes to respecting the property of the company where you work?

Recipe for Joy and Smarts. The Ten Commandments are not repressive, but liberating. They open the door to serving God and serving others. They clue the believing community about the wisest way to live. To ignore them is to invite disaster. As Walter Rauschenbusch once said, "A selfish person becomes a stupid person if he lives long enough." The Ten Laws are the humane and intelligent provision by God for humane and intelligent people.

Sentence Sermon to Remember: The Ten Commandments still cover all human relations and all spiritual relations.—Ralph Brewer.

Questions for Pupils on the Next Lesson. 1. Why must our relationship to God affect all aspects of our lives? 2. What are some of the current "goals" attracting other youth you know which are breaking their relationship with God? 3. Why is a Christian concerned about stewardship of natural resources? 4. What happened to ancient Israel when she forgot God and served other gods? Would this happen to the Church today? Could this happen to our nation?

LESSON VI—JULY 12

GOD'S WORDS IN OUR HEARTS

Background Scripture: Deuteronomy 6:1–15
Devotional Reading: Jeremiah 23:29–35

KING JAMES VERSION

DEUTERONOMY 6   4 Hear, O Israel: The LORD our God *is* one LORD:

5 And thou shalt love the LORD thy God with all thine heart, and with all thy soul, and with all thy might.

6 And these words, which I command thee this day, shall be in thine heart:

7 And thou shalt teach them diligently unto thy children, and shalt talk of them when thou sittest in thine house, and when thou walkest by the way, and when thou liest down, and when thou risest up.

8 And thou shalt bind them for a sign upon thine hand, and they shall be as frontlets between thine eyes.

9 And thou shalt write them upon the posts of thy house, and on thy gates.

10 And it shall be, when the LORD thy God shall have brought thee into the land which he sware unto thy fathers, to Abraham, to Isaac, and to Jacob, to give thee great and goodly cities, which thou buildedst not,

11 And houses full of all good *things,* which thou filledst not, and wells digged, which thou diggedst not, vineyards and olive trees, which thou plantedst not; when thou shalt have eaten and be full;

12 *Then* beware lest thou forget the LORD, which brought thee forth out of the land of Egypt, from the house of bondage.

13 Thou shalt fear the LORD thy God, and serve him, and shalt swear by his name.

14 Ye shall not go after other gods, of the gods of the people which *are* round about you;

15 (For the LORD thy God *is* a jealous God among you) lest the anger of the LORD thy God be kindled against thee, and destroy thee from off the face of the earth.

REVISED STANDARD VERSION

DEUTERONOMY 6   4 "Hear, O Israel: The LORD our God is one LORD; 5 and you shall love the LORD your God with all your heart, and with all your soul, and with all your might. 6 And these words which I command you this day shall be upon your heart; 7 and you shall teach them diligently to your children, and shall talk of them when you sit in your house, and when you walk by the way, and when you lie down, and when you rise. 8 And you shall bind them as a sign upon your hand, and they shall be as frontlets between your eyes. 9 And you shall write them on the doorposts of your house and on your gates.

10 "And when the LORD your God brings you into the land which he swore to your fathers, to Abraham, to Isaac, and to Jacob, to give you, with great and goodly cities, which you did not build, 11 and houses full of all good things, which you did not fill, and cisterns hewn out, which you did not hew, and vineyards and olive trees, which you did not plant, and when you eat and are full, 12 then take heed lest you forget the LORD, who brought you out of the land of Egypt, out of the house of bondage. 13 You shall fear the LORD your God; you shall serve him, and swear by his name. 14 You shall not go after other gods, of the gods of the peoples who are round about you; 15 for the LORD your God in the midst of you is a jealous God; lest the anger of the LORD your God be kindled against you, and he destroy you from off the face of the earth."

354

KEY VERSE: ". . . The Lord our God is one Lord; and you shall love the Lord your God with all your heart, and with all your soul, and with all your might." Deuteronomy 6:4, 5 (RSV).

HOME DAILY BIBLE READINGS

July 6. M. *Remember God's Commands.* Deuteronomy 6:1–9.
July 7. T. *Remember God's Goodness.* Deuteronomy 6:10–15.
July 8. W. *"Teach Me . . . Thy Statutes."* Psalms 119:33–40.
July 9. T. *Trust God's Word.* Psalms 119:41–48.
July 10. F. *"Incline My Heart to Thy Testimonies."* Psalms 119:57–64.
July 11. S. *"I Delight in Thy Law."* Psalms 119:65–72.
July 12. S. *"The Joy of My Heart."* Psalms 119:105–112.

BACKGROUND

In our lesson for last week, we called the Ten Commandments a flawless code and the basis of Israel's covenant with God. That is true; the Commandments stand immortal through the ages while other impressive codes have come and gone with the winds of history. But in this lesson we are to discover that there is one other, shorter statement that stands higher even than the Decalogue. It is a one-sentence statement, and it is the great fundamental confession of the Jewish faith. It puts positively what the first Commandment put negatively, and Jesus made it of primary interest when He called it the first of all commandments (*see* Mark 12:30). So, with this word from Jesus, it must be of vital importance to Christians as well as to Jews.

The Jews called it the *Shema*, and *Shema* is the Jewish word for hear.

NOTES ON THE PRINTED TEXT

I. Hear, O Israel: The Lord our God is one Lord. Deuteronomy 6:4. Our Scripture references for this lesson may be rightly divided into two sections: in section one, we are told what God is (verses 4–9) and in section two (verses 10–15) we are told what our attitude toward God should be. Part one begins with the *Shema*. "To the Jew the *Shema* is the symbol of the faith. It opens the synagogue service; it is to be said twice each day; written on parchment, it is worn in the phylactery (a tiny pouch strapped just above the eyes); it is inscribed on the doorpost. Originating in the urge to distinguish Yahweh (God) from the baals and astral deities, it has become the rallying point for monotheism everywhere—for the Jews first, and for all who ever were influenced by Judaism. The first pillar of Islamic faith is 'There is no God but Allah.' To the Christian the *Shema's* intrinsic worth is vastly augmented by the fact that Jesus made of it the supreme command."— *The Interpreter's Bible*, Vol. 2, p. 373, by permission of Abingdon Press, publishers.

One God, one Lord: that above all had to be taught every successive generation of Jewish children. The elders wore the phylacteries on their foreheads and on their arms that the children might *see* the signs of their father's faith; the fathers were told to teach their children "diligently," *every day, every hour,* that their God was a God of *love,* and that they must love Him in return.

Now this idea of God's love inviting the love of men did not originate

with the writers of Deuteronomy, but they were the first writers to make
it a matter of every-day life. God and His love should be talked about in
the family circle, in the home, as though He were the unseen guest at
every meal and hearer of every conversation. Constant emphasis upon
Him and His love should be made of this as they walked in the street,
when they went to bed at night and got up in the morning. Bind the
Shema on your forehead and fasten it to your doorpost, that they may
see; teach them, that they may *hear*. Make this one unique God so real,
so *present*, that they learn to love Him with all their hearts, and minds,
and might.

One day in Modern Israel, this editor saw a truck used to smuggle
arms—and food—to an Israel at war; on its sides were painted the words,
"Lest we forget thee, O Jerusalem." Israel has never forgotten her God,
and that is the cement which has enabled her to survive the longest and
most vicious persecution on earth.

*II. "And when the Lord your God brings you into the land which he
swore to your fathers . . . to give you, with great and goodly cities,
which you did not build . . . ."* Deuteronomy 6:10 (RSV). Israel left
Egypt as a people beaten like slaves, disconsolate and seemingly hopeless until Moses came to set their souls afire once more. When they
entered Canaan, they entered a land fertile beyond any they had known
before—a land rich in "milk and honey." In this land they built cities,
dug wells, planted vineyards and orchards of olive trees, until "the
desert blossomed as the rose."

We say "they" did all this, but by "they" we do not mean, and Moses
did not mean, the people to whom he was preaching this oration; he was
speaking of what their *fathers* had done. Those in Moses audience were
enjoying life in houses their fathers had built, drinking from wells dug
not by themselves but by their pioneers. Life was considerably better
for them than it had been for their sires in old Egypt—and they seemed
to be forgetting that! Moses warns them: "Beware lest you forget the
Lord . . . When you are full, don't forget to be reverent to him and to
serve him and to use his name alone to endorse your promises" (verse
12, *The Living Bible*). St. John, in his Gospel, put it this way: "I sent you
to reap where you didn't sow; others did the work, and you received the
harvest" (John 4:38, *The Living Bible*).

Now this ingratitude of one generation for a past generation's work
and contributions is seen in every social group and nation in the world.
We Americans pride ourselves on being the richest nation in the world,
and we are that—but it is an *inherited* wealth handed down to us from
previous generations; *we* get rich because they founded a system in
which getting rich was possible. We cry from the housetops that we are a
democratic nation—but think of what that democracy cost in terms of the
labors and sacrifices of our national fathers. We love our freedom and
pity other nations that are not so free; if you would know what that
freedom cost, take a look at the countless crosses raised over the graves
of dead Americans, who bought that freedom for us with their blood. We
love our churches, and we should, for our churches are built upon the
tombs of martyrs.

It is so easy to forget the God who has brought *us* out of the bondage of yesterday. So easy, when, as Moses put it, "we are full"—well fed, secure, with all we need and more. There is great danger threatening our faith when we are as well off as this with substance we did not earn.

There are actually three dangers involved here, in us as well as in old Israel. First, the danger of unearned material prosperity. Those of us who live on the prosperity handed down to us seldom live well or unselfishly; we merely live out our years and contribute little or nothing to the upward and onward march of the race. We may not do that intentionally; we just have so much that we forget all others but ourselves. Men who live alone are seldom happy men.

The second danger lies in our worship of lesser gods than the one God. The Israelites were tempted to worship the Canaanitish god of fertility: they wanted the fertilizing power of Baal. It took a Hosea (2:5-23) to tell the people that Israel's God and not Canaan's Baal gave them sun and rain and good soil and corn and wheat and all that they are out of the abundance of the soil.

The third danger is the most dangerous of all—it is the belief that God is really unconcerned about us, that He allows sickness and hurricanes and even wholesale disaster to afflict us. We ask, "Why?" We question God's loving care, even His presence, when we so disbelieve. And how can we worship Him, if He is as unconcerned as that?

These were questions that often "beset" the Jews, and they are still here to beset us, and to pull us away from God. Paul had the perfect answer to such questions.

Read Romans 3. Here we find Paul admitting that there are *some* who are unfaithful and with no trust in God, but they are few in number, just as the atheists in our midst are comparatively few in number. Just because *they* are unfaithful is no reason why all the rest of us should be unfaithful. Just because they broke their promises to God is no reason why we should break ours. Every man in the world may be unfaithful—but God is never unfaithful, never loses His confidence in the potentialities of men to know Him and love Him and do His will. Israel may have come near to total disaster in the wilderness, but God, according to His promise, brought them through to Canaan and made a great people of them. God never lets men down, though men so frequently let Him down! The proof of that was to be seen in God's continuing and undiscourageable love for those who so often failed to love Him. Go where we may and do what we do, we can never get out of the reach of His hand.

SUGGESTIONS TO TEACHERS

Do you remember seeing a neatly-stitched sampler with the words, "God Bless Our Home" carefully framed and hanging in the parlor? There is nothing wrong with embroidering religious themes and placing them on the wall. However, sometimes this is the extent of commitment.

God's words must be engraved in our hearts. His commandments are intended to be more than interesting religious thoughts. They are God's orders to us.

Your lesson today should stress the internal dimension of keeping

God's commandments. The key verses, Deuteronomy 6:4, 5, are the *Shema* as it is called in Hebrew (from the opening words, "Hear, O Israel . . . "), and the word *Hear* means more than simply listening. In Hebrew, *Hear* means Obey.

Develop your lesson with these questions in mind.

1. *WHO GIVES YOU COMMANDS?* Working with the scriptural material, you should impress on your class that "the commandment, statutes and the ordinances" are not a resolution presented by a committee but God's own decree. God commands. We obey. God is completely in charge. For our welfare, He has stated the ground rules laid out in Deuteronomy 6. Remind your people that God, not we, issues the orders.

2. *HOW DO YOU HEAR?* Take a few minutes to talk about what it means to "Hear the word of God." It is more than exercising your auditory apparatus. The words must be "upon your heart" (Deuteronomy 6:6). God's commands must be interiorized. Help your class to understand the deeper level of "hearing" that is meant in this passage. Present examples from your own life or others' lives of the difference between merely observing the proprieties and living the law.

3. *WHERE DO YOU OBEY?* Biblical religion is always "home-made." That is, it always takes place in the home. Have your class reflect on the ramifications of Deuteronomy 6:7–9. What specifically is each class member doing to teach and picture the faith within his/her own household?

4. *WHY DO YOU HEED?* Do not slough over the warnings contained in today's scriptural passages. Let your class understand that God's people disobey at their own peril. Dire consequences result when His people refuse to choose Him. Remind your people of how easy it is to "forget the Lord" (6:12) when everything is going well.

5. *WHAT DO YOU DO?* Have your class make lists of the requirements God lays on His people when they obey Him, such as "You shall fear the Lord," etc. Discuss what each means.

TOPIC FOR ADULTS
GOD'S WORD IN OUR HEARTS

Stamped on Every Part of Life. "Consider, for a minute, a game of bridge. To pass an evening in a trial of wits, four people agree to pretend that cards have value. They put rewards and punishments of money on the outcome. They groan at the unexpected appearance of an ace, laugh with delight when a finesse works. Then the game ends, and the cards become more colored paper again. Even in such fleeting symbolism some authority is needed to keep the symbols stably in force. There are rule books, bridge associations, and unwritten laws of etiquette. A man may signal to his partner what cards he holds—in certain approved ways. If he is caught signalling in a way that is frowned upon, he may never play bridge again in this company, and even his reputation in real life may be hurt. He gave his consent to the bridge ceremony; he violates honor by behaving unceremoniously.

"The symbols of money are more serious. They are in fact iron-rigid. A bank check is but a piece of paper and duplicates the signature of a rich man on it. If you are caught doing so, you are called a forger, your good name is gone, and your bodily freedom is forfeit for years. All you were trying to do was to get some money, which is what everybody tries to do all the time. But you did it in an unceremonious way. Your crime was not that you tried to get money by manipulating paper symbols. Financiers grow very rich manipulating paper symbols. Some people will argue that their manipulations are mere sharp short cuts to money-getting, like your forgery. But at no point in their symbolic manipulation is there a punishable lack of right ceremony. The symbols and rites of finance are backed by the state. The consent of people to take them for what they represent is automatic and universal. The aspect of ceremony quite vanishes from dollar bills, bank checks, stock certificates, and insurance policies. They seem as real, as solid, as true, as trees or children. Indeed they are, while the authority that created them and the consent that sustains them continue to exist.

"Now the laws of our religion, though no policeman enforces them, form an organic whole, a living pattern of behavior for a community and for each individual in it. The symbols and rites of the faith are stamped on every important part of life; on food, on clothing, on shelter, on time, on sex, on speech."—THIS IS MY GOD by Herman Wouk. Copyright 1959, 1970 by The Abe Wouk Foundation, Inc.

Responsibility as a Form of Love. "It's my life and I can do as I please," say some.

If you as a Christian try to give this line, God firmly answers, "No, it's not your life. It's your wife's (or husband's); it's your children's, your neighbor's now."

You are free—to love. Responsibility, in fact, is a shape which love takes.

St. Augustine summed it up well when he wrote, "Love means that I want you to be." When we remember God's Word stamped in our hearts, we assume responsibility for each other because we want each other to be!

This Is My Church. It is composed of people like me. We make it what it is. It will be friendly—if I am. Its pews will be filled—if I help fill them. It will do a great work—if I work. It will make generous gifts to many causes—if I am a generous giver. It will bring other people into its worship and fellowship—if I bring them. It will be a church of loyalty and love, of fearlessness and faith, and a church with a noble spirit—if I, who make it what it is, am filled with these. Therefore, with the help of God, I shall dedicate myself to the task of being all the things I want my church to be.

Questions for Pupils on the Next Lesson. 1. How can your congregation help parents and children to communicate with each other better about religious traditions? 2. Does God call a special group to serve Him in these times? If so, who is that group? 3. Do you consider yourself to be part of a group which is called by God? 4. What does the term, the "chosen people," mean to you? What is the biblical meaning of this term? 5. Does being a member of the Christian Church lay greater responsibilities on a person? Why and how?

TOPIC FOR YOUTH
WHICH GOD DO YOU SERVE?

Glass God. Is God allowed to rule your life? Or is He out on the edge? Do you lean on Him? Or do you depend on alcohol for release and kicks?

Nearly 25% of all students in grades seven to twelve in the United States are either heavy drinkers—five to twelve drinks on at least one occasion a week—or "moderately heavy" drinkers—two to four drinks on at least one occasion a week—according to a nationwide survey by Research Triangle Institute.

The study also found that 24.3% of all thirteen-year-olds drink enough to be classified as "moderate" drinkers. Only 27% of those 13,222 junior and senior high-school students surveyed were non-drinkers.

The survey found "indications of a strong relationship between alcohol use by teenagers and abusive drinking by adults" and a strong association between parental and adolescent drinking.

Which God do you serve? The power found in a bottle, the deity of the bombed? Or have you bet your life on the power found in the Bible, the Deity of the blessed?

Choose.

Paper God. Do you worship security? Or wealth? Is your main objective to make it big, to get rich? Are you a gambler and do you play the lotteries to grab the big prize? Will plenty of dollars bring you peace and happiness? In other words, is money your god?

If it is, watch out! Especially if you win the lottery. This is the conclusion of a pair of researchers who have studied the lives of people who have taken the big lottery prizes.

Jerry and Rene LeBlanc report the winners never seem to find the happiness they thought they'd achieve by winning the lottery. "Sudden wealth can pose many problems, and most people aren't prepared for them," the Le Blancs state. The vast upheaval in a family brought on by the unexpected windfall, their studies show, puts intolerable strains on relationships within the family, the marriage, with the neighbors and friends, with fellow workers and the society.

Few winners find that they can remain in their old neighborhoods, but must move. All report harrassment by strangers. All become suspicious and fearful of other people. Many are robbed. All the winners described feeling as if they were living in a state of siege. Most felt their attitudes toward people changing so that they began to believe that others were mean. There were a few unfortunate winners who couldn't handle the pressures of instant wealth and finally angrily ended their own lives.

Perhaps this is God's way of warning against greed. Or perhaps this is God's way of reminding us that only He is to be worshiped. Whenever we try to place substitutes in His place, these false gods succeed in destroying us.

Success God. What is "God" in your life? Big name? Impressive credentials? Important title? Making it big? Status? Honors? Acclaim? Success?

If these are what you're worshiping, take another look. Even a dog recently was able to be recognized for having attained all these!

Otis P. Albee of South Burlington, Vermont, was listed in the 1978 volume of "Community Leaders and Noteworthy Americans"—making him probably the first dog to be so honored.

A University of Vermont professor, George Albee, said that he had received an invitation in the mail to submit biographical material for the book's listing of accomplished Americans.

Professor Albee filled out the forms for his family's dog, Otis.

A few weeks later, an envelope came back addressed to "Otis P. Albee," with a paste-up of the dog's biography as it appears in the latest edition, Professor Albee said.

Otis was identified as a "retired explorer, hunter, and sportsman." His Ph.D. in animal husbandry was duly noted, as well as his status as "former leader and guide of hunting parties."

Sentence Sermon to Remember: If there is righteousness in the heart, there will be beauty in character, there will be harmony in the home. If there is harmony in the home, there will be order in the nation. Where there is order in the nation, there will be peace in the world.

—Chinese Proverb.

Questions for Pupils on the Next Lesson. 1. Does God wait for people to be perfect before He can use them? 2. What are some of the abilities which God has given you? What are you doing to develop these so that God can use them better through you? 3. Does God love people even if they do not love themselves? 4. Why is every person important regardless of his, or her achievements, possessions, or appearance? 5. What does it mean to be "chosen" by God?

LESSON VII—JULY 19

GOD CHOSE ISRAEL

Background Scripture: Deuteronomy 6:16–7:26; 9:4, 5
Devotional Reading: Nehemiah 1:4–11b

KING JAMES VERSION

DEUTERONOMY 6 20 *And* when thy son asketh thee in time to come, saying, What *mean* the testimonies, and the statutes, and the judgments, which the LORD our God hath commanded you?

21 Then thou shalt say unto thy son, We were Pharaoh's bondmen in Egypt; and the LORD brought us out of Egypt with a mighty hand:

22 And the LORD shewed signs and wonders, great and sore, upon Egypt, upon Pharaoh, and upon all his household, before our eyes:

23 And he brought us out from thence, that he might bring us in, to give us the land which he sware unto our fathers.

24 And the LORD commanded us to do all these statutes, to fear the LORD our God, for our good always, that he might preserve us alive, as *it is* at this day.

25 And it shall be our righteousness, if we observe to do all these commandments before the LORD our God, as he hath commanded us.

7 6 For thou *art* an holy people unto the LORD thy God: the LORD thy God hath chosen thee to be a special people unto himself, above all people that *are* upon the face of the earth.

7 The LORD did not set his love upon you, nor choose you, because ye were more in number than any people; for ye *were* the fewest of all people:

8 But because the LORD loved you, and because he would keep the oath which he had sworn unto your fathers, hath the LORD brought you out with a mighty hand, and redeemed you out of the house of bondmen, from the hand of Pharaoh king of Egypt.

9 Know therefore that the LORD thy God, he *is* God, the faithful God, which keepeth covenant and mercy with them that love him and keep his commandments to a thousand generations;

REVISED STANDARD VERSION

DEUTERONOMY 6 20 "When your son asks you in time to come, 'What is the meaning of the testimonies and the statutes and the ordinances which the LORD our God has commanded you?' 21 then you shall say to your son, 'We were Pharaoh's slaves in Egypt; and the LORD brought us out of Egypt with a mighty hand; 22 and the LORD showed signs and wonders, great and grievous, against Egypt and against Pharaoh and all his household, before our eyes; 23 and he brought us out from there, that he might bring us in and give us in the land which he swore to give to our fathers. 24 And the LORD commanded us to do all these statutes, to fear the LORD our God, for our good always, that he might preserve us alive, as at this day. 25 And it will be righteousness for us, if we are careful to do all this commandment before the LORD our God, as he has commanded us.'

7 6 "For you are a people holy to the LORD your God; the LORD your God has chosen you to be a people for his own possession, out of all the peoples that are on the face of the earth. 7 It was not because you were more in number than any other people that the LORD set his love upon you and chose you, for you were the fewest of all peoples; 8 but it is because the LORD loves you, and is keeping the oath which he swore to your fathers, that the LORD has brought you out with a mighty hand, and redeemed you from the house of bondage, from the hand of Pharaoh king of Egypt. 9 Know therefore that the LORD your God is God, the faithful God who keeps covenant and steadfast love with those who love him and keep his commandments, to a thousand generations, 10 and requites to their face those who hate him, by

10 And repayeth them that hate him to their face, to destroy them: he will not be slack to him that hateth him, he will repay him to his face.

11 Thou shalt therefore keep the commandments, and the statutes, and the judgments, which I command thee this day, to do them.

destroying them; he will not be slack with him who hates him, he will require him to his face. 11 You shall therefore be careful to do the commandment, and the statutes, and the ordinances, which I command you this day."

KEY VERSE: You are a people holy to the Lord your God; the Lord your God has chosen you to be a people for his own possession . . . . Deuteronomy 7:6 (RSV).

HOME DAILY BIBLE READINGS

July 13. M. *A People Holy to the Lord.* Deuteronomy 6:16–25.
July 14. T. *Chosen in Love.* Deuteronomy 7:1–11.
July 15. W. *Chosen for Blessing.* Deuteronomy 7:12–16.
July 16. T. *The Lord Is in Your Midst.* Deuteronomy 7:17–26; 9:4, 5.
July 17. F. *"Fear Not, I Will Help You."* Isaiah 41:8–13.
July 18. S. *We Are the Lord's.* Isaiah 44:1–5.
July 19. S. *A Prayer for God's Chosen People.* Nehemiah 1.

BACKGROUND

We are still reading the second sermon of Moses in this lesson—and we still find ourselves confronted with repetitions and phrases used in our previous lessons. We may wonder why Moses so often repeats himself, but we can understand why he did this; he was like the modern teacher of mathematics in a modern grade school, who makes his students repeat the multiplication table over and over and over again, so that it will be fixed firmly in their memories. They *must* be able to repeat those tables from *memory*, for all they are to study later is based on those tables.

Actually, Moses was stressing the three central themes of the Book of Deuteronomy, and of the Jewish faith: *remember, obey, and behold.* He is trying to drive these words deep into the consciousness of the people who stood before him—the people about to enter the Promised Land— but he was more concerned with the children of these people, who would need not only physical courage but a strengthening faith in their God to hold this land after they got there. Without such courage and faith, they would not last very long when they faced the embattled Canaanites who would kill every last one of them if they could.

Notice that Moses starts this section of his sermon with a reference to the children of the next generation. Preachers today often begin that way: they start with a "shocker," to get the attention of their congregations.

NOTES ON THE PRINTED TEXT

1. "When your son asks you in time to come, 'What is the meaning of the testimonies and the statutes and the ordinances which the Lord our God has commanded you?' " Deuteronomy 6:20 (RSV). "These curious little creatures," says Edward P. Blair, "are always asking 'Why?', and intelligent answers are due them." Correct! The parent who has left religious teaching to the Sunday school and dodges the embarrassing questions of his child is no parent at all; all the Sunday schools, churches, and catechism classes in the world can fail without the help of the father and mother. Many a child is a delinquent religiously, only because his parents are delinquent.

We knew a youngster once who asked his father, "Daddy, why were the first Christians Communists?" He quoted Acts 2:44 as his reason for asking *why*. Daddy's reply was, "Why do you ask me such foolish questions? Ask your Sunday-school teacher." He asked the teacher, but the teacher didn't have the answer, either. Lost, one boy.

When your son asks you why he has to obey the Commandments, said Moses, you had better have the right answer for him: "We all obey God's laws *because of what He has done for us!* If God had not brought us out of Egypt you would still be a slave. For that we promised to obey Him and His Commandments. Only then were we all really free, and really *living*. You owe God something for that, don't you?"

"For it always goes well with us when we obey all the laws of the Lord our God" (verse 25, *Living Bible*"). Remember, and obey!

II. "For you are a people holy to the Lord your God; the Lord your God has chosen you to be a people for his own possession, out of all the peoples that are on the face of the earth." Deuteronomy 7:6 (RSV). Here we have another "Why?" *Why* did God make Israel a chosen people? Why didn't He choose the Romans, who were so strong and powerful, and who ruled the world? Or why not the Greeks, the world's greatest philosophers, the famed intellectuals "who spent their time in nothing else, but either to tell, or to hear some new thing?" (Acts 17:21.) Dorothy Parker, with tongue in cheek, says:

> How odd
> Of God
> To choose
> The Jews.

She said that because, brilliant as she was, she neither knew God nor the Jews.

But God choosing the Jews is still a good question, deserving an intelligent answer. Certainly, there was little of what we might call "nobility" in the Jews at the time Moses preached this sermon. They were a band of desert nomads as they approached the gates of Canaan with none of the qualities of greatness. They had but one man great in his time: Moses. They produced no great statesmen for years to come. Egypt and Greece and later Rome had the great scholars and scientists and philosophers. Neither Israel nor Judaism, for many years to come, could boast of great thinkers; at best, they had only Philo, Maimonides, and Spinoza. They were an obscure people and of little promise in their world.

But that is exactly why God "chose" them, separated them from their more brilliant neighbors. Greece was too busy working out fancy philosophies to understand that there was but one God or to determine man's relationship with that God; the Athenians, centuries later, laughed at Paul! The Romans were too busy conquering the world, and slaughtering much of it, to give much time to God. These were strong nations—and that is one reason why God passed them to put His hand on Israel's shoulder. They simply could not easily become aware of God's grace and saving character. The Jews, a despised and suffering people, could more readily know about that.

God, according to the Deuteronomist, did not set Israel aside as His special people because they were strong; He "picked" them because their spiritual potential to truly know Him and to serve Him well. God *loved* that, for they alone among all the nations of the world could and would come to love Him alone. Time and again, Israel "went political"—time and again they struggled for political supremacy, and every time they tried it, they failed. They were not destined to dominate the world politically or militarily. They were a suffering people, and God works miracles through those who suffer. He also used Rome, in a lesser sense: this mighty Empire, in later history, this Rome, was fated to become the capital of early Christianity! God used Egypt to illustrate the fact nations drunk with power eventually fall helpless into history's gutter. And He used Israel for a nobler, more lasting purpose.

We must understand the word *holy*, in this Scripture. *Holy* did not mean that the Israelites would be a sanctified, pious, holier-than-thou people; it meant "separated"—a people separated from among all other nations, dedicated to God. This holiness involved obedience to God's laws, above the laws and customs and ambitions of other countries and peoples.

III. And repayeth them that hate him to their face, to destroy them . . . . Deuteronomy 7:10. This is a jarring note. Having pictured God as a loving God, here we find Him to be a vengeful God approving of the destruction of His enemies. The cynics and the nonbelievers love to call that to our attention!

This was written in a time when destruction of one's enemies was "the order of the day"—something to be expected. If a nation were threatened by another nation, the proper thing to do was wipe out that nation. History is full of records of cities leveled with the ground, with ghastly stories of total annihilation. If you were to visit the spot where mighty Carthage once stood, you will find nothing but ruins; that city was completely wiped out, and salt was sown in the soil, so that no people could ever live there again. It happened frequently in primitive history.

Now the Jews had a God who was "The God of hosts"—a Deity present with them in battle. God was on their side, and more than one enemy was destroyed, they believed, with God's help. But while this passage clearly refers to the elimination of Canaan, it also clearly means the destruction of Canaanitist idols, shrines, and semireligious practices. The Canaanitish god and gods of Baal (Asherah, Anath, and Ashtoreth, for instance), were a bloodthirsty lot; in self defense, the Israelite believed, they had to be wiped out with God's help. They were certain that God would help them, for God, according to Moses, "will not be slack to him that hateth him" (verse 10). Remember, these were *primitive* days in which only the strong survived.

Israel survived not because she destroyed all her enemies, en masse, but because her faith and her God were stronger than the gods of Baal. He was a God determined to conquer and destroy all worship of less than Himself. It is the destruction of non-Godly worship that is emphasized here.

SUGGESTIONS TO TEACHERS

This lesson can be easily booby-trapped by people in your class raising questions about topics which are not pertinent to *the* topic, although they may appear on the surface to be. The topic, "God Chose Israel," may tempt some to start useless discussions over whether or not present-day Jews are "chosen." The lesson topic may arouse others to embark on pointless arguments over predestination. Others may get the class enmeshed in unproductive haggling over the ethics of total warfare mentioned in Deuteronomy. Therefore, as teacher, be forewarned! You will have little difficulty if you know what the main point of the lesson is and firmly keep the discussion centered on that point.

That main point is: *We are chosen.* Although the scriptural material discusses God choosing Israel, it must be remembered that Israel means *us.* In other words, God chooses *us.*

When you emphasize that God has chosen us, you will keep the lesson on the track and not get derailed by the interesting but irrelevant questions mentioned in the opening paragraph. You can assist your people to consider what it is to be chosen by God by offering the following key points:

1. *RESCUED BY GOD.* Remember Christ's words, "You did not choose me, but I have chosen you" (John 15:16)? He does the choosing! He initiates. He has come to us, delivering us. Be sure to indicate to your class how the Deuteronomy passages speak of God bringing "us out of Egypt" when "we were Pharaoh's slaves" (6:21). Is everyone in your class aware of God's mighty rescue effort through His acts in history, starting with the Exodus and culminating with Jesus Christ? Do your people grasp that their sense of being chosen starts with remembering what God has done for them?

2. *RESPONSIBLE TO GOD.* Take a poll in your class about what folks think about being "the chosen people." Does it mean being on God's preferred list? Being considered nicer than others? Reread Deuteronomy 7:6: "God has chosen you to be a people for his own possession." We belong to God; we are His property. We exist to serve Him. Chosen-ness, in other words, means being selected for service! Insist that your people consider the obligations that chosen-ness entails.

3. *RESERVED FOR GOD.* Being chosen does not mean that we may indulge in snobbish notions that we are smarter, stronger, or better than others in any way. Look carefully at Deuteronomy 7:7. God reminds Israel in blunt terms that He has not chosen them because of any qualities they possessed. The same applies to us. The only reason for God's choosing us is His love for us! Encourage your people to comment on the place of grace—God's undeserved care—in our lives.

4. *REQUIREMENTS BEFORE GOD.* A person who realizes God's grace has been chosen. He has no choice but to love God in return and to

share that love with others. Have your class tally the demands which this love lays on each members of the chosen people. Particularly bring out the notions of trusting God and remembering what He has done which are emphasized in the Scripture passage.

TOPIC FOR ADULTS
WHEN GOD CHOOSES US

Chosen to Serve. One of the most exclusive and heroic group of heroes in World War II was a group of United States Marines known as "code talkers." Originally, there were only twenty-nine code talkers, but eventually there were 350. Each was a Navajo Indian chosen for his proficiency in English and Navajo. This elite group of Marines was attached to the Second Marine Division, and was among the first to storm ashore at Guadalcanal, Tarawa, and Saipan. The code talkers crawled through the jungle underbrush where the fighting was fiercest, carrying their radios and sending messages back to headquarters to use airplanes or artillary for companies of Marines that needed support.

This chosen outfit, transmitting in Navajo in a code which was never broken, dodged enemy fire during the "island hopping" campaigns, and helped immeasurably to save lives and shorten the war.

Being God's chosen people is like being part of an exclusive combat team. We are chosen for service not for the honor. Basically, we are selected to risk everything for the sake of obeying the Lord.

Chosen to Sacrifice. The sixty-eight-year-old field hand living near Elm City, North Carolina, limped badly from too many years backbreaking toil. Her face was wrinkled from years of exposure to the sun. She looked as if she belonged in a rest home, but she was actively involved in the voter registration program for her area. Why?

Well, she was a Christian, she replied with quiet but firm conviction, and a Christian was chosen for God's work. God's work for her meant being chosen to sign up her neighbors as new voters. Her church was a crude, unpainted wooden structure on the edge of town.

A reporter interviewing her persisted. Suppose, he asked, the Ku Klux Klan burned down the building. Wouldn't that be the end of her church?

"Heavens, no!" the woman replied with emphasis. "That wouldn't make no difference. No difference at all." She smiled. "You see," she continued, "That's just where we meets once a week."

What better illustration of the Church and being part of the chosen people!

Freedom to Be Chosen. Freedom means license, we mistakenly think. No so in the Bible. Freedom for God's people never is permission to do as one pleases. Instead, it is the kind of freedom of chosen-ness that the Lord gave Moses and Israel. Freedom means acknowledging that we are chosen by God.

Note carefully, however, that being chosen always means being selected to suffer, serve, and sacrifice. It is summed up well in Exodus 7:16 where Moses is told to go to the Pharaoh of Egypt and to announce that the Israelites are chosen: "Let my people go, that they may serve me." *God's* people and *servant* people are the key notions of being chosen people.

Questions for Pupils on the Nest Lesson. 1. Why is worship understood in the Bible to corporate instead of individualistic and private? 2. Do you understand your responsibilities to participate in the corporate worship of your church? 3. How can you give more positive support to corporate worship in your congregation? 4. What should your church do to make worship practices more consistent with the biblical concept of God? 5. What worship practices best enable Christian adults to acknowledge ownership of all they have?

TOPIC FOR YOUTH
GOD CHOOSES US

Chosen to Hang In. Christians are chosen to serve in the world, not to withdraw from it. Sometimes, we have been led to think that we are chosen to keep ourselves unsullied and untainted.

For example, the Rev. Alvin M. Stevens and his Pentecostal Faith Challengers decided they were chosen to leave the Full Gospel Temple in Freemont, California, and begin a new life. They sold their homes and belongings to raise money for a down payment for an entire town in the California rain forest 250 miles north of San Francisco. When Stevens and his "chosen" people arrived in Bridgeville, the town they bought, they found twenty-eight rundown houses, a garage, a general store and about 125 residents who were mostly young "flower children" who had fled the city to live in the wilderness. The chosen group evicted the 125 residents and suspended the alcohol and tobacco sales that had been sustained by the loggers and passers-by on Highway 36.

With the main source of income removed, however, Stevens and his chosen people quickly found themselves unable to complete payments on the $450,000 purchase. The town was put up for auction, and Stevens and the last of his Pentecostal Faith Challengers left to begin a new life somewhere else.

The biblical understanding of being chosen people, however, does not mean running away from the world. Rather, it means staying in the world as God's community to live obediently to serve.

Chosen to Sacrifice. Everyone remembers Roger Bannister as the man who broke the barrier for the four minute mile at Oxford, England on May 6, 1954. Few remember Chris Chataway and Chris Brasher. Without Chataway and Brasher, however, Bannister could never have set his record.

The three had trained together. They knew that Australia's John Landy had already had several near-misses at the record, and was journeying to Europe that summer to attempt to break the four minute mark. The trio of Bannister, Brasher, and Chataway sensed that they were going to have to make the supreme effort to set the new record that afternoon. They laid their plans carefully. Each knew that he was chosen for an important part in the attempt for the under-four minute mile.

Brasher, the 1956 Olympic steeplechase champion, was chosen deliberately to take the opening lead, with Bannister and Chataway following closely behind. The plan then called for Chataway to move ahead on the third of the four laps. Chataway, later a world record holder for the 5,000 meters, was chosen to set the pace for Bannister. Bannister was chosen to spurt ahead for the final lap. The plan worked smoothly because each runner knew he had been chosen. Although Roger Bannister took the laurels, he insists upon saying to this day, "We did it. The three of us did it."

Those who are aware that they are part of God's chosen people know that they are picked out for a team effort for a cause greater than themselves. It is always a "we-did-it" attitude, referring to the Lord and the others on the chosen team.

Chosen as Christ's. "Christ has no body on earth now but yours, no hands but yours, no feet but yours. Yours are the eyes through which Christ's compassion looks out to the world. Yours are the feet with which He is to go about doing good, and yours are the hands with which He is to bless us now."—St. Teresa of Avila.

Sentence Sermon to Remember: For many are called, but few are chosen.—Matthew 22:14.

Questions for Pupils on the Next Lesson. 1. Why should worship be with others of God's people and not by yourself? 2. Are you able to define your spiritual pilgrimage in terms of a growing relationship with God? Why or why not? 3. Why does a transforming experience of God's love motivate a person to commit his/her life to Him? 4. Does your covenant relationship with God bring you a sense of joy? 5. What should your church do to make worship experience more meaningful?

LESSON VIII—JULY 26

COMMITMENT IN WORSHIP

Background Scripture: Deuteronomy 12:1–14:29
Devotional Reading: Amos 5:18–24

KING JAMES VERSION

DEUTERONOMY 12 5 But unto the place which the LORD your God shall choose out of all your tribes to put his name there, *even* unto his habitation shall ye seek, and thither thou shalt come:

6 An thither ye shall bring your burnt offerings, and your sacrifices, and your tithes, and heave offerings of your hand, and your vows, and your freewill offerings, and the firstlings of your herds and of your flocks:

7 And there ye shall eat before the LORD your God, and ye shall rejoice in all that ye put your hand unto, ye and your households, wherein the LORD thy God hath blessed thee.

8 Ye shall not do after all *the things* that we do here this day, every man whatsoever *is* right in his own eyes.

9 For ye are not as yet come to the rest and to the inheritance, which the LORD your God giveth you.

10 But *when* ye go over Jordan, and dwell in the land which the LORD your God giveth you to inherit, and *when* he giveth you rest from all your enemies round about, so that ye dwell in safety;

11 Then there shall be a place which the LORD your God shall choose to cause his name to dwell there; thither shall ye bring all that I command you; your burnt offerings, and your sacrifices, your tithes, and the heave offering of your hand, and all your choice vows which ye vow unto the LORD:

12 And ye shall rejoice before the LORD your God, ye, and your sons, and your daughters, and your menservants, and your maidservants, and the Levite that *is* within your gates; forasmuch as he hath no part nor inheritance with you.

14 27 And the Levite that *is* within thy gates; thou shalt not forsake him: for he hath no part nor inheritance with thee.

REVISED STANDARD VERSION

DEUTERONOMY 12 5 "But you shall seek the place which the LORD your God will choose out of all your tribes to put his name and make his habitation there; thither you shall go, 6 and thither you shall bring your burnt offerings and your sacrifices, your tithes and the offering that you present, your votive offerings, your freewill offerings, and the firstlings of your herd and of your flock; 7 and there you shall eat before the LORD your God, and you shall rejoice, you and your households, in all that you undertake, in which the LORD your God has blessed you. 8 You shall not do according to all that we are doing here this day, every man doing whatever is right in his own eyes; 9 for you have not as yet come to the rest and to the inheritance which the LORD your God gives you. 10 But when you go over the Jordan, and live in the land which the LORD your God gives you to inherit, and when he gives you rest from all your enemies round about, so that you live in safety, 11 then to the place which the LORD your God will choose, to make his name dwell there, thither you shall bring all that I command you: your burnt offerings and your sacrifices, your tithes and the offering that you present, and all your votive offerings which you vow to the LORD. 12 And you shall rejoice before the LORD your God, you and your sons and your daughters, your menservants and your maidservants, and the Levite that is within your towns, since he has no portion or inheritance with you.

14 27 "And you shall not forsake the Levite who is within your towns, for he has no portion or inheritance with you.

28 At the end of three years thou shalt bring forth all the tithe of thine increase the same year, and shalt lay *it* up within thy gates:

29 And the Levite (because he hath not part nor inheritance with thee,) and the stranger, and the fatherless, and the widow, which are within thy gates, shall come, and shall eat and be satisfied; that the LORD thy God may bless thee in all the work of thine hand which thou doest.

28 "At the end of every three years you shall bring forth all the tithe of your produce in the same year, and lay it up within your towns; 29 and the Levite, because he has no portion or inheritance with you, and the sojourner, the fatherless, and the widow, who are within your towns, shall come and eat and be filled; that the LORD your God may bless you in all the work of your hands that you do."

KEY VERSE: ". . . you shall rejoice, you and your households, in all that you undertake, in which the Lord your God has blessed you." Deuteronomy 12:7 (RSV).

HOME DAILY BIBLE READINGS

July 20. M. *A Place to Worship God.* Deuteronomy 12:1–14.
July 21. T. *Do Not Go After Other Gods.* Deuteronomy 13:1–5.
July 22. W. *Give a Tithe to God.* Deuteronomy 14:22–29.
July 23. T. *Worship and Bow Down.* Psalms 95:1–7.
July 24. F. *Declare His Glory.* Psalms 96.
July 25. S. *The Lord Reigns.* Psalms 99.
July 26. S. *True Worship.* Amos 5:18–24.

BACKGROUND

In chapters 12 to 26 of Deuteronomy, we have the main purpose of the book, which was to put added emphasis upon the laws made in the wilderness and to restate some of those laws in order that the people might adapt themselves to conditions they were to find in Canaan. We might call these new laws the laws of the Land of Promise; they dealt with (1) the seat of the worship of the people; (2) with the divine government of the people, and (3) with the Land as the home of God's people.

Today we study their worship. They had problems to face as they marched into the Land—problems of dealing with the worship of the *Canaanites* who inhabited the land. To prevent any weakening of Israel's faith, it was commanded that they destroy all the shrines and altars of Canaan's gods wherever they found them—in the mountains, on the high hills, in every green tree on the plains. Smash those altars, burn those groves, where the pagans worshiped, with fire, leave nothing to remind you of Baal! (As we suggested last week, this was an order to destroy not the Canaanites but the altars and other "holy" places of the Canaanites.)

This was, to say the least, a negative approach, an approach of violence against a religious competitor. But Moses and his Israelites did not make this the *only* approach; this law of destruction. Israel was not only to tear down, but to build holy places for *their* worship.

NOTES ON THE PRINTED TEXT

I. *"But you shall seek the place which the Lord your God will choose out of all your tribes to put his name and make his habitation there*

. . . ."Deuteronomy 12:5 (RSV). More simply stated, this was the command to provide Israel with one central place of worship. This "place" is not named, in the Scripture, but it was undoubtedly Jerusalem—a city set high upon a hill, a city that could be reached by a short journey from any point in the surrounding country.

And the selection of a place so situated was a *necessity;* imagine what would have happened if every tribe and every individual was allowed to set up a temple or use any form of worship that it or he might choose! That would have been bad, for it would have left the people scattered and in danger of lapsing into the idolatrous worship of the Canaanites. One central place, one point of centralization for all Israelites, was a real necessity.

This wasn't a paricularly new idea in Israel; in its wilderness days there was a "tent of meeting," a tabernacle in which God "dwelt in the midst of his people" (spiritually, not physically), where Moses talked with God, where the precious ark was housed. This tabernacle was the "hub of the wheel," the central point about which Jewish life revolved. In the wilderness and in Jerusalem, it represented the unity of the one God, and the unity of His worship.

We all need some centralization point in our religion, some one place or organization which leads us to unity, some place in which to worship as one. Catholicism has its Rome, its Vatican; the Baptists have their associations, the Presbyterians their General Assembly, the Methodists their General Conference—all orgainzed and maintained in the interest of *unity.* Some central point is as necessary now as then. In unity there is strength; in disunity, chaos.

II. And thither ye shall bring your burnt offerings, and your sacrifices . . . . Deuteronomy 12:6. Sacrifice, in the Bible, begins with the "offerings" of Cain and Abel in Eden. It was an essential element in Israel in the time of Moses. Those who sacrificed were sincere, but the practice was often abused—as in the story of Adam's sons. Sacrifice *should* be an essential element in *our* religion, but not an act of merely sacrificing animals, as it was in Israel's early days.

Abuses of the custom were so frequent that Moses, in Deuteronomy 12, sends down the order that sacrifices should be made only in the national shrine at Jerusalem. Later, however, sacrifice was a part of the worship at other shrines—Shiloh, Gibeon, Ahechem, out in "the hinterland," where the Jews might be influenced by the sacrificial rites of the Canaanites. That was too much of a threat to the Jewish concepts of Israel, as we shall see in the condemnation of it by the Prophet Amos.

Now there were three conceptions underlying the sacrificial system. First, there was the idea that to sacrifice an animal or a share of the wheat crop was a gift man should offer to God for the good things God had provided for him. It was a recognition by men that they owed a great debt to God, and this was one way of paying that debt and to express his thanks to his God.

Then there were those who thought of sacrifice as a way to put themselves in communion with God; they divided their sacrificed animals into three sections: the fat and blood for God, certain parts of the meat for the priests and other parts for themselves. Often there was the rather selfish hope that in giving this "gift" to God, they would secure for themselves the love of God, and gifts of help and prosperity from His hand!

The third concept was the best: the worshiper, by sincere repentance, felt that his sins might be forgiven. The blood of the sacrificial victim had the power to accomplish this. We have somewhat of a counterpart of this in the sacrifice of Jesus on the cross: by His blood, we believe, are we saved, by it God's possible anger with us is wiped out, and by it a deeper fellowship with God is established. "Without the shedding of blood," says Hebrews 9:22, "there is no forgiveness of sins."

Now read Amos 5:22, 24: "Though ye offer me burnt offerings and your meat offerings, I will not accept them neither will I regard the peace offerings of your fat beasts . . . . But let judgment run down as waters, and righteousness as a mighty stream," The old prophet was condemning "sacrifice" without the works of faith. No man wins the favor of God or His forgiveness by merely killing an animal; he wins it by *sacrificial service*. He wins it in unselfish, honest tithing of his wealth and goods. The man who offers the "sacrifice" of money he can spare to the Lord and ignores the plight of the poor and the depressed gains no love from God; his sacrifice is that of a hypocrite. Two-faced sacrifice is blasphemy. God, all-righteous Himself, demands righteousness, righteousness, *righteousness!*

Sacrifice in worship took on another, more magnificent meaning with the Christ who said that the time would come when God would be worshiped not on any particular mountain, not in any particular place (such as Samaria or Jerusalem), but in spirit and in truth, anywhere the worshiper might be (John 4).

Let us examine ourselves: exactly what have *we* sacrificed lately, and for what?

III. *"And you shall not forsake the Levite who is within your towns . . . ."* Deuteronomy 14:27 (RSV). Amos would approve of this verse. The tithe paid by the Jewish worshiper was to be divided in two directions: part of it was to go to the Levites (priests), who had no other source of income, and part of it was to go to the fatherless and the widows and the strangers in the land. (This tithe was collected every three years.) This would have answered the demand of Amos that the poor and the helpless be taken care of; it lifted the whole performance of sacrificial giving above the status of a mere *ritual*, and made it a much-needed contribution to human need. It not only helped those in need; it was helpful in building the spirit of love in the giver of the tithe. The Deuteronomist claims that God's blessing falls upon those who "cast their bread upon the waters" as they give to the temple Levite and to the hungry poor man in his hut, and there have been many instances, many testimonies by generous givers, to prove that this is true. But even if it is not true, the fact remains that when the tithe is given gladly for such a purpose, the giver becomes a good steward of God, doing what God wants us all to do with our possessions. Giving, to the man who knows God, is not a duty but a joy and a sign of good stewardship.

SUGGESTIONS TO TEACHERS

Deuteronomy, the subject for this series of lessons, was originally and primarily a covenant book. It was found in the Temple (*see* 2 Kings 22, 23). It was designed for the worshiping community. So far, little has been mentioned about worship. Today's lesson deals mainly with worship.

As teacher, you will work with the background Scripture. However, you will endeavor to do more than delve into historical lore. You will help your class to move from ancient-time rules to present-day cues for worshiping. The biblical material suggests the following salient points:

1. *LET US WORSHIP* GOD. Call your class's attention to the requirement for exlusive devotion to God. Deuteronomy 12:30 states in effect, "Don't fool around with other cults and objects of worship!" Like the early Israelites, God's people today are constantly attracted by the promises of other gods. What are the "cults" which are particularly inclined to lure you and your people away from the Lord? Possessions? Security? Is it possible to give God equal time with these other gods? Notice how uncompromising Deuteronomy is about God sharing top place with others. God is the beginning and end of all true worship. Worship happens only when a person's life centers on the God who has acted and called His community into being.

2. *LET* US *WORSHIP GOD*. Take sufficient time in this lesson to get your class to understand that worship is *always* within the context of being part of God's community. Although sometimes we may pray without others beside us, we may not pray without remembering others. We may be alone, but we can never be loners. Deuteronomy 12:8 has blunt words about corporate worship being a requirement for each member of God's community. Some in your class will probably dispute this ("I can worship just as well in the woods or on the golf course." Or, "You don't have to go to church to be a Christian"). Hear them out, but remind them that the Bible, as John Wesley used to say, "knows nothing of solitary religion."

3. *LET US* WORSHIP *GOD*. The word *worship* comes from "worthship." A life focused on God and covenanted with others discovers that worship does, indeed, bring a sense of worth! Deuteronomy 12:12, 18 mention the spin-off of joy that comes from worshiping God. The background Scripture also stresses that worship is remembering whose you are. The customs of worship are memory-devices to enhance the knowledge of worth-ship God alone can bring. Have your class evaluate the worship services in your church in the light of these criteria.

4. LET *US WORSHIP GOD*. Devote some of your lesson period to the matter of religious leaders, (*see* Deuteronomy 13:1). God's community must always be leery of self-anointed "prophets" and "interpreters" who pretend to have a hot-line to the mind of God. Test the claims of leaders, lest they lure members of God's community to phoney religion. Furthermore, insist that your class talk over the necessity of discipline and order in worship, and not imagining that worship is "doing you own thing."

TOPIC FOR ADULTS
COMMITMENT IN WORSHIP

God for His Own Sake. An ancient story comes out of Strasbourg about an eccentric old woman who was seen one morning carrying a pail full of water and a blazing torch. The bystanders watched her striding down the street with her strange load. Finally, one curious soul could contain himself no longer and stopped her. Why was she carrying the water and the fire?

The woman looked at the group and answered: "I shall put out the fires of hell with the water and burn up heaven with the torch so that people would love God for Himself only, and not for fear of torture in hell or hope for reward in heaven."

Worship is loving God for Himself, and not out of fear of punishment or hope of reward.

Do you worship God solely because of your desire for a relationship with Him?

Slurred Commitment. One child came home from Sunday School eager to recite newly-learned Scripture verses. The Twenty-Third Psalm, however, was concluded with the words, "Shirley, good Mrs. Murphy shall follow me all the days of my life."

Another youngster, trying to repeat the words of the Lord's Prayer, fervently intoned, "Our Father, who art in heaven, Harold be thy name." Still another thought for years that the prayer's final petition, "Lead us not into temptation," was "Lead us not into Penn Station."

Even hymns have not been exempt. A Maine boy was certain he used to sing, "I will follow Henry Joyce," until he later found the words were "I will follow and rejoice." And "God Bless America" has had a misheard line "Through the night with a light from a bulb," in place of "a light from above."

We all hear the same sounds, but until we read the written word and understand the intended meaning, we may continue to give our interpretation. With children, it is amusing. With grown-ups, it is sad. Mistaken hearing by a six-year-old who sings, "Gladly, the cross-eyed bear," is acceptable. But a sixteen or sixty-year-old who cannot understand that it is "Gladly the Cross I'd bear" is childish.

Worship clarifies. Worship as God's community enables us to grow. Worship corrects our mishearing. Worship focuses us on the Word of God, as contained in Scripture, the written Word. Worship helps us to have a maturer faith. Worship puts the grown-up interpretation on God, on ourselves, and on life.

Double Praying. Worship is not solemn. It is intended to be joyous. God has been good to us. Jesus Christ's coming is "good news of great joy which shall be to all people."

Worship means we may sing. Those who express their commitment in worship through songs understand St. Augustine's words, "He who sings prays twice!"

Questions for Pupils on the Next Lesson. 1. Is justice the same thing as "law and order"? 2. Why must Christian adults work for the elimination of oppression? 3. Who are some of those who are oppressed in your community? 4. How may your congregation help foster respect for per-

sons and concern for their basic needs? 5. Should Christians be involved
in selecting leaders who will have concern for justice? Why or why not?
6. How is your church ministering to the poor?

TOPIC FOR YOUTH
JOY IN OBEDIENCE

One-Man Town. The prairie wind and four cats are Tim Vogelwede's
only companions on the North Dakota plains. A twenty-seven-year-old
construction worker, he is the only resident of Dover.

There is no radio, no television, no stereo, and no telephone to disturb
his solitude in the once-busy town. Carrington, the nearest community,
is six miles away. Vogelwede was born and raised there before leaving
for college.

Dover is in the wide open prairie of central North Dakota. The town
blossomed when homesteaders arrived at the turn of the century, but
small farms and small towns are fading memories these days.

Although Dover has been abandoned by its other residents Vogelwede works as a construction laborer in nearby towns.

One person, however, does not constitute a community. One person
cannot make a town. Even Vogelwede must ultimately depend on others
for his livelihood and safety.

The same is true with living a life of joyful obedience to God. We
cannot do it alone. We must be in community with others. Just as there
are no one-person cities, there are not one-person churches.

Perhaps you have thought that you could be a "hermit" Christian—a
one-person congregation worshiping God as you please, when you
pleased, where you pleased, without others. No way! Ultimately, you
must unite with others of God's family. Only then will you find lasting
joy and meaning in worship.

Scraping the Barnacles. The skippers of giant liners are instructed to
bring their ships to port for special hull-cleaning operations several
times a year. These hull-cleanings take two days and cost about $5,000.
Special brushes scrape the keel and underside of the ship, clearing away
algae, barnacles, and underwater vegetation.

A one inch growth of algae on the sides of a supertanker can create an
underwater drag that may add as much as $115,000 of extra fuel con-
sumption during a year. With fuel oil costs going up each year, it pays
ship owners to clean more frequently than in previous years. After
hull-cleaning, a ship may run at least one full knot faster, saving much in
bunker oil per voyage and cutting off days of steaming.

Worship, in a sense, is clearing away barnacles of guilt, of anxiety, of
resentment. These cause us to drag and slow down our progress. We
must scrape away whatever impedes our progress, harmony, and fulfillment as Christ's people.

God, for our own good, orders us to take time for worship. Obeying
His command to join the worshiping community of His people brings
joy and tranquility.

Loser and Keeper. "What I tried to keep in my own hands, I ended by
losing. But what I placed in God's hands, I was allowed to hold." These
words by Martin Luther sum up the meaning of commitment in worship.

Have you discovered the joy in obeying God's command to place your life and all that you have and are in His hands?

Sentence Sermon to Remember: God is to be worshiped in faith, hope, and love.—St. Augustine.

Questions for Pupils on the Next Lesson. 1. How can you evaluate whether or not authorities are acting with justice? 2. How are you expressing your faith by loving others and working for justice for others? 3. What is your class doing to discover ways to help others who are poor or oppressed? 4. What have been some times in your life when you have been aware of difficulties and limitations? If you have felt these, how are you using these experiences to empathize with others?

LESSON IX—AUGUST 2

GOD DESIRES JUSTICE

Background Scripture: Deuteronomy 16:18–17:20; 24:1–22
Devotional Reading: Isaiah 55:1–9

KING JAMES VERSION

DEUTERONOMY 16 18 Judges and officers shalt thou make thee in all thy gates, which the LORD thy God giveth thee, throughout thy tribes: and they shall judge the people with just judgment.

19 Thou shalt not wrest judgment; thou shalt not respect persons, neither take a gift: for a gift doth blind the eyes of the wise, and pervert the words of the righteous.

20 That which is altogether just shalt thou follow, that thou mayest live, and inherit the land which the LORD thy God giveth thee.

24 10 When thou dost lend thy brother any thing, thou shalt not go into his house to fetch his pledge.

11 Thou shalt stand abroad, and the man to whom thou dost lend shall bring out the pledge abroad unto thee.

12 And if the man *be* poor, thou shalt not sleep with his pledge:

13 In any case thou shalt deliver him the pledge again when the sun goeth down, that he may sleep in his own raiment, and bless thee: and it shall be righteousness unto thee before the LORD thy God.

14 Thou shalt not oppress a hired servant *that is* poor and needy, *whether he be* of thy brethren, or of thy strangers that *are* in thy land within thy gates:

15 At his day thou shalt give *him* his hire, neither shall the sun go down upon it; for he *is* poor, and setteth his heart upon it: lest he cry against thee unto the LORD, and it be sin unto thee.

17 Thou shalt not pervert the judgment of the stranger, *nor* of the fatherless; nor take a widow's raiment to pledge:

18 But thou shalt remember that thou wast a bondman in Egypt, and the LORD thy God redeemed thee thence: therefore I command thee to do this thing.

REVISED STANDARD VERSION

DEUTERONOMY 16 18 "You shall appoint judges and officers in all your towns which the LORD your God gives you, according to your tribes; and they shall judge the people with righteous judgment. 19 You shall not pervert justice; you shall not show partiality; and you shall not take a bribe, for a bribe blinds the eyes of the wise and subverts the cause of the righteous. 20 Justice, and only justice, you shall follow, that you may live and inherit the land which the LORD your God gives you.

24 10 "When you make your neighbor a loan of any sort, you shall not go into his house to fetch his pledge. 11 You shall stand outside, and the man to whom you make the loan shall bring the pledge out to you. 12 And if he is a poor man, you shall not sleep in his pledge; 13 when the sun goes down, you shall restore to him the pledge that he may sleep in his cloak and bless you; and it shall be righteousness to you before the LORD your God.

14 "You shall not oppress a hired servant who is poor and needy, whether he is one of your brethren or one of the sojourners who are in your land within your towns; 15 you shall give him his hire on the day he earns it, before the sun goes down (for he is poor, and sets his heart upon it); lest he cry against you to the LORD, and it be sin in you.

17 "You shall not pervert the justice due to the sojourner or to the fatherless, or take a widow's garment in pledge; 18 but you shall remember that you were a slave in Egypt and the LORD your God redeemed you from there; therefore I command you to do this.

19 When thou cuttest down thine harvest in thy field, and hast forgot a sheaf in the field, thou shalt not go again to fetch it: it shall be for the stranger, for the fatherless, and for the widow: that the LORD thy God may bless thee in all the work of thine hands.

19 "When you reap your harvest in your field, and have forgotten a sheaf in the field, you shall not go back to get it; it shall be for the sojourner, the fatherless, and the widow; that the LORD your God may bless you in all the work of your hands."

KEY VERSE: "Justice, and only justice, you shall follow, that you may live and inherit the land which the Lord your God gives you." Deuteronomy 16:20 (RSV).

HOME DAILY BIBLE READINGS

July   27.   M. *Provisions for Justice.* Deuteronomy 16:18–17:1
July   28.   T. *Bases for Determining Justice.* Deuteronomy 17:2–13.
July   29.   W. *Kings Must Be Just.* Deuteronomy 17:14–20.
July   30.   T. *Justice Tempered With Mercy.* Deuteronomy 24:6, 7, 10–22.
July   31.   F. *Praise for God's Justice and Righteousness.* Psalms 89:14–18.
Aug.   1.   S. *Justice and the Messianic King.* Isaiah 9:2–7.
Aug.   2.   S. *The Rule of the Messiah.* Isaiah 11:1–9.

BACKGROUND

When the American wagon trains went West, crossing the mountains and prairies to reach fertile lands upon which to build new communities, they took with them two very precious American institutions: the Church and the school. On these twin cornerstones, they built a new frontier civilization in a fruitful and beautiful land.

The Jews did much the same thing. When they came out of Egypt, they brought with them two institutions upon which they were to build a new life in the new land: the tabernacle in which to worship and the courts of law in which to disperse justice. Houses for worship and houses for justice: both were primarily important to the Jew in the hazardous days when they were putting down their first roots in their new country. The tabernacle was a first necessity; the people had to be constantly reminded that their God was in their midst, and that their basic Commandments had come from His hand. But often one or another of the Commandments or of their additional laws worked out in the wilderness were broken or disregarded, and then it was necessary to have courts of justice with which to enforce the laws that had been written. We are dealing with this legal system in our lesson for today.

Notice that in our Scripture portions, the word *law* does not appear even once, while the word *justice* appears frequently. Perhaps this was because the Jews recognized a difference between a court of law and a court of justice. There was quite a difference in their time, and there still is a difference in our time.

NOTES ON THE PRINTED TEXT

I. "You shall appoint judges and officers in your towns . . . ." Deuteronomy 16:18 (RSV). The King James Version renders this, "Judges and officers shalt thou make thee in all thy *gates.*" Both renditions are correct. The judges of the people, for a long time, held court at or near the city gates, especially in the trying of civil cases, and it is civil cases with which we are concerned today. Just how these judges and court officials were appointed is not clear, but it is generally believed that the appointments were by popular consent. Quite often they were local leaders or elders. The first (and only) requirement, at this point in their history, was that the judges "shall judge the people with *just* judgment." In our day, people are complaining that there seems to be one law for the rich in our courts, and another for the poor, and there is sad truth in that accusation. The Israelites were careful to make that impossible; they demanded that the judges be no respecter of persons. They must administer justice *impartially*. They would not tolerate any judge who took bribes, for that would make them blind to justice. They were appointed to give justice where justice was rightly to be given, and not to manipulate the law in anyone's interest.

This is an ideal that does great credit to the Jewish people; they insisted upon the basic principle that all people are equal before the law. They passed that principle down to *us*. Have we accepted it, and do we practice it, we who too often put judges on their benches by way of political appointment or fraudulent elections? Are our courts as clean as theirs?

II. *When thou dost lend thy brother any thing, thou shalt not go into his house to fetch his pledge.* Deuteronomy 24:10. Now we come to the heart of the matter: the Jews established their courts not to help rich men become richer *but to protect the poor.* Suppose a poor man borrowed a sum of money from another, richer man, and signed a pledge to repay it at a certain time. And suppose that this debtor found himself still too poor to pay off the debt when it came due. What should the man who loaned the money do? One thing he was forbidden to do: he could not enter the home of the borrower and take whatever he had for security. He must stand outside the house, and let the man in debt come out to meet him. Suppose, further, that the only "security" the poor man had was the clothes on his back. If that was all he had, the lender might take it—but he had to return those clothes before sundown of the same day, in order that the poor borrower might be protected from the cold. In our day, we have laws which are intended to deny any man the right to take from another his means of subsistence, but it does not always work; many a man is thrown into bankruptcy and poverty in spite of those laws! The Jews had a better ethic than ours in all this.

Take another situation. Suppose a certain man has the means to hire a servant, or a number of servants. Those servants, the legal code of the Jews said, should be protected against abuse or oppression. They must never have payment of their wages postponed or delayed; each hired servant must be paid *every day*, for if and when those servants were poor (as many of them were), they lived from day to day, from "hand to mouth." Prosperous landowners sometimes failed to understand that the poor lived hand to mouth, and often paid them something less than a fair, living wage; but the Deuteronomists understood it, and put laws against it in their Book. Justice for the poor! When Jesus came, centuries later, He paid less attention to the well-to-do and concentrated on the poor; in doing that, He was following Jewish law.

III. Thou shalt not pervert the judgment of the stranger, nor of the fatherless; nor take a widow's raiment to pledge. Deuteronomy 24:17. The Revised Standard Version rendition of this verse is clearer than that of the King James Version: "You shall not pervert the justice due to the sojourner . . . ." That was not an easy law for the Jews in Canaan to obey, for they had learned to be suspicious and even fearful of strangers in their midst; they feared strange faces, for it was possible that the stranger might be a Canaanite spy or enemy. But the Deuteronomist took a long step forward when he demanded justice for the stranger; he should at least be given a chance to prove that he was a friend and not an enemy. Even when he was brought into a court of law, he should be regarded as a man with rights equal to those of the Jews. Again, we see that God is no respecter of persons or race or national rivalry. All men are equal in the sight of the law—and in the sight of God. Be kind to the sojourner and do justly with him.

And be kind and just with the fatherless, the orphans, the widows, and the bondsmen. Remember, you Israelites, that *you* were once bondsmen in Egypt, and remember that God delivered you from that bondage! Do unto others (slave or free) as you would that they do unto you. If you reap a rich harvest in your fields, leave a sheaf of your harvest in a corner, so that a stranger or an orphan or a widow may pick it up. (Remember the beautiful story of Ruth?) And never, *never*, take a widow's raiment in payment of a debt.

These were ancient laws; this was ancient justice, ordained of God. And it is both Hebrew and Christian morality, based upon faith in a just and loving God. No Christian can cross it off as something primatively Jewish, for the Christian has a Jesus who not only said that the poor would be always with us, but that it would be our Christian duty to do in His name whatever we could do to relieve their poverty and lift them up. This Jesus did not have a single well-to-do man among His disciples; they were all relatively poor men. He respected the rich but He loved the poor; it was He who said, "When thou makest a feast, call the poor, the maimed, the lame, the blind: And thou shalt be blessed . . . thou shall be recompensed at the resurrection of the just." (Luke 14:13, 14).

The just! Justice!

SUGGESTIONS TO TEACHERS

"Justice," wrote Prime Minister Benjamin Disraeli, "is truth in action." Justice is fundamental to biblical faith. To this day, Arab-speaking Christians in the Middle East repeat the ancient maxim, "One hour of justice is worth a hundred of prayer."

Your lesson this Sunday examines justice. You will be studying portions of the legal code in Deuteronomy, but you should not look at these laws as curious relics from ancient times. You must assist your class in understanding the passionate concern for justice which God has. You must also help your class members to carry that understanding into practice in their lives today.

Remembering how God desires justice, you may organize the background Scripture in Deuteronomy around the following points:

1. *THE WORSHIP CONNECTION.* Take careful note of the tie between worship and justice. Worship—true worship—leads to living justly. And justice cannot flourish without a core-group of people faithfully worshiping God. Deuteronomy emphasizes that there can be no compromise with idolotry, and demands that God's people not cheat God. Here is the root for justice: honesty toward God. Our practice of justice stems directly from our desire to deal honestly with God. Indicate to your class that we Christians carry a heavy responsibility. Without us keeping alive the worship connection, the practice of justice dwindles. Do some soul-searching about worship. Is it mobilizing us to work actively for justice in our communities today?

2. *THE RESPONSIBLE COMMUNITY.* Examine the verses in the Scripture passages in the lesson calling upon each person to have a sense of responsibility to others in the community. Although the penalties may appear harsh at times, remember that the Bible insists that no one may take the law into his own hand, and, further, no one is above the law. Also let your class members digest the way Deuteronomy mandates a careful process of decision-making in order to make sure justice is done. In an age in which "Don't get involved" is the rule for many, suggest to your class that God's people act justly by being responsible to each other. Discuss the level of involvement in the community which your church has, and the level of each class member.

3. *THE RELIGIOUS COMMONWEALTH.* Deuteronomy flatly declares that the same law applies to king and commoner alike. No double standard anywhere! Even the king must have the Book beside him, and must revere God and obey Him. Remind your class that every leader is accountable to God. Justice is everyone's task. Furthermore, those in power have a particular duty to carry out justice because leaders are the pace-setters and examples for the rest of the community. Point out to your class that as members of the Christian church, each member is a leader or pace-setter or example to others. As goes the church people in the practice of justice, so goes the rest of society!

THE HUMANITARIAN CONCERN. Look at the nitty-gritty provisions for people who may stand in special need of justice such as the orphans, the widows, the homeless, the poor, the young. Have your class tally some of the rules to ensure justice for these, such as returning before nightfall the cloak which a poor man has put up as security, or leaving the edge of the field unharvested for the needy to gather. Justice means taking positive, active steps to make sure that food and warmth will be provided to every person. Justice, your class must grasp, is love applied to the entire community. Discuss what members in your community are being neglected. What concrete efforts is your church taking to meet their needs?

TOPIC FOR ADULTS
GOD DESIRES JUSTICE

Earned the Title. Samuel Jones, onetime Mayor of Toledo, Ohio, was known as Sam "Golden Rule" Jones. Once, Jones had to preside on the police court bench. One of the cases brought before him was a man who had stolen food for his family because he was broke and couldn't get a job. "Golden Rule" Jones fined the man ten dollars because he was guilty, and because Jones believed in upholding the majesty of the law.

Immediately afterward, Jones handed the bailiff the big sombrero he usually wore and ordered him to pass it among the people in the court-room, fining each of them fifty cents for living in a city where a man had to steal in order to feed his children. The hat came back full. Jones emptied it on the bench, handed it all over to the defendant and remitted his fine.

"Golden Rule" Jones combined justice and mercy, fulfilling what God desires of each of us.

Getting on With Life's Real Purposes." What do we mean by the *security* of the nation? How do we build a safer world for our children—with more and more weapons or with more ideas and imagination?

"A society can reach a point at which additional military expenditure no longer provides additional security. To the extent that such military expenditure severely reduces the resources available for other essential investment and social services, 'it can erode security rather than enhance it.

" 'Global defense expenditures have grown so large that it is difficult to grasp their full dimensions; the nations of the world are now spending over $400 billion a year on military defense. An estimated 36 million men are now under arms in regular and paramilitary forces, with another 25 million in reserves, and another 30 million civilians in military-related occupations.'

"Even public expenditures on weapons research and development world-wide, now approach $30 billion a year—more than is spent on research for the production of fuel, health, education, and food combined.

"Meanwhile, more than a billion humans in the developing countries are living in misery and degradation, and this, he (Robert McNamara) insisted, is not only a moral indictment of the rich countries, but also a missed economic opportunity, since even now the United States exports more to the developing countries than it does to Western Europe, Eastern Europe, China, and the Soviet Union combined.

"Our definition of security is out of date. Unless there is a different allocation of resources in the industrial nations from military development to human development in the poorest nations, we shall not have a peaceful world . . . . We cannot build a secure world upon a foundation of human misery.

"What have we gained by this preoccupation and increasing expenditure on military arms?

"Greater security? No. We are out of date. The concept of security itself has become dangerously oversimplified.

"It is imperative that we understand this issue clearly . . . . The point is not that a nation's security is relatively less important than other considerations. Security is fundamental. The point is simply that excessive military spending can reduce security rather than strengthen it. At these exaggerated levels (it provides) only greater risk, greater danger and greater delay in getting on with life's real purposes . . . ." Reprinted from an address by Robert S. McNamara, President of the World Bank, entitled "Development and the Arms Race," given at the University of Chicago, May 22, 1979. Quoted in the *New York Times*, Friday, May 25, 1979. c 1979 by The New York Times Company. Reprinted by permission.

Pointed Reminder. In Jewish synagogues throughout the world, regardless of tradition, worshipers regularly are reminded that God desires justice. When they come to the end of each book in the Torah, and when they reach the conclusion of each year's prescribed reading, they repeat the words in Hebrew, *"Hazak, Hazak, Vinithazak."* The words mean: "Be strong, be strong, and strengthen one another."

"Strengthen one another" is a way of passing around justice to others. It means feeding the hungry, helping the oppressed, and laboring for the helpless.

Try this kind of phrase at the close of Scripture reading instead of some of the trite and meaningless flourishes which are sometimes inserted during public worship.

Questions for Pupils on the Next Lesson. 1. How may you learn new truths about God? 2. Why must you maintain a sense of identity with the covenant community in its historical context? 3. Why are we as Christians throughout the world interdependent in our covenant relationship with God? 4. How can your class help your fellow church members understand better that each is covenanted with the rest?

TOPIC FOR YOUTH
DO JUSTICE

Everybody's Business. Dr. Theodore Cline reports an episode which happened to him on a visit to the Middle East recently. Walking down the street, he noticed sudden bright flashes and loud sizzling sounds coming from the side of a building. At first, Cline thought the flashes were caused by strobe lights or flash bulbs, or the noise and light were from a welding outfit somewhere nearby. When he strolled around the corner of the building, he discovered that a high tension wire was brushing the side of the structure. Sparks leaped and acrid smoke rose and a loud crackle occurred each time the wind blew the offending wire against the building. Ted Cline looked closer, and saw that the building was made of wood.

Rushing around to the front, he tried to enter, but found the doors locked. He hurried next door to a shop. With frantic sign language, he tried to convey the urgency of the situation to a workman inside. He finally got the workman to get his supervisor, who walked next door with Cline. This man casually looked at the dangerous wire, then turned to Cline and shrugged, "It's not my building; none of my business," he said, and walked back to his shop.

Later, almost as judgment on the lack of a sense of responsibility, the fire which followed destroyed both buildings.

Justice is responsibility for others. When we fail to live justly, we hurt our neighbor and ultimately ourselves.

Thought to Ponder. Grafitti seen on wall in Des Moines:
IT WILL BE A GREAT DAY
WHEN
OUR SCHOOLS
GET ALL THE MONEY
THEY NEED
AND THE AIR FORCE
HAS TO HOLD
A BAKE SALE
TO BUY A
BOMBER

Call for Justice Through Census Report. The latest report (U. S. Census Bureau's annual reckoning of how many Americans are "poor") issued recently was a shocker: it counted 12.3 percent of the total population—precisely 25.9 million Americans—as living at or below the poverty line, the highest percentage of poor since 1970. Worse still, there were 2.5 million more poor than in 1974 . . . .

These statistics are a call for justice. What would God have you and the Church do about these conditions?

Sentence Sermon to Remember: One hour of justice is worth a hundred of prayer.—Arab Proverb.

Questions for Pupils on the Next Lesson. 1. Do you identify yourself as part of a convenanted fellowship? Why or why not? 2. What exactly does it mean to be covenanted with others in the Church? 3. What steps are you taking to discover more about God? 4. Why does the Church here insist that it is connected with the Church in other parts of the world, including those countries which may be unfriendly to our nation?

LESSON X—AUGUST 9

THE BASIS OF COVENANT RENEWAL

Background Scripture: Deuteronomy 29:1–15
Devotional Reading: 2 Samuel 7:18–22

KING JAMES VERSION

DEUTERONOMY 29 2 And Moses called unto all Israel, and said unto them, Ye have seen all that the LORD did before your eyes in the land of Egypt unto Pharaoh, and unto all his servants, and unto all his land;

3 The great temptations which thine eyes have seen, the signs, and those great miracles:

4 Yet the LORD hath not given you a heart to perceive, and eyes to see, and ears to hear, unto this day.

5 And I have led you forty years in the wilderness: your clothes are not waxen old upon you, and thy shoe is not waxen old upon thy foot.

6 Ye have not eaten bread, neither have ye drunk wine or strong drink: that ye might know that I *am* the LORD your God.

7 And when ye came unto this place, Sihon the king of Heshbon, and Og the king of Bashan, came out against us unto battle, and we smote them:

8 And we took their land, and gave it for an inheritance unto the Reubenites, and to the Gadites, and to the half tribe of Manasseh.

9 Keep therefore the words of this covenant and do them, that ye may prosper in all that ye do.

10 Ye stand this day all of you before the LORD your God; your captains of your tribes, your elders, and your officers, *with* all the men of Israel,

11 Your little ones, your wives, and thy stranger that *is* in thy camp, from the hewer of thy wood unto the drawer of thy water:

12 That thou shouldest enter into covenant with the LORD thy God, and into his oath, which the LORD thy God maketh with thee this day:

13 That he may establish thee to day for a people unto himself, and *that* he may be unto thee a God, as he hath said unto thee, and as he hath sworn unto thy fathers, to Abraham, to Isaac, and to Jacob.

REVISED STANDARD VERSION

DEUTERONOMY 29 2 And Moses summoned all Israel and said to them: "You have seen all that the LORD did before your eyes in the land of Egypt, to Pharaoh and to all his servants and to all his land, 3 the great trials which your eyes saw, the signs, and those great wonders; 4 but to this day the LORD has not given you a mind to understand, or eyes to see, or ears to hear. 5 I have led you forty years in the wilderness; your clothes have not worn out upon you, and your sandals have not worn off your feet; 6 you have not eaten bread, and you have not drunk wine or strong drink; that you may know that I am the LORD your God. 7 And when you came to this place, Sihon the king of Heshbon and Og the king of Bashan came out against us to battle, but we defeated them; 8 we took their land, and gave it for an inheritance to the Reubenites, the Gadites, and the half-tribe of the Manassites. 9 Therefore be careful to do the words of this covenant, that you may prosper in all that you do.

10 "You stand this day all of you before the LORD your God; the heads of your tribes, your elders, and your officers, all the men of Israel, 11. your little ones, your wives, and the sojourner who is in your camp, both he who hews your wood and he who draws your water, 12 that you may enter into the sworn covenant of the LORD your God, which the LORD your God makes with you this day; 13 that he may establish you this day as his people, and that he may be your God, as he promised you, and as he swore to your fathers, to Abraham, to Isaac, and to Jacob. 14 Nor is it with you only that I make this sworn covenant, 15 but with him who is not here with us this day as

14 Neither with you only do I make this covenant and this oath;

15 But with *him* that standeth here with us this day before the LORD our God, and also with *him* that *is* not here with us this day:

well as with him who stands here with us this day before the LORD our God."

KEY VERSE: *"The eternal God is your dwelling place, and underneath are the everlasting arms. . . ."* Deuteronomy 33:27 (RSV).

HOME DAILY BIBLE READINGS

Aug. 3. M. *The Covenant with Abraham.* Genesis 17:1-8.
Aug. 4. T. *Covenants and Holiness.* Exodus 19:1-6.
Aug. 5. W. *Conditions of Covenants.* Exodus 19:7-14.
Aug. 6. T. *The Ten Commandments.* Exodus 20:1-8, 12-17.
Aug. 7. F. *The Covenant at Shechem.* Joshua 24:1-3, 14, 15.
Aug. 8. S. *The Covenant at Moab.* Deuteronomy 29:1-15.
Aug. 9. S. *The New Covenant.* Jeremiah 31:31-37.

BACKGROUND

Israel stands poised on the Plains of Moab, down along the Jordan and the Dead Sea; this is their last stopping-place before they take the final plunge into Canaan. Literally, we are told in Deuteronomy 29:2, *all* Israel was there. It was a huge mass meeting which included children, men, and women, sojourners, servants, and even unborn Israel (*see* verses 14, 15). Before them, making his third and last oration, stands Moses, the old leader making his last great public speech before he climbs Moabite Mount Nebo to die. He is not to enter the Promised Land with his people, but in his address this day in Moab he hopes to give them the strength and faith they will need if they are to survive in their new home.

Moses talked to them about covenants—old and new. He talked to inspire the grown men of Israel, and the children of Israel, and for children not yet born! And what he had to say was as important, historically speaking, as the Magna Charta or the Mayflower Compact.

NOTES ON THE PRINTED TEXT

I. . . . Ye have seen all that the Lord did before your eyes. . . . Deuteronomy 29:2. The teacher will do well to read the Home Daily Bible Readings for this lesson; he will find, there, that there was more than one covenant made between God and Israel, from Abraham to Moses in Moab. But in reading them, he will also become aware that the most important of these covenants was the one made with Moses at Horeb (Sinai).

Moses was not asking his people to make a new covenant at Moab; it was an eloquent plea for them to *renew* the old Sinai covenant and to be faithful to its obligations in a new (and dangerous) situation.

Two generations stood listening to the old hero who had brought them to this place: one generation had been with him when they left Egypt; the other generation was made up of the children of this first one, a "green," untried generation about to "take over" from their fathers. This second generation had to know "what it was all about," if they were to stay alive in a land surrounded by enemies.

Moses starts out by giving his people a history lesson; he is to be compared with a teacher instructing a class of children in American history. In order to know why they are as they are—Americans—they have to know about the forces that played upon them—about the ideals and contributions of their American forefathers. In order that the Israelites understand what they were and what they had to do, they had to know what *their* forefathers had done and thought. The history lesson, here, starts with the teacher (Moses) reminding them that they had been brought safely to the rim of the Promised Land by a God of grace and goodness.

Back in Egypt they had been nothing more than an enormous labor battalion; God wrought a miracle with them there, starting them on a long wilderness march which would have been a death march without His help. For forty long years God had sustained them, giving them food (manna) to eat, clothes to wear and shoes to wear when their old clothes and shoes wore out; whatever they needed in that wilderness, they got *from God*; they were completely dependent upon Him, and His care in providing for them should have taught them humility and obedience. But, alas, they were often proud of their own strength rather than thankful for His strength!

When they had been forced to fight wars in the wilderness, they won not so much by way of their own power and courage, but with the help of God; when Sihon the king of Heshbon and Og the king of Bashan stood in their way and refused to let them pass, the Lord had said to Moses, "Fear not, for I have delivered (them) into thy land" (Numbers 21). They passed through and possessed the land, as God had promised. Not once did God desert them; not once did God break His promises made on Sinai. Remember that, Israel: you would all have perished without the sustaining hand of your God.

We Americans, as heirs of the Pilgrim fathers and of a Washington on his knees at Valley Forge, should never forget that it was their faith in God that held them up and held them fast to their Christian convictions when disaster threatened them—and every other American in the Colonies. He who will not see the hand of God in history is in danger of losing his soul.

II. *Your little ones, your wives, and thy stranger. . . and also with him that is not here with us this day.* Deuteronomy 29:11, 15. Those who stood and listened to Moses that day—the *present* generation— were asked to renew their Sinaitic vows, to renew that contract with God, and to obey Him and His commandments in the unforseeable future. Most of them were grown men and women—but there were also children standing with them, and Moses is talking to them, of *their* future. These children, he said, share the privileges and responsibilities of their fathers by way of circumcision. He goes even further: he speaks of, if not *to*, children yet to be born in Israel, and he cries out that they, too, will have an obligation to keep the covenants made with Abraham, Jacob, and Isaac—to keep their father's promise to obey their God.

The fathers of Israel who had heard the Law at Sinai were dead when

Moses delivered this oration; they were entitled to respect, but Moses reminds his listeners that too often, thanks to their dullness of mind and heart, they did not fully understand what their part was to be in the working out of their Sinai Covenant. God had "not yet" given either them or their immediate children "a heart to perceive, and eyes to see, and ears to hear" (verse 4). Even those who stood before him had failed to understand their responsibilities to the God who had brought them safely through to this moment. The hope for the future lay in the *children*, and their children's children. The important thing here is that God made His covenant *not with individiuals but with the nation past, present, and future*. Included in that Covenant were men, women, children, masters and servants and strangers within the Israelitish camp.

To us, that may seem to be loading future generations with the burdens and mistakes of their fathers, with responsibilities that were hardly theirs. That was not the point Moses was stressing. He was only reminding them of the old Hebrew concept of tribal solidarity, that individuals in the tribes had to bear the consequences of the acts of other members of the tribe. The Apostle Paul put this concept into words when he said that "For none of us liveth to (by) himself, and no man dieth to himself" (Romans 14·7). Or, as one lesser than Paul said, "No man is an island"—a human island needing no help from others, or with no obligations to anyone else.

No man is born to do as he pleases, whatever the consequences on himself or his neighbors. "Many today feel that their sins will hurt no one but themselves, so why not indulge in one's private appetites and lusts? Both sins and acts of righteousness have social consequences: in the family, in the world where we do our work, and on generations that follow us."—Edward P. Blair.

The present owes much to the past; the children of tomorrow owe life itself to their fathers. God cannot do much in our world unless the children understand that, and contribute what they can to the common good, generation after generation after generation. When we are gone our children *must* pick up the torch.

Question: are we preparing our children for that?

SUGGESTIONS TO TEACHERS

Two years ago, the National Conference of Catholic Bishops commissioned George Gallup Associates to conduct a poll of the unchurched. The survey showed that 41% of Americans over the age of eighteen are functionally unchurched. These 61 million people, however, share just about the same beliefs as those in churches. The 41% who are unchurched, according to the poll, claim that they have faith in God and say that Jesus is God's Son. They apparently, however, just will not accept the Church as the Body of Christ.

Some in your class and some in your congregation feel the same way. Privately, they ask, "Why do I have to be part of the Church? Why can't I believe in Christ in my own way without putting up with the aggravations and sacrifices of being part of the institutional church?"

If you are honest with yourself, you undoubtedly have said something like this to yourself from time to time—especially after a particularly trying Sunday class session!

Your lesson for today should help you and everyone in your class to rethink the meaning of church membership. The title of this lesson is "Covenant Renewal." Here is the clue for both the lesson today and for your tie to the Church always. You are covenanted. You are covenanted with God and with others in Christ's family. From time to time, however, you need to renew your covenants.

The background Scripture offers rich resources in understanding the meaning of covenant renewal. Keep firmly grounded in the Deuteronomy passage, but keep your eyes on your class members and their problems with the Church. Design the lesson to assist them in renewing their commitments.

1. *RECALLING THE PAST.* God's people are able to remember. People without memories or amnesiacs are disoriented and usually unable to function satisfactorily. Those unable to recall what God has done are also helpless. You must help everyone in your class to sharpen his or her memory of God's gracious acts in his or her life. Deuteronomy 29 refreshes Israel's corporate memory. Help your people to retell the story of God's goodness, especially through Christ, into their own personal histories.

2. *STANDING IN THE PRESENCE.* "You stand this day all of you before the Lord your God," Deuteronomy 29:10 announces. A renewal of the covenant also means an awareness of God's nearness. You may tell your class that you and they can never forget their covenant together and walk away from each other primarily because God refuses to walk away from us! He is present with us. Therefore, we stand with Him and with each other. He promises to be with us, and we promise to be with Him and to keep our promises with each other—even when we may feel like quitting!

3. *LIVING FOR THE FUTURE.* Christians are a people with a tomorrow. In an era when hope for the future is scarce, covenant renewal means remembering that God empowers us to move boldly into the days to come. Take a few minutes to identify the present causes for despair over the future which your class may suggest. Ask whether any of these are too much for God to handle. Point out that the terms of the new covenant through Christ's Cross and Resurrection mean commitments by God for the future. These imply that you and your class may renew your promises to the world to be faithful for the week to come!

TOPIC FOR ADULTS
THE BASIS OF COVENANT RENEWAL

Dedicated Minority. One "whiff of grapeshot," said Napoleon, "would have nipped the French Revolution in the bud." It is usually a small minority, but a minority that has made up its mind and that knows what it wants, that manages to reach the goal. The Russian Bolsheviks furnished devastating proof of this assertion in October, 1917, when they overcame the hundred times more powerful reaction.

The same was true of the early Church. Earlier, the community of ex-slaves under Moses moved toward the Promised Land. How? They were covenanted, and they renewed that covenant with the Lord and with each other. Bound together, they could overcome regardless of the obstacles.

And so may we, the community of faith, today!

Say "We!" Years ago, in a town in Indiana, the largest church in town bought a pipe organ—the first such instrument in the area. It was an expensive organ, but, like all such organs in those days, had to be hand-pumped. To dedicate and exhibit the new pipe organ, the church decided to import a well-known musician from a nearby university.

On the big day, the virtuoso arrived and seated himself grandly at the console. He snubbed the old fellow in shirtsleeves who manned the pump beside the organ. After his first piece, he stood proudly and made an eloquent bow to the audience. "And now for my next number," the great performer announced pompously, "I shall play Toccata and Fugue in D Minor by Johann Sebastian Bach." He sat down and brought both hands down upon the keyboard. Not a sound issued. The virtuoso looked stunned.

Then came a hoarse whisper from the unseen pumper, "Say 'we,' blast it, say 'we.' "

We are covenanted together. Our harmony comes when we recognize how interdependent we are as members of Christ's covenanted community!

To Be Used. The great Paganini presented his violin to the city of Florence with the condition attached that it never be used.

Some regard the covenant as such a museum piece—merely to be preserved and viewed.

Instead, the covenant is intended to be participated in and renewed by each succeeding generation.

Have you renewed your commitment to the God who covenants with you?

Questions for Pupils on the Next Lesson. 1. What can help prompt us to recognize our need for repentance and forgiveness? 2. What are some opportunities before you and your class to experience a better relationship with God and with one another? 3. Do you understand that repentance includes both confession and a change in attitude and action? 4. Do you ever feel a need for assurance that your sin has not destroyed God's love for you? What do you do when you feel such a need?

TOPIC FOR YOUTH
COMMITED LIVING

No Christ Without the Church. We hear the criticism: "Why do we have to have an institution like the Church? Why not simply pass on Jesus' teachings without the institution of the Church?"

We forget most great human concerns are necessarily maintained and propogated by means of institutions. The home, school, and government are examples.

A monogamous marriage has been found the best institution to give a child affection and security.

You can't be religious without finding some means of *expressing* personal faith within a tradition and community to carry it out.

Reason for Huddling. T. S. Eliot's *The Rock* has a line where someone asks, "Why do you huddle together? Is it because you love each other or because you prey on each other?"

Which is it in your church?

Christ brings you and the others together as persons committed to living with Him and each other in love. Let your huddle reflect that relationship.

The Same Boat. We are bound together as Christ's people. The problems of Christians in one place are also the problems of those elsewhere. Where one hurts, all feel the ache.

When we refuse to remember that we are covenanted together, and become involved in the lives and problems of other believers, we become like the pair of shipwrecked men sitting at one end of a lifeboat. The two sat passively, watching those at the other end of the boat who were bailing frantically to keep the boat from sinking. Turning to his buddy, one of the pair of do-nothings sighed and said, "Thank goodness, that hole is not at our end of the boat."

We are in it together as people committed to Christ and to one another!

Sentence Sermon to Remember: You did something good for God last year? Forget it. What do you plan doing for Him tomorrow?—George F. Collins.

Questions for Pupils on the Next Lesson. 1. Is God always to accept you? 2. How can you show an acceptance for persons who are alienated? 3. How does the experience of forgiving others help a person to understand the meaning of repentance and restoration? 4. Why must genuine repentance include both confession and a change in attitude and action?

LESSON XI—AUGUST 16

REPENTANCE AND RESTORATION

Background Scripture: Deuteronomy 29:16–28; 30:1–10
Devotional Reading: 1 Kings 3:5–14

KING JAMES VERSION	REVISED STANDARD VERSION
DEUTERONOMY 30 1 And it shall come to pass, when all these things are come upon thee, the blessing and the curse, which I have set before thee, and thou shalt call *them* to mind among all the nations, whither the LORD thy God hath driven thee,	DEUTERONOMY 30 1 "And when all these things come upon you, the blessing and the curse, which I have set before you, and you call them to mind among all the nations where the LORD your God has driven you, 2

DEUTERONOMY 30 1 And it shall come to pass, when all these things are come upon thee, the blessing and the curse, which I have set before thee, and thou shalt call *them* to mind among all the nations, whither the LORD thy God hath driven thee,

2 And shalt return unto the LORD thy God, and shalt obey his voice according to all that I command thee this day, thou and thy children, with all thine heart, and with all thy soul;

3 That then the LORD thy God will turn thy captivity, and have compassion upon thee, and will return and gather thee from all the nations, whither the LORD thy God hath scattered thee.

4 If *any* of thine be driven out unto the outmost *parts* of heaven, from thence will the LORD thy God gather thee, and from thence will he fetch thee:

5 And the LORD thy God will bring thee into the land which thy fathers possessed, and thou shalt possess it; and he will do thee good, and multiply thee above thy fathers.

6 And the LORD thy God will circumcise thine heart, and the heart of thy seed, to love the LORD thy God with all thine heart, and with all thy soul, that thou mayest live.

7 And the LORD thy God will put all these curses upon thine enemies, and on them that hate thee, which persecuted thee.

8 And thou shalt return and obey the voice of the LORD, and do all his commandments which I command thee this day.

9 And the LORD thy God will make thee plenteous in every work of thine hand, in the fruit of thy body, and in the fruit of thy cattle, in the fruit of thy land, for good: for the LORD will again rejoice over thee for good, as he rejoiced over thy fathers:

DEUTERONOMY 30 1 "And when all these things come upon you, the blessing and the curse, which I have set before you, and you call them to mind among all the nations where the LORD your God has driven you, 2 and return to the LORD your God, you and your children, and obey his voice in all that I command you this day, with all your heart and with all your soul; 3 then the LORD your God will restore your fortunes, and have compassion upon you, and he will gather you again from all the peoples where the LORD your God has scattered you. 4 If your outcasts are in the uttermost parts of heaven, from there the LORD your God will gather you, and from there he will fetch you; 5 and the LORD your God will bring you into the land which your fathers possessed, that you may possess it; and he will make you more prosperous and numerous than your fathers. 6 And the LORD your God will circumcise your heart and the heart of your offspring, so that you will love the LORD your God with all your heart and with all your soul, that you may live. 7 And the LORD your God will put all these curses upon your foes and enemies who persecuted you. 8 And you shall again obey the voice of the LORD, and keep all his commandments which I command you this day. 9 The LORD your God will make you abundantly prosperous in all the work of your hand, in the fruit of your body, and in the fruit of your cattle, and in the fruit of your ground; for the LORD will again take delight in prospering you, as he took delight in your fathers, 10 if you obey the voice of the LORD your God, to keep his commandments and his statutes which are written in this book of the law, if you turn to the LORD your God with all your heart and with all your soul.

10 If thou shalt hearken unto the voice of the LORD thy God, to keep his commandments and his statutes *which are* written in this book of the law, *and* if thou turn unto the LORD thy God with all thine heart, and with all thy soul.

KEY VERSE: ". . . *obey the voice of the Lord, and keep all his commandments which I command you this day.*" Deuteronomy 30:8 (RSV).

HOME DAILY BIBLE READINGS

Aug. 10. M. *The Results of Breaking Covenants.* Deuteronomy 29:16–28.
Aug. 11. T. *Restoration After Repentance.* Deuteronomy 30:1–10.
Aug. 12. W. *Repentance in Josiah's Time.* 2 Kings 23:1–5.
Aug. 13. T. *"Return to the Lord."* Joel 2:10–14.
Aug. 14. F. *"Pardon My Guilt."* Psalms 25:8–21.
Aug. 15. S. *"Why Will You Die. . . ?"* Ezekiel 33:10–16.
Aug. 16. S. *Welcome to the Prodigal.* Luke 15:11–24.

BACKGROUND

The background of this lesson, based on Deuteronomy 29, is to be found in Deuteronomy 28, which reads like the description of a chamber of horrors. It is a terrifying account of what will happen to Israel if Israel will not "hearken to the voice of the Lord thy God" (28:15). It is filled with curses, destruction, threats of starvation, defeats in battle, plagues that will produce madness, blindness, rotting fields, and dying cattle, and a possible return of the people of Israel to Egypt!

Now, having been shaken up by reading this, turn to your lesson Scripture for today, in Deuteronomy 30, and see how Moses suggests that the Israelites can avoid such a day of pestilence and destruction—and read the Key Verse of the lesson, which sings another, different song.

Again, with this lesson, verse-by-verse comment seems too repetitive, so we confine ourselves to a discussion of the two central themes running through all the verses of our Scripture for the lesson.

NOTES ON THE PRINTED TEXT

Moses knew his people and loved them, but he was wise enough to know their shortcomings, their failings and foibles and imperfections. He had had plenty of that, in the long wilderness trek, and he took pains to caution them against them in his farewell speech. Particularly, he foresaw their tendency to rebelliousness and he feared their scattering among the "foreign" people they would be meeting in Canaan and the ease with which they might fall away from the worship and service of their God and bow down to Canaan's false gods and idols. That fear in Moses is behind the curses of chapter 28.

Loving them as he did, he could not leave them with those curses and drastic predictions foremost in their minds; if that happened, they would not understand that the God of Israel takes no delight in punishment (even the punishment of the wicked), but that His will and desire was that "none should perish, but that all should reach repentence" (2 Peter 3:9). That message runs through the Old Testament as well as through the New Testament. Remember, O Israel, that God's love is everlasting.

But this love on God's part calls for what we call "repentance" on the part of His children. Yes, God had destroyed Sodom and Gomorrah, but that was because Sodom and Gomorrah had not repented. This passage is not prophecy, but a conditional promise that with *true* repentance, God stands ready to offer pardon.

But just what *is* true repentance?

The Hebrew word for *repentance* means literally "to turn"; it involves a change in the inner attitude toward God and a complete change in life-style. Repentance is *not* just saying "I'm sorry," and then sinning all over again; to repent is to alter one's way of looking at life; it is to take God's point of view instead of one's own. "Repentance without amendment," said Lewis W. Dillwyn, "is like continually pumping without mending the leak."

Now there are two kinds of repentance, both of which are illustrated dramatically in two of the disciples of Jesus Christ. First, there was Judas Iscariot, the disciple who betrayed Him. Judas was the only disciple to be appointed to any office among the twelve—and the only one to die outlawed from God. He thought that in suicide he could find forgetfulness, and so he "repented" by hanging himself. This was *not* repentance; it was remorse. The fact remains that while miracles of character transformation were worked in eleven of the disciples, this man of Kerioth remained unchanged. He found no forgetfulness in self-inflicted death; he might have found mercy at the cross. It was there, waiting.

Then there was Peter, who thrice denied his Lord. In the fell clutch of circumstance he was weak; in the grip of a great conviction he cried, "Thou art the Christ." And beyond that, with his heart at last wide open to his Christ, he became the most valuable of the twelve to Christ. Peter, in true repentance, died like his Master, on a Roman cross. Peter was "turned around" in repentance, from an erratic, impulsive, humble fisherman in Galilee to one rooted deep in the Spirit, and his spirit was the Rock on which Christ built His Church. Peter knew remorse, too, but he laid that remorse at the feet of his Christ, and the remorse became power. Quite a difference there was in the "repentance" of these two.

There is a word in verse six at which we should look twice: the word is *circumcise*. If Israel will turn to God and obey His voice, then the Lord "will circumcise thine heart." The circumcised heart is the heart open to God's commands. *The Living Bible* makes this read: "He will *cleanse* your hearts and the hearts of your children and of your children's children so that you will love the Lord your God with all your hearts and souls, and Israel shall come alive again!"

Every now and then, our hearts need a cleansing—a cleansing that follows repentance. Every now and then every nation on the face of our modern world needs a cleansing, too, just as the nation of Israel needed it. But first, the nations need to *repent*—and there are no signs of repentance yet in our skies! As these words are being written, our country is bitterly protesting the actions of a Mexican government in failing to give us the oil we so desperately need. We are furious about that—but we forget that for long, long years we have treated the Mexicans as unimportant inferiors hardly worthy of our attention; now the shoe is on the other foot, and we wonder why, and we see no need of repenting our mistreatment of them. And there were those days when we refused to allow Japanese and Chinese to migrate to the United States; we thought of them only as a "market"—and that helped bring on a war that cost us dearly. But few of us will admit that our anti-immigration laws of that period had anything to do with our war with the Japanese or the rise of Communism in China. Would a little repentance help us, now? (Ask any Christian missionary to the Far East about that!)

God will work out His plan with the nations, whatever they do in disregard of His will and commands. He wilt work it out with every individual, no matter how far the individual may stray from Him. This is the heat of the message of Moses: *God never gives up.* His gate is never closed to any man or people. His case with any man is never marked "Case Closed." The door is forever open to the truly repentant.

The poet Francis Thompson once wrote a haunting poem called "The Hound of Heaven," in which he pictured a man running from God; the first lines in the poem are these:

> I fled Him, down the nights and down the days;
> I fled Him down the arches of the years. . . .

He was relentlessly followed by this mythical hound from heaven. Sometimes we think of God Himself as such a hound—tirelessly pursuing—pursuing *who?* The wicked, yes—but doesn't this God of ours pursue the good as well as the wicked, to win them by His love? If God were only "hounding" us and threatening us with punishment, He would *not* be the God of Moses or of Jesus or of any thinking Christian. God seeks us in *love* with the keys to the Kingdom held out to us in His hand.

God "pursued" Israel for centuries of victory and defeat to keep alive in them the hope of return to their homeland and to the faith of their fathers. Today we are witnessing the re-establishment of the Jews in their ancient home, and, while many of them are less than faithful to the old faith, the torch still burns and the spiritual flame of trust and faith has brought scattered Jewry home again for all the world to see. God never closed the door against them, or against that!

It works that way in individuals, too. The Father never gives up on the Prodigal Son. When the prodigal comes to realize that he has "sinned against heaven" (Luke 15:21) and that he is unworthy of forgiveness, he finds the father waiting for him at the gate of home, with open arms, forgiveness, and restoration. It will always be so, so long as there is God the loving Father.

SUGGESTIONS TO TEACHERS

Did you ever play "Truth or Consequences"? The children's game is a laugh-filled pastime in which harmless "punishments" are meted out to those who refuse to divulge the right answer.

God's kind of "Truth or Consequences" is not a childish diversion. In

Scripture, God makes it plain that He confronts His people with truth about Himself. He lets it be known that failure to comply with His truth brings consequences. However, His truth also includes mercy. The consequences of His grace mean restoration for the repentant.

Your lesson today comes to grips with the mighty theme of repentance and restoration. You will be touching a chord deep within each person as you work with the Scripture presentation discussion.

1. *LIABILITIES OF LISTENING.* According to Deuteronomy 29:19, the person hearing God's commands is constantly in danger of thinking that these do not apply in his case, and saying to himself, "I shall be safe, though I walk in the stubbornness of my heart." There are dangers in hearing God's Word! A hearer may play a "con game" with himself—and with God! Smoke out some of the deceits, excuses, and evasions which people pull to avoid taking God's commands seriously in their own personal lives. What are some occasions in the experience of your class members when they have tried to tune out God's orders in their living? Discuss how members of Christ's community, including your class, can help each other to listen more attentively to God's Word to them through Scripture.

2. *LESSONS OF LETHARGY.* Don't shrink from the rougher sections of today's scriptural passages, such as Deuteronomy 29:22–28. Apathy toward God and His commands brings consequences which are unpleasant. The biblical writers, in fact, insist that disobedience means destruction! Your class should be asked to consider some of the types of destruction which results from lethargy toward the Lord. Deuteronomy states that destruction may take such forms as natural destruction, political, cultural, and personal-family. How do those in your class react to this assertion?

3. *LAWS FOR LIVING.* Examine Deuteronomy 30:1 and the following verses. Let your class reflect on the choices placed before God's community each week. Note that God does not treat His people like pawns on the chessboard. He permits them to choose whether or not to live faithfully as covenanted people. Life is a matter of selecting "the blessing" or "the curse" which God sets before His people. Remember that God is not trying to set up His people for dire punishment. He is reminding His people (and this means *us*) that we are covenanted with Him! And He is pleading with us His people to choose to keep that covenant by living by His commands.

4. *LAND FOR LOYALTY.* God also offers unconditional pardon. He promises new beginnings. "God will gather you" (Deuteronomy 30:4). There is restoration for those who repent and return to Him. How is your church offering new beginnings to persons who have given up on life, on God, on themselves? Ask your class to relate personal experiences of times when God has opened doors of new possibilities.

TOPIC FOR ADULTS
REPENTANCE AND RESTORATION

Amazing Grace Story. John Newton was born in London, July 24, 1725. His father was a ship's captain and plied the Mediterranean ports. John never saw his father until he was seven; his mother was his constant companion. She was a devout member of the Church of England and saw to it that John attended church, prayed, and read the Bible. When she died there was no place for him to go except his father's ship and from the tender age of eight he lived amidst the cursing, drinking, and lewd talk of his father's ships.

At the age of seventeen he was seized for service on a British man-o-war but escaped and signed up on a ship in the slave trade. He soon was known as the "best blasphemer" on all British boats. He degenerated into a drunkard, murderer, and immoral sailor. In Africa, he became so drunk that he missed his boat and for a number of years was the slave of an African woman who, glorying in her power over him, made him depend for his food on the crusts that she tossed under her table.

A Portuguese slave ship rescued him and hired him in the slave trade to Charleston, South Carolina. Off Newfoundland, in 1748, a violent storm hit the ship and all hands gave it up for lost. Now twenty-three years of age, he remembered a sentence from his mother's prayers, "Lord, have mercy upon us." He cried out to God for help and, as he puts it, "The Lord came from on high and delivered me out of deep waters." When the battered ship did arrive in Ireland, he did not forget the mercy of God but quit the sea and prepared himself for ministry in the Church of England.

He served for ten years as rector of St. Mary's Woolnuth. In his congregation was Wilberforce and it is no accident that he accepted the leadership of the forces that abolished slavery in the British Empire.

Newton also wrote such hymns as "Amazing Grace," "How Sweet the Name of Jesus Sounds," and "Glorious Things of Thee Are Spoken."

Near the end of his life (1807) he met William Jay on the streets of London. As they exchanged Christian greetings, he said to his friend, "My memory is nearly gone, but I remember two things: I am a great sinner and Jesus Christ is a great Saviour."

The memorial stone erected in his honor reads:

JOHN NEWTON
clerk,
Once an infidel and Libertine,
A Servant of Slaves
in Africa, was
by the Mercy of our
Lord and Saviour
Jesus Christ,
Preserved, Restored, Pardoned,
And appointed to
Preach the Faith
he had so long
laboured to destroy.

Way to Lift the World. "Pride and humility are the poles of life," writes Soren Kierkegaard. "He who holds these two mighty forces in balance will have found what Archimedes sought in vain—a point from which he could lift the whole world, and which therefore must lie outside the world, outside the limitations of Time and Space."

Kierkegaard as a Christian knew that repentance leads to restoration of relationships with God and others, and is the only way to maintain a balance between the twin poles of pride and humility. Do you?

Prerequisite for Membership. During the Civil War, the Colonel of a Wisconsin regiment heard from his chaplain that there had been ten conversions in a rival regiment. The Colonel was incensed. "Do you really so say?" he inquired of the chaplain. The chaplain insisted it was true. Turning to the sergeant standing nearby, the Colonel barked, "Sergeant Jones! Detail fifteen of my regiment for immediate baptism!"

Although we smile, our churches sometimes show the same obsession with statistics and the same sense of competition. Annual reports of most congregations and denominations emphasize the "numbers game," or as one weary pastor puts it, "bodies and bucks—that's what seems to count the most."

It is still repentance and restoration which pleases God and which opens the door for meaningful membership within the covenanted community.

Questions for Pupils on the Next Lesson. 1. Are you sometimes tempted to interpret God's Word primarily in "spiritual" terms rather than in political, social, and economic terms? 2. What are the sources for your values? Do you ever examine these? 3. Where do you turn for help in making choices that will bear positive consequences for others? 4. Do you have the problem with the Bible in finding that you don't want to do what God asks of you rather than finding that it's too difficult to understand? 5. Does your congregation provide support for you and others in making and living out right choices?

TOPIC FOR YOUTH
GOD'S COMPASSIONATE LOVE

Power of God's Compassion. Northern Ireland has been torn by violence between warring tribal camps of Protestants and Catholics. One of the few signs of light on the horizon has been the Peace Group of Christians of all backgrounds in Northern Ireland who have been aware of God's compassionate love toward them and others.

Led by two women, Betty Williams and Mairead Corrigan, the group's purpose is to effect a peaceful solution to the conflict in that country by traveling from town to town, helping people get together to talk about ways of reconciling their political and economic differences.

Over the past year and a half, the idea has been gaining momentum all over Ireland. At a rally held on December 5, 1976, on the banks of the river Boyne (site of an historic battle that divided northern and southern Ireland), 15,000 people from both sides of the conflict joined together to pray and to hear speakers give utterance to their yearnings for peace.

The "Peace Group," as it's called, is trying to remain above the political squabbles among factions that have sprung up within the country. The unswerving focus is upon the capability of families, churches, small businesses, and farmers to do the job that political methods have failed to do.

How Much? An extremely wealthy but miserly man died. Although he was a financial tycoon, he was a spiritual pauper. He never learned the meaning of God's compassion, but harshly trampled on others. He measured life by the Dow Jones, and thought security was in stock certificates.

Following the funeral, someone asked, "How much did he leave?" The other man answered wisely, "He left it all."

Enough said.

Putting It Off. A group of wags have founded what they call the Procrastinators' Club of America, Inc. The doctrine of the group is: Never do today what you can do tomorrow," and its slogan, "Procrastinate Now!" Its 2,000 dues-paying members try to postpone payments realizing that paying dues on time incurs a 5 percent penalty. Prospective members are contacted by a form arriving in an envelope marked "Open later." At this time, the 1973 membership drive is still open. One of PCA's most successful recent projects was its demonstration against the War of 1812. The club also tries to name an annual Proscrastinator of the Year, but so far has not got around to announcing any winner. It has honored several people, including the Postmaster General.

Most of us qualify as charter members on the basis of our response to God's compassionate love. We are always getting ready to do something, but so rarely seem to follow through.

Repentance and restoration are key components to growing as members of the covenanted community. Stop procrastinating and start obeying!

Sentence Sermon to Remember: The best repentance is to get up and act for righteousness, and forget that you ever had relations with sin.— William James.

Questions for Pupils on the Next Lesson. 1. Does every choice have its consequences? 2. Did God create the world in such a way that life-affirming choices are always possible? 3. Is everyone—including you— responsible for making her/his own choices? 4. Where do you turn for help when you need advice in making choices that will bear positive consequences?

LESSON XII—AUGUST 23

CHOICE AND ITS CONSEQUENCES

Background Scripture: Deuteronomy 30:11–20
Devotional Reading: Nehemiah 9:26–31

KING JAMES VERSION

DEUTERONOMY 30   11 For this commandment which I command thee this day, it *is* not hidden from thee, neither *is* it far off.

12 It *is* not in heaven, that thou shouldest say, Who shall go up for us to heaven, and bring it unto us, that we may hear it, and do it?

13 Neither *is* it beyond the sea, that thou shouldest say, Who shall go over the sea for us, and bring it unto us, that we may hear it, and do it?

14 But the word *is* very nigh unto thee, in thy mouth, and in thy heart, that thou mayest do it.

15 See, I have set before thee this day life and good, and death and evil;

16 In that I command thee this day to love the LORD thy God, to walk in his ways, and to keep his commandments and his statutes and his judgments, that thou mayest live and multiply: and the LORD thy God shall bless thee in the land whither thou goest to possess it.

17 But if thine heart turn away, so that thou wilt not hear, but shalt be drawn away, and worship other gods, and serve them;

18 I denounce unto you this day, that ye shall surely perish, *and that* ye shall not prolong *your* days upon the land, whither thou passest over Jordan to go to possess it.

19 I call heaven and earth to record this day against you, *that* I have set before you life and death, blessing and cursing: therefore choose life, that both thou and thy seed may live:

20 That thou mayest love the LORD thy God, *and* that thou mayest obey his voice, and that thou mayest cleave unto him: for he *is* thy life, and the length of thy days: that thou mayest dwell in the land which the LORD sware unto thy fathers, to Abraham, to Isaac, and to Jacob, to give them.

REVISED STANDARD VERSION

DEUTERONOMY 30   11 "For this commandment which I command you this day is not too hard for you, neither is it far off. 12 It is not in heaven, that you should say, 'Who will go up for us to heaven, and bring it to us, that we may hear it and do it?' 13 Neither is it beyond the sea, that you should say, 'Who will go over the sea for us, and bring it to us, that we may hear it and do it?' 14 But the word is very near you; it is in your mouth and in your heart, so that you can do it.

15 "See, I have set before you this day life and good, death and evil. 16 If you obey the commandments of the LORD your God which I command you this day, by loving the LORD your God, by walking in his ways, and by keeping his commandments and his statutes and his ordinances, then you shall live and multiply, and the LORD your God will bless you in the land which you are entering to take possession of it. 17 But if your heart turns away, and you will not hear, but are drawn away to worship other gods and serve them, 18 I declare to you this day, that you shall perish; you shall not live long in the land which you are going over the Jordan to enter and possess. 19 I call heaven and earth to witness against you this day, that I have set before you life and death, blessing and curse; therefore choose life, that you and your descendants may live, 20 loving the LORD your God, obeying his voice, and cleaving to him; for that means life to you and length of days, that you may dwell in the land which the LORD swore to your fathers, to Abraham, to Isaac, and to Jacob, to give them."

KEY VERSE: "*. . . I have set before you life and death, blessing and curse; therefore choose life. . . .*" Deuteronomy 30:19 (RSV).

HOME DAILY BIBLE READINGS

Aug. 17. M. *The Religious Union of Twelve.* Joshua 24:1–7.
Aug. 18. T. *Israel Possesses the Promised Land.* Joshua 24:8–13.
Aug. 19. W. *Choose Life or Death.* Joshua 24:14–18.
Aug. 20. T. *Witness Your Own Choice.* Joshua 24:20–25.
Aug. 21. F. *Here I Raise My Ebenezer.* Joshua 24:25–31.
Aug. 22. S. *Choose to Delight in the Law.* Psalms 1.
Aug. 23. S. *Pray for an Understanding Mind.* 1 Kings 3:5–14.

BACKGROUND

A young man came home after his freshman year at college and told his father that he didn't think he would go to church any more; he had learned in college that "God is incomprehensible." His father asked, "Oh, is He? What evidence do you have for that?" His evidence was— incomprehensible.

Now in the crowd that listened to Moses' last sermon, there were many like this young man. They were not outspoken atheists, but just people who either couldn't grasp the meaning and immensity of God, or people who just didn't want to do what God was asking them to do. They had a nodding acquaintance of respect for a God they *thought* existed, but God's call did not come through to them "loud and clear." Moses saw a deadly hidden peril in that, and he threw down a challenge to them: "You will either believe, or die."

The same challenge faces us today—even more than it faced the Israelites of old.

NOTES ON THE PRINTED TEXT

Life is just one question after another, or one decision after another. What *must* we believe, and why? Yes, we think there is a God, but how can we *know* it is God speaking to us at one time or another? How can we be *certain* that it is His voice? How can we *know* what He expects of us? Isn't all this a mystery which we cannot understand? And isn't most of religion an unsolved mystery, after all?

These undoubtedly were questions in the back of the mind of the young man who thought God was incomprehensible. He wanted a test-tube God—a God who could be "proved" by scientific test, or by way of superintelligent thinking and research; he was not ready to obey a God he couldn't *see* with his mind's eye. What would you have said to him about proving God, and proving that we must, or should, obey the commandments with which He is credited?

There is uncertainty in the best of us. We tend to think of God as "something, somewhere," far removed from the earth, somewhere up there in the sky! Something, someone "hidden," or "far off." How are we to "find" such an absentee God, and why should we obey Him? Questions, questions!

Moses tells his people that God is not as far away as they think. His will is written in the heart, not in the searching mind. All the logic in the world, all the disputes of learned men, all the findings of (physical) science, will not "prove" Him or bring Him near to us. Finding God is not a matter of intellectual struggle; it is a matter of the *heart* more than a matter of the *mind*.

Israel, warned their old leader, you are looking in the wrong direction—like the Russian astronaut who said that he looked out of his spaceship and did not see any God! If the astronaut had looked into the hearts of humble people who had the spirit of God in their hearts, he might have found God! Heaven isn't made up of erudite scholars, but of the humble who have tried His way and found it good. If you want to know why you should obey God and His commandments, try practicing them, and find out! C. S. Lewis summed it up when he said, "There are two kinds of people: those who say to God, 'Thy will be done,' and those to whom God says, " 'All right, then, have it your own way.' "

The call of a living God who dwells in the heart is easy to hear: "The word is very near you; it is in your mouth, and in your heart, so that you can *do* it" (verse 14 RSV). God has brought it "near" to them in the revelation. He gave to Moses, in the Covenant which Israelites speak of with their lips and hold in their hearts. In this Covenant, in these commandments, He has told them what He wants them to know, and what to do. The choice of whether they want to do it or not is up to them.

The trouble was—and is—that we have two blind spots in our spiritual spectacles. We have a bad habit of trying to find God and get His help only when we are in trouble. We are like the little girl who prayed to God to heal her of the mumps, and who, when she was healed, said, "I don't need to pray any more. I'm well!" In the wilderness, they needed Him badly; He helped them there. But now they were to live in a land of milk and honey—and they could take care of themselves. That way, said Moses, lies *death*, and not the good life. We do much the same thing: we are quite pious at Easter and Christmas but the rest of the year our piety is not noticeable!

The other blind spot is seen in our tendency to say, "It's too difficult for us to understand just what to do about God and His commandments in our kind of world. It's so *impractical*." Recently we heard a teacher in high schoool say, "Christ demands too much of us; with things as they are, His precepts and principles are just too much for us." How does he know that? Has he *tried* Christ's way, or gone his own way?

God's way may not be easy; He never promised us a bed of roses, but He does give us, in the Commandments and in Jesus, a formula for living a life that is abundant and not lost in impossible questions and doubts. It is all amazingly simple, understandable, and practical. Even an unschooled man can read the Gospel of Our Lord and understand it—unless he complicates it all with his own intellectual wanderings and confusions. In that Gospel, God in Christ comes clear to the impossible of men. The heart of the whole matter, as Moses pointed out, is simply that we *must* love God and man if we are to live meaningful and worthwhile lives.

The stakes involved here are high: life or death. Obey God's statutes and judgments, and you will find blessedness in His promised King-dom; turn away to lesser gods and you shall surely *perish*. Life without God is scarcely worth living at all.

Now Moses has reached the end, the conclusion of his third and last oration. He might have finished it with some soft, sentimental well-wishing, or with a little flattery, so that his people would "go away happy," but he was not the sort of man to do that. He stood there with his people at a moment of crisis, and such moments call for straight, earnest talk. These people were going to be forced to make the greatest decision of their lives after Moses was gone, and he hurls a thunderbolt at them in his last words to make them appreciate the seriousness of the occa-sion: "I call heaven and earth to witness against you this day that I have set before you life and death, blessing and curse. . . " (verse 19 RSV). He may have been thinking of the procedures of the Hittites in signing treaties with other peoples; the Hittites called upon the gods of nature (winds, clouds, mountains, rivers, seas, storms) to act as witnesses to the treaties. But Moses changes this, or adapts it, to mean that the God of the Hebrews will call His whole assembly of angels in heaven and His ministers on earth as witnesses to their promise to live up to the terms of their Covenant with Him. This angelic council would testify for or against them under the direction of God as supreme Judge. If they were obedient, these witnesses would speak for them; if they were guilty of disobedience, the witnesses would *not* speak on their behalf at this final judgment.

It may just be true that God judges us every day, while we still live, but Moses is insisting that there is a *final* judgment at the hands of God when this life is done. It is by God's grace that we live and die, and we all have life and death standing before us as blessed or dreaded pos-sibilities. Therefore, Israel, choose which it shall be with you: life with God, or life with deadly sin: ". . . therefore choose life, that both thou and thy seed may live" (verse 19).

We are all faced with the decision that faced Christ's rich young ruler; we can either follow Him, or—sorrowfully—turn away. Every day, we have to choose between living by our little human philosophies or by His commands. James Clerk Maxwell puts it in these words: "I have read up on many queer religions; and there is nothing like the old thing, after all. I have looked into the most philosophical systems, and have found none that will work without a God." That is eternally right!

SUGGESTIONS TO TEACHERS

"Do I have to make up my mind?" Some prefer to defer decisions. General George B. McClellan of the Union Army, for example, had a reputation for holding off on committing himself as long as possible. When he was an engineer designing railroad bridges, he could hardly bring himself to permit the first locomotive to be driven across a newly-completed span to test the bridge's strength.

In the life of every Christian, the time comes when it is "Go!" or "No go!" Choices must be made.

How does a Christian go about making important choices?

This is your lesson topic for today. Before jumping into a free-for-all discussion, however, insist that everyone in the class saturate himself or herself in the background Scripture in Deuteronomy 30. The key decision, of course, is to choose God. Once that basic choice is made, the other decisions begin to fall into place. Therefore, be sure that you have your people understand that The Number One Choice is the decision for God.

1. *WITHIN EVERYONE'S REACH*. God helps everyone on decision-making. Making the correct choice is not an impossibility. Moreover, choosing God as the basic choice is the beginning step in all decisions. Encourage the members of your class to comment on times when they had to make difficult decisions, and how deciding first for God enabled them to get the rest of the choices in proper perspective.

2. *WITHOUT ANYONE'S RESOURCES*. Remind your class that God chooses for us. Furthermore, God is capable. God's help and God's commands are not distant and unknown. We don't have to sigh, "Who will go up for us to heaven, and bring it to us, that we may hear it and do it," (Deuteronomy 30:12). God has already approached us. As Christ's community, we know that He has come to us, deciding for us and choosing us in the person of Jesus Christ. Have your class consider how Jesus Christ is the complete expression of God's will and commands for us. Think also how Christ's nearness takes much of the guesswork out of decision-making.

3. *WITH EACH ONE'S RECALL*. You class should be encouraged to consider how important it is to remember the biblical story. Recalling what God has promised "to your fathers, to Abraham, to Isaac, and to Jacob, to give them" (Deuteronomy 30:20) is a key component of knowing what choices to make because such remembering provides input from the past. Help your people to factor in the Bible message, from Deuteronomy through to the disciples, in their choosing. Ask people in your class to relate occasions when the biblical accounts have been instrumental in pointing them to a right decision.

4. *WITHIN EVERYONE'S RESPONSIBILITY*. Have the blunt words of Deuteronomy 30:15–20 be given close attention. You can comment about our dislike for such sharply-worded either-or choices as good and evil, life and death. No sliding-scale morality here! Make sure that your class members understand how God prods each hearer to make up his/her mind about choosing Him! Eventually each must place his/her life on the line for the Lord!

TOPIC FOR ADULTS
CHOICE AND ITS CONSEQUENCES

Distinctions to Be Made. The ideological "bandwagons are coming at us more rapidly and more noisily than, I should think, at any other time since the expulsion from Eden," writes Prof. Thomas Howard. "You can't avoid them."

"They rumble and blare and loom, magnified and amplified by every kilowatt and decibel that the media can muster."

It has submitted to the steadily dinned notion of "Moral and intellectual democracy in which every idea is worth exactly as much as every other idea, and in which we are committed to giving equal time, not just on the air or in the columns of newsprint, but also in our minds—equal time, I say, to Isaiah and Beelzebub, for example or to St. Thomas Aquinas and Mick Jagger."

But to the Christian, he says that this just "will not do. . . . There is wheat and there is chaff. Distinctions have to be made. There is good stuff and bad stuff. And the only way to sort out the good from the bad is to discriminate.

"There is no question of a moral democracy, any more than there is of a gastronomic democracy. If you eat vegetables, they will do you good; if you eat toadstools, they will kill you."

Howard says that guideposts of the "Christian vision" make an adherent do some hard questioning of many of the modern vogues.

"He is not quite at liberty to let it all hang out: Indeed, he suspects that letting it all hang out is what you get in nurseries, with babies screaming and vomiting, or in mental hospitals. . . ."

Howard describes as "cults" many of the popularized attitudes, including the "cult of self," the "cult of frankness," the "cult of liberation," the "cult of the convenient," the "cult of the unstructured" and the "cult of the new morality."

As for the self-obsessed emphasis on "self-affirmation and self-discovery, self-acceptance and self-identity," he says it's a fine idea to discover who you are, but he adds:

"As for the 'cult of frankness,' with such injunctions as to 'spill it all out' and 'If you think it, say it,' he says candor is great, but adds:

"The Christian will also want to know how we propose to guard the shrine that is the other person. He will want to know, before he opens up the shrine of himself to others, just who has the warrant to come in here."

He says the "cult of the unstructured" wants occasions left loose so everyone is free to do as they please, but he says:

"Anybody who was not born yesterday knows that it is the structures and conventions that help us through chaotic and impossible situations, and that gather up and bear our flying emotions. Victory parades, music at marriages or funerals, dances of joy, liturgical processions. . . .

"If we were all left standing about vaguely in the face of huge experiences, we would soon find ourselves reduced to the feeble level—alarmingly common in our time, alas—of 'Oh, wow!' or 'Outta sight!' That is to real, profound experience what pablum is to pate.

"The cult of the new morality," he says, "contends there should be no restraints on sexual activity, but the 'Christian is stuck with all these intractable taboos again. . . . ' What's the matter with Christians? Can't they live?

"I suppose the answer here is, 'Nothing more is the matter with them than has been the matter with Jews and Moslems and Hindus and pagans all down through history who have known prefectly well that the sexual phenomenon was a high and sacred thing, to be surrounded with the most fierce strictures. . . . ' "—From an article by Thomas Howard in *Christianity Today*, 1979.

Give Him What He Wants. For our own good, God does not allow us to have whatever we wish to choose to have. He cares so much that He will sometimes warn us about our choices.

What happens when we are allowed to choose what we please! This true story may be a clue: The little one was riding on the back seat with his babysitter. The child became fretful. The mother heard the babysitter say, "No, you can't have it."

The mother instructed the sitter, "Give him anything he wants."

All was quiet for a few minutes, then the little fellow began to scream. "What in the world is the matter now?" the mother asked from front seat.

"He got it," was the babysitter's calm reply.

A wasp in the car had been sitting quietly on the window until the three-year-old was allowed to grab him.

Consequences of Choices. "A great scientist once characterized the nuclear picture of the 1950s as 'two scorpions in a bottle.' Today there are six scorpions in that bottle, and we now know that soon there will be many more; so it is becoming increasingly apparent that what any two countries may decide will not necessarily be decisive, no matter how many nuclear weapons they may possess. Any country which possesses nuclear weapons could provide a grave threat to virtually any other country, a condition which implies future danger to all nations. In any case, the nuclear genie is not out of control, and the number of scorpions continues to grow."—Stuart Symington, *QUOTE*, September 21, 1975. *QUOTE, The Weekly Digest, P. O. Box 4047, Anderson, S. C. 29621.*

Questions for Pupils on the Next Lesson. 1. Do the worship experiences in your church include praising God for His faithfulness? 2. Do you sometimes wonder whom you can trust? Whom *do* you trust most? 3. Does God's faithfulness inspire faithfulness on your part? 4. How can we distinguish between complacency and faith in God?

TOPIC FOR YOUTH
CHOOSE WISELY

Wishing They Hadn't Said It. Words have consequences. You must choose your words wisely.

Earl Butz, the former Secretary of Agriculture, told a crude joke about blacks and was forced to resign from office because of the outrage. Gen. George S. Brown, Chairman of the Joint Chiefs of Staff in 1974, appeared at Duke University Law School Forum and castigated what he called "the Jewish influence in the country." For his thoughtlessness, he received a stiff dressing-down from then-President Gerald Ford. Vice-President Nelson Rockefeller and House Speaker Carl Albert were unaware that they were in front of an open mike when they made derogatory comments about Senator Edward W. Brooke. Rockefeller and Albert had to make public apologies, but the damage was done.

Choose wisely, and start by choosing to be God's person.

Connection Between Faith and Choices. Does your faith have any tie with how you make decisions? Not if you are like most people, according to a recent Gallup poll. Perhaps this is why the choices of so many people (and possibly your decisions) so frequently turn out to be poor ones.

Roughly three out of four among the public, do not consciously connect religion with their judgments of right or wrong. "Thus God in his highest ethical dimension is denied. It would accordingly be at once possible for almost all American people to 'believe in God' and yet for society to be essentially materialistic."—George Gallup, Jr. reporting on a recent religious poll.

Almost a Hero. But for a sheriff's order tying his airplane to the ground, Clarence D. Chamberlin might have beat Lindbergh as the first to fly solo across the Atlantic.

Chamberlin was set to leave Roosevelt Field on Long Island, New York, for Germany weeks before Charles Lindbergh took off on May 20, 1927 for his record-setting flight to Paris. Chamberlin, however, had allowed himself to get into financial difficulties and found himself with a lawsuit in which a sheriff's attachment kept his plane, the Columbia, tied to the ground. Had Chamberlin chosen to be more careful, he would have pioneered. Fifteen days later, June 4, 1927, Chamberlin freed himself of the writ and did take off. He set two records: he carried the first passenger on a non-stop trans-Atlantic flight, and he established a new distance mark of 3,911 miles. Lindbergh, however, carried off the laurels and became the hero, primarily because of Chamberlin's unfortunate decisions.

Choose wisely as God's person, because every moral choice brings its own consequences.

Sentence Sermon to Remember: A man should choose with careful eye the things to be remembered by.—*The Weather Vane.*

Questions for Pupils on the Next Lesson. 1. Do you recognize that God's care should result in joyous celebration? 2. Should worship of God be limited only to certain methods? 3. What nonverbal expressions of worship can you think of? 4. Do you ever wonder whom you can trust? Whom do you trust the most? 5. How does God's faithfulness inspire faithfulness on your part?

LESSON XIII—AUGUST 30

GOD IS FAITHFUL

Background Scripture: Deuteronomy 31:30–32:14; 33:29
Devotional Reading: 1 Kings 19:9–18

KING JAMES VERSION

DEUTERONOMY 32 1 Give ear, O ye heavens, and I will speak; and hear, O earth, the words of my mouth.

2 My doctrine shall drop as the rain, my speech shall distil as the dew, as the small rain upon the tender herb, and as the showers upon the grass:

3 Because I will publish the name of the LORD: ascribe ye greatness unto our God.

4 *He is* the Rock, his work *is* perfect: for all his ways *are* judgment: a God of truth and without iniquity, just and right *is* he.

5 They have corrupted themselves, their spot *is* not *the spot* of his children: *they are* a perverse and crooked generation.

6 Do ye thus requite the LORD, O foolish people and unwise? *is* not he thy father *that* hath bought thee? hath he not made thee, and established thee?

7 Remember the days of old, consider the years of many generations: ask thy father, and he will shew thee; thy elders, and they will tell thee.

8 When the Most High divided to the nations their inheritance, when he separated the sons of Adam, he set the bounds of the people according to the number of children of Israel.

9 For the LORD's portion *is* his people; Jacob *is* the lot of his inheritance.

REVISED STANDARD VERSION

DEUTERONOMY 32 1 "Give ear, O heavens, and I will speak;
and let the earth hear the words of my mouth.

2 May my teaching drop as the rain, my speech distil as the dew,
as the gentle rain upon the tender grass,
and as the showers upon the herb.

3 For I will proclaim the name of the LORD.
Ascribe greatness to our God!

4 "The Rock, his work is perfect;
for all his ways are justice.
A God of faithfulness and without iniquity,
just and right is he.

5 They have dealt corruptly with him, they are no longer his children because of their blemish;
they are a perverse and crooked generation.

6 Do you thus requite the LORD, you foolish and senseless people?
Is not he your father, who created you, who made you and established you?

7 Remember the days of old, consider the years of many generations;
ask your father, and he will show you; your elders, and they will tell you.

8 When the Most High gave to the nations their inheritance,
when he separated the sons of men,
he fixed the bounds of the peoples
according to the number of the sons of God.

9 For the LORD's portion is his people, Jacob his allotted heritage."

KEY VERSE: *Happy art thou, O Israel: who is like unto thee, O people saved by the Lord. . . .* Deuteronomy 33:29.

409

HOME DAILY BIBLE READINGS

Aug. 24. M. *Living the Blameless Life.* Psalms 119:1–8.
Aug. 25. T. *Keeping Your Life Clean.* Psalms 119:9–16.
Aug. 26. W. *Finding Delight in God's Law.* Psalms 119:17–24.
Aug. 27. T. *Restoring One's Life.* Psalms 119:25–32.
Aug. 28. F. *Trust in the Lord.* Psalms 146.
Aug. 29. S. *Sing Praises Unto God.* Psalms 119:169–176.
Aug. 30. S. *The Steadfast Love of the Lord.* Psalms 103:6–18.

BACKGROUND

Read Deuteronomy 31 as background for our lesson today. Listen to Moses saying, "I shall not cross the Jordan with you. . . ." His work is done, and he knows it. He turns over his "command" to Joshua; he wrote down the laws he had given Israel and gave copies of them to the Levites (who carried the Ark containing the Ten Commandments) and to the elders. So much for the Law.

Then, abruptly, the great lawgiver becomes a great poet teaching a great song to the people he is about to leave; the book of Deuteronomy is to end with a song. This was appropriate, as they stand on the far banks of Jordan, for they had sung a great song long ago, when they stood on the banks of the Red Sea celebrating their release from Egypt (Exodus 15:1–8). The first song was a song of triumph; this second song, sung at Jordan, says nothing of triumph but sounds a note of warning as the people were about to enter the Land of Promise and soon (Moses believed) to prove unfaithful to their God.

The Scripture says that Moses himself wrote the song; that is possible, but scholars of the Book disagree as to the exact date when it was written. Some think that it stands as an application of Mosaic theology, rather than a composition written by him. But it doesn't matter very much that it was written before him or after him; its value lies in what it *says*. Whenever it was written, God and Moses wanted it planted deep in the Jewish heart.

The song is an eloquent assertion of the ultimate victory of God over those who oppose Him.

NOTES ON THE PRINTED TEXT

The essence of the song is found in the development of three main points or ideas that run through the whole, like a golden thread. First, there was *the greatness of God.* Can we ever grasp or fully understand and appreciate the greatness of God? Moses calls upon all in heaven or on earth to bear witness to the fact that God is the Creator of all—but most of us are too busy to stop long enough to think of that! Without this Creator—nothing! There is an old story about Napoleon and the greatness of God. Napoleon sat with a group of his officers at the foot of a pyramid in Egypt; they sat beneath the starry heavens talking about God. The officers were atheists. Napoleon did not try to answer their arguments about "the myth of God," but he pointed to the night sky and the starry lamps that lighted it, and he said, "You are very ingenious, gentlemen—but who made all that?"

The same stars that spoke of God's greatness and that inspired Napoleon still shine above us. We live in the same universe that Napoleon and Moses lived in, and modern astronomers have looked deeper and deeper into that universe and discovered new stars moving perfectly in thier courses, new planets moving within set orbits, and up there are still more and greater stars and planets than we have yet seen; we know only a little of the greatness of their—and our—Creator.

Through thousands of years, we have been awed by the mystery of His might. Leslie D. Weatherhead wrote in *The Christian Pulpit* these words: "We launched the *Queen Mary.* Oh, we felt awfully proud of that. Really it is rather like a little boy pushing a Woolworth boat along a path. In one respect, it is like that. We get very excited about it; the papers are full of it; when the vessel arrives in New York, New York goes mad, as only New York, can. And the other day God launched a new planet and nobody will know anything about it for twenty million years."

The greatness of God! Since Moses and Christ, God has been taking weak men and making them great; ever since, men have been building new lives with the help of an *almighty* God. Sidney Lanier put it well when he wrote, "As the marsh-hen secretly builds on the watery sod, Behold I will build me a nest on the greatness of God."

Moses, this day, was challenging his people to build just so in their new land—on the greatness of a God who had brought them so far, and not on the pitiful weaknesses of the lesser gods of Canaan.

When Margaret Fuller, a famous intellectual of the 1800s, said, "I accept the universe" (as though she had made some great discovery), Thomas Carlyle said, "She'd better!" We all come nearer to the greatness of God when we accept His mighty hand in every move we make.

Then there is the *justice* of God. He created different nations of men for different purposes, says Moses, but He created Israel to be an example of His justice among the nations. When Israel lived under the will of God and obeyed Him, Israel prospered, and would prosper in the future; when Israel disobeyed Him, God levied His justice upon them and punished them. He never punished the righteous, but He always punished the wicked. "Justice," said Israeli, "is truth in action." God is truth in action. When Israel erred and denied His justice, they were punished by the hand of hostile nations; when they did righteously, they were "delivered" as these nations were destroyed.

Moses speaks of this judging God as "The Rock." His truth is the *eternal* Rock of human history. T. H. Huxley was no crusading Christian, but once he wrote to Charles Kingsley, a great Christian, these words: "I am no optimist, but I have the firmest belief that the Divine Government is wholly just. The more I know intimately of the lives of other men, the more obvious it is to me that the wicked does not flourish nor is the righteous punished. The ledger of the Almighty is strictly kept and every one of us has balance of his operations paid over to him at the end of every minute of his existence."

Some writer not as famous as Mr. Huxley put it in other words "The sins we commit two by two we pay for one by one." That is justice as it should be—and it is the justice of God.

Finally, there is the *faithfulness* of God. Just the other day we heard a man say, "This world we're living in is so rotten and bad that I wonder sometimes why God doesn't just wipe it all out and start all over again with a better human race." We may all feel that way, at times, but in such times we forget the eternal, everlasting, all-out, and unending patience—or faithfulness—of God.

Israel blundered often on their way to Canaan; Israel sinned so often that we wonder why God "put up with them." But the truth remains: while Israel often insulted God, God never deserted them; *He had made a covenant with Israel,* and He kept that covenant and its promises, even when Israel went astray. Moses stresses that God is faithful, even with the worst of us! Patience, says someone, is the art of hoping and God had great hopes for Israel.

In his famous book, *The Keys to the Kingdom,* A. J. Cronin pictures a doctor dying, while his friend Father Francis sits at his bedside. Says the doctor, "I still can't believe in God." Replies Father Francis, "Does that matter now? He believes in you." He believes in us, endlessly, as He believed in Israel.

Only yesterday a representative of Jehovah's Witnesses paid us a visit. He was a very, very young Witness—sixteen years old, and very much in earnest for which we respected him. He came to talk with us about destruction. He believed that all the wicked of the earth would eventually be destroyed by an outraged God. When we asked him to tell us just who the wicked were, and of what their wickedness consisted, he replied quickly that the wicked were "those who never worshiped God." When we asked if he meant that we were all wicked who did not worship as the Witnesses worshiped, he replied. "Of course." He further instructed us that after this wholesale slaughter at the hand of God there would be only one special group left—the 144,000 mentioned in Revelation 7 and 14—which will become "the bride of Christ" and reign with Him in heaven. Furthermore, he said, these 144,000 would of course be Jehovah's Witnesses!

Now we can make any verse in the Bible mean almost anything—but in doing that we are apt to wipe out what *God* meant in His Word. God says, in this Book, that the wicked will be punished, but we may have difficulty in believing that He is a wholesale slaughterer of mankind. He is a God of *love,* who offers forgiveness up to the very end—such as the end of the penitent thief on the cross.

Wicked as they were, at times, God did *not* destroy the Israelites, even when they bowed down to their golden calf at Sinai. God is no murderer; He lets the wicked destroy themselves in refusing to abide by their covenant with Him, but He loves, and He waits, and He hopes!

SUGGESTIONS TO TEACHERS

"Things have been so bad that I think even God has given up on us," sighed a woman whose husband had suffered a crippling stroke, whose son had lost his job, whose home had been destroyed by a tornado, and who had just been informed that she would have to undergo major surgery.

People in your class sometimes feel this way. Probably, you do, too. Your lesson for this week is on the subject of God's faithfulness. You will help your class members to grow in understanding that in spite of whatever they suffer, God's promises continue to stand. He is faithful!

The Deuteronomy passages offer meaningful insights into God's faithfulness. To use the quaint Quaker expression, this Scripture "speaks to our condition" when we feel that perhaps God has given up on us.

1. *TOUCH THE RAIN.* The beautiful poem in Deuteronomy 32 likens God's Word to a gentle rain, bringing nourishment and new life. God's promises showered upon us provide fresh vitality to parched lives. You should give some time in this class period for each person to recall an example of a time when he or she could feel the "gentle rain upon the tender grass" of the Lord's Word in a time of personal spiritual drought. Emphasize that although such "dry spells" in life may come to every person, God always eventually sends a renewing shower of strength.

2. *TELL THE STORY.* "Remember the days of old, consider the years of many generations," advises Scripture (Deuteronomy 32:7). Get the big picture! See the panorama of God's activities in history. Enlarge your horizons! Review the biblical story, from Abraham and the Patriarchs, through Moses and the Exodus, through the kings and prophets, the Exile and Restoration, to the Cross, Resurrection, and Pentecost, noting how men and women discovered the refreshing promise of God within their lives. Have members of your class recount examples from Scripture of God's faithfulness. Bring the story of God's faithfulness down to these times. Discuss evidences of God's continuing faithfulness today. What signs of His faithfulness do you notice in the Church? Within your congregations? In the world?

3. *TEACH THE YOUNG.* God's faithfulness, our Scripture for today reminds us, extends to the coming generation. Our children will also know occasions when they will be tempted to think that God has given up on them. We must help prepare them for these weary times when life seems like a desert. In what ways is your community of faith enabling them to learn that God may be trusted? Is your congregation exhibiting evidence of a willingness to adventure, to take risks, be relying on God's promise? Does the ethos and do the activities of your church reflect the fact that God *is* faithful? If not, what could you do to communicate to the young that the Christian family, your church, lives by faith?

TOPIC FOR ADULTS
GOD IS FAITHFUL

Ultimatum to the Almighty. Sometimes when everything in life seems to be going terribly badly, we berate God for apparently forgetting us. Even the stoutly faithful Martin Luther in his pain doubted God's faithfulness. In February, 1537, for instance, Luther suffered from the agonies of kidney stones and other serious ailments, and was thought to be dying. The gravely ill Reformer prayed, almost as an accusation against God for permitting him to endure such discomfort and partly as an ultimatum for God to bring some release or relief, "If this illness lasts longer, I shall surely go mad." At least Luther was honest!

He added, however, shortly afterward words which reflected his trust in the Lord's faithfulness, "Even if this should happen (going mad with pain), I know that my God remains skillful and wise."

Can you say the same? Are you aware that God has given His unbreakable promise that He remains skillful and wise?

Passing on the News. Each April, thousands of runners compete in the famous Boston Marathon, the grueling 26 mile, 385 yard race through the eastern metropolitan area. Few realize the story behind a marathon. The race commemorates the great run by the greek messenger, Phidippides, who hastened on foot at top speed from the battle of Marathon in 490 B.C. to Athens, twenty-six miles away, to report that the Athenians had successfully repulsed the invading Persians.

As Phidippides staggered into Athens, the anxious citizens gathered around him for the news, and the great runner shouted in his dying breath, "Rejoice, we conquer!"

God has faithfully brought us victory thorugh Jesus Christ. Our task is to run to tell others the Good News. We are called to be faithful messengers. Life may seem to be a long, wearing marathon run, but we are entrusted with the great announcement, "Rejoice, we conquer!"

Saved by Smoke. There are times when God is faithful when we do not suspect it. Sometimes, He uses our misfortune in His faithfulness toward us.

There is an old sea tale of a sole survivor of a shipwreck who was cast up on an uninhabited island. After anxiously praying to God for deliverance, he painstakingly collected whatever he could salvage from the wreck. With pieces of the wreckage, he constructed a crude hut, and stored the few bits of valuables he had saved. Each day, he scanned the horizon for sign of a passing vessel which he could hail. God seemed to have abandoned him, however, for he sighted nothing.

One day, when he returned from a search for food, he discovered that his hut was in flames. Everything was destroyed. The worst had happened, and his situation was hopeless. Angrily, the seaman cursed God. The next day, however, a ship arrived. "We saw your smoke signal," the rescuing skipper told the shipwrecked man.

Questions for Pupils on the Next Lesson. 1. How long did it take God to create the universe? 2. What does the word *void* mean, in Genesis 1:2? 3. Is there more than one creation story in Genesis? 4. Exactly how are we created in God's image? 5. Is everything that God has made "good"? 6. If God did not create the universe, who did?

TOPIC FOR YOUTH
JOYFUL WORSHIP

Didn't Know What to Do With Riches. Police finally entered the shabby house of Sophia Easer in Pittsburgh on January 19, 1976. They found the body of the eighty-two year old recluse wrapped in rags and a floor rug, frozen to death. Investigations showed that she had refused to pay a $72 gas bill, and had had the gas shut off by the utility company. A year later, it was reported by the Allegheny Register of Wills that Sophia Easer left an estate valued at $292,000. She was surrounded by plenty of wealth, but didn't know what to do with it.

This is similar to so many of us in regard to God's faithfulness. We have the treasure of His promise, but we don't know what to do with it!

Celebrate joyfully that God has provided for us. He surrounds us with His mercy in Jesus Christ. Reach out and appropriate into your own life the greatness and goodness of God's presence around you!

What Do You Worship? A recent survey of British teenagers by the British Bible Society disclosed that nearly 75% own Bibles. However, few of them read it or know the Good News contained in it. The same survey revealed that more young people believe in Unidentified Flying Objects and life on other planets than "definitely believe" in God.

Is that about where you are? Are UFO's and extraplanetary existence more real to you than God?

The biblical message is that God remains faithful, and that He calls you to be faithful to Him. Acknowledge Him as Lord. Obey Him. And celebrate joyfully the promise that He directs your life and all life!

Plans and Cause. The universe operates by rules, not by blind chance. We may depend on the Creator-Sustainer. Even Albert Einstein again and again would comment, "God does not play dice."

Scripture assures you that God has planned and will continue to direct the affairs of this universe, including your life. His purposes are for the growth of all. He has good intentions toward you and everyone. Therefore, worship Him joyfully!

Sentence Sermon to Remember: It is not success that God rewards but faithfulness in doing His will.—Anonymous.

Questions for Pupils on the Next Lesson. 1. Why did God create man? 2. Did life begin on the land, or in the water? 3. What are the lights of the firmament? 4. Are we made in God's image physically, or spiritually? 5. How long a time did Creation take? 6. Is God still "creating" today?

This book contains lessons through August 1981. Tarbell's 1981–1982, containing lessons from September 1981 through August 1982, is on sale *now* at your bookstore.